GW00648481

The

RIVER BOYNE

Hidden legacies, history and lore
explored on foot and by boat

Anthony (Tony) Holten was born near Tara in 1945.
He travelled extensively during his marine engineering days in
the Merchant Navy prior to continuing his career working on
offshore oil and gas fields worldwide. He is the author of several
books, including; *A Stroke of Luck*, *Where Toll Roads Meet,*
On Ancient Roads, *Of Other Days* and *High Kings to Sea Kings.*
He lives with his family in County Cork.

To Joseph Stephen Holten,
11 August 1986 – 11 March 2014
Our son, brother and friend.

Mere words cannot express the loss, but these few
echo from your too brief life with us:
I was born… I lived and laughed... I learned…
but most of all I loved…
You are with us always dear Joe, God rest your spirit…

The
RIVER BOYNE

Hidden legacies, history and lore
explored on foot and by boat

Anthony Holten

First published in 2016
by Anthony Holten
ajholten@gmail.com

Text and graphics © 2016 Anthony Holten
Photographs © 2016 Anthony Holten unless otherwise credited

Anthony Holten has asserted his moral right to be identified
as the author of this work in accordance with the Irish Copyright
and Related Rights Act 2000.

British Library Cataloguing in Publication Data
An entry can be found on request.

All rights reserved. Without limiting the rights under copyright reserved alone, no
part of this publication may be reproduced, stored in or introduced into a retrieval
system, or transmitted, in any form or by any means (electronic, mechanical,
photocopying, recording or otherwise) without the prior written permission of both
the copyright owner and the above publisher of this book.

ISBN 978-0-9569911-1-9

Cover Design: edit+ www.stuartcoughlan.com
Design and setting: edit+ www.stuartcoughlan.com
Set in Adobe Garamond Pro

Printed and bound in Drogheda Co. Louth by Anglo Printers

Contents

The Middle Reaches

Acknowledgements

This book was financially assisted by:
Councillor Joe Reilly,
Navan and District Historical Society,
Meath County Council Community Heritage Grant Scheme 2016.

Special thanks to those who assisted with the research over the past five years, including: Martin Curran (who planted the seed) – Paschal Marry (a lodestone in the darkness) – Tom French ('the Humble Crowbar') – James Doherty (an anchor) – Tom and Pauline Holten – Vincent Mulvaney – John Bradley – Oliver Delany – Ethna Cantwell – Christopher (Hopper) Rennicks, Pa. Reilly Martin (Chalky) White, the late Sean Cleary and all the members of Meath River Rescue Service – Mairéad Holten – Mairéad Crinion – Bernadette Murray – Clare Ryan.

The staff of Navan Library.
The staff of the National Library and National Archives

I thank the following people whom I met along the way – and who generously provided anecdotal and other local information for these writings:

Noel Devine – Mr & Mrs Elliot, Clonkeen Mill – Brian Smyth and his mother – Mickey Creighton – Donie Halpin – Donal Bradley – Clare Ryan – Michael O'Brien – the late Mickey Morris – the late Brendan Lucey (of Clongall) – Noel French – Pat Harnett – Oliver Carty – Tom Crinion – Declan O'Connor (of Edenderry) – Ian Duggan – Phyllis (*née* Reilly) and Ultan Dunne – Martin Fagan (Dissertation on Boyne Mills) – Gerry White (contractor Kilcarn Br.) – Paul Mc'Nulty (Meath Co. Co.) – Joan Gallagher – Imelda and Mac., Craystown (boat trip) – Jimmy Geoghegan (Meath Chronicle) – Paddy Brady – Janie Quigley (Slane Mill) – Jonathan Shackleton (great grandson of Jane Shackleton) – Anthony Mc'Can – Ronnie Mc'Grane – M. Mc'Gerrity – John O'Donohoe (M.C.) – Tom Mongey – Bernadette Murray (St. Bridget's Well & Ardsallagh) – Richard Farrelly – Alan Russell (Photos) – Aubrey Martin (Aerial photos) – Ger. Cahill (Grange Bective) – Paddy Cahill (photos) – Gordon and Annie Kelly – Paddy Crinion – the late Joe Maguire – William Flood (Boardsmill) – Gerry Brady (Sally Roger's Bar) – Greg Murray – Seamus Smith (artist) – Jackie Butterly – the Markey's of the Lock-house – the Byrne family, Kate, Geoff & Frankie (Mary O'Brien's Mill, Hays.) – Patsy & Deliah Reilly of Castlefin (Reilly's) Lock – Theresa Healy – Olive Harding – Jim and Francis Tallon (Martry Mill) – Ronan and Odette Jacob (Annesbrook Mill, Mullagh) – Barbara and George Heise (Rosnaree or Molly Johnson's Mill) – the Gogan family (of 'the Leck') – Joe Mc'Donnell (Ballinacrad Fishery) – Pauline Fulham (Mc'Cullagh's Mill) – Sally Downey (Broe House & bridge) – Pat Burke.

I am grateful also to the following: Breda and the late Peter O'Leary for the view over Bantry Bay while I was writing.

My wife Marie, my late son Joseph, and my daughter Anna-Marie and Stuart Coughlan for their time and patience.

Special thanks to my son, John, for his help with editing, structuring and preparing the book for publication.

And my Mam and Dad, who took me on many childhood rambles along the Boyne banks, filling my young mind with an insatiable curiosity and a desire to discover more.

Jonathan Shackleton, Antartican, Naturalist and Forester, wrote thus of his great grandmother, Jane Shackleton, some of whose old photographs are reproduced in this book:

> *Jane W. Shackleton.*
> My great –grandmother, Jane W. Shackleton was born in Dublin in 1843 into the EDMUNDSON Quaker family who had a well-known hardware business in Capel Street.
>
> She married Joseph Fisher SHACKLETON of Anna Liffey Mills in Lucan, Co. Dublin, another Quaker family best known for their school in Ballitore, Co. Kildare (1726-1836). He was a cousin of the Antarctic explorer Sir Ernest Shackleton.
>
> Jane was an energetic and enterprising woman who travelled all over Ireland, and also visited England, Scotland, Norway, Switzerland, Germany and Algeria .
>
> She took a large number of photographs on her travels which survive today in the form of over 700 lantern slides and 40 albums. The photographs date from the 1880s until her death in 1909.
>
> Jane had a special interest in antiquities and our inland waterways with their associated structures such as mills, weirs and locks. Her photographs provide a valuable and unique record of this part of our heritage.
>
> She would have been very pleased, as are her descendents, that Anthony Holten has included a number of her early photographs in this very important book about the River Boyne.

The photographs are reproduced by kind permission of Mary Shackleton and Jonathan Shackleton.

A selection of her photographs have been published in *Jane W. Shackleton's Ireland* compiled by Christiaan Corlett, with a foreword by Jonathan Shackleton. The Collins Press (2012).

Poet and author, Tom French, following his review of the unfinished manuscript, wrote:

A Map of the River

I got this couplet from the first reach of the Boyne which appears in these pages, from upstream of Trim to Ruxton's Lock. I had never seen an otter. I may never see one again. Tony Holten gave me the title and I am grateful to him for the poem.

> The Middle Reaches
> It's taken half my lifetime to come eye to eye with an otter.
> It'll take the next half to forget how we regarded one another.

Those two lines appeared in the middle of a book published in the middle of my life. That was four years ago. Now it is late December. It has been raining for days, and half the country is under water. Two young men have just left the Local Studies room of the County Library headquarters in Navan and are heading back towards the river. They asked for 'Tom'. I didn't even get their names. The evening is mild and wet and dark already. It is that time of year again. Meath River Rescue are about their work, and these two men had been sent to find a map of the river.

I would hand them such a map with a heart and a half, that shows every bend and inlet, every shallow and deep pool. Somebody is grieving and waiting for the phone to ring. All I can do is show the two men the index map on the wall and explain what they already know. The Boyne, because it meanders through the whole county, features on too many of those sheets for there to be one map only. All I can do is direct them to the OSI's digital collection of historic mapping which, in addition to the 6" colour first edition of 1837, includes the more recent photographs taken at five yearly intervals by German jets in high summer from four miles up.

It's difficult to believe in pure coincidence. Connections are made. A coxswain of the Meath River Rescue Service who lives a stone's throw from Dowdstown reads a book about the ancient roads of Meath. Shortly afterwards the coxswain meets the author of that book and suggests the author might like to accompany the Meath River Rescue Service on one of their regular training runs on the Boyne. The author jumps at the chance to transpose some of the road history to sites observed from the river.

So it was that the author found himself on the water, and The Meath River Rescue became research assistants. I was hard on earlier drafts of this book, because I hoped it would become the good book it could be, and has become. Tony Holten will remember one meeting when I highlighted a phrase in the manuscript – 'the humble crowbar' – and suggested to him that 'NO CROWBAR IS EVER HUMBLE' could be a guide to his style in the writing of the book, that it should be written in clear capitals on a slate and put up in the room where he could see it when he was writing. He has put his heart and soul into this work.

Loss is an undercurrent in the story. In the middle of writing Tony Holten's son Joe died tragically. Loss can't help but be an undercurrent in these pages, but it is not the story. The story is of one man's passionate inquiry into a river he has always known.

Having spent his life sailing the oceans of the earth, he has come home to write. He has, I believe, written what I could not give those two young men in the Local History Room. This is the story you go out on a boat to get. This is the map of the river those men were seeking.

Tom French,
Navan, Christmas 2015.

An Introduction

Paschal Marry

To an Irish person the word "Boyne" conjures up many different images in the mind. These images may be historical, cultural, or riparian. The image does not matter but you can be assured that the mere mention of the Boyne will provoke a relatively common picture overall. Personally, up until a bright frosty morning in January 2012 my images of the Boyne would, like so many more, fall into these categories. However, since that winter's morning the mention of the word Boyne now instantaneously forms an image of the Yellow River. The reason it does so is a story that forms an integral part of this wonderful book.

On meeting Tony Holten for the first time, many years ago, I knew immediately we would be friends. Little did we know that our friendship in the future would find us on back roads, byways, rivers, streams, canals and the odd bridge or two, for the sake of historical research. Additionally, we had no idea that I would also share with him the unimaginable road of grief and loss following the death of his beloved son Joe. Unlike the deliberation posed by Robert Frost, Tony had no choice but to walk "The Road Less Taken," and face what lay before him on each step of the way. This book is a testament to an enduring strength of character, commitment, hard work and dedication in the pursuit of historical accuracy even when one has to swim against the tide. In 2011, Tony told me of the conversation he had with a mutual friend of ours, Martin Curran of Meath River Rescue Service, about the Boyne and the lack of public knowledge of its unexplored aspects. Martin and Tony invited me to take a boat trip with them on the Boyne, from its most upriver navigable point to Trim. Without hesitation I agreed and on a lovely cold, healthy morning in January 2012 I met Tony, his wife Marie and brother in law John Bradley in Johnstown. We travelled to Clongall in John's van where Tony outlined his thoughts on the possibility of a book about the less-known surprises of the Boyne.

When we reached the farm of Brendan Lucey, who sadly passed away this year (May he rest in peace), we met members of the Meath River Rescue Service team. On our many miles together, Tony and I were very fortunate to meet and become good friends with some wonderful people (you will read about them later). People whose smile and handshake are connected directly to their heart, their welcome was (and is) warm and true without any ulterior motive. The Meath River Rescue Service fall within this category without question, it is difficult to express in words the admiration and respect Tony and I hold for these wonderful people. They put their lives on hold and at risk to ease the burden of their fellow man without a second thought. In our experience we are continually impressed with their professionalism, hard work and dedication.

On that January morning I was very aware that we were guests on this training run. To that end we tried to stay out of the way and do exactly as we were told. We crossed a number of Brendan Lucey's fields on foot to reach the boat slip, where we donned our PPEs and boarded the RIB after instructions on health and safety by the MRR Chairperson Christopher Rennnicks. Martin Curran was the cox and Martin White and Richard Harding were at the bow spotting, Tony and I sat mid ship. Christopher, Marie, John and Paddy Brady followed by road as the back-up team.

As the trip commenced I began to soak in the wonderful surroundings. The river was a little narrower than the Boyne at Trim but wider than the Nanny in Duleek. I was curious about one thing though, if we had planned to navigate the Boyne from its most upriver navigable point, why were we sailing east and not west? The river at this point was equally navigable east or west but I would let the question sit for a while.

As we headed for Trim the true beauty of the environs became apparent. We were surrounded by wildlife. Two beautiful swans glided heedlessly ahead of us, but, conscious we were catching up, they took to flight, first paddling furiously along the water, then rising gracefully with wings fully extended. Water hens darted to the undergrowth of the banks for cover. A low frosty mist hung just above the water, slow burning away and the animals in the riverside fields grazed in contentment with the warm sun on their backs.

Quite suddenly, Martin slowed the RIB and I became aware of a tributary flowing from the south to join the river. While one could not describe the tributary as a river, "stream" does not describe it adequately, as it is sized somewhere in between. Martin stopped the engine and we glided slowly to the confluence. To my amazement, Tony was telling the party we had reached the "BOYNE". The tributary was called the Little Boyne and the actual river we had been sailing was the Yellow River. To prove the ancient saying "Seeing is believing," as looking at the tributary at it widest, we had reached the most upriver navigable point of the Boyne – even the single manned Boyne Currach would struggle to progress upriver from here towards the source stream or streams.

Sitting in the boat at the confluence I considered the Yellow River, while I had read many books about the Boyne, none had made such a connection. Here in Clongall, this great river which transects the ancient midlands of Bregia is suddenly, in geographical terms no more. Rather than absorbing a minor river like the Little Boyne, it in fact is absorbed by the tributary. Somewhere in the annals of history, mythology was stronger and Bóinn the lady of the river proved more powerful, why is a curious and unanswerable question.

Then and there we realized it was time to write a book and inform the public about this and other curiosities and facts about this wonderful river and record the magnificent contribution of the Yellow River to the source and waters of the Boyne.

I would take a few more trips on boat and by land with Tony, to learn more and more as we travelled; however, not all research is glamorous.

About a year later on a damp February Sunday morning, an elderly couple on the way to mass approached Garr Bridge in County Kildare. The bridge was passable by one vehicle at the time and they approached very slowly – stopping to observe one man throwing sticks into the Garr River upstream of the bridge, whilst the other was spotting for the sticks emerging from beneath the bridge on the other side. The elderly couple moved on, no wiser as to what the two men were doing, but they hardly guessed it was scientific research in an effort to find one more source of the Great Boyne.

Ballymagarvey, Autumn 2016

Elements of a Masonry Bridge

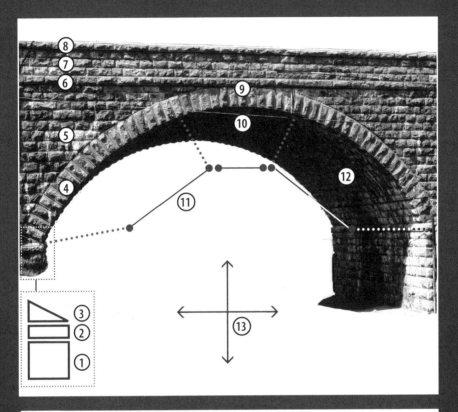

KEY

1 Vertical Riser
2 Springing Plane
3 Skewback
4 Ringstone/Voussoirs
5 Spandrel
6 String Course
7 Parapet Wall

8 Coping
9 Keystone
10 Barrel Vault
11 Segments
12 Soffit/Intrados
13 Free Waterway/Hydraulic Capacity

This arch forms part of Navan railway viaduct and is constructed from rusticated limestone blocks.

Photograph: Vincent Mulvaney. Treatment and Graphic: Stuart Coughlan

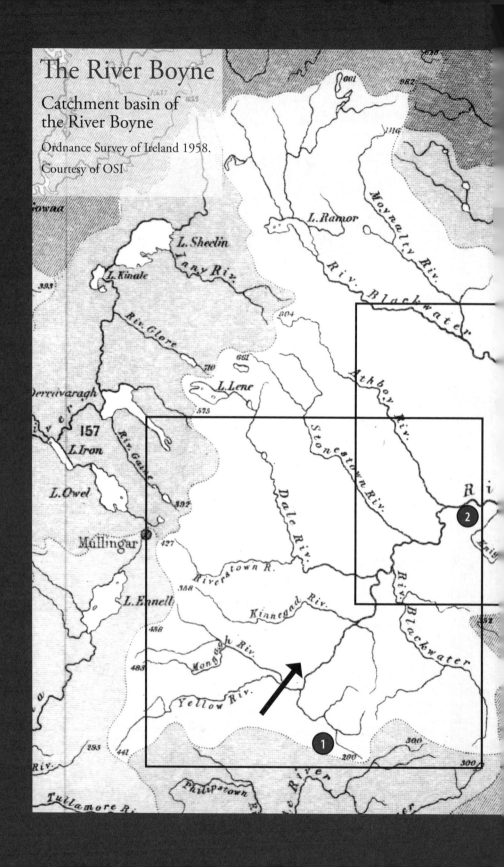

The River Boyne

Catchment basin of
the River Boyne

Ordnance Survey of Ireland 1958.

Courtesy of OSI

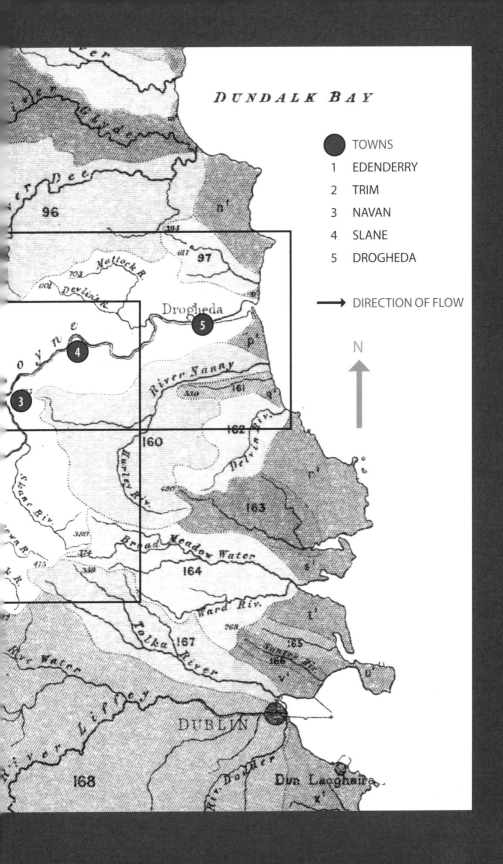

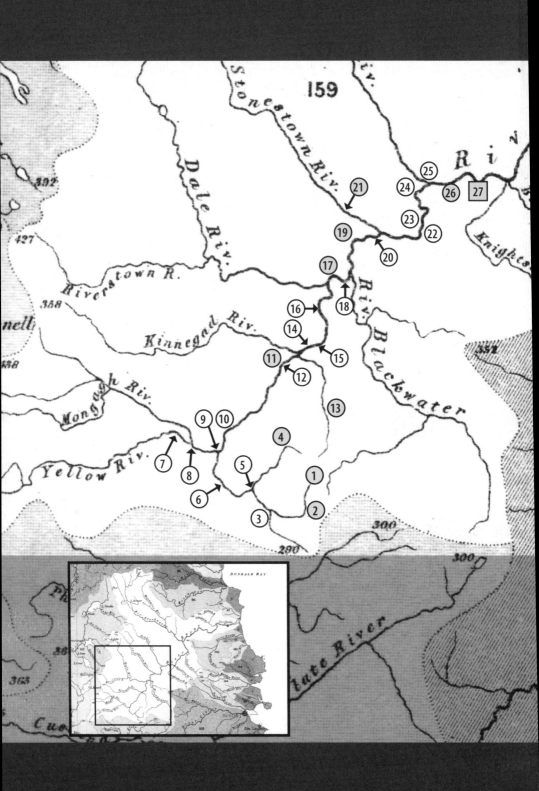

The Source of The River Boyne

Little Boyne from source to Yellow River
& Upper Reaches – Clongall to Trim

1	Carbury	15	Boyne Aqueduct
2	Newbury	16	Stonyford Bridge
3	Edenderry/Kishawanny	17	Donore
4	Garr River	18	Inchamore Bridge/Lionsden
5	Boyne Bridge	19	Portlester
6	Kinnafad Bridge	20	Scarriff Bridge
7	Sheep Bridge	21	Earls's Mill
8	Clongall Bridge	22	Boardsmill
9	Yellow River Confluence	23	Derrinydaly Bridge
10	Ballyboggan Bridge	24	Higginsbrook
11	Clonard	25	Kilnagross
12	Leinster Bridge	26	Newhaggard
13	River Glash	27	Trim
14	Ashfield Bridge		

◯ Bridge   ⬤ Region or landmark   ▢ Town

Boyne's winter landscape near Roristown.
Courtesy Tom French

The Middle Reaches

Trim to Slane

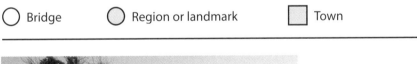

◯ Bridge   ◯ Region or landmark   ▢ Town

Goats on
Goat's/Lally's island.
Courtesy Tom French

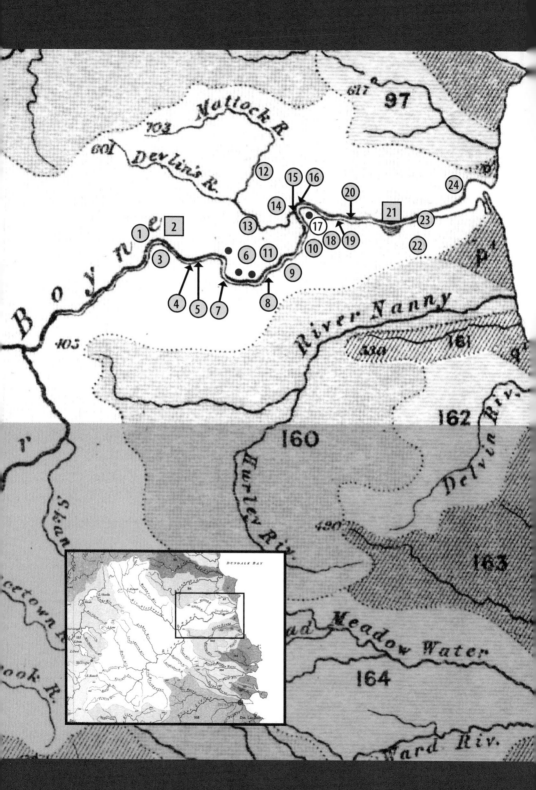

The Lower Reaches

Slane to the Irish Sea

1	Slane castle	13	Rossin
2	Slane village	14	Townley Hall
3	Fennor	15	Proudfootstown Ford
4	Rock Arch	16	The Curley Hole
5	Rosnaree Lock	17	Oldbridge House
6	Knowth, Newgrange, Dowth	18	Sheephouse
	● from west to east	19	The Sea Lock
7	Rosnaree Mill & Ford	20	The Mill Ford (Pass)
8	The Leck	21	Drogheda
9	Stalleen	22	Colpe
10	Farm	23	Mornington
11	Dowth Castle & Manor	24	Baltray
12	Old Mellifont Abbey		

◯ Bridge ⬤ Region or landmark ▢ Town

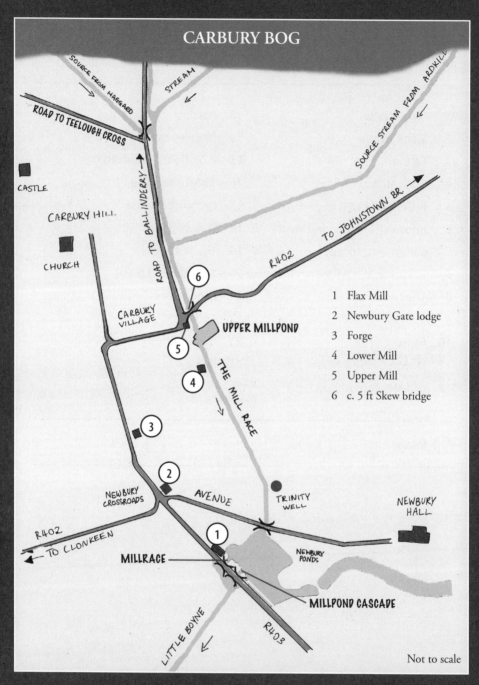

THE SOURCE OF THE RIVER BOYNE

Based on OS Map of 1837 – Drawn by Gemma Coughlan

1

The Source of The River Boyne

Divisions of the Boyne – Myth of Bóinn – Book of Ballymote & Sir William Wilde on the Legend – Summary of True Source – River Source in contemporary times – of Corn-Mills and Stone Bridges – Trinity Well & the Little Boyne – Newbury Mill Pond – Kilcooney River – Newbury Hall in 1854 – Carbury Flax Mill & Forge – Carbury Bog and feeder streams – The Haggard Stream, Sweep River & Fear English River – The MGWR & Carbury Railway Station – Haggard House – Carbury Corn Mill(s) – Carbury Hill, Castle and the Berminghams – The Pale – The Wexford Insurgent Column of '98 — Contemporary Landscape

The River Boyne, known as *an Bhóinn* in Irish (*Bóand* in Old Irish), rises near Carbury in Co. Kildare, bounds Kildare, Offaly and Meath, prior to passing solely through Meath for most of its winding journey to the Irish Sea beyond Drogheda.[1]

The river's source gave rise to several myths, and indeed caused some contention over the years; therefore, it is worth outlining the topography in both olden and contemporary times – an insight gained through considerable foot slogging and extensive cartographic study.

Before detailing the Boyne's true source, I will introduce the reader to the myth. This oftentimes repeated fable is the source of the name bestowed upon one of the most beautiful and mystical rivers in Europe.

27

In Irish tradition, the river is named after the Goddess Bóinne (Bóinn - Bóan). It is said that the earliest known use of this name was made by *Ptolemy, a* Greek/Egyptian geographer in the 2nd century AD, who named the river *Buvinda* on his map of the then known world. According to ancient scholars, this name derives from *Bou-vinda*, a compound word composed of *bó* (cow) and *vinda* denoting whiteness, brightness and wisdom, hence Boinn, the *Cow-White* (Goddess) or the *Bovine Wise* (Goddess).

Mythology places the source of many Irish rivers in holy wells or springs with magical, curative or purgative properties associated with their outflowing waters. The River Boyne is perhaps the finest example thereof, regarded throughout history as a magical and sacred river. Traditionally, the first legend of Bóinn comprises a poem, entitled *Bóand I*, composed by Chief Ollam of Ireland, *Cuan Ua Lochain* (Lothchain), whose birth date is uncertain, but his year of death recorded as 1024. A second poem, entitled *Bóand II*, appears in the ancient annals c.1000 AD; both poems relating slightly different versions of how the River Boyne came into being.

The legend of Bóinn or Bóan is preserved in verse and prose in several ancient manuscripts, including *The Great Book of Lecan* and *The Book of Ballymote* (c.1390); the following abridged (prose) version is quoted from Sir William Wilde's 1849 book entitled *The Beauties of the Boyne and the Blackwater*:

> The well of the Blessed Trinity, at which the Boyne rises, is at the foot of the hill of Carbury, anciently called Sidh Nechtain, the fairy hill of Nechtain. There was a celebrated poet and King of Leinster, called Nechtain, or Nuada-Neacht, in the first century, who had a secret well in his garden, one of the miraculous virtues of which was, that any who approached it, except the monarch and his cup-bearers, Flesg, Lesg, and Luam, was instantly deprived of sight, their eyes bursting, as the manuscripts described it. Female curiosity, however, was not to be disappointed, and Bóan, the queen, was determined to test the mystical powers of the waters; she, therefore, arrogantly, not only approached the well, and defied its powers to mar her beauty, but passed three times round it to the left, as was customary in several of the ancient incantations. Upon completion of the third round the charm was

broken, the spring rose, and three enormous waves burst over the hapless lady, mutilating her badly, and says the original, "breaking one of her eyes;" she then fled towards the sea, to hide her deformity, but the waters, now loosened from their source, still followed, till she reached the Inbher, or present mouth of the river. This Bóan was the mother of Aengus Mac An Daghda, a celebrated Tuatha De Danaan Chieftan. Dabella, the lapdog of Bóan, shared, it is said, the fate of its mistress, and was swept out on the rushing waves of the Boyne to the sea, where it was transformed into the rocks since called Da Billian.

Some legends tell of Bóan changing to a cluster of rocks close by the river mouth and others of her body being interred at the great tumulus of Newgrange. Another reputed older name for the Boyne is *Righ*,[2] supposedly bestowed on the river because the Goddess Bóan wore many golden bracelets and bangles upon her wrist or forearm, an appendage known in ancient times as *The Righ*. These ornaments, it is said, were used as gifts to her favourite bards and poets. The waters of the Boyne traditionally acquiring wisdom from hazelnuts falling in to Trinity Well from the legendary eight (or nine) hazel trees overhanging its verdant banks in times past.

Whatever the fabled queen's fate, research reveals the River Boyne, in fact, taking its rise from a bog within the Barony of Carbury, County Kildare, not from the waters of Trinity Well. The true source, as delineated on the 1837 and 1911 OS maps (traced on the contemporary local terrain), can be summarised thus: the Boyne rises from several capillaries issuing from Carbury Bog and forming two streams; these mingled north-east of Carbury Village to become a millstream powering Carbury Corn Mill(s).[3] The tailrace from the lowermost mill flowed southwards into Newbury Demesne to receive the outflowing waters from Trinity Well, and fall into a large mill pond or ornamental lake. This pond powered a flax mill, the tail race from which once comprised a stream considered as the Boyne's first flow. A secondary branch, formed by a small stream pouring over a cascade and flowing beneath the road; effectively became the pond's overflow when the mill sluices closed for operational reasons. Both streams mingled in a pool to the west of this road, then flowed south-westwards to develop as the River Boyne.

Excepting the disappearance of the mills[4] and many changes caused by

Left: Little Boyne cascading from Newbury Pond.
Right: First flow of Little Boyne beneath R403

'progress,' the above synopsis is equally valid nowadays at the river's source. The fledgling river now cascades from an overgrown pond located in woodlands within the grounds of Newberry (Newbury) Demesne, south-east of Carbury Village (circa 300 metres from Newbury Crossroads). Here the mighty Boyne is merely a one metre wide stream, flowing under a small stone bridge or gullet beneath the R403, then into another little pool alongside this road.

The pool outfalls as a small brook flowing south-westwards through the pasturelands of Ballyhagan, meandering onwards via Clonkeen and past Edenderry to its meeting with the Yellow River. The three counties of Kildare, Offaly and Meath host this confluence, which in my opinion constitutes the true starting point for one of the most scenic and historic rivers in these islands.[5] The river between Carbury and its meeting with the Yellow River is known locally (especially amongst fishermen) as 'the Little Boyne.'

Analysis of the OS maps indicates that Trinity Well is not the true source of the Boyne; a possibility noted briefly, but not explored by Wilde in the early part of his book.[6] The ancient myth being such a good story, to suggest otherwise and propose an alternative might be considered iconoclastic by entrenched historians. However, while Trinity Well outfalls to the Boyne near its source, it is but one of many streams contributing to the mighty river; flowing approximately seventy miles through the heart of Leinster to its debouchment into the Irish Sea between Mornington and Baltray.

The pond in Newbury Demesne is indicated on the 1837 map as a 'mill pond,' with its bed benchmarked at elevation 280ft above sea level. A head race taken from this pond powered a flax mill sited on the narrow neck of land separating the road and mill pond. The mill tailrace passed beneath the road via a stone arched bridge, of circa 1.5 metre span, located about 30 metres north-west of the contemporary stream outfalling from Newbury Pond; the amount of its flow once dependent on the sluice opening relevant to mill operations. The same map shows that in addition to serving as a mill pond, this body of water (circa 19.3 acres), formed an ornamental lake extending eastwards, to the front of Newbury Hall.

Trinity Well and Mill Stream in background
Courtesy Noel French

Griffith's records that Edward Wolstenholm leased Newbury Hall and 330 acre demesne from the Hon. George F. Colley at R.V. £340. The flax mill is shown as vacant, but held by E. Wolstenholm at R.V. £8. A forge sited nearby within the demesne, with house and ¼ acre garden, was leased by Thomas Mooney at R.V. £2-10s. This Smithy appears on the map about midway between Newbury Cross and Carbury Village.

The 1911 OS map shows the mill building in situ, but not recorded as a mill, and, while some ivy covered ruins are evident in the woods nowadays, these are likely to crumble away to nothing. A more tangible reminder of the ancient mill

From top:

Tailrace Br. at Carbury Flax Mill

Spur gearwheel in Flax Mill tailrace

Tank at site of Carbury Flax Mill

stands in the centre of the old millrace. When relieved of its green mantle, this unidentified object became a perfectly preserved spur gearwheel, part of the mill's machinery. The role of the two conduits feeding the Boyne are reversed; while a mere trickle passes along the old millrace, the former overflow is now the main outfall from the pond to the river, which flows onwards through the stone gullet beneath the R403.

The map shows that by 1911 the pond extension to the front of Newbury Hall was dried up and replaced by woodland, with a stream passing through its centre. The stream powered a hydraulic ram (hydrostat), before falling into the former mill pond, by then reduced to 4.9 acres.

This little brook is another contributor to the Boyne; sourced from a meshwork of capillaries located in marshy land to the north-east, not far distant from the source of the Kilcooney River.[7] It is noteworthy that although Trinity Well is benchmarked at elevation 289ft above sea level and marked as 'the source of the River Boyne' on the 1837 OS map, no such reference is included on the 1911 map.

Trinity Well is located within the demesne just north of Newbury Hall Avenue; which leads eastwards from the gate lodge opposite Newbury Crossroads and over a little bridge spanning a small stream. According to the 1837 OS map, this stream was a Mill Race, powering the above mentioned Carbury Corn Mills upstream near Carbury Village. The rill from the famous well falls into this Mill Race which in turn empties into Newbury Pond; the pond outflowing over a small cascade as the first flow of the Boyne. If the water from Trinity Well was/is the sole contributor to this Mill Race, the well could truly be described as the source of the River Boyne. As the Mill Race originates from several upstream sources in the townlands of Haggard, Knockcor, Mylerstown and Carbury to the north-east and north-west of Carbury Castle (Carbury Bog), it is more accurate; therefore, to describe it as the true source of the Boyne.

To translate the data gleaned from the maps onto the contemporary landscape at Carbury, we travel northwards from Trinity Well towards the Boyne's true source. The 1837 and 1911 maps indicate that the above Mill Race receives most of its waters from two streams. The first source (feeder) stream rises to the north-northeast of Carbury Castle from part of a raised bog known as Carbury Bog, near the convergance of Haggard, Carbury and Knockcor Townlands.[8]

Several more rills and capillaries drain the bog and marshlands hereabouts; to coalesce and form this one of the Boyne's two main source streams close by the south-western extremity of Carbury Bog. This stream now comprises a partially clogged drain flowing beneath the road to Ballinderry, south-east of the former railway station. The stream passes southwards alongside the Ballinderry road to a point just north of Carbury Village, where it joins another stream flowing from the north-east.

This is the second source (feeder of the Mill Race), which rises from a series of rills near the meeting point of Ardkill, Knockcor and Mylerstown Townlands, at the eastern extremity of Carbury Bog.[9] It flows south-westwards towards Carbury, skirting the south-eastern edge of the bog en route. From their confluence, the mingled sources flow as a single stream alongside the Ballinderry road towards Carbury.

Hereabouts, the most notable additional topographical feature on the 1911 map is the Midland Great Western Railway (MGWR) branch line. The line was opened in 1877 and ran from Nesbitt Junction, alongside the Royal Canal near Enfield in County Meath, to a terminus in Edenderry.[10] It traversed Carbury Bog from north-east to south-west, and bisected both the above streams feeding the Mill Race supplying Newbury Mill Pond. These streams are shown passing beneath the railway to continue on their previous courses and mingle as described near Carbury Village. Carbury Railway Station was sited to the south of the tracks, on the western fringe of the bog and close by the stream feeding the Mill Race. Although the branch line closed in 1963, its memory is retained by a bungalow bearing the name Station House.

Prior to the advent of the railway, the 1837 map indicates a large house, together with outbuildings and a 'pound,' located slightly north-west of the later station site and north of the Haggard Stream (directly across the road from Carbury Hill and Castle). This residence is marked Haggard on the earlier map; however, no trace of it appears on the 1911 map and it seems to have disappeared. A much larger residence and outbuildings are shown on the 1911 map; sited further to the north-west and also named Haggard, these latter buildings are still in situ.

Griffith's shows that the greater part of the 536 acre townland of Haggard, including the old house named Haggard and circa 263 acres, was leased from Viscount Harberton by Samuel Holt at R.V. £200. The incumbent Viscount Harberton in 1854 was John James Pomeroy (1790-1862).

The 1837 OS map indicates that following the confluence above the village, the stream flowed southwards beneath the Carbury to Johnstown Bridge road (now the R402). A corn mill is shown on the same map at the Ballinderry road junction east of Carbury Village. Continuing south-eastwards, the stream formed a mill pond of circa one acre, the bed of which is benchmarked at elevation 305ft above sea level on the same map. A headrace from this pond powered another corn mill further downstream; the tailrace from which is the first depiction of the stream feeding Newbury Pond as 'the Mill Race.'[11] This flows onwards through a spinney and past Trinity Well to empty into Newbury Mill Pond.

Griffith's lists one mill only on this location within Carbury Townland, a corn mill with house, offices and land totalling circa 46.26 acres occupied by William Murphy, leased from the Hon. George F. Colley at R.V. £70. It can be deduced from the above that the mill furthest upstream was likely of an older vintage and replaced later by the downstream mill; which is not shown on the 1911 map, and indeed, no traces of this mill are evident nowadays.[12]

Before departing Carbury to follow the Little Boyne's onward course, I will

Above:
Probable remains of upper corn-mill at Carbury Village (date 1776)

Left:
Bridge at Carbury Village carrying 'the Mill Race' source stream beneath the R402 upstream of Trinity Well.

mention Carbury Hill and its attendant castle. As the ancient history of this area is covered extensively in several other books, especially in Wilde's work of 1849, I give but a brief account here.

According to legend, the name Carbury derives from Cairbre, son of Niall of the Nine Hostages, whose descendants, the Cinel Cairbre or race of Cairbre, settled hereabouts. Carbury Hill was known previously as Sidh Nechtain or the Fairy-hill of Nechtain. This forms a prominent landmark, springing abruptly from the plains of Kildare and rising gradually north-westwards above the village to the ancient castle, whose ghostly silhouette provides a somewhat dramatic backdrop on the north-western horizon. Two pagan (Bronze Age) Forts or Barrows and a later Norman Motte adorn the hilltop, although not indicated on the 1837 OS map, they are shown on the latest Discovery Map which depicts the castle as a fortified house. The old maps show two disused quarries close by the castle, together with a ruined church and graveyard. Another burial ground named Templedooath is located further to the south-west; tradition holds that this was the site of Temple Doath, or Caille, the likely location of the older 6th century church of St. Muadnat.

Ancient Annals show Carbury as an important and strategic location long ago, and record many military engagements occurring in the immediate area of Carbury Hill: a combination of inter-tribal rivalry, and internecine warfare between Gaelic Chieftains and Norman invaders, resulting in much consequential slaughter.

The surrounding area comprised the furthest reaches of 'the Irish/English Pale,' a semi-fortified salient extending westward from Dublin encompassing much of the lands of Meath, Louth, Kildare and parts of several other Leinster counties. Following the Norman Invasion, much of The Pale was reputedly based upon the River Boyne, which explains the many castles, tower houses, and fortified keeps sited alongside its banks, especially near the bridges and fords. In later times; however, additional protection was provided by a deep double ditch. Specifications for the said ditch were included in an Act of Parliament, passed at the Parliament of Drogheda (Wilde on Carbury), held there in 1494.[13]

Tradition holds that the Norman Motte was constructed by Meiler FitzHenry, granted the lands around Carbury by Strongbow (Richard de Clare) following the Anglo Norman invasion in c.1170. The invaders typically building wooden castles or strongpoints atop raised earthworks, followed by construction of stone castles or tower houses nearby. The local townland called Mylerstown probably derives its name from the above Meiler FitzHenry.

Carbury Castle was built originally during the early days of the Norman Conquest, probably in the latter part of the 12th century and perhaps by Meiler FitzHenry. The castle was sacked and re-edified several times during the period between the coming of the Normans and the 1640s confederacy rebellion. Which explains why many of the surviving features, especially the chimney stacks (16-sided polygons), date from the mid-1500s; the older part to the north originates from the Early Norman Period circa 1180.

Carbury Castle from village aspect

In the 13th century, the Bermingham family (descendants of Pierce [Piers] de Bermingham) acquired the castle, which remained their ancestral home until reputedly taken for a time by the Native Irish Chieftains in the 15th century. In 1541, Sir William Bermingham was created Baron of Carbury. Upon the death of the younger Walter Bermingham in 1561, the castle passed to Sir Robert Preston (Chief Baron of the Exchequer), brother-in-law of Bermingham and ancestor of Lord Gormanstown. Sometime in the period 1562 to 1588, the Colley family (Cowley) obtained a 21 year lease on the property, which remained in their possession until the late 18th century.[14] During their tenure, the Colley's completed extensive alterations to the structure, including its conversion to a Tudor-style fortified house.

Anecdotes tell of Henry Colley's two daughters inheriting the property in the mid-18th century, and that one of these ladies (named Anne or Elizabeth), married a man named Glover and removed the roof from the castle before departing to London. The other daughter, named Mary, married Arthur Pomeroy (1723-1798) in 1747; this gentleman thereby acquiring some of

Carbury Castle from the bridge at Haggard Stream

the Colley lands in Carbury and becoming Baron Herberton of Carbury in 1783 and Viscount Herberton 1st in 1791. He did not take up residence at the supposedly roofless castle; however, but lived in Newbury Hall, designed by Nathaniel Clements in the Palladian-style and built within the newly developed demesne circa 1750.

At Carbury Hill we make our first encounter with 'the Wexford Insurgent Column' that, following the rebel's defeat at Vinnegar Hill, marched northwards through Offaly, Wicklow, Kildare and Meath in July 1798. More details of these Wexfordmen of '98 are included as we cross their line of march at Clonard, Navan, Beaupark and Slane.[15] The insurgents comprised a large body of approximately 2,000 fighting men and camp-followers which encamped on Carbury Hill during the night of July 11th 1798. During their stay in Carbury, they scavenged the area for food and arms and occupied Newbury Hall, whose owner, Viscount Harberton 2nd (Henry Pomeroy 1749-1829), was not in residence. I believe that a later claim for damages and theft was made by his Lordship's agent, Bryan Forde, in the amount of £68. The following list of goods, supposedly damaged or stolen during the raid, is quoted from the above book with the kind permission of the author:

5 new shirts at 12s. £9 – 9 squares of Muslin at 6s 6d. £2 18s 6d – 4
Lawn Hankerchiefs at 2s 2d. 8s 8d – A new Hat £1 2s 9d – A great coat
£1 15s – 2 cashmere vests £1 3s 1d – 1 pair of boots £1 9d – 4 pair cotton
stockings at 5s 5d. £1 1s 8d – 1 pair knee buckles 6s 6d – 2 suits new
clothes. £9 – 1 new saddle £1 5s 6d – 3 pair new shoes £1 2s 9d – Cash
by Sheerin an approver £1 14s 1½d – Silver watch with gold seals £9 13s
4½d – Mare broken down by the rebels and of no use to me £17 1s 3d .
. . £68 17s 11d. (sic)

In 2012 my wife Marie drove with me to Carbury in search of the Boyne's source. The month was November and the countryside covered in winter's russet hues. I find this season best suited for such ramblings; however, it has some drawbacks, as the landscape is less attractive at this time of year, with evening gloom falling much earlier. We found the Hill of Carbury and its castle without difficulty, but could find no trace of the Boyne or any sign pointing to its location. With the help of a young lady at 'the Castle Arms' pub, we proceeded back down the R403 to the lodge gate at Newbury Hall. Here, the gate was padlocked, so I risked walking upon the busy road (no footpath or hard-shoulder), and discovered the infant river hidden in the wildwood to the left of the road; not, I hasten to add, by means of any natural or man-made visual feature, but by the sound of its waters cascading from the pond.

Leaving Carbury in the gathering evening gloom, I looked upwards to the gaunt castle ruins silhouetted against the lowering sun. Then pondered over our little mystery tour of the day; wondering at the absence of a sign or plaque denoting this historic site, the source of Ireland's most mystical and historic river.

In 2012, the village of Carbury and its environs are undergoing great change due to realignment of the R402 (Edenderry to Enfield road). A new line of road is being cut near Newbury Demesne and past the site of Thomas Mooney's old forge, then over the former Mill Race to the north of Trinity Well. With many older place names omitted from the modern maps, one wonders what other landscape changes are imminent and how future generations will trace the streams and rills constituting the true source of the renowned River Boyne.

ENDNOTES

1 For convenience of narrative, the river is divided into five sections, as follows: *Source streams* and Newbury Pond – *The Little Boyne* from Carbury to the Yellow River – *The Upper Reaches* from Clongall to Trim – *The Middle Reaches* from Trim to Slane – *The Lower Reaches* from Slane to Mornington/Baltray.

2 Some traditions hold that this is the ancient name for the River Blackwater which coalesces with the Boyne at Navan.

3 The corn mills in Carbury are the first of over 130 watermills traced upon the River Boyne and its main tributaries; demonstrating the importance of these now lost heritage features to our forebears. The watermill furthest downstream was located on a small tributary river near Baltray in Co. Louth.

4 Wilde's book of 1849 describes the Boyne's sylvan beauty, ancient monuments, castles and country seats in great detail, but mentions of the river's other aspects, including its watermills, weirs and bridges are sparse indeed. A quite understandable omission, because features such as stone bridges, corn, tuck and flour mills were commonplace and almost unworthy of note then. Moreover, construction and widening of stone arched bridges, supported on wickerwork and other wooden forms, is now a dead art, but in the time of Sir William it was commonplace, providing income for many, as evidenced by Grand Jury records. Nowadays, the Boyne's landscape having changed utterly, such features and methodology, once the status quo, are largely of historic note only and rapidly becoming part of our 'lost history.' With a few notable exceptions, the watermills have vanished from the riverscape and, excepting the OS maps and Griffith's Valuation, scarcely any details recorded for posterity; the few remaining in ruins and crumbling into oblivion. Yet these were intrinsic to our history, arguably, equally important as the more recorded historical sites, an essential part of our culture. In addition to converting agricultural output to foodstuffs and clothing, our mills provided places of work and social interaction, scarce facilities indeed long ago, especially in rural areas.

5 See fuller description of this confluence in Chapter 3.

6 While most of the capillaries and feeder streams appear on the 1837 OS map, yet the direction-of-flow is not shown. Hence, to make an accurate assessment of the various sources, it is necessary to compare them with the 1911 map which includes directional arrows.

7 The Kilcooney River rises near the old north-eastern boundary of Newbury Demesne, close by the ruined castle and church in Ardkill Townland. This river flows north-eastwards, to link with the Fear English River and the Sweep River, both rising near Carbury. The mingled rivers continuing onwards to join the Kildare Blackwater at Johnstown Bridge, which has a confluence with the Boyne at Inchamore Bridge some distance above Trim.

8 Nowadays Carbury Bog (NHA 0013888) is subject to a preservation order contained in Statutory Instrument (S.I.) No. 585 of 2005. The area hosts a watershed, or water parting, as various other rivers flow in different directions from here, one of which, the Haggard Stream, passes beneath the byroad leading to Teelough Crossroads, to meander south-westwards and mingle with the Little Boyne near River Bridge at Clonkeen.

9 Yet another watershed (or parting) occurs here, the bog and marshlands are drained by at least three rivers flowing in different directions from a common source area. The Sweep River rises here, just to the south-west of Mylerstown Graveyard and castle ruins; then flows south-east to coalesce with the Fear English River, which, as described, flows onwards to the Kildare Blackwater and then to the Boyne near Inchamore Bridge. The Sweep River may derive its title from Carbury Sweep, which name is indicated on both OS maps at a nearby crossroads. The place name would appear to be almost defunct as it is not shown on the latest Discovery Map. Or perhaps the name Carbury Sweep originates from the river's name. The 1911 OS map depicts a small but very interesting and unnamed stream flowing from the same area north-eastwards through Calfstown to Ballinderry. This stream (described in Chapter Three) becomes a millrace which powered Ballyonan Corn Mill before coalescing with the Glash River that falls into the Boyne just downstream of Leinster Bridge.

10 Construction of this railway had a major impact on the drainage of Carbury Bog, as indicated by the differing capilliary layout on the 1837 and 1911 maps.

11 'The Mill Race' dropped about 25ft, between the bed of the upper mill pond in Carbury Townland and Newbury Mill Pond; receiving the water from Trinity Well en route.

12 To the east of Carbury Village (opposite a contemporary house named The Croft) the bridge carrying the R402 across the Mill Race is circa 5ft span, slightly skewed to the road and with a segmental stone arched profile. The stream was cleared during construction work on the Carbury Bypass, so this source of the Boyne is well defined at some considerable distance above Newbury Pond, and flowing strongly towards Trinity Well further downstream. A nearby stone building standing at the Ballinderry road junction may indeed be part of the older mill shown on the 1837 map. While a plaque-stone indicates a date of 1776, the remainder of the engraving is illegible. This structure is of two periods, as evidenced by its stone walls and matches the outline on the 1911 map.

13 See The Irish Pale in historical notes at back of book.

14 Legend says that a branch of the said Colley family adopted the name Wellesley (Duke of Wellington) to inherit the great estate at Daingean (Dangan) near Summerhill in County Meath.

15 The story of these brave men and their eventual fate is recorded in Eamon Doyle's well researched and most informative book, entitled *March Into Meath* (*in the footsteps of 1798*).

2

The Little Boyne
Carbury to the Yellow River

Following the unnavigable stream – Capillaries & spring wells – Ballyhagan – The Haggard Stream – Clayton Cottage & River Bridge – Clonkeen Corn Mill & old schoolhouses – The O.P.W. & Drainage Districts – old river course – Offaly Boundary – Kishawanny, its bridges & derivation of the name – Clarke's Well & Br. – Conneyburrow – Eadon Doire, 'the Brow of the Oak Wood' – Blundell's Castle & some of its history – the Colley connection – Marquis of Downshire – Downshire memorial & Castro Petre Church – Monasteroris – St. Francis Street & Downshire cottages – Edenderry & the Great Hunger – Canal Harbour & Downshire Br. – The 'Alesbury Car' & family connection with Navan – Blundell's Silver/Lead mine – Boyne Br. – Clonmeen & Tobercro – Carrick Church & castle – Carrick Hill, quarry & The Witch's Stone – The Treacherous Baron – The two Garr Rivers & bridges – Kilmore Mill – Monasteroris Monastery/Friary, Church, Corn Mill & Windmill – Kinnafad Castle & bridge – Aughramona & Roosk Togher – old road & ford – Foot Stick Ford – Grange Castle – last stretch to Yellow River.

The Boyne commences its long, winding journey to the sea by cascading from Newbury Pond, passing beneath the R403 and into a shallow pool by the roadside. The pool's outfall forms a small stream known as the Little Boyne, which flows through the flat, marshy terrain; on its way receiving tribute from innumerable other brooks, streams and rills emanating from many bogs, springs and wells. These streamlets swell the river gradually until it mingles with the much larger Yellow River at the conjunction of counties Meath, Kildare and Offaly, this confluence marking the birthplace of the Boyne proper.

Wilde mentions that in 1849 the Boyne was unnavigable for even a small row-boat from the source to Clonard. Most of the Little Boyne is unnavigable for boats larger than a one-person canoe nowadays, so the reader cannot traverse its narrow and much overgrown reaches to view the landscape from the river aspect. I will; however, describe the terrain as seen from its marshy banks, supported by data gleaned from various maps.

The myriad of small, unnamed tributaries cannot be covered in this work; however, included are some of the more noted streams and wells forming the greater complex of capillaries supplying the mighty river from source to sea.

The following wells are denoted on the OS maps alongside the short reach between Ballyhagan and Edenderry: providing an insight to the proliferation of springs dotted alongside the riverbanks and their importance to the populace long ago before introduction of rural water supplies.

Molly's Well	Carbury Townland
Black Well	To the rear of Black Well Cottage
Clayton's Well	Clayton Cottage now Clayton House
Haughton's Well	Near Clonkeen Cross Roads
Schoolmaster's Well	At Clonkeen old school, 1837 map
Moore Well	Opposite Riverstown House
Coffey's Well	Near Clonkeen Mill
Pond Well	At the entrance to Clonkeen Mill
John's Well	Kishawanny-Upper
Clarke's Well	Near Kishawanny Br.

All but one of these wells rise on the north or Kildare side of the river and many were located on, or close by properties occupied by persons or families bearing the well's name.[1]

Downstream from Newbury, the infant river flows through Ballyhagan, a townland of c.1,115 acres extending north to south from the Edenderry to Carbury road (R402) to the Grand Canal; and from Newbury Demesne westward to Clonkeen Townland. A considerable portion of this acreage comprised lands attached to Ballyhagan House; recorded by Griffith's as circa 466 acres, leased from the Rep. of Rev. Chas. Palmer by William Foote at a rateable valuation of £466.

The River Br. Clonkeen

The old maps show the river passing through bottomlands and beneath two small bridges carrying avenues to Ballyhagan House; then flowing over a dam and ford, westwards to Clonkeen. The Boyne's first significant tributary, 'the Haggard Stream,' flows from the north-east and forms the mereing with Clonkeen Townland, before falling into the river south-east of Clayton Cottage (now Clayton House). As noted in Chapter One, this stream rises on the western fringe of Carbury Bog, close by one of the Boyne's two main source streams. Clayton Cottage and land was occupied in 1854 by Thomas Tyrell at R.V. £51.

A short distance downstream, another tributary mingles with the Little Boyne from the south-east; this stream has two main sources, one an overflow from the Grand Canal at Curve Bridge (OS Benchmark at elevation 263.2ft above sea level). The other originates in a meshwork of streams draining the southern sectors of Clonkeen and Ballyhagan townlands.

Passing to the north of Riverstown House and following the river westwards, we come to the byroad linking the R402 at Clonkeen Cross Roads to the R403 about midway between Carbury Village and Derrinturn. This road crosses the Boyne (c. 6ft wide at this location) on a bridge named River Bridge, the first 'proper' bridge carrying a public road across the Little Boyne, as the other upstream structures are either private crossings or what were known in times past as 'gullets.'

The narrow byroad has traces of deep ditches on both sides, and probably dates back to at least the 1700s. The 1837 OS map indicates the parapet walls aligned with the hedgerows and a wider structure built askew to the river. The 1911 map depicts a much narrower bridge, built askew to the road and river but with the parapets spaced at road width. This profile matches the contemporary concrete structure, a probable replacement for an earlier stone arched bridge. If this is the same bridge depicted on the 1911 map, the above data suggests it may have been built prior to 1910. Although use of modern concrete (Portland Cement) can be traced to c.1850, on bridge foundations on the River Glyde in County Louth, this bridge was probably built at the turn of the century.

Both the 1837 and 1911 OS maps show a mill pond downstream, with a corn mill sited at its western end. The mill was located astride a millrace, with the Boyne flowing past as a separate stream. The earlier map shows the pond extending from the bridge to the mill and occupying an area of about two acres; while the later map indicates a much smaller pond covering only 0.611 of an acre.

Griffith's shows Clonkeen Corn-Mill occupied by Francis Rourke in 1854, who leased two properties from the Hon. George F. Colley: the first consisting of house, offices, corn mill and circa 27 acres; the second a Herd's house and c.16 acres, with the combined R.V. £36-15s. The low valuation may indicate that the mill was not in operation at the time.

The site adjacent to the old mill is occupied by a farmhouse (named Mill House) and attendant farmyard and is accessed via the former mill lane. The 1837 OS map indicates that the entrance to the mill was once part of a roadway running south-westwards and on past a large country house, now named Clonkeen House. To the south-west of the farmhouse, the road turned towards the south to disappear in the marshy lands close by the Grand Canal. Though the older road (or lane) now terminates at Clonkeen House, its outlines are etched on the contemporary landscape and can be viewed through satellite imagery.

The Author at 'the Little Boyne' beside Clonkeen Mill

In April 2013, Paschal Marry drove with me through this once pastoral scene to Clonkeen, which name possibly derives from the Gaelic 'Cluan Ceann' or Head of the Enclosed Meadow. Passing through a place, known locally as 'the High Road Gap,' and turning down the byroad towards the Boyne, we observed the many changes to the landscape caused by progress (most especially by realignment work on the R402) and reflected on the meaning of this word. Following an examination of River Bridge, we wheeled into the laneway leading to the former mill, and with kind permission of its present occupiers, Mr and Mrs Elliot, inspected the remnants of the old building.[2]

The ivy clad and roofless ruins of Clonkeen Mill stand upon the banks of the Little Boyne, occupying the footprint depicted on the old maps. The longitudinal axis of the rectangular building is at right angles to the former millrace, now mostly filled in but traceable by a deep cutting to the west. Though pierced in places by ragged openings, the circa 60ft by 25ft two storeyed structure seems sound enough. No trace of the upper floor remains and only the shell of the stone building stands on the riverbank as a reminder of its past usage.

An empty oblong aperture at low level on the millrace gable end indicates where the waterwheel shaft once spun in its wooden bearing; to rotate the long gone pit-wheel and attendant gearing, indeed, the hollow beneath the shaft entry is still obvious to the knowing eye. From the mill pond's layout, the tailrace and low level of the pit-wheel, together with the fall in the river (circa 9ft across the waterwheel as per OS Benchmarks), I would hazard a guess that the mill was powered by a breast-shot waterwheel, probably driving at least two sets of 4.5ft diameter grindstones. As no record of a kiln seems to exist, it is likely that the mill produced grist and oaten meal only, and not flour.

Standing within the silent building, I could hear the ripple and gurgling of the dark, boggy waters flowing onwards to form the most renowned and historic river in these islands. I wondered if the millers of old could hear the thumping, splashing waterwheel above the whirring gearwheels and rumbling grindstones; sounds unlikely to be heard again at Clonkeen Corn Mill.

Before our departure, the Elliots told us of an inscription above the mill's entry portal – where, following the removal of some clinging ivy, we found the date 1773 engraved on the arched door lintel keystone. An indicator that

Left: Ruins of Clonkeen Corn Mill. Right: Date 1773 on door lintel of Clonkeen Mill.

the mill probably dates from at least then, or might indeed be even older. According to Mrs Elliot, traces of the mill pond and sluices were evident when she came to live at the Mill House about fifty years earlier. She spoke also of an application made recently to the relevant authorities for funds to assist in restoration of the old mill, but none were forthcoming.

Departing Clonkeen Mill, I was saddened that such an ancient mill should be left to crumble into oblivion; and wondered who devised heritage priorities, as this is the only watermill still standing on the banks of the Little Boyne, the likes of which will never be seen again.[3]

The 1837 OS map provides some interesting data concerning the fall in the river between Newbury and an OS Benchmark just downstream of Clonkeen Mill. The pond bed at Newbury is benchmarked at 280ft above sea level, the riverbed at elevation 242ft upstream of River Bridge and at 233ft elevation circa 120 yards downstream of the mill. This represents a fall of about 9ft across the millwheel and a total drop of 47ft over the relatively short distance; a rather large fall for a river flowing through the 'flat' plains of Kildare.

On the 1837 OS map, two schools are shown in Clonkeen close by the crossroads, one sited between the cross and River Bridge, the other alongside the road to Edenderry (R402). The 1911 map; however, indicates the latter schoolhouse only, perhaps in use as a private house. Nowadays the building is modernised and known as Clonkeen Lodge, which stands opposite Edenderry Rugby Football Club. The later map does not show a building on the location of the older schoolhouse near the bridge; and where the earlier map depicts 'the Schoolmaster's Well,' an unnamed spring is indicated close by on the later map. The site of the well and schoolhouse is now occupied by a plantation, with the former Moore Well located in the middle of an open field to the west. The 1850s valuation records the newer school occupied by 'the Church Educational Society'[4] at R.V. £8-5s. and exempt from rates.

Downstream of Clonkeen Mill, the various drainage schemes altered the course of the Little Boyne completely. The OS maps reveal the many man-made alterations to the river's course between Clonkeen and Clongall/Grange during the period 1834 to 1911. The 1837 map indicates the original line of the river pre-drainage; with the 1852 revised map (Griffith's) delineating the river's original winding course, together with extra coloured-in markings representing the intended newer boundary lines for townlands and property mereings. These were formed later upon the topography by various course alterations effected during the drainage schemes.

The 1911 map indicates that the river followed the outline markings shown on the earlier map of 1852. In essence, the drainage works during the interim period (1840s to c.1908) effectively removed many of the shorter bends and twists, formed naturally over millennia. These were replaced by lengthier, man-made sweeping curves, thus enabling the river to flow more swiftly and alleviate the all pervasive seasonal flooding of the bottomlands.

The Commissioners for Public Works, known variously as the Board of Works and the Office of Public Works or OPW (and several less complimentary titles in the vernacular), was set up originally on October 15th 1831. It was formed by merging the Office of the Surveyor General of Ireland, the Barracks Board and the Navigation Board. Drainage of river basins and catchments throughout Ireland came under its remit; therefore, several Acts of Parliament were enacted to enable the various schemes planned on a countrywide basis, including the Acts of 1842, 1863 and 1866. Further legislation was enacted under the remit of the Irish Free State in 1924. The acts set up 115 Districts under the code of 1842 and a further 63 under the code of 1863, bringing the total number of Drainage Districts to 178. The various districts were put in the charge of local Drainage Boards, controlled and administered by Trustees.

This system became a very cumbersome and inefficient means of executing the myriad of proposed drainage schemes in those times, as demonstrated by the poor results obtained over succeeding years. In this context, the report of the 1938-1940 Drainage Commission is most informative in its overview of the country as a whole, and makes several references to the Boyne Catchment schemes of earlier years. The overall report reflects on past failures and places some responsibility for these upon inter alia the following causes (paraphrased for clarity):

> Failure of the District Boards, some of which had not convened for years – Failure of various District Boards to carry out maintenance following drainage schemes – Failure of communication between interacting districts – Piecemeal and haphazard execution of works – Failure to collect a drainage rate from the beneficiaries of the various schemes – The system whereby just six complainants or occupiers within a district could activate a drainage scheme without consideration of neighbouring districts' requirements – The use of the various drainage projects as employment schemes, leading to poor planning and even poorer execution – and ultimately, failure of the County Councils to carry out essential maintenance works, when these public bodies replaced the Grand Jury System in 1899.

A seemingly endless list of failures and mismanagement, not improved by the country's so-called independence from the Mother Parliament during our Dominion status, as evidenced by the following extract, which includes the period 1924 to 1948:

> We have come to the conclusion that these complaints are not entirely without justification. The principle of "assent" or "dissent", which had been an integral part of the Codes of 1842 and 1863, was deliberately excluded from the Maintenance Acts of 1866 and 1924. No consultations took place with occupiers since they had no power to object to proposed works. Inspections of Districts and arrangements and plans for the executions of works were hurried. Engineers and gangers, with practical experience of drainage works, were scarce, as little drainage work had been done for many preceding years. The scope of the operations was limited. No power existed to do work outside a

Drainage District, and in many cases, work such as the removal of rock shoals below the outfall of a District was necessary for satisfactory results. In many Districts it was found that the original works done under the Codes of 1842 or 1863 had been under-designed or that the works had not been fully carried out. In such circumstances, restoration while effecting much improvement could not eliminate flooding. Occupiers expected better results than it was possible to produce. In some Districts consideration of costs limited the extent of the work with the result that only partial restoration was effected. Charges were, however, spread over the entire Drainage District and occupiers in areas where no work was done naturally protested when called upon to contribute.

Further references to the various Boyne Drainage Schemes are made as we encounter their results further downstream, including the disastrous scheme commencing at Bellinter Bridge in 1968, and ruining the renowned Boyne Water as a salmon and trout river for close to half a century. The various drainage works resulted in the OS 1837 riverbed Benchmarks becoming irrelevant from Clonkeen to Navan, due to the OPW's attempts to canalise the river.

The short reach from north of Clonkeen House to where the river forms the mereing between Kildare and Offaly, was straightened after the 1852 OS map revision; evident from this map, which shows the old, and very tortuous course of the river from Clonkeen to the Offaly mereing. The Little Boyne forms the boundary between the two counties from the convergence of Edenderry, Kishawanny-Upper and Clonkeen Townlands upon its banks, to its confluence with the Yellow River. N.B., a minor tributary enters the Little Boyne at this junction just upstream of Edenderry – this stream is sourced south of the Grand Canal and passes beneath the waterway via a conduit named Little Tunnel.

Following the river downstream, we come to Kishawanny Bridge, located east of Edenderry. In times past, a stone arched bridge carried the Edenderry to Carbury road across the river on to a 'Y' junction upon the north-eastern riverbank; the left fork taking a small country road through Oldcourt Townland, while the right branch took the main road onwards to Carbury.

Kishawanny old Bridge from upstream

Wilde noted two bridges here in 1848; research shows that one spanned the older course and the other a newer line of river slightly to the west, suggesting drainage work being in progress at the time. In 1877 the MGWR branch line from Nesbitt Junction to the nearby terminus at Edenderry was carried across the Boyne on a metal girder bridge, located just upstream from the road bridge. To the north-east of the river, the railway line passed beneath the Carbury road at a crossing known as Clarke's Bridge. This name perhaps derived from a man named Thomas Clarke (or his family), who, according to Griffith's, had a property comprising house, offices and land totalling circa 96 acres leased from the Hon. George F. Colley at R.V. £61. The OS maps show a spring well, named Clarke's Well, sited alongside the same road close by the later location of the railway bridge (a road-overbridge).

Kishawanny (Kishavanna) is a place name possibly deriving from this long established crossing place of the River Boyne. As the letters 'K' and 'W' are not part of Gaelic, but used mostly in 'loan-words,' it is probable that the name, as spelled nowadays, is a corruption of similar-sounding words. The name Kish or Kesh is used in various places throughout Ireland to denote river crossings or small bridges; and indeed forms part of several place names, including Keshcarrigan on the Erne Navigation and Longkesh in Northern Ireland.

Kish is a name for a wickerwork basket once used as a measure for the sale of peat or turf, and indeed for transporting same. Used originally without the 'K' and spelled Ceis or Ces, it likely gave rise to the word Cesdroichet, a name for the wickerwork bridges of ancient Ireland. It was a term used also to describe wooden causeways and corduroy track-ways (or Paces) taking the older roads across boggy terrain. I suggest; therefore, that Kishawanny was once known as Ceis/Kesh an Abhainn and changed phonetically to its present form through local usage. Another possible derivation of the name Ceis/Kesh is from Clash, a name supposedly used to describe river crossings in some places (Kerry) during older times.

Kishawanny is a much changed location from when Wilde crossed its two Boyne bridges in 1848. In 2012, when my wife Marie drove with me along the R402 from Carbury, we crossed the Boyne unawares, so continued on through Conneyburrow to Edenderry. But when retracing the route, Marie's keen eye noted a housing estate named 'the Boyne Meadows,' so we knew our objective was close by. Then we spotted the old stone arched bridge, now sited on a closed off, pedestrianized road section forming the centrepiece of a reasonably well-tended roadside park. The aesthetics are spoiled by the veritable forest of signposts planted among its natural shrubbery, and hiding the Boyne from motorists passing by.

No trace exists of the earlier bridge, mentioned by Wilde in 1849, and perhaps demolished soon thereafter. I can find no written record of this bridge, a possible survivor from at least the early 18th century; as Moll's 1714 map depicts a bridge spanning the Boyne at Kishawanny, which may have dated from medieval times. Offaly County Council has surveyed all the bridges throughout the county, and assigned each a unique number. The number for Kishawanny old bridge is **OFIAR-12-004** – and the description, dated 2004, reads:

> Masonry arch bridge formerly carried Edenderry-Johnstown Bridge road over River Boyne; now restricted to pedestrian traffic. Of random rubble construction throughout. Abutment footings underpinned with concrete. Arch is of segmental profile, spans 5.2m and has dressed limestone voussoirs. Dressed string course over crown on both faces. The parapets are 6.63m apart and have dressed stone coping. Ivy overgrowth.

Appraisal:

A good example of a mid 19th century road bridge and an interesting contrast with the modern concrete bridge which now by passes it. Architectural character somewhat marred by heavy underpinning. Historical interest due to association with Board of Works and Boyne drainage scheme. Of local heritage merit. (sic)

The interesting contrast, mentioned above, is indeed striking, as the new bridge of 2003 could be described as a corrugated concrete pipe (Armco), with little aesthetic appeal in its structure; whereas the old 'retired' stone arched bridge is a testimony to the skilled stonemasons and other craftsmen of the period. The railway bridges of Kishawanny have disappeared from the landscape, together with most traces of the railway (a stark reminder of former official Myopia).

Edenderry has not expanded eastwards to include the Boyne's riverbank; therefore, it cannot be described truly as one of the Boyne's riparian towns. Nonetheless, it is well worth a visit as the charming old market town is the first major centre of population we encounter on our downriver journey, following the infant river's winding course.

The name Edenderry derives from the Gaelic Eadan Doire, which translates to 'the height or brow of the oak wood,' a name probably deriving from a hill to the south of the old town. Like Carbury Hill, though not achieving the same eminence, this hill rises rather abruptly from the surrounding plains of Kildare and Offaly, with the former market town once framing it to the north and north-west only, but now almost encircling it completely.

About midway between Kishawanny Bridge and the town, the 1837 OS map indicates a small village named Conneyburrow. A common place name in old Ireland, originating from areas noted for a profusion of rabbit burrows (warrens), when the creatures were numerous prior to their near extermination by Myxamotosis (Mixi) in the 1950s. At the village, another over-bridge, named Conneyburrow Bridge (long since demolished), carried a side road southwards across the railway, which road led eventually to the Blundell Aqueduct on the Grand Canal.

From medieval days the ancient castle, now known as Blundells' Castle, stood atop the little hill, commanding both landscape and town. Although its ruins remain, the castle no longer dominates its surroundings, the crumbling stonework a ghostly reminder of when its Anglo Norman occupants controlled all they surveyed. Similar to Carbury Castle, Edenderry Castle is sited at the outer fringe of The Pale and had a variety of owners throughout its turbulent history. The structure, a three storey tower house, built, it is said by the De Berminghams about the mid-15th century, was held by Nicholas Herbert in 1556. He was granted the lands of Monasteroris and Edenderry by Elizabeth I, following dissolution of the monastery by Henry Vlll c.1539. The castle came into the possession of the Colley family in the 1560s; at which juncture Edenderry became known as Coolestown or Colleystown.

In 1599, during the Nine Years War, Sir George Colley supposedly defended the castle against the marauding O'Neill Clan. Following the defeat at Oldbridge in 1690, remnants of the Jacobite Army reputedly attacked the stronghold in May 1691, which engagement wrecked the castle. The Colley estates in Edenderry passed to the Blundell dynasty with the marriage of Sarah Colley to George Blundell in 1642, and remained in their possession until 1786, when the Blundell heiress, Mary Sandys, married Arthur Hill, 2nd Marquis of Downshire.

All that remains of the old castle are parts of the east and south walls, together with much folklore about its chequered history; including yarns of subterranean tunnels connecting the castle to Carbury Castle, and the usual tales of intrigue associated with such ancient ruins.

Nowadays the park is adorned by at least three mementos from the past and a modern water tower. At the head of the avenue leading off J.K.L. St (initials supposedly standing for James, Kildare & Leiglin), stands the Downshire Memorial, a full sized statue of Arthur Hill (1778-1845), 3rd Marquess of Downshire; the work of the well-known sculptor Joseph Robinson Kirk in 1846.

On a higher eminence is the unusually named Castro Petre Church, the C. of I. parish church for Monasteroris Parish in which the town of Edenderry is located. This church was built and first consecrated in 1778 to replace a medieval church at the nearby monastery or friary of Monasteroris; which name, it is said, translates to Monastery of the son of Piers. Tradition holds that the monastery was built circa 1260, and that the older church may have dated from c.1290, with the name Castro Petre bestowed upon it around that time. The ruined castle of the Blundell's stands on the park's south-western sector, with the modern water tower providing a contrast further to the east.

In 1849, Wilde referred to a row of cottages on the outskirts of Edenderry:

> As we leave the town, on the road to Monasteroris, the next point of attraction, we pass through a suburb of small cottages, with well tended gardens in front of them, characterised by a degree of care, neatness, cleanliness, and, above all, by an appearance of industry and thrift quite unusual in Ireland. These cottages are given by the Marquis of Downshire to industrious tradesmen and labourers at one shilling a year rent. The general appearance of comfort in this district at once bespeaks the encouraging landlord and the admirable care of the resident agent.

In 2012, I passed along the same road, now named St. Francis Street, and noted that most of the neat cottages were replaced by modern dwellings. Several single storeyed older houses; however, still stand well back from the roadside, survivors perhaps of the forty or more cottages which so impressed Wilde in the 1840s.

Arthur Hill, 2nd Marquess of Downshire, renowned as a reforming landlord and noted anti-Unionist, had a reputation for being mindful of his responsibilities to his tenants. Considering that Sir William passed through the area in the midst of the famine, the above excerpt might suggest the area around Edenderry escaped much of the horrors of 'the Great Hunger,' a famine which ravaged the country from c.1846 to 1850. Nevertheless, a footnote elsewhere in the book mentions Edenderry Workhouse hosting 1,800 paupers (Poor Law recipients). Although Wilde expressed surprise that misery and starvation could exist in such "a fair and fertile land," he avoided a detailed description of the widespread starvation and consequent disease decimating the peasantry at the time.

On the western side of the hill, opposite St Francis Street, is the canal harbour, located at the end of the spur from the Grand Canal. It is said that in earlier times, the Blundell family opposed construction of the Grand Canal to Edenderry; but following his marriage to the Blundell heiress, Mary Sandys, Arthur Hill supported the project and paid its full cost of £692.

The Grand Canal Basin at Edenderry

The one mile long spur to Edenderry was started in 1797 and completed in 1802; it ran at the same level as the main canal i.e. no lifting lock was required, but a beautiful humped back horse-bridge (Downshire Bridge – **OFIAR-013-018**), took the Grand Canal towpath across the new spur, as it does nowadays.

The canal extension became a great boon to the locality, especially to the woollen industry, started in the early 1700s by some Quaker families. This industry is perhaps the source for the title of a little stream named Weaver's Drain, indicated on the Discovery Series Map flowing from the town to the Boyne. Edenderry has an interesting industrial connection with the town of Navan. In 1919, Daniel Alesbury who operated a woodworking business in Edenderry, took over Goodearl's furniture factory, formerly Athlumney Flour and Flax Mill, alongside the Boyne Navigation in Navan. This became known as Alesburys' Saw Mill, the precursor of Navan's famed furniture industry. As a historic footnote, at Edenderry in 1907, the Alesbury family built the first motor car manufactured in Ireland, which was known as 'the Alesbury.'

Before departing Edenderry I will refer briefly to the silver mine once operating there; and indeed shown on the 1837 OS map located close by the later site of the railway terminus. On September 28th 2011, a large hole appeared in a footpath leading across the park, near Castro Petre Church; which event turned public attention to Blundell's long gone silver mine, where miners toiled beneath Edenderry Hill in search of the elusive precious metal.

In response to the pathway's collapse in 2011, Offaly County Council initiated an investigation of the old mine workings at Edenderry. The report based on the findings from this survey included a detailed assessment of the area's geology, including the Hill of Edenderry, of which the following is a short excerpt:

> The hill is almost circular, about 500m across and rises some 20m above the surrounding landscape. The form and nature of the hill would suggest that it is an eroded Waulsortian mudbank. The "One Inch" geological map from the mid-C19th (Fig. 2) shows the hill to be mostly comprised of dolomitised 'Lower' Limestone overlain by 'Middle' or 'Upper' Limestone to the east. (sic)

The report goes on to give a detailed description of the workings investigated immediately beneath the collapsed pathway; parts of which are paraphrased here for brevity and clarity:

> That several subterranean galleries, mine shafts and adits are located beneath the hill. That in older times, some of the adits may have been driven (mined) horizontally from the quarries on the western face of the hill. That the primary purposes of the mining operations were to recover mineralised deposits (ore) of lead/silver, hosted in the sedimentary rock within the Brecciated Limestone forming the hillock. That the subsidence of the pathway in 2011, together with an earlier event in the 1980s, were caused by the collapse of previously closed-off access shafts to the underground workings.

The date of the first mining at Edenderry is uncertain, and no record of recovered ore seems to exist. The following excerpt from Sir Charles Coope's 1801 Statistical Survey of King's County; however, suggests a time line for the closure of the original workings:

> 'on the hill of Edenderry, now the church yard, there was formerly a silver mine, twice attempted to be worked, but not within these forty years.'

This entry might suggest that the mining operations ceased in the 1760s. Local history tells of mining resuming in Edenderry during the 1850s, with a company floated in 1851 by the 4th Marquess of Downshire, Arthur Wills Blundell Hill (1812-1868). As ore was not recovered during these operations, the same source suggests that this may have been a speculative device used to re-value the Downshire estates, then suffering a slump following 'the Great Hunger.' The story is supported; however, by a hand-written note inscribed upon a geological field map of the 1850s, which marks an area to the south-

The Author on Kishawanny old Bridge

west of Castro Petre Church and reads: "fruitless working made here by Lord Downshire for lead."

Standing on the retired stone arched bridge at Kishawanny, I noted the dark, murky waters of the Little Boyne flowing sluggishly towards our next destination at Boyne Bridge, about two kilometres downstream. The brownish hue of the water emanates from the many tributary streams, sourced in various bog-lands; whereas the slow movement reflects the slight fall in the riverbed. The 1837 OS map indicates the original stream-bed benchmarked at elevation 230ft close by Kishawanny Bridge, while that of the stream-bed near Boyne Bridge is at elevation 227ft, representing a fall of merely three feet over the distance.

On that December day in 2012, I noted the OPW trademark imprinted upon the river immediately downstream of Kishawanny. Here, the river is scarcely three metres wide; flowing through the bottomlands in a canal-like channel that disappeared into the wintery gloaming towards the north-west. But nature is fighting back, as evidenced by the weed growth encroaching from the eastern riverbank, leaving a clear-water channel of about one metre in places, such that even a one person canoe would find it difficult to navigate. The resilient alders, sallies and willows are struggling hard to restore the natural order; however, reaching out over the modest stream to entangle with the shrubbery on the opposite shore.

Leaving the town of Edenderry, we drove north-eastwards along the R401 to Boyne Bridge; where the river turns in a great, sweeping curve to head westwards towards Kinnafad. We won't follow the river just yet, but linger awhile at the bridge to discuss its structure and explore several other notable sites in the vicinity.

The crossing of the Edenderry to Kinnegad road (now the R401) and the Little Boyne forms a shape that could be likened to a giant 'X' or scissors; with the road continuing north-eastwards to cross the river again at Ballyboggan Bridge. As mentioned, the 1852 OS revised map, in some locations shows both the older and newer river lines. Cross-referencing this map with the 1837 and 1911 editions suggests the older and now defunct bridge was located circa fifty yards south-west of the present structure, which replaced it during the drainage schemes of c.1842-1844. The new bridge is included in the Offaly County Council's list of bridges, and assigned the number

OFIAR-012-003 2. The following is an excerpt from same:

Survey date   28/07/2004

Skew masonry arch bridge carries Edenderry-Kinnegad road over Boyne River. Abutments of roughly-dressed limestone blocks, randomly laid and underpinned with concrete. Shallow buttress, similarly detailed, to abutments. Arch is of segmental profile and set skew to the river; span is 3.84m (as measured orthogonally). Arch ring is of rusticated blocks. Soffit comprises skewly-laid limestone blocks. Spandrels and parapet are of random rubble, embellished with dressed string course and copings. Ivy covered.

Appraisal:

This bridge is architectural interest and of historical merit due to its association with the Board of Public Works and Boyne drainage scheme. It is also of technical interest on account of its skewed span. Of local heritage significance. (sic)[5]

At the bridge, the Little Boyne forms the mereing between the townlands of Ballygibbon-east, Ballygibbon-west and Edenderry; similar to Kishawanny, the river here is very overgrown, with lush vegetation and overhanging trees almost entirely blocking the waterway.

Following the R401 north-eastwards, we come to Clonmeen House, a large stone built country house standing to the east of the road. The 1911 OS map shows the house on this location, while the 1837 map indicates a house bearing the same name located directly opposite, to the west of the road (now Clonmeen Farm). Further north along the R401, is a road junction, where the eastern section of Carrick Road branches to the right and runs south-eastwards to Oldcourt.

The holy well named Tober-cro (Tober-croagh-neeve or 'the Well of the Holy Cross'), is located at the south-eastern sector of this junction. The well, dedicated to a sacred cross, burned it is said, on orders of King Henry VIII following dissolution of Ballyboggan Priory. Although this well is overgrown and almost unknown nowadays, it was once a highly venerated place of pilgrimage for the area.

Church on Carrick Hill

North-east of the well on the lower slopes of Carrick Hill, is the ruined Carrick Church and attendant graveyard, overlooked from the north by the crumbling remains of Carrick Castle (or Carrickffeoris). Tradition holds that both the castle and church date from the 13th century and that the church measured 60ft long by 25ft broad. The origins of the castle is attributed to the De Bermingham family and thus known locally as Carrick-Oris. Originally a three storeyed keep or tower house approximately 30ft square, only part of the south-western section survives and stands in a field close by the roadside (R401). Local folklore includes a tale of treachery; of how, on Trinity Sunday in 1305, Pierce de Bermingham (Sir Pierce Mac Feoris), thereafter known as the treacherous Baron, and Jordan Comin supposedly invited Murtagh O'Connor, King of Offaly, and his brother Calwagh, together with 29 members of the O'Connor Clan to dine at the castle, where they were murdered.

To the north-west of the castle, the western section of Carrick Road branches to the left and winds across the southern flank of Carrick Hill, or 'the Hill of the Rock.' To the north, the hill towers above the road and

Carrick Castle on Carrick Hill

forms the horizon in that direction, the hilltop dotted by bushes, with many whitish-coloured sections of rock outcropping through its green, grassy sward (in geological terms Carboniferous Limestone, part of the Edenderry Oolite formation). The origins of the name Carrick, meaning 'rock' in Gaelic, can be attributed to these outcrops.

It is said that an ancient building (traces of which were mentioned by Wilde in 1849) once stood atop the hill, supposed remnants of some long gone monk's cell. A large quarry is located on the hillside's northern flank, with a laneway linking it to Carrick Road. A nearby spring, named Scully's Well, is shown on the OS maps north-west of the quarry road.

Griffith's indicates that the quarry of 1.3 acres, together with circa 353 acres were leased from the Reps. of Wm. L. Palmer by Henry Mathers at R.V. £280.

Carrick Hill is the source of several legends, including that of the Witch's Stone; named after a chunk of rock, supposedly hurtled from Croghan Hill by an evil witch, aimed at some Saint resident upon Carrick Hill long ago.

The source of this legend was a large cluster of boulders or rock mass, once sited on the south-eastern quarry rim, only part of which remains; because, as Wilde states, some 'mischievous quarryman split the stone by blasting.' For which deed, legends say, the offender was forced to leave the district forever.

The stone is said to consist of 'trap-rock' (known also as Greenstone), laid down much later in geological time and gathered mostly within fissures and faults of the bedrock, hence the title trap-rock. Several such rock formations were located near Dowth Tumulus, at the Big Bend, mentioned later as we pass on downriver.

The Kildare County Geological Report describes the Witch's Stone thus: 'a glacially transported quartz porphyry erratic known as the Witches Stone can be seen near these outcrop exposures.'(sic) The 1837 and 1911 OS maps indicate the Witch's Stone on the hillside, with the latter map showing a Limekiln on the northern rim of the quarry.

Another interesting stream, named the Garr River, enters the Little Boyne at Boyne Bridge; indeed, according to the old maps, two rivers bearing the name Garr rise in the same area, then flow in different directions to coalesce with the Boyne several miles apart. As indicated on the maps, the stream entering the main river at Boyne Bridge rises in a meshwork of capillary streams sourced in Nurney and Fearavola Townlands; then flows westwards to Buggans Wood, where its course turns southwards. From here to Rinaghan Townland, the 1837 map names the stream the Garr River. Its upper reach; however, is named variously the Garr River and Garr Screens River on the 1911 map, while its lower reach is shown only as the Garr River on the same map. At Rinaghan, the river turns to flow due west, forming the townland mereing to Carrick Road; where it passes beneath Garr Bridge and flows onwards to mingle with the Boyne at Boyne Bridge.[6]

The 1837 OS map indicates an 'old millrace' branching from the Garr River at Rinaghan, to flow due south to Brooke Ville House; opposite which the same map indicates a ruined mill in Kilmore Townland, near Oldcourt Crossroads. This mill site was close by the contemporary location of High Field Golf Club. The mill tailrace ran on south-westwards to fall into the Boyne just upstream from Boyne Bridge. Although the mill is shown on the map accompanying Griffith's 1854 valuation, I could find no record of it in the valuation listings.

According to the 'direction of flow' indication arrows on the 1911 OS map, another stream rises to the west of Buggans Wood; then flows north-westwards through Lucy's Wood and 'the Bog Wood' to a byroad leading from Ballindoolin to Cloharinka. It continued north-eastwards beneath another bridge named Garr Bridge, where it turned to flow due north through Clushabona Wood and onwards past Toberall (Toberaulin or the beautiful well) to Nule's Bridge. From here it flowed north-eastwards to mingle with the Boyne above Ballyboggan Bridge. This river is named the Garr River on the 1837 map, but is unnamed on the 1911 edition. To add to the confusion, the river appears to be named Garr River on the latest Discovery Map, from Nules Bridge to Boyne Bridge.[7]

The Little Boyne continues south-westwards for some distance, before swinging to the north-west in a great curve towards Kinnafad. Just north-west of Edenderry; another tributary mingles with the river from the south-west. Following this stream upriver we come to Waterstown Bridge, which nowadays carries the R441 across the little river. To the south are the ivy covered ruins of a church, standing within a graveyard dominated by a large Celtic Cross. This church and burial ground once formed part of the Friary/ Monastery of Monasteroris, the remains of which stand upon and close by a nearby wooded mound in the midst of a field. The OS maps indicate a well named Toberhola sited by the roadside to the north-west of the churchyard. Wilde says of these ruins in 1849:

> Sir John de Bermingham, Earl of Louth, founded an abbey in the year 1325, for conventional Franciscans, at Tatmoy, in Offaly, the ancient name of this territory; and from the Irish name of this chieftain it was called Monaster-Feoris. In 1511, Cahir O'Conor, Lord of Offaly, was slain near this Monastery. It was a place of considerable strength, as the remains of the building still testify, and sustained a lengthened siege by the Earl of Surrey, Lord Lieutenant of Ireland, when he marched into Offaly at the time of his expedition against the O'Moores of Leix, who, with other Irish chieftains, had invaded the borders of the Pale.[8]

The 1837 OS map indicates a millrace flowing from swampy lands to the south-west, near the Grand Canal. This race passed beneath the road (R441) south of Waterstown Bridge; then flowed through the monastery grounds to power a corn mill located to the east of Monasteroris in an area named Mill Mount. Griffith's indicates that this mill, together with kilns, offices and land totalling 316 acres was occupied by Richard Gilliard, and leased from Robert Lucas at R.V. £50. The map shows a ruined windmill sited on a slight eminence south of the water mill and to the rear of the contemporary industrial estate.

Downstream from Monasteroris, the Little Boyne continues on its north-westerly course to flow beneath Kinnafad Bridge, which carries the Jonestown road north-eastwards through Grange and Rahan (Rahin) to Glyn Crossroads, near Ballyboggan Bridge. The name Kinnafad derives from the Gaelic Ceann Atha Fada or in English, Head of the Long Ford. A title that suggests this was an ancient crossing place, and indeed may explain the presence of the nearby castle; probably erected to defend the strategic location. Wilde covers the area in great detail, and mentions that many artifacts, consisting mostly of spearheads and suchlike weapons, were recovered in the vicinity, sketches of which are included on page 38 (2nd edition).

The bridge spanning the river at Kinnafad is another of those built during the drainage schemes of 1844-1862; now assigned the number OFIAR-004-004 1 by Offaly County Council. The description reads:

Survey Date 11/08/04

Single arch masonary bridge carries road over Boyne River at county boundary. Abutments are of rock-faced limestone blocks, regularly laid. They have projecting rounded ends and are coped with a finely dressed string course (which extends around the ends). The bottom of the abutments are underpinned with concrete. Arch is of shallow segmental profile and spans c.5.40m. Its voussiers are of rusticated margined blocks and the soffit is of dressed blocks. The spandrels are detailed as abutments. By contrast, the parapets, which are spaced at 6.40m, are of squared random rubble. They terminate in out-projecting piers detailed as the spandrels and with rusticated and margined quoins. A finely dressed string course runs over the crown and continues around the parapet piers. The parapets and piers are also coped with finely dressed limestone blocks with curved tops. Slight curve to deck.

Appraisal

This bridge is of high architectural quality as evidenced by its contrasting finishes and embellishments. It is also of historical interest, being associated with the Boyne drainage scheme undertaken by the Board of Public Works. It is the most impressive of the attested Board of Works bridges recorded in the Boyne catchment within Co Offaly. Of regional heritage significance, meriting inclusion in the Record of Protected Structures. (sic)

The remains of Kinnafad Castle stand in a 7.5 acre field close by the bridge and to the south-east of the road. The castle is a rectangular three storeyed, 14th century Keep measuring about 50ft by 40ft, and although the eastern wall is missing, the remaining structure seemed fairly sound from my vantage point by the roadside gateway. The structure is yet another of the many De Bermingham castles decorating the landscape of the Boyne.

We now travel north-eastwards along the byroad; to where, approximately half a mile north of Kinnafad Bridge, the 1837 OS map depicts the hamlet of Grange, comprised of a cluster of dwellings to the left of the road. Slightly north of the hamlet is Grange Castle, standing on the opposite side of the road in a salient of Grange-West Townland. Although Wilde does not give a date for its construction, contemporary local history holds that this was another of the De Berminghams' castles, built c.1460. The castle is described as a tower house, later embellished with Jacobean battlements and chimneys in the early 17th century. The castle's history records successive generations of its owners completing many alterations to the structure, including the addition of a great hall, restored recently and named Fallon Hall.

It is said that Walter Bermingham sold the castle to Thomas Tyrrell, whose family retained possession of Grange until 1988; at which juncture the late Robert Tyrrell transferred ownership of the tower to the Government Agency, Duchas. Thought the castle as such is not recorded in Griffith's, the Tyrrell family name appears frequently as occupiers and lessors of many properties in the district.

The Little Boyne is slightly broader at Kinnafad, its stream much cleaner and free of the clogging vegetation, due to drainage work completed in recent times. The comparison with a canal is more evident hereabouts, both upstream and downstream of the bridge; in 1849, Wilde also likened the river to a 'small modern canal' because of the recent drainage work.

Beyond the bridge, the river continues on its north-westerly course to a place named Aughramona on the old maps, where the Little Boyne makes its last major turn to the north-east. On the western riverbank, the 1837 OS map shows a road running alongside a small stream, flowing from Roosk Bridge (located south of Roosk Togher), and onwards to the Boyne at Aughramona. While no bridge or ford is evident, the same map indicates this road continuing eastwards and linking with the byroad leading from Kinnafad Bridge to Grange just south of the hamlet. Although only the eastern section of the road is shown on the 1911 map, a 'foot stick' (or footbridge) is indicated crossing the Little Boyne at Aughramona. These clues provided by the old maps, suggest that a ford may have existed here in times long gone, and give rise to conjecture that the name may once have been Ath Na Moin, or 'the Ford of the Bog.' Perhaps this long gone roadway superseded Roosk Togher, an ancient causeway (or Pace) that crossed the bog-lands nearby.[9]

From here, the Little Boyne flows the short distance to its meeting with the Yellow River. Where we will board the boats, kindly provided and crewed by the Meath River Rescue Service, and take the reader along the river's course through the heart of County Meath, to view the many and varied aspects of the Boyne on its winding journey to the sea.

ENDNOTES

1   Griffith's provides an explanation for the names given to some of the above listed wells: Haughton's Well being named after John Haughton (or his family) who resided close by Clonkeen Cross Roads; while Coffey's Well was named after Patrick Coffey (or his family), occupier of a house on a 125 acre holding directly across the Boyne from Clonkeen Mill.

2   When we arrived, Mrs. Elliot was hand-milking a newly calved cow. Emerging from the cowbyre, she placed the bucket of beastings in the middle of the farmyard, to greet us warmly and show us around the old mill. This encounter evoked fond memories of my youth, when such hospitality was the norm in the Ireland of the day.

3   North of the river and directly opposite the corn mill (near the northern edge of the mill pond on Patrick Coffey's 1850s farm), the OS maps indicate the site of a castle, not a trace of which structure existed upon the landscape, as so stated by Wilde in 1849.

4   NLI – The Dublin University magazine: a literary and political Journal, pp. 628-646, 1844.

5   The skew-building of the arch was necessitated by the relative angles of river and road. In my view, such structures are an engineering marvel, considering the basic tools and equipment available, and as such are a lasting testament to the skilled craftsmen of times past. Unfortunately, during the best-forgotten Celtic Tiger era, I have seen several similar bridges flattened, with their painstakingly measured, skew-cut and shaped stonework buried beneath modern developments.

6   On a visit in April 2013, I noted that the tiny river was very overgrown, with a mere trickle of water passing south-westwards beneath this Garr Bridge on Carrick Rd. (a small bridge or gullet); located north of Highfield Golf Club at the junction of Rinaghan, Ballygibbon-East and Carrick Townlands.

7   In April 2013, I confirmed also that this other stream (the northern Garr R.) passes north-eastwards and under the second Garr Bridge (located in Ballindoolin Townland near Beaghan's Well), then continues onwards to flow briskly beneath Nules Bridge (a skew built stone bridge with a span of c.12ft). It commingles here with a smaller stream flowing from the direction of Grange Castle; exactly as depicted on the 1911 OS map. I could find no trace of Toberall (or Toberaulin), as shown on the same map at the eastern end of the bridge. See further mention at Ballyboggan Br.

8   Other sources maintain that the Annals of the Four Masters suggest the monastery was founded about 1260, with a church built nearby in approximately 1290. It is said that the O'Conor Clan used the old building as a fort or stronghold for a time, and that Cromwell removed the Franciscans from the Friary during his reign of terror c.1650s.

9   Moll's Map of 1714 shows a bridge spanning the Boyne in the vicinity of Kinnafad/Aughramona. The crossing may have been at either location as it is impossible to pinpoint the exact site due to the small scaling of this map.

3

The Upper Reaches
Yellow River to Clonard

The Yellow River – Source – Derryiron Corn-Mill – Garr Townland and other Garr Br. – Sheep Bridge – Castlejordan/Mongagh River – Rochfort Bridge, Dooneen fort & Adhoul Lough – Castlejordan & mill – Clongall Bridge – Lucey's Farm & Skregg Hill – Our boat journey begins – Confluence of Yellow River & Little Boyne – Grange West & Tobernakill – Rahin/ Rahan – Russelswood – The northern Garr River – Ballyboggan Priory & mill – Ballyboggan Bridge and altered river course – Ticroghan Fortress & mill – The Belly of the Boyne – An encounter with two swans – Clonard Monastery, old & new Leinster Bridges – The Bull's Ring – Turnpike roads, toll-houses & Messers. Hogan & Flood – Tyrrell's House – Battle of Clonard & the Wexford Insurgent Column.

According to the OS maps of 1837 and 1911, the *Yellow River* rises in the boggy, marshy lands of Derryarkin, Ballyfore, Bunsallagh and Derrycoffey Townlands, located north-west of Daingean (formerly Philipstown) in County Offaly. The source is augmented by a series of capillaries forming a river, named Big River on 1911 map, which joins(ed) the Yellow River where it formed the border with County Westmeath for a short distance. However, the older topography has been altered considerably hereabouts by drainage/ reclamation works.

From its source, the river meanders mainly eastwards to mingle with the Boyne at the conjunction of Clongall, Clonmore and Grange-West Townlands, located in Meath, Offaly and Kildare respectively. On its c. twenty-mile long course, I found one watermill recorded upon the old maps, Derryiron Corn Mill (**OFIAR 004-011**), marked on the OS maps in a townland of the same name.

The mill headrace was taken from a sluice on 'the Big River' near the source, to run south of the Yellow River for a considerable distance to the mill. In Derryiron Townland, the millrace branched to run south-eastwards to Toberdaly Bridge, where it supplied feed water to the Grand Canal. The tailrace fell back into the mother stream below the corn mill (at Garr Bridge). While some traces of this old millrace can still be discerned in the extensive bog-lands of Derryiron, little or nothing remains of the mill or kiln. Griffith's records this property as follows: corn-mill and kiln, leased by John and Thomas Mooney from Francis Dame @ R.V. £4 for the buildings only; such a low valuation perhaps indicating that the mill was not in use at the time.[1]

Starting from Sheep Bridge, we follow the lower reach of the Yellow River to its confluence with the Boyne, about three miles downstream. This bridge links the townlands of Ballyfore and Castlejordan on the Meath side to those of Killowen and Clonmore on the Offaly riverbank. While the origin of the name is uncertain, the contemporary bridge is an 1850s OPW replacement for an earlier 18th century structure (located closer to Castlejordan) demolished during the drainage schemes of 1844-1862. The newer structure is included in the Offaly County Council's Heritage listing as **O.F.I.A.R. 004-003** with the review reading thus:

> Sheep Bridge on Yellow River
>
> Survey date 11/08/2004
>
> Masonry arch bridge carries minor road over Boyne River at county boundary. Abutments are of dressed limestone blocks, laid randomly. They have slightly projecting rusticated and margined quoins and are embellished with a finely dressed string course (which extends around the ends). The bottoms of the abutments are underpinned with concrete. Arch is of segmental profile and spans 4.56m. Its voussoirs are of rusticated margined block and the soffit has dressed blocks.

The spandrels and parapets are detailed as abutments. The latter are spaced at 6.45m and terminate in out-projecting piers detailed as the spandrels. A dressed string course runs over the crown. The parapets are coped with dressed limestone blocks with curved tops. Curved deck. Ivy overgrowth.

Appraisal
Although of modest scale, the architectural quality of this bridge and its historical association with the Board of Public Works and Boyne drainage scheme makes it of local heritage significance. (sic)2

About halfway between Sheep Bridge and the Boyne confluence, we come to another tributary, named variously the Castlejordan River and the Mongagh River. This stream is sourced from bog-lands in Derrygreenagh and Farthingstown Townlands to the south-west of Rochfortbridge in County Westmeath, it then flows approximately twelve miles north-northeastwards to mingle with the Yellow River south-east of Castlejordan. Taking its initial rise from capillaries draining the bogs surrounding Dooneen Fort and Adhoul Lough (a boggy marsh), it passes beneath a bridge, named Rochfort Bridge on the 1837 OS map and Mongagh Bridge on the 1911 map. Perhaps the former name derived from the nearby town of Rochfortbridge. I cannot discover the origins of the name Mongagh, one possible derivation is from Moin Gagach, meaning Chink or Crack in the Bog (which would describe the river admirably); another could mean Moin Ath or Bog Ford. The former stone arched bridge (**O.F.I.A.R. 003-001**) was demolished in recent years and replaced by a concrete Armco pipe.[3]

On its passage through Kildangan Townland the stream's name changes to the Castlejordan River. The river flowed through the village and once powered a corn mill located close by the ruined castle, the origins of the place name Castlejordan.[4] There is a dwelling on the mill site nowadays named Mill House. Griffith's indicates that this mill was occupied by John McNamara, who leased it, together with house, offices and land totalling c.12.6 acres from Robert Jolly at R.V. £20-10s.

A short distance downstream from the Castlejordan River is Clongall Bridge, the last crossing on the Yellow River before it mingles with the Little

Boyne. This is a relatively new bridge, as neither it nor the contemporary road running from Castlejordan across the river to Clonmore Crossroads is shown on the 1837 OS map, but the bridge is included on the 1882 map under the name Russel's Bridge.

Construction of a bridge at this location is recorded in the Grand Jury Presentment Book of 1860 – an outline of the intended route is etched on the 1852 revised map, indicating earlier plans for its inclusion in the road network, from the village to the river. The bridge is included on Offaly County Council's heritage listing as **O.F.I.A.R. 004-005**, with the description reading thus:

> Clongall Bridge (Russel's Bridge 1882 OS map)
>
> Survey date 11/08/2004
>
> Masonry arch carrying minor road over Yellow River at county boundary. Abutments are of dressed limestone blocks, laid randomly and underpinned with concrete. Arch is of shallow segmental profile and spans 6.68m. Its voussoirs are of dressed stone blocks. The spandrels are of squared random rubble, but the parapets are detailed as the abutments. A finely dressed string course runs across the crown. The parapets are spaced at 5.57m and are coped with dressed stone with rounded tops. The north-east approach wall has collapsed. Ivy growth on upstream (west) face.
>
> Appraisal
>
> A typical mid-19th century bridge, but of no special heritage merit.

The Edenderry and Castlejordan Angling Association, which controls the fishing on the rivers hereabouts, state that the Mongagh River holds a good stock of small wild brown trout and a number of fish up to 2 pounds in weight – and that the Yellow River has a good stock of small trout, with the stretch below Clongall Bridge holding trout up to 2 pounds in weight.

And so we take to the boats: to share the riverscape of the Boyne with our reader, who can join us now on this stage from Clongall to Ashfield Bridge, part of a memorable series of waterborne journeys, exploring the river channel from source to sea.[5]

Black swans cavorting at Lucey's refuge Clongall

We gained access to the river via Brendan Lucey's farm on the County Meath side, through fields adjoining the Yellow River opposite the animal rescue/refuge centre run by Brendan's mother. While awaiting the arrival of the lads with the boat, we were entertained by the antics of several 'rescued' ducks and two black swans cavorting in a small pond nearby.

This area of Clongall is named Skregg Hill on the 1911 map, the origins of which name eludes me and seem to be lost in the mists of time. Brendan and his brother kindly provided their tractor to pull the rescue service jeep, complete with trailer and our river chariot, across several soggy fields to reach the river; while the remainder of us trudged up Skregg Hill and down to the riverbank, pursued by a bunch of very curious bovines.

The Yellow River's course traverses a green, grassy valley running through low, undulating hillocks swelling from a narrow enough floodplain. The water flowed about two metres below the riverbank hereabouts, largely due to drainage works performed by the OPW over the years. Manoeuvring the boat to the river via one of the modern-day cattle-drinking cuttings in the steep riverbank; we cut the restraining barbed wire with a pair of pliers and launched the craft into the briskly flowing water. Then it was all aboard our RIB (rigid inflatable boat) on our first voyage of discovery; the driver and support crew were Paddy Brady and Christopher (Hopper) Rennicks, with the boat crewed by Martin (Chalky) White, Richard Harding and Martin Curran as 'Cox. of the Boat,' with Pascal Marry and I as supernumeraries.

The reach of river between our entry point and the Boyne confluence is about 25/30ft wide and overhung by a variety of naturally-seeded scrub trees, including alder, willow/sally and hawthorn. Variations in passage width were caused by a combination of scrub growth and riverside sedges encroaching sometimes to midstream. The lowermost tree limbs hanging over the water and creating major obstruction to boat passage, making the stream unnavigable in places and causing the craft to hang-up at times. On such occasions, Chalky and Richie hopped overboard to free the boat, sometimes from nature's clutches and occasionally heaving us over Board of Works Ripples i.e. rocky ledges created during the various drainage works executed by that public body. Of which creations the reader will learn more as we progress downriver to Navan. Here and there, the low-hanging limbs caused 'beaver-dam-like' blockades in the stream, formed initially by intertwining of tree branches

From top:

Paschal Marry at Russelswood

Martin Curran (Cox) at confluence of Little Boyne & Yellow River

Hopper Rennicks at Lucey's Slip

and weed growth, but these naturally occurring barriers were oftentimes consolidated by various items of colourful flotsam and jetsam, detritus cast aside by our wasteful society.

Soon our boat reached the confluence, where the much larger Yellow River receives tribute from the Little Boyne. I use this description advisedly, as I am well aware that the Yellow River is considered a tributary of the Boyne, but from the river aspect such is not the case. At the meeting point, the Yellow River is at least treble the size of the Boyne, both in volume of water and in width of stream, and has flowed about double the distance from its source. But although it is a greater river than the Boyne in the parameters generally used for such comparisons, it does not have the myths or legends of the more renowned river associated with its history, hence the name has faded into near oblivion.

Whatever the merits of such speculation, the 'meeting of the waters' is a difficult place to discover and even more awkward to access. As no public road passes close by, a lengthy trudge across private lands is necessary to acquire a close-up view of the confluence, but the best vista is from the vantage point of a boat.

Downstream from the confluence, the Boyne turns in a great curve to head northwards, forming the mereing between Meath and Kildare en route. The reach of the now enlarged river, especially from Clongall to Ashfield Bridge, was altered completely by the several drainage schemes completed by the OPW over the years. Most of these course alterations were planned or executed in the period 1842 to 1846 and 1848 to 1862; as evidenced by a study of the Commissioners of Public Works, Ireland, 17th report (1848) and cross-referencing the 1837 OS map with the revised 1852 edition. Such a study reveals many of the river's twists and turns eliminated, with the new course (hereabouts varying between 40 and 80 feet in width) altered to lengthy straights and great sweeping curves to allow an easier passage for the river waters.

These adjustments to the river's course presented problems with the existing bridges; however, causing some to be demolished and rebuilt spanning the newer line of river. Several of the longer crossings, such as Ashfield, Stonyford, Inchamore, Scarriff and Derrinydaly Bridges having some of the central arches and pillars removed, with larger central spans inserted within their existing structures to increase the aggregate free waterway. These bridges are discussed in detail when encountered on our downriver boat journey. In summary, this reach of the river, presented on the 1911 OS map, is totally different to that depicted on the OS map of 1837.

Leaving the confluence, our boat continued downstream on a flat calm reach of deep, dark water. It was a bright, cold November day, but as the wind blew from the south-east, the high riverbank on our right flank sheltered us from most of the rigours of its icy blast. This riverbank formed the boundary of Grange-West Townland in Co. Kildare, upon which was an ancient spring-well known as *Tobernakill,* sited in the field immediately adjacent to the river confluence. This name translates from Gaelic to mean 'the well of the Church' (Kill or Cill being an old name for a church in the native Irish tongue). The well is marked on the Discovery Map as a Holy Well, with no name applied or no trace of its rill draining to the Boyne.

From here to Ballyboggan Bridge, the Boyne is relatively deep and its channel almost unobstructed, the floodplain on the Meath side mostly flat and rising only slightly to form the horizon in the near distance. This almost featureless plain comprises the riparian parts of Clongall, Harristown, Ballynakill and Ballyboggan Townlands. The two-tiered riverbank is a couple of metres above the river level, limiting our perspective, with further visual obstructions presented by riverside sedges and reeds. The Kildare shore of this reach provides more of interest to discuss; therefore, I will focus attention on the south-eastern bank as we glide downriver towards Ballyboggan.

We passed by a large area of woodland on the Kildare riverbank, obscuring the nearby Rahin (Rahan) House from the river aspect. The 1837 OS map shows a wooded area in this vicinity, but located further from the river; while the 1911 edition indicates a larger woodland named 'the Glade Wood' lining the riverbank hereabouts.

Wilde refers to planting of the new demesne in Rahin being still in progress when he passed this way in 1849. A combination of wildwood and conifer plantation now lines the shore from upstream of Rahin House to the great north-eastwards sweep of the Boyne through Russelswood Townland. The riverbank of Russelswood is covered by a modern plantation, extending downstream to Ballyboggan Bridge; most of this c.151 acre townland is, in fact, now overgrown by woodland. On the day, we exchanged pleasantries

The placid Boyne at Russelswood

with several people walking along the riverside pathway, taking advantage of the fine weather and wonderful setting.

Griffith's indicates that Rahin House, together with 567 acres was held in fee by the Rep. of William L. Palmer at R.V. £490. The valuation indicates also that much of Russelswood Townland was held by the same person.

Our boat glided downriver on this deep, still stretch of the Boyne, with inverted reflections of Rahin Woods mirrored from the darkened surface. This riverscape came close to matching or even surpassing any vista in Ireland; images of mirror-like river, evergreen and deciduous wildwood and verdant pasturelands stretching to the near horizon, a scene of sylvan beauty, contrasting with and complementing the otherwise drab winter landscape.

Sheltered from the biting wind in the deep recess of the river, we were warmed by the pale winter's sunshine. These balmy conditions, together with the beauty of the setting causing one of the lads to exclaim aloud "God, that's a beautiful day, I'd love to live again."

From mid-river, we could see remnants of stone buildings atop a slight ground eminence rising gently from the northern or Meath riverbank at the end of the long, straight stretch, where the Boyne sweeps eastwards to flow beneath Ballyboggan Bridge.

Ballyboggan Priory ruins

These are the ruins of Ballyboggan (Ballybogan) Abbey or Priory, a distinctly English or Anglo Norman institution, described in detail by Wilde in 1849. Tradition holds that the priory was constructed in the 12th century for canons of the order of St. Augustine by Jordan Comin, and named originally 'the Priory de Laude Dei.' In a footnote on page 52 of his book (2nd edition), Wilde speculates that this may be the same Jordan Comin, who, with Piers De Bermingham massacred leaders and members of the O'Connor Clan at Carrick Castle in 1305, and states that should this be so, the priory must have been founded in the 13th century.

Mention is made also that in the year 1446/47, a great plague ravaged Meath, Leinster and Munster, taking the lives of several hundred priests, including that of the Prior of Ballybogan.

Amongst its reputed vast holdings of about 5,000 acres, the priory had many and varied possessions, including several dozen Messuages, extensive woodlands, meadows, arable land and one thousand acres of pastures – a water mill and six eel weirs are included in the inventory. At the dissolution of religious houses commencing in c.1538, Henry Vlll granted much of the possessions of Ballyboggan Priory to Sir William Bermingham, later Lord Carbery. Towards the end of the reign of Elizabeth l, these lands were bestowed upon Edward Fitzgerald (of Ticroghan?). Entries in the County Louth Archaeological Journal of 1955 indicate that the six eel weirs in the Manor of Ballyboggan were granted to Sir William Bermingham on 17th July 1542.

Wilde mentions also that *Tobercro* was named after a famous cross from this priory, burned by order of King Henry in 1538. Griffith's records circa 242 acres of land, including the site of the priory and graveyard, being leased from the Marquise of Landsdowne, by Frederick H. Langan at R.V. £226. Other entries indicate that the same Mr Langan held the Toll rights of the nearby Fair Green at R.V. 15s. (located north-west of the Priory).

On the Meath riverbank to the south-west of the ruined priory, the 1837 OS map shows a mill (of unspecified usage) and millrace upon a little stream flowing from the north-west and falling into the Boyne at the place where the river now curves eastwards.[6] This stream is sourced in a series of capillaries draining from Moydrum Bog (named Loughnabuoy Bog on Larkin's Map) to the north-west. No trace of this mill is shown on the 1911 map, or indeed exists on the modern landscape. One might well wonder; however, if this was the remnants of the mill listed in the ancient annals. As a point of interest, no eel or fish weirs are indicated on the old OS maps in the area of Ballyboggan, perhaps an indication that these were eliminated by earlier drainage works.

Nule's Bridge. KE- R401 - 004.00 - on R401 Northern Garr River

A small stream falls into the Boyne on the Kildare side, directly across from the site of the above mill; this is the northern section of the Garr River, previously mentioned in Chap. 2, which river takes its rise close by Buggan's Wood in Ballydoolin Townland. Towards its north-eastern end, the stream flows past an ancient burial ground and long disappeared castle in Brackagh Townland, then beneath the stone arched Nule's Bridge (close by Toberall or Toberaulin), and through Russelswood to the Boyne. As detailed in the earlier chapter, this stream is named differently on the various maps. From my reading of these, there appear to be two rivers flowing in different directions to the Boyne, and both named Garr River; thus accounting for the two Garr Bridges in County Kildare as shown on the maps.

The river crossing at Ballyboggan was perhaps associated with the monks of the nearby monastery, as per custom and practice of earlier times. It is likely, indeed, that this was a ford originally, first replaced by a wooden bridge or wickerwork *Cesdroichet*, and then by a stone arched structure following the Norman Invasion in the latter half of the 12th century.

Garr Bridge - on the northern Garr River in Balindoolin Townland Co. Kildare

The bridge spanning the Boyne here is an obvious OPW replacement for an earlier structure, as a bridge is depicted at this location (but not named) on the Taylor & Skinner map of 1778. The contemporary bridge links the townlands of Russelswood and Ballycowan on the Kildare side to Ballyboggan on the Meath riverbank. The road crossing the river (R401) connects Edenderry to Kinnegad; in the immediate vicinity it runs from Glynn Crossroads, past *Lady Well* to the Boyne. The contemporary Ballyboggan Bridge was most likely constructed during the drainage schemes of 1848 to 1862, as its design conforms closely to that of many other bridges built by this public body at the time.[7]

At time of writing, neither Meath nor Kildare Co. Councils seem to have completed heritage listings and detailed descriptions of their bridges similar to that of Co. Offaly, I cannot; therefore, include a professional assessment of the structure. However, I will provide my own impressions of the bridge, as observed on our downriver journey and during later visits by road. Without, I may add, the benefit of measuring equipment, so the following figures are approximate only:

Ballyboggan Bridge

From river aspect:

The bridge comprises a single shallow stone arch of segmental profile, with a span of about 25/30ft which abuts vertical stone columns on each riverbank at a height of c.10ft above mean water level. Outside the springers, these columns rise to parapet level, forming a rectangular pillar about 5ft x 2.8ft at all four corners. The arch rings/voussoirs are of rusticated limestone blocks, as are the spandrels, with the abutments and pillars constructed from rusticated limestone blocks laid to a regular pattern. The soffit (intrados) appears to be of dressed limestone blocks in regular lines and the abutments are underpinned with concrete to compensate for deepening of the river channel during drainage work. A dressed string course runs atop the arch crown, and continues around the out-projecting parapet piers.

From road aspect:

The approach to the bridge, on both riverbanks, comprises an embankment buttressed by stone walls, which rise to about 3.5ft above road level and have battlemented tops. The approach on the Meath side is much longer due to the wider floodplain – midway along its length this embankment is pierced by a c.16ft arch of near semicircular profile, which appears to be of an older vintage than the river span, and may indeed be part of an earlier bridge. All four of the previously described pillars are approximately the same height and constructed of dressed limestone blocks, laid in regular pattern and topped with two differently sized dressed coping stones, embossed with rusticated centres. Each parapet wall is the same height as and sandwiched between two piers, being c.0.8ft thinner than the out-projecting piers. The parapets are spaced at circa 22ft and are coped with dressed limestone slabs with rounded edges. The western parapet wall is heavily overgrown by ivy.

Left: Ballyboggan Bridge downstream.   Right: Ballyboggan Bridge flood eye.

Similar to other places along its course, the old maps show a very different River Boyne at Ballyboggan. Here, the 1837 and 1852 revised edition depicts the river's winding course splitting into two streams, with one channel running to the north of the floodplain, the other to the south along the Kildare boundary. Between the two channels were several islets, two of the smaller isles located in the vicinity of the bridge, with one larger island downstream of the crossing.[8] The previously described other stone arch of near semi-circular profile is located between two sloped buttresses about mid-way along the approach embankment on the Meath riverbank. This arch is high and dry nowadays and its c.16ft span is partly blocked by the western buttress. While possibly built as a flood-arch, it could be a survivor of the earlier bridge spanning the northernmost river channel. Various drainage schemes transformed the river such that the main channel was realigned to form the contemporary course running to the south of the floodplain and beneath Ballyboggan Bridge.

Before departing this area, we will take a diversion northwards along the R401, then follow a byroad leading north-eastwards to a forked road junction in the midst of Ticroghan Townland. The 1837 and 1911 OS maps depict a series of earthworks located in a large (circa 22 acres) field north-east of the road junction. Further to the north-east, both maps show a walled-in graveyard, within which is a ruined church named Chapel of Ease. The earthworks are named Ticroghan or Queen Mary's Castle (site of) on the OS maps – Larkin's Map provides only a graphic depiction in the form of a diamond-shaped rectangle, with four out-projecting bastions on its corners; all four nearly aligned to the cardinal points of the compass. The contemporary OS Discovery Series map names this location a 'star shaped fort.' Wilde gives the following description of this ancient stronghold, as noted in 1849:

> About a mile beyond the bridge of Clonard, towards the west, we find the ruins of the old fortress of Ticroghan, or Queen Mary's Castle, as it is sometimes styled; it can be seen from the Ballybogan road, upon the left bank of the river, and may be visited in that route. We cannot, however, stop to record the annals of every feudal or monastic pile that attracts our attention on this passage down the Boyne; but we may here remark, that Lord Ormonde retired to this castle, from Trim in 1649, shortly before the siege of Drogheda, and that, "after a well regulated defence," it was surrendered by Lady Fitzgarret, in 1650, to Colonel Reynolds and Colonel Hueston. In its vicinity some remains of an ancient church and a burial ground, which formerly contained an ancient font, also exist; but even within our own memory portions of the walls of the castle have been torn down to supply building materials. De Lacy built a castle at Clonard, but, if this was not it, we cannot find any trace of it.

In a footnote on the same page (75 - 2nd Edt.), he adds:

> *The peasants in the neighbourhood relate a story that the siege was about to be abandoned when the besiegers discovered that the soldiers in the fortress were firing silver bullets; encouraged by this proof of the extremity in which the beleaguered were, the Parliamentary forces continued the attack with renewed energy, and soon succeeded in reducing the castle.*

Other references state that the fortress of Ticroghan (Tycroghan) became one of Owen Roe O'Neill's midland garrisons for a time during the Confederacy Rebellion in the 1640s; his son Henry being married to Helena (or Elena), daughter of Sir Luke Fitzgerald of Ticroghan Castle.

North-westwards from the forked junction at Ticroghan are remnants of a large tree and brush covered mound, sited in a field to the right of the road.[9] This unnamed fort covers circa one acre and is delineated on both OS maps as a diamond-shaped, double-embanked mound (from the southern aspect). Perhaps this ancient earthwork was a precursor of the much larger fortress to the south-east?

Former RIC Barracks at Ticroghan Crossroads

Left: Ticroghan - graveyard and chapel of ease.
Right: Old building - potatoe garden on site of Ticroghan - Queen Mary's Castle - fortress.

The 1837 OS map shows an 'old mill' sited on the approximate location of Ticroghan Castle's southern bastion, close by the road junction. This mill is not shown on Larkin's Map or the 1911 map, and is unrecorded in Griffith's 1850s valuation. The millrace is shown on the older OS map, fed from a little stream flowing from the north-west and sourced in a bog to the south of Ardnamullen Townland (near the long gone ruins of Ardnamullen Castle). This townland name suggests a connection with a mill as it translates to 'the height or rise of the mill.' The mill tailrace flowed southwards forming the eastern mereing of Ballyboggan before mingling with the Boyne east of Ballyboggan Bridge. Across the road from this mill was the Constabulary or RIC barracks, on which site a beautifully presented stone house enhances the rustic scene nowadays.

I noted several bovines grazing contentedly on the lush grass amidst a myriad of wildflowers and sedges, growing on the site of this long gone fortress. Its strong bastions once dominated the landscape and withstood the ebbs and flows of our turbulent history. However, like Ancient Bablyon, its time came and went, with little trace remaining nowadays of the mighty outer defences or inner castle walls; except to the knowing eye, which may observe the ground ridges and occasional variation in colour of the meadows. A study of the 2005 OS ortho,' and other satellite imagery, reveals the outlines of some foundations, especially those of the northern bastion. The little stream that once powered the mill continues to flow beneath the road, but no trace of the mill is evident in the farmyard now occupying the site. The ivy covered ruins of the old Chapel of Ease still stand within its enclosing stone walls; however, as no plaque or other such sign is evident, a stranger passing along the road might never know that this seemingly empty stretch of ground once hosted so many important events.[10]

The river aspect changes once again below Ballyboggan Bridge. Passing beneath the great arch and continuing on downriver, when looking back upstream, the forested banks of Russelswood could be seen through the window of the stone arch, with the remains of the old priory silhouetted on the Meath riverbank against the setting sun. But, returning my gaze to the downriver aspect, no such landmarks were evident within my limited range of vision from the deeper cleft of the river.

This section of Boyne is somewhat wider from Ballyboggan to Clonard, with the stream flowing between high, grassy banks rising about three metres or so to flat riverside meadowlands. Despite all the earlier drainage works, the river course winds and twists its erratic way through the flat plains of Meath and Kildare, with the occasional willow, sally and alder trees drooping over its slow moving waters. This area was known in times past as Bolg-Bóinne or 'the Belly of the Boyne,' because of the many great serpentine bends in the river's course.

There are several supposed derivations of the place name Clonard. In the Annals of the Four Masters it is named Cluain Iraird or Erard, which reputedly means 'the retirement on the western heights' – while John O'Donovan calls it Erard's Lawn or Meadow in the 1836 Field Notes. Here, in 530 (or 544) AD, Saint Finian founded a monastery which became famous throughout the then known world, and attracted scholars from far and near to study at this centre of learning. Supposedly some of the many students of Saint Finian were: St. Kieran of Clonmacnoise – St. Columbkille – the two St. Brendans (Birr & Clonfert) – St. Molua – St. Canice and many others.

The Annals of Clonard indicate that the town and monastery were plundered and burned several times throughout their turbulent history, these outrages being carried out variously by tribal chieftains and foreign invaders such as the Danes and other Norsemen.[11] The first recorded attack on the monastery and town by the Normans is in 1170, when Dermot Mac Murcha, King of Leinster, assisted by Earl Strongbow, sacked and burned both it and the town. The annals state also that the said Mac Murcha died (within a year)

Left: A determined pair.   Right: Elegance in flight.

of an insufferable and unknown disease which turned his flesh putrid while he was still living.

The site of the ancient monastery is located about a mile north-west of Leinster Bridge, it lies to the north of the Clonard River in the townland of Clonard-Old; St. Finians Church (old c.1808) is supposedly built upon part of the ancient site near the contemporary village of Clonard.

On these sluggish, tranquil stretches, we made the first of many encounters with a pair of swans frequenting the Upper Boyne reaches. These noble denizens of the river took umbrage at our noisy intrusion into their habitat; expressing their indignation by cruising slowly ahead in two-abreast formation down midstream, such that we could not pass and were compelled to slow to their more sedate pace. This continued for some little distance, until they tired of the sport and took flight; giving us a spectacular view of raw power and natural elegance in flight from our ringside seat in the boat. Then with a hop-skip and jump they landed again about one hundred metres ahead of the boat; where the slow manoeuvres were repeated, followed by an encore of the take-off.

Thus we continued along this sector of the Boyne, with the two mighty birds providing an enthralling sideshow to keep our attention occupied on this otherwise rather mundane river reach. When nearing the M4 Motorway Bridge at Clonard, the two creatures disappeared into the riverside sedges. We passed on under the concrete bridge; the raw, unaesthetic lines of the structure less than inspiring, even on such a beautiful day.[12]

A few hundred yards downstream, an older version of Clonard Bridge is much more appealing to the eye of the beholder. The triple stone arches providing yet another glimpse of how skilled craftsmen, using mostly rudimentary tools and equipment, could erect such elegant structures during those frugal times.

The bridge carries the former N4 (now the R148) across the Boyne, linking the townland of Mulpheder on the Meath side to Clonard-New on the Kildare riverbank. This became the line of the Dublin to Kinnegad turnpike (tollroad) from 1731; the turnpike road being extended to Mullingar and then to Athlone in 1733. In 1856 all such tollroads were abolished by Act of Parliament. Because many of its features are in character with several other Boyne bridges built by the OPW, it is likely that this bridge (erected and opened by 1831), was financed by a combination of the Meath and Kildare Grand Juries, and built by or under supervision of engineers later employed by the Commissioners of Public Works.

I could find no detailed professional assessment of this structure; hence, the following description is based on my own observations during the river trips beneath its arches and my many crossings of it over the years:

Leinster Bridge

From river aspect:
The bridge comprises three medium rise stone arches of segmental profile, each with a span of about 25/30ft: the outer arches abut vertical stone columns on each riverbank at a height of circa 9ft above mean water level. Two mid-river columns or pillars are circa 6ft in width and form a combined support for these and the central arch. The two central pillars have rounded (bull nosed) cutwaters both upstream and downstream. The pillars and cutwaters terminate at springer level and are topped by a dressed string-course, with the cutwater extensions topped by conical stone cappings; the abutment pillars are detailed in similar fashion. The splayed abutments commence from out-projecting piers at the extremities of each parapet and extend for about 20ft inland. All visible stonework appears to be of dressed limestone, laid in regular pattern. The arch rings/voussoirs are of dressed limestone, as are the spandrels. An unusual pair of interlocking cut-stones (similar to a mortise & tennon joint) is included in the spandrels above each central pillar. The soffit appears to be of dressed limestone laid in regular pattern. The abutments and

river pillars are underpinned with concrete to compensate for deepening of the river channel during drainage work. A dressed string-course runs atop the arch crowns, and continues around the out-projecting parapet piers. The waterway of the two riverside arches was partly obstructed by encroaching vegetation, hence unnavigable for our boat.

From road aspect:

The contemporary road crosses the bridge from Kildare in the south-east to Meath on the north-western bank: the approach to the bridge on both riverbanks is comprised of an embankment topped variously by rail fences and hedgerows; the embankment on the Meath side being much longer due to the wider floodplain. The circa 3.5ft high parapet walls are of dressed limestone blocks and spaced at about 32ft; they are coped with dressed, double-chamfered limestone interlocking blocks and overgrown by ivy in places. At each end, the parapets have wing walls, which flare out such that the approach roadways have hard shoulders and grass-margins. The spacing of the parapets at circa 32ft is consistent with the specifications for turnpike/post road bridges of the period. The remains of the turnpike or tollhouse (known locally as 'the coffin house' because of its oddly-shaped roof) stands to the south-west of the road about 200 yards from the Kildare riverside, on the apex of the contemporary road to Edenderry – this house was probably built contemporaneously with the new bridge in 1831.

Left: Leinster Bridge from upstream
Right: Stonework detail onKildare side of Leinster Bridge.

The Leinster bridge of 1831 was built during one of many realignments of the Dublin to Kinnegad tollroad or turnpike. It replaced an older structure (then in poor condition) of nine arches, once located about two hundred yards upstream, not a trace of which remains. The older bridge is named Clonard Bridge on Molls' 1714 map,[13] the Taylor & Skinner maps of 1778 and on Larkin's Map of 1812. I can find no record of why the newer bridge of 1831 was called Leinster Bridge, but it was perhaps named such to distinguish it from a nearby bridge, named Clonard Bridge, which spans the Clonard River.

The entire road system was very different in those days prior to the advent of the present day bridge, I will; therefore, devote some space for describing the old layout, to portray a clearer picture of events that unfolded here during the rising of 1798.

The pre 1798 road layout in the vicinity is depicted on page 62 of the Taylor and Skinner 1778 book of road maps. This is an important insight to the locality, as the later OS maps indicate both of the bridges and some of the old defunct roads, which presents a rather confusing image of the scene. A study of the Taylor and Skinner map shows that the Trim to Edenderry road

From page 62 of the Taylor and Skinner 1778 book of road maps

ran from the east at Ashfield Bridge, westwards, alongside the Boyne and linked with the Dublin to Kinnegad turnpike (contemporary N4/R148) at a 'T' junction south-east of the river in the townland of Clonard-New.

The junction was located just west of the previously mentioned later (1831) tollhouse. The road continued on a common line south-eastwards for about 300 yards, then split at a forked junction, the turnpike road turning at 90 degrees to run northwards across the river via the old bridge, with the lesser road turning southwards towards Edenderry (contemporary L50001). A small hamlet, including several thatched cottages and the old tollhouse, clustered around this road junction; with the road across the old bridge controlled by a lockable gate to enable collection of the tolls. Directly opposite, on the Meath or western riverbank was a Coachman's Inn, used as a staging post (or relay station), where horses were kept in readiness to relieve those drawing the coaches on the section.

A study of the old maps and Griffith's 1854 valuation provides some further insight to various other topographical features adjacent to Leinster Bridge in times past. On the Meath side, the 1837 map indicates the Post Office located on the new line from the bridge towards Clonard, due north

Newer tollhouse (Coffin House)

from the old Coachman's Inn on the older line of road. The PO is not marked on the map of 1911. A field of 2 acres 2 roods 10 perches, shaped rather like a truncated tundish or funnel (from the southern aspect), can be identified from Griffith's Valuation as the former Fair Green of Clonard; occupied at the time by Elizabeth G. Magan and leased from Lady Catherine Rich at R.V. £2-10s. The same Elizabeth G. Magan was assessed for the tolls of the Fair Green, valued at R.V. of £8. She is listed also as occupier of a larger property with several vacant houses, this included the site of the PO and comprised 336 acres of land, together with a Herd's house and offices, leased from the said Lady Rich at R.V. £222. It is likely that this Herd's house was indeed the old Inn and staging post of former days.

Traces of an older road can be discerned on the 1837 OS map, leading westwards from the Fair Green; the now defunct route linked with the byroad running from the vicinity of Clonard Church to the Ticroghan to Clonard road. This was perhaps the remains of an older line of the Drogheda/Trim to Athlone Norman road, prior to the advent of the turnpike in 1731.

To the east of the hamlet near the old bridge and tollhouse on the Kildare riverbank, the 1837 OS (coloured) depicts an enclosed ovid (egg) shaped section of land, which it names 'the Bulls Ring.' The enclosed area is lined by trees and surrounded by a water filled moat or trench, supplied by a stream sourced in a field to the south. The outflow from the moat fell in to the mereing drain that divides Clonard-New and Kilrathmurry Townlands. The 1911 map; however, indicates only the drain or ditch, with 'the Bulls Ring' gone from the landscape. I can find no record of this curious feature or its former usage other than its depiction on the 1837 and 1852 editions of the OS maps, but if one walks in these fields, the mereing drain is still evident where it falls into the Boyne just upstream of Leinster Bridge.

Griffith's indicates that a 179 acre 1 rood property, including the southern end of the old bridge, the old tollhouse and half the hamlet, together with the memorial site at the Croppies Grave, was leased by Edward Ledwich from William Ledwich at R.V. £93-10s. This included a 'Steward's House' and offices, which may have been the former tollhouse. An adjacent property to the east, comprising a house, offices and land totalling circa 6.76 acres (including most of 'the Bulls Ring'), was leased from William Ledwich by Thomas Tyrrell at R.V. £4; with William Hughes occupying a nearby house on a site of 5 roods, leased from Thomas Tyrrell at R.V. 5s. These houses comprised most of the hamlet near which 'the Battle of Clonard' unfolded in 1798, hence they apparently survived the conflict only to disappear from the landscape post 1854.[14]

The entire townland of Clonard-New comprising 63 acres and 3 roods, together with a Herd's house, is shown on the 1850s valuation to be leased by Thomas Flood (from ....Tyrrell) at total R.V. £41. The new toll house and offices are shown in the valuation to be occupied by Messrs. Flood and Hogan, and leased from the 'Trustees of the Turnpike Trust' at R.V. £1, with the tolls of the turnpike road at R.V. £10.[15]

Before we leave Leinster Bridge, I will give a brief account of events that unfolded here in July 1798; thus explaining previous references to 'the Croppies Grave/Memorial' and 'the Battle of Clonard.'

To the east of the old tollhouse and Boyne Bridge stood Tyrrell's stone built fortified house, commanding both the bridge and these two road junctions. On July 11th 1798, this house became the focal point of an engagement between the military and the previously mentioned Wexford Insurgent Column, which skirmish became known as 'the Battle of Clonard.'

Although there are several and varying accounts of this engagement related, I will mention only one; because it provides an important historical context to the event. A detailed account of and background to this almost forgotten episode of our history is given in Eamon Doyle's insightful book entitled *March Into Meath* (*in the footsteps of 1798*).

The book traces the origins of the conflict, from the start of the 'new' penal law era, through religious repression by the ruling elite and the rise of the United Irishmen movement. It records also the deliberate goading by the authorities (and others) to provoke an uprising, which they felt could be readily suppressed by superior military might. Most of the goading consisted of general rapine by the regular military, ably assisted by local militias and yeomen. Their summary executions, floggings, pitch-cappings and burning of homesteads sowed the wind, now about to engulf the land in the whirlwind of insurrection. The narrative tells of how mass executions (30 prisoners in Dunlavin Co. Wicklow and 28 in Carnew on May 24th and 25th) fanned the already smouldering embers of righteous anger into the searing flames of rebellion in Wexford on May 26th 1798. It traces the campaign in Wexford, from the engagement with Bookey's yeomen at The Harrow, through Oulart Hill, Tubberneering and Vinegar Hill to formation of the column and its trek northwards into Wicklow; the ill-fated meeting with the Wicklowmen at Whelp Rock and on through Kildare to the encounter at Clonard Bridge.

We cannot include Eamon Doyle's riveting account of the engagement, or the many local anecdotes included in his book. A summary of the event; however, shows that Thomas Tyrrell, incumbent High Sherriff of Kildare, when recognizing his family's vulnerability during earlier hostilities, had moved them from his own house in nearby Kilrainy to his kinsman's (John Tyrrell) residence beside the Boyne Bridge. He converted this house to a near impregnable fortress by closing up the lower openings and stockpiling large quantities of arms and ammunition within. The house, and a turret or tower in the outer courtyard, formed vantage points from which Tyrrells' musketeers could rain a constant fire down upon anyone approaching either place with hostile intent.

When the insurgent column of about 2,500 men, consisting mostly of Wexfordmen, some from Wicklow and a few from Kildare and other disparate groups, arrived in Clonard, they came upon what was effectively a well prepared trap, set and ready to be sprung. Although their numbers were vastly superior, over two thousand against the forty-odd defenders, a closer examination of the facts shows that the odds were stacked against them. Exhausted by their long trek and many skirmishes en route, and armed mostly with pikes, some swords, pitchforks and a motley array of firearms with sparse amounts of powder and shot available; they were, in fact, ill prepared to do battle with a well fed and armed foe, that, though fewer in numbers, held near impregnable positions.

Legends say that the column's main objective on the day was merely to cross over the bridge and head northwards to link with insurgents in Down and Antrim, not to do battle with the military. It is said also that the insurgents might have passed on had not one of the teenaged Tyrrells shot dead a leader of the rebel group (known as Captain Farrell), when he approached the house to parley for passage across the locked-off bridge. Whatever the truth of this speculation, battle was engaged following this shooting, with the affray lasting for several hours.

The Croppy memorial

Little doubt exists as to the bravery displayed by both sides in the conflict, with the insurgents mounting a myriad of attacks across open ground in the face of withering musketry fire from the house and tower, and the defenders holding firm against the odds. The rebels scored a limited success by taking the tower, but sustained heavy losses, supposedly 160 men were killed and many more wounded during the entire affair.

Some accounts say that the battle ended with the arrival of a small contingent of yeomen and about a dozen Fencibles from Kinnegad. However, as Eamon Doyle remarked in his book, such doughty warriors as the insurgents, having proved their undoubted valour on many a battlefield in the southern campaign, were unlikely to have taken flight at the arrival of the yeomen. It is more likely; therefore, that withdrawal of the rebels towards Carbury had commenced before the advent of the men from Kinnegad, who, according to another version of events, merely discharged a couple of desultory volleys from the safety of the Meath riverbank.

The victory was supposedly commemorated by composition of an Irish reel named 'the Kinnegad Slashers;' however, as stated in the old proverb "paper never refuses ink," so perhaps this tune was a truer reflection of their hubris following the victory at Clonard, rather than any valour shown on the field of battle.

On our downriver trips and more recent visits on terra firma, I noted the Boyne flowing ever onwards through the changing landscape; its dark hued,

Limekiln and mound at site of Tyrrell's fortified house

boggy waters unperturbed by the slaughter that took place here beside its green banks all those years ago. Little trace remains of Tyrrells' House, its surrounding courtyard wall, the tower where so many rebels expended their life's blood; with no obvious signs of the tiny hamlet or the old tollhouse now evident to the searching eye. Mother Nature is continuing to wrap her forgiving mantle over the scene, the few remaining ivy covered stone walls and some earthen embankments providing tantalising glimpses of what was there in '98. The one tangible reminder of what happened here is the Croppy Memorial, standing in the field close by the former route of the road over the long gone bridge.

Therein is a strange irony: although the Tyrrells' and their military friends won the victory on the day, no commemorative plaque or monument to their name stands at the scene; yet the defeated croppies are remembered by a Celtic Cross and plaque with some of their names inscribed thereon. A fitting memento to those brave men, who, though vanquished in this battle, reignited the flame of religious and personal freedom for future generations… and perhaps a reminder of history's judgement on the justice of their cause.

ENDNOTES

1 The above-mentioned Garr Br. (an 18th century stone arched structure **OFIAR 004-012**), is not to be confused with the two Garr Bridges spanning the Garr River(s) in Co. Kildare: in this instance, the bridge is named after the townland of Garr in Co. Offaly, which bridge carries a byroad across the Yellow River.

2 Though the above survey states that Sheep Bridge spans the Boyne River, it does, in fact, cross the Yellow River. Sheep Bridge is named such on Larkin's Map of County Meath, surveyed in the period 1804 to 1810 and published in 1817 – a bridge is shown at this location on the Taylor and Skinner maps of 1778.

3 A small tributary named 'the Milltown River' joins the Mongagh River at Derrinch. This stream rises at the fringe of the Brosna Basin catchment, east of Lough Ennell – it flows eastwards through Milltown Pass, then through bog-lands named Mongagh and Clash in Pass of Kilbride Townland, upstream from its confluence with the Mongagh River. While Mongagh Bog is reclaimed, both are shown on the 1837 and 1911 maps draining to the Milltown River via a small stream named Clash Drain.

4 Perhaps derived from Jordan Comin, reputed founder of Ballyboggan Priory in the 13th century – note previous mention of his supposed involvement in the massacre of the O'Connor Clan at Carrick Castle in 1305.

5 We covered the entire route of the Boyne, from the Yellow River to the estuary at Mornington, during the winters of 2011-2012 and 2012-2013. The harsher winter months were chosen to ensure sufficient water depth for passage across the many shallows, rapids, weirs and other obstructions encountered en route. The various stages of our journey being determined also by the demands placed upon the lads of the Meath River Rescue Service, who kindly slotted us 'amateur historians' on board as supernumeraries during their many training exercises upon the river. Thus the trips were not always completed sequentially e.g. the first trip described in the book, from Clongall to Ashfield, was, in fact, completed on Nov. 7th 2012. This was one of the last in the series dedicated to research for these writings. But to avoid confusion and for ease and continuity of narrative, all subsequent sectors are recorded as though they occurred in a continuous sequence.

6 The mill near Ballyboggan Priory is depicted also on Larkin's Map of County Meath (published 1817) as a multi-spoked wheel, the standard symbol used on this map to mark watermills.

7 The bridge at Ballybogan is depicted on the Taylor and Skinner map of 1778 upstream of the Abbey/Priory – whereas the contemporary bridge is located immediately downstream of this structure. As the road configuration is similar on the map to that prevailing on the landscape, this is likely to be merely a mapping error.

8 The large island mentioned above is depicted on Larkin's Map immediately downstream of the river crossing – Ballyboggan Br. is not indicated on this map – which is not unusual as Stackallan Br. is omitted from the same map downstream of Navan.

9 The byroad, nowadays running south-westwards from Clonard, past the site of Ticroghan Castle and onwards to join the R401 near Ballyboggan Priory, formed part of the great (Norman) road linking Athlone to Drogheda via Trim. The section from Trim to Phillips-

town (Daingean), which includes Ticroghan, can be traced on page 247 of the Taylor and Skinner maps of 1778.

10 A narrow salient of Ticroghan Townland extends southwards to form a short section of riverfront between Ballyboggan Bridge and Clonard; thus making this one of the Boyne's riparian townlands.

11 A comprehensive history of Clonard and its ecclesiastical institutions is included in Anthony (Dean) Cogan's 1862 *The Diocese of Meath Ancient and Modern*.

12 On this river reach and within Kilrathmurry Townland on the Kildare riverbank, the 1837 OS map indicates an 'old' mill race, which ran from the Boyne for a considerable distance parallel to the river and terminated close by the place where Rathmurry House (Rathmurry Demesne) is depicted on the later 1911 map. No mill is shown and I could not find any record thereof on Griffith's 1850s valuation.

13 The Down Survey 'County' Map of 1656 depicts this bridge in text only, and names it Clunard Bridge – whereas a graphic depiction of twin parallel lines crossing the Boyne appears on the Moyfenragh Barony map, which names the crossing Clunard Bridg (sic). This graphic depiction appears elsewhere at the known locations of several bridges such as Trim, Kilcarn and Slane.

14 The former tollhouse (newer), known in the vernacular as 'the Coffin House,' stands on the north-west apex of the Edenderry road's (L50001) junction with the N4/R148. On the opposite or south-east apex of this junction stands an old limekiln, immediately behind which is a small, scrub and weed covered low, oval shaped knoll comprised mainly of gravel. These features are located immediately north of the old Tyrrell House and within its former curtilage. Although the outline of the knoll is marked on the 1911 OS map, it is not recorded as a mound, nor is the limekiln marked as such on the map.

15 It is interesting to note that Thomas Flood and Edward Hogan are listed in Griffith's 1854 valuation as occupiers of the land upon which the Dublin and Slane/Dublin and Drogheda turnpike roads were constructed. In this instance the valuation lists the 'Trustees of Tolls' for these roads as the lessors. This is an interesting link between two separate turnpike roads, and suggests that Messers. Hogan and Flood were private toll collectors – yet again emphasising the truth in the old adage that "little new exists under the sun," as many of our contemporary tollroads are operated in a similar manner.

4

The Upper Reaches
Clonard to Inchamore Bridge

The River Glash, its source & watermills – Bunglass & Ballyonan Mill – The Kinnegad, Kilwarden & Clonard river (Blind River) – The 'condemmed canal' – Ashfield or Screeboge Townland – Ashfield Br. – Access slipways, 'cow slips' & end of a perfect day – Farewell Kildare – MGWR rail bridge, Boyne Aqueduct & Richard Evans canal engineer – a changing riverscape – Moneymore Weir – Stonyford (Boyne) Br., older & newer – River Deel & its sources – Upper Boyne Lakes – Mills upon the Deel and its tributaries – Killyon Corn Mill – Donore Friary, chapel – Donore Castle – Inchamore Br., older and newer – old road network & Rourkestown Br. – Lionsden (Lion's Den), hamlet, dispensary, forge, corn-mill, Anne Daly's house – The Enfield/Kildare Blackwater, its source, tributaries & watermills – some history of the 'new' Trim/Longwood road (R160)

Passing beneath the central span of Leinster Bridge, we continued our boat journey downriver. The Boyne hereabouts is broad, deep and unobstructed, sweeping in a series of chicane-like curves, cutting through the broad floodplain which slopes gently to the horizons. On the Kildare riverbank, about three hundred metres below the bridge, a small, partly clogged tributary enters the Boyne. This is the River Glash (or Green River), connected to the little stream, mentioned in Chapter One.[1]

On the 1911 OS map the stream is unnamed near its source, from where it flows north-eastwards through Calfstown to Ballinderry; then on to Clonuff Bridge-South and beneath a side road, where it powered a corn mill (occupied by Matthew Flanagan in 1854) near Kilcandrick House in Garrisker Townland. It continues onwards to pass beneath Clonuff Bridge-North (on L1002). From here it is named 'mill race' on the old maps and flows onwards across the River Glash via an aqueduct to Broadford Bridge. The 'mill race' flowed alongside the River Glash to Bunglass and powered Ballyonan Flour Mill, then fell into the River Glash; which once rose near Broadford and has a confluence with the Boyne below Leinster Bridge. The convoluted course of this little river reflects the considerable skill and ingenuity of the old-time millers in utilising the various smaller streams to power large mills such as Ballyonan Mill.[2]

The stream, once known as the 'mill race,' still flows from its source to Broadford, but through a vastly changed landscape. Although Kilcandrick House occupies the same site by the little bridge, it now overlooks a huge quarry and the stone arched bridge is replaced by a concrete structure. Matthew Flanagan's mill seems to have disappeared entirely from the landscape, its site now fronted in the new millennium by several modern dwellings and a business premises bearing the name Maguire's Tyres. The former mill is alive in local tradition; however, as a nearby house bears the name 'Millfield' and a housing estate is named 'Mill Race Lawns.'

But from Broadford to Ballyonan Mill, much of the old 'mill race' has disappeared, some of it beneath new developments and part of it is buried under the M4 Motorway. The water that once powered the flour mill at Ballyonan now appears to coalesce with the Glash River close by its source near Broadford. Perhaps the entire stream, from its rise near Carbury to the Boyne at Leinster Bridge, is known as the Glash River nowadays, but the old maps tell a different story.

Downstream from the Glash River, the Boyne flows to the north-east on a relatively straight, deep stretch for several hundred metres, then commences on a long gentle curve taking it due east under Ashfield Bridge. At the start of this eastwards sweep, another major tributary merges with the main river from the north-west. This stream is named variously the Kinnegad River, the Kilwarden River and the Clonard River as it meanders through these districts, and on Larkin's Map it is named 'the Blind River.'

The ruins of Ballonan Flour Mill

The confluence of the Kinnegad - Clonard river

The tributary rises in the vicinity of Knockaville in Co. Westmeath, where several small rills and capillaries flow from various bog-lands to form the stream. The embryonic river continues in a south-easterly direction, forming the mereing between Enniscoffey or Cartan & Hightown Townlands for a considerable distance. About a half mile from its source, the old OS maps depict a mill pond and corn mill situated on the river's edge within Hightown Townland.

Griffith's records the mill thus: corn-mill, house, offices, kiln and circa 110 acres of land (plus 24 acres of bog), leased by Peter Flynn from Charles Tuthill at R.V. £79-10s.

Further downstream, in the townland of Rattin (part of Clonfad), the maps show a complex series of mill races and sluices associated with another mill pond and corn mill situated some distance to the east of the stream. Griffith's describes the mill thus: house, offices corn-mill, kiln and land totalling circa 50 acres, leased by Denis Hagerty from Rev. John Fetherston H. at R.V. £37. These two mills were once powered by this tributary river, the only mills I could find along its course as depicted on the OS maps.

The name Kinnegad River first appears on the maps within Rattin Townland, from where the river flows in a predominantly east-northeasterly direction to Kinnegad. Flowing south of the town, it then turns northwards towards Aghamore Townland; on this stretch it crosses a very interesting landscape feature oftentimes the subject of discussions by historians.

The 1837 OS map shows a large trench/earthworks, running almost uninterrupted from the edge of the Kinnegad to Thomastown road north-west of Kinnegad. It passes in a great loop north of the town and north-eastwards through Kilwarden on a course parallel to the Royal Canal. This cutting can be traced to just east of 'the Hill of Down' Canal Bridge; where it links to the southern bank of the existing canal in the townland of Molerick (at Molerick Bog). The said map names this feature variously 'condemned line of canal' and 'former intended canal.' Cross-referencing the older map with that of 1911 indicates that most of it had merged with the landscape by then. Some of the old line can still be traced through satellite imagery; however, including a large section located between the Kinnegad River and the Trim road to the east of the contemporary water treatment plant. Almost the entire line of this landmark is indicated also on Larkin's Map of County

Meath; on which it is marked as 'first proposed line of canal.'

This was an older line intended to take the canal to Thomastown via Kinnegad; the preferred route of the earlier Royal Canal Co. as surveyed by their engineer, Richard Evans, and partly executed in the 1790s. Following an enquiry into delays and cost overruns on the project, the Company abandoned the original route. It was replaced by the contemporary canal line, proposed and surveyed by engineer John Brownrigg in the early 1800s. Brownrigg was an assistant to Evans on the Upper Boyne Navigation project in c.1792.

In Aghamore, the Kinnegad River coalesces with a small stream (the Kilwarden River) flowing from a bog north of Drumman, and assumes the name of the lesser stream. Turning in a great loop, it flows southwards and crosses the line of the 'condemned canal' again, before passing beneath the R161 at Kilwarden Bridge. Flowing south-eastwards from here, the river continues onwards to Monagalliagh north of Clonard. It then passes under Clonard Bridge, which carries a minor road linking the village to the site of the ancient abbey of Clonard. From here to its confluence with the Boyne the tributary is named 'the Clonard River.'[3]

Continuing our boat journey through an unaltered Boyne riverscape, we round a slight curve and arrive at Ashfield Bridge. A bridge is shown here on the Taylor & Skinner maps of 1778, linking the townland of Ballynakill on the Kildare side to the townland of Ashfield or Screeboge in County Meath. The same map indicates that Ashfield House, located south-east of the bridge, was then owned by Ash Esq., perhaps explaining the first name of the townland. In that era, Ashfield Bridge carried a road across the Boyne linking the Dublin to Kinnegad turnpike (now the R148) from a junction at Ballynadrumny, to the former Norman route from Drogheda, through Trim. This crossed the Boyne at Stonyford Bridge, and continued westwards through Clonard and Ticroghan, then to Athlone; therefore, Ashfield was an important bridge at the time.[4]

Nowadays the bridge carries a minor road from the R160 at Ballynakill Crossroads, across the Boyne to link with another byroad running from Stonyford Bridge to Clonard-Old. This junction is located a short distance south-west of Blackshade Bridge on the Royal Canal.

Ashfield Bridge is comprised of seven stone built arches, three of which on each riverbank are survivors of an older structure. The central span is another fine example of those built by the OPW during the drainage schemes of 1844 to 1862.

The centre section is very similar to the single span bridge built by the same public body upstream at Ballyboggan. There are some notable differences; however, because the new central arch is incorporated within the fabric of, and became part of an older bridge. Although it is a well-designed and elegant structure, the newer arch alters the aesthetics somewhat, spoiling the original symmetry by its different size and shape. The following description is based on my own observations during our river trips and several later site visits.

ॐ

Ashfield Bridge

From river aspect: Newer centre span

The section comprises a single medium/shallow stone arch of segmental profile, with a span of circa 25/30ft which abuts vertical stone columns at a height of about 8ft above mean water level on each end of the arch. The columns are built of rusticated limestone blocks, laid to regular pattern and faced both upstream and downstream with rounded cutwaters (bull nosed). The cutwaters are topped at arch springer level by a dressed string-course, which continues around each column, forming the arch springing plane. These two columns are circa 8ft wide and form mid-river pillars that carry the entire new structure and support the arches of the older bridge at the ends of the newer span. At each of the four corners, a circa 2.5ft x 6ft out-projecting pier rises from the cutwaters to parapet level. The arch rings/voussoirs are of rusticated limestone blocks, as are the spandrels, which are laid to a regular pattern. The soffit (intrados) appears to be of dressed limestone blocks in regular lines and the pillars are underpinned with concrete to compensate for deepening of the river channel during drainage work. The underpinning projects beyond the upriver cutwaters as wedge shaped extensions. A dressed string-course runs atop the arch crown, and continues around the out-projecting parapet piers.

Ashfield Bridge upstream

The older bridge from river aspect:
The three original arches on each side of the newer central span are of semi-circular profile, with their arch crowns about 2ft higher than that of the newer span. All the older openings span c.10/12ft and one on each side is open to the river, but at time of writing these are partially blocked by river sedge such that they are unnavigable; the other four are high and dry and could be described as flood arches. The inter-arch pillars are circa 6ft in width, and form vertical columns to springer level, as do the upriver and downriver cutwaters, which are of semi-circular profile and topped by conical cappings. The soffits/intrados of the three openings on the Meath riverbank are plastered, with several of the original corbel stones still in place (used for supporting construction timber or wickerwork forms). The arch ring-stones/*voussoirs* are of dressed stone, the spandrels of randomly laid rubble as are the parapets. An inspection of the unplastered arches on the Kildare riverbank, shows that the soffits/intrados are of randomly laid, dressed rubble stone. Some of the ring-stones are in poor repair and require pointing to avoid further degradation. One opening on the Kildare bank is partially blocked off by a mass-concrete wall. The abutments on both sides are formed by the approach embankments/retaining walls which are topped by battlemented walls/parapets of randomly laid, dressed rubble stone.

The complete bridge from road aspect:

The approach to the bridge, on both riverbanks, comprises an embankment buttressed by stone walls, which rise to about 4.5ft above road level and have battlemented tops. Both of the older sections have a distinct humped back appearance, with the newer span forming a flatter road section at midpoint of the bridge. The newer parapets, spaced at circa 20/22ft, rise about 3.5ft above road level and have rounded cut stone cappings. The four piers at the corners project circa 8in. beyond the parapet walls. I could find no label stone or plaque mounted on any part of the structure.

The older part of the bridge probably dates from the early to mid-1700s or possibly from a slightly earlier period. Judging by the symmetry of the original structure and the dimensions of the span built by the OPW, the newer section perhaps replaced two arches and one pillar similar in size to those surviving from the original.

Following our discussion and detailed inspection of the bridge (in which our support party participated also), Chalky and Richard pulled the RIB out to midstream and we set off downriver again. As it was now late afternoon and the light fading towards evening, our Cox., Martin Curran, decided to call it a day. This was the most sensible course of action, because we were not equipped or prepared for nighttime roaming on the river. Safe, accessible entry/exit points are few and far between on the Boyne; the nearest to us at that time being at Dixon's private residence just downriver from Ashfield Bridge.

Ashfield Br. from Kildare riverbank

At Dixon's Slip (Clockwise from top) Recovering the boat, Tom French and a friend and 'Suiting up', left to right; T. French, M. Curran, P. Marry, C. Rennicks, P. Brady and M. White

In this instance, the lads manoeuvred the boat in to one such drinking slip, where we disembarked into the mass of muck and cow-dung constituting these locations, especially in wintertime. While clambering up the slope to the lush green paddock on the riverbank, I slipped on a 'cow-pat' and fell flat on my face in the mire, thus gaining a different perspective to the flower known as the cowslip.

With kind permission of Ray Dixon, the Rescue Service uses this facility for training exercises and indeed at times for response to emergencies. Here we pulled the boat from the river onto the trailer, then changed out of our sodden kit in Ray's garage.[5]

So ended a day's exploration of the historic River Boyne and we departed the scene to go our separate ways... we amateurs to our homes, the lads of the

Rescue Service to their temporary base in Navan; where they still had work to do cleaning the boat and preparing equipment for the next callout.

About a fortnight later towards the end of November, we set out from the same improvised slip with two boats, this time bound for the mill at Bective Bridge.

Following a welcome cup of tea and snack in Dixon's kitchen, we suited-up in the garage and clambered through the mud to board the boats; deployed on the river and awaiting our departure for the downriver reaches. Martin Curran was 'Cox. of the boat' once more, with Hopper Rennicks and Martin (Chalky) White acting as lookouts on the bows; Tom French, Paschal Marry and I made up the numbers as supernumeraries. The second boat was crewed by Pa. Reilly, Richard Harding, J. Rennicks and M. Boland, with Oliver Delany as an extra hand. Paddy Brady and Eamon Quinlevan drove the jeeps and comprised the support group that kept in touch with the boats by radio and made contact at the various bridges en route.

Dixon's slip is directly opposite Ashfield House, where the river is relatively deep and about sixty feet wide. Looking upriver from the boat, we had a good view of Ashfield Bridge; with winter's bright, watery sunlight gleaming through its seven arches, lighting them up like windows against the darker rain clouds massing in the sky to the west.

Heading on downriver, we passed the mereing of Boolykeagh Townland on the southern shore. According to the 1836 Field Notes, this name translates to 'blind or dark dairy,' but it has a greater significance in terms of the River Boyne's course. From here the river flows solely through County Meath to Marry's Weir at Oldbridge; where it first touches County Louth at Townley Hall on its upper tidal reaches.

Just below this mereing, we rounded a slight curve and came upon one of the most impressive man-made features on the Upper Boyne; the twin, stone arched structures built to carry the Midland Great Western Railway and the Royal Canal across the Boyne. The former a three arched railway bridge, the latter a massive aqueduct known as 'the Boyne Aqueduct.' These stone viaducts carry railway and canal across the river, from Boolykeagh Townland on the south bank to Ballynabarny Townland on the northern shore. According to the 1836 Field Notes, the latter name translates to 'the town or place of the gap.'[6]

Clockwise from top: Boyne Aqueduct and Railway Br. from downstream.
Ivy clings to the Aqueduct's magnificent stonework.
Boyne Aqueduct from downstream - with railway Br. in background.

An assessment of The Boyne Aqueduct in Ronald Cox's Heritage Civil Engineering Works (HEWs) listing, No. 3128 N 692 453:

> The Boyne Aqueduct was completed in 1804 and carries the Royal Canal over the River Boyne near Longwood in County Meath. The river at this point is about 40ft wide and flows through the central arch of the aqueduct.

The designer, Richard Evans,[7] was faced with the problem of providing a structure capable of withstanding not only the forces applied by the canal water, canal traffic and the dead weight of the masonry, but also the considerable lateral forces resulting from the river when in flood. The resulting viaduct in rusticated ashlar limestone masonry has three arches spanning the river and its floodplain.

The arch profiles are three centred and are each about 40ft span with a rise of about 16ft. The voussoirs in the arch rings are 2ft deep and the tops of the spandrel walls terminate in a cornice running the length of the aqueduct. The 6ft piers have a simple architectural feature rising from curved cutwaters. The massive abutments are splayed at the base to a width of 107ft 6in.

This stretch of the canal is about 35ft wide and narrows to 20ft over the aqueduct, the total length of which is 132ft. There are 8ft 9in. wide towpaths on each side of the waterway.

The main Dublin to Galway Railway runs alongside the canal and crosses the river on a parallel masonry arch viaduct, built in 1849, which has three flat elliptical arches of rise to span ratio of around 0.25 and of similar span to those of the aqueduct.

To the south of the Boyne, the old road from Bunglass joins the R160 at Ballynakill Crossroads, which road passes over Roe's Bridge and continues north-eastwards to pass beneath a single stone arched railway bridge (former MGWR line). About fifty metres further on, the R160 passes under a single stone arched aqueduct carrying the Royal Canal, then continues onwards to Longwood, about one kilometre to the north-east.

Nowadays the Boyne is about 60ft wide upstream of the railway bridge; however, the river narrows to about 40ft and flows through the central arch only. The other two arches on both bridges are isolated from the unflooded river by banks approximately 6ft higher than the mean water level; therefore, they act essentially as flood arches. Although no trace remains of the transverse weir, indicated on the 1837 OS map immediately upstream of the aqueduct, a pronounced ripple on the river surface indicates its former location about midway between the two bridges.

Because of the constriction, our boats were carried rapidly through both arches on the torrent, such that we had little time to admire the magnificent stonework. However brief the transit, we noted the pillars of both bridges were underpinned in concrete, and the structures overgrown by ivy and other greenery. The adjacent riverbanks are returning to Mother Nature's welcoming embrace in the form of sally, willow and other scrub timber, growing profusely around the stonework and overhanging the channel in places. In these frugal post Celtic Tiger times, some of the tax revenue, extracted from the long-suffering taxpayers, could be spent by our government in giving these magnificent structures a much needed facelift.

The river broadens below the aqueduct, and we noticed a subtle change in the riverscape between here and Stonyford Bridge. From here onwards, the riverbanks rise to perceptibly higher ground on both shores; the upriver marshy bottomlands change gradually to more verdant pastureland, and from the river aspect the Boyne appears to be flowing along a shallow valley rather than winding through a flat plain. The river passes between steeper banks, larger stretches of which are two-tiered. These layered riverbanks resulting from the spoil, generated by the many drainage schemes, being spread such that a higher embankment is formed further back from the river; the lowermost ledge possibly representing the original level of the bottomlands. A greater amount of river growth and sedge becomes apparent hereabouts, with a corresponding increase in the profusion of scrub and riverside alders, sally and hawthorn, all tangled together on the riverbanks.

In the townland of Moneymore,[8] opposite Moneymore House, the Boyne turns almost 90 degrees from its course to flow in a more north-northeasterly direction towards Stonyford Bridge. Here, the 1837 OS map depicts a zig-zag shaped weir crossing from bank to bank, with a large island occupying the centre of the river. As there is no mill shown in the locality, and as evidenced by its shape, this was perhaps a fishing or eel weir in times past, of which I can find no record. On our journey downriver, we became aware of this unknown weir when the boat hung up, whereupon Hopper and Chalky took to the water and hauled us across.

This rocky ledge or shoal is what remains of 'Moneymore Weir.' The remnants of the island, shown on the map, are still evident upon the Boyne, and take the form of several small, rocky islets and shallow shoals impeding

Clockwise from top: A conference near remnants of Moneymore Weir and island;
Hopper frees our boat at Moneymore; Unnavigable river.

river passage. Hopper and Chalky were very busy on this stretch between
Moneymore and Stonyford Bridge because of the many obstructions,
shallows and overhanging trees encountered en route. A profusion of gravel
pits occupy much of the eastern riverbank alongside this section of the Boyne.

Stonyford (Stoneyford) Bridge crosses the Boyne and links the townland
of Drummond on the western bank with that of Monyfin on the eastern
shore. The name can be somewhat confusing as another bridge with the same
title spans the Stonyford River, a tributary mingling with the Boyne further
downstream.

The origins of the name are uncertain as no such place name exists close by
the bridge; however, the title may derive from a river ford, perhaps a precursor
of the bridge. From our experience of the stony riverbed hereabouts, this ford
was most likely named 'the Stoney Ford.' Local lore attributes the place name

to a series of stepping stones, supposedly providing a river crossing here at one time. The 1911 OS map shows a large house named Stoneyford House at the south-east end of the bridge and a group of buildings across the road is shown as Stoneyford; Larkin's Map depicts a small hamlet at the latter location. No trace remains of a transverse weir, depicted on the 1837 OS map spanning the river about fifty metres above the bridge.

Like Ashfield Bridge upstream, this is a two-generation bridge i.e. it contains elements of an older and newer bridge within its structure. Although the newer section seems to be located entirely at the eastern extremity, it is possible that another one or two smaller arches are buried by river-drainage spoil or hidden in dense scrub on this (eastern) riverbank. During our river boat trips, I noticed the tops of two older arches peeping above the western bank, but the eastern bridge approach was hidden by dense undergrowth; therefore, invisible from the boat.

This prompted my return on terra firma to carry out a further inspection in April 2013; however, I could not gain access to this section of riverside as it is located on private property. The following assessment is based on this visit and observations made during the earlier boat trips.

૪

Stonyford Bridge

Newer OPW built span

The section comprises a single shallow stone arch of segmental profile, with a span of about 45/50ft which abuts vertical stone columns at springer level about 8ft above mean water level on each end of the arch. The columns are built of rusticated limestone blocks, laid to regular pattern. There are no obvious cutwaters, but if present, they are hidden by the riverbank which abuts both upstream and downstream facades of the base columns. On all four corners and circa 3ft from the outer edge of the columns, circa 6ft wide out-projecting piers rise from the foundation to parapet level, where they are capped by dressed, embossed stone slabs. The pillars have a pronounced batter, being much thicker at the base and tapering to about 2.5ft at parapet level. The arch rings/voussoirs are of dressed/rusticated limestone blocks, as are the spandrels, which are laid to a regular pattern. The soffit (intrados) is of dressed limestone blocks laid in regular lines. Both support columns are underpinned with concrete to compensate for deepening of the river channel during drainage work. A dressed string-course runs atop the arch crown, and continues around the out-projecting parapet piers. The downstream façade is coated heavily in ivy, with much less greenery clinging to the upstream pillars and parapets.

N.B., an extract from the Commissioners of Public Works, Ireland 17th report of 1848 states: "Stonyford Bridge commenced 9th May – Arch keyed 17th of August – Bridge opened to traffic 1st Sept. 1848" (paraphrased for clarity).

The older bridge from downriver aspect
as viewed from north-western riverbank only:

Starting from the north-western pillar of the newer span, the older bridge is comprised of the following: circa 12ft abutment/retaining wall, constructed of random rubble which supports both older and newer spans: semi-circular profiled arch of circa 10/12ft span about 8ft high, this opening is blocked by plywood sheeting at upstream and downstream ends – circa 5ft wide pillar – semi-circular profiled arch of c.10/12 span about 8ft high, this opening is blocked off downstream with a 3ft trellis fence and is open to the private garden upstream: it appears to be in use as a shed – circa 5ft wide pillar – semi-circular profiled arch about 08/10ft span and circa 8ft high, this opening is blocked by stone masonry, such that it is almost invisible except for its ring stones, which are of roughly dressed rubble as are those of the other two arches. The spandrels are of dressed rubble, randomly laid: the one visible soffit, that of the central arch; is of randomly laid rubble, with many gaps and small fissures visible between individual stones. The western approach to these three arches is comprised of a stone buttressed circa 25ft long embankment (with a discernible lean to the east), at the outer end of which is a small semi-circular flood arch of circa 6ft span and approximately 4ft in height (blocked by masonry) which forms the westernmost extremity of the bridge. There are no cutwaters on any part of the older bridge. About midway along this embanked section, approximately 10ft of the parapet wall has collapsed such that the resultant pile of rubble may, in fact, be obscuring another flood arch.[9]

From road aspect

On the east side, the approach road is straight and approximately 14ft wide, with narrow grass margins on each side. The 3.5/4.5ft high, randomly laid rough stone walls are covered extensively in ivy and topped with a mixture of concrete caps and stone battlement; reflecting many repairs carried out over the years. The road rises sharply at the newer span and narrows such that the parapets are spaced at c.16/18ft and topped with double-chamfered, dressed stone blocks on the newer span. A label stone on the northern wall is illegible to the naked eye. The parapets on the older bridge are of randomly laid rubble stone. The northern wall is battlemented and runs westward over the inter-bridge abutment, the three larger arches, the embanked buttress and the smaller flood arch (note previous mention of breach at this end). The southern parapet has a concrete capping and terminates just above the third arch (walled up circa 08/10ft), where the road drops again, to swing south-westwards in a sharp curve. This part was probably demolished to improve visibility through the blind bend. The ground level on the southern side has been raised such that most of the bridge, from the 08ft blocked arch to the smaller flood arch at the end, is now buried and invisible from upriver. The sharp drop at each end gives this bridge a distinctly humped back appearance.

Approaching Stonyford Bridge with support group keeping watch

The earliest record I can find of a bridge at this location is on Molls' Map of 1714. As mentioned, the Taylor and Skinner road maps of 1778 show a bridge spanning the Boyne here, which carried an ancient line of the (Norman) road from Athlone, via Clonard and Ticroghan to Trim: this road ran onwards alongside the Boyne through Scurloughstown, Bective and Dowdstown, where it parted from the river to continue on through Duleek to Drogheda. In my opinion, the older sections of Stonyford Bridge may date from the 1600s or possibly from late medieval times. The newer span dates from 1848; it probably replaced three or possibly four arches of similar size and profile to those still surviving on the western riverbank.[10]

Considering its antiquity and structural condition, it is somewhat surprising that a weight restriction has not been imposed to date.

Left: Dogs watching me through collapsed parapet of Stonyford Bridge.
Right: Rough water near Donore.

Below the bridge, the Boyne passes through a landscape very similar to the stretch between Ashfield and Moneymore. The river flows due north before sweeping eastwards in a great curve, then turning to continue north-westwards. The bulge or salient enclosed between these great sweeps includes much of the townland of Ballyadams on the western riverbank. At the most northern point of this townland, another major tributary, the River Deel coalesces with the Boyne opposite the townland of Ballymahon. The Boyne, from Stonyford Bridge to this confluence, runs between high banks covered liberally with scrub timber including the prolific alder, sally, birch and hawthorn; some of which encroach upon the stream and provide obstructions to boat passage. The many shallows and shoals, together with rocky, sedgy islets, while enhancing the beauty of the scenery, provided challenges to our progress downriver. Thus Hopper and Chalky spent most of their time in the water lugging the heavy RIB across the various obstacles.

The River Deel forms a mereing between the townlands of Ballyadams and Donore where it falls into the Boyne just downstream of Killyon House. The Deel, sometimes known as the Dale, takes its main rise from a group of small and medium sized loughs in the hinterland of Fore and Collinstown, County Westmeath. These are known as 'the Upper Boyne Lakes' and parts of some are located within Meath. While many other rills, streams and several unnamed minor lakes contribute to the Deel, these loughs constitute the main sources and are comprised of three distinct groups with individual outlets that combine to form one of the Boyne's major tributaries. The groups of loughs are known variously as the Ben Loughs – the Glass Loughs and Lough Lene.

Starting with the most north-westerly group, the Ben Loughs, we will follow the various source streams, depicted on the 1837 and 1911 OS maps, as they grow to form the River Deel downstream of Lough Adeel. The most northerly lake in the group is Lough Annagh or White Lake, which outfalls through a series of tiny lakes named, Rushy, Oldtown, Crockdoo and Carrick into Ben Lough. This in turn falls into Ben Lough Middle, which flows into Ben Lough South. The stream from here continues south-eastwards to coalesce with another brook flowing south-westwards from Lough Bane; which lake receives the waters from Glass Lough North and Glass Lough South. These combined streams flow south-southeastwards to Cummerstown Townland and mingle with a brook outflowing from Lough Lene (famed for its 'gin-clear' water), located further to the west.

The developing river continues south-eastwards and flows in to Lough Adeel, which outfalls near its north-western end to form the River Deel proper. As the section from the lough to Drumcree is the first part of the river bearing the title of River Deel on the OS maps, the name probably derives from the title of this lake.[11]

The river continues from Drumcree on a south-eastwards course past several small loughs, including: Kennedy's Lough, Long Lough and Black Lough (now dry). Continuing on past Lough Hoo and beneath Mooretown

Bridge, it flows into Lough Analla and outfalls to flow through the upper and lower Dysart Loughs and on past Dysart Taly (site of an ancient abbey?).

Below here, the river turns southwards to flow beneath Ballynacor Bridge and onwards to Cummer Bridge; then mingles with a small tributary flowing from the west through Killagh. Continuing southwards to Raharney, it turns to the south-east and coalesces with the Riverstown River in the townland of Grange Beg, near Derrymore Lough about a mile below Raharney. Near Annadruce Bridge, the Deel turns eastwards to flow beneath Inan Bridge and enter Co. Meath; then mingles with the Curris River and turns to flow south-eastwards through Killyon to fall into the Boyne.

The following list of mills located on the River Deel and its tributaries was compiled from data gleaned from the 1837 and 1911 OS maps and Griffith's 1850s valuation:

⁂

Watermills on the River Deel and catchment (10 of)

Carrick Townland

Below Lough Bane: house, offs, corn-mill & kiln and land occupied by Arthur Dempsey, leased from William Fetherston H. @ R.V. £18-10s.

Cummerstown Townland

near Lough Lene: house, offs, corn-mill & land occupied by Anne Murtagh, leased from trustees of Wilson's Hospital @ R.V. £117-5s

Gormanstown Townland

at Drumcree below Lough Adeel: corn-mill, tuck mill, offs & land occupied by Edward Tormey, leased from Robert Smyth @ R.V. £21-0s.

Glenidan Townland

near Lough Glass South: corn-mill, kiln & offs occupied by Thomas McDaniel, leased from Patrick E. Murphy @ R.V. £29-0s.

Grangetown Townland

East of Drumcree Br. below Lough Adeel: house, off's, corn-mill, tuck mill, land, leased by Thomas Martin from William E. Smyth @ R.V. £168-0s.

On small tributary at Killagh Br.

house, off's, corn-mill, tuck mill and land occupied by Maurice Hagerty, leased from Sir John Nugent Bart' @ R.V. £94-0s.

Raharney-Little Townland

in Raharney Village: house, off's, mill & land occupied by Christopher Keefe, leased from Knight of Kerry @ R.V. £50-0s. N.B., the title Knight of Kerry was bestowed on John Fitzgerald's sept following the Acts of Settlement in the 1660s – their main ancestral home was in the Barony of Iveragh in south Co. Kerry.

On Riverstown River in Mill Land Townland

flour mill, off's & land occupied by Benjamin Hannan, leased from Earl of Longford @ R.V. £80-0s.

On Riverstown River in Cushinstown Townland

mill, kiln & land occupied by William Garty, leased from Captain John Nugent @ R.V. £25-0s. N.B., the tailrace from this mill returned to the Riverstown River in Thomastown T/L, close by the Royal Canal feeder water supply to Thomastown Lock.

The last mill identified on the River Deel is located in the townland of Ballyadams to the south-east of Killyon Bridge and downstream of Killyon House. The mill has gone long since, but a dormer bungalow occupying the site is named Old Mill House. The millrace for this mill was taken from the Deel upstream of a weir located within Killyon Demense, which local tradition holds was named 'Magan's Weir.' This race is long gone, but traces of it can still be found near the road bridge (R161), close by the bungalow named 'Old Mill House.' Killyon/Ballyadams Mill is recorded thus on Griffith's Valuation: house, off's, corn-mill & land occupied by John

Treacy, leased from Elizabeth G. Magan @ R.V. £10-10s.[12] A windmill is indicated on Larkin's Map to the south-east of Killyon Br, between the road and the Boyne.

Fishing on the River Deel is controlled by the Deel and Boyne Angling Association, which includes the following information about the river in its brochure (not verbatim)):

> The River Deel is a limestone river and it is characterised by the clarity of its waters. There are excellent hatches of fly life on this river including various upwing species, sedges and dipthera. This river fishes best in the early part of the season before its luxuriant growth of weeds gets firmly established. This river is deep and is best fished by wading, so chest waders are essential. There is good fishing at Cummer Bridge upstream of Raharney and at Clondalee and Killyon bridges below Raharney. Parking is generally off road and the best access is from the bridges.'

In the area of the Deel confluence, the 1837 OS map indicates the Boyne's course laced by a series of islands with an eel weir near the southern bank, and both rivers shown encroaching onto much of the broad floodplain. The 1911 map depicts the scene altered similar to other locations upstream, and reflects the contemporary course.

During our downriver passages, we noticed the strong flow issuing from the mouth of the Deel (25/30ft wide at the confluence); which current causes an almost whirlpool-like effect upon the more placid Boyne water. Hereabouts a change takes place to our river because of the additional waters contributed by the Upper Boyne Lakes. Although scarcely noticeable initially, one becomes aware gradually of some subtle differences; the Boyne, less tinted by the brownish waters of the upland bogs, assuming a more vigorous aspect, its clearer water reflecting the winter's pale sunlight.

While drifting across deeper pools, here and there we noticed an increased activity of the river denizens, as the fish broke the mirror-like surface to become acquainted with the many flies clustering in the deep cleft of the river. On one occasion, Chalky almost 'poached' a large trout or perhaps a

The River Deel's confluence with The Boyne

small salmon. While dipping the portside oar, I heard him exclaim in surprise and saw a glint of silver as the big fish slithered off the rising oar back to its habitat… and wondered who was the most startled. On this reach we became reacquainted with our pair of swans, whose antics kept us entertained for a considerable distance downriver.

The Boyne continues on its north-easterly course between the townlands of Donore to the north and Ballymahon to the south, until it turns south-eastwards at a great sweeping bend close by the easterly mereing of Donore. When he passed this way in the late 1840s, Wilde described an old ruin on the riverbank at this bend:

> In the demesne of Killyon, on the northern bank of the river, about midway between Clonard and Trim, are the ruins of an old church and friary, originally founded by St. Liadhan or Liedania, the mother of St. Kieran of Saighir, who is still the patroness of this parish. From some of the inquisitions and Burke's *Hibernia Dominicana* we learn that the Dominican monks of Trim retired to the Friary of Donore, as it is sometimes called. The two walls which now remain are picturesquely situated on a sloping ground, surrounded by some patriarchial ash trees.

The 1837 OS map names and indicates the ruins in outline, but the map of 1911 marks the spot with the inscription 'Friary & Chapel (site of),' an indicator that the old friary had disappeared entirely by then. Nowadays the ancient site is marked only by a circular clump of trees adorning the small field, with no sign on the roadside indicating its former presence.

Similar to other places we passed by, the 1837 OS map depicts a very different river here; with the waterway much broader and divided by two large islets upstream of the great curve at Donore, while downstream, the Boyne is sprinkled by many tiny islets. But despite all the drainage works executed throughout the years since then, the river continues to fight back, as evidenced by the many shoals, islets and shallows we encountered en route.

Rounding the curve, we caught our first glimpse of Donore Castle from the river aspect; in 1849, Wilde wrote of this place:

> Below the friary, on the northern bank the square border castle of Donore forms a conspicuous object, as its ruins are in better preservation than most of the other castles of the Pale, particularly those on the northern side of the river. We have not been able to collect any accurate information with reference to this building, which does not appear to be any older than the fifteenth century. It was probably built by some of the Anglo-Norman soldiers, who spread themselves over the fertile valley of the Boyne for two or three centuries after the English invasion. There are several Donores, both in Meath, Westmeath, and Kildare; and two of these – McGeogehegan's castle in Westmeath, and Donore Hill, from where James beheld his defeat at the Boyne – are memorable locations.

It would seem that little more clarity as to the origins of Donore Castle exists nowadays, than did in Wilde's era. Although anecdotes are related of how over fifty of the McGeoghegan clan were massacred here during the Cromwellian campaign, there seems little substance to these yarns. This is perhaps yet another foul deed attributed to 'the Great Protector,' that possibly never occurred, at least not in the area mentioned. Wilde's reference to the several locations of the place name Donore possibly provides a solution to this particular riddle; as McGeoghegan's castle in Donore, near Horseleap in Co.

Donore Castle from the river aspect

Westmeath fell to Parliamentarian forces c.1650. Regarding the ownership of this particular Donore Castle in the turbulent years of the Confederate Rebellion (Wars of the Three Kingdoms); I believe that one Garrett Lynch possessed this castle at the outbreak of hostilities in 1641, and that the same gentleman applied for restoration of his property during the Acts of Settlement in the 1660s.[13]

The castle is a three storeyed rectangular keep or tower house standing close by the northern riverbank, its four corners orientated almost exactly to the cardinal points of the compass. There are several unusual features within its fabric, including three corners of rounded profile, with the fourth or south-western corner nearest to the river encompassing a round tower for access to its upper storeys. The single entry portal is located on the western wall immediately north of the tower. Directly above this entrance is a well preserved machicolation, constructed at parapet level and accessed from the roof.[14] A crack is discernible on the western wall at third floor level, and the walls are pierced at random by embrasures and several window slots, with some larger window openings higher up on the tower. The battlements are of ornamental stonework and appear to be in reasonable condition. Access to the building can be gained across a field, via a wooden stile leading off the nearby R161.

Beyond Donore Castle, the Boyne's course continues south-eastwards to where Ballymahon Townland adjoins the townland of Lionsden on its southern shore. Here the river turns again and flows due north to Inchamore Bridge at the northern extremity of the latter townland. This is a very scenic reach, the deep cleft made by the river cuts through a pastoral landscape, with the riverbanks dotted here and there by alder and sally trees, sometimes encroaching partly over our waterway. Hopper and Chalky had time to relax, as the Boyne flows broad and deep here between its two-tiered banks. Approaching the bridge, we noted that the river passes close by the old Trim to Longwood road and that some residents of nearby houses used the riverbank for boating access. An occasional small private riverside arbour could be seen nestling beneath the willow trees.

Inchamore Bridge is yet another hybrid, with a newer section built by the OPW within the fabric of an older structure. Nowadays the bridge carries the Trim to Kinnegad road (R161) across the Boyne, linking the townlands of Lionsden and Donore. The R161 runs on the southern side of the Boyne from the Wellington Monument in Trim, through Boards Mill and on to Castlericard Townland. Here it swings to the south-east and crosses Rourkestown Bridge[15] spanning the River Blackwater (named variously the Enfield Blackwater and Kildare Blackwater), which has a confluence with the Boyne about half a kilometre downstream of Inchamore Bridge. In Lionsden the road splits at a 'Y' junction, the R161 veers further to the south-west and crosses the Boyne via Inchamore Bridge, with the old line of the Trim/Longwood to Edenderry road continuing alongside the river as a minor road.

The earliest map record of a bridge at this location (upstream of the Blackwater confluence) can be found on Molls' 1714 map. Pratt's map of 1703 indicates a bridge crossing the Boyne just below its confluence with the River Blackwater a short distance further downstream, and the road running onwards along the north-western riverbank towards Donore Castle. The Taylor and Skinner map of 1778 shows the road crossing the Boyne below the confluence (perhaps by a ford); however, it depicts a branch road crossing the Blackwater and continuing alongside the Boyne to Stonyford Bridge (the old Norman road from Drogheda to Athlone). Larkin's Map of 1812/17 and both the old OS maps reflect the contemporary road layout.[16]

The scaling of Molls,' Pratt's and the Taylor and Skinner maps is very small; therefore, not suitable for tracing exact road layouts. But they are the best available maps prior to the advent of Larkin's Map and the first Ordnance Survey, and, in fact, provide clues to a very different road layout here in earlier times. If one studies the 1837 OS map, an ancient roadway can be traced from the Boyne's western bank, opposite the old church and graveyard of Clonee on the eastern shore. This road ran south-westwards through Donore Townland towards the castle. Nowadays the same road is a narrow laneway (known in the vernacular as Conneyberry or Conneyburry Bohereen), leading off the R161 just east of Donore Castle. It can still be travelled upon to within a few hundred metres of the Boyne, and terminates at a private dwelling. Perhaps this was an earlier access route to/from the castle, which crossed the river via a ford to connect with the road running alongside the Boyne in Clonee.[17]

Further insight to this complex river crossing can be gained by cross-

The River Boyne from Taylor and Skinner's, 1778 Maps of theRoads of Ireland

1 Clonard Bridge	2 Ashfield Bridge
3 Stonyford Bridge	4 Inchamore Bridge
5 Rourkestown Bridge	
6 Scariff Bridge	7 Derrinydaly Bridge

referencing the OS map of 1837 with those of 1852 and 1911. This exercise shows that many alterations took place to the courses of the Boyne and Blackwater hereabouts, especially in the area close to the old corn mill in Lionsden.

While Inchamore Bridge is listed in 'the National Inventory of Architectural Heritage' as No. 14404106, no great detail is provided of the newer structure, and the older part is merely referred to as 'flanking' sections of a medieval bridge. The following description is based on my observations from the boat trips and other inspections from terra firma:

Inchamore Bridge

(Inchymore – Anchimore on some Grand Jury records) – OPW built span of 1848 (almost identical to the newer span of Stonyford Br.).

The section comprises a single shallow stone arch of segmental profile, with a span of circa 45/50ft; which abuts vertical stone columns at springer level about 6ft above mean water level on each end of the arch. The columns are built of rusticated limestone blocks, laid to regular pattern. The base columns extend about 4ft upstream and downstream of the bridge facade. On all four corners and about 2.5ft from the outer edge of the columns, circa 6ft wide out-projecting piers rise from the foundation to parapet level, where they are capped by dressed stone slabs. The pillars have a pronounced batter, being thicker at the base and tapering to about 2.8ft at parapet level. The arch rings/voussoirs are of rusticated limestone blocks, as are the spandrels, which are laid horizontally to a regular pattern. The soffit (intrados) is of dressed limestone blocks laid in regular lines. Both support columns are underpinned with concrete to compensate for deepening of the river channel during drainage work. A dressed string-course runs atop the arch crown, and continues around the out-projecting parapet piers. Both façades are clear of ivy.

N.B., an extract from the Commissioners of Public Works, Ireland 17th report of 1848 states: "Inchamore Bridge commenced 11th April – Arch keyed 6th

June – Bridge opened to public 1ˢᵗ July 1848" (paraphrased for clarity). This report also names the area 'Little Inchimore.'

Western end of the older bridge from the south-western aspect:
Starting from the upstream or south-western pillar of the newer span, the older bridge is comprised of the following: c.15ft long abutment constructed of random rubble which supports both older and newer spans. Semi-circular profiled arch of c. 12/14ft span and about 8ft high:[18] circa 25/30ft long sloped buttress, from ground level to base of parapet wall (N.B., from the symmetrical appearance of the bridge, it is likely that this buttress, which is replicated on the downstream façade also, obscures another arch of similar size) – semi-circular profiled arch of c.10/12ft span about 8ft high – c.10/12ft pillar of random rubble – semi-circular profiled arch of circa 6/8ft span about 5ft high: 45/50ft long stone lined embankment of random rubble construction. Semi-circular profiled arch about 6/8ft span and 5ft high (flood arch), which has a sloped surrounding buttress on its opposite or downstream end: these arches are plastered internally and each has at least two tie-bars with iron strong-backs to prevent the structure spreading: several such tie-bar arrangements are located at random on the older part of the structure. Some of the arch rings are plastered, with those visible formed from dressed rubble stone.

Eastern end of the older bridge – from the south-eastern aspect:
This end of the bridge consists of a stone lined embankment rising gradually to abut the newer span; the structure, built from random rubble, is approximately 70ft long and topped by battlemented walls: near its eastern extremity, it is pierced by a single arch of semi-circular profile, which spans c.10/12ft and is circa 5ft high. There are three tie-bar and strong-back arrangements supporting this arch, which may have been built originally as a conduit for the tailrace of the nearby corn mill.

From road aspect:
On the east side, the approach road is straight and approximately 16ft wide, with narrow grass margins. The 3ft high, randomly laid rough stone walls are topped with a mixture of concrete caps and stone battlement – about 20ft of

the northern wall has collapsed. The road rises gradually to the newer span and narrows such that the 4.5ft high parapets are spaced at c.16/18ft; these are topped with double-chamfered, dressed stone blocks on the later section: the four piers are capped with dressed, embossed stone slabs. A label stone on the northern wall reads *Inchamore Bridge 1848*. The parapets atop the western end of the older bridge are of randomly laid rubble stone; both walls are battlemented and run westward over the inter-bridge abutment and the remainder of the older bridge as described above.[19] Like Stonyford Bridge, there are no cutwaters on the older parts of this bridge, and the drop at each end gives it a distinctly humped back appearance.

Clocckwise from top left:
Beneath Inchamore Bridge; Rooted ivy, nature's artwork on the bridge stonework and former millrace arch on Inchamore Bridge.

The 1837 OS map depicts what appears to be a seven arched bridge at this location, with the arches in a continuous sequence from the western end; where the river is shown widening in a bight and flowing through all the openings: this seven arch sequence does not appear to include the single arch at the eastern extremity of the structure. The 1911 map reflects the current bridge layout.

Because of the discrepancies in the earlier maps, it is difficult to place an accurate date on the original bridge, but in my opinion, the older sections of Inchamore Bridge may date from the 1600s or possibly from late medieval times. The newer span dates from the OPW 1848 drainage scheme, and perhaps replaced two (or three) arches and two pillars of similar size and profile to those surviving on the western riverbank.

Considering its antiquity, it is surprising that a weight restriction has not been imposed upon the structure to date.

Lionsden (referred to in the 1836 OS Field Notes as 'a fancy name'), was a populous place in pre famine days; with the 1837 OS map showing two weirs on the Boyne immediately upstream of the bridge, a corn mill and a hamlet of circa twelve houses located close to the bridge. Griffith's records a lady named Anne Daly listed as Lessor of several properties, including a corn mill, dispensary and a forge, as follows:

> Corn-Mill & kiln (listed as vacant) – Rateable valuation £2-0s.
> Dispensary – Leased to Guardians of Trim Union – Rateable valuation 15s: "N.B. half rent rateable."
> House, Forge & garden – Leased by Michael Grogan – Rateable valuation £1-10s.

The corn mill was located alongside the old road to Longwood, about three hundred yards south of the bridge, between the road and the Blackwater (which flows almost parallel to the Boyne hereabouts). Alongside the same road and immediately south of the mill was a large house, built as a 'hollow square' i.e. a quadrangle of buildings surrounding a central courtyard. This house is recorded by the valuation as occupied by Anne Daly and leased from one Godfrey Meade Swift (of Lionsden House) at R.V. £31.

The mill was powered by the Blackwater, as evidenced by the 1837 OS map; which indicates what appears to be a millpond to the south of Anne Daly's house, connecting to the Blackwater via a broad channel. Though not delineated clearly on the maps, it would appear that the tailrace ran under the Longwood road at the 'Mill Bridge.'[20] It then flowed between this road and the Boyne, passed beneath the aforementioned arch at the eastern end of Inchamore (Boyne) Bridge and onwards to the Boyne at its confluence with the Blackwater.

The configuration of the Boyne and Blackwater rivers together with that of Lionsden Mill, as depicted on the older OS map hereabouts, explains the following somewhat cryptic comment in John O'Donovan's 1836 Field Notes on the name Inchemore: "the river insulates a part of the land here, hence the name." This is a probable reference to the name meaning 'Big Island,' which meaning can be extrapolated thus from a study of the former topography:
This millrace and river layout effectively formed an island between Boyne and Blackwater; thus giving rise to the above name Inchemore or 'the Big Island.' The 'island' included Lionsden hamlet (or Rourkestown), and was accessed via Inchemore (Boyne) and Rourkestown (Blackwater) Bridges. The name Inchemore is now meaningless to this location and cannot be interpreted from the contemporary Boyne landscape because the millrace has disappeared.

The OS Field Notes of 1836 state that "Lionden Corn Mill was doing good business, with plenty of water available."[21] The 1911 map indicates that Anne Daly's house had disappeared, together with much of the mill buildings. A vacant small dwelling (which may have formed part of the mill) stands on the site of Lionsden Corn Mill; this building is surrounded by stone walls that appear to match the curtilage of the long gone mill.

The old dispensary was located directly across from Anne Daly's house, sandwiched between the Longwood road and the Boyne, upstream of the now overgrown WWll Pillbox. This building is not shown on the 1911 map and has disappeared entirely. Michael Grogan's forge stood by the roadside in the approximate centre of the old hamlet, next door to the contemporary Margo Bye's farmhouse, between Inchamore and Rourkestown Bridges.

The two long gone weirs on the Boyne present somewhat of a mystery as they were not used to power the mill. The upper weir, located about five hundred yards upriver from the bridge, ran askew across the river from south to north. This weir directed water into a channel running alongside the western riverbank to a point just upriver from the bridge, which channel narrowed and terminated in another weir. As the maps do not indicate the usage of these man-made works, it is reasonable to propose that they were once used as fishing weirs.

And so we arrive at the Boyne's confluence with the Enfield or Kildare Blackwater, a tributary rising in an area to the north-west of Prosperous in County Kildare. The OS maps show the river is sourced in a series of rills and capillaries draining the bogs and marshy lands of Hogestown and Gilltown to the west and south-west of Staplestown Village. The 1837 OS map depicts several of these streamlets gathered into at least three mill ponds that powered a corn mill close by Gilltown House. The largest of these former ponds now comprises an area of woodland adjacent to the entry gates of this house. In the 1850s, the mill, house, offices and land were occupied by James Murray, and leased from Conway R. Dobbs at R.V. £63-10s (the mill is shown as disused on the 1911 map).

From the mill, the infant River Blackwater flows northwards between Monarua and Ballinamona bog-lands (now mostly drained) and beneath a byroad named 'the Range.' Continuing northwards, it passes under Blackwater/Derrycrib Bridge in Derrycrib Townland to flow onwards to Newtown and turn to the north-west.[22]

Following the north-westerly course, the river flows beneath the oddly named Bishop's Chair Bridge,[23] then under New Bridge and through the grounds of Knockanally House (now Knockanally Golf Course), where it once supplied a series of ornamental lakes. From here, the Blackwater continues its north-westward course to Dunfierth Townland, and turns due west to Johnstown Bridge to mingle with the Fear English River flowing from the south. Upstream from its confluence with the Blackwater; this river powered a corn/flour mill in Metcalfe Park within the townland of Gorteen. According to Griffith's, this mill, kiln, house, offices and land were occupied by Patrick Dempsey, and leased from George R. Magrath at R.V. £20-10s.

From Johnstown Bridge, the Blackwater flows north-westwards to 'the Big Island' (formed by an older river diversion), then passes beneath the M4 Motorway (where the Edenderry Branch Railway line once deviated from the main line at Nesbitt Junction), and turns to flow alongside the MGWR railway line for a short distance. About a half kilometre to the west of the now defunct rail junction, the river turns to flow almost due north beneath the railway and the Royal Canal. Further north, the river once swept in a great curve to the north-west beneath the older stone arched Blackwater Bridge carrying the former Dublin to Kinnegad turnpike road across the river; nowadays it flows beneath a concrete bridge bearing the realigned, newer edition of this road (R148) westwards to Moyvalley.

Continuing on its generally north-westerly course, the Blackwater receives 'the Aleckafin River,' flowing from the south. In the townland of Clonguiffin, south-east of Longwood, the Blackwater turns onto a north-easterly course taking it beneath the road at Clonguiffin House. The 1837 OS map depicts a corn mill close by this house, which mill is not listed in Griffith's and, indeed, is not shown on the 1911 map.[24] A mill appears at this location on the 1656 Down Survey Barony maps. Traces of the old mill races can still be discerned on satellite imagery.

The river sweeps around Longwood Village in a great semi-circle, taking it beneath the 'new' Trim/Longwood road (now the R160) and turns north-eastwards to flow beneath Castlericard Bridge.[25] Passing between "two very perfect tumuli," mentioned by Wilde in 1849, the river forms the mereing between the townlands of Lionsden and Castlericard from here to its confluence with the Boyne.

Fishing on the Kildare/Enfield Blackwater is controlled by the Longwood Angling Associatrion, from Johnstown Bridge downstream to the Boyne – the river has a good stock of wild brown trout ranging from ½ pound to 1½ pound in weight.

ENDNOTES

1 This stream rises near Ardkill and Mylerstown Townlands, close by the Boyne's source at Carbury Bog – where the Sweep River rises also, but flows in the opposite direction to coalesce with the Fear English River and Kildare Blackwater.

2 The four-storeyed Ballyonan Flour Mill, occupied by Matthew Flanagan in 1854, still stands alongside the old Dublin to Kinnegad turnpike road (now the R148) just west of Bunglass, where the road from Trim (via Longwood) joins it at a 'T' junction. The name Bunglass probably derives from Gaelic, with *Bun* meaning the *bottom* or *base* and *Glass* representing the name of the little River Glash (Small or Green River): the name thus translating to 'the Bottom of the Glash/Green River.' which describes the place admirably. This area is situated a few hundred metres south-east of Tyrrell's House, the epicentre of the Battle of Clonard in 1798. The previously described 'mill race' once fell into the River Glash downstream from the mill, then, passed beneath Bunglass Br. on the turnpike road and into the Boyne as described. Perhaps this is the same mill race mentioned in Wilde's description of the said battle.

3 Cross-referencing the OS map of 1837 with that of 1911 indicates that this tributary's course was greatly altered in the interim period. The 1656 Down Survey 'County Map' depicts a bridge spanning this river at Kinnegad, with the Barony of Moyfenrath map also indicating a bridge close by Kinnegad Castle. In his *The Dublin to Navan Road and Kilcarn Bridge*, Peter O'Keefe states that although partly filled in, three of the arches from 'Kinnegad old Bridge' were still surviving in the early 1990s, and that this bridge dated from 1662. Research indicates that the old bridge carried the Dublin/Kinnegad (later turnpike) road across the river immediately east of the contemporary bridge just outside the village and that it was bypassed during early drainage works, probably in the 1840s. I am uncertain if any of the old structure has survived more recent realignment of this road (R148). The 1836 OS Field Notes say the following about this bridge: "an indifferent bridge of four arches on the Mail Coach Road."

4 The 1837 OS map and Larkin's map of County Meath indicate a byroad leading north-eastwards from a point close by the northern end of Ashfield Bridge. This road led on past Ashfield House and turned northwards to link with the aforementioned road from Trim to Ticroghan just south-west of Stonyford Br. This connecting road was cut off by construction of the Royal Canal. Nowadays its western end comprises a private entrance to Ashfield, other dwellings and the railway 'level crossing.' Its northern section forms a minor road/laneway, leading to some farms and dwellings, and terminates at the towpath alongside the banks of the Royal Canal in Ballynabarny Townland.

5 The almost complete absence of proper access slipways to the various rivers and waterways

is a major problem for the River Rescue Service. The lack of such facilities imposes unwarranted hardship and hazards upon this volunteer service; whose members are obliged frequently to haul and drag heavy boats and equipment across mucky fields and down overgrown laneways to reach the riverbanks. There to manhandle the boats into the water via equally mucky cattle-drinking slips liberally coated with cow-dung. In addition to the obvious inefficiencies of these methods, which may cause delay in response to emergencies, the lads tell me that severe damage is oftentimes caused to their equipment and vehicles.

6   Ruth Delany's *Ireland's inland Waterways*, contains a graphic account of the Royal Canal and some of the political shenanigans that took place during its construction in the troubled era from c.1790 to 1817.

7   Richard Evans (c.1740? to 1802), was a very talented but somewhat controversial Welsh engineer who worked on the Irish canal system from the 1770s until his death in Jan. 1802. During his time in Ireland he was involved in many projects (sometimes simultaneously), including: The Grand Canal 1770s to 1789, when he was dismissed – The Royal Canal 1793 – Ballyshannon/Erne project – Newry Canal. From 1793 until its completion in c.1798, he was involved in construction of the Upper Boyne Navigation from Carrickdexter Lock to the summit level in Navan: the surviving remnants of this canal are a lasting tribute to his engineering skills. The date given for completion of the Boyne Aqueduct indicates that he passed away before it was opened in 1804.

8   Named Meenymore on Larkin's Map of County Meath

9   'Google road view' shows that this breach was present in June 2009 and unfenced then; however, though still unrepaired in April 2013, the gap was fenced off by a wooden paling, giving one the distinct impression that it was now a permanent feature and not listed for immediate attention by the powers-that-be: perhaps an indicator that those in charge of such matters are not overly interested in preserving this ancient bridge.

10 In the Lent Assizes of 1807, Grand Jury presentments were made for some major repair work to this bridge, including work on parapets and 'Pinning' of the arches; which term I believe was used at that time instead of the more modern word 'Pointing.'

11 Another stream outfalls from the south-eastern end of Lough Adeel; then flows south-westwards to join the above stream flowing from the north-western sector of the same lake: this confluence is located close by Drumcree Village, just to the south of the contemporary R396. However, whereas the stream flowing from the upper end of the lake is marked as the River Deel on the old OS maps, the opposite situation pertains at time of writing. Nowadays the other branch outflowing from the lower or south-eastern end of the lough bears the name of the river; as evidenced by a sign at the bridge where the 'Deel' passes beneath the R396 to the east of Drumcree Village. The OS maps depict this branch of the river coalescing with a small tributary that flows from Loughnasaggart to the north-east, then past a corn mill in Glenidan Townland.

12 Regarding the old 'Coachman's Inn' and the tolls of the Fair Green in Clonard, note previous reference to Elizabeth G. Magan, who was lessor of various other holdings around Clonard. The Magans owned/occupied extensive properties in counties Meath, Kildare and Westmeath, and were noted for large cattle drives from the West of Ireland.

13 (Ref. Noel French)

14 A feature on many such castles of The Pale; it consists of a walled platform (or chute) supported by stonework corbelled from the main wall. These were used by defenders to rain missiles and perhaps boiling water down upon the heads of attackers attempting to gain access via the only doorway. On other castles of The Pale, a similar feature, known as 'the murder hole,' was incorporated within the base of the access tower. For further information see Chap 06 (Riverstown Castle) in *On Ancient Roads – Recollections, History & Folklore of Co. Meath* by Anthony Holten.

15 Rourkestown Bridge is an OPW replacement for an earlier bridge, and was perhaps built during the drainage schemes in 1848-1849. The bridge spans circa 35/40ft and mimics most of the features previously described on other upriver bridges. Although I can find no such place name in the area immediately adjacent to this location, the name possibly derives from the O'Rourke (or Rourke) Clan, occupiers of vast holdings in this area during times past. From its proximity to the bridge, the hamlet in Lionsden (mentioned later in this chapter) may indeed have been named Rourkestown.

16 On p. 26 of *The Dublin to Navan Road and Kilcarne Bridge*, in his description of Derryinydaly Bridge, Peter O'Keefe includes the following rather cryptic reference: "The next upriver bridge crossing was Inchimore Bridge removed in 1769 for £63." This information perhaps derived from Grand Jury presentment records, and may indicate demolition of an earlier bridge at Rourkestown?

17 Perhaps the same crossing shown on the Taylor and Skinner map.

18 I noted that this opening was home to a somewhat disgruntled ram, tethered (or spancelled) to a free-moving wooden post.

19 The Lent Assizes of 1807 show the following presentment for work on this bridge: *to Thomas Swift, James & Michael Cox to build battlements to Anchimore Bridge, on lands of Anchimore Mill, road from Trim to Kinnegad wages included £14-12s- 3d.* (sic)

20 The following Grand Jury presentment to the Lent Assizes of 1807 tends to prove the existence of this bridge: *to Edward Daly, James & Michael Cox to build battlements to Anchimore Mill Bridge on lands of Anchimore, road from Trim to Edenderry wages included £13-13s-8d.* (sic) Underlined by author.

21 An explanation for Lionsden Corn Mill being listed as vacant in 1854 can be found in the Commissioners of Public Works, Ireland 17th report (1848), which states that the water power of this mill was purchased and the falls/dams removed. This mill; therefore, became defunct in 1848 because of the drainage scheme.

22 The Commissioners of Public Works, Ireland, 17th report of 1848 states that Derrycrib Br. was "thrown down" on 15th June 1848; construction of the new bridge commenced June 17th, with the bridge opened to the public on June 27th. This is a remarkable achievement by any standards.

23 Built originally in 1745 by Josiah Hort, Archbishop of Tuam.

24 Clonguiffin corn mill was omitted from the 1854 valuation because the Commissioners of Public Works purchased the water power and removed the falls/dams. This mill; therefore, became defunct about 1848 because of the drainage scheme, which completed major rea-

lignments to the River Blackwater hereabouts, with a new bridge built to conduct the river beneath the Longwood to Blackwater Br. road.

25 This road (now the R160) did not exist in 1837 as shown on the OS map. However, in the 1852 revision accompanying Griffith's Valuation, the road appears here and there in outline only (two dotted lines). From its junction with the Summerhill road outside Trim, the new line is traceable on the 1837 OS map through Dogstown to Newtownmoynagh, east of Boards Mill. Here the road ceases on the earlier map but is shown on the 1852 rev. as a series of double-dotted lines on its contemporary line through Brannockstown – where it linked with an existing road running on to Tobertynan Townland. No trace of the contemporary road line from here to Longwood appears on the earlier OS maps.

5

The Upper Reaches
Lionsden to Trim

Portan & Muchwood Townlands – old riverscape – Battle of Portlester & Charles Moore's lost head – Pass or Ford of Portlester Mill – Scarriff Bridge, older and newer – Stonyford/Stonestown River, its sources & watermills – Misset's & Earl's Mills – Brannockstown & Derrinydaly islets & weirs – The Tromman River, Kill Mill & Boardsmill – a lost fish weir – Derrinydaly (Drinadaly) Bridge, older & newer – Blackwater Drainage District & Scheme 1844-1849 – Bellewstown fishing weir – Higginsbrook tuck mill – the factory road – Tremblestown/Athboy River, its source and mills – Ardglassan Cottages & Lady Island – Kilnagross, Mitchell's Weir & mill – Newhaggard, its great mill & tower – the highway from Trim to Clonard – the rocky river – Kennedys' Weir, millrace & mills – The Watergate & town walls – older & newer Watergate Bridges – old race course, Trim Gaol, old gasworks & Sally Rogers' Bar.

Passing beneath the great span of Inchamore Bridge, we continued on downriver. Drifting by the mouth of the Blackwater, the arch of Rourkestown Bridge loomed from the misty eastern shore, like a darkened opening leading to another world.

The Blackwater hereabouts forms the mereing between the townlands of Lionsden and Clonee, with the Boyne flowing generally north-north-

Kildare Blackwater joins the Boyne - Rourkestown Br. in background

eastwards between the latter townland and Donore to the west. Where the previously mentioned Conneyberry Bohereen once met the Boyne, a small salient of Portan Townland (c.100 metres wide) forms the left or western riverbank. Beyond this is the townland of Muchwood to the east of Ballivor Village. At the northernmost end of Muchwood, a three hundred metre or so sector of Portlester Townland fronts the Boyne, which turns 90 degrees here and flows onwards to Scarriff Bridge in a series of serpentine-like curves.

The 1837 OS map depicts a glebe of 22 acres extent on the eastern riverbank, including the graveyard and ruins of Clonee Church. This map shows also that from here to Scarriff Bridge, the Boyne flowed through a broader floodplain, divided into many islets formed by the myriad channels cut by the river through the alluvial plain. Several of these little islets were planted, adding an extra dimension to the river's sylvan beauty during those times. The various drainage schemes removed most of these features, and by 1911 the river had been altered such that it flowed through a single and much narrower channel. During our downriver passage, we encountered remnants of these islets in the form of shallows, rocky ledges and the all-pervasive 'board of works ripples.' Despite these alterations, it is still a most attractive riverscape from the aspect of a boat.

Left: Kildare Blackwater joins the Boyne - Viewed from Rourkestown Bridge.
Right: Swans in a row

Muchwood, or Coill Mhore in Gaelic, means 'the big wood,' and it is tempting to say the place was named after the large tract of woodland, shown on the 1837 OS map covering the Boyne's western banks for most of its passage through the townland. These areas of forestry extended along the river through Portlester and on into Moyfeagher. The name; however, is much older than the era of the great wooded demesnes that burgeoned throughout Meath and elsewhere during the 1700-1800s, as it is named such on the 1656 Down Survey map. The 1837 OS map indicates a graveyard located between two old ringforts in the approximate centre of the townland, close by some unnamed buildings. The buildings occupied the site shown as Muchwood House on the 1911 map, which does not mark the two forts and indicates the graveyard as 'site of' only.

Portlester was the scene of a military engagement during the Confederacy Wars of the 1640s. The event reputedly occurred on June 7th 1643 and became known as 'the Battle of Portlester.' I understand the 'battle' was fought close by a place called 'the River Boyne Pass' or 'Ford of Portlester Mill.' This skirmish involved, I believe, Confederacy of Kilkenny forces led by Owen Rua (Roe) O'Neill (supported by a unit of Alistair MacColla's Scottish Highlanders) on one side; opposed by Parliamentary Army contingents, led by generals Montgomery and Charles Moore (2nd Viscount of Drogheda). Anecdotes say that O'Neill, chastened by an earlier defeat at Clones, placed his men behind an earthen breastworks guarded by cannon, and then invited the Roundhead forces to attack his fortified position. These tales relate also that Charles

Moore was decapitated by a cannon ball (supposedly fired by O'Neill); which event routed the attackers and won the day for the Confederacy.

Portlester is mentioned in the aftermath of another major event during the Confederacy Wars. Following the defeat of confederate General Thomas Preston's Leinster Army by Michael Jones' Dublin garrison at Dungan's Hill (Battle of Drumlargan), near Summerhill in August 1647, tradition holds that: Owen Roe O'Neill's Ulster army marched through the Pass of Portlester Mill to mount an effective rearguard action, routing Jones' advanced brigade and enabling survivors of the Leinster army to escape.

The Down Survey maps show that the boundaries and river frontage of Portlester (named Portlestown on the older map) have remained relatively unchanged from the 1650s, so it would seem that Portlester Mill Ford was located along this section of the Boyne.[1] But I cannot find any trace of the ancient crossing depicted on the old maps, or a record of a mill upon the Boyne in this area. The various drainage schemes altered the riverscape such that no trace now remains. In the north-west of the townland, a rather odd landmark may be connected to the ditched fortification supposedly thrown up by O'Neill for the battle of Portlester. Just south of the contemporary R156, to the east of Ballivor Village, is a section of double ditch about 350 yards long and 20ft wide, now overgrown by a row of mature trees. This feature is depicted on the 1837 and 1911 maps and is somewhat unusual, because it is not connected to other landscape features. Perhaps it originated in and once formed part of the breastworks thrown up by Owen Roe O'Neill all those years ago.

Although several mentions are made of 'the castle in Portlester' in the various accounts of the battle, I cannot find any depiction of this edifice on the older maps, including the 1656 Down Survey Barony maps. There are many records; however, of 'the Manor of Portlester,' which may be one and the same building.

Passing on downriver towards Scarriff Bridge, we noted that the vast woodlands of Muchwood have disappeared, so perhaps the name is no longer relevant to the townland. The woods of Portlester are gone also, but less dense woodlands cover the riverbank of Moyfeagher most of the way to the bridge.

Scarriff Bridge is another hybrid structure, carrying the contemporary R156 (former L4) (Dunboyne/Summerhill/Ballivor road) across the Boyne from Batterstown/Ballymulmore in the south-east to Moyfeagher on the north-western riverbank. The following is a summary of Scarriff Bridge, an extract from the book by Peter O'Keefe and Tom Simington entitled *Irish Stone Bridges – History and Heritage*:

Scarriff Bridge – Grand Jury record for construction of earlier Br.

> There is a most informative entry concerning this bridge in query book for the Meath grand jury 1761-76 in the National Archive: Summer Assizes, 1760: Item 35. Whether £160. 2s. 6d. be raised and paid to George Nugent, Walter Dowdall and James O'Reilly for 915 perches of mason work at 3s. 6d. a perch towards finishing and completing a new bridge now building over a ford on the River Boyne, commonly called Scarivenaharna on the great road leading from Castlepollard to Rathmullion and the same being necessary to complete and finish said bridge over and above the sum of £200 already granted by the county for building said bridge, work doing. (sic)

Description of contemporary structure (newer and older) by Peter O'Keefe circa late 1980s, from *The Dublin to Navan Road and Kilcarn Bridge*:

> The OS half-inch map shows the crossing was on the Rathmoylon Road (L4) and marked Scarriff Bridge though it is not a townland. I had an opportunity to visit the bridge and was surprised to find it high and dry in a field but still carrying the L4. The Boyne had been diverted into a new channel about 15ft below the old one and a new bridge built abutting part of the original. There is a plaque on the new bridge: "Drainage, under the Acts 5th and 6th Vict. Cap. 89, 1849." Closer examination showed that the new bridge had been underpinned as part of the Boyne Arterial Drainage Scheme of the 1970s. Three townlands meet at the bridge – Moyfeagher, Batterstown, Ballymulmore. The derivation of the anglicised, phoenetic version of the crossing place in the query book is best left to experts, but the shortened Scarriff does not accurately represent the terrain as it is difficult to imagine it ever having been a rough rocky crossing place like Enniskerry.

The 1849 Scarriff Bridge of 60ft span has a rise of 9ft, a ratio of almost 7 to 1. It was a daring arch for the period and it is obvious that the talented team of engineers in the Office of Public Works were insistent on avoiding piers in the river and obtaining maximum hydraulic capacity. The piers however had to be very substantial to withstand the high lateral thrust. An interesting feature of the bridge are the joints in the spandrel masonry which are a continuation of the voussoir joints. This type of appareil is also found on some of the 18th century bridges on the Shannon, such as Shannonbridge. Most of the other 1840 bridges in Meath have horizontal joints. The 1840 arches in both Drinadelly and Scarriff have been listed for strengthening by Meath Co. Council following recent examination and assessment.

There are four arches of the 1760 bridge left. It would appear that the original had at least seven and that three were removed to make way for the 1849 bridge. The roadway is 18ft wide between parapets. The piers are 7.5ft thick with substantial triangular cutwaters fore and aft. All the cutwaters are brought up to form pedestrian refuges in the parapets. The span of what was the central arch is 18ft flanked by two of 14ft and a 10ft end arch. The intrados are segments of circles. The ring stones are 15in deep, well cut and slightly wedge-shaped of varying thickness but almost true voussoirs. There are no proper skewbacks and the springing plane is formed by a tilted stone.[2]

I noted the bridge has a distinctly humped backed appearance from the road aspect, especially from the northern approach. The parapets are of different periods, constructed mostly from rough stone, with several sections repaired in mass concrete. The western wall is heavily overgrown by ivy, and the pedestrian refuges clogged by greenery (one playing host to a telegraph pole), such that they are mostly unfit for purpose. All the older arches on the northern bank are reinforced by tie-bolts and strong-back arrangements, which appear to be of an older vintage and not the work suggested by Peter O'Keefe to be imminent in the early 1990s. Some concrete buttressing was evident on the downstream north-eastern extremity, beyond the 10ft end-arch, now blocked by wooden sheeting and possibly in use as a shed. Perhaps

From top: Scarriff Bridge downstream - old and new and from upstream.

home for a pair of donkeys, observing me with undisguised curiosity while I clambered around the structure. No traces of iron reinforcing systems were evident under the ivy covering the newer 1849 span.

Passing beneath the mighty arch, we headed on downriver and came to the confluence of the Stonyford River, located about five hundred metres downstream. The intervening rocky, layered riverbanks show substantial deepening of the river here during the various drainage schemes. Several

Left: Stonyford River joins the Boyne. Right: Curious donkeys at Scarriff Bridge.

'fisherman's gaps' at the parapets and the well-trodden banks, indicate that the Boyne hereabouts is a favourite spot for anglers.

At its confluence with the Boyne, the Stonyford River forms the mereing between the townlands of Moyfeagher and Monkstown. This river takes its main rise to the south-west of Oldcastle, and then follows a generally south-easterly course to its meeting with the Boyne. The 1836 and 1911 OS maps indicate that the river is first named the Stonyford River below the convergance of Sranaboll Townland, County Meath with the townlands of Cavestown and Mulliganstown, County Westmeath. Here, two main source streams mingle; the smaller one from the direction of Archerstown Lough (now dried up) in Archerstown Townland, County Westmeath. The other stream constitutes the major source, and rises in the boggy/marshy lands close by Loughcrew to the south-west of Crossakeel, County Meath.

We will follow the route of this main source stream, depicted on the OS maps, as it develops to form the Stonyford River. To the south-east of Loughcrew, just south of the former Knochlough Crossroads and the contemporary Diamor Crossroads, several small capillaries combine to form a stream flowing south-eastwards.[3]

In the townland of Diamor, near a hamlet named Roachtown, the stream fed a mill pond, which powered a watermill, shown on the earlier map as a corn mill and named on the 1911 map as Diamor Corn & Saw Mill. From here the developing river flows south-eastwards to a small, boot-shaped lake, named on the 1837 OS map as Ballure Lough and on the later map Newtown Lough.[4] The stream outfalls from the 'toe' of the boot and flows almost due south to an unnamed place/hamlet on the mereing of Stirrupstown and the townland of Boherard, as shown on the earlier map, but named Killallon on the 1911 map (N.B., this area is located within the civil parish of Killallon).

Here, a glebe, together with a graveyard and church are shown on the 1837 map, across the road from a motte or ringfort. The church is marked 'in ruins' on the later map, which shows a windmill (at the site of a contemporary pub named Killallon House) and also names a nearby road junction Darcy's Cross Roads.

The river splits below Killallon hamlet, in the townland of Killacroy (church of the round hill), with the most western branch flowing through a tiny lake named Stillafiddler Lough on the OS maps. The eastern branch formed a millrace that powered Killallon Mill, located also in the townland of Killacroy. While this mill is depicted on the 1837 map, it is not shown on the 1911 edition, and the oddly named Stillafiddler Lough appears to have dried up (supposedly named after a local fiddler who operated a Poitin Still).

The two river branches re-join below Killallon Mill and the stream continues its course south-eastwards to the townland of Clonever at its mereing with that of Newtown Townland in County Westmeath. From here it flows south-westwards, mostly forming the border between Meath and Westmeath to the meeting point of the three townlands, Sranaboll, Cavestown and Mulliganstown. On this stretch, the burgeoning stream receives the outflow from Freehan Lough, fed from Lough Shesk further to the north.

The other stream, mingling with the Stonyford River here, drains the hinterland of Archerstown in County Westmeath, including the former Archerstown Lough and the area around the manor house, both of which features have disappeared. A corn mill is depicted on the 1837 OS map, just south-east of the lough. Although the mill buildings are shown on the 1911 map, they are gone now, replaced by a modern dwelling fronted by an old stone wall, which perhaps formed part of the mill's former curtilage.

From here the stream is named the Stonyford River on the OS maps, and flows past the ruins of Clonarney Church before continuing onwards through Rosemead Demesne. Then it meanders south-eastwards to the townland of Balrath South (near Southhill), where it receives a tributary flowing from the environs of Delvin in County Westmeath. Below this confluence, the river turns and flows eastwards through the townland of Stonestown; receiving the waters of Ballyhealy Lough before passing under Stonestown Bridge, and turning southwards to flow beneath Lisclogher Bridge (named Wooden Bridge on the 1837 OS map).[5]

Further downriver, just upstream from Cloghbrack Bridge, a millrace is taken from the river to power a corn mill located nearby in the townland of Ballynadrimna. The tailrace from this mill continued flowing south-eastwards alongside the Stonyford River, to power Earl's Mill, about three kilometres further downstream.

Rathkenna Bridge is the next bridge we encounter following the river's south-easterly course to Earl's Bridge, where the aforementioned mill race once re-entered the river as the tailrace from Earl's Mill. This mill is depicted as a corn mill on the 1837 OS map, but not shown on the 1911 edition. A visit to the site, located alongside the Ballivor/Kildalkey road, shows that apart from the remnants of the mill race stream, no trace of this mill now exists, or indeed any signs of the miller's house which once stood directly across the road from the mill. The river flows onwards from here, beneath Shanco (old hollow) Bridge and past Portlester House, then onwards under Stonyford Bridge to merge with the Boyne.[6]

The following list of mills located upon the Stonyford River and its tributaries was compiled from data gleaned from the 1837 & 1911 OS maps and Griffith's 1854 valuation:

Watermills on the Stonyford River and catchment (05 of):

Diamor Townland

below Diamor Cross: house, offs, corn-mill, kiln and land occupied by Richard Goodwin, leased from William B. Wade @ R.V. £13-0s-0d. N.B., nowadays the former mill site is occupied by two modern/modernised stone built dwellings.

Archerstown Townland (Co. Westmeath)

below Archerstown Lough: house, offs, corn-mill, kiln and land occupied by John Ball, leased from Robert Smyth @ R.V. £54-0s-0d. N.B., Archerstown Lough (now dried-up and reclaimed) is listed in the valuation as occupying 11 acres 01 rood and 28 perches.

Killacroy Townland

below Killallon (Killallon Mill): house, offs, mill and land occupied by Thomas Glennon, leased from the Earl of Annesley @ R.V. £41-0s-0d.

Ballynadrimna Townland

North-east of Cloghbrack Bridge (Larkin's Map): house, offs, corn-mill and land occupied by James Potterton, leased from Owen B. Cole @ R.V. £59-0s-0d. According to the 1836 Field Notes, local tradition holds that the lands hereabouts (Barony of Lune) were granted by Hugh DeLacy to a Knight named Robert Misset following the Norman Conquest, and that this mill was once known as Misset's Mill. In ruins by 1870.

Corballis Townland (the odd town J.O.D. 1836)

Ballivor/Kildalkey road, Earl's Mill: house, offs, corn-mill and land occupied by Michael M'Garry, leased from Earl of Darnley (Sir John Duncan Bligh – 1778-1872: Envoy to Hanover 1838-1856) @ R.V. £61-10s – while it is possible that the mill's name derives from the said Earl of Darnley, the 1836 Field Notes state that local tradition holds that this mill was once occupied by one Gearoid Iarla. In ruins by 1878

Below the Stonyford confluence, the winding course of the Boyne continues in a mostly south-easterly direction to a point about midway along the riparian sector of Brannockstown on the southern shore. Here it turns and flows north-eastwards past Boards Mill to Derrinydaly (Drinadaly) Bridge. About midway between the confluence and the big bend at Brannockstown, the 1837 OS map depicts a group of about ten islands, with the largest sized at 4.5 acres.

The original river spread across the wider floodplain here, with two main channels flowing past on either side of the larger island; two skewed weirs are shown bisecting both channels, and linking the islands to both riverbanks. As no mill is recorded on the location, these were most likely fishing weirs, of which I can find no record. Both the townland of Derrinydaly on the northern shore and Brannockstown on the opposite bank, have small salients (outward bulges) in their boundaries, effectively encompassing parts of the islands within their respective townlands. The owner of Derrinydaly must have wielded more political influence; however, as the townland mereing includes most of the islands and both weirs within Derrinydaly.

Boards Mill is a place name, the origins for which I can find no definitive explanation. It is located on a narrow salient of Brannockstown extending alongside the Boyne to the mereing of Newtownmoynagh Townland. The place is named such on the old maps, including Larkin's (1812/17) and both the 1837 and 1911 editions of the OS. While all three maps indicate a mill on the location, the OS maps specify that it was a corn mill and not a saw mill (as the title 'Board' might suggest). The 1836 Field Notes say the following of this place name: "Muilean an Chlair – Mill of the Board" and go on to state emphatically "the name does <u>not</u> signify Board's or Borde's Mill" and mention that Beaufort's Map (1797) names the place as Boormills. John O'Donovan concluded that the name should be spelled Boardsmill.

The mill occupies the same footprint shown on the OS maps; it is now a well maintained stone built, two tiered barn standing at an angle between the road and the Boyne just south-west of the RC church. The higher building, now an empty shell, once consisted of three storeys and a loft, and comprised the operating part of the mill, probably containing at least two sets of grindstones. The lower profiled part of the building housed the drying kiln.

This mill was not powered from Boyne water, but driven by a small stream known variously as the Millstream, and the Tromman or Boardsmill River. The stream takes its rise from several capillaries and rills sourced in the area south-east and south-west of Kilballyporter Townland ('wood on the way past'), which lies to the south-west of Rathmoylon. One of these streams is part of a complex of millraces which once powered a corn mill named Kill Mill, located close by Kill Bridge.[7] Griffith's shows that this watermill, with attendant house, offs and land was occupied by Richard Keefe, who leased the property from Robert Fowler at R.V. £54. From here the stream flows westwards in a great curve forming the mereing of Tromman Townland, hence the name given to the stream.[8] Flowing beneath Tromman Bridge, the river continues onwards through Castletown to its meeting with the Boyne at Boards Mill.

The old maps show that the Tromman River split into two streams on the eastern side of the road (now the R161) across from the mill. Here, a weir once provided water-head to power the mill, with excess water diverted through a spillrace flowing alongside and then passing beneath the road (at 'the Minister's Br.') into the Boyne about three hundred metres upstream from the mill. The water powering the millwheel passed through a sluice and directly beneath the road, then through the wheel, with the tailrace running on downstream and falling into the Boyne at the mereing of Newtownmoynagh. All this has changed, the river now flowing along the course of the old spillrace, with no traces of the weir and old headrace remaining.

On a visit to Boards Mill in Jan. 2014, I spoke to William Flood, and with his kind permission examined the old corn mill and its layout on the riverbank. He told me that his family operated the mill until its closure circa 1954-1957, at which time it ground wheaten and oaten meal. Like others living alongside the Boyne, he had many less than complimentary comments to make about the OPW and their blinkered approach to the post 1968 drainage scheme; which, he said, ensured that his mill would never again operate as a water-powered corn mill. He went on to explain how the spill weir was ripped out by the draglines, thereby closing off the sluice and mill race that powered the mill, operated by his family for several generations; and of his legal battles with this public body to clear drainage spoil from his land. In addition, removal of the weir deprived the family, who also run horse stables, of the deep upstream pool once used as a swimming/hydro pool for the equines.

Parts of the old gearing and several redundant millstones lie in the yard and adorn the eastern gable of the stone building. While nothing remains of the waterwheel or headrace, remnants of the tailrace can be traced from the mill, where it turned north-eastwards to run alongside the Boyne. The largest part of the gearing remaining intact is the 8/10ft diameter cast iron 'pit-wheel.' The surviving millstones are about 4.5ft in diameter and are likely formed from granite; quarried in single pieces and not segmented French-Burr-type stones contained within iron hoops. I noted one 'bedstone' and two 'runner stones.' The latter stones had two different drive profiles, one with the older (and rarer) three-pronged drive slots, the other with the four drive slots; an indicator that both the triple pronged and four pronged rynd (rind) or mace-head were used at this mill.[9] Although eroded with the passage of time, the visible faces of the millstones appear to be dressed for use as grist stones i.e. for grinding meal and not flour.

Pitwheel and triple prong drive runner stone at Boardsmill

Griffith's records the mill thus: house, off's, corn-mill, Herd's house and land totalling circa 215.6 acres, leased by William & Jas. Flood from Charles B. Leslie at R.V. £175-0s-0d. William Flood told me that the mill was operated by his Great Grandfather during this era.

On our downriver passage from the Stonyford River, we saw no trace of the cluster of islets and two interconnecting weirs, once located between the townlands of Derrinydaly and Brannockstown. On this reach, I believe there is a place on the river known as Lugnahulla, a whirlpool once a favourite bathing place for locals.

Passing by the mouth of the Tromman River and on by Boardsmill, we came to where the tailrace from Flood's corn mill once fell into the Boyne. Here, the 1837 OS map depicted a series of small islets connected by a weir skewed towards the northern riverbank. As these islets and the weir were laid out in a similar fashion to the great fish-weirs on the Lower Boyne, such as the Cherry Islands, Broe, Ballinacrad and Stalleen, it is reasonable to suggest that this combination at Derrinydaly was once an ancient fishing weir; perhaps 'Crooked Weir,' mentioned in the Commissioners of Public Works 1848 report on drainage works carried out near Derrinydaly Bridge.

The Tromman River at Boardsmill

All traces of this complex had vanished by the early 1900s, as evidenced by the new river channel depicted on the map of 1911.

I reflected that in 1849, Wilde noted the profusion of places named after the river hereabouts e.g. Boyne View, Boyne Bank, Boyne Lodge. Rounding a slight curve in the broad, sedgy river reach, we saw the great arches of Derrinydaly Bridge silhouetted against the grey wintry skyline to the north.

Travelling along this broad reach, our boat developed problems with the engine, which caused it to fail eventually. This provided an opportunity for the lads to practice their towing skills, which expedient took us downriver to beach the boat at an improvised cattle slip beside the bridge. While the two crews worked on the ailing engine, the rest of us inspected Derrinydaly Bridge.

Similar to the upstream bridges, this bridge contains elements from two different periods. Nowadays it carries a minor road across the Boyne to Derrinydaly Townland on the northern shore, linking the R161 in Newtownmoynagh to another minor road running from Kilnagross Cross Roads to the R156 Ballivor Road. This byroad was/is known in the vernacular as 'the Factory Road,' the reason for which nickname will become clear when we visit Higginsbrook Tuck Mill further downriver. According to the 1836

Approaching Derrinydaly Bridge

OS Field Notes, the name Derrinydaly derives from "O'Daly's little oak wood." The Down Survey map of 1656 names the townland Drinadaly, which accounts for this variant of the name in the vernacular and on some maps.

In his *The Dublin to Navan Road & Kilcarn Bridge* (published in 1994), Peter O'Keefe writes of Derrinydaly Bridge:

> In 1845, E. Russel C.E., an engineer employed by the Commissioners of Public Works, reported that this bridge had six apertures with an aggregate waterway of 87ft. and was supported by piers 9ft thick. To increase the waterway the two central arches and the pier between them were removed and replaced by an arch of lower rise.

He includes also the following snippet from the earlier history of the bridge:

> In 1761 the Grand Jury presented "£36 to be raised and paid to George Nugent, Alex Wood, Myles Dowdall in part of the sum of £360 for the erection of a new bridge over the Ford of Drinadely on the River Boyne on the great road leading from Johnstown Bridge and Rathmoylan to Athboy, Finny, Castletowndelvin and

Castlepollard, which will require 1600 perches of mason work @ 4s. 6d. per perch." The information on the line of the road here is more historically important than the rest because Elizabeth 1 had given an adventurer named Patrick Cullen a large land grant in 1600 AD for erecting Johnstown Bridge, replaced in the 1840s. It was a very strategic crossing. The presentment also indicates that there was a ford at Derrinydaly.

This assessment of the bridge derives from our river trips and several subsequent visits:

Derrinydaly Bridge – Newer OPW built span of 1848 (almost identical to the newer spans of Stonyford Bridge and Inchamore Bridge).

The section comprises a single shallow stone central arch of segmental profile, flanked by two semi-circular profiled arches of the older bridge on each side. It comprises a span of circa 35/40ft which abuts vertical stone columns at springer level about 6ft above mean water level on each end of the arch. These columns are incorporated as inter-arch pillars between the older and newer spans. The columns are built of rusticated limestone blocks, laid to regular pattern. The base columns/pillars are rounded (bullnosed) and extend as cutwaters about 4ft upstream and downstream of the bridge facade, they are topped by rounded stone cappings.[10] On all four corners, circa 6ft wide out-projecting piers rise from the pillar cappings to parapet level, where they are capped by dressed, embossed stone slabs – the piers have no obvious batter and are circa 2.8ft thick at parapet level. The arch rings/voussoirs are of rusticated limestone blocks, as are the spandrels, which are laid horizontally to a regular pattern. The soffit (intrados) is of dressed limestone blocks laid in regular lines. Both support columns are underpinned with concrete to compensate for deepening of the river channel during drainage work. The concrete underpinning has pointed profiles, extending about 2ft both upstream and downstream of the rounded cutwaters. A dressed string-course runs atop the arch crown, and continues around the out-projecting parapet piers. Both façades are clear of ivy. The strengthening work predicted by Peter O'Keefe in 1994, has been put into effect as evidenced by the five tie-bar & strong-back arrangements on the upstream and downstream spandrels and arch rings.

Older 1761 sections flanking the newer central span on both riverbanks – these are very similar on both banks; therefore, I will give details of the section abutting the northern bank only:

> These two arches each have a waterway of c.14.5 ft in width, they have a semi-circular profile, and are of similar rise; both appear to be symmetrical, with all the older arches presenting a level profile from the river aspect. The innermost arch is open to the unflooded river and springs almost vertically from the support column; back-to-back with the arch springers of the newer span. The outer arch is not open to the unflooded river, but acts as a flood arch circa 3ft above mean water level. The triangular-faced 9ft wide inter-arch pillar is underpinned in concrete. This pillar is continued upwards to form pedestrian refuges on both the upstream and downstream bridge facades. The arch rings/voussoirs are of dressed stone, the soffits/intrados are plastered such that their stonework cannot be evaluated. The spandrel walls, pedestrian refuge risers and parapets are of dressed rough stone, some laid to regular pattern and some randomly. The parapet walls are battlemented. Several tie-bolt & strong-back arrangements are fitted to support the older arches/approach embankments and buttresses.

The bridge from road aspect:

> On both riverbanks, the approach road to the bridge is carried on a stone faced/buttressed embankment which rises gradually to the older sections, giving the bridge a distinctly humped backed appearance. The older approach walls/parapets are circa 3ft high and of rough stone construction with battlements and four triangular pedestrian refuges approximately three feet deep. The newer parapets are spaced at about 20ft, built of dressed limestone blocks and circa 3.5ft high,

they are capped with rounded, dressed limestone blocks. The road is about 18ft wide with a narrow grass verge. A great upstream and downstream vista of the Boyne unfolds from the bridge apex (at the arch crowns); with the old graveyard of Derrinydaly located close by to the north-east.

Reconstruction work on Stonyford, Scariff and Derrinnydaly bridges was executed under the Drainage Act of 1842 (5 & 6 Vict, Cap. 89). This was part of the Blackwater Drainage District (Meath & Kildare), including sixteen miles of the Blackwater from Staplestown to Lionsden, and circa three miles of the Boyne from Stonyford Bridge to Higginsbrook below Derrinnydaly. The extract from the Commissioners of Public Works, Ireland 17th report of 1849 (signed by Commissioners Harry D. Jones & William T. Mulvany) is very informative, and provides a great insight to those post-famine times. The report includes an account of the 'final awards' i.e. details of the cost of the work completed under the scheme and the source of the funds.

The total cost of the scheme was £12,115, of which £1,839 would be recovered from the County by means of Grand Jury Presentments; which element covered the costs of reconstructing the bridges etc., this amount would in turn be recovered from land occupiers by means of the County and Barony Cess or property tax.[11] Private individuals contributed various sums as follows: S. Coates, Ballyvoneen £228-13s-2d – Mr W. Murphy, Ballyvoneen £238-10s-2d – Mr Thomas Kearney, Ballynakill £253-16s-6d – from the wording of the report it appears that these sums may have been private investments in the scheme. The remainder of the costs amounting to £9,555-1s-1d was borrowed at an interest rate of 5% per annum.

Having no success with the engine, the lads decided that we supernumeraries would transfer to the other craft and continue the journey downriver with Hopper as 'Cox. of the boat.' The other boat, with Martin as Cox., would attempt the remainder of the trip using manpower on the oars. This venture was abandoned some distance downstream and the lads joined the support team for the rest of the journey. So we departed the scene, going under Derrinnydaly Bridge and heading on downriver, passing on by Kenastown on the eastern shore, a townland which runs close to the Boyne hereabouts, but has no riparian sector.

The author at Derrinydaly Bridge

This reach of the Boyne evoked an emotive response from Wilde in 1849; in particular the many wooded islets enhancing the riverscape. Though the islands are gone now, the river flows onwards through a pastoral landscape. From the deep cleft of the river we observed groups of horses and cattle; some gazing back with equal curiosity, perhaps wondering at the origins of these brightly clad invaders of their domain. Here and there we encountered clumps and rafts of weed and river sedge in midstream; with occasional groups of willow, birch, alder and hawthorn drooping from the two-tiered banks and obstructing the waterway.

The boat rounded the great loop in the river and passed by Roristown House on the eastern bank (built c.1778); and according to the OS Field Notes occupied by C. Drake in 1836. We continued on through Bellewstown and came to where the river turns through 90 degrees and flows north-eastwards towards Newhaggard. Here in times past was another complex of islets and weirs, now disappeared. This was a combined fish and mill weir; the fishing weir traceable back to at least 1611, with records of the mill included on the Blackwater drainage report of 1848 and Griffith's 1854 valuation.

As shown on the 1911 OS map, the weir was built askew to the river and ran in a great curve from the eastern bank to a long, narrow island or rampart close by the opposite riverbank. This arrangement directed water from above the weir to a head race running between the island and the riverbank. About mid-way along the island, the 1911 map indicates a building of unspecified usage; when cross-referenced with the map of 1837 this building is seen to be a tuck mill. On Griffith's the mill is described thus:

> Bellewstown Townland – house, off's, woollen mill and circa 4.56 acres of land occupied by Simon Browne, leased from Frederick Higgins @ R.V. £16-0s-0d.[12] The mill was defunct by 1896.

Larkin's Map of 1812 depicts this mill by a multi-spoke or cogwheel symbol, the standard used on this map to denote watermills.

The above landowner's name perhaps explains the derivation of the first part of the place name 'Higgins Brook'; the second part most likely derives from a small tributary flowing from the west and falling into the Boyne just upstream from the mill. This place name applies also to the adjacent residence in contemporary times.

The Commissioners of Public Works, Ireland, 17th report includes the following entry concerning work executed on the Boyne at Higginsbrook Mill in 1848:

> At Higginsbrook the completion of the weir was effected and the fish-pass finished satisfactorily; the dams and the remains of the old weir above, however, have not been removed for the same reason before assigned for not finishing the other portions of the work.
>
> The special work ordered at the factory has, however, been carried out, and the concern now enjoys all the benefits which can be conferred on it, the excavations being carried to the full extent ordered by Commissioner Mulvany, and the conduit built in the manner approved of, which has been since subdivided by the owner, and a smaller wheel hung than was originally intended.[13]

Ruins at site of Higginsbrook Tuck Mill (the factory)

The 1953 Louth Archaeological Journal informs us that the Civil Survey (1650s) records the following entry concerning the weir at Higginsbrook in Bellewstown:

> '*another fishing weir was situated at Bellewstown, upstream of Newhaggard for on the 21ˢᵗ February 1611 Sir James Carroll obtained a grant of the manor of Trim with, inter alia, 2 shillings out of a fishing weir on the Boyne near "Bedlestown" (Bellewstown), from Richard Misset, and on 23ʳᵈ December, 1624 the same possession was granted to Richard, Earl of Cork.*' (sic)

On our downriver passage through this broad, sedgy reach, we saw the partly roofless remains of the ancient mill standing high and dry upon the riverbank between the river and 'the Factory Road,' but no trace of the more ancient fish-weir of Bellewstown remains to enhance the landscape of the Boyne. On a later visit to the site via Trim and Kilnagross, I noted the ruinous building on the riverbank; but a stranger might never know its history, because no plaque or other sign denoting its former usage is mounted there to inform the curious eye.

The Boyne above Newhaggard

Following the Boyne's north-easterly course, about a half kilometre downstream we come to another bend where the river sweeps in a great curve and flows due east towards Newhaggard. Here, the last major tributary above Trim, the Tremblestown (Trimblestown) or Athboy River falls into the Boyne; to which tributary's source I will now take the reader, exploring its reaches and following them to their meeting with the Boyne at Kilnagross.

The source can be traced on the 1837 and 1911 OS maps. These show that several rills and streamlets, draining the marshy lands in the townlands of Corstown, Ballynamona, Balrath and Phillipstown, coalesce in the townland of Belview to the west of Ballinlough. As depicted on the above maps, the infant stream flows to the south-east from here as 'the Belview River,' passes through Dogstown, then onwards to Ardglassan Bridge to the west of Ardglassan Cottages.[14]

Continuing southwards through a long, narrow woodland named Rampart Wood, it passes beneath Martinstown Bridge located about a mile to the west

Athboy skew Bridge

of Crossakeel (now on the L2801). It then flows through Creevagh Townland, passes on by Creevagh House and onwards to Milltown Bridge. Below the bridge, to the west of Kilskeer Village, it receives a small tributary flowing from the direction of Clonmellon, before passing close by Crocknaree; the summit of which is marked as an OS triangulation reference point on the 1837 map.

Flowing south-eastwards from here, the river takes a complex course through the townland of Drewstown-Little; passing onwards to the north-east of Triermore House and south-west of Jonesbrook Cross Roads, then beneath Drewstown Bridge. It continues eastwards from here, flowing to the north of Drewstown House and walled garden; where it receives the waters of a small stream draining from Girley Bog to the north-east.

The river then turns towards the south-east and exits the demesne in a big looping twist taking it due south to Clonleasan Townland. It is noteworthy that Jonesbrook Lough, depicted on the 1837 OS map to the north of the demesne, is not named on the 1911 map, and, indeed, has disappeared from the contemporary landscape.

Other features of Drewstown Demesne are White Lough and Black Lough, the latter lake is circular in shape with a small island in its centre. According to the 1837 map, the outflowing stream from White Lough powered a 'water engine,' the first such we have encountered so far on the Boyne or its tributaries.

Continuing south-south-eastwards, the river is first named 'the Athboy River' on the 1911 map in Gillstown Townland; from where it flows on through the townland of Hospital Land to Athboy Bridge, upstream of which it is split by a longitudinal weir. The main river takes the most westerly course and passes beneath the single arched bridge; a segmental arch of about 18ft span built askew to the road. The easterly branch forms a millrace that powered Athboy Corn & Flour Mill, then flowed beneath the twin arched bridge (both of semi-circular profile) to re-join the main stream further to the south.

The 1837 map shows the river exiting Athboy Village between Danson's Court and the Fair Green; the 1911 map depicts the former as Danes Court, with the railway terminus to the east. Beyond this lay 'the Fair Green' and an oddly named townland called Eighty Eight Acres (actually 156 acres 1 rood 8 perches). From Athboy, the river continues southwards to Clifton Lodge Demesne and onwards to Tullanoge Townland, where it is first named 'the Tremblestown River' on the maps.

On its western bank and within a narrow salient of Kildalkey Townland, the 1911 map depicts a section of double ditch, named 'The Pale' – it is noteworthy that the 1837 map shows this as a single line or hedgerow. Local tradition holds that this extensive length of double ditch was part of the medieval defensive line around the environs of Dublin known as 'the English Pale.'

Then onwards the river flows to Tremblestown Bridge, and past an old graveyard close by Tremblestown Castle ruins (ancestral home of the Barnewall family), thence to Lady Island, a small townland consisting of 2 acres 3 roods 5 perches.[15] From here it flows almost due east to pass beneath the Trim to Kildalkey road at Kilnagross Bridge, and fall in to the Boyne just below this bridge. It is somewhat remarkable that Tremblestown Townland does not have a riparian section on the Boyne; the OS maps indicate that it was cut off from the river by a salient of the 118 acre Kilnagross Townland extending downriver to Dunleever Glebe.

The following are details of the two watermills found on the Tremblestown/ Athboy River:

Martinstown Mill.

The mill located on the tributary of the Athboy River in Martinstown to the north-west of the town is described thus on Griffith's 1854 valuation:
House, office, corn-mill & kiln and land occupied by Michael M'Cormick, leased from the Governor's of Stephen's Hospital at R.V. £15-15s.
N.B., all that remains of this mill are some ivy mantled stone walls standing at the roadside (R154) beside the old bridge.

Newman's Mill.

Athboy Flour and Corn Mill, located on the Athboy River at Townparks in the town of Athboy, described thus in the valuation:
House, corn-mill, office and garden (31 perches), occupied by John Webb, leased from the Earl of Darnley at R.V. £85-0s-0d: local tradition holds that a family named O'Keefe (or Keefe), supposed last operators of Keely's (Kiely's) mill in Trim, moved to Athboy at the end of the 19th century to help Newmans operate the mill there. I recall visiting Newman's Mill several times with my father during the 1950s to collect loads of pigmeal. The old mill is gone now, the former millrace dried up beneath the twin arches and several apartment blocks occupy the site, with florists and visual aid shops where once we drove through the mill gates in our Ford-ten van. The skewed bridge is listed under the Meath Heritage Project as MH-N51-001-00.
N.B., Lady Island is shown by the valuation to be held 'in fee' by Thomas Hart at R.V. £2-5s.

At Kilnagross Bridge, in a nook formed by the Tremblestown River stands a modernised stone built dwelling; in the adjacent farmyard is a castellated building occupying part of the footprint of the former Kilnagross House. The 1837 map depicts this house as a quadrangle with inner courtyard, similar to the abode of Anne Daly in Lionsden. While uncertain of its earlier history, I believe that in the mid-20th century this place became known in the vernacular as 'the Dutchman's,' because a man of that nationality established a vegetable processing industry in the farmyard, where several local people were employed.

Another mill is shown on Larkin's Map and depicted as a corn mill on the 1837 OS map about three hundred yards below the Tremblestown River's confluence with the Boyne. This mill is not indicated on the 1911 map and no traces of the mill or its attendant house remain. The vanished mill is known in the vernacular as Mitchell's Mill. While the mill is not included on Griffith's, the site upon which it stood is listed thus:

> Lot No. 2a – house, office and land totalling circa 11.6 acres, occupied by Patrick Mitchell, leased from Lord Trimblestown at R.V. £7-10s.

Jim Reynolds' *A Life by The Boyne* relates some folklore of the area including a tale of how Mitchell's Corn Mill came to be abandoned:

> About three quarters of a mile downstream from Higgin's Mill, and less than four hundred yards upstream of Newhaggard Weir was Mitchell's Mill. For the couple of years it took to rebuild this huge weir and mill, all grinding of corn ceased at Newhaggard Mill with the result that Mitchells became a very busy place. The Mitchells knew when this weir was completed that it would leave their mill inoperable, which indeed was the case. The waters backed up and left them swamped.
>
> Tradition tells us that when Newhaggard Mill was closed every horse and cart the Mitchells could muster was on the roads as often as possible. Although most of the time they were loaded with sacks of chaff, they travelled around Tremblestown, Bective Drinadaly and the Rock, all the time passing through Trim creating the impression that they were doing twice as much business as they actually were. (sic)

The story goes on to relate how the Mitchells sued Newhaggard Mill for compensation and were awarded £800 by the courts – and how the family took to supplying hay to the Dublin market thereafter. Though the veracity of the traditional tale cannot be established at this remove, the topography of the location suggests that the raising of Newhaggard Weir did indeed make Mitchells' Mill inoperable through loss of differential water-head across its waterwheel.

A close study of the terrain and the OS maps indicates that a solution for this problem may have been attempted by taking a millrace off the Tremblestown River from a higher elevation upstream of Kilnagross House. The maps depict a small stream taken from the river and flowing to the rear of Kilnagross House, then beneath the Trim to Kildalkey road and onwards to the Boyne just above Mitchells' Mill. Although badly overgrown nowadays, the course of the stream is still evident on the landscape.

We pulled the boat ashore close by the old mill site, to rendezvous with the back-up team for refuelling; this operation being supervised by a pair of curious equines, now in occupation of the empty field where once the ancient corn mill stood on the riverbank.

Back in midstream, we continued on downriver, drifting past several sedgy islets in this broad reach before rounding a curve and observing the great bulk of Newhaggard Mill emerging from the mist shrouded southern shore. The 1656 Down Survey Barony of Moyfenrath map indicates a castle here, with *A Mill* shown both graphically and in text immediately upstream. The same

Refuelling at Kilnagross

The Ruins of Newhaggard Flour Mill

map depicts a row of dots running from "New Haggert" Castle westwards to Castle Rickard church, which is marked *The Highway From Trim to Clonard.*

Newhaggard Mill was the largest mill located on the Upper Boyne reaches, as evidenced by its footprint on both the 1837 and 1911 OS maps. Although the later map shows that the buildings were extended in the interim period, the mill occupied mostly the same curtilage in both eras, with the earlier map showing it as a flour mill while the later map names it a corn mill.

There are major differences in the layout of both the head and tail races. The earlier map shows the weir running askew from the northern bank and connecting to the building nearest the river on the opposite shore. This weir elevated the river level and directed water through the headrace flowing between the newer and older buildings on the southern bank. Another weir (perhaps a salmon leap) extended across the river from the skewed weir to the northern riverbank.

The later map indicates a different layout, with the weir running in a curve from the northern bank to a narrow islet or rampart in the river's centre; breached at intervals by small spill weirs or slots and connected to the mill building closest to the riverbank. This arrangement also directed water through a gap between the buildings, where the long gone waterwheels were most likely located in millwheel housings. This map shows the chimney in situ, with two footbridges straddling the millrace between the buildings, and that the cross weir (salmon leap) had vanished.

The work executed in building the newer weir probably caused the problems with Mitchell's Mill upstream. As the OS revised map of 1852 depicts the older weir layout and because local tradition tells us that thirteen pairs of millstones were "being worked vigorously" in 1860 (Jim Reynolds), the weir was most likely altered in the period 1852 to 1860.

The earlier tailrace is shorter, and shown re-entering the river opposite a large island (3.612 acres on 1911 map) located just below the mill. The later map shows the tailrace continuing on downriver for a distance of about 750 yards from the mill. This tailrace extension was obviously part of the work completed to improve the water-head across the millwheels, thereby increasing the operational capacity of the enterprise.

Tradition holds that the massive six-storeyed building still standing on the riverbank was built about 1760, to take advantage of the newer Corn Acts, which paid subsidies for road transport of flour to the city of Dublin. Lewis' Topographical Survey (1837), commenting upon the area around Trim says of this mill: "on the River Boyne about a mile to the west are very extensive mills called New Haggard Mills, the property of Mr. Nangle, producing about 40,000 barrels of flour and oatmeal." Different sources name the mill's owners as Matthew Devereux, James Connolly (c.1770) and Charles Nangle. Griffith's gives the following details of this mill:

> Lot No. 1 h, house, offices, stores, flour-mill & garden (1 acre 3 roods) & land totalling 24 acres 3 roods 21 perches, occupied by Richard and Michael Odlum & Co., leased from John Connolly @ R.V. £260-0s-0d.
> Lot No. 3a, Miller's ho., offs & gar. (2 perches 30 roods), occupied by Messers. Richard & Michael Odlum & Co., leased from John Connolly @ R. V. £2-5s-0d.[16]

On a visit to the site in January 2014, I noted that most of the buildings of the older or more landward part of the mill have disappeared; some of the old stone walls undoubtedly absorbed into the fabric of the many modern farm buildings now occupying the site. The outline of the old walled garden, mentioned on Griffith's Valuation, can still be observed to the south-west of the former mill. The mighty weir, its eel houses and tail race have vanished, victims of the OPW post 1968 drainage scheme. The huge rectangular building (constructed c.1760), with castellated gables and tall stone chimney still stands on the riverbank; its myriad of empty, gaunt window openings overlooking the Boyne from the roofless, empty shell yet another testament to the wastefulness of mankind.

From Kilnagross to the medieval stone arched Bridge of Trim, the Boyne flows in a relatively shallow cleft between two-tiered banks winding through a broad floodplain. The 1837 OS map depicts the three great mill weirs along this reach, together with a series of islets, some of which are covered by plantations. The 1911 map shows a similar layout except that Mitchell's Mill and weir have disappeared, Newhaggard Weir is altered and most of the riverbanks straightened.

The new bridge at the Watergate is shown on the later map; this bridge will be discussed presently, together with the weir for the 'town mill' i.e. Kennedy's Corn/Flour Mill. The Boyne riparian townlands on this section are Dunleever Glebe, Crowpark and Townparks-North on the northern shore, with Newhaggard, Commons (1st division) and Townparks-South forming the southern riverbank.

Back on the boat and commencing our run down the stretch of river once occupied by Newhaggard Mill Weir, it soon became apparent that this reach contained several sections of white water. These are caused by the many OPW ripples, together with rocky shoals and shallows, relics of the former great weir. Dredging operations were still in progress hereabouts, as evidenced by the many fresh piles of rocky spoil adorning both riverbanks. This work, I believe, is an attempt at deepening the river to provide river amenities for water sports. One might well wonder why such a possibility was not considered prior to the great weir being torn from the riverbed; this is yet another example of official dearth of foresight, now costing a fortune to redress.

Going on downriver past the ruins of the mighty mill (an even more imposing and spectacular sight from the river), and on by the remains of the old tower house of Newhaggard (on the southern riverbank), we come to the spot where once another great weir provided water-head to power the

The new Watergate Bridge

long gone mill near the old Gaol of Trim. This weir was built askew to the river, from the Commons near the former site of St. George's well on the southern shore, to the old mereing of Crowpark and Townparks-North just downstream from St. Patrick's Well.[17] The weir connected to a series of islets or ramparts running alongside the northern shore,[18] which enclosed a mill headrace that ran for about 550 yards to the mill located just upstream from the contemporary Watergate Bridge.

This bridge spans the river Boyne from the site of the old Watergate on the southern riverbank. The earlier bridge once crossed the rampart and mill tailrace to link with Mill Lane in Townpark-North. Apart from the bridge, all these features are gone now; the weir, millraces and mill have vanished, with scarcely a trace of their former presence evident to the unknowing eye. The remaining traces of the former mill workings comprise some stubs of stone walls at the western end of Mill Lane; together with a rocky shoal causing a line of white water across the Boyne at the approximate midpoint of the old weir.

Although the OS maps (including the 1852 Rev.) depicts the mill in Trim Town variously as a flour and corn mill; Griffith's lists two mills on the site, one described as a tuck mill the other as a flour & corn mill. The 1854 valuation lists these mills thus:

Townparks North – Mill Lane, Lot 3: house, offs, flour, corn and tuck mill and yard occupied by Patrick Kennedy, leased from Edward E. Chambers @ R.V. £55-0s-0d.

Townparks North – Mill Lane, Lot 4: flour and corn-mill, offices and yard, held in fee – R.V. £10-0s-0d. N.B., no portion of land was listed as being attached to either mill.

Cross referencing the above valuation listings with the various maps reveals that both mills were probably housed within the footprint of the one building depicted on the maps. As this building straddled the millrace, it is probable that one mill was located on the rampart section, with the other housed in the portion of the building located to the north of the millrace. As a point of interest, the 1911 map shows that Kennedy's Mill was in ruins at the time.

The Watergate was an old stone arched gateway providing entry/egress through the town's ancient western defensive wall. Some historians conclude that it opened onto the original fording point of the Boyne; which gave the town its name Baile Atha Truimm (Troim) in Gaelic, or Ford of the Elder Tree. Perhaps it also led to the 'Highway from Trim to Clonard,' shown on the 1656 Down Survey Map.

The walls of Trim once enclosed the medieval town, which included sections on both riverbanks. In addition to the Watergate, the OS maps show that the wall was pierced by four other gateways including the Athboy Gate (Black or North Gate), Navan Gate (or Rogue's Gate), Sheep Gate and the Dublin Gate. These gates and the line of the wall are depicted on the 1837 OS map, but the later OS map indicates only parts of the Watergate and Sheep Gate structures, together with several sections of the wall existing at the time. Fortunately, the Shackleton Collection contains a photograph taken by Jane Shackleton in 1896, prior to construction of Watergate Bridge. This remarkable picture was 'snapped' from the contemporary line of Watergate Street and depicts the arched gateway together with five youths; four boys sitting atop the partly crumbled structure, and a well-behaved girl standing demurely next to the western pillar. The background, as seen through the arch, provides a rare and fascinating glimpse of the Boyne as it was in Trim long ago, with the mill weir and Kennedy's long gone mill clearly visible against the backdrop of the Townparks riverbank.[19]

Shackleton 1896 Watergate

Another landscape feature I noted on the map of 1911 was a race course located on the southern riverbank; an oval-shaped track following the mereing of Manorland and the Commons on its northernmost leg, then sweeping close by the Kinnegad Road to the south, near Gallow's Hill ('the Gallops' nowadays). A viewing stand was located near the southern sector, just to the north-west of the contemporary OPW offices.

Maelseachlan Statue - the footbridge and Trim Castle

The first Watergate Bridge was built across the Boyne in 1904. This bridge is listed in Main Record (County Meath) as No. 14328043, and described thus:

> Four span road bridge, built 1904, consisting of four cast-iron spans resting on concrete piers. Triangular cutwaters on both upstream and downstream sides of the bridge. Plaque on road side elevation.
>
> This bridge is an excellent example of late nineteenth and early twentieth century construction. Cast-iron and concrete construction dating from this period is unusual in Ireland. Date from plaque on west side of bridge reads: 'Watergate Bridge 1904 built by J.H. Moore G.S. Collins & Newman. Contractors.'

The bridge was demolished in the early years of the new millennium and replaced by a single span metal bridge carried by two bowstring trusses; this bridge was opened in 2004/5. The new bridge, with a budget of 1.2 million Euros, was designed by Roughan & O'Donovan of Galway and described thus in their literature:

The new Watergate Bridge comprises a pair of slender tapering pentagonal arch ribs crossing the river in a single span of 35m, carrying two lanes of traffic and cantilever footpaths. The width of the bridge is 15.15m.

All traces of the rampart and Kennedy's Mill tailrace have now disappeared from the Boyne at Trim.

The last major landmark upstream of Trim Bridge was the 'Old Gaol;' now vanished and replaced by private dwellings. In 1854, these buildings were listed in Griffith's as: Old Gaol, offices & yard held in fee by Edward Blake at R.V. 10s. Two workmen were tragically killed during demolition of this structure in the 1950s. Directly across the river, on the southern bank, was the former gasworks, downstream of which is a licensed premises now known as Sally Rogers' Bar.[20]

ENDNOTES

1 From the various accounts of the Battle of Portlester, it is apparent that some confusion exists as to whether the skirmish took place at this mill ford on the River Boyne, or at a ford on the Stonyford River to the north of Portlester Townland. While the latter location has a corn mill marked on the 1837 OS and Larkin's Map, it was located in Corballis Townland and local tradition places the long gone mill (Earl's Mill) as dating from the early 1800s only. There is no mill shown in this townland (old spelling Corbolys) on the 1656 Down Survey Barony map. Near the former site of the ford on the Stonyford River is a stone arched bridge named Earl's Bridge. The mill and bridge were possibly named after the Earl of Darnley (Bligh), owner of the former Portlester estates. Local tradition says also that a bush, known as Moore's Bush, once grew close by here, at the supposed spot where Charles Moore was decapitated by a cannon ball.

2 The following informative snippets are from a report by Richard Gray, district engineer for the Upper Boyne Drainage District in 1849: "the masonry executed during the season consisted in the erection of a new arch at Scariff in place of the old bridge which had been formerly underpinned for the Blackwater drainage. The arch has a clear waterway 60ft in width; the abutments are founded 6ft below the old underpinnings and the bottom of the waterway is now 4ft below the general range of the gradient line, and 2ft below the dishing line, falling gradually to this depth from 20 perches on either side of the bridge. The roadway was opened to the public on the 23rd of November and the temporary bridge removed and stored; on the 5th of December one parapet was nearly finished and half the string course set in the opposite side when the order to stop was received; there was a railing set up to protect the thoroughfare." N.B., this report commenced by Gray stating that during the first five months of 1849 no work had been done for lack of funds. In the Scariff Division the average number employed was 187 per day with a peak of 376. The reference in this report to an earlier draining of the Meath/Kildare Blackwater may be to the scheme executed under the Drainage Act of 1842 (5 & 6 Vict, Cap. 89).

3 This area has a profusion of ringforts and marshlands, one such marsh bearing the title of Red Bog.

4 Not the much larger Newtown Lough to the west of Clonmellon, which outflows to the south of Clonmellon towards Killua.

5 From this bridge to the mereing with Woodstown, the reach of the Stonyford passing through Lisclogher Great Townland is named 'the Lisclogher River.'

6 This Stonyford Br. is located on the river of the same name, close by the contemporary Kilmurry water treatment plant. A plaque on the northern parapet declares that the bridge was constructed by the OPW in 1877. The engineer in charge is named James Dillon.

7 The OS maps depict a ruined windmill in a field to the south of Kill Mill; at time of writing, the remnants of this stump can be viewed from the road beside the National School. I could find no record of this windmill on Griffith's Valuation.

8 Keegan's vast quarry complex now covers much of this townland.

9 These rynds/mace-heads (part of the runner stone driving and balance mechanism) vary from place to place on the Boyne and tributaries. The millstones observed on the Lower Boyne, e.g. Rosnaree, Roughgrange and Stalleen, having a four-spoked or cruciform-shaped profile, while those at Bective Mill, Kilcarn Upper corn mill and the ancient King's Mill in Lismullin (on the River Gabhra) had triple-spoked rynds for driving their *runner stones*. The only watermill still operating in the area, Martry Corn Mill on the River Blackwater outside Navan, has a three pronged profile on its millstones.

10 These columns are probably formed from the original 9ft thick pillars, described in E. Russel's 1845 report; as it would have been almost impossible to support the remaining flanking arches in a river environment (without cracking) during reconstruction work in 1848.

11 The County Meath presentments were made to the Grand Jury at Trim Assizes on 12th June 1849 – the County Kildare presentments were made to the Kildare Grand Jury in Athy on 2nd Aug. 1849.

12 Local tradition holds that this mill was known as 'the factory' and contained two pairs of millstones in addition to being a tuck or fulling mill; one pair for shelling grain, the other for grinding corn. It is said also that plenty of water was available to maintain the mill in full operation for up to nine months in the year and that the diameter of the waterwheel was 11.25ft.

13 This report indicates that the Commissioners of Public Works built the new weir at Higgins Brook Mill c.1848; ironically, the same public body demolished the weir just over a century later.

14 A quaint village comprising two terraces of stone built, slate roofed cottages (total 15) – built for the workers of the Arglassan Estate in c.1830. The little village, complete with green areas and chestnut tree, appears as if by magic while one motors along the country road; like an oasis from the past amidst the surrounding desert of modernity.

15 'The Down survey Barony of Navan map of 1656 depicts a bridge crossing the river immediately downstream of Tremblestown Castle.

16 The valuation shows also that John Connnolly had circa 560 acres of Newhaggard leased from Lord Tremblestown at R.V. £575-0s-0d, including Newgaggard House and gate lodge and all the mill curtilage. The 'Miller's ho.' listed on the valuation was sited just downstream of the tower house ruins, close by the riverbank and accessed by a laneway leading from the mill.

17 A holy well venerated annually by a Pattern. In 1995, Sister Assumpta initiated a pilgrimage to the site, the 20th anniversary of which was celebrated on St. Patrick's Day 2015

18 According to Jim Reynolds, two of these islets were named Hoggs' Island and Sherry Island.

19 The best information available suggests that The Watergate was demolished c.1902. Local tradition holds that a 6th gate named the Bridge Gate may have existed, and was possibly sited close by the drawbridge to the castle.

20 Formerly known as The Bridge Bar, named such by Gerry Brady in honour of a lady named Sally Rogers; owner of a newspaper shop across the road, at the town end of Trim Bridge: supposedly the only such shop in Trim at the time. According to Gerry, before her demise about 1990, she bequeathed the premises to him. Gerry related the tale to me one day when I called to take some photos of the bridge from his riverside balcony. I believe that Sally is interred in the nearby Newtown Cemetery.

Athboy R.

Killbrie

25 Garnett C.

Cas. Ru.ˢ

Trimleston

L. Trimleston

24

Kells Rᵈ
P. 263

Jullingar Rᵈ
P. 244

23

Charter
School

22

TRIM
Ch. Ruˢ

Navan R.
P. 246

Knightsbrook

21

Percivall Esqᵗ

Boyne R.

Bective Rᵈ

Scurlockstown

6

The Middle Reaches
from Trim to Bective

Bridge of Trim – Ancient routes – The Non navigable Boyne – Land route from Trim to Drogheda – Historic sites – Boyne Cottages – Mel Gibson & Trim Castle – Millenium Br., Leper Stream & Maudlins – Hamilton's Island – Maudlins Br. – The Drawbridge & unfinished canals – Magee's Island, Smart's Weir & mill – Newtown Priory, Cathedral & Dillon Tomb – St. Peter's or Newtown Br. – Marcie Regan's Pub – St. Johns Priory & Crouched Friars – Shiels/Kiely's Weir & mill – Iffernock Fishing Weir & lost mill of Loganstown – Knightsbrook, Moynalvey, Clonymeath & Dangan River – Dinells Brook & Mrs. Delany – A Foot Br. in Freffens & Scurlocks Br. – Old routes to Dublin – Knock Mills – Old Waterworks – Wilde & Scurlockstown Church, Castle – Boycetown/Derrypatrick River – Scurlockstown Br. & Cassidy's Mill – Dunganny Fishing Weir – Tribley Rail Br. – Changing river – Bridge of the Grange – Rathnally Weir, Mills & townland – Corn Bounty – Trubley/Tribley & Lally's Island.

On that cold November day in 2012, our boat passed by the *Mael Seachlain* equestrian statue standing on the right riverbank. Continuing onwards beneath the wooden footbridge, we passed under the new Watergate Bridge towards the old bridge of Trim[1]. Here the Boyne flows between stone lined banks constricting its channel on the approach to the medieval bridge.

177

The passage through the old arches is tricky due to the stronger flow, with the broad concrete skirts surrounding the mid-river pillars providing an additional impact hazard.

Thus we had little time to linger beneath the ancient arches, to admire the structure and provide a spectacle for the few dedicated tobacco smokers braving the wintery conditions on the balcony of Sally Rogers' Bar. So we carried on through to the downstream side. Here the boys held the boat steady in mid-river while we viewed the bridge from the river aspect.

Peter O'Keefe and Tom Simington give a full technical description of this bridge in their *Irish Stone Bridges – history and heritage,* where they write:

> The bridge is founded on rock. The bed under the arches was lowered by an average of 4ft as part of the 1970s Boyne Drainage Scheme. The piers were left intact perched on solid rock but with the footings protected by reinforced concrete 'pontoons'.

The authors conclude that the contemporary bridge replaced an older structure (built c.1200 AD), shortly after it was supposedly swept away by a great flood in 1330 AD.[2] This is perhaps the oldest original (un-widened) masonry road bridge being used in Ireland today. During our brief interlude at the bridge I noted some of the irregularities mentioned by O'Keefe in his technical review; including the double row of ringstones, and several places where the outer ring of the arches are irregular, possibly due to slippage of the wickerwork/wooden forms of long ago.

The downriver façade has a clearer aspect than the upriver face, which is more encrusted by moss and lichen, with several shrubs sprouting from its stonework. The Boyne flows from north-west to south-east here and is spanned by the bridge at an almost perfect right angle to its course. It is remarkable that this structure survived so many floods over the centuries. The aggregate width of its waterway is about 64ft, while the original free waterway/hydraulic capacity of Derrinydaly Bridge upstream was circa 87ft in width, considered inadequate by the Office of Public Works in 1848.

Its survival is more remarkable when one considers that the Boyne receives the waters of the Tremblestown River immediately upstream of Trim, and the constricted passage of the river at Trim, imposing greater stress on the ancient

The upstream facade Trim Bridge

bridge. Its future seems more assured; however, because of the work executed by the OPW in recent times, with the deepening of the riverbed effectively increasing its free waterway capacity.

Trim (Town) Bridge H.E.W. No. 3157

The bridge is comprised of four segmental, pointed arches (similar to Babes Bridge); each spanning circa 16ft and the inter-arch piers are about 8ft wide, and faced by triangular cutwaters. The three upstream cutwaters have tapered cappings extending to just above the arch crowns; while one downstream cutwater rises to road level, the other two extend to just above the arch springers. The springing planes/skewbacks are masked by the cutwaters which are incorporated with the piers to that level. The spandrel walls are of random rubble, partly coursed. The keystones are uniform with the arch ringstones, which consist of roughly dressed, rectangular stones of varying thickness from about 3in. to 6in. The face to face width of the bridge is circa 21ft. The road width is about 16/17ft between 18in. thick parapets, which are capped by heavy, dressed flagstones.

Nowadays the bridge carries the routes from Trim to Navan, Kells and Athboy across the Boyne. In former times, the main routes (coach roads) from Dublin to Sligo via Athboy and Oldcastle and from Dublin to Granard via Finae passed over this bridge. These routes shared a common line from the Black Bull Inn via Scurlockstown to Trim; the section from the Black Bull to Athboy being turnpiked (or tolled) from c.1731 to 1752, when it ceased as a toll road, the first turnpike road in Ireland to become a 'free road' during that era.

This is an opportune juncture at which to address the myth of the Boyne's navigability from Trim to the sea in times past. While there are various interpretations of the term *navigable,* the most commonly found in dictionaries, as applicable to waterways and rivers, is: '*sufficiently wide or deep to provide free passage for vessels, ships or boats.*'

Similar to the myth placing the Boyne's source in Trinity Well, this myth may have evolved through many (unproven) references to various saints, such as St. Patrick and St. Loman, plying the river to its upper reaches long ago. On p. 82 of his book (2nd edition), in a reference to St. Loman's adventures on the Boyne, Wilde writes:

> 'he (Loman) waited another forty days, out of obedience to Patrick.
> Then, according to the order of his Master (the Lord being his pilot),
> he came in his boat against the stream, as far as the ford of Trim…'

These and other such references to the saints' upriver travels perhaps caused the myth to perpetuate and evolve. Thus resulting in the contemporary, widely held view that the Boyne was navigable between Trim and Drogheda during medieval times; a notion seemingly rooted in the belief that the Normans based their stronghold at Trim because of its accessibility via the River Boyne.

This concept is portrayed pictorially in tourist brochures and graphics at Trim Castle, with a large sailing vessel depicted moored in the adjacent harbour; supposedly having delivered a cargo of 'stores' from Drogheda at 'the River Gate.' However, these graphics and pamphlets fail to convey details on how this miracle of water transportation was achieved. The proposition fails to stand up under close scrutiny, and I believe that Trim became a bastion town for the Norman Conquest/settlement due to its location on the River Boyne, traditionally the north-western boundary of The Pale.

The following assessment of the Boyne's navigability is based on a study of its geography and topography, rather than the romantic notion that Norman ships plied its reaches between the walled towns of Trim, Navan and Drogheda:

The 1837 OS map shows that the River Boyne, from Trim to Navan, spread across most of the floodplain between the higher banks swelling to the surrounding eskers and hillsides.[3] Consequentially, in many places the river's course divided into a series of small streams, rivulets and rills, forming a myriad of channels flowing around the numerous islets obstructing the main river course. At such locations, these small, narrow streams increased water velocity and formed white-water shallows at the rocky ledges constituting the riverbed; these conditions making upriver passage well-nigh impossible for unpowered craft of the period.

In addition, as evidenced along the river's course nowadays, such narrow passageways are liable to blockage by fallen trees and river debris forming beaver dam-like structures across their waterways. The many naturally occurring obstructions were exacerbated by man-made structures such as bridges, fishing weirs, *kidills* (staked fences) and mill dams blocking free navigation of the river.

The same map depicts the Boyne's course between Trim and Navan littered with clusters of islets and narrows; most notably at Iffernock, Dungany, Rathnally, Trubly (Tribley), Balsoon, Bellinter, Ardsallagh and Upper Kilcarn. Except during periods of very elevated water levels, this section of river is still unnavigable (as defined earlier), for modern small high-powered propeller driven, shallow draught RIBs, despite massive drainage works executed by the OPW from 1968 to the present day.

During our downriver trips in the winters of 2011-2012 and 2013-2014, we experienced great difficulty negotiating the river even during elevated water levels: our lightly laden craft hanging up on the many shoals and shallows, having to be hauled across these obstructions; a very labour intensive operation, impossible to execute on an upriver passage against the strong current

Non navigability is not a modern phenomenon caused solely by drainage works. When attempting the navigation extension from Navan to Trim in the period 1790 to 1798, the constructors chose an overland canal routed towards Rathnally. An indicator that the 'river navigation' was less attractive due to the Boyne's many obstructed sections, and to difficulties posed by riverside landowners. It is evident from research that these problems were more acute during medieval times.

Regarding the river reaches from Navan to Slane and Drogheda, a study of the Boyne Navigation indicates that the river was far from navigable pre-1750. In this context, it took circa forty years and a vast amount of funding to construct a navigable waterway capable of lifting barges and lighters from the tidal reach at Oldbridge to the summit level at Navan, 113ft above mean tide level. When completed in 1800, ten sections of lateral canals (totalling circa 11.25 miles) circumvented various obstructions, including: fords and bridges, mill weirs, rocky shoals and rapids, clusters of islets and fishing weirs. Apart from the many weirs, the worst natural barriers were located in the reaches between Stackallan and Slane, Slane to Rosnaree, Broe to Stalleen Lower and Oldbridge.

A more cogent and convincing case can be made that the main transport link between Trim and Drogheda was the road running from Trim through Scurlockstown, Bective, Ballymagarvey and Duleek; a much shorter and less hazardous route than the Boyne passage. This old road became part of

the main route from Athlone to Drogheda. The section from Trim towards the sea was protected by a line of strategically positioned castles, keeps and tower houses. Starting at Trim, those known formed a near continuous defensive line alongside or close by this road and are/were located as follows: Saint Johns (at Newtown Br.) – Scurlockstown – Trubley – Bective – Balsoon – Asigh – Riverstown – Castletowntaragh – Philpotstown – Walterstown – Kentstown – Balrath – Athcarne and Duleek. This route ran some distance inside the supposed outer defensive line of The Pale, based upon the River Boyne. Why then

Scurlockstown Castle (woodcut)

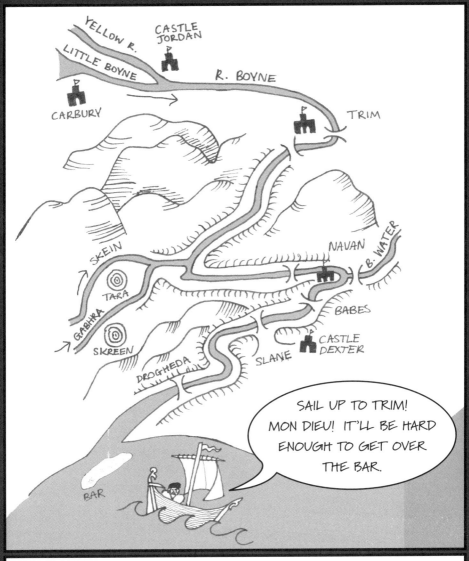

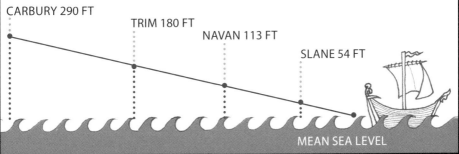

Illustrations: Gemma Coughlan. From a sketch by the author and Marie Holten from an idea by Paschal Marry

would the militarily astute Norman invaders become dependent for supplies on an unnavigable river forming part of their outer defensive line?

While the Boyne, from Trim to Navan and Drogheda, was non navigable in any practical or commercial sense during the period from the Norman Conquest to the advent of the Boyne Navigation c.1750-1800, many of the short, deeper sections were used by various sized craft for different purposes. The Boyne coracle being employed locally all along the river for fishing and used for transporting people, animals and smaller goods along short sections and indeed across the river.

Larger craft were known to have been used for sailing on the maintained river sections close by big country houses and the various castles. Trim Castle most likely fell into the latter category, with the Boyne reach made navigable locally. In the absence of compelling evidence to the contrary, it is reasonable to conclude that the several historical references to the River Boyne being navigable from Trim to the sea, pre 1750, are mistakenly based on this local boating activity.

As Trim and its main heritage sites have been discussed and recorded extensively in other writings, I will mention only some of these and concentrate mostly on the Boyne's landscape hereabouts. Starting with the north-eastern or left riverbank, a cluster of historic sites crown the hillside just east of the mereing (a defined boundary)[4] of Townparks North and Porch Field. These include Nangle Castle, the Yellow Steeple (part of the former Augustinian Abbey of St. Mary's), Talbot Castle and Sheep Gate. The first three sites are located within the area of the old town wall, while Sheep Gate supposedly provided access through the wall for brethren of the Newtown Abbeys.

The name Porch Field (Porchy) may derive from an older form for the name of this gate (Porchgate). The 1837 map shows that the name Porch Field is given to an area of 278 acres and 21 perches, bounded to the north by the townlands of Blackfriary and Lackanash, with the River Boyne forming the southern boundary. Downstream from the Porch Field is another cluster of historic sites, including Newtown Abbey and church, sited just above the ancient bridge of Newtown.

Immediately below Trim Bridge, in Townparks South on the opposite or south-western riverbank, stand a row of six artisan-type dwellings named Boyne

Cottages. While their origins are uncertain, they may have been constructed during the mid to late 1800s as workers' cottages for Lord Dunsany, whose family (Plunkett) once owned the castle and grounds, together with extensive properties in Trim. South of these is the old courthouse, formerly used by the Meath Grand Jury to hold bi-annual assizes, which pronounced judgement upon supposed lawbreakers, and decided on presentments for construction and repair of the many bridges and roads throughout the county.

Left: The Boyne Artisan Cottages. Right: Trim Castle (keep) from the river, seen through the curtain wall at the harbour-basin.

Further downstream in the townland of Manorland (1st Division) stands the imposing pile of Trim Castle (King John's Castle), construction of which commenced under Hugh de Lacy in the late 12th century, and which was completed in the early 13th century. The inner castle or keep (donjon), with its many-cornered projections, is partly surrounded by a bastioned curtain wall, which, on its southern aspect is pierced by a gateway (once the drawbridge over the moat) protected by a barbican outwork. The 1837 OS map shows that the curtain wall surrounded the castle and bailey completely at that time, but the later map indicates the riverside section of this wall had mostly disappeared. In 1994, Trim Castle was used to shoot scenes for Mel Gibson's *Braveheart*; in which film Gibson played the star role of William Wallace in his 14th century struggle to free Scotland from the 'yoke of English oppression.'

South of the castle, the 1837 OS map depicts the New Gaol (built in 1834); a remarkable construction shaped rather like a fan, with five oblong radial blocks surrounding a circular central hub. The 1911 map shows this building, together with a Bridewell and Industrial School occupying the same site, with the Union Workhouse on a site to the south in the townland of Manorland.

Resuming the river journey, our boat left the ancient arches of Trim Bridge and passed on downriver towards the Millennium Bridge; a single span wooden, beamed and latticed footbridge mounted upon concrete riverbank abutments. As the name suggests, this bridge was erected by Trim Town Council to celebrate the new millennium, and spans the river from the castle complex on the south-western shore, to the Porch Field on the opposite riverbank. Downstream of the footbridge, the Boyne flows over rapids and on past the castle, before turning south-westwards towards the bridge at the Maudlins.[5]

Until removed during the post 1968 drainage scheme, a small islet, named Hamilton's Island, was located in mid-river immediately below the castle's curtain wall. This was named after famed Royal Astronomer Sir Rowan Hamilton, who camped there frequently and swam in the Boyne hereabouts as a youngster. On the adjacent south-western riverbank, the 1837 OS map depicts two small parcels of land; the most upriver of which is named Commons 4th Div'n., the other shown as 'part of Maudlin,' a detached portion of the nearby 105.5 acre townland of Maudlin, which has no other riverside sector.

The map of 1911 shows the Fever Hospital located on the Commons' site; and depicts a short length of stream or rill entering the Boyne just downstream from the south-eastern flank of the castle's curtain wall. This is perhaps the 'Leper Stream,' (or Water of Luppard), a small river that according to local tradition took its name from the leper hospital at the Maudlins and once maintained a water level in the castle moat. Old Corporation records indicate that this stream, which rises to the west of Gallows' Hill, was culverted during the 18th century. Currently, part of the former castle 'harbour' or moat near the River Gate, is inundated by a small stream of water, pumped from the Boyne close by the Millenium Bridge.

The bridge at the Maudlins crosses the Boyne from Friar's Land (3rd Div.) on the southern bank, to Porch Field. Built c.1978-1982, it is of concrete construction and anchored by two riverbank abutments. The triple span bridge, supported by longitudinal mid-river columns, incorporates riverside pedestrian ways (sub-road) on each bank. The structure carries the R154 across the river, to link with the northern section of the R161 leading from Trim to Navan.

Passing along the deep stretch upstream and beneath the central span, we observed a ragged stone arch perched on the bank in the Porch Field immediately downstream. The little structure, known in the vernacular as 'the Drawbridge,' was built c.1750-1790 and had nothing to do with the nearby castle, but in my view was once part of the uncompleted section of the Boyne Navigation intended as a water transport link between Navan and Trim. 'The Drawbridge' spans circa 15ft and has a width of about 7ft; very similar dimensions to those of Ruxton's Bridge, a horse-bridge spanning the canal at Navan.

Most of the ringstones are missing, and if equipped with parapets originally, it was most likely a footbridge providing access to a tiny islet (1.408 acres), referred to colloquially as Magee's Island (named after a family who owned the Porch Field). The islet was formed by a short section of canal bypassing a weir called Smart's Weir, which historically provided water-head to power a tuck mill on the southern riverbank.

According to Jim Reynolds' *A Life by the Boyne*, this canal section had a two-lock system designated as number eight lock. I have been unable; however, to find any records on the maps or discover other written sources that support this proposition – or that the No. 7 lock was located further downstream below Newtown Bridge.[6] The post 1968 drainage scheme filled in this canal, incorporating Magee's Island within the riverbank. This explains why the crumbling stone arch stands forlornly at the bottom of the Porch Field, high and dry beside the Boyne.

Smart's Weir ran askew across the Boyne, from the eastern tip of Magee's Island to the opposite riverbank at a narrow salient of Friarspark Townland (1st Div. 23 acre 4 perches), extending to mid-river between Commons 5th & 6th Divs. It connected to a river rampart/islet via a set of sluices and eel traps. The 1837 OS map indicates extensive buildings located on this Friarspark salient, with the tailrace falling back into the Boyne directly below the mill.

Griffith's records the following of this mill in 1854: house, offs, and corn-mill, occupied by John Smart, leased from Edward E. Chambers @ R.V. £18-10s.

The mill is depicted on Larkin's Map by the standard cog wheel symbol and shown on the 1837 OS map as a tuck mill. Local tradition has it that this was a dual purpose mill, with two pairs of stones for grinding and one set for shelling corn; powered by a waterwheel 14ft in diameter and 3.5ft wide, and that the tuck mill was powered by a wheel 12ft in diameter and 2.5ft wide. It is said that sufficient water was available to keep the mill in operation throughout the year, with the eel traps in use until c.1940, long after the mill(s) becoming defunct.[7]

Flowing across some shallows at the site of Smart's Weir, the Boyne's course swings to the north-east, and we followed this deeper reach, on past 'the Echo Gate' towards Newtown Bridge.[8] The northern riverbank is formed hereabouts by the Porch Field, which rises gradually towards the Navan road at Lackanash. Nowadays a footpath winds along the shore, from Newtown to the Drawbridge and onwards to Sheep Gate; from which eminence a wonderful vista of the ancient town, the castle and Yellow Steeple unfolds against the river backdrop. A cluster of old, grey-hued stone buildings is visible from mid-river, standing on the mist shrouded northern shore at the farthest end of this river reach; remnants of the ancient abbey of Newtown, together with the equally old cathedral, graveyard and parish church.[9]

The drawbridge arch

Newtown Abbey from the river.

Here, in 1206, Simon de Rochfort, a Norman Bishop, founded an Abbey of Canons Regular of the Order of Saint Victor (an Augustinian institution). In doing so he transferred the *See of Clonard* to this beautiful spot by the River Boyne. The monastic settlement, named the Abbey of Saint Peter and Saint Paul, flourished and supposedly became one of the wealthiest institutions in the land. In 1486 its prior, Thomas Scurlock, became the order's treasurer for all of Ireland. The monastery was suppressed by King Henry VIII around 1540.

The bridge at Newtown (formerly Peter's Town) consists of five stone arches and is one of the oldest Boyne crossings in use today. Although unsure of its exact age, I believe it was built sometime in the 15th century. The crossing links the townland of Saint Johns on the southern shore to that of Newtown on the northern riverbank. Traditionally, the bridge was sponsored by William Sherwood, Bishop of Meath (later Lord Deputy), and erected in the period 1460 to1475. It was supposedly used as a toll bridge for a time by the monks at the nearby monastery. The earliest map reference I can find is the 1656 Down Survey map of Moyfenrath Barony, on which it is named 'Johnstowne Bridg', while the Barony of Navan map names it Newtowne Bridge.

Viewed from the road, the bridge is distinctly humpbacked, with a slight dog-leg leading on to its southern end. This effect is caused by the southernmost and smallest arch being built slightly askew to the main structure (about 0 to 5 degrees). The four main arches cross the river in a straight line, and are not 'curved upriver towards the current,' as suggested in other writings. The bridge is now single carriageway and carries a local road across the Boyne, linking the R154 with the R161, but in olden times it formed part of the route from Dublin to Sligo via Athboy and Oldcastle.[10]

ॐ

Newtown or St. Peter's Bridge - H.E.W. No. 3158

Upriver aspect

Starting from the northern end, the bridge is comprised of the following: circa 30ft long, splayed abutment constructed of random rubble and flared towards the north-west – circa 6ft wide semi-circular cutwater with conical/rounded capping terminating at arch crown level – (**No. 01 arch**) a segmental profiled arch of c.18/19ft span and c.10/12ft high: the spandrel wall at the abutment end of this arch is noticeably corbelled, to allow flaring of the parapet at the bridge end – circa 8/9ft wide pillar of coursed stone, faced by triangular/rounded cutwater, with conical/rounded capping terminating at arch springers: a smaller conically topped pillar extends upwards to arch

---

Newtown Bridge and the fortified part of St. John's Abbey

Left: Loganstown shore through No. 02 arch of Newtown Bridge.
Right: corbelled detail on southern arch.

crown level – (**No 02 arch**) a segmental profiled arch of c.18/19ft span and c.10/12ft high – c.12/14ft wide pillar of coursed stone, faced by triangular/ rounded cutwater, which extends upwards to parapet level and forms the one (oblong) pedestrian refuge located near the bridge centre – (**No 03 arch**) a segmental profiled arch of c.17/18ft span and c.10/12ft high – c.10/12ft wide pillar of coursed stone, faced by triangular/rounded cutwater with tapered capping rising from springer level to mid-parapet level – (**No 04 arch**) a segmental profiled arch of 15/16ft span and c.10ft high – circa 7/8ft wide pillar of coursed stone, faced by triangular/rounded cutwater with tapered capping rising from springer level to mid-parapet level – (**No 05 arch**) a segmental profiled arch of c.12/13ft span c.10ft high: this arch is more circular and of significantly different profile to the other four arches – circa 8/9ft wide rounded cutwater of coursed stone rising to just above the arch springer level, and mostly buried in southern riverbank – circa 20ft splayed abutment constructed of random rubble and flared towards the southeast.

Downriver aspect

The aesthetics are spoiled somewhat by a sewer pipe and watermain attached to the eastern façade. There are no cutwaters on this side; as a consequence, a pronounced batter is noticeable on the downstream pillars and spandrel walls. The concrete underpinning is of squared profile, with no pointed ends. The skew construction of the most southern arch is very clear from this aspect, with an out-projecting section, corbelled from the spandrel stonework, demonstrating the skill of stonemasons long ago. The latter feature, like that on the opposite end of the bridge, was executed to allow flaring of the parapet wall towards the southeast. The difference in construction methods, arch profile and techniques used, may indeed be an indicator that this section was built at some other time than the remainder of the structure.

General

The arch rings are formed from dressed stone oblong blocks of varying size and have well defined keystones. Several iron tie-bar and strong-back arrangements are installed on the structure. The spandrel walls are of dressed stone construction throughout as are the parapets; the river pillars are built upon solid rock and are of coursed block construction. Some corbel stones, used to support original construction forms/wickerwork, are still in situ beneath the arches at springer level. The undersides of the soffits are coated with sprayed-on concrete, thereby making it difficult to note details of intrados and skewbacks/springers. The river pillars are underpinned, with upriver pointed extensions formed into concrete pontoon-like rafts that make navigation more difficult. The estimated free waterway/hydraulic capacity is circa 85ft, about the same as Derrinydaly Bridge and approximately 20% greater than that of Trim Bridge.

Passing below the ancient arches, Marcie Regans' public house is visible, perched on the Newtown riverbank directly across from 'the Hospital or Priory of Saint John the Baptist.'

This ancient set of ruins cluster upon the southern bank immediately below the bridge. They comprise a combination of monastic buildings and a defensive-type keep, similar to the many tower houses and castles of The Pale elsewhere along the riverbanks; perhaps it once formed part of the outer defences on this main approach to Trim. The religious institution, from which the townland name probably originates, was founded here in the early 13th century, possibly in the period 1202 to 1220 AD. It was occupied by an order of Cross-bearers, whose monks were known by the title of 'Crouched or Crutched Friars' (*Fratres Cruciferi*) whom, it is said, wore a habit embroidered with a crucifix and supposedly carried staffs or croziers topped with an ornate cross. Brethren of the order reputedly spent their time caring for the sick, but,

The Abbey of the Crouched Friars – St. John's

similar to the Order of Saint Victor across the river, it was supressed by Henry VIII circa 1540.

On the adjacent site downstream, the town sewerage plant stands upon the riverbank a short distance upstream from the new water intake supplying domestic water to Trim and its environs.

Continuing on downriver, we passed over shallows where once Kiely's Weir crossed the river from the northern bank at Newtown to the opposite shore in the townland of Iffernock. This weir provided water-head to power Kiely's Tuck and Corn Mills. I believe that a family, named O'Keefe (or Keefe), were the last operators of Kiely's Mill (Ref. Jim Reynolds). In earlier times, the weir and mill combination was known as Shiel's Weir and Mill.

Griffith's records the mill thus:

> house, offs, mills and land totalling circa 9 acres, leased by John Shiel from Samuel Gerrard @ R.V. £63.

The weir ran askew across the Boyne from just downstream of Newtown Bridge, and was tied to the southern or right hand riverbank via the most upriver of a set of islets, linked together by a series of sluices and spillways. The two mills were about midway along the lengthy millrace; with the 1837 OS map showing the tuck mill located on the island or river rampart, and the corn mill on the mainland. As the weir and mill buildings are depicted on the

The riverscape below Newtown Bridge

1911 map, the weir was probably demolished subsequently during the post 1968 drainage scheme. The mill site is now occupied by a stud farm, which location was once named 'the Ponderosa Stud.'

On this stretch the river is wide and sweeps further to the south-east, with the left or north-eastern bank rising towards a low ridge forming the Loganstown shore. The right bank hereabouts is flatter on the Iffernock[11] side (named Teaguestown on Larkin's map); the former line of the Trim to Black Bull turnpike road (now the R154) runs alongside the river to Scurlockstown, where the older line of the Trim to Drogheda road branches towards Bective.

Descending this steeper section, we grounded several times upon rocky shoals; remnants of the many shallows, fishing weirs and islets removed during the several drainage schemes carried out by the OPW. Towards the end of this reach, just above the confluence of the Knightsbrook River at the great bend of Scurlockstown, the OS maps depict a series of islands and weirs, once known as Iffernock Fishing Weir, and mentioned by name in the Civil Survey of 1656.

The 1837 OS map shows a weir running askew from the right riverbank to a large elongated island located in midstream; on the same map, another weir runs from the island's mid-point to the north-eastern riverbank at Newtown Park (Demesne) in Loganstown Townland. According to Jim Reynolds, an eel house was located on the bank close by the latter weir.

This was also the location of a corn mill listed on Griffith's in Loganstown and marked as vacant. The building, with a £10 R.V., was owned by 'the reps of Sir Charles Dillon,' but is not marked as a mill on the OS maps. A ruined stone building standing on the riverbank nowadays may be part of the old mill, and may have been used as the above eel house in later times.

As shown on the OS maps of 1837 and 1911, the Knightsbrook (or contemporary Glearnog) River is named variously the Moynalvey River, Clonymeath River and Dangan River as it flows through these districts to its confluence with the River Boyne at Iffernock, just upstream of Scurlockstown. Though difficult to discern clearly, the Down Survey Map of Moyfenrath Barony names it Binells or Dinells Brook; perhaps the name of the Norman Knight after whom it was named originally.

The stream is sourced from three separate capillaries which coalesce south-west of Culmullin to form the infant river. The northernmost rill rising in the townland of Baltrasna, the middle stream in Leonardstown (near Kilmore House), while the southern branch rises near a ringfort in the townland of Newtownrathganley, south-west of Paget Priory (now the Glebe) near Mullagh Crossroads (R125-R156). This stream flows past Piper's Well and onwards, to the north-west of Kilmore Crossroads. All three source streams coalesce in Kilmore Townland just south-east of Moynalvey.

From here, the stream flows north-westwards as the Moynalvey River to Moynalvey Bridge; near which an 'old corn mill' is depicted on the 1837 OS map. Then onwards the river flows to Clonymeath Bridge, where it assumes the title of Clonymeath River; then continues north-westwards to Clonmahon Townland, where it becomes the Dangan River. Continuing north-westwards to Dangan Bridge in the townland of Ginnets Little, it turns west to Gibraltar within the great demesne of Dangan. Where many features, such as 'the Battery,' 'the Obelisk' and 'the Quay' are shown on the 1837 OS map, together with remnants of a great artificial lake and a wide canal close by the castle.

Mrs. Delany – *nee* Pendarves (Mary Granville), in her memoir entitled: *A Memoir 1700-1788*), tells of an interesting visit paid to Dangan, 'Lord Mornington's place,' in 1748. Lord Mornington's only son, Garrett Wellesley, was the father of the Duke of Wellington, and Mrs. Delany's godson. She writes from Dangan on October 15:

This place is really magnificent; the old house that was burnt down is rebuilding. The gardens and park consist of six hundred Irish acres. There is a gravel walk from the house to the great lake, which contains twenty six acres and is of irregular shape, with islands for wild fowl. There are several ships, one a complete man-of-war. My godson is governor of the fort and Lord High Admiral; he hoisted all his colours for my reception, and was not a little mortified that I declined the offer of being saluted…. He [Master Wellesley] is a most extraordinary boy; he was thirteen last month, he is a very good scholar.

Flowing onwards to the townland of Umberstown Great, the stream morphs into the Knightsbrook River and flows to Laracor (of Jonathan Swift fame); where it turns eastwards past Knightsbrook House and ornamental lakes to flow through Freffans. Passing beneath the multi-arched footbridge (or packhorse bridge),[12] the stream forms a millrace that powered the Knock Mills (Nock in the vernacular), before passing beneath the old turnpike road (R154) and falling into the Boyne at Iffernock.

The ruined mill, which hosted the Scurlockstown Olympiad in more recent years,[13] was once a thriving local industry. This was one of the few watermills

The Seven Eyed or Knightsbrook footbridge

on the Boyne catchment system powered by an overshot wheel. Larkin's map shows the headrace for this mill running alongside the Knightsbrook River from about a half mile upstream beside 'the Rock Road' or L2204, where it is taken from the main river course just below the footbridge.

The 1837 OS map also shows the long headrace, together with a weir, artificial lakes and a complex series of water channels close to Knightsbrook House. These appear to be part of the water source to the nearby Knock Mills. The elevated headrace explains how the mills obtained the water-head to power the overshot wheel.

The mill is set well back from the old turnpike road and is accessed by a laneway leading off the road to Laracor (the Rock Road). The 1837 OS map indicates that this lane joined the turnpike road at a crossroads near Newtown. It was probably part of the older line of the Dublin to Trim road, reputedly running atop the Galtrim Esker prior to the road becoming a turnpike in 1731.[14]

The same map names the mills at this location 'Knock Mills' (corn) and shows the buildings, together with a mill dam. Griffith's records this location as lot No. 12a of Iffernock Townland and says of the site: house, offs, flour mill & land totalling circa 20 acres, leased by Richard Keefe from the Hon. T. Rowley @ R.V. £80. The OS Field Notes of 1836 reference this mill as follows:

> 'On the N.E. of the td. are Knock Mills, the property of Mr. Keefe; they are extensive and well supplied with water which flows in a wooden channel over the wheel. This td. is the property of Lord Langford.' (sic)

From a study of the maps and inspection of the derelict buildings at time of writing, it is evident that two millwheels were once in use at this mill; the over-shot wheel, mounted near the centre of the main building on its north-eastern façade, the other, perhaps a breast-shot wheel, located on its south-eastern gable towards the river.[15]

For many years the old waterworks supplying Trim had an intake located on the Knighsbrook River close by Knock Mills, in addition to being supplied by a prolific spring well source. The 1911 OS map depicts a site to the south-east of the mill, marked Springs (Trim UDC). In more recent times; however,

Above:
Knock Mills (an artist's impression)
Courtesy of Annie Kelly

Left:
Scurlockstown Bridge older & newer

a new works was constructed and takes its source directly from the River Boyne near the Knightsbrook confluence.

On his visit to Scurlockstown about 1847 or 1848, William Wilde mentions an ancient motte in this nook of the Boyne Valley. He wrote that it was 'dug out for 'manuring' the local fields;' with the remains of the central chamber or 'kisvaen' the sole reminder of its former presence. In earlier days, manuring was done by using limestone gravel, the main building material used in many of these ancient mottes or forts. Unfortunately, over the years a great number of the ancient raths all over the countryside were destroyed in this manner, especially on the nearby Hill of Tara.

The ruined church and graveyard are very old; with the church reputedly built by Walter de Lacy, son of Hugh de Lacy, in the 12th century on the site of an older church. It was granted later to Saint Thomas' Abbey in Dublin in the early 13th century. Wilde remarks on the ruins, noting the circular chancel arches and the remains of an ancient stone cross, used as a headstone in the cemetery.

Boycetown-Derrypatrich River and Motte – Site of Scurlockstown (Cassidy's) Mill

At the old Scurlockstown Crossroads another small stream flows under the road and eastwards into the Boyne close by the road to Bective. This watercourse is known as the Boycetown River, which rises to the south-east near Culmullin (the corner of the mill J.O.D 1836) and on its route to Scurlockstown is named the Derrypatrick River for some distance along its meandering course.[16]

Flowing north-westwards from its source, it passes beneath Derrypatrick Bridge and onwards to Boycetown Bridge near Kiltale. Here it becomes the Boycetown River, the stream continues to Milltown Bridge on the mereing of Walterstown and Milltown Townlands near Pike Corner.[17] From here it flows to Scurlockstown Bridge, where the river divided into two streams; the westernmost forming a millrace which passed beneath the road, the other branch passing under another two arches to flow onwards towards the Boyne.

Downstream of Scurlockstown Crossroads,[18] the Boycetown River millrace flowed on by the ancient church and motte, and then powered a corn mill before rejoining the main stream and falling into the Boyne. The 1837 OS map depicts this corn mill close by its confluence with the River Boyne; known as Scurlockstown Mill, it is oftentimes confused with the Knock Mills nearby.

Griffith's records the following of Scurlockstown Mill: house, corn-mill, kiln, offices and land totalling circa 15.6 acres, leased by Thomas Cassidy from Christopher Drake @ R.V. £27. I believe this mill was destroyed by fire in 1857.

On the Bective road close by, the valuation records a forge, house and offices leased by James Mooney from C. Drake at R.V. £1-0s.

This landscape is changed utterly today. The 1911 map shows that the buildings at Cassidy's Mill,[19] together with James Mooney's forge had vanished by then, and that the entire millrace was filled in. The main road is realigned, isolating the old Scurlockstown Bridge, which now forms part of a feature park beside Jack Quinn's hostelry to the west of the new line.

Travelling eastwards along the Bective road (now the L2203), about three hundred metres from the old Scurlockstown Crossroads, we come to the place where the dark bulk of Scurlockstown Castle once towered above the road. However, because I have been unable to find information about this edifice readily available, I am reliant on Wilde's description of this old tower house (or watchtower of The Pale) and its condition when he travelled the road in 1847-1848.

Larkin's Map, the OS map of 1837 and the sketch map in Sir William's book all show the site of the castle to the right of the road, about halfway between the crossroads and the place where the railway line from Kilmessan ran in later years. This was opposite the little laneway leading down to Cassidy's Mill. Not a trace of the castle remains today and I cannot discover what happened to the structure or when it was demolished; it would seem to have vanished into thin air.

History records its construction in 1180 by William de Scallog, an Anglo-Norman Fief of Meath, but it does not show who removed the old building or why. Wilde mentioned that the eastern wall was cracked from top to bottom and that this was supposedly caused by 'the balls of Cromwell,' whose army, legends say, met stiff resistance here on their way to deal with Trim following the sacking of Drogheda. While no mention is made of cannons, let us assume 'the balls' referred to are cannon balls. He states that the castle was a donjon, or square keep, with round towers on the diagonal corners and that many of the barrel-vaulted stone floors were in good repair. The accompanying woodcut engraving would seem to suggest that the castle was built diagonally to the road.

Passing on by the Knigtsbrook and Boycestown rivers, our boat rounded the great bend of Scurlockstown, heading north-eastwards into the teeth of a biting wind. A short distance downstream, we grounded upon some rocky shoals at the upper end of a long stretch of white water. Hopper, Richard and Chalky were very busy for some time thereafter, hauling our craft across these shallows. So much for the river being navigable during Norman times, thought I, while heaving my cold, miserable and water-soaked body from one gunwale to the other in an attempt to stabilise the RIB. These shallows are located where once Dunganny Weir ran askew across the Boyne from Loganstown to Scurlockstown on the right or eastern shore.

This fishing weir is mentioned in the Civil Survey of the 1650s, and referenced in the Louth Archaeological Journal of 1953 as follows: On 11th February, 1669 one Samuel Bull was granted a moiety of the great mill at Scurlockstown with 'ye moiety of ye great fishing weir.' While the OS map of 1837 shows the weir running askew across the river and linking a series of islets, the 1911 map indicates just the islands dividing the Boyne into a series of narrow channels for some considerable distance.

Having freed our boat from the shallows, we continued on downriver through a wide, deep reach of the Boyne, and then came to a dressed-stone pier standing about two metres above the water in mid-river. This is a remnant of Tribley Railway Viaduct that once carried the MGWR line

Tribley Rail Viaduct.

across the Boyne from the townland of Finglagton Great to Loganstown on the opposite riverbank. The bridge was built circa 1862-1864 as part of the railway extension from Kilmessan Junction to Trim and Athboy; it was dismantled and sold for scrap when the railway closed down in the early 1960s.

The structure was of latticed cast iron construction, resting on expansion rollers set upon massive, flared stone abutments on the riverbanks and two intermediate piers; one in mid-river, the other built on the western floodplain. I came to know about the rollers because a local man rescued one such during demolition of the bridge. Many of the limestone blocks from the riverbank abutments and western pillar were rescued also; some of these can be seen adorning gate piers and ornate walls alongside roads near Dunderry and Bective Station.

During my youth I passed beneath the bridge many times while cycling along the old Tribley road on the way home from Trim. The narrow road descended to the river's edge under the bridge, next to the big stone abutment forming an acute blind corner, around which the road curved and climbed to the higher riverbank. The River Boyne flowed under the bridge in close proximity to the low wall by the roadside; where, reaching over, one could touch the water. It was a peaceful place of rippling river and dappled shade under overhanging trees.

Left: Margaret Kellly holding baby (unknown) and Bridget Gannon on the now defunct railway near Tribley *c.* 1940s. Right: Midstream remnants of Tribley Viaduct pillar.

All this is gone now. The road reverted to its original line before the advent of the railway, and the area where we once dipped our hands in Boyne water became a rubbish dump (now closed). A local woman named Annie Kelly installed a model house upon the site, which has become a landmark and a great attraction for visiting tourists.

Downstream from the railway viaduct, the Boyne flows wide and deep between wooded banks rising more steeply above a narrower floodplain; with the riverbank two-tiered in places where the OPW drainage scheme dragged spoil from the riverbed. Hereabouts the Boyne begins a further transition, bidding farewell to the upland bogs, and morphing gradually to flow through a deeper valley; meandering through verdant meadows and loftier banks formed long ago by eskers laid down by the last ice age.

Here, one of the earliest bridges spanning the River Boyne was supposedly built at the Grange of Scurlockstown. Not a trace remains of this bridge nor has there been such for many years. The Down Survey County and Barony Maps of the 1650s and Petty's map of 1685 indicate the bridge, but because of the poor scaling it is difficult to be precise about the location. Cross-referencing the Barony of Deece map with that of the Barony of Navan provides more information. The former map indicating the unnamed bridge crossed the river from the Grange of Scurlockstowne, just downstream of the boundary of Great Finlaghtowne (Finglaghton Great); while the map of Navan Barony locates the bridge close by the mereing of Rahanally (Rathnally) on the opposite shore.[20] A study of the later OS maps places the bridge approximately 200 to 300 metres below the former Tribley Viaduct.

While none of the other maps show this structure, a clue can be found in the old road network. The 1837 & 1911 OS maps and the latest Discovery map show that the road from Trim to Rathnally has a 'T' junction near Littlerath. One leg of the 'T' ends in a cul de sac. This truncated road leads along the Rathnally/Loganstown mereing in the direction of the Boyne and towards the supposed location of the ancient bridge.

On the other side of the river, beyond the Grange, two cul de sac roads lead off the Kilmessan to Pike Corner road and pass through Curtistown and Creroge towards the Boyne at Grange. Perhaps these were once connecting links to the ancient bridge. Larkin's map shows a cluster of buildings on the riverbank close to the location of the probable eastern end of the bridge.

Though there is now no trace of the old structure, an official written record survives in the calendar of state papers for Ireland, which referenced events supposed to have taken place during the Nine Years War (1594-1603). The reference was discovered by Richard Haworth (MAHS) in a very detailed report from a spy to his paymaster, outlining a proposed invasion of The Pale by the armies of O'Neill and O'Donnell; the report was dated October 1599. It stated that O'Neill's foot soldiers intended to cross into The Pale at the bridges of Slane and Kilcarn and O'Donnell's men were to cross the bridge at the Grange, while the horses were to use the various fords should they be passable.

As history records, the proposed invasion did not take place at that time. In 1600, O'Neill, with an army of 3,000 departed south in an attempt to unite the warring chieftains in Munster; where he was defeated at the Battle of Kinsale in 1601 (Jan. 1602 Gregorian Cal.). The record is a very useful marker, identifying as it does the three ungarrisoned bridges over the Boyne between Trim and Drogheda.

Below this location, we encountered quantities of reeds and river sedge growing in mid-river, making progress slower in the steadily worsening weather. Downstream of the weed beds, a large island presented us with a choice, to take the left and narrower channel, or the wider passage near the Tribley shore. As it transpired, the 'island' was merely part of the rampart for the great weir of Rathnally, and the left channel once formed part of the millrace that powered the mighty flour mill.

Rathnally Mill, left; from the river and right; impression of the downstream facade by Liam Fox, sponsored by Eithne Cantwell.

Local tradition holds that from early times a mill stood on the riverbank at Rathnally (Ref. Jim Reynolds). I believe a record exists indicating the presence of a mill on this site since the 14th century. Master of the Rolls, Sir Thomas Carter, owned the Rathnally estate and mill in times past;[21] when the mill and estate employed a great number of local people and a settlement developed in the area to house the many workers. During the mid-18th century, the Irish Parliament passed an Act subsidising land transport of grain and flour to Dublin; a typical bounty paid at the time being three pence per mile for 5cwt (or 40 stone) of flour. This bounty had a huge impact on corn milling and hastened construction of many large industrial mills like Rathnally.

The 1836 OS Field Notes say of Rathnally Mills and crop yield:

> convenient to the house, on the brink of the Boyne, are two corn mills, whose wheels are both undershot. The diameter of one is 18ft. and its breadth 14ft.; of the other the diameter is 14ft. and the breadth 5ft. They are the property of Mr. Thomson. The soil of this td. is light yellow clay, and produces of wheat 9 barrels, of oats 14 barrels, and of potatoes 60 barrels per Irish acre. (sic)

While 381 acres of the total 394 acre townland of Rathnally is recorded in Griffith's 1854 valuation as occupied by Robert Thomson, who leased the property from the Reps. of John Thomson (in Chancery), no listing is made of the flour mill in the valuation. It would seem; therefore, that in this instance, the term 'in Chancery' meant that the property was within the jurisdiction of a 'Court of Equity,' and perhaps not subject to valuation as a consequence?

The weir is delineated on the OS map of 1837, running askew from the eastern bank at Grange to a river island/rampart on the Rathnally side; a long headrace is depicted running between this rampart and the riverbank. The two mills were combined in one near 'L' shaped structure (four storeyed & loft) standing on a smaller island/rampart at the downstream end of the headrace. The 1911 map shows the layout in greater detail, with the following description based upon details gleaned therefrom and several site visits:

The mill (with the larger wheel) is furthest downstream and laid-out at right angles to the headrace and river, with its eastern gable towards the river. The other adjoined mill with the smaller wheel is built at a slight angle to the river and runs longitudinally to the line of the headrace, with the millwheel housing located on the upriver gable. The 1911 map shows the larger wheel supplied through an opening in the centre of the transverse building, with the smaller wheel fed through a sluice diverting a side flow through the wheel located on the other building's gable end.

On a recent site visit, I walked along the Boyne Meadows following the line of the old headrace, filled in during the post 1968 drainage scheme. Little else remains except a small stone arched footbridge, which once provided access for mill workers to operate the sluices. The mill building is mostly intact, but the roof is gone and it is now an empty shell held together by ivy. Both millwheels were undershot (as per 1836 Field Notes) and are still in position but only the metal frames are intact. The main wheel seems to be dimensioned as per the Field Notes. It is located underneath the easternmost building, with the shaft and part of the broken main pit wheel metal gearing still in position. The second wheel seems to be of a newer vintage and is approximately 14ft in diameter and about 5ft wide, as per the Field Notes, and constructed from several 'V' shaped cast iron sections.

This wheel is located on the western end wall and is of an overhung design and supported by a thick stone buttress wall to carry a tail-bearing assembly, now gone. None of the gearing is on site for this unit, just a large hexagonal iron shaft about one foot in cross-section. The miller's house is restored and presently occupied. The buildings that housed the kilns and grain store are still intact but unused at present. The famous walled garden of Rathnally can still be seen, located across the road from the mill buildings, with Rathnally House standing in spacious grounds just east of the mill.

Rathnally lies in the heart of a beautiful and pastoral landscape alongside the River Boyne, and the mills once formed the epicentre of a thriving community. Legend says that almost two hundred people were employed at the mill, the gardens and the manor house. Additionally, hundreds of horses were stabled there, utilised at harvesting, equestrian work and as draught animals hauling flour and meal to Dublin.

As referenced in endnote No. 6, a section of canal, from Newtown Bridge to Rathnally, locked-out to the Boyne via Brennan's Lock just above Rathnally Weir. This was part of the unfinished Boyne Navigation from Trim to Navan, which crossed the deep water above Rathnally Weir to the opposite shore. Here, a short section of canal was cut on the Tribley/Trubley or south-eastern riverbank, to by-pass the weir and stretches of shallow water below. If completed, this would have made the Boyne navigable from Newtown Bridge to Bective Weir further downstream. Research indicates that this was the likely route chosen, which I believe was intended to link with an overland canal (unfinished), routed from the Ludlow Lock (at Leighs Brook) in Navan, via the Commons and Balbraddagh, to intercept the Boyne between Rathnally and Bective.

Jim Reynolds mentions in *A Life by the Boyne*, that the canal, from Trim to Navan, was completed except for installation of sixteen pairs of gates on its eight locks; however, this is not confirmed by my research. While Ludlow Lock and Ludlow Bridge (in Navan) were completed to a certain extent, the canal was cut only in short sections located between Navan and Balbraddagh. These cuttings are indicated on the 1837 map and Preston's Bellinter estate maps, and indeed, can be traced on the landscape nowadays (in Gainstown and Balbraddagh). I found no evidence suggesting that cutting of the section linking Balbraddagh to the Boyne, between Rathnally and Bective Weir, was ever attempted, or of the navigation being completed and used between Trim and Rathnally.

Goat's – Lally's Island from upstream

The canal cutting at Tribley isolated a portion of land (2.348 acres), accessed by a stone arched bridge built over the canal; a lock was located near the eastern end. This lock was used by the local populace for many years as a bathing place; until Rathnally Weir was dragged from the river and this canal filled in during the post 1968 drainage scheme.[22]

Making our way across the shallows where the great weir once provided power to drive the mighty flour mills, we took the wider channel alongside the Tribley riverbank. Then progressed downriver to a natural barrier across the waterway; formed by several trees fallen from the shore, through which we threaded our way most carefully to the open water again. While negotiating the section downstream of this first island, the gaunt grey stonework of Rathnally Mills was visible from the river aspect, glimpsed through twisted willow, black birch, alder and pine trees growing on the former millrace rampart.

We glided on downriver; negotiating a reach passing through a narrow floodplain, which on the left (or Rathnally bank) inclines gradually from the wood-fringed river towards the R161, hidden on the misty hillside. The right

The rocky reef at Ballyna Ford.

208

(or Grange bank) rises more steeply through verdant pasture and tilled fields towards the L2203. About midway along, we came to a small island near the left riverbank, which the maps indicate is sited just across from the mereing of Trubley Townland.

Trubley, or Tribley, as we know it, was both a parish and a townland and supposedly named after a family that came here during the early Norman Period. In the 1836 Field Notes, John O'Donovan refers to the name as follows: *Trubley, a family name of English origin – they came from Glamorganshire to trouble ye Bregians of old.*[23] At one time a castle stood here upon an eminence above the River Boyne on the south-eastern side of the river. Local tradition holds that Oliver Cromwell spent a night at the castle while his forces attacked the town of Trim; some historians say that he was never near Trim, but sent minions to do his work.

During his travels in the area, Wilde concluded that this castle (ancient seat of the Cusacks) was yet another watchtower of The Pale and similar to Scurlockstown and other such castles. In his time, the remains of two circular towers were visible, together with a well-built dovecote (pigeon house).

Bective Mill.

Above:
Bective bridge

Facing page:
Bective Br. c. 1890s
Note the house to left near Horan's
Limekiln & thatched dwelling at
the Turries to right of Bridge.
Courtesy Gordon Kelly

Left:
The boat negotiating an arch of Bective bridge.

Hot soup at Bective Mill, from left to right: O. Delany; Tony Holten (author) P. Reilly, M. Curran, C. Rennicks (Navan River Rescue Crew) Tom French (Navan Library).
Photo Courtesy John Bradley

Griffith's records the following of the farm close by Trubley Castle: house, offs, gate lodge and land totalling circa 203 acres, leased by Matthew Fulham from Thomas E. Taylor @ R.V. £200.

We came to another island at the end of the reach just below the site of Trubley Castle, now the home of the Lally family. The island, formerly named Sheep or Goat Island is now titled Lally's Island after its present occupiers. The OS maps indicate that the island once consisted of three smaller islets, which seem to have merged to form the present island of circa three acres. Although partly blocked by trees and other debris, we succeeded in finding a navigable passage down the Tribley side, en route observing several goats peering curiously from the island's undergrowth.

Then we motored along another broad reach, heading onwards to Bective Mill. Here we partook of a most welcome hot meal in the kitchen of the former miller's house; previously used as a forge by the Smyth family in the early years of the 20th century.

ENDNOTES

1 This footbridge spans the river between Commons 1st Div. and Townparks North. I believe it was erected prior to construction of the new Watergate Br. to provide pedestrian access.

2 The reference (pp 116/117 of Grace's Annals) – possibly an extract from the Laud Manuscript) states: 1330. Most violent storms, by which a house was blown down which killed the wife of Milo Verdon and his daughter. There was also a great flood, especially of the Boyne, by which all the bridges *on that river*, except Babes, were carried away, and other mischief done at Trim and Drogheda. (sic) This subject is discussed further in the chapter on 'the Bridge of Slane' because of the similarity in historical context.

3 Although experts conclude that the tidal levels were about 4 metres higher in circa 3,000 BC, other evidence suggests that the contemporary (unflooded) mean water level was the status quo during the Early Norman Period.

4 Ref. Sheetlines: The journal of *The Charles Close Society* for the study of Ordnance Survey Maps – Sheetlines, 70 (August 2004), pp.8-9.

5 This name derives from the Middle English word Maudelen, defined in dictionaries as meaning Mary Magdalene or 'the penitent sinner.' The name (as used at Trim) applied to a medieval leper hospital once located on the site and named after the said Mary Magdalene. The 1911 OS map shows Maudlin Graveyard located on the adjacent downstream site in Friars-land (3rd Division). In the 1970s, a local committee installed a statue of the Blessed Virgin on this site, named appropriately *Our Lady of Trim*. The name Maudlins is shown on the 1656 Down Survey Barony of Moyfenrath map downstream of Trim.

6 My own research suggests that the canal at Magee's Island formed part of the unfinished canal extension from Navan to Trim; this section is shown on Larkin's Map and the 1837 OS map. Another lateral canal ran alongside the northern bank of the Boyne, from the mereing of Newtown and Loganstown Townlands, opposite Kiely's/Shiel's Mill, to the Rathnally/Loganstown mereing. Here it locked-out to the river via a lock known locally as Brennan's Lock, immediately below the long gone railway bridge at Tribley. This canal section bypassed the fishing weir at Iffernock and another known as Dunganny Weir, located downstream of Scurlockstown. The 1837 and 1911 OS maps show the old canal and the weirs on the river hereabouts.

7 While this tradition may indicate that Smart's Mill diversified to include corn grinding facilities, it may be confused with Shiel's/Kiely's mill further downstream, which is depicted on the maps as a tuck & corn mill. As Smarts Weir is shown intact on the 1911 map, it was probably demolished during the post 1968 drainage scheme.

8 The 1837 OS map depicts another island (unnamed) about midway between the former site of Magee's Island and Newtown Bridge. This islet is not shown on the map of 1911.

9 Just east of Newtown Cathedral, in the body of the ancient parish church is the famous Dillon Tomb, known as 'the Tomb of the Jealous Man and Woman.' Named after the stone effigies of a man and woman laid-out atop the monument; it is the supposed last resting place of Sir Lucas Dillon and his wife Lady Jane Bathe. Local tradition holds that the title of the tomb derives from the 'Sword of State' deployed on the male effigy, perhaps signifying separation of the couple in the afterlife… and, it is said, reflecting Sir Lucas's

displeasure at his Lady for a previous affair. This tomb reputedly possesses the cure for warts, invoked by rubbing the affected part with a plain pin, which is then deposited in the earth near the monument.

10 The road across the bridge is about 13.5 to 14ft wide and the parapets are of mixed construction, reflecting the various repairs completed during its long life. The one pedestrian refuge is upstream and about 8/10ft long by 3ft deep. From old photographs studied, it seems that no refuge existed in the 1890s, but one is depicted on the 1911 map. The contemporary refuge would appear; therefore, to have been built atop the cutwater between No. 02 and 03 arches sometime in the interim period.

11 Defined on the 1836 Field Notes as Iath Fearnog or 'Land of the Alders.' These notes also mention that 'Mr. Nagle has a good corn mill on the river' (in Iffernock), a possible reference to an earlier operator of Shiel's/Kiely's corn mill? Larkin's Map of 1812/17 depicts a race course to the west of the old turnpike in a townland named Teaguestown (Iffernock).

12 A bridge is shown on the OS maps at the easternmost end of the Knightsbrook lake system. This bridge is known nowadays as the Knightsbrook or Seven Eyed Bridge and consists of seven stone built arches, which mostly span dry land. It is a very unusual structure, with the near flat (elliptical) segmental arches varying in size and of multi-centred profile. The old bridge is approximately five feet wide and has a single parapet wall on the downstream side, which reduces its passage width to just over three feet. Some suggest that it was either a footbridge or perhaps a bridge for packhorses, although the narrowness of the passage would seem to be unsuitable for the latter purpose. Its origin is uncertain, but legend says that it was once part of an ancient right of way leading into the town of Trim. On the OS map of 1911, a foot path can be traced from Rock Lodge, in the townland of Freffans Little, across the Knightsbrook River via this footbridge, and on to Friarsland (3rd Div.), near the old Union Workhouse at the Maudlins. Like many such structures in Ireland, the bridge is in poor condition.

13 I competed in a road cycle race during the inaugural event held here in 1967/68; and well remember the shindig held in the old mill yard afterwards. Where a makeshift overshot millwheel was mounted on the front façade of the building, and ostensibly driven by water supplied from the Knightsbrook River through a wooden flume, but, according to local tradition, it was actually driven by a hidden electric motor.

14 The Down Survey Barony of Moyfenrath map of 1656 depicts a bridge, named 'Scurlocks Bridg,' spanning Binells/Dinells Brook (Knightsbrook River) at the later location of Knock Mills in Iffernock. The Barony of Deece map shows a pair of parallel dotted lines running from the direction of Trim, crossing the brook, and then running on through Branganstown and Kiltale to the south-eastern edge of the barony at Knockmark. These depictions most likely represent an older line of this road, and suggest that the old bridge at Knock Mills could be Scurlocks Bridg.

15 In the 2008 edition of *Riocht na Midhe*, Anthony McCan, writing of his great-great-grandfather, John Henry McCan in c.1820 (who had the flour mill at Rathnally leased in the early 1800s), says: 'It was at this time that John started on the path of rapid expansion which was ultimately to lead to disaster. It began with a short lease on a flour mill at

Iffernock in Trim, about 12 acres containing the flour mills, dwelling house and out offices lately in the possession of Mr. Ross Fox.' The valuation books show that the mill's 5 pairs of stones were almost idle by 1879.

16 This river rises just west of one of the River Tolka's sources, indicating another watershed (or parting) in this area.

17 The Down Survey Barony of Deece map depicts a mill hereabouts in 1656, the probable origins of the townland name Milltown.

18 An important junction in olden times, as it formed the intersection of the ancient route from Athlone to Drogheda and the turnpike from Black Bull to Athboy. This was once part of the main route from Dublin to Granard and Sligo via Trim, Athboy and Finae (Finnae). The 1656 Down Survey Barony of Deece map depicts a watermill on the location of Cassidy's Scurlockstown Mill. In contemporary times a hostelry stands at the crossroads, which in older days I seem to recall was thatched. It was later owned by the famous Meath footballer, Jack Quinn; many people refer to the place as Jack Quinn's Cross nowadays.

19 Research shows that the Cassidy family at Scurlockstown Mill were connected to the Andrews family that operated mills at Roestown near Slane and at Clatterstown near 'the Four Knocks' at Bellewstown.

20 The map of Navan Barony also notes the bridge here as 'A decried Bridg.' While difficult to discern clearly, I interpret this to mean that the structure was 'condemned,' an indication that the bridge was ruinous at the time.

21 In the 2008 edition of *Riocht na Midhe*, Anthony McCan, writing of his great-great-grandfather, John Henry McCan, who had the flour mill at Rathnally leased from 1812 to May 1828 says of this lease: in the year 1812, four years after the birth of Francis and five years after his arrival in Navan, John McCan started out in business on his own when he leased the mills of Rathnally from Anna Maria Thomson. The lease dated 5 October 1812 tells us that the mill had been built in 1755 by the Hon. Thomas Carter. Included with the mill were a dwelling house, stores, barns and 24 acres plantation measure of land. The lease was to run 21 years commencing on 1 November 1812, and the rental was £450 sterling. The lease was terminated early because John Henry McCan became bankrupt.

22 For more information on Rathnally Mills and canal, see *On Ancient Roads*, pp 38 to 42. Also Chapter 10 of this book; – Navan and the Confluence; for more details on Ludlow Lock's location.

23 In pre-Norman Ireland, Brega (Bregia) was an area in the north east of Meath, Ua Cellaig country, which also encompassed some of Louth, much of the Boyne Valley and parts of several bordering counties. Other versions of the Trubley name existed, including Tubberville and Turburvyle. Trubley Castle is shown on the 1656 Down Survey Barony of Deece map, Larkin's Map and the OS maps of 1837/1911. The remains of the towers described by Wilde in 1849 are no longer visible on the landscape.

7

The Middle Reaches
Bective to the Skein

Bective & its various names – Fair Green & Fairs – The Street – Arriving by river – Rocky ledges & ancient Ford – Ballina – Bective Mill & a disappearing weir – A lost millrace – the Saw Mill – missing millstone – The lost mill of Bective & the Turries – Horan's Limekiln & Harvey's Mill – Bective Bridge, its history & possible predecessor – the L.D.F., four mines & a pillbox – freezing rain & Bective Abbey – Balsoon & Ripperstown – river shallows & a precipice – River Clady, its source & ancient Br. – Wilde on Clady Church, bridge & ancient 'Beehives' – Cletty – Modern neglect of ancient site – Asigh (Assey) Ford, castle & graveyard – Asigh Weir & ancient mill – George Briscoe's Railway Viaduct – Bellinter Estate & House – A disappeared riverscape – Bellinter Bridge & Lord Tara – Ardsallagh Corn Mill and Eel traps – Skein confluence.

In 1836 Bective Parish consisted of the following townlands: Balbradagh, 'town or place of the thieves;' Balbrigh, 'place of the lea or meadow;' Balgill, Bective, Cloncullen, Dunlough, Gillstown and Grange. For more details of Bective and its environs refer to *On Ancient Roads.*

Legends say that the name Bective derives from Begteach, meaning 'the Little Palace.' Supposedly, the High King's household transferred to Begteach following the priest's cursing of Tara, 'Teachmor' or the big palace, in the middle years of the 6th century AD. Other anecdotes tell of the name deriving from the small beehive structures near the Clady Churchyard. However the name evolved, it has several variations to both its spelling and meaning; including Bectiff, Begty, Beigthigh and Ballyna (Ballina). Another name proposed by John O'Donovan in the 1836 OS Field Notes is Mainistir an Aonaigh, or Monastery of the Fair. Some historians refer to the area as 'the place of the crosses,' while several of the old maps name it as Bridgeend; therefore, there are many names and anecdotes from which to choose.

Arriving by road from Tribley (Trubley), one passes between Ballyna (Ballina) on the left and the townland of Ballynavaddog on the right; the latter name translates to 'the town of the plovers.' Larkin's Map and the 1837 OS map show the Fair Green near the corner of this townland, occupying the south-western sector at the crossroads. Traditionally two fairs were held here annually; on May 16th a fair for dry cows and heifers and on November 1st a fair for cattle and pigs. It is said also that during the earlier fairs in May the practice of hiring Spalpins (Spalpeens) was widespread; Spalpins were known also as 'penny a day men.'

Griffith's records the Green as follows: the Fair Green, consisting of 9 acres 3 roods 35 perches, occupied by Henry Williams, leased from Thomas E. Taylor at £6-10s. R.V. – tolls of the Fair Green were set at R.V. £15.

The crossroads at Bective was formed by the intersection of the main road from Dunshaughlin to Athboy (now the L4010) and the old Norman road from Trim to Drogheda (now the L2203). During the ordnance survey of 1836, between thirty and forty houses stood in the village which had a population of about 140 people. Turning left and proceeding downhill towards the river brings one to a place known in bygone days as The Street and to others by the nickname Duck Street.

Arriving at Bective via the river presents one with an entirely different perspective of this beauty spot. Below Lally's Island, the Boyne (at mean level), although narrowed somewhat by encroaching sedge, swings more to the north-east and flows deep for about 250 metres, then drops suddenly across two rocky ridges running in parallel across the entire river channel. These ledges are about 6 metres apart, with each causing the river to fall about a ½ metre, and are most likely products of the post 1968 drainage scheme.

On the day, our boat hung up on the upriver ledge, causing the craft to list heavily and turn sideways-on to the current; a tricky situation indeed and fraught with danger, but overcome eventually by the handling skills of the well-trained River Rescue lads.

The river flows deep again downstream for about 250 metres, then runs over another shallows, formed here by three transverse ledges across the channel. The most upriver of these ridges is at near right angles to the river, while the other two run slightly askew to the channel. Since the demise of the mill weir further downstream, this has become a favourite local bathing place because of the deep pool formed in the Boyne above the uppermost ledge. The wide reef created by these rocky ledges is the probable site of the ancient river ford, giving the title Ballina (Ballyna) to the 170 acre townland on the southern riverbank. The name derives from Gaelic and translates to Beal An Atha, or 'the Mouth of the Ford.' Two ancient forts (or duns) once overlooked this crossing, with remnants of the military-type mound on the northern bank still in situ, while that on the southern shore is gone long since.[1]

The mill most commonly referred to as Bective Mill stands on the north-western riverbank about 250 metres upstream of the bridge. This is shown on Larkin's Map of 1812/17 by the standard cog wheel symbol denoting watermills; on the 1837 OS map it is depicted as a corn mill and on the 1911 map as a saw mill. The footprint of the buildings, their layout and water power source are shown to be very different on the two OS maps.

The 1837 map shows the small, rectangular mill building on the riverbank, built at right angles to the river, but no weir is indicated, making this the only watermill I have noted upon the main stream of the Boyne without a weir providing the water-head. The map delineates the following arrangement, perhaps providing water-head to power the mill instead of the more conventional weir or dam system: a chain of three islets ran downriver from a point about 270 yards above the mill, to terminate below the mill circa 60 yards from the bridge. A stream flowed around the most upriver islet, through a narrow channel to the millwheel and re-entered the main river downstream of the lower islet. This is obviously the millrace channel, possibly utilising the natural fall of the Boyne hereabouts to turn an under-shot or paddle wheel. Not a very satisfactory or reliable arrangement, I would suggest, as it most

Clockwise from top: Bective Mill,
Our crew examining millstones at Bective Mill 2012 - Courtesy John Bradley
A pair of Flour stones at Bective Mill - Courtesy John Bradley

likely provided limited power and was more dependent on the vagaries of the river. I found no mention of the mill in the 1836 OS Field Notes, maybe an indication that it was not in use at the time.

This map indicates also an alternative power source was used, or in the process of development during the Ordnance Survey c.1828-1836. A circa 20ft wide channel is delineated running along the floodplain and parallel to the river for about 450 yards upstream, from the head of the millrace to the reef or ford athwart the river. Having studied the layout extensively, it is my belief that this channel was, or was intended to be used as a millrace. If true, this represented an ingenious use of natural features; employing as it did the deeper water upstream of the reef, which indeed constituted a natural or sunken weir. But we shall never know for sure, as the post 1968 drainage scheme drastically altered the entire riverbank around Bective Mill.

Griffith's 1852 revised OS map depicts the same layout as that shown on the map of 1837; including the mill footprint, the system of islets and the artificial channel running parallel to the river from the millrace to the reef upstream. Griffith's records the following of Bective Mill: house, offs, corn-mill and land totalling 36 acres 6 perches, leased by Thomas Byrne[?] from Richard Bolton @ R.V. £70. The high valuation is a good indicator that the mill was in use at this time. The mill holding included the parallel channel/millrace running from the mill to the upstream reef.

The 6 inch and 25 inch OS maps of 1909-1911 (surveyed c.1886); depict an entirely different layout at Bective Mill. Although situated at the same location, the mill occupies a much larger 'T' shaped footprint. A weir runs askew across the Boyne from the bank at Ballina to the most upriver of the three islets, which have merged to form a river rampart; with two sluices to spill excess water from a new millrace flowing from the weir to the millwheel. The parallel channel is shown to be dried up and the mill is depicted as a Saw Mill. From cross-referencing the various maps, it is probable that reconstruction of this mill took place during the period c.1852 to c.1886, but as to when it first converted to a saw mill is a moot point.

The building has four storeys, with a loft increasing its overall height to five. The original slated roof is gone, but is replaced by one of galvanised, corrugated iron. An inspection of the building indicates that the smaller mill of pre 1837 vintage is probably included within the fabric of the newer structure. This older building was perhaps three storeyed and comprised the central part of the present mill, with the waterwheel mounted upon its river-facing gable. The joints where the upstream and downstream extensions were added on are visible, with little or no interlocking stonework apparent. It is likely that these extensions were built and the height of the original mill increased as part of the mill's upgrade during construction of the skewed weir, perhaps in the period 1852 to 1886.

The saw mill section was located on the lower level to the east of the pit-wheel and associated metal gearing.[3] I recall visiting the mill as a young boy with Dad and my brother Tom about 1952, to have some hurling sticks cut from ash trees. The sections of trees were placed on the big sawbench; which was then trolleyed along on rails to move the logs into the reciprocating saw. The bench dwarfed our relatively tiny ash stumps as it could handle trees up to four feet or more in diameter. We watched the big horizontal crosscut saw cut into the log, converting it into thick slices or boards; the crisp rasping of the crosscut and zinging of the nearby bandsaw rang out loud and clear, almost drowning the other sounds of the mill. The crosscut saw was about eight feet long and driven by an oiled, wooden crank-rod; in turn powered by a wheel driven by a belt from a layshaft: the primary source of power being the waterwheel thumping and splashing away outside. The saw could be swivelled and used in the vertical position, like a conventional crosscut sawing logs.[4]

On the floor above are mounted four sets of grindstones, three of French-Burr-type segmental construction (with shrunk-on iron hoops), at least one of these sets being manufactured by Pierces of Dublin in 1857. Each one of the 4th pair is quarried from a single piece, maybe of Donegal Granite; these were perhaps used for shelling grain and not for grinding meal or flour. The 'runner-stone' from the 4th set is now missing; I believe it was taken away some years ago to be used as an ornamental feature in the garden of famous author, Mary Lavin. I understand that Oliver Delany is attempting to return this stone to its home, as part of ongoing efforts to restore Bective Mill. Like elsewhere on the Boyne, the millstones at Bective were driven by the triple pronged Mace-head Rind (or Rynd), and are the only sets of stones, complete with driving gearing, still intact and in situ upon the entire River Boyne.

It is difficult to establish an accurate history for this mill because of a dearth of written records. Based on research to date, I estimate that the older mill was built in the early to mid-18th century (c.1700-1750). Some conclude that the mill stands on the site of a monastic mill of the nearby abbey, but although possibly true, I consider it unlikely for reasons to be outlined later. While no clarity exists as to when the mill first became a saw mill, it perhaps changed to a combined operation (corn and sawing mill) following construction of the 2 metre high skewed weir. I believe that Phillip Smyth[5] bought the mill in 1904, whereupon it was re-equipped with a German-made sawing system and sawing timber became its main function, with corn grinding as a secondary source of income.

During the early phase of the post 1968 drainage scheme, the skewed weir was dragged from the river and dumped upon the riverbank as spoil; with the mill races filled in and the mill left high and dry about two hundred feet from the Boyne. The then proprietor, Bill Smyth, attempted to keep the operation going utilising electric power, but failed on account of the increased costs, and the mill shut down for good around the mid-1970s.

This takes us to the story of Bective's Lost Mill. Directly across the Boyne from Bective Mill, on the south-eastern riverbank, is a small paddock of just over half an acre, once known as 'the Turrey Gardens' or 'Turries.' A gap in the south-west corner leads into a long, narrow field running westwards at a raised elevation alongside the Boyne floodplain. This field is about 100 metres wide by 400 metres long, with the lower boundary alongside the floodplain formed by a deep, dried up ditch. The field's western boundary consists of a small stream known in the vernacular as 'the Versheen River,' which presently flows down a steep slope from the Bective to Trim road (L2203), then turns sharply at the north-western corner of this long field and falls into the Boyne above Bective Mill. The 1837 OS map depicts the Versheen River flowing as described, but connecting also to the now dried up deep ditch, which it names Old Mill Race. This millrace is shown running eastwards to 'the Turries,' where it flows past a large 'T'-shaped building (probably once the old mill), then beneath the road close by Bective Bridge and onwards to fall in to the Boyne near the Ballina/Balsoon mereing.

The 1911 map shows a similar layout, with the stream to the west blocked off, the other branch flowing eastwards through the 'old mill race' and onwards through the Turries to the Boyne at Balsoon, as described. This map depicts also what appear to be some ruins of the 'T'-shaped building in the paddock.

In 1854, Griffith's records six people residing in plot No. 4 which comprised the Turries i.e. Lot (a) Michael Mahon, Lot (b) Thomas Gonsen and Lot (f) James Clark. Three others seem to have resided in part of the old mill, which appears to be listed as three individual houses without gardens, each leased from Henry Williams at R.V. 5s-0d – the listed residents are: Lot (c) Patrick Clarkans – Lot (d) Jane Clarke and Lot (e) Patrick Cassidy.

Left: Buried tailrace arch of Bective's lost mill at 'the Turries'
Right: Horan's Limekiln - 2014

In 2007, when searching the fields by the roadside I found the small stone arched bridge once taking the tailrace of 'the Lost Mill' beneath the Bective to Robinstown road (R4010) and into the Boyne downstream near the site of Horan's Quarry. Though overgrown in 'the Turries' paddock on the Trubley side of the road, the well-defined keystone and the arch crown are visible from the field on the downstream side of the bridge, situated about 50 metres from Horan's Limekiln.[6] As it is possible to see only a small portion of the buried arch, the exact size of the bridge is difficult to determine, but appears to be about 1.5 metres in span (river width).

The above anecdotal and topographical details were obtained during research for my previous books and further on-site investigations conducted for this work. The data gleaned from various maps, together with extensive studies of the terrain and anecdotal recollections of local people, especially Mickey Creighton and Mickey Morris, leads to the conclusion that a mill of unspecified usage once stood on the south-eastern riverbank close by Bective Bridge.

Local tradition names this Horris' Mill, perhaps named such after a family of that name residing at 'the Turries' in more recent times. This tradition holds also that it was driven by the waters of the little stream flowing from close by Kilcarty Demesne, through Knockstown to Ballina, and that prior to more recent OPW excavations, its steep banks and those of the Old Mill Race were lined with hewn stonework. As mentioned, this small river was named the Versheen, with the mill supposedly powered by a horizontal waterwheel with vertical drive-shaft. Having found no written references to the stream or 'the Turries,' I am unsure of the correct spelling for either name; however, a local anecdote tells of the stream being named after a Norman Knight.

Several small dwellings of mudwall and stone construction occupied the road frontage of the Turries paddock below the old mill, and formed part of 'the Street of Bective.' But, apart from some small sections of their roadside walls, all traces of these and the old mill have vanished, removed, I am told, by the OPW during the post 1968 drainage scheme.

I consider that the above research shows the story of the Lost Mill is indeed true, and it was likely of ancient origins. The Barony of Deece Down Survey Map of 1656 depicts a millwheel on the south-eastern riverbank, perhaps on this very site, while no mill is shown upon the opposite riverbank at Bective on any of the Barony Maps. Before the advent of the larger industrial mills in the 18th century, many of the more ancient mills were built upon and powered by the smaller rivers; hence this may be the former location of Bective's monastic mill.

The third mill in the vicinity was located in an old stone building on Bagnall's Farm (once Mackeys), slightly east of Tribley near the townland of Ballynavaddog. It was reputedly a small corn mill known as Harvey's Mill; possibly powered by the waters of several small streams collected in a millpond, with the tailrace falling into the Versheen River. I cannot find any record of this mill on the maps or from written sources, the only reference is in local folklore, but no recollections are within living memory. From the descriptions given, it would seem that this was not a commercial mill, perhaps producing flour and meal only for its owners. On a visit to the site I examined the old stone building, although it is in good condition, no trace remains of the machinery, millwheel or sluice systems. The 1837 or 1852 revision maps do not show a mill on the site, and while the building is depicted on the 1911 OS map, it is not marked as a mill. However, a small stream is shown feeding a pond of 0.207 acres adjacent to the supposed former mill. Griffith's reveals the source of the name Harvey, as it records the following of this site, listed as lot 2a: house offices and land totalling circa 257.5 acres, leased by Richard Harvey from Thomas E. Taylor at R.V. £105.[7]

The Boyne Bridge here is a twelve arched stone structure with battlemented parapet walls and a road width of about 18ft. It has a more pronounced humped back aspect from the south-eastern approach, with the other end leading

Bective Bridge and Abbey c. 1976 - Note mill tailrace arch - Courtesy John Bradley

onto a steep hill at Bective Abbey. While walking across the bridge recently accompanied by Mickey Creighton, I stumbled over a 'pothole,' whereupon he laughed loudly. He then pointed out three other such depressions, and explained that although reappearing frequently, they were dug originally by the Local Defence Forces (or L.D.F.) during 'the Emergency' as part of the 'Boyne defensive line' in World War ll. Four mines were planted in the holes and kept under observation from the 'pillbox' located near Horris' Mill; their purpose to blow up the bridge should an Allied Army or the Wehrmacht come marching down the hill. Ironically, the four explosive devices were marked prominently by large red-painted arrows pointing to their 'secret' location!

No certain date for construction of Bective Bridge seems to exist, as no record was found to date. Peter O'Keefe concluded the bridge was probably built early in the 18th century. None of the earlier maps, including Moll's 1714 map and Petty's Map of 1683, shows a bridge at Bective, although Pratt's Map of 1702 provides a clue. This map marks the road from Killeen to Bective, but indicates the river cutting the road at Bective, whereas it shows the bridges at Trim and Kilcarn cutting the river. Thus it would seem that no bridge spanned the Boyne at Bective when Pratt's Map was surveyed previous to 1702. At the contemporary location of Bective Village, the 1656 Down Survey Barony of Deece map shows a townland named *Bridgent*, bordered to the east by a small parcel of land named *Bridgent plo* (ploughland). These place names suggest that a bridge across the Boyne existed at Bective previous to the 1650s, perhaps a clue to the derivation of the later name Bridgeend.

An OPW engineer informed me that while underpinning the pillars and abutments of Bective Bridge during the drainage scheme in the 1970s, the original stone pillars and abutments were discovered to be founded upon wooden bases, and not on rock or glacial till (boulder clay). He added that this was a common enough feature on old bridges especially in boggy terrain.

ॐ

Bective Bridge – H.E.W. No. 3160
(upriver aspect)

From the north-western riverbank, the bridge comprises the following:
A circa 50ft long slightly splayed approach embankment/retaining wall of roughly coursed, dressed rubble stone; pierced midway by **No I arch**, a circa 6.1ft span segmental profiled mill tailrace arch – (**No. 2 arch**) c.11.4ft span segmental arch, with vertical pillars rising to springer level @ circa 3.5ft above concrete underpinning (N.B., this arch has a flatter profile than the other arches on the bridge) – about 5.5ft wide pillar, faced by triangular cutwater, with tapered capping rising to bottom of parapet wall – (**No. 3 arch**) c.12ft span segmental arch, with vertical pillars rising to springer level @ circa 5.5ft above concrete underpinning – about 6.5ft wide pillar, faced by triangular cutwater, with tapered capping rising to bottom of parapet wall – (**No. 4 arch**) c.12ft span segmental arch, with vertical pillars rising to springer level @ circa 6.4ft above concrete underpinning – about 7ft wide pillar, faced by triangular cutwater with trapezoidal pillar built atop, which extends upwards to form an oblong pedestrian refuge in parapet wall – (**No 5-6-7 & 8 arches**) four central arches of c.14ft span and segmental profile, with vertical pillars rising to springer level about 7ft above concrete underpinning (N.B., these four openings have three inter-arch circa 5.5ft wide pillars, faced by triangular

cutwaters, with tapered cappings rising to just above arch crowns) – about 6ft wide pillar, faced by triangular cutwater (damaged by flotsam/trees) with trapezoidal pillar built atop, which corbels out and extends upwards to form an oblong pedestrian refuge in parapet wall – note, the cutwater between No 7 & 8 arches has sustained impact damage from flotsam/trees – (**No. 9 arch**) c.12ft span segmental arch, with vertical pillars rising to springer level @ circa 5.7ft above concrete underpinning – about 6.5ft wide pillar, faced by triangular cutwater, with tapered/rounded capping rising to bottom of parapet wall – (**No 10 arch**) c.11.5ft span segmental arch, with vertical pillars rising to springer level @ circa 7ft above concrete underpinning – about 6ft wide pillar, faced by triangular cutwater, with tapered capping rising to bottom of parapet wall – (**No. 11 arch**) c.10ft span segmental arch, with vertical pillars rising to springer level @ circa 5.7ft above concrete underpinning – c.10ft wide pillar, faced by triangular cutwater, with sloped capping rising to bottom of parapet wall (N.B., this pillar/cutwater is high and dry on the riverbank) – (**No. 12 arch**) circa 8ft span segmental/near-pointed arch, with vertical pillars rising to springer level just above current ground level (N.B., this arch does not appear to be newly underpinned with concrete rafts, it is about 7ft high from its current base beneath the road centre) – about 50ft long slightly splayed abutment/approach embankment, constructed from roughly coursed, dressed rubble stone.

Assessment of above data

Apart from the No. 1 smaller mill tailrace arch and the different profile of No. 2 river arch, this end of the bridge is symmetrical, with the arch crowns increasing progressively in height from the north-western end to No. 4 arch. The four mid-river central spans, numbers 5-6-7 & 8 are approximately the same height and similar in span. No. 9, 10 & 11 arches do not have the same symmetrical progression as the north-western end; however, with No. 9 arch-crown at a noticeably lower elevation than No. 10. The dry No. 12 arch seems to be of different construction, being of near-pointed segmental profile and built of rougher stone – perhaps added as an additional flood arch or is possibly part of an earlier, unrecorded structure. I suggest that the obvious anomalies apparent on the south-eastern end raise the possibility of an earlier stone bridge at Bective than the contemporary structure.

General

The arch rings are formed from dressed stone oblong blocks of varying size and have some well-defined keystones. The spandrel walls are of roughly coursed, dressed stone construction throughout as are the parapets, the river pillars are of coursed block construction. Several corbel stones, used to support original construction forms/wickerwork, are still in situ beneath some arches at springer level. The underside of No. 2 arch soffit is coated with sprayed-on concrete, the others appear to be of roughly coursed, dressed stone. The river pillars are underpinned in concrete, with upriver pointed extensions and downriver squared profiles. The estimated free waterway/hydraulic capacity of the arches open to the unflooded river is circa 110ft, with an additional c.14ft flood capacity provided by arches I &12, when clear of debris. At time of writing, fallen trees lie across arches No. 8, 9 and 10, which may cause additional problems to their already damaged cutwaters.[8] There are no downstream cutwaters and no pronounced batter to the structure.

Bective Br. from downstream

Following the welcome meal at Bective Mill, we boarded our boat and set off into the teeth of the gale, heading on downriver towards Navan. The freezing rain carried by the scything east wind drove pellet-like into our faces as we passed beneath the old arches, to see the more ancient pile of mist-shrouded Bective Abbey standing atop the elevated north-western riverbank.

As this abbey is covered in many historical works, and indeed, detailed extensively by Wilde on pp. 108 to 112 of his book (2nd edition), I will give only a brief account here: the abbey, it is said, was founded by Murchadh O'Melaghin (Mael Seachlain), King of Meath in c.1147, as 'Daughter House' to the great Cistertian Monastic establishment of Mellifont.[9] It flourished until suppressed in c.1536 by Henry Vlll. Following the dissolution, the abbey and lands came into the possession of one Thomas Asgarde, and was then owned by the Wyse family and later by the Dillon dynasty. Griffith's records the following of the abbey's immediate curtilage, with no buildings included: Lot No. 7b, plantation occupied by Richard Bolton in fee.

The abbey, re-edified several times during its monastic occupation, was once almost three times larger than the contemporary structure. The surviving buildings consist of a defensive tower house (possibly part of the original abbey), cloisters,[10] part of the monastic church and cells of the monks, and

Bective Abbey seen from the river.

the ruined Tudor Mansion; perhaps erected post dissolution by the Asgarde or Wyse families. While tradition holds that some stones and the roof timbers from the missing sections were "used to reinforce the walls of Trim and build the King's Mills," I suspect some were employed to construct Bective Bridge.

Below the abbey, the Boyne swings north-westwards, and then turns to flow due east towards Assey. Within this great loop on the right bank lies the old C. of I. Parish of Balsoon, once noted for its old castle and churchyard; tradition holds also that in ancient times the area was associated with the King's household on the nearby Hill of Tara. In the OS Field Notes of 1836, John O'Donovan stated that Balsoon translates to 'the place or town of Samhan,' which he concluded meant 'the town of the Sorrel.' In local lore, a less complimentary name for the area was 'Ripperstown.'

A Norman family named Ussher owned Balsoon from about 1300 to 1713, with Archbishop Ussher supposedly building (or rebuilding) the castle in the 1590s. A member of this family became the first Assistant Provost of Trinity College in Dublin. It is said that in 1643 Owen Roe O'Neil captured the stronghold (a tower house of The Pale) in one of his raids during the Confederate Wars. The castle was demolished about 1830, with the stones used to build the new residence, part of a barrel vaulted structure being the sole indication of its former existence. On the OS maps, the track of an old road can be discerned running north-eastwards towards the Boyne at the Assey end of the parish (still visible on the contemporary landscape). This was known in the vernacular as Bothar na Mhuillin or 'the road to the mill,' which name perhaps derived from a mill formerly located downriver in Assey.

Leaving the abbey astern, our boat forged its way downriver against the strengthening gale, crossing over several OPW ripples en route; then passing beneath Balsoon House perched atop its eminence on the eastern riverbank. Just below the house, the 1836 OS map depicts a series of islets in midstream, with the river divided into several smaller channels. High above on the western riverbank, the same map shows a precipice towering over these islets, near which lofty location Mary Lavin resided in later years. Although the islands appear on the map of 1911, they are gone now, being dragged from the river during the post 1968 drainage scheme; but their former location now forms yet another set of white water shallows, where we grounded again, so the lads had some more fun dragging us across.

Clady River joins the Boyne

Clady River

Just downstream of these shallows, we came to where the Clady River falls into the Boyne; according to the 1836 Field Notes, the name Clady or Cladach means 'the river with muddy banks.' Two tiny rills form the initial source of the Clady River, one taking its rise near the ancient Rathmore Abbey (near Athboy) and flowing eastwards; the other stream rising close by the old school at Rathcarn and flowing to the north-east, to coalesce with the first at the eastern mereing of Clonymore Townland. Flowing eastwards through Tullaghanstown and then southwards through Meadstown, the river turns towards the east and passes beneath Dunderry Bridge (built 1905), where it is first named the Clady River on the 1911 OS map. From Dunderry, the river continues south-eastwards to Balbrigh Bridge (built 1905), then north-eastwards to the newer (c.1840s) line of the Trim/Navan road. Continuing onwards, the river passes beneath the semi-circular arch on the old line of the Trim, Kilcarn to Drogheda road (now Bective House avenue), then past Clady Church/Graveyard and under the ancient twin arched Clady footbridge to the Boyne.

Semi-circular arched Br. on Clady river - old line of Trim to Drogheda road
now Bective House Ave.

Wilde says of this church in 1849:

> "the church, which is now a complete ruin, was originally a
> parallelogram, with a projection at the south-eastern side – a sort of
> transept – and a bell-turret upon the western gable; but although we
> are able to trace the outline of this building throughout, the only
> portion of much interest spared by the hand of time is a very beautiful
> window, in the south chapel, the stone frame-work of which is quite
> perfect. It consists of two cinquefoiled arches, in the "early English"
> style, separated by a light shaft. The carvings on the round capitals are
> rich and tasteful."

Of Clady Bridge he says:

> "the adjoining stream is crossed by an ancient   stone footbridge,
> about thirty yards in length, and supported by two arches of different
> shapes. It is about five feet in breadth and does not appear to have ever

Gateway to Clady graveyard hidden in Bective woods - May 2014

had a parapet. It is one of the very few foot-bridges which we have ever seen or heard of in this country, and if it is coeval with the church to which it leads, and which in all probability it is, it cannot be denied that this is the most ancient stone bridge existing in Ireland."[11]

And of the subterranean chambers at Clady, he wrote:

"in an adjoining plantation, and not above a stone's throw from the church, were lately discovered two subterranean chambers. Each of these crypts is formed entirely of un-hewn stones, arranged in the shape of a beehive dome, but without mortar or cement, the arch being formed by each tier projecting… They differ from the sepulchral caves in that the dome springs directly from the floor, and not from a course of upright pillars, such as we find at New Grange, Dowth and elsewhere…"

More details of Clady Church, graveyard, bridge and the fabled *House of Cletty* are given in William Wilde's book, pp. 112 to 116 (2nd edition).

233

Left: Clady ivy covered church and overgrown graveyard - 2014
Right: Ivy clad author standing atop the ancient Clady footbridge
Note rubbish skip decorating this heritage landmark

In his detailed account of these ancient chambers, Wilde states that the structures date from pagan times, and possibly were part of a troglodyte village used by the Firbolg or Tuatha De Danaan. In general, he opined that Clady was the more likely site of the fabled 'House of Cletty' (or Cleiteach, home of infirm High Kings), than that of the motte near Stackallan, considered by many of his contemporaries as the location of this mythical kingly residence.

I noted that in his book, Wilde lauded Mr Bolton, the then incumbent owner of Bective House, for enclosing Clady Churchyard within his new demesne, thereby protecting its stonework from "the loitering peasantry," whom, he said, were wearing it away by using it as whetstones for various tools.[12]

One wonders what impression the honourable gentleman would have of Clady in these progressive times; with the tumbled, overgrown church surrounded by tottering and flattened tombstones enmeshed in a wilderness of weeds, tangling briar and shrubbery. The eyes of the ancient Clady Bridge are blocked by a mass of flotsam and fallen trees, hidden from view by the same tangled mess. But, although not caring a whit for its heritage value, as evidenced by the all-pervading neglect, the present caretakers have assiduously blocked the ancient bridge with a rubbish skip, lest some "loitering peasant" or wandering fisherman use it as a shortcut home.

Raindrops falling from Asigh Graveyard gate

Passing onwards by the Clady, our boat rounded the great sweep beneath the bluffs at Bective House (built c.1820-1830), heading into the broad reach towards Asigh (or Assey), located a short distance downriver on the southern shore. Here we clambered ashore amidst the wind and rain to inspect its crumbled churchyard. The place name derives from the Gaelic *Ath Sidhe* or 'the Ford of Sidhe.' At which place, the Annals of the Four Masters records that Sidhe, son of King Dian, was killed during a battle in 524 AD, with the place (possibly Kirb originally), thus named after him. This ford was the likely crossing place of one of the fabled five great roads of Tara, *An Slighe Mor* (Mhor).

The remains of the ancient church and attendant graveyard stand on the grassy bank above the Boyne; upstream of which a glebe of about three and a half acres is shown on the 1837 OS map. This was part of the townland of Assey and once owned by Lord Trimblestown (Tremblestown).[13] Nowadays this site is home to the Crinion family, whose residence is located close to the old churchyard. Beside the house and close to the Boyne stood the ruins of Assey Castle, another watchtower of The Pale. Anecdotes tell of how the remains of this former landmark were demolished in recent years by the OPW because of the dangerous state of the structure; with the stones dumped and used as filling for an access road to Warrenstown College. Another reflection on the official mindset towards preservation of our uniquely historic landscape!

Wilde gives a description of this castle as seen in 1849, concluding it was similar to the castles in Trubley and Scurlockstown, a square keep with flanking towers on the eastern and western corners. Though the date of its construction is uncertain or who resided therein, it was probably erected in or around the late 12th century. Local tradition holds that the Plunkett family owned the castle for a time, as their coat of arms was supposedly carved on stonework in Asigh graveyard.

The 1837 OS map depicts a weir located on the Boyne, running askew from immediately below Bective House across the river to the mereing of Balsoon and Assey Townlands. This weir is rather unusual, as it is shown with a rectangular-shaped construction or contrivance on its northern end at the Bective riverbank; this may represent a set of fish passes/traps.[14]

The 1656 Down Survey Barony of Deece map shows a church, a tower house and a mill close by the River Boyne in Assey, below 'the Road to the Mill' in Balsoon, This mill is displayed in text as *A mill*, rather than shown as a graphic of a water wheel; the 1656 Civil Survey also records a corn mill in Assey. While the weir had vanished from the riverscape by 1911, the map of that year depicts a series of islets and a channel running parallel to the river in Asigh. Nowadays a small stream, known as the Bonfield River, falls into the Boyne at the former site of this ancient mill.

Passing over several rocky ledges, our boat continued onwards in the blinding wind-driven rain, through which haze we glimpsed the grey portals of Asigh Railway Viaduct's great arches looming above the darker cleft of the Boyne. The railway viaduct was constructed as part of the Dublin & Meath Railway's branch line to Navan, which line was built by Moore Brothers under contract. Although much delay occurred on the Trim to Athboy branch due to disputes with landowners, the Navan line opened in 1862. The bridge is built slightly askew to the river and links the townland of Assey to that of Grange (Bective) on the northern shore. The line was closed to passenger traffic in 1947 and restricted to freight and the occasional 'football special,' then closed finally in the early 1960s, with track pulling commencing in 1963.

Asigh (Assey) Railway Viaduct

This bridge, consisting of six segmental profiled, high rise stone arches, is a smaller version of the seven-arched Navan Railway Viaduct, with two lesser abutment arches of about 25/30ft span and four river arches of circa 35/40ft span. The pillars are circa 6/7ft wide, and faced by upriver and downriver cutwaters, topped by tapering/rounded cappings which rise to springer level at about 8/10 above mean water level. A dressed string course runs above the arch crowns for the entire length of the structure, atop this is built a circa 2ft high parapet wall coped by dressed stone slabs. The pillars were underpinned with concrete during the post 1968 drainage scheme, which also narrowed and deepened the main channel, thus leaving three of the arches high and dry. The viaduct is comprised throughout of dressed/rusticated limestone blocks laid to regular pattern, and is circa 27/30ft wide. It carried a single track during its operational days, but is now privately owned.[15]

Below the viaduct, our boat took us downriver between the townland of Grange-Bective on the left bank, and the townland of Bellinter on the opposite shore. In the 1836 OS Field Notes, John O'Donovan interpreted Ballinter as meaning '*Baile an tSáoir*,' or 'the town of the carpenter'. The Down Survey map shows that part of Bellinter, from the River Skein (Skeene) to the River Boyne, was located in the Barony of Lower Deece and named Ballniteeran in those times.

From top: Bellinter House from the water; The Boyne above Bellinter Bridge.

In the 1650s, John Preston, son of Hugh Preston from Bolton in Lancashire, came into possession of vast land holdings in Counties Meath and Laois, totalling almost eight thousand acres; these properties included Bellinter and its extraneous estates. He supposedly acquired most of this land from mercenary soldiers and adventurers who campaigned with Cromwell and received confiscated land as payment for their services to the Parliamentarian Army. Much of this land hereabouts was seized from the Nangle family, one of the prominent former Norman families in County Meath (aka De La Corner).

Bellinter House was designed in the Palladian-style by renowned architect, Richard Cassells, for the incumbent John Preston in 1750. John Joseph Preston (who died without male issue, I believe) bequeathed the estate(s) to a friend named Gustavus Briscoe c.1896. A family named Holdsworth acquired the property from 1957 to 1966, when it was taken over by the Irish Land Commission, and divided into small farms. Bellinter House lay idle for several years until occupied by the Sisters of Sion, and then sold on in 2004, when it was converted to a 34 room luxury spa hotel.

The river reach from Asigh to Bellinter Bridge runs north-eastwards in a well-defined channel cut between floodplains of varying width. The left or Grange riverbank rises steeply to level pasturelands, whereas the right bank ascends more abruptly to an escarpment, which in turn swells gradually towards the Hill of Tara in the near distance to the south. About midway along, Bellinter House stands atop the high bluff, overlooking this once majestic river reach; the first of many such wooded, craggy hillsides we encounter from here to Drogheda. I believe this part of Bellinter Demesne became famous for its riverside vistas following construction of the avenue from the house to Bellinter Bridge. The 1836 and 1911 OS maps depict one large island and many smaller islets dotting the river immediately below the house. Most of these were covered in woodland, and must have presented a very pleasant aspect to those gazing down from the eminence of the gravelled driveway.

The handiwork of the OPW is evident here again, as all these islets were dragged from the river and dumped upon the banks c.1968. On our passage downriver, we encountered their remains in the form of rocky shoals and shallows, interspaced with profuse growth of river sedge, saplings and weeds. Near the eastern end of this reach, about 200 metres above Bellinter Bridge, a small tributary named *Abainne na Sceile/Sceillig* falls into the Boyne from the north-east. This stream rises near Balbradagh and flows eastwards through Farranderry to the Boyne in Ardsallagh.

Prior to commencement of the Boyne arterial drainage scheme at Bellinter Bridge in 1968, the OPW removed the commemorative plaque from its original position on the south-western abutment, and replaced it upon the

Stone footbridge (the Butler's Br) on old line of River Skein at Bellinter.

western parapet wall, where it can be observed nowadays. Engraving on the stone declares that it was laid on July 1st 1813 by John Preston, Lord Baron Tara, the first and only holder of this title; one of the so-called union peerages bestowed prior to the Act of Union in 1801. The honour was awarded to Preston in 1800, ostensively for his leadership of the Navan Cavalry during 'the battle of Tara' in 1798. However, tradition holds that these titles were handed out to members of the gentry for their support in the dissolution of the Irish Parliament, thereby effectively disenfranchising the majority of the Irish population.

Bellinter Bridge is a crossing with six main arches, one secondary (or millrace) arch and battlemented parapet walls. The width of the bridge is thirty feet, face to face and it is over two hundred feet long. Peter O'Keefe estimated that 1300 perches (1 perch equalling 24 cubic feet) of stonework were used to build the structure. Presentments for its construction were made to the Meath Grand Jury prior to 1812, which were traversed, possibly because of the cost or perhaps due to political intrigue. A further presentment was made to the summer assizes of 1812 and certified by that sitting. This presentment is numbered item 60 and reads:

We present £.1,418,, 7,, 11 to be raised as before and paid to Lord Tara Joseph Maguire Rev'd Philip Barry Richard McGlew & Pat Springer To build a bridge over the River Boyne Wages £70,, 16,, 6 Amount £.1489,, 6,, 5 Certified at Summer 1812. (sic)

The same presentment appears in the Lent assizes of 1813. I note that, unlike many other presentments of the time, the townland, road name and location of the bridge are omitted. Whatever problems caused the traversing of the previous presentments were seemingly overcome by the addition of extra names to the summer of 1812 edition; the presented costs being reduced also from £1510-7s-6d to £1489-6s-5d.[16]

ॐ

Bellinter Bridge

from upriver aspect

Starting from the Ardsallagh end, the bridge is comprised of the following: A circa 20ft long slightly splayed approach embankment/abutment of coursed, dressed stone – circa 9.5ft span multi-segmental (elliptical) profiled arch (this arch was most likely used as part of a headrace for Ardsallagh Mill further downstream) – circa 300ft long retaining wall/buttressed elevated approach embankment of coursed, dressed stone – (**No I arch**) 28ft span segmental profiled, medium rise arch with vertical pillars rising to springer level @ about 6ft above concrete underpinning – circa 6.5ft wide pillar, with triangular cutwater and cappings rising to arch springer skewbacks – (**No. 2,3,4 & 5 arches**) four central segmental profiled, medium rise arches of 35ft span, with vertical pillars rising to springer level @ about 6ft above concrete underpinning (N.B., these four openings have three inter-arch circa 6.5ft wide pillars, faced by triangular cutwaters, with cappings rising to arch springer skewbacks – circa 6.5ft wide pillar, with triangular cutwater and cappings rising to arch springer skewbacks – (**No 6 arch**) 28ft span segmental profiled, medium rise arch with vertical pillars rising to springer level @ circa 6ft above concrete underpinning – circa 50ft long slightly splayed abutment/ approach embankment, constructed from coursed, dressed stone.

Top: Bellinter Bridge *c.*2006.
Below, left, the bridge from upstream and right, as seen from downriver.

General

The arch rings are clearly defined and formed from dressed stone oblong blocks of regular size, with well-defined keystones rising above arch crowns. The spandrel walls are of coursed, dressed stone construction throughout as are the parapets, the river pillars are of coursed block construction. The corbel stones, used to support original construction forms, are still in situ about one foot below springer level. The arch soffits appear to be randomly laid, and the river pillars are underpinned in concrete, with upriver and downriver pointed extensions. The estimated free waterway/hydraulic capacity of the arches open to the unflooded river is c.140ft, with an additional 56ft flood capacity available from the two dry abutment arches. Many of the cutwaters, both upriver and downriver, are in need of maintenance, especially pointing. Several small trees have taken root in various parts of the structure. The upriver walled embankment has some stones missing, while parts of the sub-structure are starting to crumble in places. The downriver side is mostly inaccessible, but many small trees are rooted in the various gaps and joints.

Left: The hidden millrace arch on Bellinter Bridge.   Right: Leaving Bellinter Bridge.

The 1837 OS map shows a weir immediately upstream of Bellinter Bridge, which weir was most likely built originally to provide water-head for a corn mill located about 600 metres downstream in Ardsallagh. Although no weir is shown on the 1911 map, a stream/millrace is depicted crossing the floodplain from the Boyne to the smaller (9.5ft span) arch at the Ardsallagh end of the bridge. This stream continues beneath the arch and flows on downriver to a channel, formed by a series of islets that led to the corn mill depicted on the earlier map. Despite all the drainage work, a shallow depression, once the course of the millstream, can be seen on the north-western floodplain above the bridge. It is possible also that the *Abainne na Sceile/Sceillig* was once diverted through this arch to supplement the millrace.

An estate map of Ardsallagh, drafted by J.J. Byrne in 1843, shows a "Proposed Mill Holding" of circa 24.6 acres, but does not give details of the millrace.[17] Other interesting details are shown on the map, including: the mill and several associated buildings – 'proposed sunk fence' – 'proposed new avenue & lodge' (later built) – a road running to the mill from the north-western end of Bellinter Bridge – a weir upstream of the bridge – and six 'proposed labourers houses/gardens,' to be sited on the riverbank, on the opposite side of the Grange-Bective road at the same end of the bridge.

Though shown as a corn mill on the 1837 map, there is no record of Ardsallagh Mill in Griffith's 1854 valuation or the 1911 map, but the eel weir/traps are indicated at the former mill site on the later OS map, opposite the Skein's confluence with the Boyne. Indeed, I recall the sound of Boyne water thundering through the eel traps during our boyhood picnics on the banks of the Skein long ago. This is all gone now, as the OPW were active

243

Top:
Passing throught the weed beds below Bellinter Bridge and approaching the M3 Boyne Bridge
Photo Courtesy John Bradley
ß
Below, from left:
M3 Boyne Bridge seen from the northern arch of Bellinter Bridge

New -v- old at Bellinter from downriver aspect.

here during the post 1968 drainage scheme; dragging the old weir, traps, islands and thousands of tons of riverbed out to be deposited as so much rubbish on the banks of the Boyne.

In the continuing foul weather, we passed through the portal of No.3 arch, then on by Oak Lodge we went and through the myriad of rushy islets towards the new M 3 Boyne Bridge;[18] a three span integral concrete and metal bridge built about 2008. Somewhat aesthetically less pleasing than that crafted by master tradesmen like Joseph Maguire, Richard McGlew and Pat Springer all those years ago. Continuing on past the mid-river discharge from the sewage plant now resident in the former Clooneen Wood at Castletown Tara, our boat negotiated the many rocky shoals and shallows above the River Skein's confluence with the Boyne at Dowdstown.

ENDNOTES

1 Wilde mentions this sepulchral mound, once sited alongside the old Norman Trim/Drogheda road west of Bective Village. He notes that much depredation was done by the peasantry seeking treasure, but notes also the damage caused by road contractors executing Grand Jury work.

2 Ancestor of the Byrne family, who operated several barber shops in Navan for many years.

3 This is significant, because wooden (or metal and wooden) gearing was used in corn and flour mills, to alleviate the risk of explosion and fire. An explosive atmosphere was often generated within such mills from the tiny particulate matter (dust) of the grinding process; which could be ignited by sparks created by metal-to metal-gearing.

4 For a fuller account of this mill visit, see *On Ancient Roads*, Chapter 4, pages 54 to 58.

5 I believe he was a cousin of the famous Parnellite and Navan mill owner, Luke Smyth (once owner of Ludlow St. Mills). The Valuation Cancellation books list various lessors/occupiers of Bective Mill, including: 1855 to 1866 Richard Harvey – 1866 to 1869 Richard Bolton 'in fee' (N.B., Richard Bolton died c.1868) – 1869 to 1874 John Fagan – 1874 to 1875 Luke Smyth – 1875 to 1887 John Fegan – 1887 Reps of John Fegan/Thomas Fegan 'in fee' – 1899 Thomas Fegan – 1899 & 1913 Phillip Smyth. I believe the 1821 Census records James Gosan (Gonsen?) and his son John living in Bective – both are listed as millers but are not shown as working at Bective Mill.

6 This Limekiln is still in good condition and sited in a yard about 150 metres from Bective Bridge. I believe it was used by the Horan family up to the middle of the 20th century, with the stone for burning taken from the quarry downstream.

7 The Valuation Cancellation Books show that Richard Harvey had the corn mill at Bective leased from Richard Bolton, together with 36 acres 6 perches of land, at R.V. £30 for buildings & £40 for the land. The lease ran from 1855 until 1866, when it was cancelled, leaving Richard Bolton holding the property 'in fee.'

8 At time of writing, the parapet walls at both pedestrian refuges are badly cracked, leading one to suspect that their support structures are giving way. These appear to be quite flimsy, being corbelled off spandrels above upriver cutwaters, the most south-eastern of which is damaged and crumbling. Construction of these refuges may have formed part of the following 1807 Grand Jury presentment for Bective Bridge: *To Skeffington Thomson & John Young Esq., John Sherlock & John Martin to build and repair the battlements of Bective Bridge over the Boyne road from Athboy to Dunshaughlin, wages included £14 0s 9d.* (sic)

9 Wilde refers to Bective Abbey as the Abbey Beatitudine and states also that it was known in Irish as Sendrede, or "the Old Bridge."

10 A footnote on p. 153 of Harold G. Leask's book entitled *Irish Churches and Monastic Buildings*, includes the following: *Cloister fragments, culled from Bective, are to be seen at other places not far distant from the abbey: in Clady graveyard and in the tower face of the modern R. C. church at Johnstown, near Kilcarn bridge. This piece has a fine relief carving of a King in the same style as the abbot at Bective.* (sic) N.B., following an examination of both carvings, I have little doubt that the Johnstown engraving originated at Bective. One wonders; however, what became of the carvings that once adorned the other arches in the cloisters of Bective Abbey?

11 The present length of Clady Br. is about 35/40ft. Research has located two other such narrow stone bridges within a 3 mile radius of Bective. Note earlier reference to the seven arched stone foot-bridge in Freffens on the Knightsbrook River. Another twin arched stone foot-bridge is located on an old line of the River Skein at Bellinter – refer to p. 98 of *On Ancient Roads*. So far I have failed to discover any records of the origins or age of Clady Bridge, but consider it was possibly used as a 'pack-horse bridge,' for transporting materials to and from Bective Abbey. It may well have been utilised to convey stones for the various reconstruction phases of the abbey, from c.1200 to the dissolution in c.1536; note the several quarries shown downstream on the 1837 OS map.

12 Wilde was particularly critical of the wear and tear to the ancient baptismal/waterfont, once located in the Clady Church, but moved to Bective House and supposedly used by Bolton as a garden feature (flowerpot). As this vessel matches closely the description given by Wilde in 1849, one might wonder if it is the same ancient font now resident in the nearby Robinstown Church, which I believe was presented to the Robinstown Parish from Bective C. of I. church when it was converted to an art gallery in recent times (c.1994). Tradition holds that this church was built by Bolton in c.1850s… within which he perhaps found a home for the old Clady font, rather than his garden?

13 The former parish of Assey consisted of the townlands of Assey (with the glebe), Ballinter and Balgeeth.

14 The Louth Archaeological Journal of 1953 records the following of Bectiff Fisheries: *the last abbot surrendered, inter alia, a water-mill and a fishing weir on the Boyne valued at 6s. 8d. Andrew Wyse was granted this fishing weir in 1552 and the following year, on 22nd February, 1553, he was given license to alienate the property to Richard Dillon, John Wycombe and Richard Fox: much earlier in its history the abbey of Bectiff had a fishing weir in Balkyndroght which I have been unable to identify.* (sic)

15 The beautiful bridge barely survived the ravaging lion of progress in the 1960s, being spared an ignominious fate by local landowner, the late George Briscoe, who bought the structure from CIE for £60, prior to this far-seeing public body blasting it from the landscape with explosives. Asigh rail-overbridge, spanning the Trim/Drogheda road close by was not so lucky, as it was demolished several years ago by a building contractor for its valuable stonework. Local tradition holds that during the early days of the railway, some trains used the viaduct as an 'unofficial halt' – where servants from Bective House de-trained and walked to the big house along a scenic pathway through the estate, known as the Bo (or Bow) Walk. Some say that the Boltons insisted on this procedure because they did not wish to have people of low status observed walking along the road from the nearby Bective Station; while others see it as a kindly gesture to avoid the longer route from the station!

16 For further information on Bellinter Bridge and the road developments in the area, refer to Chapter 9 of *On Ancient Roads.*

17 The map also indicates that the existing mill holding was occupied by people named Byrne.

18 The Down Survey Barony of Skreen map shows a small townland named Phillips Towne within the parish of Dowdstown (Dowestowne). The tiny enclave was roughly 'L' shaped and clearly marked as a separate entity to the remainder of the parish. Its boundary ran from the later Dowdstown Bridge to the future site of Bellinter Crossroads, from where it followed the Barony boundary (a stone-lined double ditch dividing Skreen & Lower Deece) to the Boyne below Bellinter Br. The eastern boundary was possibly formed by the River Skein. The map shows the townland of Dowestowne as number 58, the townland of Phillpottstowne as number 59 and Phillips Towne as number 58(2). The route of the M3 is gouged through this former enclave, in the centre of which a pre-construction archaeological dig during c.2005/2006 uncovered an ancient circular motte and a square bailey-like enclosure – described to me by the archaeologists on site as dating from 700 A.D. to one thousand years B.C. For more information on this, see *On Ancient Roads* chapter 10, P.145 and NRA Publication, entitled *Places Along the Way,* which includes details of excavations made in Ardsallagh Townland.

J. Taylor Map of 1802 – showing the area from Tara to Navan. N.B., the canals depicted from Navan to Dublin, Kells & Trim were never built – The 'new Turnpike Road' shown was the 1796/98 new line from Dunshaughlin to Dillon's Bridge – refer to *On Ancient Roads*.

8

The Middle Reaches
Dowdstown to Kilcarn Mill

River Skein and its mills – The Gabhra, its name, source and mills – Lismullin, the Nith Stream and the King's Mill – the wells of Tara – Big Bend at Dowdstown – the River Nanny & its source – the Black Hole & Boyne Deeps – Ardsallagh Parish, demesne, ancient monastery, castle/house – Ardsallagh Mill & eel weir – St. Bridget's Well & a lost ford – Dowdstown Demesne, House & Taylor dynasty – Norman Church, limekiln, turnpike road & Brian Boru's Bridge – Dalgan Park – Upper Killcarn Weir, mill & limekiln – Kit & Mary-Jo Meehan – recollections of a former riverscape – Lower (Greater) Kilcarn Weir & millraces – The Big Mill & Miller's House – Kilcarn Waterworks … a neglected & destroyed heritage site – over Kilcarn Weir – an ancient riverbed, rocky shoals & O.P.W. ripples – the sunken weir – Kilcarn new bridge – beneath Kilcarn old bridge – known history of the old bridge.

The contemporary spelling of the river's name as Skane appears first on the 1837 OS, this version probably deriving phonetically through vernacular usage. I cannot trace the current spelling directly to any source except a province in Southern Sweden. The name is spelled variously Skeene, Skreen, Skiene and Skein on Grand Jury records and upon the Down Survey Barony of Deece map. In my youth, we spelled it Skein, which I believe was the river's original name that may derive from the shape of a skein of geese or wool;[1] a form the meandering river assumes on its passage through the landscape around Tara. Alternatively, it may derive from a variant name for the Barony of Skreen, as the river formed the mereing between the baronies of Deece and Skreen for some considerable distance.

In the USA the term *Skein* is used to describe the spawn-carrying membrane/roe-sac of salmon and trout, which is cured and employed as bait for catching the same fish – a practice now outlawed here.

The Skein takes its initial rise from Gaffney's Well, once located at Supple Park in Dunshaughlin, from where it is culverted and surfaces again south-west of the Community College. At the mereing of Leshemstown and Drumree Townlands, it coalesces with several other rills, the largest of which flows northwards from the townland of Merrywell. Immediately west of Drumree Bridge, the 1837 OS map shows a millrace taken from the Skane to power a mill at Knockmark further downstream. These features had vanished from the landscape by 1911, as they do not appear on the map of that year. Continuing onwards on a course almost parallel to the Navan/Dublin Railway Line, the Skein is joined by a small stream sourced in the townland of Redbog (east of the Dublin/Navan road). This stream forked near Smithstown House, with the western branch powering Clowanstown Corn Mill (close by Killeen Castle and known to some as Clavinstown Mill), the eastern leg powering Leshemstown Corn Mill; the two tailraces entering the Skein as separate streams.

Further downstream, the river flowed beside the railway, forming the mereing with the townland of Warrenstown, before entering the wooded demesne at Dunsany, then flowing on beneath Dunsany Bridge.[2] Downstream, near 'the Cricket Field,' the Skein receives the waters of a small stream that powered a corn mill near Ganzey Village; which 'village' is not marked on the earlier OS map. The river continues onwards, flowing north-westwards beneath Athronan Bridge (road), then on to Swainstown where it passes beneath a bridge on the long defunct road from Batterjohn-Little Crossroads (later the back-avenue to Swainstown estate).

In Lambertstown, the river split to form a millrace, flowing westwards around Kilmessan Village to drive a corn mill at the mereing of Kilmessan and Balreask Townlands.[3] The main branch continued past the Glebe and

Rectory, then on by St. Mary's Church to Kilmessan Bridge, north-east of the village.[4] Flowing north-westwards from the bridge, the river re-joined the tailrace of Kilmessan Mill beside the millpond, then, turning north-eastwards, flowed towards the former footstick ford of Riverstown,[5] shown on the 1911 map.

From here the river turns north-westwards, to flow in a great loop (or Skein) around the former Cluide Wood of Bellinter and on to Ambrose Bridge.[6] N.B., close by the Royal Tara Golf Course 12th 'Tee-box,' is the emergency dump (or kickback) valve for the so called state of the art Dunshaughlin sewerage tertiary treatment plant, located in the former Clooneen Wood at Castletown Tara – when in operation, this system dumps largely untreated sewage into the River Skein just above Ambrose Bridge, effectively turning the last mile of this once beautiful river into an open sewer.

The Skein continues onwards to pass beneath the M3 Motorway and coalesce with the River Gabhra upstream of Dowdstown Bridge.[7] The 1837 OS map depicts the river forming the long gone ornamental lake within Dowdstown Demesne, then flowing across a crescent weir and under the avenue (former 1729 line of the Navan/Dublin turnpike road), then onwards to the Boyne just above the 'big bend' at Dowdstown – see *On Ancient Roads* chapters 08-09 and 10.

Mills on the River Skein and catchment (05 of):

Knockmark Mill

A mill is depicted graphically here on the1656 Down Survey Barony of Deece map: Griffith's records the following of Knockmark Mill: house, offices, corn-mill & land totalling circa 20.6 acres occupied by John Boylan, leased from Eliza Johnson @ R. V. £20.

Leshemstown Mill

Griffith's records the following of this mill: Herd's house, offices, corn-mill & land totalling circa 13.26 acres occupied by Patrick McNamara, leased from Hans H. Wood @ R.V. £22-5s.

Clowanstown Mill

(Known also as Clavinstown or Teelin's Mill, near Killeen Castle). Overshot wheel. Griffith's records the following of this mill: house, offices mill & land totalling circa 9.26 acres occupied by Patrick McNamara, leased from Earl of Fingal @ R.V. £32.

Dunsany Mill

(North of later Ganzey Village) Griffith's shows no record of the corn mill shown at this location on the 1837 OS map and the map accompanying the valuation; however, it records the following of the site: house, offices & land totalling circa 20.27 acres occupied by Phillip Hughes, leased from Lord Dunsany @ R.V. £18.

Kilmessan (Arnold's) Mill

Griffith's records the following of this mill: house, offices, corn-mill, kiln & land totalling circa 27.76 acres occupied by Christopher Arnold, leased from John Preston @ R.V. £20. (Mill shown as disused on 1911 map).

The course of the River Gabhra was changed utterly by construction of the M3 motorway through its valley (c.2005/2010), and the historic river now flows through a landscape altered drastically by road developments. The following description is based upon my own recollections and the river's course as depicted on the OS maps of 1837 and 1911.

Until controversy erupted over construction of the motorway, many people considered the Gabhra as merely another unnamed stream. In my boyhood I heard the stream referred to as the Gowra or Gabhra, and most people thought it was named after a goat, or *gabhar*. The name seemed to exist in the vernacular only and rarely appeared in written form until recent times. However, I was familiar with the name in the context of the Fianna and the battle reputedly fought on *The Fields of Gabhra*; therefore, it is worth devoting some space to this near forgotten stream, so central to the myths and legends of Tara in olden times.[8]

The Gabhra rises in the vicinity of Branstown near the former Lock Gabhair or Lough Gower,[9] close by the old road to Trevet Graveyard[10] and the former Collierstown Bog. From here it flows east of Clowanstown (Clownstown-

Left: Old Dowdstown parish church. Right: This image, taken before the motorway was built shows where the Gabhra meets the Skein at Dowdstown Bridge, the Hill of Tara is visible in the background.

Skryne) and through the Commons, following a meandering course to the north-east. Flowing under the Ross Cross/Oberstown road, it enters the townland of Baronstown, to flow past the site of Maryville House. Passing beneath the little bridge in Baronstown on the old road from Meagher's Cross to Skryne, the stream enters Lismullin, where it receives a brook flowing under the N3 from the slopes of Tara. Although known by several names, this brook is mostly referred to as the 'Odder River' or the 'Nith Stream,' which rises near Castleboy and receives outflowing waters from three of the legendary five (or seven) wells of Tara.

According to the sketch map in George Petrie's 1837 paper entitled *On the History and Antiquity of Tara Hill*, the first of these wells is named Taeg, the second Neamnac(h), or the Chrystalline Spring, known variously as 'Saint Patrick's Well,' 'Dark Eye' and 'Well of the White Cow.' The third well was located near Tara Hall or Newhall on the eastern slopes and named 'Cabnac Chormac.'

In Lismullin, the Gabhra continued on by the Brick Field, then turned to flow almost due north past the site of the long gone Augustinian Nunnery named 'the Priory of the Holy Trinity.' Continuing past Lismullin Manor and towards the Skryne road, the river passed beneath Lismullin Avenue Bridge and turned northwards towards the gorge.[11]

A dam and sluiceway were once located hereabouts, forming a circa 3.5 acre ornamental lake upstream towards the Manor, but these features have disappeared in recent years. Emerging from the wooded glen (Gabhra Gorge) the river flows past Crockatanney or 'Hill of the Fox,' where in olden times its waters powered Lismullin Mill (the 'King's mill').[12] From the former mill site, the Gabhra flows to the north-west towards Dowdstown. Along this stretch it commingles with the small stream flowing down from Clonardran and under the bridge at Garlagh Cross. Then passed under Dillon's Bridge (demolished in c.2008 to enable construction of access road to M3) on the main Dublin to Navan Road and merged with a small stream flowing down from Jordanstown through Boxer Daly's old farm.

At the site of the long gone Sally Wood in Dowdstown, the Gabhra split and formed two branches; thus creating the Gabhra Island upon which stood the water mill shown on Larkin's Map. Before the advent of the M3, the Gabhra flowed through several fields below the island to merge with the Skein at Dowdstown Bridge; but nowadays it passes beneath the motorway and through a totally altered landscape to join with the same river.

Mills on the River Gabhra (03 of):

Lismullin Mill

The corn mill at Lismullin is described thus in the 1836 Field Notes:
The little river Gabhra flows westwards along its northern border. On this river the first water mill in Ireland is said to have been erected on the orders of the High King Cormac Mac Airt to relieve his concubine from the labour of grinding corn with tha quern. On the supposed site of this ancient mill now stands Lismullin Mill, of which a man named Christopher Byrne is the miller. His mother's name was Hand, and she claims descent from the founder of the first mill, who came to Ireland from Scotland. (sic)

Griffith's records that in 1854, the lessee of the premises was Patrick Byrne and that the rateable valuation for the mill, the house and the 26 acre farm was £36-15s-0d. The last miller was John Byrne, known as Long John Byrne, reputedly evicted in 1883 and the mill demolished by its then owners, the Dillon family, because of non-payment of rent.

Blundelstown Mill

This mill is depicted on the 1837 OS map as an Old Mill, the ruins of which were still evident on the riverbank beside Dillon's Bridge during my younger days. Extensive research suggests that this was a Fulling or Tuck Mill, the known details of which are presented in *On Ancient Roads*. The following extract was gleaned from an old issue of Riocht na Midhe:

It was recorded at Navan, in 1636, "that the mill at Blundelstown had been owned by William Rowles of Dublin, who on the 22nd March 1624, made it over by treaty to George Devenish of Dublin, Robert Plunkett and William Pallice of Dublin, and, Will' Archbold of Crookestown Co' Kildare, and his heirs. The Civil Survey of 1654/56 lists the mill as part of the goods of William Malone of Lismullin, an Irish Papist." (sic)

The mill at Castletown Tara (Castletowntaragh)

The third mill on the Gabhra was located at Castletown Tara, the only references to which mill I discovered in the Civil Survey of 1654/56 and the cogwheel symbol on Larkin's Map of 1812. Although no other records could be found, the pre-motorway topography of the area supports the proposition that a mill was located there long ago. More details of this location are included in Chapter 13 of *On Ancient Roads*.

Just below the Skein confluence, we come to the great bend in the river at Dowdstown, the closest the Boyne comes to Tara, located circa two miles to the south-east. Here the river turns almost 90 degrees from its north-easterly course, to flow north-westwards towards Navan. This river turning is significant in both geological and topographical terms, as it causes the commingling of the Boyne and Blackwater at Navan. And may indeed solve the mystery of why no salmon 'run' the river Nanny, other than the oftentimes repeated yarn that St. Patrick cursed some contrary fisherman at Laytown.[13] In his book entitled *The Making of Meath*, Robert Meehan writes about the interconnection of the rivers Boyne and Nanny thus:

The lower Boyne Valley stretches from the base of the Hill of Tara at
Bellinter, where the river becomes incised into the landscape in a deep
meltwater channel, as far as Mornington. The Boyne and the Nanny

flow generally eastwards and there is some evidence that the Nanny was a former course of the Boyne during the end of the last ice age. The river catchments are separated by a high watershed at Realtoge-Redmountain-Donore, where high ridges of shale and limestone occur. Both the Boyne and the Nanny are flanked by flat-topped terraces which record the high relict floodplain of the former rivers during deglaciation.

The source of the River Nanny is located on the south-eastern slopes of the above up-thrusting ridge at Realtoge. One of several source streams in this area rises from a spring named *Gregory's Well* (now unmarked); at the conjunction of Harristown, Mooretown and Alexander-reid Townlands, and then coalesces with a series of small rills emanating from the south-eastern slopes of Carn Hill. The stream flows generally southwards through Crollege to join a brook taking the outflow from Tobermurry, a well in Realtoge. The developing river flows onwards beneath Follistown Bridge on the Navan to Kentstown road; it mingles with other rills sourced in Gerrardstown, Staffordstown, Brownstown, and Glenuaignagh to form the 'Nanny Water' above Daly's Mill.[14]

A study of the topography shows that the two rivers are in close proximity at Dowdstown, with the Boyne passing within circa two miles of the Nanny's source as the crow flies. The Gilltown/Follistown River, which falls into the Boyne opposite Ardsallagh House, rises at Corballis Vale/Gilltown, from where several other streams flow in the opposite direction towards the Nanny. These features tend to support Robert Meehan's suggestion that "the Nanny was a former course of the Boyne during the end of the last ice age." The obvious corollary to this being that the Boyne found an alternative path by turning and 'incising' a newer course to join an existing river (now the Blackwater) during those cataclysmic times. Which infers also that the Blackwater once formed the main channel to the sea, with the other river (now the Boyne) flowing through the contemporary Nanny estuary to the sea.

Peter O'Reilly's *Rivers of Ireland*, mentions that sea trout are found in the Nanny only as far upriver as Julianstown Bridge, and brown trout up to Dean's Bridge (Follistown Bridge) near the source. Jim Reynolds wrote thus of the Nanny's dearth of salmon: "although large enough to hold salmon one has never been seen or caught in it." From these and other references, it is apparent that the mighty fish do not use the river as a *run* to spawning grounds. The solution to this riddle perhaps lies in the previously mentioned river's course alteration; the wise salmon, like the eels eternally finding their way back to the Sargasso Sea, retrace their roots to the *redds* in the spawning grounds of the upper Boyne and Blackwater reaches.

At the apex of the great bend, on the Dowdstown shore, a bight or small bay once indented the riverbank, which feature is shown on the older maps, including the 1656 Down Survey maps and the various OS maps; yet another ancient landmark to disappear from the riverscape during the drainage scheme.

In local lore, this was a fearsome place known as 'the Black Hole,' supposedly deep and bottomless, into which, it is said, a horse and cart once fell, never to be seen again. Rounding the great bend, our boat headed north-eastwards along a wide, deep stretch known locally as the Boyne Deeps. Here, the wooded escarpment above the Dowdstown riverbank partly sheltered us from the rain scything across the valley on the east wind. The floodplain on this side consists of two fields, called the upper and lower Boyne Meadows, stretching from the river bend to the old Kilcarn Townland mereing directly opposite Ardsallagh House.

The old demesne of Ardsallagh forms a great salient around which the Boyne flows beneath its high, wooded plateau. In the 1836 Field Notes, John O' Donovan states that if the name was spelled Ard Salach it would mean 'the dirty height' and says also that Ardsallagh means 'the height of the Sallows,' which word possibly derives from an old English word *salh* meaning 'a small willow tree.' Others say it could be interpreted as 'the boggy height.'

Most historians seem to agree with O'Donovan and conclude that it means 'height of the Sallies.' I am of the opinion; however, that a ford once existed here at the Boyne shallows, linking Ardsallagh with the Dublin/Navan turnpike road running along the heights just across the river in Dowdstown. I believe; therefore, that another slight spelling change such as to *Ath Sallagh*, could alter its meaning to 'Ford of the Sallies.'[15]

The former parish of Ardsallagh included the townlands of Kennastown (Cannistown), Philpotstown, Macestown, Williamstown or Bawn, Farranderry and Ardsallagh. It is said that in the 6th century AD, Saint Finian of Clonard built the monastery of Escair Branain (Ard Bren nDomhnach) somewhere within this area. While no definitive trace of this institution has been found, some historians conclude it was located close by the site of the ancient 12th century church sited alongside the old line of the Trim/Drogheda road.[16]

St. Bridget's Well. Courtesy Bernadette Murray

Tradition holds that this church (dedicated to St. Bridget) was built in the early 13th century by the Anglo Norman family of de Angulo (Nangle), reputedly to compensate local people for their seizure and occupation of Ardsallagh, together with its church sited close by the Boyne near St. Bridget's Well. Shortly after the Norman Conquest, the Nangles built a castle or tower house close by the Boyne. From here, in my opinion, the Ford of Ardsallagh once provided access to the main Navan/Dublin road (turnpike) across the river in Dowdstown; which was probably built atop the line of the ancient road from Tara, *An Slighe Asail*.

Following the Cromwellian confiscations, Ardsallagh came into possession of the Preston family, who intermarried with the Ludlows. The incumbent owner, George James Ludlow, died c.1842 without issue and bequeathed the estate to 'Lord' John Russell, Duke of Bedford, (later Prime Minister from 1846 to 1852 and from 1861 to 1862), who had the new residence constructed c.1843-1844.[17] The estate was leased for several years until coming into the ownership of James McCann MP c.1903. It was purchased by Cormac Murray c.1938, whose descendants live there today.

In the mid 1700s, Mrs Delany (*née* Pendarves/Mary Granville) waxed eloquently about the splendours of Ardsallagh Demense, its riverside arbours and sunken gardens.[18] Likewise, in 1849, William Wilde was fulsome in his praise of the estate, perched on its eminence above the beautiful Boyne reach – mentioning in particular the many pathways lined by yew, lime and splendid beech trees, together with the great variety in form and colour of its flora, further enhancing the landscape. He was; however, less impressed with the newly built mansion, which he described thus:

we wish we could say as much for the house, which looks as if it was in a state of half mourning, being built of very dark – almost black – limestone, with all the quoins, chimneys, and ornamental portions nearly white. Time, however, may greatly assist to remedy this, and soften the glaring effect it now presents.

Left: Sombre and dark, Ardsallagh House   Right: Dowdstown house

On the opposite shore is the contemporary townland of Dowdstown (Dowestown), the 'propriators' (sic) of which are shown by the Civil Survey of 1654 to be Lawrence Dowdall of Athlumney and "Wm" Baggott of Dublin – both Irish Papists. The survey shows that the townland was one-third part of a 'plowland' and consisted of 184 acres.

Other sources say that neither of the previously named gentlemen resided there; the estate being run by a steward, living in what was described in the Down Survey as a cottage-style residence, possibly the original part of Dowdstown House. Dowdall, having forfeited his lands during the confiscations following the Cromwellian wars, regained them upon Charles II being restored to the throne; but lost them again after the Battle of the Boyne in 1690.

Thomas Taylor, the first of this family to hold land in Ireland, was an assistant to Sir William Petty who conducted the Down Survey in the 1650s. The primary purpose of which survey was mapping of lands seized from its owners, thereby enabling its appropriation and reassignment to soldiers and mercenaries for services rendered to the Parliamentarian Army. It is said that Taylor sold his estates in Sussex and came to Ireland where he obtained over twenty thousand acres at this time; including vast properties at Kells (later the Headfort estate) and substantial lands around Bective.[19] He may have gained possession of Dowdstown then, but the best information readily available suggests that property seized from the Dowdalls was assigned to Robert Rochfort (1652-1727). The Taylors perhaps came into possession of Dowdstown in the second half of the 18th century, possibly around the 1770s.

The ancient graveyard and ruins of Dowdstown Church stand on a hillside adjacent to the former old Navan/Dublin turnpike road, nowadays used as the back avenue. This site commands the once beautiful vista of the River Skein's confluence with the Boyne. Very little remains nowadays, except parts of the square belfry and a more modern wall surrounding the churchyard;[20] with a couple of ancient gnarled beech trees brooding over the scene.

The church was supposedly built in the 1180s by a Norman knight named Sir Walter Duff, and once contributed part of its tithes to the Cistercian Order of Saint Mary's in Dublin. Tradition holds that the townland name derives from his surname and was called Duffstown in older times; equally it may have been named after Dowdalls of Athlumney. Several more supposed derivations of the name exist. The old building was once the church for the parish of Dowdstown, comprised of Dowdstown and Philpotstown Townlands which no longer form a parish but are part of the larger conjoined parishes of Johnstown and Walterstown.

As depicted on the 1837 OS map, the footprint of Dowdstown House occupied a quadrangle, built to a hollow-square pattern surrounding an inner courtyard, accessed via a wide, arched portal on the eastern wall. This building matches the contemporary northern wing, and may indeed contain parts of the original 1650s cottage-style residence within its fabric.[21] The same map indicates a long, narrow right-angled building attached to the southern end of the quadrangle, which appears to be an unfinished extension.

The map of 1911 shows the footprint of the contemporary building, including the original quadrangle and enclosed courtyard; together with the multi-gabled, turreted sections forming the southern part of the building. While there are many local yarns about the origins of this later neo-Jacobean extension, a study of the maps (and other sources) indicates that it was most likely constructed in the period 1870 to 1880.

The Columban Fathers bought the 560 acre Dowdstown property from the Taylor estate in 1927 for the sum of £15,000. It is said that as the deeds prohibited sale of the property to *papists*, some adroit manoeuvring occurred to circumvent the ancient prohibition. Dalgan Park College was built in the 1930s and opened in 1941, with about one hundred and seventy students attending there at its peak.

The name Dalgan Park originated from the Columban's former house near Shrule on the Mayo/Galway border. Dowdstown House remained the international headquarters for the Columban Fathers until 1967, when this organisation moved to Dublin. Nowadays the house is named after Father John Blowick, one of the founder members of the Columban Society. Since 1981 it has been leased to the Meath Diocese and is used as a retreat and conference centre.

Passing on by St. Bridget's Well on the left bank,[22] our boat hung up on the rocky reef immediately below Ardsallagh House, hence the lads took to the water to free us once more. Despite much blasting and removal of innumerable tons of rock, the river is still shallow hereabouts; which supports the proposition that this reef formed a river ford in times past. The new line of the Gilltown/Follistown River (altered during the post 1968 drainage scheme) now falls into the Boyne just below the rocky reef at Ardsallagh. Should we follow this stream eastwards across the Boyne Meadows and into the Dowdstown Woods, we encounter first a well-preserved limekiln, and then an ancient bridge that once carried the Navan/Dublin turnpike road across the little stream, the former old mereing of Dowdstown and Kilcarn.[23]

Left: Limekiln in Dowdstown. Right: Brian Boro's Bridge in Dowstown woods

Below Ardsallagh, we come to the site of the mill weir that once provided water-head to power a corn mill at Upper Kilcarn (Little Kilcarn), the drop across this weir reflected still by the fall in the riverbed hereabouts. The weir ran askew across the river, from the Ardsallagh bank to a river rampart on the Kilcarn shore; the 1837 OS map shows a corn mill here, with one section built on the rampart and the other on the main riverbank. The mill tailrace, formed by a series of linked islets, fell back into the Boyne several hundred metres downstream, below Upper Kilcarn House. While the map of 1911 depicts the weir, the islets, millraces and sluices, no trace of the corn mill is evident.

Although completely overgrown during my younger days in the 1950s, this landscape had changed very little since 1900. The post 1968 drainage scheme altered the entire scene; however, dragging the weir, islands and all traces of the old mill from the river, such that posterity will never know what was there in times past.

During many boyhood walks along the Boyne, my brother Tom and I often visited the site, taking the pathway through the woods from Brian Boru's Bridge, and following the line of the old turnpike road to the farmhouse occupied by Mary Jo and her husband Kit Meehan. The old miller's house, of mudwall and stone construction, stood on the north-eastern edge of the ancient road; near the corner of the laneway leading up to the newer line of the Navan/Dublin turnpike road (now the R147), which replaced the old turnpike line in c.1814.

Here, in the flagstone-floored kitchen, we shared many a pot of tea with the Meehans, being regaled by tales of how the house and yard were used as a staging post in times long gone, and of the many 'car-men' and coach passengers who may have trodden the same flagstones long ago. Most traces of this ancient setting were removed from the riverscape during the best-forgotten Celtic Tiger era; the site no longer welcoming to Boyne ramblers, now sealed-off by electronic gates and occupied by one of the many mini-mansions of that period.[24]

I could find no record of this mill in the 1654/56 Civil Survey, but a mention is made of a corn mill at Upper Kilcarn c.1702, in Cyril Ellison's *The Waters of the Boyne and Blackwater* – refer to details of *The Big Mill* at Greater Kilcarn later in this chapter. Griffith's records the mill as follows:

> lot 19a, house, offices, corn-mill and land totalling 5 acres 1 rood 2
> perches, leased by James Ledwich from Charles Barry @ R.V. £12-10s.
> – limekiln & quarry leased @ R.V. £5.[25]

While drifting on downriver through this greatly altered landscape, I reflected upon several boat trips made along this reach many years before. In the 1960s, my friend John Bradley took me upriver from Kilcarn Waterworks in a flat-bottomed boat, used for fishing and river maintenance at the works. Leaving the deeps above the great weir at Lower Kilcarn, we rowed beneath a canopy of chestnut trees lining the Ballagh and Ardsallagh riverbank; their branches spreading down to the river, with blossoms and leaves almost touching the water. The boat floated through and brushed aside a blanket of water lilies, with saucer-sized blooms spread across our path in the shade of the trees. The near flat lily pads contrasted with the tall, straight riverside rushes swaying and rustling in the light summer's breeze. On a bright sunny day and a wisp of warm air on one's face, boating on this stretch of river with its magnificent foliage and sunlit water, was a unique experience, the most perfect you could wish for in a lifetime.

Continuing on up the Boyne, occasionally disturbing the musings of a basking frog or nesting coot, we came to Upper Kilcarn. Here the river divided into several streams to flow around the scrub and briar covered islands. Passing through the narrow channels to the sound of Boyne water thundering through gaps in the ancient mill weir; we emerged from the reeds to see the line of white water pouring across the falls of Upper Kilcarn.

Although these features are all gone now, and the river flows through a broad canal-like channel, the riverscape retains much of its former beauty. On the left bank, the wooded heights of Ardsallagh and Ballagh (Boynehill)[26] rise abruptly above a broad floodplain, while on the opposite shore, the ground rises gradually towards the heights of Kilcarn and Oldtown.

The old Navan/Dublin turnpike road ran alongside the river from the mill yard at Upper Kilcarn, and on past Upper Kilcarn House (now O'Kelly's stud farm), to link with the newer (1814) line just upstream of Kilcarn Bridge. The north-eastern end of this old road forms the contemporary Mill Lane.[27] On the heights above, the ruined Norman church and beautifully restored

Left: Ballagh or Boynehill.   Right: Over Kilcarn Weir in flood Jan 2014

graveyard of Kilcarn stand beside the old line of the Trim/Drogheda route via Cannistown, Kilcarn and Oldtown. This old church once hosted the ancient and decorative baptismal font, now resident in Johnstown Chapel.[28]

Due to the foul weather, very little of this beautiful vista was visible from the boat as we motored down the sluggishly flowing reach towards the weir at Lower or Great Kilcarn. The slow rate of flow is caused by the water backing up above the mighty weir, the sole surviving mill-weir on the Boyne above Navan. One would think that this weir should be preserved for posterity; however, it survived destruction in the 1970s only because of intervention by Jimmy Bradley, my father-in-law, who persuaded the OPW dragline operative to desist from demolishing the ancient structure, lest the citizens of Navan be deprived of their water supply.

Kilcarn Weir runs askew across the Boyne from Boynehill, and connects to a stone built rampart on the Kilcarn side. This upper or headrace rampart runs for about 80 metres downstream, forming a circa 20 metre wide, partly paved channel; on its other side lined by a stone river-wall fronting the main riverbank. About mid-way along, the rampart is breached by a 'spill' sluice gate, used to control the mill water-head during its operational days.

The headrace was/is split in two by a triangular-shaped cutwater at the downstream end. The right'-hand' race flowing beneath a stone arch to power the smaller upstream millwheel; the other race flowing through a screen (rack), then diverting via a sluice and around the upper gable wall to turn the larger millwheel. Below the waterwheels, the two races combined in a circa 8 metre wide tailrace, separated from the river by a rampart of rough-hewn stone. This rampart ran on downstream for about 500 metres

The rack and split millrace at Kilcarn Mill *c.* 1976 - Courtesy John Bradley

to Kilcarn Bridge (old), where it abutted a wider pillar separating the two easternmost or millrace arches from the remainder of the structure. There is some evidence to suggest that the mill tailrace continued for a considerable distance below the bridge in older times.

Kilcarn Mill was a two storeyed over basement stone built structure, with a slated roof above open rafters. The main entry/exit (for grain) provided by a doorway on the upper floor, in later times known far and wide as 'the loft.' Because the building abutted against the steep hillside, the elevated doorway opened onto a wider space fronting the former Navan/Dublin turnpike road, now the Mill Lane. The mill's footprint is nearly identical on both the earlier and later OS maps, the only difference being a small extension projecting from the southern wall, as shown on the 1911 map.

The orientation of the mill is east to west in plan, and the main building is of rectangular shape, with a smaller oblong annexe on the north-western corner projecting about 18ft into the headrace and 8ft further downriver – the main rectangular section measures about 70ft long by 35ft wide, with the annex increasing these dimensions as outlined above. An undershot waterwheel approximately 12-14ft in diameter by 3-4ft wide was 'hung' in a stone, semi-circular shaped housing located in the nook upstream of the projecting annex. On the gable of which was mounted the main waterwheel, also of undershot design and about 18-20ft in diameter by about 6ft in width.

Likewise, the miller's house and old granary are laid out in similar fashion on both maps. There is one major difference between the maps; however, whereas the 1837 map depicts the site as a 'Corn & Flour Mill,' the map of 1911 names it Kilcairne Pumping Station (Navan UDC).

Clockwise from top: Stephanie and Eilleen Bradley boating on the millrace, Kilcarn Mill to the left, the Mill House on the right; A young Jimmy Bradley at Kilcarn *c.* 1938; Stephanie and Eileen (Pidge) Bradley boating on the Boyne at Kilcarn Weir *c.* mid-1930s; Stehanie Bradley with Maura and James Kelly - boating on the Boyne at Kilcarn *c.* 1938.

This brings us to the chequered history of 'the Big Mill,' a tale, which I believe, is a sad reflection on the true attitude towards preservation of our industrial heritage.

Griffith's records Kilcarn Mill thus: house, offices, flour mill and land totalling 5 acres 3 roods 18 perches, leased by James McCann from --- White and others @ R.V. £93.

The following synopsis of Kilcarn (Kilcarne) Mill's earlier history is gleaned from a fuller account in Cyril Ellison's book entitled *The Waters of the Boyne and Blackwater – A Scenic and Industrial Miscellany* (Paraphrased for clarity):

The lands of Upper and Lower Kilcarne in the Barony of Skryne have had a long association with the family of Barry of Santry, Co. Dublin, a branch of the Barrymores…" - Richard Barry, Mayor of Dublin, had a grant, dated 2nd March 1627, for the tithes of Great and Small Kilcarne. - "The Civil Survey shows that there was a mill on the Boyne at Great Kilcarne but none in Little Kilcarne. But when Henry, 3rd. Lord Barry of Santry, leased the estate in 1702 to Charles Barry for lives for ever, it included the Mill at Little Kilcarne and the Mill at Great Kilcarne near the bridge, known locally as The Big Mill…" - In May 1771, Thomas Williams, then in possession of Great Kilcarne, together with its Flour Mills, Watercourses, Mill Holme,[29] Kiln, Dwelling House and Offices and the little Park adjoining, apparently included Hamlet and Allen Wade as partners in the lease. - In the year 1776-1777, this partnership benefitted from transporting nearly 13,000 cwt. of subsidised flour to Dublin (c. 650 tons – the 3rd highest total in the country), and received the sum of £713 in bounty payments. - "The mill was later worked by Fay & Co. of Navan, succeeded by Francis Hughes, a Dublin merchant. Then in 1822 the property was sub-let to James McCann of Stalleen. Mr. McCann negotiated a 999 year lease in 1851 and for many years Kilcarne Mill was run in conjunction with the family business, John McCann & Sons, Millers and Bakers, 15 West Street, Drogheda. The Field Names Book of 1835 mentions Kilcarne as 'a large corn and flax mill, so evidently diversification had taken place with the decline in the demand for flour…" - "In 1896 an agreement was made to sell

Kilcarne Mill as a going concern to Luke Smyth of the Boyne Mills, Navan. The agreement apparently never took effect, for in 1898 the McCann interest was sold to Navan Town Commissioners for £400 in order to provide an intake and pumping station for the town water supply. The contractor for the water works was a Belfast man, William McLarnon as was the engineer John Swiney."

While I could find no inventory of Kilcarn Mill for 1898, it is reasonable to conclude from the above records that the mill was at least partly operational when bought by Navan Town Commissioners. Anecdotal recollections of the Bradley family show that the larger and smaller waterwheels, with their associated gearing and power trains were still in situ then,[30] but no information is available on the number of grindstones used in the mill or their eventual fate.

During conversion to a pumping station, the smaller waterwheel and associated gearing were removed to facilitate installation of water intakes. The pumps were installed at basement level, and belt-driven from lay shafts, powered by gearing driven by the 18/20ft diameter waterwheel. Back-up power was provided by a reciprocating steam engine, supplied from a steam boiler installed in the extension shown on the 1911 map.

Construction of water intakes, raw water settling tanks and three slow-sand-filters was completed within the mill curtilage (or holding); with a storage reservoir built atop a nearby hill at Oldtown. From here the treated water gravitated to Navan via the first water main leading from the new works to the town, completed in 1900. This was routed across Old Kilcarn Bridge, following the line of the Navan/Dublin road, to feed a new pipework system, together with an older water supply built by Bishop Nulty in Athlumney c.1860s (see Chap. 11).

The back-up steam engine was installed because of the intrinsic unreliability of waterwheels as a primary source of power, due to fluctuations in river levels. Family legend tells of Jimmy senior's wife Ellen stoking the furnace to keep up a head of steam when he was occupied elsewhere. The steam plant became redundant in 1932, being scrapped and replaced by a diesel engine of mid-1920s vintage. Although modest enough in power output, this was a relatively huge engine, with a flywheel approximately 10ft in diameter and a 'donkey-engine' starting system.

Clockwise from top:

Kilcarn Mill, Miller's House and grannary or pumphouse (now demolished) *c.* 1976;

Reconstruction of waterworks 1931; Flooding at Kilcarn Mill *c.* 1977;

Mill entrance from old Turnpike road *c.* 1977;

The 'slow' sand filters and Mill House at Kilcarn Waterworks *c.* 1977.

Photographs courtesy of John Bradley

This unit became redundant in turn, being removed from the premises c.1953, and installed at Stafford's Sawmills near Kilmainhamwood, where it powered the plant well into the second half of the 20th century.[31] On Dec. 8th 1954, the old mill was inundated by the greatest flood of the Boyne within living memory, when the plant was knocked out of action.

During this period, the local Fire Brigades kept Kilcarn Waterworks going by using portable pumping systems. Following this incident, the waterworks was redesigned, with modifications completed and new plant commissioned by c.1956. The most significant part of this operation involved removing the pumps from the mill and reinstalling them at a higher level in the old lofted granary, located to the south of the Miller's House.

With various modifications, this system remained in service until the 1970s, when Kilcarn Waterworks was replaced by a new plant, commissioned by Meath Co. Co. at Liscartan on the River Blackwater. Due to initial unreliability of the new works; however, the plant at Kilcarn was returned to service: thereafter, until decommissioned around the turn of the new millennium, the old waterworks was used as extra capacity and back-up for the burgeoning town of Navan.

In c.1912, the mill loft was leased from Navan UDC by R.C. Metge of Ratholdren, for storage of grain and tobacco, the growing of the latter crop being then a thriving industry around Navan. As recorded in the minutes of various UDC meetings, this was a strife-torn relationship, with the council attempting to rescind the lease as early as 1914; ostensively because of concerns about insurance… Mr. Metge was much aggrieved at their offer of £5 in compensation; however, claiming that he was due at least £10 on foot of the improvements made to the premises.

An amicable agreement seemed to have been reached; however, as a Major Metge was still in occupation when another row erupted over holding of dances on the loft in 1925. The mill features also in tales related of the period 1918 to 1922 (Irish War of Independence), when men on the run used the buildings as a weapons cache and hideout; one yarn telling of how the Black and Tans directed a fusillade of shots at the mill, fired from their lorries parked on Old Kilcarn Bridge.

Kilcarn Mill, with attendant Miller's House and granary at Lower or Great Kilcarn is one of the oldest such mills upon the River Boyne, with a history perhaps dating back to the 1500s. The site has been in charge of two publicly funded bodies, namely Navan UDC and Meath County Council, from 1898 until time of writing in 2014. Care of the site during this tenure does not reflect its important heritage or historical value. The two councils' stewardship, in the context of the mill's preservation as a heritage site, is a record of destruction and neglect, which, if perpetrated by others, could be described as scandalous.

The earlier neglect/destruction of heritage items includes: disposal of ancient machinery and mill wheels for scrap: demolition of the mill roof and loft to avoid cost of repair/rates, breaking down of ancient walls/kilns for convenience, and so on; a seemingly endless list of apathy and indifference. While this earlier damage and neglect may be attributed to ill-informed officialdom, there is little to excuse the Council's failure to include the remains of the mill, house and granary on its own Record of Protected Structures (RPS).

Had this site been protected, infliction of further damage might have been avoided in the new millennium; such as complete destruction of the original waterworks facilities – neglect of the Miller's House, now in an advanced state of disrepair. Demolition of the ancient lofted granary for no obvious reason, and I believe, use of sledgehammers to break up the old Pearn pumps for scrap metal; poor recognition indeed of this unique heritage mill site, and for services it provided for a century when serving as the waterworks.

Back on the boat we continued along the deep, still water above the great weir in steadily worsening weather, and entered what was once the great maw of the millrace powering the *Big Mill*. About midway along, we came to a newly formed gap in the weir; through which we passed over (or through) the circa 6ft high weir without major difficulty.[32] Leaving the turbulent water below the falls, we headed on downriver towards the new bridge of Kilcarn.

Similar to Upper Kilcarn, the river hereabouts descends surprisingly steeply in a series of shoals or ledges, formed and re-formed over millennia by calcified lime depositing upon the underlying rocky bottom. This constitutes a unique habitat for fish, other aquatic organisms and plant life; a somewhat rare attribute of the Upper Boyne nowadays, because the post 1968 drainage scheme tore the heart out of the riverbed elsewhere.

The small section survived only because the old mill weir remained in situ to provide deeper water for Kilcarn Waterworks' intake. During dry seasons, it is possible to wade across the Boyne hereabouts, but quite dangerous as the soft deposits tend to crumble underfoot. The calcified ledges continued for approximately two thirds of the distance from the weir to the new bridge, and terminate at the ancient shallows known as the Sunken Weir.

During the drainage work and construction of the new bridge, the shallows were dug out and the river draglined from just above the new bridge to Navan. As a result, the riverbed nowadays consists mostly of sandy mud and other silts, trapped by the myriad of rocky ledges formed by the OPW during the Boyne catchment drainage. They caused major problems on this section at Kilcarn, with the RIB hanging up frequently; the lads spending most of their time in the water lugging the boat across these obstructions.

We carried on downriver and passed beneath the new concrete bridge, designed by Donald Murray and constructed by the firm of Murray Engineering. The bridge was opened to traffic in 1977, relieving a choke point and altering a road configuration existing since medieval times. The shoaly river bottom continued to just above the old bridge, where several small islets are re-forming in the river despite the best efforts of the OPW draglines.

Approaching the western end of the bridge, we viewed the three c.11ft span medieval arches there, and then headed for No. 4 arch, the westernmost of the four mid-river wider spans of circa 22ft. The ice-cold rain, borne on the wind scything downriver from the south-east, made conditions very unpleasant as our boat passed beneath the ring stones of the ancient arch. While we examined the stonework in the gloomy interior, a combination of paddles and the engine running full astern held the RIB in position against the vortex of water tearing through the tunnel-like, darkened eye of the bridge. It was not a place to linger, so we took some photos and passed on; exiting the arch and heading downriver over the shallows and OPW ripples towards Navan on the misty horizon.

Kilcarn Br. in flood c. 2015 - Courtesy Audret Martin

ぞ

Kilcarn Bridge (H.E.W. No. 3159)

This ancient bridge spans the River Boyne from west to east, and links the townland of Balreask-Old, on the western riverbank, to that of Kilcarn on the eastern shore. The bridge carried the Dublin to Navan turnpike (or tollroad) across the river from its inception in 1729 until the dissolution of the Irish turnpike system in 1855/56. In the immediate vicinity, this road ran alongside the Boyne to Dowdstown, across the Hill of Tara, through Killeen and then to Dunshaughlin. Tradition holds that in earlier times the road from Tara to Kilcarn ran atop the line of one of the ancient roads of Tara, *An Slighe Asail*. Two less-known roads once crossed this bridge, namely, an older line of the Trim/Drogheda road, routed from Rathnally to Grange-Bective and onwards through Cannistown, Johnstown, Oldtown, Kentstown to Duleek; and the Athboy/Drogheda road, passing through Dunderry, Curraghtown and linking with the aforementioned Trim road, via *An Bothair Álaing* (beautiful road), at its contemporary junction with the Cannistown road.

The antiquity of this river crossing is reflected in the names given to two townlands on the western riverbank. The 1837 Ordnance Survey map shows the older name of Balreask-New as Ballybatter or in English *the town or place of the road*; while that of Boynehill is shown as Ballagh, which translates to 'the Place of the Ford or Pass.' In addition, the importance of the crossing point, from the Anglo Norman perspective, is emphasised by the conjunction of Ballybatter, Balreask-Old, Athlumney and Kilcarn Townlands in the immediate vicinity. The bridge is depicted on the Down Survey Barony of Skreene Map of 1656, which map shows the townlands of Ballybatter and Ballagh named Batterstown and Rallagh respectively.

A full technical description of the bridge is beyond the scope of this work; however, Peter O'Keefe's *The Dublin to Navan Road and Kilcarn Bridge*, includes the most detailed account of the bridge available to date. The booklet was compiled in support of the 'Save Kilcarn Bridge' Committee, formed in 1981 by Elizabeth Hickey and other history/heritage enthusiasts in response to the proposed demolition of the bridge following opening of New Kilcarn Bridge in 1977. Although pedestrianized at this juncture, the bridge has been poorly maintained in the interim period, and at time of writing is in obvious need of a facelift due to the ravages of weather and time. This description is based upon the above publication and my own research.

The surviving bridge possibly contains elements of several distinct structures as follows:

> Original bridge – possibly dating from 12th century – and its post-1330 replacement.
> Mid-period bridge, dating from late 16th century.
> Upstream extension, dating from c.1729.
> Contemporary structure, dating from late 17th or early 18th century.

Unknown original pre-1330 Br. & 9 arched replacement post-1330.
Some historians believe a reference in the Laud Manuscript (replicated on pages 116/117 of James Grace's Annals Hibernia), stating: "that all bridges upon the Boyne, except Babes," were destroyed by a great flood in 1330, sets a marker for construction of the replacement bridge at Kilcarn sometime after this date – O'Keefe concludes that it may have been built during the 1400s. It is my opinion that these ancient references should be treated with caution and examined more critically, as many later assumptions are predicated upon their veracity, which cannot be proven readily in other ways. I believe that if a stone bridge existed here prior to 1330; sections of it possibly survived

and may indeed form part of the surviving bridge. From the evidence available, the replacement bridge was c.13.5 feet wide and constituted of nine segmental profiled arches. It is likely that the three downstream arches nearest the western or Balreask-New riverbank are survivors of the original pre-1330 structure.

Mid-period Bridge (13 Arches)

Peter O'Keefe concludes that the earlier 9 arched bridge was extended eastwards during the 16th century – the extension included two river arches, a circa 20ft pillar or retaining wall and two millrace arches abutting the eastern riverbank.[33] The additional arches were of similar segmental profile to those of the earlier bridge, with each spanning c.11ft and linked by three 7.5ft wide piers. The lengthening of the structure involved considerable alteration to the eastern riverbank and realignment of the road. The structure carried the highway atop the slightly flattened arch crowns, thereby giving the road a more level aspect similar to the stone arched bridges at Trim and Slane.

Upstream extension

While no record was found in the Grand Jury presentments or Turnpike Trustee books, to date, it is reasonable to propose that this bridge was widened to its current dimensions (circa 23ft face to face) when the Dublin/Navan road converted to a turnpike in 1729, or shortly thereafter. During research, I examined the underside of several arches, including No. 3 and 4 (courtesy of Meath River Rescue Service), and noted the following: the upriver extension was constructed as a separate entity, with no ties to the original stonework – that it is approximately 9.5ft wide and built mostly of smaller stones, some of which are undressed – the courses of old and new sections are unaligned and the gap between the extension and the older bridge is quite pronounced, being sufficiently wide to place my hand within the joint in several locations. Impressions of the old supporting forms (possibly wickerwork) are visible in the mortar on sections of the older structure. The upriver extension is symmetrical, with all the arches of segmental profile. On this façade, most of the triangular-shaped cutwaters extend (or once extended) upwards to form pedestrian refuges within the parapet walls.

Contemporary Bridge (11 Arches)

Viewed from downriver, the contemporary bridge consists of eleven arches, laid out in three distinct groups as follows: starting from the western or Balreask-Old riverbank, a group of arches numbered 1, 2 and 3 – these are most likely survivors of the original bridge, and as described above they each span c.11ft and are connected by two piers of 7.5ft width. Another 7.5ft pier on the eastern flank of No. 3 arch supports the first span of the mid-river section, which comprises four arches numbered 4, 5, 6 and 7 – these are much larger openings, each with a span of 22ft and the crown about 4ft higher than the smaller arches at either end. A circa 7.5ft pier abutting the eastern flank of arch No. 7 supported the above described 16th century extension of two river arches, a circa 20ft pillar or buttressed retaining wall and two millrace arches abutting the eastern riverbank. These are of similar segmental profile to those of the earlier bridge, with each spanning c.11ft and linked by 7.5ft wide piers. The piers are faced by triangular profiled cutwaters extending upwards to circa one metre above the ringstones of the smaller arches and to the crown of the larger spans. There is one exception; however, with the pier/cutwater linking No 6 & 7 arches extending to form the one pedestrian refuge within the downriver parapet wall. With the two millrace arches open to the river, the bridge has an aggregate free waterway width/hydraulic capacity of circa165ft, but with the two millrace arches presently closed off from the unflooded river, this is reduced significantly to circa 143ft. Which, to say the least is unwise, and poses extra hazards to the structure's survival due to increased stress imposed during flooding.

Assessment of structure

Measurements taken by Peter O'Keefe during the 1990s indicate that the outline of the contemporary eleven arched bridge fits within the footprint of the 16th century thirteen arched structure. From this and other research, he speculates that six of the smaller arches carried away in a flood during the late 17th or early 18th century – and suggests that these six arches were replaced at the time by the four larger spans, which effectively increased the free waterway or hydraulic capacity of the bridge. It is possible; however, that the structural alteration was completed on a planned basis, but as no record is available, this aspect will remain a moot point. The structure at this

Clockwise from top:
Old Kilcarn Bridge, Jan 2015; Joint in old Kilcarn Bridge and Refractory tiles from Kilcarn mill drying kiln

period still had a face to face width of circa 13.5ft, which carried a roadway approximately 10.5ft wide – the higher rise of the central spans caused a slight incline towards the bridge's mid-point.

Most of the Big Mill is gone, with much of the millrace vanished and the tailrace filled in; a stranger passing now might well wonder what was here before. If not cherished, this ancient bridge spanning the Boyne for centuries past, bearing disparate travellers such as Norman Knights tramping from Drogheda to Trim, Isaac Butler on his 1740s journey to Lough Derg, crowds to the monster meetings at Tara and hosts of football supporters taking Sam Maguire home, will disappear entirely from the landscape.

The Hearth in the Old Mill House

Elizabeth Marie Bradley/Holten

On winter mornings in the old mill house, I awaken to hear sounds of Dad cleaning out the fireplace downstairs. The clang of metal against metal as the poker and shovel clear out the remains of the previous night's fire. Into a bucket – shovel after shovel – go cinders, ash and memories of a warm hearth the night before.

Then… sounds outside of the old shed door being unbolted and shovels of coal scooped up from its cement floor – echoing into the crisp, cold air, amplified by the water of the River Boyne flowing alongside the old mill.

Sometime later the smell of burning kindling and coal come wafting up the stairs, intermingled with crackling sounds – and the inward eye sees a glowing fire in the hearth downstairs. A warm hearth again and its tales of a new day and night begin.

During the day ahead as mother goes about her housework, she pops in and out of the sitting room to check on the lighting fire and add coal as needed. While doing this she takes advantage of a quick warm for herself, as the old Mill House is very cold while moving around doing daily chores.

On washing days as the clothes are taken in from the line outside, they are laid across a clothes-airer – yet another chance for a little warmth as the clothes are placed in front of the open fire. Come end of day, clothes taken away and folded – the hearth is now open to all and many a bum is warmed as the family arrive home. Now the hearth comes into its own, as stories of everyone's day are told.

One of my two brothers liked to repair gadgets, whether they be fishing rod reels, parts of waterpumps or various other mechanical objects, as he is a plumber by trade and a keen fisherman. As a result many a 'gadget' was brought in and held across the open hearth to our father sitting on the other side – often by two very 'greasy/oily' hands, to be shown and talked about as to their faults and ways of mending them. Many a discussion took place like that between father and son in front of that warm hearth – problems solved between an older and younger head and in doing so a love and admiration shared, a lasting bond formed.

Mother, her day's work around the old house done, would sit down beside the fire. Her place given up by whoever was sitting in it, and lest we forgot, our father was ready to say: 'up out of there and let your mother warm her feet.'

At end of day her place was next to the fire on the couch beside father: her tasks of washing, cooking, cleaning, sewing and looking after us all and the old house, done for another day. Before we got television, and even afterwards, she would take out her knitting, sewing or lace-making and chat away as she went about it. I learned many a craft from her hand, sitting in the heat of that old hearth. Sometimes a neighbour would call and share their knitting skills or maybe for a chat.

In later years, we kids started to move out and have our own families and homes. My older brother being first to do so would drop by most nights to chat to mother and father about his day, his family and the news he had to share… yet again around the old lighting hearth.

As grandchildren arrived, they too warmed their cold bums, hands and knees in front of the hearth. Many a time after snowball games out in the yard, then into the hearth they would run to dry out and tell their tall tales to doting grandparents, who made sure there was a good warm fire and open arms to welcome them.

Cousins would meet and play together in the heat of that old hearth. Many a doll's hair dried and combed there, toy trucks and cars were driven beside it, sometimes too close for comfort.

Over the years, parents, children and grandchildren enjoyed the warmth of that old hearth – many a family pet too – four generations of our family, and a number of other families before our time. That old hearth could tell many a warm tale.

The old Mill House is no longer lived in, its hearth not lit and warm, maybe one day it will be again. The old hearth once more warm and inviting, many more tales then told in its warmth.

❧

ENDNOTES

1   See *Where Toll Roads Meet* and *On Ancient Roads.*

2   A bridge is depicted here on the 1656 Down Survey Barony of Skreen map (probably Dunsany Br. or its predecessor).

3   The OS maps show many variations to the river's course at Kilmessan, between 1837 and 1911; however, these are too complex to describe in this work.

4   Kilmessan Bridge was rebuilt c.1900 to replace a structure swept away during a flood in 1898-1899. I note from Meath County Council's early records that they were seeking tenders of under £70 to replace the bridge.

5   Another water mill was possibly located near the concrete bridge that replaced the Foot-stick-ford at Riverstown c.1929. Many river course alterations took place hereabouts, with traces of a possible millrace and pond evident until removed by developments of recent times.

6   Built by local Stonemasons Pat & Ambrose Lynch c.1814 for the sum of £114-15s-8d, with the bridge named after Ambrose Lynch – see *On Ancient Roads* p. 128.

7   Dowdstown Bridge is covered by two Grand Jury presentments to the Lent & Summer Assizes of 1802 (spelled Doubstown Br. in the presentments). These show that the bridge was built c.1802 by local Stonemasons, John & Ambrose Lynch at a cost of £166-14s-9½d, for more details see *On Ancient Roads* pp. 120/121.

8   John O'Donovan's 1836 Field Notes on the parish of Templekeeran say of this river: - "*Gowra River – local ……. Gabhra, the genitive case of Gabhar largely used as nominative. c.f. Gabhar Aichle, Gowra of Aichle, now the Hill of Skreen, near Tara. This little river rises in a bog near Stranstown (sic) in Skreen Parish. It flows along the northern border of the detached portion of Templekeeran ph. and continues westwards to join the Boyne at Ardsallagh. Note Of the name Gabhair or Gowra, Eoin Mac Neill could find no definition in any dictionary or glossary; but from a study of its usage he concluded that it meant "a low broad ridge between two river valleys." (see phases of Irish History, p. 107). The Templekeeran River probably takes its name from the neighbouring Gabhar Aichle, the ancient name of the Hill of Skreen. "* (sic)

9   The Great Red Bog of Lagore, where many ancient artifacts were discovered during drainage works in the early 1800s. The name Lagore probably derived phonetically from the more ancient title Lock-Gabhair/Lough Gower, and may indeed be connected to the name of the River Gabhra.

10 One of the oldest Norman burial grounds in Ireland.

11 This section of Lismullin Avenue and bridge (now bypassed) was once part of the main route from Summerhill to Drogheda. It was superseded in c.1803/04 by a new line running from Batterjohn (big) Crossroads to Rathfeigh (from west of Dunsany – on the old line of the Black Bull/Trim turnpike road, now the R154). The old line through Lismullin Park from the Dublin/Navan turnpike road (N3/R147) was 'stopped-up' by C.D. Dillon and Thomas Carberry for the grand sum of 5-shillings, as recorded in the Grand Jury Lent Assizes of 1808.

12 For a more detailed account of the three mills once located upon the River Gabhra, see *On Ancient Roads*, Chapter 13 p. 90 *The Mills of Gabhra*.

13 This bend in the river intrigued me since my boyhood by the Boyne, and I wondered at its origins. However, local historian, Paschal Marry of Ballymagarvey (who is researching the River Nanny's ancient history), recently drew my attention to Robert Meehans informative book.

14 (Daly's Mill pp 214/216 *On Ancient Roads*) – As described in chapter 11, the millrace powering Chadwick's Mill in Athlumney, sourced near Shane's Well on the invert of this watershed, flows in the opposite direction to enter the Boyne at the Athlumney/Fargans-town mereing below Navan.

15 See *Where Toll Roads Meet*, pp. 62 to 65.

16 This ancient road was routed through Bective Demesne, Cannistown, Kilcarn Br., and onwards through Johnstown, Oldtown to Duleek. It was the only main route passing by Ardsallagh Townland prior to cutting of the 'new line' of the Summerhill/Navan road c.1809/15. The new road ran approximately three miles from Castletown Tara to Can-nistown Village, and included construction of Bellinter Boyne Bridge and Ambrose Bridge spanning the River Skein. For more details, see *On Ancient Roads*, Chapter 9.

17 The 1837 OS map shows the footprint of Ardsallagh House to be entirely different to that of 1911, and that the gate lodge at Bellinter Br. or the avenue from there to the house had not been built at the time. A firm indicator that the above J.J. Byrne's estate map of 1843 was commissioned as part of John Russell's upgrade of the estate, including construction of the new Elizabethan Mansion in 1844, just south of the former castle site.

18 Her husband, Mr. Delany, supposedly designed and laid out the gardens and woodlands of Ardsallagh in the early 1700s.

19 The title Marquis (Marquess) of Headfort was another of the so-called Union Peerages, created in 1800 and granted to Thomas Taylor, 2nd Earl of Bective – the Marquess also holds the subsidiary titles of Baron Headfort and Viscount Headfort in the Irish Peerage and Baron Kenlis in the U.K. Peerage (created 1831), which entitled the holder to a seat in the House of Lords.

20 Reputedly built by the Board of Guardians circa late 1800s/early 1900s.

21 Many big houses of the period were built to this hollow-square design, perhaps reflecting a quasi-defensive attitude still prevalent within the psyche of the ruling elite during those turbulent times.

22 For more details of this well, see Sir William Wilde's *The Beauties of the Boyne and the Black-water*, p. 128 (2nd edition).

23 The bridge, known in local lore as Brian Boru's Bridge, appears to have been widened at least twice, perhaps once c.1729 for the initial turnpike and again c.1796/98 during realignment of the turnpike from Dunshaughlin to Dowdstown, with the centre section built in an earlier period: it is likely that prior to the road becoming a turnpike in 1729, the bridge was part of the more ancient route from Tara to Kilcarn, Navan and Teltown, which followed part of the reputed line of *An Slighe Asail*. Although this could be one of the oldest surviving stone bridges in County Meath, its very existence is almost unknown

as it is ignored by historians, hence has fallen from the radar screens of history. Some private restoration work was completed several years ago, but the western extension is mostly crumbled away since, and the surviving structure needs urgent attention. Like many other items of heritage interest, this bridge will disappear from the landscape if not preserved for posterity. For more details of the bridges & turnpike road in this area, see *On Ancient Roads*, chapters 9 & 10.

24 Although all traces of the mill have vanished, a pair of well-preserved, French-Burr type millstones survived and are stored at Tallon's Martry Mill – the story of these stones is related in *Where Toll Roads Meet*, pp. 51 to 53.

25 This limekiln was on the site of and adjacent to the old corn mill at Upper Kilcarn, not the one mentioned earlier sited close by Brian Boru's Br. in the Dowdstown Woods.

26 A small tributary enters the Boyne here (Ballagh River). This stream rises in Balreask-Old and passes beneath the road at Cannistown into Boynehill – where it once enhanced the former magnificent walled gardens.

27 The line of this old road can be traced via satellite imagery – for more information on this road, see *Where Toll Roads Meet*.

28 For details of this font's history and carvings/inscriptions thereon, refer to William Wilde's book pp. 129 to 131 (2nd edition).

29 Middle English from Norse: meaning an island or low, flat land near a river.

30 The Bradley family name became synonymous with Kilcarn Mill/Waterworks after James Bradley Sen. took up residence in the old Miller's House as first caretaker of the waterworks at the *Big Mill*, shortly before the turn of the century in 1900. Born in 1871, he was fondly known as 'Little Jimmy Bradley' or 'the Auld Chap in later years.' An experienced fitter, employed previously in Mason's Metal/Engineering Works, Academy Street Navan, he operated Kilcarn Waterworks and completed most mechanical and other associated maintenance work. Auld Jimmy continued on as waterworks superintendent until 1932, when his son, James, assumed the superintendent's role. He remained on as assistant for several years, and resided at Kilcarn until his death in 1966, aged 95 years; a remarkable man with a long service record spanning so many years. James Bradley Jun. worked as superintendent of the plant to his retirement in the 1980s, but remained in residence at the Miller's House until his death in 1996, aged 88 years, thus ending a remarkable family lineage at Kilcarn Mill.

31 An old log book from Kilcarn Waterworks records details of this engine thus: "National Horizontal Cold Starting Heavy Oil Engine" installed and started 1st February 1932." This was a National 100hp, single cylinder unit operating on black diesel circa 200 Seconds Redwood Viscosity. Other interesting details of the power plant and pumps included in the book, are: "Pearn" 40 & 8 hp turbine pumps installed 1933: Electric lighting and D.C. Dynamo installed Oct. 1935: Works changed over to electric power 10/4/1937 – that in the three year period from March 30th 1934 to March 31st 1937, the diesel engine pumped 236, 520, 000 (236.520 million) gallons at a cost of £1,328-14s-5d (£1 for every 178,000 gallons, with fuel costing 1s-10 ¼ d per gal.) … in the period March 1940 to March 1943, 256, 232, 296 (c. 256.296 million) gallons were pumped by electricity at a cost of £1, 587-

12s-1d (£1 for every 161. 000 gallons).

32 I cannot discover what caused this breach; some say it was made by fishery interests to help salmon gain the Upper Boyne reaches, others that it was made by flotsam/trees during a flood. But if not repaired soon, this breach will succeed where the OPW failed in the 1970s... and Kilcarn Weir will be no more. This ancient setting holds precious memories for numerous folk, including me – in my youth, I often swam at the skewed weir, indeed, my wife Marie taught me to swim there in exchange for driving lessons in my old Ford Anglia. In those days it was a beautiful, near idyllic setting, a veritable Mecca for many people, some local but others from Navan and elsewhere, who came to swim in the reasonably clean river waters of the day. On the hot summer evenings, the grassy banks at Boyne Hill and the stone 'river wall' by the mill might be thronged with old and young bathers, many mothers bringing offspring for their weekly bath; a never-to-be-forgotten mixture of Sunlight Soap and Boyne Water. The laughter, merriment and ecstatic screaming of excited kids filled the summer air. But like elsewhere, modernity has caught up with this place also. Now the new waterworks is like a WWll Stalag, enclosed within electronic gates and security fencing, no longer welcoming to all; considered unfit for such social activities but seemingly fit-for-purpose as a source of drinking water, despite the sewerage works disgorging massive quantities of effluent into the Boyne upstream at Dowdstown. So in the summer evenings the place is quiet now; except for the sullen roar of Boyne waters tumbling across weir and incessant drone of passing traffic on the nearby N3. In my memory I can still hear the merry laughter of the children, as they cavorted in the waters – and once more wonder at the hidden price paid for progress.

33 The Civil Survey records a mill at Kilcarn in 1656, not depicted on the Down Survey map of the same era. Grand Jury records show the mill in Lower Kilcarn was known as *the Big Mill*, perhaps to distinguish it from a smaller corn mill at Upper Kilcarn. If Kilcarn Mill, in fact, dates from the 1500s, it was one of the oldest mills powered by the Boyne – the 1837 & 1911 OS maps give clear depictions of the mill tailrace running from Kilcarn Mill and passing beneath the two easternmost arches of the bridge. The Longfield estate map of Kilcarn Demesne (c.1822), gives very clear details of the mill, the bridge and tailrace layout at Kilcarn.

9

The Middle Reaches
from the Big Mill to Navan

Athlumney Parish, Townland & Demesne – Johnstown, Bailis & the Double Ditch – P.P. Metge, Guernon's Wall & the Passage – Boyne View & the Souterrain – Ballybatter & Balreask-Old – The Smithy & old road network – Post famine Balreask-Old Hamlet – The New Line & the Scelp (Sceilp) – Saint Columb's Church, Dr. Maurice Neligan & the Wexford Men of '98 – The Swan, Swan Bridge & Swan Lane – Fair View & Belmount – Limekilnhill – The Slip & Athlumney Ford – Limekiln-street, the Butter Stream & Boylan's Lane – Dillonsland – The Great Flood of 1954 & John Boylan's High Water Mark – Mellows Terrace.

Below Kilcarn Bridge the Boyne flows north-westwards towards Navan; with Athlumney on the right and the townlands of Balreask-Old, Limekilnhill, Dillonsland and Townparks forming the left or south-western bank. From Kilcarn to the mereing with Ardmulcnan Parish just below Babes Bridge, the river encloses the 'old parish' of Athlumney within a wedge-shaped sector, with the town of Navan located at its westernmost point. The parish of about 2,453 acres, included the townlands of Athlumney (592 acres), Johnstown, Bailis, Alexander-reid (Alexander Reid), Mooretown and Ferganstown & Ballymacon.

John Bradley fishing the Boyne at Kilcarn. John, a successful angler & flytyer, is acknowledged in Peter O'Reilly's book, *Flies of Ireland*.' Courtesy P. Cahill

Hereabouts Athlumney once consisted of wooded pastureland rising steeply above a narrow floodplain to a low escarpment; crowned by manor houses, ancient fort and ruined castle, their inverted images all reflecting from the river. This scene is replaced by another reminder of the Celtic Tiger era; with modern developments dominating the new landscape, and mirrored from the Boyne waters.

We will first travel along the Athlumney shore, starting from its mereing with Kilcarn about fifty metres north-west of Kilcarn Bridge.

This section, once Athlumney Demesne, forms a narrow salient enclosed between the river and the townlands of Johnstown (123 acres), and Bailis (127 acres). Athlumney Townland broadens beyond Bailis, where the boundary runs eastwards along the 'old' Athlumney/Drogheda road; then turns westwards to the Boyne opposite Blackcastle Demesne. The enclosed area forms a giant 'V'-shape between the two river reaches, with its apex at the confluence of the Boyne and Blackwater in the town of Navan.

The western mereings of both Johnstown and Bailis Townlands were once formed by a remarkably well preserved trench known as 'the double-ditch;' some of which has disappeared beneath developments comprising the 'new village' of Johnstown. The deep gripe, traditionally considered as part of The Pale, ran north-westwards from the Kilcarn/Johnstown road,

Clockwise from top: Between the bridges 2012, Section of Taylor & Skinner 1778 - Kilcarn to Navan Map, Carved stone removed from Bective Abbey Cloisters - now inset on tower of Johnstown Chapel - referred to in Chap. 07.

to terminate abruptly in a field just south of the old Athlumney/Drogheda road.

Athlumney House is situated about mid-way along the riverside demesne; overlooking the Boyne from atop its high, grassy banks, the vista enhanced by the stone arched bridge of Kilcarn in the foreground, with the nearby Hill of Tara providing a perfect backdrop. The house was built in the late 17th or early 18th century by a Hugenot family named Metge. This family rose to prominence in the district, with several older place names in Navan deriving from their name e.g. Metge's Lane and Metge's Lock. A new road, named Metge's Road, bisects their old demesne and leads to the 'concrete jungle' comprising the new landscape of Bailis and Johnstown.

In 1854, Peter Ponseby Metge held the 130 acres Athlumney Demense in fee at R.V. £168. The demesne was covered by woodland in the nook within the area close by Kilcarn Bridge and the Johnstown road, with enclosed gardens and a fish pond located between the house and 'the double ditch.' The 1911 map indicates a sawmill in the yards to the north of the house; which I believe was powered by a water turbine driven by a small stream that rises in Brannanstown and flows down through Johnstown.

A building contractor, named Benny Mc'Entaggert, acquired the house in the 1940s and his family resided there for about fifty years. Following initial proposals by its new Quango owners to demolish the structure, it was renovated extensively and is now part of a business park and occupied by 'de-centralised' government departments. During my childhood I recall a member of the Metge family residing in Balreask-Old, directly across the river from Athlumney House. Named Major Metge, he seemed to be clad most times in old fashioned knickerbockers, otherwise known as plus-fours; a nickname deriving from the extra four inches of cloth required to cover one's knees.

Previous to recent realignment of the road from Kilcarn Bridge to Johnstown, the access avenue to the demesne ran from the main gate (located close by the 'new' crossroads on the Johnstown road), to Athlumney House and yards. Prior to 1820, the avenue or roadway continued north-westwards, passed through the grounds of Boyne View House and joined the old Athlumney/Drogheda road close by Violet Hill. An important junction in the context of Navan's history, as I believe it once connected this old road to the ancient ford of Athlumney.

The avenue/roadway passed between the two properties, through a gap in a high stone wall known as 'the passage.'[1] Local legends tell of the stone wall being named Guernon's Wall; however, I could find no reliable derivation for this name. The new road, leading from Metge's road (new) to the modern bridge on the Boyne beside the Swan River, runs alongside the former path of Guernon's Wall, from 'the double ditch' to the Boyne.

In a gravel pit, once located in a nook between Guernon's Wall and the Boyne,[2] an ancient souterrain or subterranean stone chamber was unearthed circa 1848. Wilde made a brief note of this discovery on the eve of his book's printing in 1849, but included little detail. More information on this find appeared in William F. Wakeman's *Handbook of Irish Antiquities*, published by Hogges, Figgis, and Co. in 1891 – the relevant text, with an accompanying sketch, reads thus:

> An excavation which, some forty years ago, was accidentally discovered upon the grounds of P. P. Metge Esq., in the vicinity of Navan, may be described as a good example.
>
> The chamber is of an oval form, and measures in length 11, in height 6, and in breadth 9 feet; B is a passage or gallery (in length 15 feet), which has fallen in at C, D D are niches set into the sides of the gallery, which, like the chamber, is lined with uncemented stones, laid pretty regularly. (sic)

Athlumney souterrain 1891 - Wakeman Handbook. Plan courtesy V. Mulvany

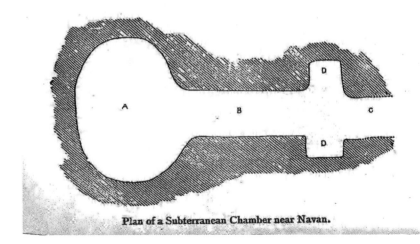

Plan of a Subterranean Chamber near Navan.

This chamber, likened by Wilde to similar structures at Clady near Bective, probably dates from pre-Christian times. No further information can be gleaned by using modern scientific techniques; however, because the relic was dug out together with the gravel pit, perhaps to satisfy an insatiable need of gravel for construction of the railway. At the time, considered to be mankind's ultimate solution to transport problems, but later discarded in favour of road motor transport. Leading to a similar destructive cycle during the Celtic Tiger years, when the latest panacea for our travel woes became tolled motorways; touted incessantly and mantra-like by vested interests to a credulous public.

At the western end of Kilcarn Bridge, the Navan to Dublin turnpike road entered Balreask-Old and ran northwards to the mereing with Limekilnhill, formed by the Swan River. The townland mereing between Ballybatter and Balreask Old runs along the centreline of the road to the midpoint of Kilcarn Bridge, whereas the eastern end of the bridge is located entirely within Kilcarn Townland.

The road layout in the vicinity of Kilcarn was vastly different in the times prior to construction of 'the Big Mill' and the first stone bridge; I believe the earlier crossing was via a ford, perhaps located at the above-mentioned upstream shallows once known as 'the sunken weir.' This theory would explain the various older road configurations, gleaned from studies of the maps.

Dignan's shop and pub - *c.* 1890s - former location of Kilcarn Turnpike

The old road network is covered extensively in *Where Toll Roads Meet* and *On Ancient Roads*. In summary, the older Dublin to Navan road ran across the Hill of Tara, through Dowdstown and alongside the Boyne, first to the ford and then to Kilcarn Bridge when construed during the Early Norman Period. The road assumed the pre 1977 configuration within the Kilcarn area with its development as a turnpike or toll road in 1729. The turnpike from Dunshaughlin was realigned circa 1796-1801 to by-pass Killeen and Tara and again in 1814 to avoid the choke points at Brian Boru's Bridge in Dowdstown and the mill in Upper Kilcarn. This new line is effectively the contemporary N3/R147.

The junction at Kilcarn Bridge (Balreask Old) was an important crossroads, forming a link between the Dublin to Navan turnpike (tollroad) with the earlier main route from Trim to Drogheda via Rathnally, Balgil (Balgyl), Cannistown, Johnstown, Oldtown and Kentstown. In addition, the old main route from Athboy to Drogheda, via Dunderry, Curraghtown and *An Bothair Álaing* joined this road about three hundred metres to the south of Kilcarn Bridge. The old OS maps show Balreask Old to be a well occupied hamlet.

The Preston Bellinter Maps – Prepared from a survey of the Estates of Lord Tara (John Preston), conducted in 1810 by James Vaughen from Athboy. Courtesy of the late George Briscoe.

No. 2
1 The hamlet at Balreask – Old
2 old road to Drogheda via Oldtown
3 Kilcarn Mill

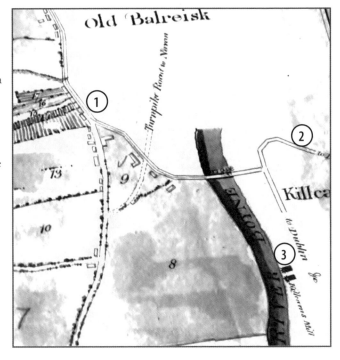

These, and other sources, indicate that the hamlet included several dwellings, a public house and the toll-house immediately adjacent to the junction; with a gate blocking the road, where tolls were collected from travellers on the turnpike road. Larkin's Map of County Meath displays a cluster of dwellings surrounding the ancient road junction.[3]

The 1837 map shows all the buildings, except one, located within Balreask-Old Townland, with the mereing between Ballybatter and Balreask Old running to the south-east of the Cannistown road. The Dublin to Navan road operated as a tollroad from 1730 to 1856, when all such tollroads in Ireland were dissolved by Parliament. The toll-house ceased operation at that time and became the local post office and grocery store for a time.

A Smithy or forge started at the crossroads sometime after 1854, as it is not listed on Griffith's Valuation of that year, but is indicated on the 1911 map. Indeed, the Smithy was still active during my early childhood years; when I well remember the roar of bellows and rhythmic ring of hammer on anvil as 'old' Mick Markey, the blacksmith, shaped iron shoes for fitting on our cob pony named Polly.

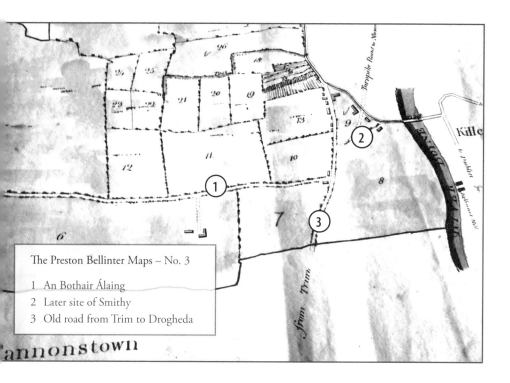

The Preston Bellinter Maps – No. 3

1 An Bothair Álaing
2 Later site of Smithy
3 Old road from Trim to Drogheda

The newer line of the road from Kilcarn Bridge to 'the Scelp' was cut circa 1807, at which time the older turnpike line, winding up the hill and through Balreask Old became defunct as a main route. It reverted to the status of a byroad, known as 'the Old Road' thereafter. The new line is about one statute mile in length, and runs from the former turnpike house (toll-house), now the Old Bridge Inn, to Swan Bridge. In the Grand Jury Query Book for the Barony of Skreen, I found two presentments covering construction of the one bridge on this line. The presentments were recorded under the summer assizes of 1807 and listed as items number 430 & 431 – they indicated that William Johnson, Charles Montague and Richard McGlew received £18-16s-3d for constructing the arch and £20-3s-8½d for building the battlements.

The bridge carried the new line across a little stream rising in Balreask Old, then passing through a small glen before falling into the Boyne north-west of Kilcarn Bridge. This bridge was demolished and replaced by concrete pipes in March 2010; to facilitate construction of the new road from Kilcarn, now feeding the M3. Development of this new road system involved a deep cutting being driven through the line of 'the Old Road,' which, apart from a pedestrian bridge and a difficult-to-find exit road (with lockable gate), is truncated for the first time since its turnpike days in 1730.

Referring to the place name, the Scelp or Skelp, I suggest that this unusual name is sourced from the local idiom and topography pertaining during construction of the new line in 1807. Collins' Irish Dictionary defines the meaning of the Gaelic word *Skeilp* as a slap or glancing blow; it was used also in the vernacular to describe the action of cutting something e.g. "take a scelp off the door to make it fit." The term is used now to describe a little hill on the 'new line,' at its junction with 'the Old Road' beside Swan Bridge. I believe the name applied originally to the new road between Kilcarn Bridge and the Swan, as this is built almost entirely upon a ledge, formed by the road builders 'taking a Skeilp' from the sloping hillside above the Boyne.

A section of land adjacent to Swan Bridge and located at the junction of the old and new lines is shown on the 1837 OS map as a glebe. This glebe land of circa ten acres included an area extending from the Old Road to the Boyne, bisected by the 'new line' in 1807. On the south-western corner of the glebe, the same map indicates a rectangular plot marked 'Site of old church & burial ground' (directly across from the contemporary Navan Rugby Club),

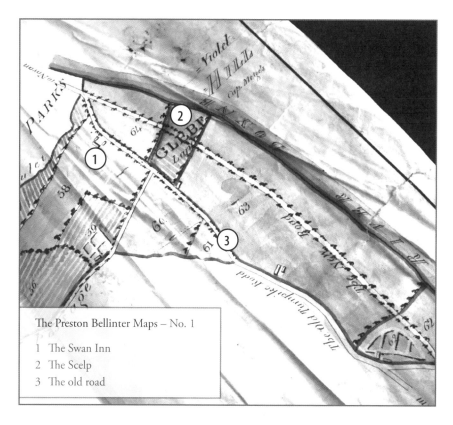

The Preston Bellinter Maps – No. 1

1 The Swan Inn
2 The Scelp
3 The old road

while the 1911 map depicts it as 'Burial Ground (disused)'. The site of this long gone churchyard, bulldozed several years ago, is now covered by modern housing. The following footnote in Dean Cogan's 1862, *The Diocese of Meath, ancient and modern* (Vol.1 p. 231), identifies this ancient ecclesiastical site:

> There was a church in the parish of Navan, situated between Navan and
> the bridge of Kilcairne, on the townland of Balreask, called by tradition
> "St Columb's Church." There was a burying ground around it. All the
> stones have been taken away. It is at present "glebe land". (sic)

Local tradition holds that the bodies of several Croppies, killed in the area during the rebellion of 1798, were interred at the old churchyard;   k n o w n to some as the Croppie's Graveyard. These may have fallen at the so-called 'Battle of Tara' on May 26th 1798 or more likely were victims of the savage reprisals inflicted by local Militias and Yeoman Cavalries in the immediate aftermath of the rebels' defeat at Tara. In this context, it is alleged that the Yeomen organised pursuits similar to their fox hunting exploits of more peaceful times, to chase down the rebels, many of whom, when captured, were shot out of hand or hanged from the nearest tree without due process being observed.

Another source for the legend may be the previously mentioned Wexford Insurgent Column, which, following the rebel defeat at Vinegar Hill on 21st June 1798, marched northwards through Wicklow, Kildare and Meath. In addition to 'the Battle of Clonard' (described in Chap. 3), the column fought many skirmishes with the military en route; including a battle at Knightstown Bog near Wilkinstown, which the rebels lost to vastly superior forces. This was the last major engagement, following which the column scattered; with a small group of horsemen heading back southwards across the Boyne, to be defeated finally at Ballyboughill in North County Dublin.

Eamon Doyle's book names over thirty wounded Croppies, reputedly taken to the Meath County Infirmary in Navan, where they were treated by Dr. Maurice Neligan, surgeon to the Meath Militia. The book (1911 edition pp. 76-77) lists some 32 wounded rebel prisoners submitted to the surgeon's care between 12th July and 22nd Aug 1798. The incursion into County Meath began with the Battle of Clonard Bridge (beside Leinster Bridge) on 11th July, where the rebels withdrew after fierce fighting failed to take the heavily fortified Tyrrell house. It effectively ended with the defeat at Knightstown on July 14th and the dispersal of the column.

These dates coincide with the above lists in the book. The first wounded prisoner being admitted to the surgeon's care on 12th July, the day after the battle at Clonard Bridge; where the rebels incurred heavy losses, including about 160 dead and many others wounded. The remaining wounded could be accounted for by the military operations in pursuit of fugitives from the column.

According to Dr. Neligan's report, replicated in Eamon Doyle's excellent and well researched book, all the prisoners in his care were 'cured's of their wounds and ailments, which covered the full spectrum from gunshot wounds, through fever to rheumatism. Considering the much recorded ferocity of the military towards prisoners and civilians alike prior to, during and after the rebellion of '98, one wonders at their subsequent fate and if some were buried in the reputed mass grave at the defunct cemetery near the Swan Inn in Balreask?

The Boyne is very shallow downstream of Kilcarn Bridge, so the lads were kept busy hauling our craft across the many obstructions. The foul weather continued, causing very unfavourable conditions on the boat and rendering recording, sightseeing and photography impossible. The previously described riverbanks, rising to Athlumney House on the north-eastern shore and to 'the Scelp' towards the south-west, were mostly obscured as we drifted along the Boyne in our small bubble of visibility. A narrowing of the south-western floodplain; however, announced our arrival at Swan Bridge, where the original turnpike road, now 'the Old Road,' swept down Swan Hill to run alongside the river towards the town of Navan.

The name of this bridge derived from a hostelry named The Swan, which once stood on the site now occupied by the Ardboyne Hotel. It is probable that the name originates from the location's proximity to the Boyne and the many swans frequenting its banks. The old Inn, perhaps predating the 1730 turnpike, was a former Carman's hostelry, providing sustenance and overnight lodgings for drivers of the coaches once plying the highway. The Toffs probably frequented the more upmarket inns in Navan, such as the Black Lion Inn sited close by Halpin's Entry on Market Square.[4] The old building still stood there in Balreask during my youth, when I recall helping my father while he worked in the sheds nearby; previously used as stables during its heyday as a hostelry.

The front wall of the stables adjoined 'the Old Road,' its high stone wall forming the boundary for about fifty yards, with two tall, cut-stone piers at its western end providing an entry to the former Inn. If memory serves, the old building was rectangular in shape, with a small porch on its front façade; it was two storeyed with a slated roof, and a pronounced batter to the walls giving it a pyramid-like profile. The old hostelry, together with the stables was demolished in the late 1960s or early 1970s; yet another part of our heritage to disappear without trace.

In 1854, Griffith's records the site of the old Inn, comprising offices and about 38 acres, leased by Mary Rogers from John Jos. Preston at R.V. £41-10s. The land adjacent to The Swan was used in the early 1900s as a nine holed course, known as Navan Golf Course. This club shifted to the former

Deerpark of Bellinter in the early 1920s and became Bellinter Park Golf Club (now the Royal Tara).

The title given to the old hostelry spawned several other place names and is reflected in some contemporary developments. The most abiding of these is Swan Lane (or Swan's Lane); which derives from an ancient roadway leading south-westwards from the former site of St. Columb's Church. This old route once connected the Dublin/Navan turnpike road (and Athlumney Ford) to the old line of the Trim road leading through the Commons and Robinstown. Prior to cutting of the new line from Navan to Trim via Balreask to Balgil in 1814, Swan Lane ran through Balreask Old, linking with the old Trim road just south of Commons' Bridge.

The stream flowing beneath Swan Bridge is largely unnamed but known to some as Swan River. Rising in a series of rills and streamlets draining the marshy lands beyond Duncanstown and Hanlonstown in the former Commons, the brook flows eastwards, forming the mereing between Balreask-Old and Limekilnhill Townlands from the old line of the railway to its confluence with the Boyne.

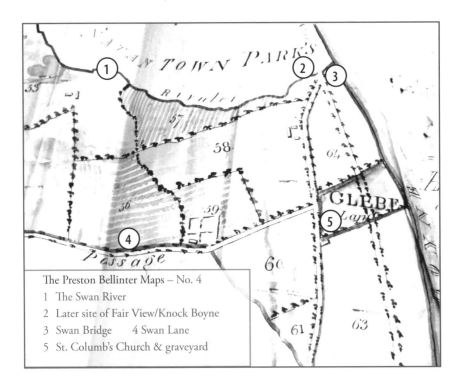

The Preston Bellinter Maps – No. 4
1 The Swan River
2 Later site of Fair View/Knock Boyne
3 Swan Bridge   4 Swan Lane
5 St. Columb's Church & graveyard

Back on the boat, we passed by the old Swan Bridge on our left, and then beneath the new bridge across the Boyne, linking the N3/R147 (former turnpike road) to Metge's Road in the 'new village' of Johnstown. Travelling onwards between the shores of Limekilnhill and Athlumney, we crossed a modern weir, built to record water levels in the Boyne; then manoeuvred through shallows where the R147 passes close by the river and a slipway once provided access to the water. Here the river curved slightly north-eastwards away from the old road line, this divergence forms a wide spit of land, where the first riverside buildings of Navan town stand. Downstream from the slip, the river curves slightly north-westwards again, revealing the stone railway viaduct looming from the misty riverscape at the edge of visibility.

The left or south-western riverbank includes the townland of Limekilnhill from Swan Bridge to 'the Butter Stream,' which little brook forms a mereing with Dillonsland. The small stream rises in the fields to the south of the now defunct Greenmount House, and runs alongside a laneway (once known as Boylan's Lane) to the Dublin road at the town end of the former Limekiln-street. Here it passed through a gullet beneath the road and flowed onwards to the Boyne. Traditionally, the name of the stream derives from the local custom of placing 'country butter' to cool in its clear waters; a common enough practice in the days before refrigerators.

Two manor-type houses are located on the higher ground overlooking this stretch of riverbank, both within the townland of Limekilnhill; which townland consisted of c.154 acres and included about ten acres of 'Abbey Land' on its western extremity. The residence nearest the Swan Bridge is named Fair View on the 1837 OS map and indicated as Knock Boyne on the 1911 map. The No. 22 milestone is shown on the latter map located to the left of the road near the entrance to the house; indicating that this place was 22 Irish Miles distant from the gates of Dublin Castle. Installed originally in 1733, shortly after this road became a turnpike, the milestone stood by the footpath throughout my youthful years. It disappeared in recent times, lifted by the Urban Council, I believe, and taken to its yard in Navan for safe keeping. Griffith's indicates that Fair View was occupied by Patrick Nicholls; the property consisting of house, offices and land totalling circa 8 acres being leased from Luke Byron at R.V. £12.

The other big house is named Belmount and located closer to the town.

The residence had two entrances from the Dublin road, one, complete with gate lodge, opposite the slip to the river, the second located at the town end of the property beside the later E.S.B. transformer/switching station. This was occupied for many years by the Spicers, a well-known family of millers and bakers, who operated the Boyne Navigation in the early years of the 20th century. In 1854 the property consisting of house, offices and land totalling c.11 acres was held in fee by Rev. Maurice Neligan; perhaps a relative of Doctor Neligan who treated the insurgents of '98 a half century previously.

A large gravel pit is shown on both OS maps, close by the roadway and between the two properties. 'The Boiler McGuiness,' a famous Meath footballer of the 1948-1954 era, lived in a house built in later years near the site of the ancient pit; perhaps once the former location of the limekiln from which this townland name derives.

Which takes us to the old ford of Athlumney: named and spelled variously as Ath Luimnigh, the Ford of Luimmeach; Ford of the Bare Place, St. Loman's Ford and Ford of the Herds. A more recent derivation describes it as Ford of the Mantled Place. The ford has been named also as Navan Ford and Nuad Ath or the New Ford. While many variants of the name and its meaning are recorded, little doubt exists as to the derivation of the name *Ath*, this being the Gaelic name for such river crossings e.g. *Ath Sidhe* further upstream near Bective.

Similar to Asigh, the townland of Athlumney derives its name from the ancient ford, the exact location of which has disappeared in the mists of time. From my youthful memories of the area; however, together with extensive research of the ancient maps, I venture the opinion that the ancient crossing place of the Boyne was located close by the aforementioned slipway leading into the river directly opposite Belmount gate lodge.

Athlumney ford was the nearest upstream shallow crossing prior to construction of 'the New Bridge' carrying the old Athlumney/Drogheda road across the Boyne opposite the town centre. A trip to Kilcarn Bridge was required in times of high water, or indeed to make any dry-shod transit of the river without a horse, boat or wagon. A similar return journey on the opposite riverbank, made the round trip from the square of Navan to Athlumney Castle approximately three Irish Miles. The most likely alternative route, used to bypass the ford, was the previously described road (the later avenue) running through Athlumney Demesne and atop the north-eastern riverbank. This once led from the Johnstown road, via Athlumney House, 'the passage' through Guernon's Wall and onwards to the junction with the old Athlumney/Drogheda road near Athlumney Castle.

In the early days of the Norman Conquest, the route from the ford probably led from the north-eastern bank via the Norman motte or fort,[5] to link with the old Athlumney road beside the ancient graveyard, south of the castle. In later times it led directly from the ford to the road (later avenue) linking Kilcarn Bridge to the said castle, via Athlumney House and 'the Passage.'[6] In support of this suggestion, Larkin's Map indicates the earlier roadway leading from the vicinity of the motte to the north-eastern riverbank opposite the slip; with a cluster of dwellings or hamlet shown on the Athlumney riverside at the suggested site of the ford.

Babes Bridge formed the nearest downstream crossing during medieval times; however, research reveals this structure in poor repair from about 1460 and perhaps impassable by the mid-1500s. Kilcarn Bridge; therefore, was the only reasonable alternative to Athlumney Ford prior to construction of 'the New Bridge' in the period 1735 to 1756.

The slipway or *slip*, as it was known to some, has disappeared from the Boyne, indeed, it is erased almost entirely from public awareness nowadays. But I remember it well, as it formed an opening in the riverside boundary, where the lower concrete wall ended and a higher wall marked the deviation point of road and river. I recall the lower wall was topped by a rusting pig-wire fence, with the Boyne rippling over the shallows at its base. These sights and sounds registered on my psyche while walking along the footpath, on the days I spent (or misspent) my 3d bus fare buying ice pops or Bull's Eyes in the Seven Dwarfs Café; hence, faced the five mile homeward trek and the wrath of my mother. In the times of the horse and cart, locals used the slip for taking carts, traps and wagons into the Boyne to soak the wooden wheel felloes (or felly), thereby preventing shrinkage that caused the iron hoops to fall off.

My final thoughts on the ancient ford are: it is quite likely that some enterprising persons had boats or rafts (perhaps ancient Boyne Currachs or Corracles) engaged in ferrying operations at Navan. Or maybe an early version of a taxi service operated at the ford; with a wheeled-wagon employed to carry townsfolk dry-shod across the river.

Excepting Limekiln-street, the old maps show that the section of land between the waterfront and the Dublin road was sparsely populated, from 'the slip' to the site of Murphy's old distillery in Academy Street. The floodplain broadens from the slip northwards to the railway viaduct, and is bounded towards the south-west by an esker ridge forming the higher ground of Limekilnhill and Dillonsland. The 1837 OS map indicates only Limekiln-street located on this section of floodplain, which street could be described then as a separate hamlet adjacent to Navan.

Limekiln Street thatched houses with Butterstream 'slated row' and viaduct in background.

Larkin's Map indicates a similar layout, with a cluster of dwellings shown at the same location; which may suggest that Limekiln-street developed as a hamlet because of its close proximity to the ancient ford of Athlumney. During my youth, I can recall only two major buildings located on the stretch between the slip and the old street: Hogg's Furniture Factory (Crannac Furniture in 1961 [Gael-Linn] – later Worker's Co-Op), and Jack Callaghan's Garage (Riverside Motors). When the old Smithy at Kilcarn closed down in the 1960s, blacksmith, 'young' Mick Markey, started up a business manufacturing wrought-iron gates and railings in an old building at the Kilcarn end of the street.

Griffith's 1854 valuation names the following people leasing and in occupation of houses in Limekiln-street at the time:

No.	Occupier	Lessor	Property	R.V.
01	Julia Barrett	Rev. Robt. Hamilton	House & Garden	£2. 15s
02	James Meehan	John Barrett	House	£0. 15s.
03	Thomas Rogers	Rev. Robt. Hamilton	House, offices, garden	£4. 0s
04	Anne Crosbie	Ditto	House & Garden	£1. 0s
05	Margaret Lyons	Anne Crosbie	House	£0. 10s
06	Patrick M'Glue	Rev. Robt. Hamilton	House & Garden	£1. 10s
07	Silvester Curran	Ditto	House, offices & garden	£4. 10s
08	James Clarke	Ditto	House, offs & sm. garden	£3. 0s
09	Michael Fox	Ditto	House, offs, small garden	£1. 5s
10	Julia Hammond	Ditto	Ho, offs, & sm. Garden	£1. 10s
11	Anne Caffrey	Ditto	House & small garden	£1. 0s
12	Thomas Quinn	John Donohoe	House	£1. 5s
13	Joseph Sullivan	Ditto	House	£1. 5s
14	John Donohoe	Duke of Bedford	House, offices & garden	£3. 0s
15	Mary Pemberton	John Donohoe	House	£0. 15.
16	Thomas Dowd	Ditto	House & small garden	£1. 0s
17	Patrick Smith	Ditto	House & small garden	£1. 0s
18	Owen Rounn	Ditto	House & small garden	£1. 0s
19	James Smitrh	Ditto	House & small garden	£1. 10s
20	James Rogers	Duke of Bedford	House & small garden	£2. 10s
21	Patrick Downes	Ditto	House & small garden	£1. 10s
22	Patrick Rogers	Ditto	House & small garden	£1. 5s
23	Mary M'Donagh	Ditto	House & small garden	£1. 10s
24	Patrick Rogers	Ditto	Ho, offs, & sm. Garden	£2. Os
25	Rose Hanly	Ditto	House & small garden	£0. 15s
26	Sylvester Curran	Ditto	Offices & small garden	£2. 5s
27	Patrick Blake	Mary Crosbie	House	£0. 15s
28	Thomas Meehan	Ditto	House	£0. 15s
29	Mary Crosbie	Duke of Bedford	Ho, offs, & small garden	£2. 15s
			Waste of houses, yards, streets, &c.	

The OS maps show that Dillonsland comprised a townland of 77.5 acres and extended from Limekilnhill at the Butter Stream to the Leighs Brook. Where it formed a mereing with Townparks; which townland comprised about 324 acres, extending from the long gone Brady's Building (in Robinrath), to Poolboy Bridge and included much of the old walled town of Navan.

Griffith's shows that in 1854, Rev. Robt. Thomson held two plots in Dillonsland (in fee), one consisting of about 52 acres and the other comprising of house, offices and land of 1 acre 3 roods 34 perches at total R.V. £116 – the latter lot was probably Greenmount House.

Rev. Thomson was a member of the Skeffington Thomson family that owned Rathnally near Trim and several other properties in the area.[7]

A row of two storeyed houses occupies the higher ground in Dillonsland opposite Butterstream. This site, once known locally as 'Sheridan's Field,' was named after the Sheridan family; who owned much property in Navan including Greenmount House, Navan Engineering Works and two hardware shops. The fourteen houses were built by Navan U.D.C. in the period 1932 to 1934 and occupied by 1935. It is called Mellows' Terrace; named in honour of Liam Mellows, a prominent Republican activist in the Irish War of Independence. On Dec. 8th 1922 during the Irish Civil War, Mellows

The railway houses & spa fountain – Courtesy Vincent Mulvany

was shot by firing squad, together with three fellow anti-treaty Republican prisoners, Rory O'Conor, Joseph McKelvey and Dick Barrett; as a summary reprisal by the Free State Government.

To date I have been unable to establish a date for construction of the row of houses constituting the roadside terrace known as Butterstream. Local anecdote tells of the cottages being owned by the railway company at one time, which is perhaps true. Although the terrace was not constructed until a later date, Griffith's indicates that part of the land upon which the houses now stand was held by the Dublin and Drogheda Railway Co. in 1854. The valuation map marks a plot numbered 10, which included grounds containing the GNR railway station, the viaduct and remnants of the distillery and a strip of land south-east of the railway.

If the railway company built the houses in the latter half of the 19th century, this perhaps explains the old right of way running on the south side of the viaduct, from Academy Street towards the old GNR railway station; which nowadays provides a pedestrian access to Woodlands housing estate.[8]

On the Feast of the Assumption, the 8th of Dec. 1954 (the 32nd anniversary of Mellows' execution), the River Boyne burst its banks and flooded vast areas of the valley from source to sea. Much of Navan was flooded, including Academy Street, where the water rose to almost windowsill level on the Butterstream houses. The inundation level is recorded in stone – by a line John Boylan carved on a wall at the last house on the former Limekiln-street. Following John's death in the late 1950s or early 1960s, the old house (one of the original thatched dwellings) was demolished and replaced by a modern bungalow; the high water mark (or Plimsoll Line) being transferred to the new boundary wall, where it can be seen at time of writing.

This was the worst flood of the Boyne and its tributaries within living memory, which inundated vast tracts of County Meath, causing evacuation of houses alongside the river in Trim and Navan. I recall vividly the massive overnight wind and rainstorm causing flooding of the River Skein in Dowdstown on the same day. My most abiding memories are of a full sized haycock being carried downriver on the flood, the water level rising to our back door and the tremendous sucking noise caused by the flood at Dowdstown Bridge; where it rose above the eye of the arch, thereby forming a vortex or suck-hole.

I believe the storm we witnessed on that memorable day in 1954 emanated from a series of weather systems, touring the North Atlantic Ocean that winter in the aftermath of Hurricane Hazel. Which storm made its landfall in Ontario on October 15/16, causing catastrophic damage to Toronto and its environs.

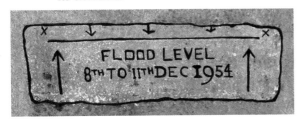

The old laneway (named Boylan's Lane) started from forninst John Boylan's later high-water mark at the former Limekiln-street; from where it ran alongside the Butter Stream up to the fields in Dillonsland. The marked wall fronted an old house, set further back than the remainder of the houses on the river side of the ancient street. During my youth, the house next door (on the Kilcarn side) was occupied by a Joss Butcher, otherwise known as 'the Dirty Butcher,' who collected dead animals from the district and dissected them in the yard to the rear of the premises.

The foregoing pages describe the landscape on the Boyne's approach to Navan. Including its researched history, and my own recollections from early childhood in the late 1940s until my teenage years of the 1960s; at which juncture Navan began to change utterly.

Above: Plaque commemorating John Boylan's 'High water mark on Dec. 8th 1954

ENDNOTES

1   Tradition holds that 'the passage' became the subject of a lawsuit when closed in the early 1820s. It is said that this lawsuit resulted from a dispute over the right of way between the Metges of Athlumney, for whom it provided a short cut to Navan, and James Williams, occupant of the adjoining property of Boyne View. Williams supposedly 'stopped up' the opening between the two massive stone-built gate piers. I believe this situation prevailed until the new millennium when developers demolished both the wall and piers.

2   In 2014, Meath Co. Co set up headquarters in a building once intended to be the head office of Quinn Insurance – this structure is named Buvinda House, and stands close by the destroyed heritage site of the souterrain.

3   Griffith's 1854 valuation indicates 44 tenants occupying properties at the junction and within the circa 2.5 acre triangular plot, located on the elevated ground above the turnpike house and bounded by the old road network. The lessors of these houses included John Ballard (10 of), Mary Casey (7 of), Brigid Monaghan (2 of), John Carty (2 of), William

Byrne (2 of), J.J. Preston, John Farrelly and Henry Coglan one each; while the Commissioners of Public Works held the turnpike house in fee. This is a remarkable population density for such a small area in post-famine Ireland; and indicates that sub-letting was alive and well at the time.

4   In Slater's 1824 directory, Cath. Halpin is listed (under the heading of Inns) as proprietor of the 'Black Lion' – perhaps an explanation for the derivation of the contemporary name Halpin's Entry.

5   I believe that this feature is known in the vernacular as 'the King's Belllybutton'

6   The road leading from the ford and its alternative route via Kilcarn Bridge linked originally with the old Navan/Drogheda road close by the ancient church and graveyard in Athlumney. In a later period, the 1837 OS map shows a house named Violet Hill occupying the site of the former junction, which is shown located further to the east on this map. Griffith's Valuation indicates that the Meath County Surveyor, Samuel Searancke (1811-1885), occupied this house in 1854. This place became known as 'Searanckes' rather than Violet Hill – I believe that local folklore once contained a myriad of tales about strange occurrences hereabouts, leading to the area being considered with some dread and shunned by locals. The 1911 OS map indicates that the Convent laundry was built upon the site in later years.

7   Development of Dillonsland and the northern section of Limekilnhill, from about 1830 to 1911, is traceable by studying the old maps and cross-referencing the different periods. No buildings are indicated on the 1837 OS map between Murphy's old distillery, located on the southern extremity of Academy Street, and Limekiln-street; which commences at the Butter Stream and continues to the approximate later location of Callaghan's Garage. The street consisted of a continuous row of houses (thatched cabins) on each side of the old coach road; with the name originating from the townland name of Limekilnhill. The map accompanying Griffith's 1854 valuation, shows the railway viaduct crossing both road and river and bisecting the old distillery, but it, too, indicates no buildings on either side of the road between the remnants of the distillery buildings south of the viaduct, and Limekiln-street. The 1911 OS map; however, shows a few changes on the approach road to Navan, including: some of the dwellings on the river side of Limekiln-street are gone, with open spaces between the houses – the remains of the distillery buildings to the south of the viaduct have disappeared, replaced by three houses alongside the road and another larger house recessed well back towards the river. The greatest change of all; however, was a row of fifteen dwellings shown along the river side of the road, from upstream of the recessed house to the Butter Stream, thus joining Academy Street to Limekiln-street. This row of small dwellings became known as Butterstream (or 'the Slated Row or Range'); an unofficial place name, not recorded on any maps until relatively recent times.

8   A terrace consisting of sixteen cottages (described in the Meath Chronicle of 1911 as *artisan dwellings*) of similar size and shape was constructed alongside Railway Street c.1900 to 1908. Another local legend says that the latter houses, together with the fifteen dwellings in Butterstream were known as Lady Kesterman's Houses, which lady resided in Greenmount House in the second half of the 19th century.

Bective Abbey.
Aerial view from the North-east. In the background is the River Boyne and Bective Bridge, with the farther riverbanks formed by the riparian sections of Balsoon and Ballyna Townlands. Courtesy of Aubrey Martin

Athlumney (Aylesbury's) Weir. Aerial from downstream.
In the background is 'the Ramparts,' with the Boyne Navigation Canal alongside.

Courtesy of Aubrey Martin

From top:
Members of Meath River Rescue Service outside their new headquarters in Navan. Courtesy
Paddy Cahill. Recovering the 'Titanic' R.I.B. at the Curly Hole.

From top:
The author (and slash hook) at No. 01 milestone on 'the Lost Navigation' in Cruicetown.
Marie and Seán Óg at Rosnaree Mill

Stackallan (Lugaree) Weir.
Aerial view from upstream, left to right; Cocker's Wood, Stackallan Guard Lock, Lugaree Pool,
Weir and salmon leap and the Millrace and Cotton (Woolen) Mill.
In the background, the Boyne turns to flow through Dollardstown and Cruicetown to Slane.
Courtesy of Aubrey Martin

10

The Middle Reaches
Navan and the Confluence

A different landscape – the bypass 'through town' – Navan Railway Viaduct – the souterrain & Viking Hoard – Mason's Engineering Works – a 'buried bridge' and its rediscovery – Ludlow Bridge & Lock – the 'V' weir – Ludlow St. or Navan Boyne Mills – a great fire in 1919 & demise of Spicer's Boyne Mills – Navan Power Station & its water turbines – the light on St. Mary's Church clock & a street light at 'the Round O' – Nash Foundry & buried heritage – a frozen river – Boyne Navigation, Metge's Lock, & Navan Lightering Works – 'V' weir, the Rack & millraces – the New Bridge – Athlumney Boyne Mills – the confluence – River Blackwater, its lakes & mills – Poolboy Bridge – a snapshot of Navan, before, during and after The Great Hunger – Mr. & Mrs. Hall on Navan in 1844 – are we learning from our history?

Beyond the slip, the first street lights of Navan twinkled through the gathering gloom as the boat carried us downriver between the misty riverbanks. But this is a different landscape nowadays, altered utterly and forever in the mid-20th century. Our craft now passed beneath banks adorned with modernistic buildings, mirroring the glass cages clinging to many a riverbank in far-flung, distant lands, whose alien waters I travelled during my seagoing days.

Ladies gathering rushes on the Boyne, with remnants of Murphy's Distillery upstream of Railway Viaduct *c.* 1902. Courtesy Donie Halpin

This is especially so on the south-western shore, where high rise flats, potential slums of the future, greet visitors to Navan with their ugly, graceless silhouette. The opposite shoreline of Athlumney has retained much of its former beauty; however, where green slopes, dotted by occasional trees, rise towards the motte and Athlumney Castle, thus obscuring the more distant rash of development from the immediate river aspect.

The massive changes to the centuries-old riverscape of Navan commenced with a 'temporary little arrangement' i.e. construction of what became known as 'the Inner Relief Road' through the heart of old Navan.

This project began in the 1970s with adoption of the strange concept of building a bypass road through the town centre; rather than a more effective and less destructive ring road around the outskirts. In my view, the failure of this so-called visionary concept led to a domino effect: first causing a major choke point in the town, leading to a hue and cry during the impatient, hubristic Celtic Tiger era spawning the M3 motorway and its tolled bypass to Kells. Moreover, the ring road (which should have been built originally as a first option), is being constructed in piece meal fashion and still unfinished, thirty years later. All of this poor planning and myopia succeeded in destroying most of Navan's industrial heritage, in addition to creating a huge tax burden for future generations.

Murphy's Distillery bisected by rail viaduct. Note the chimney and riverside 'Privvys' of Butterstream. *c.*1890s

Despite intense local opposition, the scheme was bulldozed (quite literally) through the old town, with the new road constructed along the riverbanks during the first half of the 1980s. At times leading to scenes reminiscent of post famine Ireland; with the Sherriff threatening evictions and battering rams the order of the day, as the town's ancient mills and vintage machinery were pummelled into the ground, providing filling material for the grand project.

Drifting onwards through this modern and 'progressive' landscape, I reflected upon the changes to the old home town during my own lifetime. And I wondered if we truly understood the meaning of this frequently used, or misused word, *progressive*, and its inevitable consequences for the survival of our human species on Planet Earth. In his *Mere Christianity*, C.S Lewis penned the following, enduring and timeless gem of wisdom:

We all want progress. But progress means getting nearer to the place you want to be and if you have taken a wrong turning, then to go forward does not get you any nearer. If you are on the wrong road, progress means doing an about-turn and walking back to the right road; and in that case, the man who turns back soonest is the most progressive man. We have all seen this when we do arithmetic. When I have started a sum the wrong way, the sooner I admit this and go back and start over again, the faster I shall get on. There is nothing progressive about being pigheaded and refusing to admit a mistake. And I think if you look at the present state of the world, it is pretty plain that humanity has been making some big mistakes. We are on the wrong road. And if that is so, we must go back. Going back is the quickest way on.

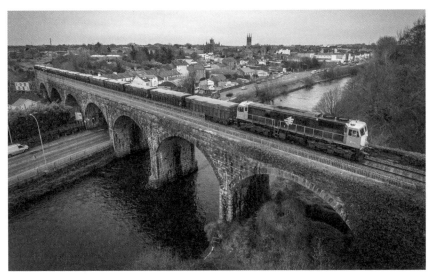

Train on Navan Viaduct - Courtesy Aubrey Martin

Passing between the new riverbanks, the left shore now formed by stone-filled wire baskets (Gabions) buttressing the new road, we glided on by the former back gardens of the Butterstream houses and beneath the mighty fifth arch of the railway viaduct.

The railway viaduct spanning the River Boyne in Navan, constructed in the period 1848 to 1850, carried the Drogheda/Navan branch line and Kells extension across the river from Athlumney to the station in Dillonsland. This line formed a spur for the Dublin & Belfast Junction Railway Company (later the Dublin & Drogheda Railway Co.), which became part of the Great Northern Railway (GNR) following a later amalgamation.

The bridge was designed by John Macneil (born near Dundalk) and built under contract by Moore Bros' at a reputed cost of £3,326. It is 406ft long, constructed of rusticated limestone blocks throughout and comprises seven medium rise segmental profiled arches of varying sizes; the three south-westernmost each spanning 49ft (Academy St. end), the central arch 52ft and the three north-easternmost each spanning 50ft. Although the viaduct carried only a single track, its width of 27ft incorporated part of the track layout for the attendant station.[1]

John Macneill, originator of the overall concept, designer of the Navan Viaduct and the more famous Boyne Viaduct at Drogheda, was engineer in charge of the railway construction. He later received a Knighthood for his work on the Dublin to Belfast railway project. The bridge was completed c.1850, when it opened to traffic. Nowadays the line is operated by Iarnród Éireann and carries freight traffic only. The river pillars were underpinned with concrete during the post 1968 drainage scheme and the riverbed deepened. The unflooded Boyne now flows beneath two of the 50ft span arches, with the third such, or north-eastern abutment span, effectively utilized as a flood arch. The Inner Relief Road runs alongside the river and beneath the 52ft central span.

Local tradition holds that a souterrain was discovered here c.1848, during excavations associated with construction of the Viaduct. This reputedly consisted of an underground passage over 50ft long, with two branches at right angles, and included a pair of circular beehive-shaped chambers; similar to those mentioned previously in Athlumney Demesne (Wakeman 1891) and Clady. The entrance to this souterrain has, unfortunately, since been lost.[2]

Other archaeological discoveries consisted of some human remains and artifacts, later to become known as *The Viking Hoard*. These included a horse's skull, bridle and horse trappings of iron, bronze and silver, bosses (discs with protuberances), iron rings plated with bronze, small bronze buttons and 7 ornamental plaques of gilt and bronze. These artifacts have been dated to the 9th/10th centuries and are now in the National Museum.

On the left bank, just below the viaduct, is the former site of Mason's Engineering Works. A William Mason is listed at this Academy St. address by Griffith's in 1854 and in Slater's 1894 Directory is described as a Blacksmith & Farming Implement Maker (I believe they also built their own bicycles here). It is said that their products included farm machinery such as horse-drawn ploughs, reapers, tumblers and rakes. Cast iron seats from such equipment can still be seen at heritage events, and one made by Mason's of Navan is considered as very rare indeed.

The previously mentioned, 'Jimmy Bradley Sen.' worked here as a fitter before transferring to Kilcarn Waterworks in 1898. Family tradition holds that one of the jobs he recalled working on for Masons entailed fabricating and installing new railings for St. Mary's Church (C. of I.) during the 1890s. I believe Mason's had a jetty or dock on the riverside for transhipment of their new machinery products to the Port of Drogheda via the Boyne

The Leighsbrook outfalls to the Boyne near Circular Road in Navan

Navigation Canal. The site was taken over by Gilbert Bros. in the early years of the 20th century and run as a general engineering business until the 1980s.

Immediately downstream is what I call 'the buried bridge of Navan,' located where the Leighsbrook falls into the Boyne near the junction of Circular Road and the former Navan to Dublin turnpike road at Bridge St. This bridge was built in 1798 -1799, as part of the western extension of the Boyne Navigation to Trim, and included a lock; the name given the combination was Ludlow Lock and Bridge. While the lock disappeared many years ago, the bridge survived intact until the early

The 'V' Weir in Navan - Mullen's Mill to fore with Byrne's (later Spicer's) Ludlow St. Mill and New Br. in background c. 1902. Courtesy Donie Halpin

THE WEIRS, NAVAN.   PUB. BY MEATH CHRONICAL LTD.

The 'V' Weir in Navan

1980s, when it was 'entombed' in tons of concrete, then buried as part of the Inner Relief Road scheme. The bridge now lies beneath the new junction at the former site of Navan Engineering Works,[3] with a tiny section of its north-eastern parapet the only visible proof of its existence.[4] Somewhat ironically, it was the cause of some excitement when 'discovered' during a sewerage augmentation scheme in 1999, whereupon an archaeological survey ensued, with a report issued to the same County Council that interred the structure originally.[5] For more information on the unfinished Boyne Navigation extension from Navan to Trim, see Chapter 3, Rathnally Weir.

The river descends quite sharply hereabouts, where once the former magnificent 'V' weir diverted the Boyne waters to power the two Ludlow Street Mills, the electricity generating station and the Athlumney Boyne Mills on the opposite riverbank. The weir was built more like an 'A', with its pointed-end invert to the river's flow and the cross-bar formed by a salmon-leap linking the two skewed side weirs. The left or western weir ran from mid-river to a rampart forming a circa 300 metre long, narrow island abutting 'the New Bridge' at the pillar between No. 2 arch and the now entombed No.1 arch (see bridge details below).

The millrace thus formed was about 20ft wide and powered two mills, known variously as Ludlow Street Mills, Navan Mills and Boyne Mills. The smaller four storey upriver mill was built entirely upon the rampart and accessed via a bridge straddling the millrace. There are noticeable differences in the footprints of both mills as depicted on the OS maps of 1837 and 1911; perhaps reflecting increased activity in Navan milling during part of this period. The two mills shared a common entry from Ludlow Street, which, for reasons that will become self-evident, was known later as Foundry Lane. Navan Boyne Mills – Ludlow St. Mills (02 of).

No. 01 Navan Boyne Mill (upriver building)

1837 OS map corn mills – (1854 valuation): Lot 18 corn-mill, kiln, offices and yard, leased by James Mullen from Francis Murphy @ R.V. £66. N.B., I could find no further detailed records of this mill or its owners, but it may have been operated by Luke Smyth prior to 1881, as he is listed in Slater's 1881 Directory as miller at Boyne Mills and again in 1894. He was a noted Parnellite who died in 1899, and mentioned earlier in the context of his own and family's connection with Bective Mill. It is probable that the mill had a riverside jetty close by the head of the weir, for transhipment of cargoes to and from the Port of Drogheda as it had access to the Boyne Navigation via Medge's Lock. I believe the four storey building was used in the 1960s-1970s by Hugh Hilliard for fabricating tubular furniture, and survived until the early 1980s, when it was demolished to make way for the route of the Inner Relief Road.

No. 02 Navan Boyne Mill (downriver building)

This mill was located immediately downstream on the same millrace; it was a much larger, six storey building, straddling the millrace, with sections built upon both the rampart and the main riverbank. On the 1837 OS Map it is recorded together with the above mill under the heading 'corn mills' – (1854 valuation): Lot 19 corn-mill, offices & yard, leased by Patrick Byrne from Francis Murphy @ R.V. £70. N.B., it would appear that John Spicer occupied the premises in 1870, as his name is listed on Slater's 1870 directory as miller at both Blackwater Mills and Boyne Mills.[6] In the early years of the 20th century it was known as Spicer's Boyne Mills, its generators supplying electrical power to the County Infirmary, which supply was extended to the new County Council Offices c.1912. On 19th June 1919, the Meath Chronicle reported that this mighty mill was destroyed by a fire in the early hours of the previous Monday morning:[7] going on to add a detailed description of the conflagration, which, but for a favourable wind and heroic efforts by various Fire Brigades (including one from Tara St. in Dublin), might have engulfed all of Ludlow Street. The building was wrecked by the fire, and later demolished, with the loss of some fifty jobs.

In 1923, the new Navan Power Station, erected on the site of Spicer's Boyne Mills, straddled the former millrace also and was accessed from Ludlow Street through the old mill yard. Navan Urban District Council operated the station, equipped with three water turbines powered by the old headrace, with an auxiliary semi-diesel (hot bulb) engine as back-up. At the time, this station produced Direct Current (D.C.), and supplied Navan Town only. The aforementioned Jimmy Bradley Jun. was employed here from 1925 until 1932, when he transferred to Kilcarn Waterworks.

In Dec. 1925, Jimmy commenced work with Comairle Baile Na h-Uaime (Navan UDC) at age 17, serving a seven year electrical apprenticeship at the generating station. He related many stories of the times spent at the old

Opening of the new Hydro Station Oct. 1923: at controls Sean MacNamidhe, Chairman of Navan UDC, with his son Eamonn and members of the Councils and business community. Courtesy G. MacNamidhe

station by the Boyne, including how he installed his first electric light over the clock in St. Mary's Church at Church Hill and Navan's first street light beside the contemporary 'Round O' pub at Flower Hill. In c.1932, Navan connected to mains electricity from 'The Shannon Scheme,' and the Ludlow St. power station ceased supplying the town, but I believe remained operational. Jimmy Bradley was offered a post at Pollaphuca Works, but opted to take up the position at Kilcarn Waterworks.

In the early 1930s, the Nash Manufacturing Co. Ltd., a subsidiary of Elliot's' Saw Mills, set up a foundry on the island or rampart between the power station and 'the New Bridge.' The enterprise was initiated to manufacture metal heads for tools such as forks, shovels and other farm/ garden implements, then in short supply due to the 'economic war' with Great Britain. This range of tools, fitted with wooden handles manufactured at the saw mill on the Blackwater, was one of the mainstays of the business. The foundry buildings consisted of a large, off-white coloured metal shed,[8] and included the masonry built generating station; the water turbine-generators, I believe, supplied D.C. power to the works until hook-up of mains electricity to the foundry in the late 1950s. All this area was flattened during construction of the Inner Relief Road in the 1980s; Mullen's Navan Boyne Mill and the old generation station, together with its turbines being used as waste material to fill in the millrace… minders of our heritage indeed?

The deep section of the Boyne above Navan Weir was frozen-over several times during the years, the most noted occasion being in the winter of 1940; which event is recorded for posterity by a photograph in the Meath Chronicle 100-year book. Many tall tales are told of this period, including one relating how local garage owner, Barney Allen, drove his taxi upriver on the ice and beneath the Railway Viaduct. While this tale is creditable enough, the story about horse-drawn hay-carters taking a 'shortcut' to Dublin via the ice-covered river beggars belief; as one might well wonder how they progressed through the arches of old Kilcarn Bridge and over Kilcarn Weir! If memory serves, a coating of ice and snow encrusted the still water above the weir in the hard winter of 1962/63, during my employment as an apprentice in Navan Engineering Works.

At the head of the 'V' weir, a fairway led from the deeps into the Boyne Navigation at Metge's Lock, located on the opposite or eastern riverbank.

Left: Lighter under construction at Navan 1902 - 1903. Courtesy Donie Halpin
Right: The Rack. Courtesy N&DHS

The navigation provided an average lift/drop of 94.6ft, varying according to tidal conditions in the estuary below Oldbridge. Although the lift/drop per lock varied also, the total figure was divided between 13 locations, from the tidal lock below Oldbridge to the summit level, controlled by the 'V' weir at Navan.[9] This peak was once indicated at elevation 113.8ft above mean sea level by the OS Benchmark on the upper gate stonework at Metge's Lock, where the canal locked-out to the river. Details of each lock and lateral canal are included as encountered on our downriver journey from Navan to Drogheda.

In 1902, James McCann, MP, took over the Boyne Navigation between Navan and Drogheda when he leased the waterway for a period of seven years, and renamed it 'the Meath River Navigation.' Many improvements were effected on the canal around the turn of the century (1894 to 1904), including upgrading of locks and installing more user-friendly operating mechanisms on the lock gates throughout the system. In 1902, a boat building facility was set up beside Metge's Lock – this venture cost £1,196, as so stated in a report to Meath County Council in 1914.

The boat yard, named Navan Lightering Works, consisted of a dry-dock and a large shed constructed in the area between Metge's Lock and 'the New Bridge,' to the east of the area now known as Andy Brennan Park. This building housed carpentry workshops, foundry and blacksmithing facilities and other support systems for boat building and repair. Vessels constructed in the dockyard were built in the open spaces next to this shed, and then launched via a slipway to the river above the great weir. Three boats were built at this works over a period spanning 1902-1903, and became known as 'the Boyne Lighters.' These vessels, the only such built at Navan, were named the *Teltown, Saint Patrick of Navan* and the *Tara* – being built and launched in that order.[10]

The dock was isolated from the river and converted to a swimming pool in the late 1950's or early 1960's, when I recall many children sporting and playing on the riverbank, then descending the serried rows of blue-painted steps to swim in the Boyne water within the oblong pool. These facilities have long gone from Navan, as the entire area was decimated by the OPW during the post 1968 drainage scheme; with the lock and former dry-dock filled in, such that little trace remains nowadays of James McCann's efforts to raise Navan's industrial profile.

The right or north-eastern branch of the great weir linked to an island or rampart, abutting the New Bridge's upstream façade. The various available maps, from Thomas Williams' 1756 sketch map of Navan town, to the OS editions of 1837 and 1911, depict differing configurations of the mid-river islands upstream and downstream of the bridge. It is difficult; therefore, to assess accurately the old layout based upon these maps alone. Aerial photographs from 1966 provide the final clue; however, enabling the following conclusions to be drawn: this bridge had eight arches of varying span; six open to the river below the 'V' weir, with No.1 arch (now entombed) abutting the town riverbank providing a tailrace conduit for the Ludlow St. Mills. The river pillar of No. 8 arch, now buried on the Athlumney shore, was linked to the upstream island/rampart, thus forming a headrace flowing through No. 8 arch and beneath the road (R153) to power Athlumney Boyne Mills; a flour & corn mill complex located immediately downstream of the bridge.

The entry to the latter millrace became known as 'the Rack,' a name once given to the sluice and screen system, sited about 200 yards upstream of the bridge at the head of the race. Here, the 1656 Down Survey Barony of Skreen map depicts a mill in graphic form; while the 1837 OS map shows an 'old corn mill' on the edge of the canal immediately upstream of Somerville Bridge. I can find no other record of a mill at this location, but note the 'old corn mill' is replaced by a row of four houses on the 1911 map, which houses are in situ at time of writing.

Onwards we went in the boat, passing by the new generation glass cages adorning the riverbank behind *Tobar Oran* (Tubberorum) to the rear of the former Tholsel (Market House) and later courthouse, sited on the left bank above 'the New Bridge.' The weather was appalling, so we paused only briefly beneath No. 3 arch to examine its structure; during which brief interlude I noted that the bridge had been widened twice in times past – with both extensions located on the upriver side.

The New Bridge

The New Bridge was the first recorded stone bridge built across the River Boyne in Navan town, and links the townland of Townparks to Athlumney on the opposite bank. It was constructed sometime between 1735 and 1756, as the town entered a time of prosperity with the growth of mills and milling. Although doubts exist as to its origins, tradition holds that it was built by the old Corporation, which had originally opposed its construction.

The bridge is a stone arched structure of segmental profile; consisting of eight arches originally, one, a c.19ft span, is entombed beneath the Inner Relief Road at the town end, another, a c.15ft span, is buried close by the entrance to Andy Brennan Park.[11] On the contemporary configuration; therefore, six

Upriver facade of 'the New Br.' before it was cleaned in July 2015

arches remain open to the river and in service. In its early days, the bridge carried a road across the Boyne, which divided on the Athlumney riverbank, one branch taking a more easterly route to Drogheda via 'the Little Furze' (near Athlumney Castle), Realtoge, Kentstown and Duleek. The other followed the southern bank of the Boyne through Haystown, Rosnaree and Donore.

As recorded in Grand Jury records, the contemporary road running from 'the Fingerpost' to Kentstown, was cut in c.1814-1816, as part of a new line, named in the Grand Jury presentments 'the Navan to Balbriggan Road.' Nowadays the R153 crosses the River Boyne via 'the New Bridge' and at the Fingerpost connects to the Boyne Road, which continues onwards as the L1600 on the older route through Haystown and Donore to Drogheda.

꙳

Contemporary structure from downriver aspect

Starting from the western or town end, the bridge is comprised of the following: Original c.10.5ft inter-arch pillar, now forming the bridge end abutment (N.B., this is reinforced by splayed concrete rafts, included during construction of the relief road – (**No I arch**), circa 20ft span segmental profiled arch with vertical pillars rising to springer level @ about 6ft above mean water level – circa 9ft wide pillar of coursed stone, faced by rounded cutwater and capping terminating above arch crowns – (**No 02 arch**) c.17.5ft span segmental profiled arch with vertical pillars rising to springer level @ about 6ft above mean water level – c.10ft wide pillar of coursed stone, faced by rounded cutwater and capping terminating above arch crowns – (**No 03 arch**), c.17ft span segmental profiled arch with vertical pillars rising to springer level @ about 6ft above mean water level – circa 28ft long embankment/ retaining wall of coursed stone (N.B. this wall once abutted a mid-river downstream island, now gone – (**No 04 arch**) c.15ft span segmental profiled arch with vertical pillars rising to springer level @ about 6ft above mean water level – circa 20ft span embankment/retaining wall of coursed stone, faced by a circa 6ft wide rounded cutwater with tapered capping terminating above arch crowns – (**No 05 arch**) c.16ft span segmental profiled arch with vertical pillars rising to springer level @ about 6ft above mean water level – c. 7ft wide pillar of coursed stone, faced by rounded cutwater and capping terminating above arch crowns – (**No 06 arch**) c.16ft span segmental profiled arch with vertical pillars rising to springer level @ about 6ft above mean water level. N.B., the upstream extensions are misaligned with the original arch here, possibly an indication of slippage during construction, or sinkage of the original structure. The eastern end consists of the buried millrace arch, with the lower part of the old millwheel housings forming the river wall downstream of the bridge.

General

The upriver extensions are constructed as two separate entities, with no obvious ties to the original stonework on the arches we examined. The first is 7.75ft (93in.) wide and the second, or upriver extension, is on average 11ft (c.122in.) wide above the 'batter' line of the upstream façade. They are built mostly of randomly laid, roughly coursed stones, some undressed: the courses of old and new sections are unaligned, with pronounced gaps between each extension and the original bridge. The ringstones are noticeably different, those on the upriver façade being constructed from dressed stone, oblong blocks with clearly defined keystones, while these aspects are less pronounced on the downriver rings. The cutwaters are smaller also, being more rounded than triangular, with conical cappings terminating at the bottom of the spandrel walls below the arch crowns. The spandrels and parapet walls on the extension are built of more cleanly dressed stone than those downstream, which appear to be more randomly laid than evenly coursed. The contemporary bridge is 36ft 1in. wide, face to face (excluding the batter) with no pedestrian refuges in the parapets. The original bridge was on average 17ft 4in. wide and carried a c.14ft wide road across the Boyne, a slightly narrower bridge than Bective and Stackallan Bridges. The free waterway width/hydraulic capacity of the contemporary bridge is c.101ft; effectively increased during the post 1968 drainage scheme, when the pillars were underpinned and the riverbed deepened. During our sojourn beneath No. 3 arch, I noticed a large zig-zag diagonal crack in the intrados stonework – running from the foundation, through the arch springers and upwards across the crown to the opposite side… and wondered at its cause.[12]

Left: Hopper Rennicks examines uneven joint in upriver extension of 'the New Br.'
and, right, the crack on Jan. 4th 2015

Exiting the arch, we entered the short, broad river reach between the
two ancient bridges of Navan, the last few metres of the Boyne before it
coalesces with the Blackwater, their combined stream then turning to flow
due east towards the Irish Sea. This section was widened during the post
1968 drainage scheme; with the wooded island dug out and piled upon the
bank as heaps of spoil. On the eastern riverbank, and built up close to the
downstream façade of 'the New Bridge,' stands a four storey stone building,
with a c.14ft diameter (now decorative) metal waterwheel overhanging the
filled-in millrace from its riverside frontage. This is now an apartment block
(River Mill View), which in my youth was part of William, 'the Bard Welsh's/
Walsh's,' mill, and sole surviving section of the large complex of mills once
known as Athlumney Boyne Mills.

Athlumney Boyne Mills (02 of)
Athlumney Townland: (1837) corn mill & flour mill) – (G.V.1854) Lot
29 (2) flour & corn-mills, offices and yard, leased by George Mullen from
Sir Wm. M. Somerville Bart @ R.V. £185. The valuation records also that
Patrick Delany had some attached buildings leased from Sir Wm. Somerville
– Slater's 1846 directory records Laurence and Patrick Delany as millers at
Athlumney Mills. N.B., as noted, this was a complex comprising at least two

mills, one fronting the river (the contemporary stone building), which had two wheel-houses originally, and was perhaps powered by a pair of undershot waterwheels, hung in series formation, driven by a millrace flowing within an enclosed breakwater. The second mill was located to the rear, in the space between the riverside mill and the canal basin just below Somerville Bridge. This mill was likely powered also by the millrace sourced from the eastern branch of the 'V' weir, which passed thr ough 'the Rack' and beneath the now buried No. 8 arch of 'the New Bridge.' The headrace was probably covered over downstream of the bridge, as it is not shown on the maps, but the tailrace from this mill is depicted on the 1837 OS map, falling into the Boyne below the confluence and immediately above Ruxton's Lock. From about the late 1930s or early 1940s, Bard Welsh/Walsh operated a furniture manufacturing business from these premises for many years; the nickname 'Bard' I believe originated from his penchant for humming the famous song '*the Bard of Armagh.*' In the 1970s, many of the buildings were used by Mullagh Co. Op. as a Hardware Shop and Builder's Providers. During the Celtic Tiger era, most of the site was cleared and several apartment blocks erected thereon, with the stone building converted to residential flats.

Entering the confluence, we turned up the River Blackwater to pass beneath Poolboy Bridge. The strong current tearing through the confines of the ancient arches prevented us making the full passage to the upstream side, so Hopper and the lads held the RIB in position while we inspected the underside of the arch. This bridge, too, was widened twice, but, unlike 'the New Bridge,' by extensions added to both the upstream and downstream sides of the structure.

Observing the mass of brownish water mingling with the Boyne and forming a whirlpool at the confluence, I wondered at the origins of this mighty torrent. A close study of the OS maps reveals that the River Blackwater, known as the Kells Blackwater, rises in County Cavan, to where the reader is now invited to join in a brief trip to its meeting with the Boyne. For convenience, the Blackwater is divided into two distinct sections i.e. the Upper Reaches from the headwaters to Lough Ramor (Lough Muinreamhar), and the Lower Reaches from Virginia to Navan.[13]

Aerial view from the mid 1960s showing the weir, the New Bridge and the surviving mills.

1. Confluence
2. Approx site of second Athlumney Boyne Mill
3. Blocked arch / culvert at basin
4. No.1 arch New Bridge
5. No. 8 arch New Bridge
6. George Mullen's Mill 1854 / Bard Walsh
7. Somerville Bridge
8. Nuns' Yard
9. The 'Rack'
10. Foundry Shed
11. Old HEP Station
12. James Mullen's Mill 1854
13. Western weir / millrace
14. The Salmon Leap
15. Eastern weir / millrace
16. Dry dock / swimming pool
17. Metge's Lock

River Blackwater Upper Reaches (Rampart/Murmod River).

The river takes its first rise from a series of rills near the townland of Crossmakeelan, north-east of Baileborough in County Cavan. These coalesce in Bracklin Townland to form the initial source stream; which flows south-westwards to Laurel Mount, and receives a tributary sourced from the three Gartnaneane Loughs, consisting of North Lough, South Lough (now dry) and the most easterly of the group Gartnaneane (Gortnaneane) Lough. The tiny Blind Lough, once part of this group, seems to have dried up by 1911, and now appears to be part of a swampy field.

From here it flows south-westwards past Altagreenan Fort and onwards to Lear Bridge, then northwards to fall into Castle Lough. From the north-west, this lake also receives the waters of three interconnected lakes, namely, a tiny lake also named Blind Lough, which flows to the largest lake in the group named Skeag Lough Upper; this in turn flows to Drumkeery Lough, the entire system then emptying into Castle Lough via a small tributary.

Outflowing from the southern sector of Castle Lough, the river passes to the east of Baileborough Castle, and receives the waters of Bog Lough before turning in a series of great loops to flow through Crocknahattin Townland. Two corn mills, a weir and a series of millraces are depicted here on the 1837 OS Map.

Continuing onwards in two great loops, the river flows through Spear Vale, to fall into Parker's Lough. On this stretch a bleach mill appears on the 1837 map, whereas the 1911 map shows a large building named Vale Mills (disused) and a flax mill. Both located in the townland of Galbolie, close by Galbolie Lough, which empties into the Blackwater source stream also.

Outflowing from Parker's Lough, the river continues onwards and passes beneath Parker's Bridge, then flows on past a brickyard to Galloncurra Lough. Flowing southwards from here, the river continues on to Carricknaveagh Townland, where it turns to flow due north and power a corn and tuck mill in Cleffin Townland; depicted as a corn mill only on the 1911 map. From Cleffin, the river flows in a great loop to Killinkere Bridge, and then turns north-westwards to fall into Gallon Lough.

Outfalling southwards from this lake, the river continues beneath Stranaquery Bridge, receives the outflow from Lisgrea Lough and continues through Murmod Townland. Here the 1837 OS map depicts three eel weirs, a corn mill (recorded as a flax mill in 1911), Tobar Finn and Finn McCool's (Finn McCumhail) House. Below Murmod Bridge, the developing river flows south-eastwards to Virginia, and falls into Lough Ramor close by the old ferry landing stage.

Lists compiled using data gleaned from the 1837/1911 OS maps and Griffith's 1850s valuation:

Upper Blackwater Mills in County Cavan (08 of).

No. 01 – Crocknahattin Townland

(1837) two corn mills – (G.V.1854) Lot 23 house, offices, corn-mills, kilns and land totalling 29.75 acres, leased by Samuel Simpson & Son from Sir John Young Bart @ R.V. £50-10s.

No. 02 – Galbolie Townland (Spear Vale)

(G.V. 1854) flax mill – bleaching mill, offices and land totalling 10.25 acres held in fee by Sir John Young Bart @ R.V. £21-10s. N.B., the 1911 OS map shows a large building named Vale Mills and marked as disused, with a flax mill further downstream near Vale House.

No. 03 – Cleffin Townland

(1837) corn mill/tuck mill (G.V. 1854) corn & tuck mill, offices and land totalling circa 2 acres, leased by Andrew McLlwain from Lord Farnham @ R.V. £8. N.B., corn mill only shown on 1911 map.

No. 04 – Greaghadossan Townland: 1911 OS map

flax mill shown on a small tributary river, but not recorded on 1837 map or Griffith's 1854 valuation.

No. 05 – Murmod Townland

(1837) corn mill & tuck mill (G.V. 1854) Miller's House/Herd's House & 2.76 acres, leased by James and Michael Bride from Joseph Story @ R.V. £2-10s for each property.

No. 06 & 07 – on Park River in Correagh Glebe

(1837) corn mill (G.V. 1854) Lot 15c corn-mill, Miller's & kiln-man's houses and land totalling 3 acres, leased by Bernard and Edward Brady from Rev. Henry Hunt @ R.V. £6. --- in Fintawan Townland (1837) corn mill (G.V. 1854) house, offices, corn-mill and land totalling 31.25 acres, leased by Matthew Brady from Lord Fulham @ R.V. £20.

No. 08 – on Bureen River in Ballaghanea Townland (1837) corn mill & tuck mill (G.V. 1854) Lot 27a: house, offices, corn-mill/ tuck mill and land totalling 35.76 acres, leased by Walter Tormey from the Reps. of the Marquis of Headfort @ R.V. £31.

River Blackwater Lower Reaches (Lough Ramor to Navan).

The river outflows from Lough Ramor at the Nine Eye Bridge, and is first named River Blackwater on the OS maps at the mereing of Ryefield and Stramatt Townlands. In Ryefield, a tributary river (known as the Cross River) powered a corn mill at Ryefield Cross Roads just upstream from its confluence with the Blackwater. Flowing on eastwards to Daly's Bridge, the Blackwater powered a corn mill upstream of this bridge in Pottlereagh Townland, and continues on past the Motte of Derver and over several eel weirs to Castlepole Townland, to power a tuck & a corn mill in this townland.

The Blackwater forms a fishing hole known as Sheep(s) Hole, then flows beneath Claven's Bridge[14] and onwards past a corn and flour mill (at Ballintubber House) to the ancient Mabe's Bridge. From here the river continues to Cakestown Glebe; where the 1837 OS map depicts an 'old corn

Headforth Bridge. Alan Russell

mill' immediately above Maudlin Bridge. Passing beneath this ancient bridge, the Blackwater flows on to Headfort Demesne south-east of Kells; formed a series of ornamental lakes and flowed beneath Headfort Bridge, to depart the demesne in a south-easterly direction.

At Bloomsbury, the Blackwater receives the Moynalty River, named variously the Baroro (Bororo) and Owenroe River from its sources near the townlands of Tanderagee, Lisnalea and Lurganbane in County Cavan. On the OS maps the river is named the Barora from the source to Mullagh Bridge, and from there to the Boyne is named the Owenroe or Moynalty River.

Mills, weirs and heritage features on the Barora/Moynalty River:

No. 01 – Lisnalea Townland, Co. Cavan
(1852 & 1911 maps) Steam Flax Mill – Not recorded on Griffith's.

No. 02 – Cormeen Townland, Co Meath
Corn Mill – Tuck Mill (Cloggagh Mills 1911)   near Cloggagh Lough. Griffith's – leased by Patrick Clinton from Kemp Sturgeon, house, offs, mill, kiln & 100 acres @ R.V. £70.

No. 03 – Greaghnadarragh Townland, Co Cavan
Corn Mill (1837 only, not recorded on Griffith's).

No. 04 – Skearke Br. Three Eel Weirs.

No. 05 – Skearke Townland Co. Meath
Annesbrook Corn Mill (on 1837 map) – Annesbrook Corn & Saw Mill (on 1911 map) – Overshot wheel powered by a small tributary stream via millpond. Griffith's – leased by John Rathburn from Joseph Rathburn, house, offs, mill, kiln & stores, including 79acres – 3r – 10p @ R.V. £85-10s.

No. 06 – Mullagh Br. – Fish Weir.

No. 07 – Old millrace upstream of Moynalty Village
(1837 only).

No. 08 – Donore Townland Co. Meath
Old sheep fold (1837 only).

No. 09 – Newtown Townland, Co. Meath
Two Fish Weirs & Eel Weir + Ornamental Lake.

No. 10 – Balreask Steps
(1837) & Eel Weir at Fyanstown Br.

Passing on south-eastwards and beneath Bloomsbury Bridge, the Blackwater continues to Teltown and powered Tallon's Corn Mill (or Martry Mill), one of the few remaining operational watermills in Ireland. Passing over the site of Teltown Ford, the river once powered another corn mill in Teltown immediately below the ford. Continuing onwards in a series of tortuous loops, an 'old mill' is depicted on the right bank in Tankardstown just upstream from Donaghpatrick Bridge.

Martry Mill gearing

Clockwise from top: Mortimer's/ Elliot's Mill;
Martry Mill undeshot wheel;
Runner stone from Upper Kilcarn Mill stored at Martry Mill.

Flowing south-eastwards to Tatestown, the Blackwater receives the Yellow River; a tributary of which once powered a corn mill at Wilkenstown. Passing south-eastwards, the river flows by the ruins of Liscartan Castle on the right bank and then past Ratholdran Castle on the left bank, opposite which it once powered Liscartan Corn Mill. On the descent from here to the confluence with the Boyne in Navan, the Blackwater fell about 24ft, powering a series of six mills and two distilleries.

Lower Blackwater Mills (10 of) – Lough Ramor to Liscartan.

No. 01 – Ryefield Townland, Co. Cavan – Ryefield Cross Mill 1837) corn mill – (G.V. 1854) house, offices, corn-mill and land totalling circa 68.6 acres, leased by Hugh Porter from trustees of Marquis of Headfort @ R.V. £58-10s.

No. 02 – Pottlereagh Townland Co. Meath – Daly's Cross Mill (1837) corn mill – (G.V. 1854) house, offices, corn-mill and land totalling circa 100.5 acres, leased by John Daly from James Naper @ R.V. £128.

No. 03 – Castlepole Townland: (1837) corn mill/tuck mill – (G.V.1854) house, offices, corn-mill & tuck mill and land totalling 100 acres, leased by Henry Dyas from James W.L. Naper @ R.V. £148. N.B., this site is depicted on the 1911 map as corn mill only.

No. 04 – Townparks Townland (at Ballintubber House 1911 map) (1837) Flour & corn mill – (G.V. 1854) Lot 1a - house, offices, corn-mill, kiln & land totalling 74.75 acres, leased by Thomas Farrelly from the Marquis of Headfort @ R.V. £100. This mill is shown as disused on the 1911 map.

No. 05 – Cakestown Glebe: (1854) the 'old corn mill' shown here on the 1837 OS map is not listed on Griffith's 1854 Valuation.

No. 06 – Martry Mill in Martry Townland: (1837) corn mill – (G.V. 1854) corn-mill, offices and land totalling 6.76 acres, leased by William Welles from John Tisdall @ R.V. £22-15s. N.B., the adjacent miller's house is not included in the valuation. I believe the Tallon family took over the lease from a man named McDonagh in 1859, and have operated the premises ever since. In contemporary times, the mill is powered by a waterwheel supplemented by an electric/hydraulic power drive, and produces flour and oatmeal.[15] The present miller, James Tallon, is descended from a long lineage of corn millers; therefore, has many tales for interested tourists visiting this unique site. For more details of this mill and the two millstones that <u>would not</u> grind corn at Martry, when taken here from the mill at Upper Kilcarn, see *Where Toll Roads Meet*, pp. 51 to 53.

No. 07 – Teltown Townland

on the north-side of the river at the site of the Teltown Ford: (1837) corn mill – (G.V.1854) corn-mill, offices and land totalling 3.6 acres, leased by John Kellet from Louise Garnett @ R.V. £11.[16] N.B., Larkin's map depicts a road crossing the Blackwater here by a ford, and linking the Navan/Kells road to the road from Donaghpatrick Br. to Teltown.

No. 08 – Tankardstown Townland

on the south-side of the river, 'old mill' on 1837 OS map: no mill recorded on Griffith's valuation of 1854.[17]

No. 09 – Liscartan Townland:

(1837) corn mill – (G.V.1854 *In Chancery*) house, offices, corn-mill and land totalling 4.6 acres, leased by James Cullen from Thomas Gerrard @ R.V. £84. According to Ellison, this mill was owned by Lord Cadogan.

No. 10 – Wilkinstown Mill – on a tributary of the Yellow River

(1837) corn mill – (G.V. 1854) corn-mill, offices and land totalling 28.6 acres, leased from Sir William Somerville Bart by Thomas Fegan @ R.V. £136.

Navan's Blackwater Mills (06 of).

No. 01 – Mill Brook – Abbeyland South:

1837 OS map – Paper & Frieze Manufactory – (1854 Valuation): Lot 2a offices and land totalling 3.6 acres, leased by James Forde from Earl of Essex @ R.V. £6-15s. N.B., although local tradition holds that James Forde manufactured woollen goods at Mill Brook from 1842 until 1866, when it was taken over and expanded by the Clayton Bros. of Yorkshire, the low valuation is a good indicator that there was no mill operating here in 1854 – perhaps this is a confusion with Forde's Wool Mill at the Mollies further downstream (ref. mill No. 3 below).[18]

Thomson, on page 51 of his statistical survey of 1802 says of this mill: Mr McDonnell has also erected on this river (immediately above Mr. Fay) a paper mill, which is worked to very great extent; in it are manufactured all kinds of brown and lapping paper,[19] paper for hanging, and some letter paper; but the demand in the country being chiefly for the coarser kinds, they are, consequently, the principal sort manufactured. He has also erected machinery for stamping paper-hangings, & c.; and in several branches of his manufactory, from the gathering of the raw materials of which the paper is composed, to the delivery of that paper when manufactured, he employs a number of persons of all ages and sexes. (sic)

The earliest cartographic reference to a mill on this site is on Thomas William's 1756 sketch map of Navan town.

No. 02 – Fay's/Skelly's Mill

In grounds of Blackwater House – Abbeyland South: 1837 OS map – Distillery & Flour Mill, in ruins – (1854 valuation): Lot 4a house, corn-mills, offices and land totalling 36.2 acres, leased by R.H. & J. Skelly from Earl of Essex @ R.V. £135. N.B., according to a plaque on the building, dated 1783, these mills were operated in earlier times by Messers. Conelly/ Clark & Fay – they later became Spicer's Blackwater Mills – Slater's 1870 directory lists John Spicer as miller at Blackwater and Boyne Mills, while the same directory in 1881 names John & Joseph Spicer as millers at Blackwater and Boyne Mills. Thomson's Statistical Survey of 1802 comments that this mill, in point of storage, had perhaps the greatest such capacity in Ireland, and that had it commanded a greater water head, "could work machinery to any extent."

The survey records the following of Fay's flour milling operation: this concern forms an oblong hollow square, two sides of which are 216 feet each, and the other two are 157 feet from out to out, enclosing a space 167 feet by 88. In this space Mr. Fay has erected a double kiln 80 feet by 24. This square consists of a flour-mill, corn stores, malt-house, brewery, and distillery; that side running parallel to the river has seven lofts and the other three sides have five lofts each. (sic)[20]

The earliest cartographic reference to a mill on this site is on Thomas William's 1756 sketch map of Navan town.

No. 03 – Forde's Mill

Abbeyland South, at 'the Mollies' – upstream from Cavalry Barracks/former site of Navan Abbey: 1837 OS map – corn mill – (1854 valuation): Lot 3a wool mill, offices, gate lodge, yard and land totalling 3.1 acres, leased by James Forde from R.H. & J. Skelly @ R.V. £45.

The earliest cartographic reference to a mill on this site is on Thomas William's 1756 sketch map of Navan town.

No. 04 – Bradley's Mill

Abbeyland South – some mystery attaches to this mill, as it is not depicted graphically on the 1837 or clearly on 1854 OS maps – a caption on the site, reading Mill & Distillery, applies to Morgan's Mill across the river. It is recorded as Disused Corn Mill on 1911 map – (1854 valuation): Lot 1 house, corn-mill, offices and garden 1 acre 1 rood 30 perches, leased by Patrick Bradley from Earl of Essex @ R.V. £50. Slater's 1870 directory lists Bernard Bradley of Watergate St. as a miller. Part of this mill was used as a furniture factory by Moran Bros. in the 1960/70s – the mill and its landmark brick chimney were demolished c.1982 to make way for the Inner Relief Road.

No. 05 & 06 – Morgan's two Blackwater Mills.

Two sets of mills were located upon a narrow salient of the Blackcastle Demesne which extended above Poolboy Bridge on the northern riverbank, and included the Mill Lane and Navan Gas Works.[21] Like Bradley's Mill in Abbeyland South, some confusion of location exists here also, as the mills are depicted differently on the various maps, as follows: 1837 & 1854 maps, upper mill opposite the old Cavalry Barracks is shown as 'mill in ruin' – lower mill is depicted graphically but is named by the caption Mill & Distillery displayed on Bradley's Mill site across the river. – 1911 map depicts the upper mill as Saw Mill and the lower mill is shown as a Corn Mill. Griffith's 1854 valuation records the following of this site: flour mill, corn & scutch mill (Gallen's in 1919), offices and land totalling 2.6 acres, leased by William Morgan from trustees of Richard Fitzherbert @ R.V. £125.[22] Slater's 1870 directory lists a William Morgan as miller of 'Poolboy Mill, while the 1881 directory records a William Morgan as Miller of 'Blackcastle Mills,' these were obviously the same mills listed under different place names.

The site of Poolboy Bridge is the oldest recorded bridge location in Navan, with a bridge reputedly spanning the River Blackwater hereabouts from the Early Norman Period circa 1200 AD. The present structure contains elements from three periods; the original centre section perhaps dating from the 14th century or earlier, with the two extensions being added in the early 18th and early 19th centuries. This bridge was known variously as Navan Bridge (on 1656 Down Survey map), Swyne Bridge (because of the pig market beside the Bridewell) and Poolbwee/Poolboy Bridge, this name reputedly deriving from yellow-tinted, muddied water pouring downslope from Flower (Flour) Hill.

In earlier times, the bridge carried the 'great road to the north' (now the R162) via Nobber and Cootehill. This road forked at the contemporary 'Round O,' and formed the northern route (now the N51) alongside the Boyne to Drogheda via Slane, where it linked to 'the Great North Road' from Dublin to Derry (now the N2). During its turnpike era, the section from Navan to Nobber was tolled c.1735 and remained as a turnpike road until discontinued as such by Act of Parliament c.1767 – the turnpike or tollhouse for this section was sited at the 'Round O' Bar.

ॐ

Some technical details of Poolboy Bridge.

General structural features

Apart from varying dimensions and cutwaters, many features of this bridge appear to be remarkably similar to those of the nearby 'New Bridge,' and Poolboy may indeed have been used as a model for the later bridge on the Boyne. The contemporary structure is comprised of seven arches, with similar segmental profiles on six of the upriver and downriver facades. Six arches span c.16/18ft and the interconnecting pillars vary also in width. The seventh arch, abutting the Blackcastle riverbank, conducted the tailrace from Morgan's Blackcastle Mills beneath the road and has two completely different profiles – the upriver arch is of very low rise, multi-segmented (elliptical) profile with vertical riser walls, while the downriver arch has a segmental

Poolboy Bridge

profile similar to that of the main river arches. This arch exits the bridge through a wing wall that once formed the riverside gable of the old Militia Stores, but now supports a shop/apartment block, towering above the ancient structure. Near the north-eastern end, the 1911 OS map depicts a breakwater running for about 50 yards downriver from the bridge pillar separating the fourth and fifth arches; although this structure has disappeared entirely, it was likely part of the Boyne Navigation works at Blackcastle Quay. The present bridge is circa 35ft wide, face to face, which, with the exclusion of the two extensions, indicates that the original structure was similar in width to the unaltered New Bridge, and carried a road of similar size (c. 15ft between parapets) across the Blackwater.

Underneath the Arches.

The upriver and downriver extensions are constructed as two separate entities, with no obvious ties to the original stonework; the upstream is about 7ft wide and the downstream circa 8ft, both are built mostly of randomly laid, roughly coursed stones, some undressed. The courses of old and new sections are unaligned, with pronounced gaps between each extension and the original bridge. The soffits (intrados) of the original central spans, as viewed on inspection, are plastered, thereby obscuring the stonework; which appears to be of much rougher construction than that of the two extensions. Several downstream extension arches have a pair of corbel stones protruding from the vertical risers, about midway between mean water level and the arch springers. The ringstones are different also, with those on the upriver façade of an older vintage and less pronounced, the downriver rings are constructed from dressed stone, oblong blocks, some with more clearly defined keystones. The free waterway/hydraulic capacity of the bridge effectively increased during the post 1968 drainage scheme, when the pillars were underpinned with concrete and the riverbed deepened.

Downstream extension.

During research of the Grand Jury query and presentment books, I found the following entry, which may apply to the downstream extension of Poolboy Bridge. While difficult to decipher exactly due to faded text, the following was included in the 1801 Summer Assizes record of 'the County at Large' presentment book:

> Item 129 – Wher £310-10s-18d bal. of £391-6s-2d & £19-11s-4d wages raised as before and acc. for in Old 2u (?) 315 acc. for by Tm. Ruxton Esq. Cha. Drake Dillon Esq. Rev: D : Hamilton Esq. Chs. Cusach Esq. Chas. Morgan Edw. Morgan Thom. Everard Esq. to widen & repr. the bridge of Pulboy over the Black Water at Navan road from Navan to Drogheda. (sic)

The date of the above record suggests this extension being added to the bridge in c.1800, concurrent with completion of the Upper Boyne Navigation to Navan and development of Blackcastle Quay. The extension is constructed in a style contrasting to the upriver version, the stonework dressed to a finer quality, with parapets and spandrels more evenly coursed. The cutwaters are also more decorative, being of trapezoidal profile and ascending to parapet level, forming oblong, shallow pedestrian refuges, an unusual and attractive feature.

Top: 'the New Br. from Poolboy. Ludlow St. (Spicers) Mill to left. - The thatched building to the right was probably part of the old tannery. *c.* 1890s.
Below: Ruxton's Bridge from the confluence - *c.* 1890s

Upriver bridge extension.

No record of this bridge extension was found in the Grand Jury records to date. While this could mean the record has been lost, it is more likely that the extension predates these records, diligently maintained only from c.1760 onwards. The extension perhaps was built concurrent with construction of the new military barracks on the site of the old Navan Abbey in 1717, to enhance the supply line from the Port of Drogheda before the advent of the Boyne Navigation, almost a century later. The stonework of this extension is obviously older than that of downstream, and the cutwaters built to the triangular profiled design – these rise to parapet level and incorporate pedestrian refuges within the parapet walls.

Poolboy Bridge is an elegant structure, capable of enhancing any landscape; however, some aspects, such as the slovenly laid plastic drain pipes protruding from jagged holes, cut by 'tradesmen' through its ancient stonework, the silted up and debris-blocked arches etc., provide further evidence of our inability to cherish such heritage features.

Turning away from this medieval bridge, we passed back through the confluence and on downriver into the teeth of the howling wind and rain towards Ruxton's Lock; where we pulled the boat ashore, thus ending this leg of a memorable trip on the River Boyne.

❧

A snapshot of Navan before, during and after the Great Hunger.
(and its echoes in contemporary times)

This, the largest town in County Meath, held various titles over the years including Navan, An Uaimh, Nuachongbhail and was known in times past by several other names. The variants of this name having exercised the minds of many historians, and caused much contention amongst learned scholars over the years, I will not add to the confusion. Suffice to say, though born and raised in Dowdstown, I am honoured to regard it as my old home town of Navan, where I attended school and spent my youth before departing on many global rambles.

Navan developed in phases from a small, medieval town controlling the confluence of Boyne and Blackwater, through a period as a walled Anglo Norman market town with a Royal Charter, Tholsel or Market House, a Portreeve and Corporation, to a thriving centre of industry and commerce, with corn, tuck and flax mills, a paper mill and three distilleries. Post famine decline; however, brought much poverty to the area until it was rejuvenated with the birth of the furniture trade in the late 19th century. A detailed history of the town is beyond the scope of this work, but for those wishing to learn more about this ancient place, I recommend the journals of the Navan and District Historical Society, entitled *Navan – Its people and its past*.

I note with disappointment that in his book, entitled *The Beauties of the Boyne and Blackwater* (1849), Sir William Wilde mentions very little about

Navan or its people, in fact, although he travelled the land in 1847-1848 in the midst of the Great Hunger, apart from some footnotes, little or no mention is made of this cataclysmic event or its disastrous consequences for the peasantry of the era. In his brief discussion of the town; however, he writes the following about Navan:

> The inhabitants, like those of most towns through which a river flows, have turned their backs upon the stream, scarcely a glimpse of which can be seen from any of its narrow streets. There is here a picturesque weir, and immediately below the bridge which crosses it on the Drogheda road, the Boyne receives the Blackwater, which is there nearly as large as the stream into which it flows. There are also two valuable and extensive flour mills at this point.

His reticence about the plight of the cottiers, peasantry and townspeople is perhaps explained by the following:

> As we only engaged to present our readers with scenes of beauty or of interest, we cannot be expected to devote much of our space to a description of Navan! – a dirty, ill built, straggling collection of houses, boasting the honour of having been half a county-town. (sic)

Referring to the statement that the people of the town 'have turned their backs upon the stream,' the omission of the equally valid corollary that: 'they did so to use the river for powering their essential industry,' is astonishing for such a learned man as Sir William. This omission is especially noteworthy when one considers that in those long gone so-called primitive times, at least twelve major mills, three distilleries and other smaller enterprises extracted hydro power (nowadays the elusive green energy) from the Boyne and Blackwater within a one kilometre radius of Navan. How our so-called *greens* of contemporary times would drool at the prospects of using all that *sustainable, renewable energy*. And perhaps gnash their teeth in frustration at the thought of it being wasted nowadays, because blinkered officialdom demolished the 'picturesque weir' (the 'V' weir) mentioned by Wilde, in addition to several other weirs in the region.

Top: Murphy's Distillery *c.* 1890s
Below: 'the New Br.' - the two Ludlow St. Mills to L. One Athlumney Boyne Mill to R. -
Bradley's Mill in mid-background. A Boyne Lighter, the dry-dock & Metge's Lock in mid-pic.
*c.*1903

An account of any area in Ireland, purporting to represent a true picture
of the place during the 19th century, is incomplete without any mention of
the Great Hunger, which decimated the country between the years 1846 and
1850.

Several years earlier, in 1844, Mr and Mrs Hall travelled the land and
scribed a book entitled *Hall's Ireland* – but, unlike Sir William, they were
not 'shy' about writing of the people or the plight of the peasantry in County
Meath. As these writings were a grim harbinger of the horrific famine about
to engulf the lower classes, I consider a lengthy extract therefrom is a timely
reminder of this poorly recorded, darker aspect of our relatively recent history:

There is, indeed, no part of Ireland where an Englishman will find himself so completely at home, for; added to great natural beauty, he sees on all sides the beneficial results of careful cultivation, and marks in every direction the ordinary consequences of industry directed by science; while the poverty and wretchedness that are everywhere forced upon his attention is here seldom perceptible; and "the clamorous voice of woe" rarely "intrudes upon the ear." Much of this apparently prosperous character is, however, hollow and unsubstantial: the large farmers are indeed wealthy, but of small farmers there are few or none; the policy of the "graziers" has for a long time been to devote the produce of the soil to the raising of cattle; and the clearing of estates" in Meath has, therefore, been proceeding at a disastrous rate. We quote the words of a common labourer with whom we conversed on the subject – "The land is given over to the beasts of the field!" The small plots of ground are "wanted for the cattle;" and as the cabins cannot exist without them, they are in rapid course of removal. The consequence is, that although misery is not to be encountered upon highways, or adjacent to pleasant meadows, the towns into which the poor have been driven are thronged with squalid countenances; starvation stalks at noon-day through their streets; and perhaps in no part of the world could be found so much wretchedness "huddled" together into an equal space; as the tourist may note in the single town of Navan. All about the suburbs, the cabins are filthy to the last degree; a very large number of them have no other outlets for the smoke but the broken windows; the roofs of many have partly fallen in; and we examined several from which every available piece of wood had been taken for firing, at periods when the pressure of immediate want had rendered the unhappy inmates indifferent to the future. We entered some of these hovels – within a dozen steps, be it remembered, of the centre of a town, and not hidden by distance and obscurity from the sight of sympathising humanity – and were shocked to find their condition wretched almost beyond conception, and certainly beyond credibility. The scene appalled us the more because of the lovely and plentiful land we had previously passed through; the fat cattle feeding on pasture so fresh and green; the huge stacks; the full barns; the comfortable houses, midway between mansions and farmsteads – the air of luxury, indeed, that pervaded every object within our ken! It was a sad contrast; to be witnessed without heartache only by those who have become familiar with it, and have learned indifference from habit. (sic)

In the context of the Great Hunger 1845-1850, Grand Jury records show that under the prevailing system, pre-famine public works were financed by the baronies and not by crown or government grants. The money for these works being extracted from tenants by means of the County and Barony cess or tax, the poorer cottiers; therefore, had fewer resources available for food. The population increased and social conditions deteriorated greatly during this period, while the County and Barony cess increased six fold… was this merely a coincidence? Although many other factors contributed to the disastrous famine, the relentless increase of the cess had a huge negative impact upon the largely agrarian population; many being forced into dependence on a single-crop diet – the humble spud or potato. History records the dire effects of the Great Hunger consequent to the persistent failure of this crop, and the impact these had on the Irish psyche: the horror and deep sense of loss remaining indelibly imprinted upon the national conscience and causing a long-term schism in Anglo-Irish relations.

Referring to the 'clearing of the estates' in County Meath, which had a large bearing on the causes and consequences of the famine throughout the county: these clearances drove cottiers off their small holdings and into the towns and appalling living conditions, described so vividly by Mr and Mrs Hall. Were these to occur nowadays, they would evoke international outrage, with an ensuing worldwide clamour to drag the perpetrators before an international tribunal; there to be charged with crimes, including genocide and 'ethnic cleansing.' But in those dark times, the lower orders had no recourse to such justice; being dependant entirely on their own meagre resources and the magnanimity of the ruling elite – many of whom, in fairness, were equally horrified at the catastrophe unfolding in their midst and responded with great generosity.

But others took advantage of the situation by cynically accelerating 'cleansing' their estates of the now unwanted 'cottier' tenants, to make way for the more profitable bovines and horses. These landlords oftentimes used brutal and heavy handed methods on the starving cottiers; the Sherriff and his Bailiffs being guarded by well-fed members of the local militia and constabulary, while they demolished the humble cabins with sledgehammer and battering ram.

This dark period of our history has never been addressed properly, recorded or dealt with on a national level; therefore, no healing process occurred to remove the resultant sense of horror from our national psyche. Even during my early childhood in the 1940s, I was aware of this dark event, resonating as it did down through the generations; in relative terms it was still a recent event almost within living memory.

It is somewhat ironic that the former Russell Arms Hotel and Bedford Place in Navan were named in honour of a prime minister whose government oversaw the near total extinction of Irish Cottiers by starvation and disease during the Great Hunger. 'Lord' John Russell, Duke of Bedford, was successor to Robert Peel in 1846 and held office until 1852; which period included the worst years of the famine. Though Russell was not a member of the Meath gentry, and indeed rarely visited Ireland, he inherited much of the Ludlow estates in the vicinity of Navan, from a member of that dynasty who died without issue.[23]

The above excerpt from the Hall's account of pre famine Navan, makes for disturbing reading in these uneasy times of the post Celtic Tiger economic collapse; it reflects poorly upon the ruling elite of the period. Many of these were absentee landlords, especially following the *Act of Union* in 1801; which amongst many other ill effects, removed whatever sovereignty we had at the time, effectively disenfranchised the lower orders and transferred power to the Mother Parliament in London.

All of the above bear an uncanny resemblance to the events of contemporary times from circa 2008, when our 'Republic' likewise lost its sovereignty. This time to our European 'friends,' and the lower orders of our society once again bore the brunt of the storm following the failure of our *own* incumbent ruling elite. The same elite decreed that the lower orders would carry the burden of official ineptitude and systemic failures, by imposing *Local Property Tax,* in my opinion a most unfair tax upon the family home and family – not on property; followed quickly by the unfolding debacle of the 'water tax.'

Our rulers seem to have a strange inability to learn from history, as these taxes originate from the same mindset that spawned 'the *cess*,' 'fire-hearth tax' and 'window tax,' imposed in the 1600s. It is difficult to understand; therefore, how our new taxes are deemed to be 'progressive,' as they mimic closely a most regressive and punitive system from long ago. These earlier taxes, in their initial form, were borne by property owners, but changed by the ruling elite's influence in Parliament, to be paid only by the property *occupier* – the same as our 'new' taxes. This caused massive deprivation to the lower orders; that comprised the vast majority of the population in both urban and agrarian areas. As a consequence, the word *cess* was uttered like a curse that passed down through the generations, because I heard the old folk using it many times during my youth e.g. "bad *cess* to your so-and-so."

One wonders what curse future generations will apply to the present situation and how their historians will record this dark period of our history, for which, this time blame cannot be attached to the usual suspects, "the bloody English."

ENDNOTES

1   A rectangular profiled brick chimney once stood in the former distillery yard immediately
    downstream of the viaduct. This stack rose above the bridge parapet and remained a feature
    on the landscape until demolished in relatively recent times. Although some mystery at-
    taches to its later usage, it perhaps originated as part of Murphy's Distillery, located on this
    site before the advent of the railway. I believe it may have been part of a later steam powered
    pumping system from the 1850s to around 1900, supplying water from the Boyne to the
    nearby GNR Railway Station for the steam locomotives. A fountain (known by some as
    'the Spa') is located upstream, integral with the bridge inter-arch pillar on the river side of
    the old Dublin Road. There are differing opinions as to the water source for this outlet, but
    tradition holds that during construction of the viaduct, the water was piped by the Railway
    Co. from a spring in Athlumney (or Dillonsland), as drinking water for the residents of
    Academy St.

2   A confusion of site-location may exist here, perhaps explained by the following, somewhat
    unclear reference on P.135 of Wilde's 1849 book (2nd Edition): "While these pages were
    passing through the press, a most extensive souterrain was discovered in the cutting of the
    railway on the western bank, just under Athlumney, consisting of a straight passage fifty-
    three feet and a-half long, eight broad, and six high, branching into two smaller passages
    which run off at right angles from it, and ending in two circular bee-hive shaped chambers,
    precisely similar to those at Clady, together forming the figure of a cross. The walls of this
    great cave having risen to a height of four feet and a half, they then begin to decline, and
    the roof is formed by enormous flag-stones laid across; these stones are all rough and un-
    dressed, and are placed together without mortar or cement. This extensive cave, so recently
    discovered, will form an additional object of attraction to tourists. A few bones of oxen
    are all that have yet been found in it." N.B., in a footnote to the reference, Wilde writes:
    "A somewhat similar cave may be seen in the grounds of Mr. Metge, not far distant from
    Navan," – a reference to the chamber located in the gravel pit near Athlumney House, re-
    corded in Wakeman's Handbook of 1891. Due to the poor communications of the period,
    one may well wonder if these 'two' sites were one and the same?

3   Once occupying the site of the Navan Academy (St. Finians) opened here in 1802 by Rev.
    Eugene O'Reilly. The culverted section of the Leighsbrook runs beneath Academy St. here,
    and empties into the Boyne through a circa 6ft diameter concrete pipe.

4   Tradition holds that Thomas Curry, the noted local sculptor, used the eye of this bridge as
    an improvised workshop during the mid-1800s. Beneath this arch, he reputedly sculpted
    inter alia the Celtic Cross (dated 1864), now standing outside St. Mary's RC Church in
    Navan, and the concrete statue of St. Patrick that stood on the Hill of Tara for a century.
    Before being, it is said, surreptitiously removed and 'dumped' for a while at the OPW
    yard in Athcarne – during which process, I believe our Patron Saint's head was broken off;
    however, it is currently being 'restored' by the OPW at Trim. For more information on this
    arch, see *On Ancient Roads*, p.41.

5   Reference Excavations 1999, edited by Isabel Bennett – pp. 239-240 *Summary Accounts of
    Archaeological Excavations in Ireland*. This information was 'unearthed' by local historian

Vincent Mulvaney, to whom I am indebted for assistance provided on the Boyne and other research projects.

6   The 1870 directory also lists Lawrence Byrne as miller at Navan Mill.

7   This report, too lengthy for full inclusion, contains the following interesting snippets: "The local Fire Brigade, commanded by Capt. Crotty, was summoned after 5 o'clock a.m., and immediately proceeded to the scene, where they found flames issueing from two floors in the vicinity of the dynamo room in which Captain Crotty believes the fire started…" - "all that remained of Spicer's mills from which so many workers received their livelihood, and of which Navan was justly proud, were four cracked, blackened and tottering walls…" - "the Fire Brigade turned their attention to adjacent buildings, from many of which, the panic-stricken occupants were removing their households goods in momentary expectation of the flames spreading…" - "a call was sent through to Dublin Fire Brigade at six o'clock a.m. and in response to the call Captain Myers, of the Dublin Fire Brigade, arrived on the scene with an engine and crew at 7 a.m. …" - "as the mills are situated on the banks of the Boyne, there was no dearth of water, and the pumps of the five and a-half ton engine from Tara Street…" N.B., the one hour response time from Tara St. to Navan seems incredibly fast even by today's standards!

8   Part of this old shed survived, and was used to house a concrete products manufacturing business near Kells.

9   Starting from the tideway and moving upriver, the lifting/lowering locks are named Old-bridge Lower, Stalleen Lower, Broe Lower, Rosnaree (double), Slane Castle Weir, Carick-dexter, Cruicetown, Castlefin (Reilly's), Deerpark, Thomson's, Taaffe's, Rowley's and Metge's – Ruxton Lock is located in Navan but did not increase the overall lift of the navigation, because it provided side access only to the Boyne at Blackcastle.

10 For more information on Navan Lightering Works and the boats built there, refer to *Navan its People and its Past* – Volume 2 pp. 181 to 196 – the journal of the Navan and District Historical Society. Volume 3 of the same journal (2015) contains more information on this area, including its mills and 'the New Bridge.'

11 I believe this arch was not visible on the downstream façade because of the millwheel housing. As noted above, a study of the OS maps and old photographs indicates that the arch conducted a millrace (fed from the eastern branch of the great 'V' weir), which powered Mullen's Athlumney Boyne Mill (later Bard Welsh's Mill) and another mill in the yards close by the canal – these were part of the mill complex shown on the 1837 OS map as a corn & flour mill. The tailrace from the latter mill flowed to the west of the canal and fell back into the Boyne above Ruxton's Lock. Another smaller 9th arch (feeding this millrace) may have been located between the 8th arch and the abutment of Somerville Br. If this arch existed, it is buried long since and no definitive evidence of it exists either on the landscape or maps.

12 The Meath Chronicle of 1919 reports (with tongue-in-cheek due to prevailing censorship) on an incident occurring at this bridge during the Irish War of Independence. It states that part of the parapet wall was damaged, and speculates that 'the Shinners' might have attempted to demolish or otherwise disable the structure. Other anecdotes tell of a loud bang being heard, which supposedly caused nearby houses to shake violently. This occurrence

was later attributed to one of Spicer's Bakery vans losing control on Timmon's Hill and colliding with the bridge. But like most tales of those troubled times, we are still awaiting an explanation for the 'real cause' of the event! N.B., the bridge was closed to all road traffic in July 2015, and the crack(s) repaired by means of metal sleeves, pins and grouting (similar to 'rock pinning').

13 Although many people consider Lough Ramor to be the source of the River Blackwater, the true source is located further north beyond Baileborough; a proposition made also by Wilde in 1849. Lough Ramor is fed by several tributaries and many natural springs. The most significant tributaries emptying into Lough Ramor are the Park River (from N.W.), the Bureen River (from S.E.) and the Rampart or Murmod River. While the Park and Murmod rivers each are large enough to be considered as the main source of the Blackwater, I have chosen the latter, as it appears to be the most prolific source stream, fed by a multitude of loughs and minor tributaries. The river flows from Murmod Townland through Virginia from the north-east, and then turns southwards to fall into the lake at the former ferry landing. As a moot point, I will consider this to be the Blackwater's true source and follow its winding course to Lough Ramor, then onwards to its confluence with the Boyne in Navan. N.B., the Park River is fed by a series of interlinking lakes (near Billis Br.), known as Nadreegeel Loughs, while the Bureen is sourced in Cuilcagh Lough.

14 This multi-arched stone bridge is bypassed nowadays. The realigned Kells to Carnaross road passes over the Blackwater on a modern bridge (Loyd Br.) just to the east. In 1897, Kells UDC built a new waterworks about a ½ mile downstream. This works consisted of slow-sand filter beds, with two Francis water turbines supplying the power. These were 24 inch diameter impulse/reaction turbo wheels, each of which yielded c. 7.5 h.p. at the water head available. The water for the works being obtained from a weir immediately above the bridge and controlled by a sluice gate, which diverted a raceway beneath a smaller arch on Claven's Bridge, then onwards via a c. 6ft wide channel to the works. The waterworks has been restored in recent times by a group of heritage enthusiasts led by Ronnie Mc'Grane, despite less than enthusiastic support by officialdom.

15 Following the post 1968 drainage scheme, I believe the river hereabouts no longer provides enough power to drive the millwheel during times of elevated water levels – this is caused by loss of 'differential-head' across the wheel due to alterations of the riverbed during the drainage works. So the mill, powered by the Blackwater for several hundred years, finally fell victim to the OPW draglines in the 20th century.

16 In his book, *The Waters of the Boyne and Blackwater*, Cyril Ellison says of this mill: In the 16th century the Hospitalliers had a mill in Kilmainhambeg, near Kells and another near Teltown, described as 'thrown down and unprofitable.' The latter was again in use in the 19th century and known as Martin's Mill. It was later bought and demolished by the McCanns.

17 In the same book Ellison says of this mill: Tankardstown Mill near Donaghpatrick Bridge once operated beside the imposing fortified mansion built by the Luttrell family early in the 17th century. The story goes that Oliver Luttrell lost all his gold in the river in his hurry to escape Cromwellian forces. In more peaceful times the mill was rebuilt by William

Sterling of Adamstown in 1731. The mill has disappeared and the castle has given way to a modern residence.

18 On page 49 of his book, Cyril Ellison gives more details of Mill Brook's history, from the early 1700s to its time as Clayton's Mill, which closed down in the 1960s.

19 For sanding/polishing.

20 Three advertisements in 'the Freeman's Journal' of 1817 (discovered by Ethna Cantwell of N. & D.H.S.), throw some light on the history of Blackwater Mills: the first Advert' names Eliza Fay, John Fay & Richard Fay as Bankrupts and states that their properties will be sold by auction in the Royal Exchange Coffee House at 3p.m. on Oct. 1st 1817. It lists the properties as follows – New Wheat & Flour Mills with dwelling house and upwards of twenty acres, held by lease with 46 years still remaining, at yearly rent of £115-13s.-1d., to be sold with several encumbrances. A second Advert' appeared at a later date in the same journal listing this property for sale at the same venue on Nov. 20th 1817. The third Advert' on Nov. 14th 1817 (with Mrs. Fay of Flower hill as reference) sought either a Partner to operate the excellent Distillery and Brewery located at Blackwater Mills, or a person with relevant experience to let the premises as a going concern. Whatever the results of these exchanges, it would seem that Blackwater Mills came into the possession of R.H. & J. Skelly, sometime after 1837, when it is listed as 'in ruins' on the OS map, and 1854, when recorded as a going concern on Griffith's Valuation.

21 The Gasworks buildings occupied a site between Gallen's Flax Mill and Poolboy Br. It was fronted by Mill Lane and backed onto the tailraces (flowing through a channel within a breakwater) downstream of Morgan's Mill complex. From 1856 onwards, this became a favourite resting place for tramps and other wayfarers – it was known to such folk as 'the Hot (or Warm) Walls, because of the heat emitted by the coal-fired gas generating furnaces and retorts. (see also footnotes in Chapter 11).

22 Richard Farrelly in Navan and District Historical Society Volume 2 Journal, gives more details of these mills, summarised as follows: In 1851, the upriver ruined mill was rebuilt by William Morgan, son of James Morgan (owner of the mill further downstream), the upriver mill operated as a corn mill until c.1908, when it was converted to a saw mill by Joshua Elliot and Thomas Mortimer, whereupon it became known as Mortimer's Mill and later as Elliot's Mill – it ceased operations in the 1960s. The mills further downstream near the bridge had a chequered history, sections of the complex being operated variously as a corn mill (James Morgan), flax scutching mill (Gallen's Mill) and saw mill (Darker's Mill & Furniture Factory).

23 *Expenditure of vast amounts of money and resources on construction of roads and public build-ings in the years preceding the Great Hunger of 1845/1850 is oftentimes confused with famine relief works; that in 1847 forced an already starving population to earn a pittance of Trev-elayan's Corn by performing public works which included building roads to nowhere. Charles Edward Trevelyan (1807-1886) was assistant secretary to the treasury in the Whig Government led by Lord John Russell. Trevelyan was a devout Christian professing to believe that famines were sent by Almighty God to prevent the lower orders from overpopulating the earth... not exactly the best credentials for a man charged with relief of famine in Ireland!*

SKETCH PLAN OF
THE UPPER BOYNE NAVIGATION
CARRICKDEXTER — NAVAN

1 Mortimer's/Elliot's Mill
2 Morgan's/Darker's Mill
3 Gasworks
4 Bradley's Mill
5 Bridewell/Town Hall
6 Militia Stores
7 Round 'O'
8 Blackcastle Quay
9 Sophie's island
10 Old Athlumney Road
11 Ludlow Br. (buried)
12 Ludlow St. Mills
13 Smith's Bridge/Bishop's line

14 The Fingerpost/Crossways
15 Bazzer Nulty's Br.
16 Factory Village & millpond
17 Athlumney Mill
18 Chadwick's Corn Mill/Bacon factory
19 Farrell's Lodge
20 Donaghmore Round Tower
21 Babes Br.
22 Dunmoe Corn Mill
23 Sharpe's Bridge
24 Mary O'Brien's Corn Mill
25 Dollardstown Mills
26 Carney's Tuck Mill
27 Carrickdexter Weir and Lock c. 1 mile

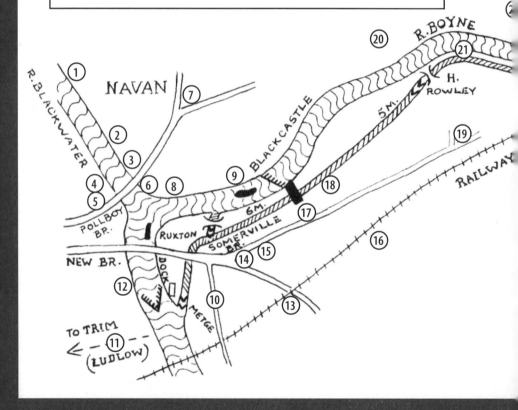

ELLISON'S SKETCH

Original sketch from Cyril Ellison's

The Waters of the Boyne and Blackwater

(A Scenic and Industrial Miscellany) – 1984

COUNTY

MEATH

11

The Middle Reaches
Navan to Rowley's Lock

The Valley – Blackcastle Fisheries of old – Boyne Navigation – Metge's Lock – Ruxton's Lock & Horse Bridge – Blackcastle Quay & Navan Gasworks – Somerville Bridge and the Basin – The Ramparts – Blackcastle Demesne – Bishop Nulty's waterworks & Smith's Bridge – Athlumney Weir – Athlumney flour, flax and corn-mill – Factory Village – Birth of the furniture trade – Chadwick's Mill & McCann's Bacon Factory – The Bathing Pond at Bailis – Shane's Well, Gregory's Well & Tobermurry – Source of Nanny Water – Knock-a-Raymon, Tober Ruadh & Fanning's Holy Well – Swinnerton Fish-Weir and Boyne Meadow.

On this sector of the middle reaches below Navan, the vista changes again as the Boyne, swollen by the Blackwater, passes through a more dramatic landscape. Excepting the navigation's dereliction, the river remains largely unchanged along this reach since William Wilde traversed its banks during the late 1840s. The phenomenon occurred because the Office of Public Works (OPW) was prevented from doing major work on this section during the earlier upriver schemes of the 1800s, which reshaped the Little Boyne and Upper Boyne reaches forever.

Future generations are especially fortunate that during the drainage scheme, inaugurated with much fanfare at Bellinter Bridge in 1968, the OPW 'dogs

Left: The other Tony Holten beneath 'the New Bridge' in Navan 4th January, 2015.
Right: Ruxton's Bridge and lock from the river aspect

of war' or draglines were not unleashed to wreak havoc upon the middle and lower reaches below Navan. Hence the river valley, from Navan to Oldbridge, retained most of its aesthetic appeal during these destructive times. Hereabouts the Boyne flows through a pastoral landscape; where rapids, canal ramparts, wooded heights and deep gorges combine with old manor houses, churches, castles and keeps to form a riverscape of great beauty.

In 1913, Augustus Grimble's The Salmon Rivers of Ireland, enthused thus about the Boyne reach below the confluence:

> Between this junction and Drogheda, a distance of about fifteen miles, lie the various celebrated rod fisheries of the Boyne. With a course of seventy miles and draining one thousand and forty square miles of country, while receiving the surplus waters of fifteen large tributaries, whose total length is two hundred and sixty miles, it is therefore not surprising that between Navan and Drogheda the river varies in width from sixty to one hundred yards, its banks in some places resembling those of the Tay above Perth, where it flows through the Scone and Battleby estates, although the Boyne is not nearly so rapid as the Scotch river... *he goes on to say of Blackcastle Fisheries:* the best of the pools on the upper water, which is now let on lease to Sir Francis Ley, Bart, Epperstone Manor, Nottingham, are Mill Sharp, Tunnel, Beech Tree, Hut, Narrows (north side), and Sclam, while there are fully half a dozen others. On the lower water there are Long Sharp, Head of the Island, Old Bridge, and White Rock, with others. The best flies are

Flys and equipment used on the Boyne post 1940s. Courtesy John Bradley.

Jock Scot, the Blue Jock, the Claret, Lemon and Grey, and the late Major J. P. Traherne's noted killer, the Blue Boyne; while, as all these flies are standard patterns, it has not been thought necessary to describe them for the flie-tier.(sic)[1]

Because of the multi-faceted and complex nature of the Boyne Valley between Navan and Stackallan, the various aspects are described individually, starting with the Boyne Navigation canal.

The navigation between Navan and Drogheda was not a true canal, but comprised of several navigable river sections linked by lateral canals. A series of artificial waterways, varying in length from a few hundred yards to several miles, were cut to bypass river shallows, rapids, fish-weirs and mill weirs. In addition to raising some existing weirs, several navigation dams were built, increasing the river levels to a navigable depth, on the Boyne Navigation averaging 3.5 to 4.5ft. The system was developed in two distinct phases spanning over a half century, from circa 1748 to 1800. Construction of the first phase, known as the Lower Boyne Navigation, commenced at Oldbridge Lock near Drogheda in 1748, and was completed to Slane by 1763.

Although some crude canals were built between Slane and Stackallan during the 1750s, competing interests and political shenanigans delayed the project until the 1790s; when building of the Upper Boyne Navigation, from Carrickdexter to Navan began in earnest, under supervision of engineer Richard Evans assisted by Daniel Monks. A base was set up at Stackallan; with construction operations carried out concurrently downstream to Carrickdexter and upriver to Navan. The canal was completed to Navan and officially opened in April 1800, to the great satisfaction of that town's business community; whose persistence in advocating the benefits of the navigation had been rewarded finally.

Between Navan and Stackallan the navigation consisted of one continuous lateral canal with five locks. These locks were named and situated as follows: Metge's Lock at the summit level above the 'V' weir in Navan (as described),

Ruxton's Lock opposite Blackcastle, Rowley's Lock in Ferganstown (Farganstown), Taaffe's Lock (or Bective) in Ardmulchan and Stackallan or Thomson's Lock in Ardmulchan Parish. Four locks, namely, Metge's, Rowley's, Taaffe's and Thomson's provided a total lift/drop of circa 21.5ft between Stackallan (OS Benchmark 91.5ft) and Metge's, OS Benchmark at elevation 113ft above sea level on the heelstone (or hingestone) of the lower gate. The section; therefore, had three pound levels, where the canal water was trapped or penned between the upper gate of the lower lock and the lower gate of the upper lock.

Metge's Lock was described by some as a guard lock, the primary purpose of such locks being to protect the canal from flood damage and safeguard the lower locks should an emergency occur. The other guard locks on the navigation had no lift/drop function; however, the benchmark level of 107.9ft on the upper gate stonework of Rowley's Lock suggests that the summit lock (Metge's) provided a lift of circa 4 or 5ft to take the navigation from this pound level into the deep water above the 'V' weir. This arrangement was perhaps designed as a feeder system and to optimise water depth in the lateral canal between Navan and Stackallan, even during most seasonal fluctuations of the river levels – possibly achieved by keeping the sluices (or paddles) on both lock gates open during non-operational periods.[2]

Metge's Lock was named after a family who occupied Athlumney Demesne and served as Trustees of the navigation. A team headed by James Morgan constructed the lock in the period 1792 to 1798; with Ruxton's Lock built during the same period by James Costello & Co.

The canal passed from the summit lock and under Somerville Bridge, carrying the Boyne Road (R153) eastwards across the canal towards Beauparc and Drogheda, as described. Some history of this bridge can be traced from the label-stones: the original bridge being constructed by John Nowlan under supervision of chief engineer Richard Evans in 1792; it was then re-constructed and lowered by J. Navagh (contractor) in 1879, under supervision of John Henry Moore (1844-1912), Meath County Surveyor.[3] Concrete upstream and downstream extensions were added by Meath County Council in 1936, under supervision of County Surveyor E. J. Duffy. The reconstructed arch of 1879 springs from vertical walls at either end and has a high 'span to rise' ratio, giving it a distinctive, flattened and almost elliptical profile.

Ruxton's Lock c. 2015 - Courtesy Aubrey Martin

An extra arch allowing for the passage of draught horses and hauliers, included within the fabric of the original structure, is bricked-up nowadays, as the darkened opening provided a haven for nefarious activities. While exploring the ramparts during my schooldays, I recall passing through this dank cave-like passageway; dodging water dripping from the old stonework and wondering what horrors lay waiting in the darkness.

The canal immediately downstream of Somerville Bridge became known as 'the Basin,' because it formed a broader reach from the bridge to Ruxton's Lock several hundred yards downstream. Some of the wrought iron mooring rings can be seen affixed to the stone canal wall opposite Spicer's Bakery. This filled-in canal bed is accessed nowadays through *Andy Brennan Park* and under the dried-up main arch of Somerville Bridge. The upper gate to Ruxton's Lock is located at the north-eastern corner of the Basin; in 1852 the OS Benchmark on the lock stonework indicated it sited at elevation 110.2ft above mean sea level.

This lock provided side access only to and from the Boyne, where barges and lighters crossed the river to discharge and load cargoes at Blackcastle Quay. The Militia Stores were located close by, adjacent to Morgan's Mill tailrace arch of Poolboy (Poolbwee) Bridge on the River Blackwater.

Previous to 1815, Blackcastle Quay included an extensive coal yard and corn store, occupied by Peter Daly, a Navan Innkeeper.[4] In earlier times, Daly formed a partnership with John Ruxton of Blackcastle, Thomas Everard and George Armstrong to operate a vessel, known as the Union Lighter, for carriage of goods and passengers on the navigation. Perhaps this vessel was so named to celebrate the Act of Union in 1801. In 1815, the quay and stores were leased by John and Francis Chadwick, millers and coal merchants of Drogheda, operators of a nearby corn mill.[5]

Blackcastle Quay was a very busy place during the heyday of the canal in the 19th century, and indeed at the dawning of the new century in 1900. Hence the crossing from Ruxton's Lock must have been used frequently. The oftentimes told story of the towing horse being placed aboard the barge and the vessel 'poled' across the river, is less than credible to those familiar with such operations. While this method was possibly used on less turbulent crossings downriver at Slane, Rosnaree and Broe, it was likely inadequate at Navan and Stackallan due to strong river currents prevalent at these locations. The crossing to Blackcastle Quay was particularly difficult and hazardous because of the rip current-like effects of the confluence. This situation being complicated further by the two millraces from the upstream Athlumney Boyne Mills pouring into the river immediately above Ruxton's Lock, and the tailraces from Morgan's Blackwater Mills exiting the breakwater below Poolboy Bridge, immediately adjacent to the quay. In my view, some type of cable/pulley system must have been used to propel the unpowered craft across the current and upriver against the strong flow setting towards the east. This subject is discussed further in the chapter dealing with Stackallan.

Below the lock, Ruxton's Bridge spans the canal's former spur to the river; the only such horse-bridge we encounter on the Upper Navigation. These bridges were built to allow towing horses and pedestrians cross the canal at various locations along the waterway. The bridge was built under supervision of Richard Evans, engineer in charge, as so declared by the beautifully crafted label-stone adorning its parapet. These stones for the Upper Boyne project were shaped and carved by Simon Austin and John Colwell.[6] This lock and bridge were named in honour of the Ruxton-Fitzherbert dynasty, owners of the 2,000 acre Blackcastle estate and also members of the Boyne Navigation Trustees. The 1837 OS map shows that the portion of Blackcastle estate located between the Slane road and the Boyne, including the demesne further downstream at Swinnerton, enclosed an area of 395 acres extending from the town of Navan to Dunmoe.

The towpath runs from Ruxton's Bridge to Stackallan Bridge upon a rampart separating the artificial waterway from the river. The section between Navan and Athlumney Mill has a high, wooded bank overshadowing the canal and rampart alongside the river. This area, so eloquently praised by Wilde in the 1840s, is still appealing to the eye; the soft green hues of its woodlands in springtime and russet autumnal tints providing a beautiful sylvan-like setting for pleasure walking nowadays. The navigation milestone No. 6 was located about mid-way along this stretch; an indicator that the place is six miles upstream from Carrickdexter Lock, official starting point of the Upper Navigation.

Other features of the navigation are discussed as encountered on our downriver journey.

On November 11th 2011, a cold, dry day with fitful, wintry sunshine breaking through the lowering clouds, Marie and I drove through Navan, crossed 'the New Bridge' and swung into the car park located between Spicer's Bakery and the old 'Fingerpost' road junction. Here we rendezvoused with the group involved in the Navan to Slane leg of our Boyne trip.

This time two of the River Rescue boats turned up, together with nine men, including: Martin Curran, Pa. Reilly, Hopper Rennicks, Chalky White, Declan Murphy, Sean Cleary with supporting team and drivers, Ted Boland, E. Quinlevean and Jamie Rennicks; the supernumeraries were Tom French, Oliver Delany and me. Kieran Maguire took some photographs of the group assembled on and around the elegant arched structure of Ruxton's Bridge.

Launching the two boats, we set off on the next leg of our journey; first going upriver to have a further look beneath the arches of 'the New Bridge,' given only a cursory examination on the previous trip due to inclement weather. Passing back downriver and through the confluence, we made a few sorties against the strong current tearing beneath the arches of Poolboy Bridge, then, headed back downstream alongside the Blackcastle shoreline towards Slane.

The remains of an old limekiln stand on the northern riverbank, opposite and slightly upstream from Ruxton's Lock. This kiln is shown on the 1911 OS maps, together with an attendant quarry, the probable source of the limestone burned at the kiln to produce powdered lime. Used for many purposes in those days, including whitewashing buildings, making mortar and manuring acidic land. The main riverbanks are stone-lined hereabouts, an indication that this area of the Boyne was well-tended in former days. Passing by the burned-out shell of Blackcastle House, I noted a small stream falling in to the canal from the high southern riverbank, directly opposite the house.

This little river once played an important role in Navan's history and provides an interesting insight into how things were done in days gone by. The 1911 OS map indicates that the stream rises in a small 0.288 acre circular pond located nearby, in a field east of the avenue leading to Boyne View House. Another small tributary joins it from close by the old village of Athlumney named the Little Furze: it passes beneath Smith's Bridge on the Navan to Kentstown road, then under Athlumney road bridge (once known as Bazzer Nulty's Bridge), and falls into the canal as described. Grand Jury records show that Smith's Bridge was built in 1816 at a cost of £160; during construction of the new road linking 'the Fingerpost' or Crossways junction in Navan to Kentstown. To the south of this bridge, an old ivy-covered concrete pillbox-like structure stands beside the little stream; this provides the most tangible reminder of what was known locally as the Bishop's Waterworks or the Bishop's Line.

This water supply system was built by Bishop Nulty during the 1860s, to service the ecclesiastical establishments of the town, including convents, parochial house, St. Mary's RC Church and other public facilities like schools and hospitals. The concrete structure housed two hydraulic rams or hydrostats, which were powered from the dammed-up stream. These pumped water to a brick-built storage tank mounted atop the nearby tower house of Athlumney Castle; from where the water gravitated to various facilities throughout the town. Another concrete pump-house was built, but not completed, and stands on a site close by the Bazzer Nulty's Bridge, which name derived from a family of that name living beside the bridge. The two concrete structures were interconnected by a stone built water duct, filled up long since.

The original ram-house and dam for the Bishop's Line are located within the grounds of a bungalow occupied by Donie Halpin, while the unfinished structure stands near the residence of Mrs. Connolly. These two relics of past engineering works are perhaps some of the oldest surviving concrete structures in the town. As this stream seems to be unnamed, 'the Bishop's Brook' might be an apt enough title for same.[7]

Clockwise from top: Ayelsbury - Chadwicks Weir; Stephanie Donohoe (later Bradley) and baby Betty Reilly on Boyne rampart above Aylesbury's Mill 1935; Shackleton Photo of Alyesbury's (Blundel's) Mill *c.* mid-1890s.

We re-joined the second boat and carried on downriver towards Athlumney Mill and fish weir; the first of many such we encounter on the journey to Slane and Drogheda e.g. a total of four weirs are located on the Boyne within the precincts of the Blackcastle estate between Athlumney and Dunmoe.

The OS maps show Athlumney Weir (known also as Chadwick's Weir) starting from the northern riverbank and running askew across the river, to terminate at the former millrace rampart near Athlumney Mill. The 1911 map indicates salmon traps located at the upper end where the weir connects to the Blackcastle bank, and a fish-pass (built in the 1880s) about midway along towards the mill. These fish-passes were sometimes referred to as 'the King, or Queen's Gap.

The mill in Athlumney had a complex history and was known by several names, including Athlumney Mill,[8] the Flour Mill, the Flax Mill, the Saw Mills and Alesbury's Mill; all of which titles reflect the many functions of the mill over its varied existence.[9]

According to the 1837 OS map and Griffith's 1854 valuation, the main mill in Athlumney was a Flax, Corn and Flour Mill. Though exact details are difficult to obtain at this remove, it seems that flax and corn processing operations were conducted within the one structure, with a reported output of 15,000 barrels of flour in 1860. The 1837 OS, in addition to the map accompanying the valuation, show the combined mill was built mostly upon the rampart between the river and canal, with a smaller section bridging the waterway and extending eastwards.

The millrace split immediately upstream of the mill, one part driving the larger undershot wheel in a separate housing alongside the river; the other channel diverted beneath the building and powered two smaller breast-shot wheels. The latter wheels drove electric generators in addition to other machinery; their tailraces exiting the mill via an arched tunnel on the building's downstream façade. The housing for the huge, undershot waterwheel (of cast or wrought iron construction 12ft dia. by 20ft wide) extended north-westwards, supported on the riverside by an extension to the weir. The 1911 OS map and photographs from the Shackleton collection of 1894 show the mill straddling the canal on a stone arch incorporated within the structure's fabric. This extension included a chute on the downriver façade for loading produce onto canal barges and lighters. On the upriver or south-western gable of the main building was a bell cote, housing a bell for summoning the millworkers and announcing various items in the mill's daily routine.

The six storey building cost over £20,000 to build originally, and was one of the first buildings in Ireland designed to be fire resistant. The floors, internal walls and critical elements of the structure were lined with sheet iron and no combustible material used in exposed locations. The site was leased from the River Boyne Co. to a Lancashire man named John Blundell, with the mill built immediately alongside the canal in 1806. The location provided ready access for loading goods directly onto barges without the necessity of more costly road transport. Some products were shipped downriver to domestic outlets, others onward bound to foreign markets via Drogheda Port. In 1809,

Blundell leased land in Athlumney from John and Richard Ruxton as a site for a yarn factory; which site became the subject of a lawsuit that Blundell lost subsequently.

John Blundell died in 1811 and I believe his administrator, Christopher Blundell, passed away slightly later in the same year. In 1814, the trustee of the estate, Blaney Balfour (Townley Hall), leased the mills to Nicholas Hamil and Matthew Wade. In later years, the firm of Chadwicks and Blundell of Drogheda became involved in the mill, together with Francis Blundell & Co. of Dublin, sack, canvas and yarn manufactures. The enterprise prospered and employed 250 persons by the 1850s, many of whom lived in Athlumney Village (or the Factory Village), consisting of 75 small houses and several larger dwellings at the time. Then followed post-famine decline and the once prosperous mill experienced hard times, being idle by the turn of the century.

Griffith's records Messrs. Gradwell, Chadwick & Co. as occupier of house, offices, spinning mill and land totalling circa 5 acres at R.V. £6-15s. This low valuation perhaps an indication that Athlumney Mill was not in use at that time; the site was held in fee by 'the Boyne Navigation Co.' and included another corn mill further downstream. Slater's 1846 Directory records Francis Blundell as a flax spinner in Navan Flax Mill.[10]

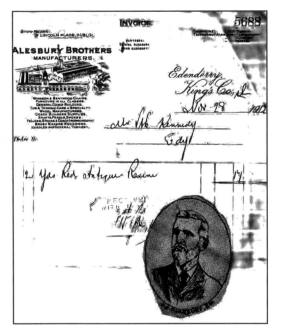

Athlumney Mill was taken over by James McCann MP and converted to a modern sawmill in the declining years of the 19th century. The enterprise flourished even though James McCann passed away in April 1904 and by 1906 was listed as Navan Sawmills and Furniture Factory Ltd. This represented the birth of Navan's great furniture manufacturing tradition, providing the mainstay of employment in the town for many years thereafter. The factory turned out some items of

Aylesbury 1919 billhead

top quality furniture, many of which were displayed at the Irish International Exhibition in 1907. Other products made from wood were manufactured here, including, elm coffins, felloes (felly) for wheels, components for drays and carriages, fencing, wooden buildings, some of these being exported to England via the Boyne Navigation.

Goodearl Brothers, from High Wycombe, acquired Athlumney Sawmill in 1915 and commenced production of high quality Windsor cane-seated chairs. During WWI, they produced tent pegs in vast quantities and other timber goods; with the business managed by Percy Goodearl and Wilfred Dean, who lived locally. Political events during the Irish War of Independence caused the firm to close and the business was taken over in 1919 by Daniel Alesbury, owner of Edenderry Timber Mills. This firm continued woodworking operations at the mill and installed a steam engine c.1924 to supplement the power generated by the waterwheels. The mill employed about one hundred staff, with the production line specialising in wood-spoked wheels for the English car market, high class furniture and wooden horse-drawn vehicles, together with many other more mundane products for the domestic market.[11]

Similar to the supposedly 'unsinkable' *R.M.S. Titanic* in 1912, the 'indestructible' Athlumney Mill met its fate in March 1933; shortly after the spring blizzard of that year provided Navan residents with a memorable end to winter's cold grasp. The internals of the huge building were gutted by a fire, which took a mere four hours to consume the supposedly 'incombustible' mill. In fairness, the rapid spread of the conflagration was assisted by many apertures in the floors, walls and ceilings, cut during numerous modifications completed throughout the mill's lifetime. These breached the fire-integrity of the building and sealed its fate once the fire started in the upper floors.

The structure, though damaged by the fire, stood on the site by the river until its demolition in the 1970s; yet another reminder that nothing made by man is indestructible. During my schooldays in the brother's school, I oftentimes heard of how the mill was 'burned down by the boys from Edenderry,' and wondered at the source of the tale. The Alesbury's connection to that town perhaps supplies a clue to the origins of this particular yarn.

Apart from a few stubs of stone walls, the most tangible reminder of the mighty mill is the stone arch spanning the canal. This was not built originally as a bridge, but formed the mill's eastwards extension over the canal. Used for

Aylesbury's Mill main arch and secondary millrace arch (tunnel) mostly buried 2014

taking raw materials to the mill, it is one of only three locations where the towing path passes beneath the main arch; the others are Thomson's Bridge at Stackallan and Rock Arch near Rosnaree.

Part of the old multi-segmented arch is used to carry a lane across the canal onto the former towpath, elevated nowadays by debris from the old Athlumney Mill. This c.15ft wide lane now provides access to the ramparts from the Boyne Road opposite the old factory village. The remainder of the arch (circa 25ft wide) is grassed-over nowadays; considered unfit for purpose as a load bearing structure due to a large hole in the arch crown, perhaps caused by falling debris during the mill's demolition.

It is one of the most unusual stone arches remaining alongside the Boyne, the ring stones are of dressed limestone, each with pointed top and chamfered edges, such that its face stands out boldly. Every second stone is tied deeper in to the intrados/soffit, which is constructed of dressed rubble stone. The central stone (keystone) on the downstream arch ring has the following engraved upon its face: *BM & Co 1807*.

Alongside the main arch stands the downstream secondary tailrace opening, an arch of almost flat segmental (elliptical) profile, but mostly buried beneath the rubble now forming the river rampart. Hopefully the guardians of our heritage will soon take steps to preserve the remnants of Athlumney Mill, former spearhead of the industrial revolution in Navan.

Another mill once standing adjacent to the canal further downstream is often confused with the previously described Athlumney Mill. The original mill hereabouts would appear to have been a corn mill, perhaps named Grainger's Mill. Little is known of this mill, the origin of which is uncertain, but it may be one of several corn/tuck mills recorded upon the Boyne within Athlumney by the Civil Survey of 1656. The Down Survey 1656 Barony of Navan map depicts a corn mill in Athlumney on the south-eastern riverbank just downstream of Navan. Slightly further downriver, the same map depicts a landmark, quaintly titled '*a tree in ye river.*'

The suggestion that this was a mill of some antiquity is supported by its layout on the riverbank and the water source used to power the large overshot wheel, one of the few such waterwheels immediately adjacent to the Boyne. Prior to introduction of the Corn Bounty in the mid to late 1700s, which caused proliferation of larger industrial mills; many of the mills upon the Boyne catchment were located on the tributary rivers, such as the Deel, Stonyford, Knightsbrook, Skein/Gabhra, Blackwater and the Mattock, to name but a few. Watermills located on larger rivers such as the Boyne, required the construction of massive weirs; expensive to build and very often beyond both the financial means and engineering skills of private millers. Flooding created an additional problem, causing loss of differential head across the millwheel. Mills on the smaller tributaries; however, were generally more economical to build, and when operated via millponds, could work for longer periods because of the greater fall towards the larger river. The generally larger water-head enabled use of overshot or back-shot millwheels, producing considerably more power than undershot or breast-shot waterwheels.

The 1837 OS and Griffith's 1854 map names this as a corn mill, and shows the small sized mill building located between the canal and the Drogheda road; but set well back from the waterway with the tailrace flowing into the canal. This location casts some doubts on previous descriptions of corn and flour being offloaded from the building directly onto barges upon the canal.

Other writings state that the mill was powered by an overshot wheel, "fed by a millrace running at right angles to the river from a reservoir in the townland of Bailis, known as the Bathing Pond." In fact, the headrace was supplied from a millpond located across the road and adjacent to the previously described Factory Village; the millstream from this pond forming a boundary between the townlands of Athlumney and Ferganstown & Ballymacon.

The 1837 OS map shows the Bathing Pond located within Bailis on the eastern edge of the double ditch forming its mereing with Johnstown. I cannot find any map delineating a connection between the Bathing Pond and the corn mill in Athlumney. The 2005 OS ortho' indicates the pond site now lies buried beneath one of many developments in the area (new Johnstown Village).

The stream (or millrace), forming the main source for the millpond at the Factory Village, rises a couple of miles further east close by *Shane's Well* on the north-western slopes of Carn Hill (known to some as Harristown Hill).[12] Flowing southwards from the source, this stream passes under the Navan to Kentstown road and turns westwards, to flow beneath the Johnstown road south of Casey's Cross.

Turning north-westwards it runs under the new and 'old' Athlumney roads, to flow due west for several hundred yards, forming the northern mereing between Bailis Townland and Athlumney, before flowing north-westwards again and falling into the millpond at the Factory Village. The 1911 map depicts the section between the pond and the 'old' Athlumney road as the Mill Race, and shows a footpath running alongside. While most other streams sourced in this hilly area, turn eastwards to 'the Nanny Water' catchment, it flows westwards towards the Boyne, thereby indicating a watershed in the area of Mooretown and Morrell (the Manor).[13]

Griffiths indicates that in 1854, Athlumney Corn Mill was leased from Messrs. Gradwell, Chadwick & Co. by John and Francis Chadwick at R.V. £30, with no land included in the record. Slater's 1846 Directory records that John and Francis Chadwick were millers at Boyne Mills, with Michael Worthy registered as their manager (this could be confusion with the upstream Athlumney Boyne Mills beside 'the New Bridge'). The valuation records that the Boyne Nav. Co. leased plantations totalling 5.6 acres and 10.76 acres of canal banks and water from Richard Ruxton Fitzherbert at total R.V. of £3.

Later records (including the 1911 OS map) indicate that the main Athlumney Corn, Flax and Flour Mills, together with the corn mill operated by the Chadwick's, were listed under the generic heading of Athlumney Mills – some writings tell of the corn mill processing oatmeal only.

James McCann took over Chadwick's Corn Mill as part of the greater scheme for developing the Athlumney woodworking facility, and it seemed to have been enlarged and incorporated into this operation. Cross-referencing the 1911 map with that of 1837 shows an increased mill footprint on the later map, with part of the newer structure located alongside the canal. On this map, the millpond is sited on the canal side of the Navan to Drogheda road within the mill site, with the former pond at the Factory Village defunct. In 1902 part of the corn mill was converted to McCann's Bacon Factory, its trademark depicting the round tower and church belfry of nearby Donaghmore.

The former corn mill, known as Chadwick's Mill, has vanished from the Boyne's landscape, but the little stream that once powered its overshot waterwheel still passes beneath the road; flowing alongside the ancient mereing of Ferganstown & Ballymacon and Athlumney, now the south-western boundary of St. Mary's Cemetery. As this stream seems to be untitled, I would propose 'the Millstream' as a suitable name for this brook.

Back on the boat, we passed by Sophie's Island on the Blackcastle side where the Boyne turns north-eastwards approaching the skewed weir in Athlumney.

Left: Chadwick's Millrace Br. upstream arch - just below the old mill pond.
Right: Millrace Bridge downstream arch - note the pointed profile contrasting to rounded profile of upstream arch

Legend says that this little wooded islet was named after Sophie Fitzherbert of Blackcastle. Hugging the shore by the canal rampart, we followed the narrowing channel towards the former great maw of the millrace. The River Rescue lads decided that we supernumeraries should vacate the boat for the passage across the mill weir, which had a drop of approximately 6ft to the white water beneath. Martin pulled the boat alongside the riverbank and we scrambled ashore through the sedges onto the canal towpath.

From the more solid platform of terra firma, we viewed the splendour of the riverscape. The scene retains much of its sylvan beauty, though marred somewhat by the old sewage works on the opposite bank and the rash of Celtic Tiger era developments glimpsed through the sparse winter foliage. Thankfully, nature will wrap its forgiving mantle around the old works eventually and cover the scars inflicted by our careless society. The foul odours of mankind's waste products are not as intense here nowadays, this minor miracle achieved at the expense of the area adjacent to Rowley's Lock further downstream, where the new works sit above the riverbank, pouring effluent into the river.

Despite the intrusion of modernity, Athlumney weir still appeals to both audio and visionary senses, the Boyne's constant murmur subdued hereabouts by muted roar of water cascading over man-made falls. On the bright, sunny day, a Heron perching precariously upon a log caught across the weir disdainfully ignores our presence while gazing at the ever-flowing river passing towards the sea.

Walking onwards along the towpath with the lads, I reflected that in 1849, on the riverside immediately below the mills, Wilde noted an abrupt bank, which he named *Knock-a-Raymon*, and said of this place:

> A few years ago, a vast quantity of animal remains, and some sepulchral urns in small kistvaens were discovered. It was evidently one of the barrows of the aborigines.

He goes on to state that the site was no longer important because it was then a mere potato garden, and mentions also that a sacred well named Tober Ruadh (Red Well ?) was located nearby. Extensive research of the OS maps and other sources failed to disclose the location of these sites.

In Aug. 1976; however, Wilde's observations about the ancient burial site were confirmed, when a mechanical digger uncovered an intact cist burial in the same location across the road from St. Mary's (New) Cemetery. Unfortunately, the tomb, later dated as originating from at least the Iron Age, was badly damaged in the process. The burial cist (containing a female skeleton), sited within a one metre high earthen mound of fourteen metres diameter, was located near a quarry and marle pit indicated on the 1837 OS map between the canal and road.

This map shows a laneway leading south-eastwards from the road for a fair distance into the fields and coming to a dead end near the old Church of Killagrin. I believe this was called Fanning's (or Fannen's) Lane because a family of that name resided about mid-way along its length. Following the railway's arrival circa 1848, a level crossing provided access across the tracks, and more recently the lane formed the north-eastern boundary of the new cemetery (St. Mary's). In a field close by the residence was a holy well, named Fanning's Well in the 1938 'School Folklore Scheme,' which cites a description of this well, related by an older man named Simon Mulvany. The well, surrounded by a capped stone enclosure, had the cure for several ailments, invoked by the applicant dropping a pin into the water; perhaps this was a newer name for the sacred well referred to by Wilde as Tober Ruadh?

We waited below the weir while the lads bailed out the boat, swamped when caught in the white water under the falls, then re-boarding our craft, headed on downriver through this beautiful setting. Downstream from Athlumney, the Boyne sweeps due north, then turns again to head north-eastwards

Left: Swinnerton Lodge from towpath *c.* 2007. Right: Swinnerton from the river aspect 2012

around the great curve at Swinnerton Lodge on the northern bank. This side of the river includes the long, narrow salient of the old Blackcastle Demense, running downstream to Dunmoe Townland. The rash of developments disappears hereabouts, with some tall, stately trees towering above the lesser woodlands of the old demesne. The bank is covered by wildwood alongside the river's curvature, with Swinnerton (Swynnerton) Lodge perched mid-way along in a clearing upon a grassy ledge overlooking this reach of the Boyne.

The 1837 OS map shows only some small buildings at the site of the lodge, whereas the map of 1911 indicates a much larger establishment; together with the salmon hatchery alongside the access avenue from the Slane road. The hatchery, established circa 1894, was fed from a stream rising in Batterstown and flowing beneath Donaghmore (road) Bridge. The lodge was inherited and occupied by Samuel Fitzherbert in the late 18th century following the death of his mother, Letitia Fitzherbert. This lady married John William Ruxton in the 1740s, thereby establishing the Ruxton Fitzherbert dynasty. When Samuel died in 1825, Swinnerton passed to his nephew, Richard Ruxton Fitzherbert, inheritor of the greater Blackcastle estate.

The right or south-eastern bank, from the mereing at Chadwick's Mill to below Rowley's Lock, is included within the combined townland of Ferganstown & Ballymacon. The Athlumney riverbank is covered by dense wildwood, thinning out where the Boyne swings northwards towards the lodge. Here, the canal continues on a straight line north-eastwards; the divergence between river and canal thus forming a separate sector of land, divided into three fields. The largest of which comprised 15.25 acres and

Left: P. Reilly in boat at Swinneton Fish-Weir 2011. Right: The Boyne between Swinnerton and the Boyne Meadows. Photos courtesy Tom French

is named the Boyne Meadow on the 1837 OS map.[14] It is evident from the same map that extensive drainage work took place here during construction of the waterway, with several of the deep ditches still in situ; these fields are accessed via the old towpath.

Passing on downriver through sylvan surroundings, we noted several people walking along the towpath, enjoying the fine weather and magnificent setting. Continuing on by the site of Donaghmore's Mass Rocks on the left bank, we went on past the lodge and approached the fish-weir.

This weir is reverse 'Z'-shaped, with a longitudinal extension downriver to the fish-traps on the Blackcastle side. Though forming merely a ripple upon the Boyne's surface with no great fall on the downstream side, the weir still represents a considerable obstruction to river navigation; hence Pa. and Hopper jumped into the fast-flowing water to manhandle our boat safely across. I believe that the old traps are used to capture eels on their nocturnal downriver migrations to the far distant Sargasso Sea. This weir is recorded on the 1837 OS map as described above, but the 1911 map shows a curved extension running from the traps to the opposite riverbank alongside the Boyne Meadow, which extension seems to have disappeared entirely.

Ancient records show that this is perhaps the weir recorded in the Louth Archaeological Society's 1953 (Vol. 13) paper as follows:

> Above Dunmoe we come to the famous Blackcastle fishery, now well known as a rod fishery. On 3rd August 1402, James le Botille, Earl of Ormond, granted his manor of Blackcastle to Katherine, his wife, daughter of Gerald, late Earl of Desmond, together with fisheries, etc. By an indenture between James, Earl of Ormond, and John Tallon of Blackcastle, the earl granted, inter alia, the water of Boyne and fishing thereof for twenty one years, on 30th April 1543 and in the next month (12th May, 1543) the same earl leased a house "with appurtenances in Donamore," a little upstream in Blackcastle, but the water of the Boyne and the fishery were excluded from the lease. The Civil Survey again gives us information that in Blackcastle there was a fishery weir and mill. This is, no doubt, the predecessor of the weir used until 1938 to capture fish to stock the hatchery in the Blackcastle demesne. (sic)

Clockwise from top left: Concrete wall blocking lock for flood protection 2007; Rowley's Lock & Lock-house with Crockminnan or 'Kid's Hill' forming background *c.* 1902; Rowley's Lock Bridge in 2007.

Another weir of similar size and shape is located a few hundred metres further downstream; crossing between Ferganstown and Blackcastle. The weir is not indicated on the 1837 OS map, but appears on the 1911 edition and can be identified by satellite imagery. No fish-traps are evident on the river or maps, so its origins and purpose are uncertain, but it was perhaps constructed as part of Blackcastle Fisheries sometime in the mid to late 1800s. This weir caused considerable obstruction to our downriver progress, providing the lads with another opportunity for water sports.

The south-eastern floodplain narrows just below this weir, with the canal rampart and towpath constructed closer to the Boyne and the riverbank swelling to a steep, wooded ridge above Rowley's Lock. John O'Donovan's 1836 OS Field Notes name this ridge *Crockminnan, Cnoc Mionnan, hill of the kids* and say of the hillock:

> This is a ridge, which extends N. from Rowleys Lock along the Canal
> and the River Boyne, standing some height above them.

Wilde notes a minor tumulus crowning the hilltop, of which no trace can be found on the OS maps. The official mind-set and appreciation of this unique landscape is demonstrated, once again, by the large sewage treatment plant atop the eastern riverbank. I believe that when started up several years ago, this plant disgorged its foul, untreated contents across the local fields and into the canal, instead of to the Boyne as intended.

ENDNOTES

1   The hut mentioned is not the one standing on the south-eastern riverbank at Dunmoe Weir nowadays, but was located on the opposite bank in front of Swinnerton lodge – the Old Bridge pool is probably at Babes Bridge.

2   Research suggests that a culvert was taken from the Boyne Deeps just above Metge's Lock. This probably ran alongside the canal and powered a waterwheel/pump, which partly supplied Bishop Nulty's waterworks in 1879. The culvert perhaps ran beneath the Athlumney Road (R153), then passed under the Boyne Navigation Co. (or B.N.C.) premises at the old bakery yard, and fell into the canal at the south-western end of 'the Basin.' The walled-up exit of this culvert (perhaps also used as a feeder stream for the canal); can still be seen at low level on the eastern wall of the old canal basin. Refer to 'the Bishop's Line,' later in this chapter and Vol No. 3 (2015) of the NADHS journal *Navan – its People and its Past.*

3   On a point of interest: the Meath County Surveyor's salary was £600 in 1899 – during research I found an entry, dated October 23rd 1899, recording the said J. H. Moore accepting a pay rise of £40 which raised his salary to £640 per annum. The entry records also that he received an annual allowance of £10 for stationery and postage to carry out the functions of his office.

4   In later years, coal supplies to the nearby Navan Gasworks were shipped from Drogheda via the Boyne Navigation to Blackcastle Quay. The gas was manufactured by 'cooking' the coal in furnaces, with the produced gas (laden with Carbon Monoxide or CO), passing through scrubbers / retorts, and then to the gasometer located on the riverbank above the works. The by-product, coke, was sold to local industries and used also as domestic fuel.

5   Navan Gas Company (Limited) was registered on April 12th 1856 – it had Capital of £4000, in 400 shares of £10 each. I obtained this information from Share No. 31 (Courtesy of Declan O'Connor – Edenderry), which share was issued to John Clarke of Navan on Aug. 6th 1856 and signed by Mat'w Kelly, Secretary.

6   Ellison.

7   Another interesting relic of Navan's history can be seen nearby, where, between 'the Fingerpost' and Bazzer Nulty's Bridge, the outlines of several stone windows and doorways are incorporated within the roadside wall. These are remnants of a five house terrace standing between the Boyne Road and the canal banks; supposedly condemned and demolished in the mid-1930s. The houses, known as 'the Long Houses,' are shown on OS maps with their gardens extending to the edge of the navigation. Old records of St. Mary's RC Church (researched by Vincent Mulvany) confirms this as an official address; an entry from June 1836 recording John O'Brien, miller, of Longhouses contributing 5 shillings towards the fund for construction of this magnificent building.

8   These mills are sometimes confused with the previously described Athlumney Boyne Mills (1854 George Mullen's flour & corn), located in Athlumney Townland just below 'the New Bridge,' above the Boyne's confluence with the River Blackwater.

9   The principle sources for this description of Atlumney Mill are the 1837 and 1911 OS maps, Cyril Ellison's *The Waters of the Boyne and Blackwater* and Griffith's 1854 valuation. Secondary sources are Larkin's Map and miscellaneous notes in M.C.L., together with

many on site explorations.

10 Griffith's records a circa 7.15 acres site located between road and railway, and another c.16.1 acres site, directly south of the railway, leased by Francis Blundell from Wm. M. Somerville Bart. Preceding the railway's arrival circa 1848, the 1837 map indicates a schoolhouse alongside the roadway leading to the larger plot; on which it marks a factory and several smaller buildings – the place now known as 'the Factory Village.' The 1852 map includes the names Factory and National School separately within the smaller field; which school-house was leased by the Commissioners of National Education from Francis Blundell at R.V.13s. County Council cottages were built alongside the road frontage of this field in the mid-20th century, and many of these modernised dwellings occupy the same site nowadays.

11 One of the first Irish-built motor cars was constructed by the Alesbury Brothers at their Edenderry works, with the vehicle being exhibited at the Dublin Motor Show in 1907. A light motorcar, reputedly with chassis and body built entirely of Irish wood; it was powered by an 8/10 HP Stevens-Durea twin cylinder engine. I believe that the four-seater car was fitted with a three-speed gearbox and had solid rubber tyres. It was manufactured in 1907 and 1908 only, but I cannot ascertain how many were produced in total: the car, known as The Alesbury, was listed as one of the earliest Brass-Era vehicles (courtesy D. O'Connor).

12 John O'Donovan's 1836 Field Notes record that *Skahan's* or *Shane's Well* was called after an old man named Shane McCaffry.

13 As described in chapter 7 (in the context of the River Nanny's source), the outflow from a nearby spring named *Gregory's Well*, links with a complex of small rills emanating from the south-eastern slopes of Carn Hill: these combine to form several small streams that coalesce and flow southwards through Crollege, to join an outflow from a well named *Tobermurry* in Realtoge, and pass beneath Follistown Bridge and flow onwards to become the Nanny Water.

14 I believe that Fitzherbert's of Blackcastle purchased the Boyne Meadows from Taaffe's of Ardmulchan in 1870.

12

The Middle Reaches
Dunmoe to Stackallan

Rowley's Lock – Crockminnan or The Kid's Hill – Farrell's Lodge & The Bush – Moran's cows & The Long Acre – Donaghmore Round Tower, Francis Ledwidge & the McGoona family – Babes Bridge, the old road network & Graig's Cross – Dunmoe Cottage – Ardmulchan House – Beauty of the Boyne Deeps – A Fishing hut on Railway Wheels – Dunmoe Mill Weir – A visit to Dunmoe Mill – Dunmoe Church & D'Arcy's Castle – Ardmulchan Church, Bells & Ringforts – Crocknagoney & Lug-Gurrum – Taaffe's Lock – The Broad Bay – Broadboyne Bridge. Teach Collan or Stackallan – The lost village & church of Stackallan – Fu Manchu & Broadboyne Br.

Rowley's Lock is named after a landed-gentry family of that name.[1] As declared by the inscription carved on its label-stone, the lock was constructed under supervision of chief engineer Richard Evans in 1792.[2] Its purpose to lift vessels traversing the waterway circa 7.9ft, from the pound level above Taaffe's Lock downstream (OS-B.M. at 100ft), to that of the pound level extending upstream to Metge's Lock in Navan. The benchmark on the lock's lower gate heelstone is at elevation 108.1ft and on the upper gate stonework at elevation 107.9ft. The Lockkeeper's house was built by Nicholas and Peter Taaffe, with the lock gates made and supplied by John Monks at £26 for each pair. According to the account in Cyril Ellison's book, the gates were floated in the Boyne at Stackallan and pulled by bullocks to their upriver destination.

The lock is located immediately below the escarpment, with the Lockkeeper's house sandwiched between canal and *Crockminnan.* A laneway once led from the front of the house across the fields to a place on the nearby old Navan to Drogheda road named 'the Bush' on the 1837 OS map. Though this name perhaps applied to a house in the locality, tradition tells of such place names deriving from resting places of tramps and other wayfarers in times past. The same map shows a place named 'the Beggars Seat' located close by on the road between Crollege and Realtoge. Next door to 'the Bush' was 'Farrell's Lodge,' named thus on the OS maps, but I cannot trace its residents on Griffith's Valuation of 1854. The lodge stood directly opposite the avenue to Ferganstown House. John O'Donovan's 1836 Field Notes say of Farrell's Lodge:

> In the td. of Ferganstown and Ballymacon, on the west side of the road that leads from Navan to Drogheda, about 1½ miles from the town of Navan, and near the border of Ardmulchan ph.
>
> This is a neat Cottage with some ornamental grounds of small extent attached to it.

The list of Lockkeepers in Cyril Ellison's book indicates that Robert Timmins was the keeper here in 1793. In 1854, Griffith's records the Boyne Nav. Co. as lessor of the house, occupied by Brigid Nally at R.V. 10 shillings.[3] The valuation indicates also that the same company held 6.25 acres of canal water and 12.6 acres of canal banks in fee at R.V. £2-10s.

The Moran family were the last occupiers of the Lock-house in this lovely, isolated spot by the Boyne, and, indeed, many older residents of Navan know the place only as Moran's Lock. I believe Julia Moran was the last official occupant of Rowley's Lock-house, residing there with her brother Stephen until the early 1960s; following his death, Julia departed the house to live in Navan. It is said that the Moran's owned two cows, one 'timed' to calve in the springtime, the other in autumn, thus providing the family with a constant supply of fresh milk. The cows foraged along the canal banks between Athlumney and Ardmulchan; the ultimate 'long acre.' A colloquialism sourced in the practice of un-landed cottiers grazing the family cow by the

Rowley's Lock-house 2014

roadsides in olden times, and indeed prevailing during my childhood days of the 1940s and 1950s.

Pulling the boats ashore below the Boyne Meadow, we scrambled onto the bank and walked along the towpath to the lock, and discovered yet another scene of decay and waste of a potentially valuable and unique amenity. The bridge label-stone, the lock and Lock-house are smothered in clinging ivy; which will lead to their destruction if not checked. The lock gates have rotted away, with the upper pair replaced by a chevron-shaped concrete wall, mimicking its pattern; a feature added to most of the locks following closure of the navigation in the 1930s, to prevent the canal banks washing out during severe flooding.

The once comfortable and scenically located Lock-house still stands beneath the towering wood of *Crocminnan*; but only just, the roof now collapsed and almost gone entirely, with dark, empty door and window openings overlooking the river. Gaunt reminders of the old building's past, when the Lockkeeper's family gained warmth from the now cold and uninviting hearth; and lighters plied the waterway, with bargeman's whip-crack and 'gid up' cry to the towing horse echoing along the valley... sights and sounds unlikely to return to this quaint setting.

North-west of the Boyne, the round tower, old church and graveyard of

Donaghmore (Donoughmore) stand near the road from Navan to Drogheda. These are the remains of an ecclesiastical settlement supposedly dating from the time of Saint Patrick. The church was re-edified in the 13th century during the Early Norman Period; which explains the church belfry, a common feature of such Anglo Norman places of worship. As this establishment is well recorded and indeed, covered in forensic-like detail by George Petrie in 1837 and by Wilde in 1849, there is nothing more I can add to the fount of knowledge.

Over the years, the McGoona family were custodians of the churchyard and possessed a wealth of folklore and information on the locality. In earlier years, the family operated a limekiln nearby, supplying lime to the area, including the Blackcastle estate.[4]

Close by the McGoona's house was a vast orchard, once known as 'the Cherry Orchard,' with a wide range of other fruit trees, including plum, pear, several varieties of apple and many of the smaller fruits.[5] Tradition holds that the renowned local poet, Francis Ledwidge, often sat musing beneath the fruit trees when composing his poetry.

Great credit is due to the local community/committee who, inspired by the Dungan family, maintain the old graveyard in pristine condition, together with promoting local history and folklore.

Rose and Eric Brady (who now occupy the site) have the following to say of this unique heritage site:

> Since we purchased McGoona's back in 2005 we are trying to restore the site and orchards to their former prestige.
>
> The old limekiln, built in the 1700's, was used as part of the quarrying activities in the surrounding area. Rock removed from the local quarries was reduced to limestone dust by heat treatment in the limekiln, and then used as a land fertilizer and the main constituent of lime mortar.
>
> The orchards, known as 'McGoona's Cherry Orchards,' played a vital

part in the life of the great Slane bard Francis Ledwidge and his best friend Mattie McGoona. It was also a source of community outings for local families from the town and surrounding areas at fruit harvest time.

With the passage of time the orchards have become unmanaged and need replenishment and renewal; it is our intention to restore the site to a level of its former glory. A rare oasis of tranquillity in the hustle and bustle of a noisy environment, the orchard overlooks the Boyne Valley, exuding a magical peace in the shadow of the monastic ruins and the round tower of Donaghmore.

Left: McGoona's Limekiln 2014, and right, in 2016

Many old legends tell of the round towers being constructed solely as refuges for monastic monks and their treasures during the era of the Norsemen's raids upon our shores; this idea being drilled into our simple minds in those distant days, when rudimentary history was taught by rote the same as catechism. But my childish brain struggled with the concept even then. I often wondered at the practicality of the proposition; of how an entire community could be housed within the tiny space, how elderly monks climbed the vertical edifice, and figured that the whole lot could be smoked out by the attackers lighting a large fire around the base.

My youthful misgivings were well founded, as the brethren at nearby Slane and Monasterboice found to their cost; because, legends say, that they, together with their monastic possessions, were burned within their respective strongholds during some of the many Viking raids up the Boyne.

Seemingly, the halls of academia had similar misgivings to that of my simple and more plebeian mind. George Petrie (1790-1866), in his gold medal winning essay *Ecclesiastical Architecture anterior to the Norman Invasion*, sheds some light on this much mooted topic. Written to the Royal Irish Academy and published in 1845, it reveals a veritable war of words between academics and antiquarians of the era regarding the origins of these ancient structures. The writings reflecting differing schools of thought amongst these august persons; some maintaining their origins could be attributed, amongst others, to the Phoenicians, the Pagans and the Danes, with their uses described variously as fire temples, sepulchral monuments and watchtowers or beacons.

Donaghmore round tower towards sunset (Pic by John Holten)

Petrie debunked many of the more exotic claims about the round towers. His own view being that they were built during the Christian period as multi-functional appendages to monastic churches; primarily as belfries (*Clog-Theach* or *Bell-Houses*) to warn of impending danger and summon people from afar to worship at the monastic church. He believed also that they were used sometimes as refuges and perhaps as watchtowers.

I understand that contemporary thinking tends to concur with Petrie's views that the round towers were used mainly as belfries. Their great height of circa 100ft causing the pealing bells to be heard at greater distances; with their secondary purpose being to provide refuge for valuables and people. The lofty access portal is explained by the need for a massive, heavy foundation to counteract the cantilever-effect of the tall towers, and render access difficult for attackers.

The River Rescue lads returned to the boats, while the remainder of us made the hike along the towpath to Babes Bridge; located a short distance downriver above the next bend. The single surviving arch stands in the midst of a chestnut grove between the canal rampart and the Boyne. It is shown as a dotted line across the river and named Donaghmore Br. (in ruins) on the 1837 OS map; while the 1911 map depicts outlines of the arch and two mid-river pillars but does not name the structure. The remaining arch spans circa 17ft and its width is approximately 16ft. With experts concluding the pillars were 6.5ft wide and allowing for the parapet walls, these dimensions suggest the bridge carried a 12ft wide roadway, from Ferganstown across the river to Donaghmore on eleven arches. The segmental pointed arch design indicates construction of the bridge dates from the Early Norman Period (circa 1200); therefore, it is one of the earliest stone bridges upon the Boyne.

The structure was known variously as Babes Bridge, Ferganson's or Farganson's Bridge and Robber's Bridge; the last name derives from tales of the area being a favourite haunt for highwaymen and cattle thieves in times past. The original title for the bridge seems to derive from a Norman named John Baub or Balbie, perhaps its builder in earlier times. A statute of 1413 reputedly decreed that lands be set aside to pay for maintenance, but these were somehow misappropriated by corrupt officials in Dublin Castle – if

Babes Bridge

true, confirming yet again that 'little new exists under the sun.'

Peter O'Keefe states that ancient records indicated the bridge was ruinous in 1463 and had collapsed by 1500; casting some doubts upon folklore telling of Oliver Cromwell's 'new model army' marching across the bridge during his murderous campaign of the 1640s and 1650s. Local legends (*Dean Cogan 1862*) say that following Phelim O'Neill's Ulster rebellion in 1641, Sir Richard Grenville's henchman, Captain Wentworh, massacred hundreds of 'protected people' hereabouts as a prelude to the arrival of 'the Great Protector.'

References in the ancient annals (Laud Manuscript/Peterborough Chronicles), to the effect that all the bridges on the Boyne, except Babes, were destroyed in the great flood of 1330 are examined in the chapter on Slane Bridge, which has a similar historical context to Babes and Trim old Bridge.

The only recorded dry crossing point (stone bridge) on the Boyne between Kilcarn and Slane in earlier days, Babes Bridge was obviously an important and strategic location. Yet no trace of the road leading to the bridge's south side is evident on the landscape immediately adjacent to the structure. During research for *On Ancient Roads*, I studied the older road network in the area and came to the following conclusions:

At Johnstown Village, the main route crossing Babes Bridge branched from the previously described old Trim to Drogheda road via Cannistown, Kilcarn Bridge and Oldtown. It headed due north from Johnstown to the old Alexander Reids Cross Roads (now Casey's Cross).[6] Here it intersected the old road from Navan through 'the Little Furze,' (later Athlumney Village), which route led across Realtoge Hill to Kentstown, and from there to Drogheda via Duleek. From the crossroads, the old route to Babes Bridge continued northwards past Killagrin (*graveyard of the tree* J.O.D. 1836), through Ferganstown, then across Babes Bridge and through Dunmoe to Graigs Cross, from where the route continued on as the ancient road to Nobber via Kilberry.

On our downriver journey, Pa. Reilly described an old stone paved roadway running in the woods alongside the Boyne from the lodge close by Blackcastle Quay to Dunmoe. He came upon many traces of this old route when fishing along the riverbanks and noted that it was well defined and constructed from a type of cobblestone.

Studying the OS maps confirms his observations, as the track is denoted by a series of double, dotted lines leading from Blackcastle to the road near Dunmoe Old Church and castle. While this may have been merely a cart-way or woodland trail connecting various elements of the Blackcastle estate (such as the four fishing weirs), it is possible that the track was laid atop a more ancient road leading from Navan to Dunmoe and connecting with Babes Bridge. For example, the avenues of several other demesnes in the vicinity, Slane, Somerville, Lismullin and Dowdstown, are traceable to older roads rerouted by the Grand Jury.[7]

It is my opinion that the old road went eastwards alongside the Boyne from Babes Bridge, then turned northwards, passing through the long gone village of Dunmoe. From where it led to Graigs Cross (1837 OS) or Craigs Cross (1911 OS) on the Slane road, to link with the older road to Nobber via Kilberry and Wilkenstown.

The variation in the names recorded on the maps is quite significant because Craig is a family name, whereas John O'Donovan's 1836 Field Notes define Graig as a Gaelic name for a village. The name; therefore, might indeed be connected either to the lost village of Dunmoe or the nearby townland of Graigs.

The family name Craig is not recorded in Griffith's 1854 valuation of Dunmoe Parish or Graigs Townland; but three small dwellings close by the crossroads were occupied variously by Laurence Gibney, James Lynch and Catherine Reilly. These houses were leased from Joseph Mc.Loughlin who in turn had 840 acres of Dunmoe leased in two lots from John R. Corballis at a combined R.V. of £752. In addition, he had several small dwellings sub-let to

Remains of ancient fish-weir at Dunmoe

The fisherman's hut at Dunmoe Weir

various tenants. The valuation and map records Mc.Loughlin residing nearby in a large building with attached out-offices (described as a Herd's house), adjacent to the site where Dunmoe House is shown on the 1911 map.[8]

On that mid-winter's day in November 2011, our little group stood on the crown of the old arch and held an impromptu meeting; discussing its history and wondering about the future. These ponderings prompted recollections of my many rambles along the towpath while recovering from a stroke. At the time I drew inspiration from the arch's very existence, while sitting beneath the chestnut trees listening to the soothing sounds of the river flowing through its ancient stonework. Thankfully, the intervention of Peter O'Keefe (then road engineer with Meath Co. Co.) and others in the 1980s ensured its survival into the new millennium... but what now? The several trees, rooted within its ancient joints, are likely to accomplish what the mighty River Boyne failed to do over many centuries; by knocking the sole surviving arch, thereby erasing this memento of our past from the landscape of the Boyne.

Downstream from Babes Bridge, we crossed the last fish-weir, which on its northern side is located within the precincts of Blackcastle. The southern half is built on the boundary of Ferganstown and Ardmulchan; therefore, its location could be described as sited in either townland. It is shaped differently to the other upstream fish-weirs, being of roughly 'C'-shaped configuration in the centre of the river, with trap slots shown on the OS maps adjoining both riverbanks. Though the weir is not very high, the boats required manhandling to cross the obstruction it causes to river navigation.

We glided past the boundary of Blackcastle Demesne and Dunmoe just

Aerial Boyne at Dunmoe *c.* 1958 showing the limekiln, mill and castle. Courtesy M.C.L.

downstream from the weir and travelled on downriver through yet another scenic riverscape; the Boyne reach above Ardmulchan Church, described by Wilde as 'Rhine-like.' Dunmoe is a parish consisting of about 995 acres, which is not subdivided into townlands. In a nook at its north-western mereing with Blackcastle is a house named Dunmoe Cottage on the OS maps, the first of two such named places we encounter within the parish. Griffith's describes this as a Herd's house and offices, and indicates also that it was leased by Thomas Martin from John R. Corballis, together with 13 acres of land at R.V. £15-5s. On the riverbank just downstream from the cottage stand the ruins of Dunmoe Corn Mill. Griffith's indicates that in 1854, Edmund Commons had the mill, with house, offices and land totalling c.18.76 acres leased from Thomas Martin at R.V. £30. Other records show that this mill was operated by the same family until circa 1920.

Directly across the Boyne from Dunmoe Mill, the imposing bulk of Ardmulchan House stands on an eminence overlooking this majestic reach of river valley. The house and stables form part of Ardmulchan Demesne and estate, long associated with horse breeding and equestrian events. The original house was the ancestral home of the Taaffes, landed gentry who had other holdings in the area.

About 1900, a Scottish family named Fletcher acquired the property. They demolished the old house and built the present Edwardian-style mansion

Left: A discussion at Dunmoe Mill ruins.
Right: Hopper Rennicks and Martin Curran at Dunmoe Mill wheelhousing

on its site, using much of the material from the older structure, together with bricks from nearby Skahanassey (Tully's Brickyard) and other material imported from Scotland. The Fletcher family owned the property until 1950, when it was sold to Anthony Riddell Martin, whose name became legendary in the context of his association with the horse racing industry and his many exploits around Navan. A German family bought the estate in the 1960s, and though it has changed hands several times since, I believe it maintains strong ties to horse breeding and racing traditions. A long tier of steps leads down from the house to the canal banks, where a private footbridge spans the waterway. This is a beautiful location, with a magnificent view of Dunmoe Castle across the valley.[9]

Travelling by boat down this river reach between Babes Bridge and Dunmoe Weir was a memorable experience; although I walked the riverbanks many times over the years, the mid-river perspective is very different. From the towpath, the vista is curtailed by trees or perhaps one's inability to obtain the perfect vantage point. Whatever the reason, the view from midstream seemed more appealing, almost three dimensional. Ahead towards Dunmoe I saw bright water stretching onwards between high banks covered in winter's russet foliage; with low-angled sunshine reflecting from the river, highlighting the grey mist rising above the murmuring falls. Looking aft towards the darkening woods of Blackcastle, a different scene unfolded; Boyne's darker waters here reflecting wildwood towering over its banks, inverted images mirrored from

Contrasts at Dunmoe Weir

the glassy surface, like portraits hung upside down in nature's art gallery.

Drifting along on these placid river deeps above the weir, I noted the mostly deciduous wildwood of Blackcastle changing to the evergreen hues of conifer plantations; in eye-catching contrast to the endless rim of Boyne water pouring across the falls into the cauldron of white foam beneath. On the opposite shore, the green-painted fisherman's hut, overlooking the weir, stood out in bold relief against the backdrop formed by the high, wooded slopes of Ardmulchan. I recalled that during their ramble along the river in 1978, Seamus Heaney and his travelling companion, Anthony Bailey, took advantage of the hut to rest awhile and admire the beauty of the scene.

I reflected also on my own rambles down 'the Ramparts,' while re-learning to walk following a stroke in 1999, that I too, used the same hut's rickety chairs to ease aching limbs while my eyes absorbed the charming riverscape of Dunmoe.

The hut is mounted on what appears to be an old railway bogey, its flanged metal wheels buried in the soft loam of the riverbank nowadays. Although unfamiliar with its history, I presume it was wheeled out along the towpath from Navan some years ago and may be a relic of the Dublin/Navan Railway, once known as *the Meath Road*.

Dunmoe Weir is a mill weir, running in a great crescent across the river

Dunmoe Mill Weir - Courtesy Alan Russell

to the northern bank, where it leads in to the headrace that once powered Dunmoe Mill. Although not a fish-weir, a set of eel traps were located in the millrace near the mill; this was common practice in all the Boyne mills, with the millers supplementing their sometimes sparse income with revenue from eels. Moreover, the tough, leathery eel skins were commonly used as bindings for various appurtenances and items of mill machinery, including drive belt jointings.

The other boat shot across the weir while Martin and the boys pulled ours in to the bank above the millrace, where we scrambled through dense undergrowth to an old laneway; in my opinion the former route of the ancient road leading northwards from Babes Bridge. Nowadays this links with a cul de sac leading to the Slane road near Graigs Cross. The old maps indicate a cluster of houses standing alongside this ancient roadway between the mill and the crossroads, perhaps remnants of what was once known as Dunmoe Village.

The riverbank and lane close by the mill are mostly overgrown, so we beat our way through weeds and briars, past the remains of the old ivy covered limekiln and on to the mill ruins, standing on the riverbank above the weir. This was one of the smaller mills on the Boyne, not a larger industrial flour mill of the type that flourished following enactment of the 'new' Corn Laws in the mid-18th century. Which might suggest that Dunmoe Corn Mill could be a building of some antiquity, the original perhaps dating from late medieval times. But, like many other old buildings alongside the Boyne, the partly crumbled and roofless mill seems to be held together by ivy, clinging to most parts of its ancient but reasonably sound stonework. Other buildings to the north and east of the mill, possible remnants of the millers' house and former granaries, could not be examined because of dense briars and vegetation.

The mill straddles the millrace, with the remains of the eel traps located on the little island separating river and headrace. The millwheel housing is on the southern gable and incorporated as part of the building's main structure. The dimensions of the housing, together with the height and configuration of the head and tailraces, suggest that the millwheel was circa 12 to14ft in diameter and 3 to 4ft wide. The remains of the wheel hubs, the apron-board slots and low abutment wall, further suggest that the millwheel was a breast-shot, overhung type, supported by a pedestal bearing mounted on the low wall. Two cast or wrought iron, six-spoked hubs lie on the floor within the remains of the stone housing. Rusting relics of the days when this mill ground corn and provided a place of social interaction for the local community, a time that has well and truly passed on in the new millennium.[10]

The story of Dunmoe Mill has a little sequel, related to us by Hopper Rennicks during one of our trips down the Boyne. Several years earlier, an East German named Willie Eigeman acquired the site and established basic living quarters within the old mill. Restoring and operating the eel traps, he set up outlets exporting eels to the German market; also bringing fishing enthusiasts from Europe to fish the Boyne and River Moy in Mayo. He had greater plans

Left: Part of millwheel hub Dunmoe Mill. Right: The author at Dunmoe Mill.

for Dunmoe; however, so dismantled an old sugar refinery in Austria, shipping its greenheart timbers to Navan for use in restoring the mill. Unfortunately, he passed away before bringing these plans to fruition, so the enterprise died with him. But on our visit we saw his simple quarters set up in the old building, and wondered if some other enterprising person will carry on the ancient tradition of eel harvesting from the Boyne at Dunmoe Mill.

Boarding the boat again, we made our attempt to cross the weir near its southern end, but hung up about midway across. Following some slagging from the other boat's crew and more acrobatics by Pa. and Hopper, we floated away from the white water, albeit very wet and with a boat half full of Boyne water. Passing beyond the weir, we could see the great bulk of Dunmoe Castle, and hear the wind whistling through the empty windows and across its crumbling walls. The castle, one of many tower houses on the fringes of The Pale, was supposedly built by Hugh De Lacy circa 1200, during the early years of the Norman Conquest. The building was gutted by a great fire in 1799, which perhaps caused much of the structural damage referred to by Wilde in the following account of this castle and attendant church in 1849:

> "Dunmoe Castle stands on a commanding eminence, above one of the fords upon the Boyne, and must have been originally a position of great strength. The stones, however, with which it is built, are remarkably small, in consequence of which it is yearly crumbling into a shapeless mass of ruins. It is an oblong pile, with circular flanking towers on its river face, which measures seventy-three feet. It was originally built, it is said, by De Lacy, but the present structure bears the evidence of an Anglo Norman keep of the sixteenth century. It has had many masters and stood several sieges in its day…" "This castle was re-edified and inhabited while James ll. was in Ireland. Its last lord was D'Arcy, whose name is now usually associated with it…" "Within the adjoining enclosure is a small chapel containing the mausoleum of its last lords; it is now a filthy dungeon exposed to the atmosphere, and strewed with the bones and coffins of the descendants of this once noble family. Some twenty years more, and the traveller will have to inquire for the site of this castle of the Pale."

Dunmoe castle

The above assessment of the castle is very accurate except for one small detail. Although much of the northern section has gone, the castle's river-facing façade, which Wilde predicted would disappear entirely within twenty years, still stands prominently upon the Boyne's northern bank over one and a half centuries later – its crumbling structure an object of great interest for tourists strolling along the canal towpath on the opposite riverbank.

The Boyne flows due east for a short distance below Dunmoe Weir, then sweeps in a graceful curve north-eastwards beneath the high ridge at Ardmulchan; named *Crocknagoney* (hill of the rabbits) in the 1836 Field Notes. Atop this eminence are the ancient ruins of Ardmulchan Church and belfry and an earthen ringfort; commanding an unspoiled vista of wooded canal and rampart, winding river and brooding castle, framed by the rolling, pastoral landscape of County Meath.

The name Ardmulchan has several different spellings e.g. Boundary Sketch of 1829 *Ard Mullachain*, the height or hill of the little summit; Annals of the Four Masters *Recte Ard-Maelchon*, Maelchu's height or hill; Civil Survey 1656 *Ardmulchain*. John O'Donovan agrees with the Civil Survey spelling and adds the following to his 1836 Field Notes: "Mr. Taafe has put the correct spelling of this name on the winkers of his horses" – presumably a reference to the incumbent Mr. Taafe in Ardmulchan House.

The Annals of the Four Masters tell of a great battle fought near Ardmulchan circa 968 AD, in which the southern Hy-Neill were defeated by a combined force of Leinstermen and Danes, under the leadership of Amlaff (Olaf) Cuaran. Other tales are told of the old church and three-storeyed belfry on the hilltop being built upon the fabric of an ancient castle of the Tyrrells, and that Ardmulchan belonged to the Earls of Kildare (Fitzgeralds) for a period. The history of this place is covered in greater detail by several historians, including Elizabeth Hickey, an extensive excerpt from whose work

Ardmulchan Church overlooks the 'Rhine-like' Boyne & Navigation from Crocknagoney (the author c. 2007)

is included in *Yellow Furze Memories,* by Conor Brennan. So we will not tarry further, but continue our journey downriver towards Stackallan.

We passed beneath *Crocknagoney*[11] and on the northern riverbank observed an old railway wagon, sometimes used as a refuge for rod-fishermen. Further downstream we came to a series of weed covered islets running askew across the river, from the Dunmoe bank to the canal rampart directly below Ardmulchan Ringfort. These are what remain of the ancient manorial/monastic fish-weir of Ardmulchan, granted to Donat (Donough), Earl of Thomond in March 1593 as part of the possessions of Ardmulchan. The record shows also that they were eel weirs but in ruinous condition. Though ruined for many years, the weir still represents a major obstacle to navigation, overcome eventually by manhandling the boat through the old trap slots near the southern riverbank. During these water sports, Pa. snagged on a submerged object, from which he experienced some difficulty getting free; doing so eventually and floating on downriver in hot (or cold) pursuit.

Just below the weir is a deep pool, known as Lug Gurrum or 'the Blue Pool,' into which, legends say, the three bells of Ardmulchan Church were thrown following the Reformation in the mid-16th century. This event supposedly occurred to prevent Protestants being called to worship at the former RC Church, acquired by 'the new religion.' If true, one might wonder are the bells still lying on the muddy riverbed beneath.

The Boyne curves north-eastwards beyond this weir, with the canal and

Above:
Remnants of
Ardmulchan fish-weir
- possibly dates from
1500s

Right:
Taaffe's Lock c. 1896
- from Shackleton
collection

Facing page:
Boyne Nav' Taaffe's
Lock gates 2007
(the author 2007)

rampart following the same line. About mid-way along the curve we come to Taaffe's or Bective Lock, constructed c.1792. The former name deriving from the Taaffe family of Ardmulchan, the latter from the Earl of Bective, a member of the Taylor (Headfort) dynasty and one of the Upper Boyne Navigation trustees. Griffith's shows that in 1854, the Boyne Navigation Co. held 53.76 acres of canal banks in fee at Ardmulchan at R.V. £3-9s., including the area from the townland mereing below Babes Bridge to Stackallan Bridge.

Beside the lock, an aqueduct carries/carried the canal across a stream flowing down through a small, wooded glen truncating *Crocknagoney*. This stream rises in a series of springs on the north-eastern slopes of Carn Hill, and flows past the old monastic settlement of Ardmulchan; perhaps forming its main water supply in days long gone. As I could find no local name for the river, I suggest 'Ardmulchan Stream' as a suitable title.

The Lock-house at Taaffe's Lock was occupied in 1854 by Thomas Murphy at R.V. 11s., the lessor being the Boyne Navigation Co. (B.N.C). The OS maps show two buildings adjacent to the lock; one on a small plot of land (0.540 acre) to the south of the canal, the other located between the rampart and river. I could find no trace of the latter building, which was, I believe, an outbuilding or shed and later used as a fishing hut. The site on the opposite

Lower Dunmoe Fish-weir at No. 3 milestone - probably dates from at least 1500s

or south side of the canal is densely overgrown, so cannot be searched for remnants of the Lock-house; once accessed via footbridges on the lock gates.[12]

The OS Benchmark on the lower gate's heelstone is at elevation 99.9ft, and on the stonework of the upper gate at 100ft. This lock provided a lift of about 8.5ft from the pound level above Stackallan or Thomson's Lock at 91.3ft elevation, to the pound level of circa 100ft, the approximate operating level between here and Rowley's Lock upstream. The ivy covered, rotted remnants of the wooden gates are in situ at time of writing. After clearing some greenery, I found the old rack and pinion sluice operating mechanism; though the gears are missing, it is evident that this lock was equipped with the improved double-reduction system, capable of operation by one person. The visible stonework seems sound enough; however, the label stone has now disappeared beneath the ivy and scrub, covering the old lock below the high ridge of Ardmulchan.

Rounding the curve and passing by the No. 3 navigation milestone, we came to another old 'C'-shaped weir athwart the river about 50 metres downstream of the marker stone. This obstruction we crossed with little difficulty. It was obviously a fish-weir in olden times, as the river torrent pours at great speed through the former trap slots near the southern bank. This may be the remains of a weir in Dunmoe, recorded in the Civil Survey of 1656 and later the subject of a grant to George D'Arcy in 1684. Passing onwards through the white water, signs of Mother Nature re-establishing supremacy were evidenced by a small willow tree, clinging limpet-like to rocks forming the ancient traps.

Further downstream, the Boyne sweeps to the north-east through a short, 'S'-shaped reach, then continues towards Stackallan. The river is sprinkled hereabouts with sedgy clumps and flows through a broadening floodplain beneath grassy, tree-dotted pastureland rising towards high ridges on both sides. But the canal follows a straight line, to re-join the riverbank close by Stackallan Bridge; this divergence isolates a c.14 acres section of meadow bottoms (water-meadow) between navigation rampart and river. Prior to the advent of the canal, the wider floodplain became known as Broad Boyne; which in even earlier times was called 'the Broad Bay of Ardmulchan.'

Looking eastwards from our boat along 'the broad bay,' we could see the greyish stone arches of Stackallan Bridge emerging wraith-like from the wintry haze at the head of the wide reach. The bridge crosses the Boyne from south-east to north-west, connecting the townland of Ardmulchan to both Stackallan and Dunmoe; the road running northwards from the bridge to Wicker's (Wigger's) Crossroads forming the mereing between Dunmoe Parish and Stackallan Townland. In the north-east corner of Dunmoe and close by the bridge is the other residence named Dunmoe Cottage on the OS maps. Griffith's shows that in 1854, this house, with offices and land totalling c.10 acres was leased by Rev. Robert Hamilton from James Aylmer at R.V. £19-10s. On the opposite shore, in the nook formed by the intersection of canal and road, are the remains of another ancient ringfort; reputedly employed in older times as a training camp for the Meath Militia, but more recently used as a gravel pit.

The bridge is a magnificent structure and described variously as the Bridge of the Boyne, Broadboyne Bridge and Stackallan Bridge; in the mid-18th century it was known as Bray Bridge and recorded as such on Grand Jury presentments. The other three titles can trace their origins to the several names used for the area; however, the name Bray poses something of a puzzle.

Above:
Broadboyne Bridge

Right:
Hidden 7th eye of Broadboyne Br. - in grounds of Dunmoe Cottage

While some say it may derive from a composite of the words forming the name Broad Bay; I would suggest as an alternative that it perhaps derives from the Scottish word Brae, meaning a slope or hillside, possibly translating to 'the Bridge of the Slopes' or 'Bridge of the Hills.' A title fitting the location admirably, as the bridge connects the hillsides on both sides of the river.

The age of the structure is uncertain, but it was probably built sometime after 1714, as it does not appear on Pratt's 1702 map or Moll's Map of 1714. Grand Jury presentments were made for major repairs to its battlements and replacement of coping stones in 1760; therefore, it was possibly constructed during the interim 46 year period. The bridge consists of six 30ft span medium rise segmental arches, with five inter-arch 6ft wide pillars, and heavy stone abutments at each riverbank:[13] it is 24ft wide face to face and about 18.5ft in road width, being built originally to carry an old line of the Dublin to Carrickmacross/Ardee or Kells road across the River Boyne. All the pillars have triangular cutwaters, both upstream and downstream, extending to parapet level and including pedestrian refuges. While examining the underside, we noted this structure was not widened in times past; and that shuttering corbels protruded from the arch-springer stonework.

Researching Grand Jury presentment books of the 18th and 19th centuries, I noted many requests for funds to replace bridge parapets and coping stones throughout the county. In several instances, the record indicated that the stonework was *stolen*; perhaps an additional reason for use of iron dowelling to secure the stonework, from both the ravages of nature and the thieving hands of man. Local people tell me that some of the bridge stonework was stolen in recent times.[14] The contemporary 4ft high parapets were constructed c.1812, as evidenced by the following presentment submitted to the Meath Grand Jury Lent Assizes of 1812:

> "We present £204-13s-9p, to be raised, as before, and paid to Gus Lambert, Michael Brownwell, Robert May and J.M. Grainge to repair a bridge on lands of Stackallen on the road from Carrickmacross to Dublin, overseers' wages £10-4s-9d., Amount £214-18s-6d."

An extension to the bridge was built on the southern riverbank in 1792, to carry the road across the new canal. Richard Evans designed this structure, as evidenced by the label stone adorning the parapet, which informs us also that the bridge is named Thomson's Bridge. From the distinctive style of the carving, it is apparent that this stone was engraved by the same craftsman who completed the label stones on the bridges at Rowley's and Ruxton Locks. The segmental, low profiled arch springs from vertical walls on each side, the structure merging with the abutment of the larger bridge; with a slight hump back rising above the flattened line of the existing crossing. The rampart ascends steeply to road level between the two bridges, where the towpath passed through a gateway, approximately 10ft wide, and crossed the road to a similar opening in the opposite parapet wall. This provided access to a narrow spit of land running downriver to Stackallan or Thomson's Lock.

Stackallan is a parish and townland located on the northern riverbank. In 1836, John O'Donovan concluded that the name Stackallan derives from the

Right: Furrows in stonework of Thomson's Br. - created by tow-rope friction

Gaelic *Tigh Collain* or *Teach Collan* (St Conain's house) – and quotes Bishop Ceternach (early 10th century), as follows:

> It is curious to remark, that in some of those districts, colonised by the Danes and English, the Teach or Tigh, of the Irish, was made Sta or Sti as in this instance [Stackallan], and in Stickell, Stagonnell, Stillorgan, in Irish Tig Chillin, Teac Chonnell, Tig Lorcain. *(sic)*

O'Donovan includes the following pertaining to the long disappeared village and church of Stackallan, located circa one mile north of the bridge:

> In the W. part Stackallan td. , 4 ½ miles N.E. from Navan.
> A small village of some 10 ground-floor, thatched cottages, adjoining the N.E. of Boyne House demesne. The parish church, a small and apparently old building, is at the S. end of the village, from which it is separated by a small stream. A Boys' school is held in a room in the west end of the roof of the church; the average attendance is said to be 30, but on the day I visited it there were only 19 boys present, of which 3 were Protestants and 16 R. Catholics. The scholars pay 2s. a quarter for being taught spelling and reading, and 3s per quarter for writing and arithmetic. The Rev. Mr. Disney gives 5 guineas a year for the support of the school. In the village there is a girls' school, a small neat building; it is supported by Lord Boyne's family. The church can accommodate 100 persons; its average attendance is 40. Over the church door is a small tablet bearing an inscription very difficult to decipher and a knight's helmet in demi relief with a crest that appears to be a Phoenix in a nest of flames. The shield that should accompany the helmet has been removed or defaced. On the eastern side of the door of the church, and close to it, is an old flat tombstone embedded in the ground. There is writing on it in in old English characters.

These notes were compiled by H. Tucker Lt., R. E.,18th April, 1836.
The above excerpt from the OS Field Notes provides an excellent insight to Stackallan Village of long ago, and paints an important picture of pre-famine times in rural parts of the Boyne Valley. When the old church was

demolished a few years ago, I believe that several artifacts were removed to the church in Slane.

I have abiding memories of Broadboyne Bridge and its beautiful landscape because of my peripheral involvement in an incident that occurred there during my teenage years. A series of films depicting the dreaded Oriental archvillain, *Fu Manchu,* appeared on cinema screens worldwide during the 1960s; one of these *The Face of Fu Manchu,* included scenes filmed at Broadboyne Bridge.

Sometime in the summertime of 1964, while working as an apprentice-mechanic in Navan Engineering Works, I accompanied Sonny McNally in the breakdown truck (the only such vehicle in Navan equipped with a crane at the time) out to Stackallan, where the bridge was part of a film set. Being merely nineteen years of age, I was greatly excited while driving in the old Ford F.600 V8 (c.1956 Petrol model) pickup over 'the New Bridge' and out the Boyne Road towards Haystown. Though oblivious to the name or content of the movie, I was looking forward to my involvement, be it ever so simple.

At the scene, I noted a crowd of film technicians clustered on and around the bridge at the bottom of Sharpe's Hill; where an old 1930s Austin 10 lay

Ford F600 V 8 truck used in 1964 during filming of the scenes from film 'the Face of Fu Manchu' - Courtesy D. Woods

canted over on its running board, tilted towards the Boyne side of the canal rampart. Though my memory of the event is dimmed by the passage of over forty years, I recall the sense of amazement at the scene presented to my youthful and inexperienced eyes. The stuntman stood next to the old car, all padded up like an American Footballer; the inside of the old Austin was padded in similar fashion and reinforced by ironwork, to avoid injury to the driver. This caused me to hold a jaundiced view of Hollywood's super heroes' 'feats of derring-do' in future years. A coat of black paint covered the car's bright metalwork to avoid dazzling the film camera.

The first shoot had failed because the old car, being so heavy, refused to cooperate by rolling down the canal rampart into the river. Our job now was to pull the Austin up the slope to the road; which we did and awaited with interest for a second shoot. The sequence formed part of a car chase set in 1930s England, hence the unspoiled setting of Stackallan. I watched while the set-carpenters replaced the smashed *Balsawood* (Hollywood) gate; the director considering it not prudent to have the car crash into the stout old oak gate, where once the draught horses passed through the gap between the round stone piers set in the parapet wall.

All being ready, the Austin came tearing down Sharpe's Hill, crossed the hump on Thomson's Bridge, then, with an almighty screech of brakes, performed a handbrake-turn and smashed the flimsy new gate to smithereens – but this shoot was a failure, too, because the car still refused to roll down the slope.

So on it went, for the next several days the film crew tried to get the perfect shoot; but all their efforts failed because the cumbersome, old car lost too much momentum in the right-angled turn, required to take it through the narrow gateway onto the rampart. But I didn't care, as I lay basking in the warm summer sun, a very welcome interlude in the tedium of a mechanic's life.

The story had a postscript; however, the old Austin lay rusting in the vacant lot beside Navan Engineering Works for a long time thereafter. I cannot recall its eventual fate; maybe it was scrapped or perhaps claimed by some vintage car enthusiast to be lovingly restored. Time passed as did my memory of the events at Broadboyne Bridge; until one day, while serving somewhere on the high seas with Shell Tankers, I watched the movie *The Face of Fu*

Dunmoe Castle - Ardmulchan House and the Rhine-like Boyne from Ardmulchan -
Courtesy Alan Russell

Manchu. This scene, the source of so much excitement in my life all those
years earlier, took less than thirty seconds to unfold on screen; the director
having overcome the Austin's failure to cooperate by cutting the action as the
car crashed through the gate.

During my cycling days in the 1960s, I used Sharpe's Hill while training
for the annual Ras Tailteann – puffing and panting my weary way past the old
'Emergency pillbox,' set about mid-way up near the ancient ringfort, perhaps
once part of 'the House of Cletty.' Though short enough, the hill provides
one of the toughest climbs in County Meath because of the steep ascent; but
all the effort was rewarded by the magnificent view across the Boyne Valley
from the hilltop.

ENDNOTES

1 In July 1800, Clotworthy (Taylor) Rowley (1763-1825) was created 1ˢᵗ Baron Langford, supposedly as an inducement to change his vote to one in favour of the Act of Union, passed in 1801 – another of the so-called Union Peerages.

2 The bridge at Rowley's Lock was not built as a horse-bridge, but to access the towpath and lands cut off by the canal, such as the Boyne Meadows – see comments later in the chapter concerning ancient roads leading to Babes Bridge.

3 A list of Lockkeepers, compiled for Meath Co. Council's Road Committee in 1913 during a review of the navigation's proposed liquidation, names A. Dowdall as keeper at this lock, and shows him in receipt of a quarter-annual salary of 10s and 6d.

4 The Meath Chronicle records litigation taking place regarding right of way access to this kiln. One hearing on Aug. 26ᵗʰ 1924, the other on July 3ʳᵈ 1926 – in both instances the judge's decision favoured the McGoona's. Interesting historical snippets emerged from these hearings, including: that no lime was burned at the kiln since the 1870s, and that another hearing had taken place earlier before a 'Republican Court,' which also found in favour of the McGoona's.

5 In 1854 the area including Mc'Goona's house, orchard and limekiln is recorded on Griffith's Valuation thus: Lot 16a – house and land totalling 3 acres 2 roods 9 perches, leased by Matthew M'Gowran from trustees of Richard R. Fitzherbert @ R.V. £5-15s. N.B., I believe M'Gowran was an older form/spelling of McGoona.

6 This old junction is named Alexander Reids Cross Roads on the 1837 OS map. It was a 'staggered' junction prior to building of the new road from the Fingerpost (Crossways) junction to Kentstown in 1814/16. Larkin's Map depicts both the older and newer road lines in the vicinity of this crossroads, many of the older roads have since been erased from the landscape.

7 Thomas Williams' 1756 sketch map of Navan Town depicts a short length of truncated road, running eastwards along the Boyne from the later site of Blackcastle gate lodge at the north-eastern end of Poolboy Br. This old roadway is marked 'Road to the Fields' and is traceable on the 1824 estate map of Blackcastle.

8 The foregoing snippets are included as an indicator of how some place names have changed down through the years, thereby losing their significance, context and relevance to the local topography and landscape – and as a snapshot of the prevailing local agrarian system, perhaps an interesting insight of rural Ireland in the immediate aftermath of the Great Hunger.

9 More details of Ardmulchan House and its history are given in Yellow Furze Memories, whose author, Conor Brennan, worked on the estate for its various owners over the years.

10 Note the reference in the next chapter to Stackallan/Ardmulchan Corn Mill further downstream, operated in 1791 by a man named John Martin. Perhaps he was related to Thomas Martin who leased Dunmoe Mill to Edmund Commons in 1854 – it is noteworthy that some people also referred to Dunmoe Mill as Martin's Mill.

11 A wooded, truncated-spur-like ridge petering out as a rocky outcrop above Taaffe's Lock

12 A list of Lockkeepers, compiled for Meath Co. Council's Road Committee in 1913 during a review of the navigation's proposed liquidation, names John Murphy as keeper at this lock (Ardmulchan), and shows that he was in receipt of a quarter-annual salary of 10s-6d. Another entry in this report states that the Lock-house at Bective Lock was leased as a fishing lodge in 1914.

13 Another smaller segmental arch pierces the upstream façade on the north-western river-bank, hidden from the river by a sloping stone buttress. This opening was most likely used as a flood arch in times past, but its downstream end is walled up by masonry. The arch is c.10ft wide by about 6ft high and is now high and dry due to increase of surrounding ground levels. N.B., a professional assessment of this bridge, and more Grand Jury information are included on pp. 23/24 of Peter O'Keefe's The Dublin to Navan Road and Kilcarn Bridge.

14 At time of writing, the parapets were damaged by vehicular impact, and have been repaired, not very well, may I add, with the 'repairs' sticking out like 'sore thumbs' compared to the stonework executed by the stonemasons of long ago!

13

The Middle Reaches
Stackallan – Hays – The Navigation

Conor Brennan & Cottonmill Road – Boyne Lighters – Thomson's Lock & bridge – Sir William Wilde & Lugaree Pool – House of Cletty — Martin's Mill & Stackallan Weir – Fagan's Sibin – O'Brien's Corn Mill – Bride's Well, the bent railway & the Famine Br. – Darling Lilly & The Pink Panther – Green Lanes & Farrell's Smithy – Seamus Heaney & Triffids – Draught horses & barges – Stackallan Guard Lock & hidden canals – Deerpark Lock – Castlefin (Reilly's), Cruicetown Locks & Carney's Tuck Mill – Carrickdexter Lock & the lost canal of Ligpulse – the grand pool of Lagpolse.

This takes us to the crook in the Boyne, referred to as Stackallan Weir. Conor Brennan's *Yellow Furze Memories* provides a vivid picture of country life as it was here in the first half of the 20th century; and indeed a unique insight into earlier times.

The book is an invaluable source of local history and folklore, providing snippets difficult to find elsewhere; including a tale of three canal lighters, moored alongside the Boyne at Stackallan. These old canal boats, used as platforms for swimming and fishing, disappeared from landscape and memory over the passing years. He tells of how the former Youth Hostel was once Fagan's Pub (closed in 1927, it became a shebeen [sibin] in later years),

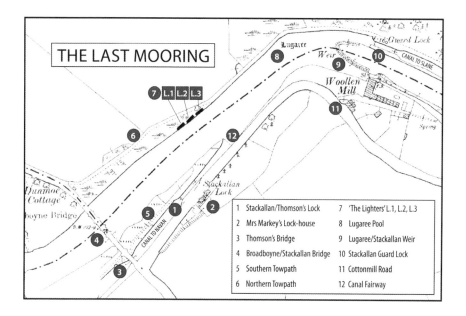

and many other tales of the locality; including names of families living in the terrace of seven worker's houses at the old cotton mills.

This book emphasises the importance of local history and folklore, and how it provides mortar for binding together the many complex strands of mainstream history.

The above lighters were the last of James McCann's (later John Spicer's) fleet that plied the waterway in the early years of the 20th century.[1] Note the following excerpt from Cyril Ellison's book referencing a submission from John Spicer to the Board of Trade c.1915, in an attempt to save the waterway:

> He was prepared to allow his firm's boats to be taken over by any new company. The fleet at that time consisted of three wooden lighters bought from McCann and repaired in the dry dock and a 'fine iron boat in perfect order,' perhaps the same one entered in the 1884 accounts with a book value of £250 and named the Wasp.

Back on the boat and passing under Broadboyne Bridge, we lingered awhile beneath the ancient arches to examine and admire the older-style craftsmanship, then continued on downriver. The towpath ran along the spit of land forming the canal rampart, from the bridge to Thomson's (Stackallan)

Clockwise from top left: The Fu-Manchu gate; Thomson's Canal Bridge; Broadboyne and Thomson's canal Bridge - Shackleton Collection *c.* 1896

Lock. This is the first of three public road crossings we encounter on the entire navigation between Athlumney and Drogheda.

Here the towpath had a choice of two routes; one taking the path up the incline and across the road via 'the Fu Manchu gate.' The other line veered right and ran on a ledge beneath Thomson's Bridge, with both paths re-joining and leading to the lock. The latter route was obviously used extensively, as evidenced by several 'rope furrows,' worn into the bridge pillars by the barge tow ropes. In 1854, the spit of land (I acre 2 roods 3 perches in area) forming the rampart downstream of Broadboyne Bridge, was leased by Peter Taaffe from the B.N.C. at R.V. 6 shillings. An indication that perhaps this part of the rampart had become defunct as the towpath, and Cottonmill Road, from the bridge to the lock, was employed as the canal track-way. I believe that the Markey family from the former Lock-house used this section of land as a vegetable garden during WWll, but the little peninsula is overgrown nowadays, presenting a challenge to the hardiest of Boyne rod-fishermen.

Stackallan or Thomson's Lock is located on the right or southern bank approximately three hundred metres below the bridge, where the lateral canal from Navan locked-out to the open river. An attendant Lockkeepers' house is sited across the road; beneath a high bluff and still in use as a pristine, modern residence. The lock was so named after Skeffington Thomson from Rathnally; one of the canal trustees, whose family also owned property at Dillonsland in Navan.

The title of this lock can cause some confusion, because, although shown as Stackallan Lock on the maps and sketches, its actual location is within the parish and townland of Ardmulchan (old). Griffith's indicates the Lockkeepers' house occupied by Bryan Fagan in 1854 at R.V. 15s., while Cyril Ellison's book shows it occupied by Bridget Crinion in 1860. It is worth noting that the 1854 valuation indicates Bridget Crinion in occupation of the Lock-house further downstream at Deerpark Lock,[2] on the opposite riverbank. While the lady may have moved abode in the interim period, it is more likely that this may be an example of the confusion caused by the lock's title.

Conor Brennan's book provides additional anecdotal snippets regarding the Lock-house at Stackallan/Thomson's Lock. He tells of how, in the early years of the 20th century, the house was home to a well-known character named Johnny Murphy; whose antecedents supposedly lived there and operated the lock for many years beforehand. They were related to the Murphy family residing at Taaffe's Lock further upstream. Johnny, an accomplished rod-fisherman, acted as gillie for several local fisheries and 'visiting gentlemen.'[3]

The following is quoted from Conor's recollections of an old cottage that once stood close by the Lock-house in Ardmulchan (Thomson's Lock):

Lock-house at Thomson's (Stackallan) Lock

Reminiscences

Just above Mrs. Markey's house on the same side of the road I remember a little thatched cabin owned by a Mrs. Farrell or Farrelly, a tidy little old lady, she had a little shop and she was called "the Bunch". It was a great treat to be brought in and handed a penny toffee or six "bulls eyes". A few years later we could quietly purchase a single "woodbine" for one penny. That is now 74 years ago and still remaining is a white rose-bush which blooms each year as it did long ago around the door of the little house.

The Meath Chronicle of March 10th 1900 reports on a tragic drowning occurring on the night of 27-28th Feb. 1900. The inquest heard that on the night in question, the Lockkeeper, John Murphy, was informed by his next door neighbour, Margaret Lynass, of someone falling into the lock and shouting for help. When searching the chamber, he discovered a body in the water, which he recovered by using his fishing rod – though the male victim, a resident of nearby Haystown, showed signs of life, he failed to respond to resuscitation and expired some time later. The jury, whose foreman was Mr. Matthew Mullen, found that the deceased came by his death at Ardmulchan due to drowning and added the following rider to their verdict:

> We the jury, wish to call the attention of the authorities who are responsible for the demolition of the protection wall of Ardmulchan Lock, to have the same secured in such a way as to protect life.

The wall protecting the lock may have been demolished to allow usage of Cottonmill Road as a towpath for draft horses taking barges to the lock, as suggested earlier. The canal authorities seemingly paid scant attention to the jury's recommendation; because the lock remains unprotected by a roadside wall at time of writing over a century later.

The OS Benchmark on the stonework of this lock is at elevation 91.5ft at the lower gate heelstone and at elevation 91.3ft on the upper gate stonework. The lock had a lift/drop of approximately 6ft; from the navigable river level of circa 86.6ft above Stackallan Weir, to approximately 91.3ft, the pound level to Taaffe's Lock further upstream. The 1837 OS map shows other buildings sited on the opposite roadside above the lock. These may have survived from the operations base, set up here during construction of the Upper Boyne Navigation, from Carrickdexter to Navan in the period 1790-1800.[4]

Below Thomson's Lock and immediately above the weir, the 1837 OS map depicts a place named Lugaree; which name translates to 'the King's Hole,' known to some as 'the King's Shear.' The latter name may derive from a medieval (14th century) law, obliging owners of fish-weirs to provide a 24ft wide gap enabling 'the King's boats' traverse the river without obstruction. This free passage was known in olden times as a Watersarde (further reference to this is made in the chapter on Oldbridge). Wilde states that the pool was a sacred place in pagan times, a tradition maintained during the Christian period. A Patron or Pattern (a religious ceremony) was conducted annually until the early 19th century; whereby it became customary to swim cattle and horses across the river as a charm against fairies and diseases. It is probable that the name Lugaree derives entirely from the King's Shear or Watersarde and not from legends of the Pattern, which may be sourced in more ancient mythology.

Wilde mentions that some historians considered the fort or rath, overlooking the river from Sharpe's Hill, once formed the fabled House of Cletty (abode of infirm High Kings), but opines that Clady was the more likely site of this mythical kingly residence. The renowned antiquarian refers to the nearby well, *Tobar Padraig*, as the possible location of an ancient well named *St Sinchen's Well (Tobar t-Sinne)*.

A fisherman at Lugaree weir

Stackallan or Lugaree Weir provides one of the most peaceful and spectacular vistas on the River Boyne; in 1849, Wilde described the horseshoe-shaped weir thus:

> The river here forms a smooth, glass-like sheet of water, and below the bridge affords us one of those striking effects which the weirs upon the Boyne exhibit, of a long unbroken line of liquid, bent into a graceful curve, goldened with the sunshine, as it glides in swift but silent track over the long horse-shoe fall, and then breaks into a million streams – its spray dancing in the sunshine, and its bubbles reflecting all the prismatic colours of the rainbow, as it again springs onwards in its course.

The navigation crossed the river here to the northern bank, with the draught horses led over Stackallan Bridge and down the towpath to the next canal section, starting above Stackallan Weir. The river's unflooded navigable or pound level between Thomson's Lock and the weir is circa 86.6ft (above sea level), controlled by Stackallan Guard Lock and weir. The towpath on the northern riverbank is mostly inaccessible now, and passes through a privately owned and almost totally overgrown woodland named Cocker's Wood. Renowned poet Seamus Heaney's attempt to pass this way in 1978 is recounted later in the chapter.

Lugaree Weir and cottonmill from Stackallan Guard Lock

The weir provided water-head to power the adjacent cotton mill, built by a man named Coxon in 1802. In 1815 the mill was owned by a Lancashire family called Grimshaw who supposedly employed about three hundred people in the weaving section. I could find no record of this mill in Griffith's 1854 valuation, suggesting that the buildings were not in use during that period. I believe that James Forde, who operated a woollen mill in Navan's Abbeylands, restarted it as a textile mill about 1860 – it became part of Clayton's Navan Mill Brook woollen operations c.1866.

A corn mill is shown on the 1837 OS map (Ardmulchan Corn Mill), located close by the site of the former *An Óige* youth hostel (earlier Sibin) but is now long gone. Griffith's records the operator of this mill as Patrick Dunne; it was leased from the reps' of William Pack at a rateable valuation of £30, for the mill, kiln, waste of houses, house and small garden. The remains of the large cotton mill (and later Clayton's Woollen Mill) still stand on the riverbank. The road known as Cottonmill Road runs alongside the Boyne from the bridge, past the lock, the textile and corn mill at Lugaree to the Haystown road, and provides a beautiful riverside setting.

David Jebb, owner of Slane Mill, refers to Stackallan Weir as Martin's Mill Weir of Legoree in his 1779 engineering report on the canal works. The report stated that this weir had been raised two feet since the 1750s, which, he claimed, caused most of the damage to the original canal works between Stackallan and Carrickdexter Weir some distance downstream. Moreover, he stated that this weir prevented salmon from ascending to the Upper Boyne reaches... not 'his' mill weir at Slane.

A reference to Martin's Mill is included in one of the Longfield estate maps (No. 16 dated 1791), which depicts Stackallan Weir with two fish-passes, including a mill and headrace on the above described site of Dunne's Mill. Some text on the map indicates that the mill and 2 roods 20 perches were leased by John Martin from Lord Boyne for a fee of ten shillings.

From the foregoing, one could deduce that this was perhaps the same corn mill operated by Patrick Dunne in 1854.[5] A snippet in Conor Brennan's book may provide a clue to the descendants of this seemingly lost mill's owners. In describing the Cottonmill Road, he mentions a well-known family, named Martin, occupying two small fields between the Cotton Mill yard and Coyle's Corner and residing in a two-storeyed thatched house thereon: Ned Martin, a noted gardener and the last of this family living in the homestead, passed away in the 1920's.

I have been unable to find a definitive record for the origins of Stackallan/Lugaree weir. Perhaps the snippets from Jebb's report indicate that it was indeed built to power Martin's Mill, located as shown on the Longfield Map of 1791. If so, this suggests the existence of a corn mill in Ardmulchan since very early times. In his submission to Parliament, '*A scheme of the navigation of the noble River Boyne*,' Markes Plunkett mentions a sluice (an older name for a weir) at 'King's Mill' in Ardmulchan. As this submission was made in

Clockwise from top left: Stackallan Cotton-Woolen Mill worker's houses; Stackallan millrace at rear of worker's houses; Byrne's Cottage winter scene at Haystown - Courtesy Alan Russell

1710, it lends credence to the proposition that a mill here possibly dated from the late medieval period.

Because the area surrounding Stackallan is steeped in history and folklore, it is worth taking a detour from the Boyne to visit other sites of interest in the locality.

Another corn mill is shown alongside Cottonmill Road on the 1837 OS map; located between the contemporary Stackallan Railway Bridge and the old quarry near the Boyne (Coyle's Corner). The mill was powered by a small, unnamed stream flowing down the valley from Dollardstown and beneath Bridewell Bridge, which carries the old road from Navan towards Drogheda. The property consisting of a mill and kiln, a house, together with land totalling circa 2.1 acres, was located in the townland of Haystown & Carnuff Little, and leased in 1854 by Mary O'Brien from the Earl of Mayo (of Haystown House) at a rateable valuation of £23-15s.

While no trace of the mill remains, a walk around surrounding fields reveals the probable location of at least two mill ponds, not shown on the OS maps. Because of the smallness of the stream the mill would have been dependent on a pond (or ponds) for continuity of operations. The coming of the railway in 1847 probably caused the mill to cease working, as the rail line is built through both of the pond locations and the mill stream was re-routed. The low valuation of 1854 supports the proposition that the mill was defunct at the time.

A cottage now occupied by the Byrne family is located close by the former site of Haystown Corn Mill. Geoff, a member of this family, told of how he provided assistance to a film crew, shooting scenes for the 1968 movie *Sinful Davey*. This movie, directed by John Huston, starred John Hurt, Pamela Franklin, Fionnula Flanagan and a cast seeded with Irish actors. According to Geoff, one scene required transportation of a horse onto an island in the Boyne, formed by the old canal rampart below Stackallan Weir. Following various shenanigans with boats and several fruitless other attempts, he suggested that the animal be moved across the canal via an improvised causeway. When Geoff built the temporary Kesh and the horse successfully landed on the rampart, he recalls John Huston handing him a one-pound note as reward for his efforts.

Bridewell Bridge is a stone bridge with a single arch of segmental profile,

Clockwise from top left:
Cottage now standing on site of Mary
O'Brien's Mill - with Byrne family and
James Doherty; Odd shaped stone in
roadside bank at Byrne's cottage;
Bride's Bridge near Katie Harte's Corner.

it is circa 12ft in span, with the arch crown about 6ft above mean water
level. The name derives from an ancient well named Bride's (or Bridie's) Well,
supposedly named such after St. Bridget (Tobar Bridghe) and located on the
north-west corner at the junction of Cottonmill Road and the old Navan to
Drogheda road, once known as Katie Harte's Corner.

The late Doctor Beryl Moore tells in her writings of an annual Pattern or
Patron being held at this well from the early Christian period to relatively
recent times, which probably continued ancient pagan fertility rites.
Nowadays the well is overgrown by tangled vegetation, but an old iron gate
(turnstile), now absorbed by the hedgerow, once provided public access.
Dollardstown (Dullardstown) Church was located on a hillock close by the
well at the north-west corner of this road junction.[6]

Two nearby mounds date from prehistoric times; one remains almost
undisturbed, the other excavated by the archaeological team performing
survey work on the Hill of Tara during the 1950s. I believe that this dig
unearthed a burial Cyst (stone-lined chamber), together with several
'crouched skeletons,' now in the National Museum.

From left: The Famine Bridge, Plaque on famine Bridge.

Stackallan Railway Bridge (built in 1847), is actually located in the old townland of Haystown, it carries the former Dublin & Drogheda Railway, later the G.N.R. or Great Northern Railway branch-line from Drogheda, which ran onwards through Navan and Kells to Oldcastle. Part of this line is still used nowadays, transporting processed ore from the lead and zinc mine in Navan to Drogheda. Local legends tell of 'the bent railway,' of how the owners of Haystown Demesne (Bourkes) refused to cede land to the railway company because, it is said, of the company's decision to relocate the station from its original site at Turnpike Bridge (on the Slane/Dublin road), to its later location in Beauparc. Thereby forcing them to 'bend' or re-align the permanent way closer to the Boyne; which diversion caused construction of extra bridges and the huge embankments of the present day. But I cannot delve deeper into this intriguing yarn in these writings.

Movie makers used this line as a location for action sequences in at least two films; scenes from *Darling Lili* were shot in the area adjacent to Beauparc and Slane during the late 1960s. The movie, released in 1970, starred Julie Andrews, playing the role of female spy Lili Smith (or Schmidt), with Rock Hudson playing Major Larrabee, an American air-ace and Jeremy Kemp. Set during WWI and loosely based on real life exploits of Mata Hari, the famous or infamous female spy, it was directed by Blake Edwards and included many action scenes and dog-fights involving triplanes and biplanes of that era. I recall one scene being prepared at a railway siding in Navan; involving a 1960s C.I.E. train complete with dark hued orange livery and equipped as an old style corridor-train – headed by a steam locomotive but hauled by a diesel

Clockwise from top:
Photo taken in 2016 outside Drogheda on Belfast line - Courtesy Aubrey Martin

Culverts under railway on Mary O'Brien's Millstream

The milestone at Haystown

Convenience Railway Br. near former millpond for Mary O'Brien's Mill

engine in disguise. Preparations included using screwdrivers to puncture hundreds of (bullet) holes in improvised plywood panelling.

While the train 'puff-puffed' along the tracks, it was attacked and strafed by German air ace 'the Red Baron,' but American hero Bill Larrabee (Rock Hudson) chased him away, flying in his vintage biplane above the green fields of… Beauparc, not Flanders as depicted in the movie. The strafing scene was made more realistic by hundreds of mini explosive charges or fire crackers being discharged, giving the impression of bullet-churned earth… Hollywood heroes indeed.

The other scene was filmed for one of the Pink Panther movies (*Return of the Pink Panther*) directed also by Blake Edwards, and included a helicopter drop to a moving train, again on the tracks close to Beauparc.

The railway bridge is known locally *as* 'the famine bridge,' because it was constructed in '*Black 47*,' the worst year of the Great Hunger. Local legends tell about many people dying of hunger and disease during the construction work, and their bodies buried in unmarked graves in the roadside ditches nearby. Other tales are told of a leper colony located on the high ground above the glen, overlooking Coyle's Corner; these legends cannot be authenticated readily, as I believe they are sourced from the Schools' Folklore Scheme of 1937-1938.

On the 1837 OS map, both road junctions in Haystown are named Green Lanes. The railway bridge located between Haystown crossroads and Broadboyne Bridge is named Sharpe's Bridge on the 1911 map, as it is nowadays; possibly called such after the Sharpe family, recorded as residents of the area on Griffith's 1854 valuation. A police barracks (Constabulary Force) is marked slightly to the east of the crossroads on the 1837 map. Here also can be seen what I believe is the one remaining milestone on this line of the old Navan to Drogheda road. The stone stands on the south side of the roadway to the east of the cross and reads Navan 3 miles/Drogheda 9 miles; these distances are measured in Irish Miles comprising 2,240 yards.

Until recent times, Farrell's Smithy was located near Haystown Crossroads alongside the road to Deanhill (Upper Green Lanes). This Smithy was operated by successive generations of blacksmiths bearing the name James Farrell; from the early 19th century to mid-20th century. They were renowned for their iron cart/wagon axels and farm gates, bearing the initials J.F. stamped within a circle, which were sold throughout County Meath and further afield.

The River Rescue boys pulled the boats ashore to stretch cramped muscles and take lunch break at this scenic place beside the once sacred pool. Chewing our soggy sandwiches (survivors of the downriver trip), we surveyed this pastoral landscape from the grassy banks alongside Cottonmill Road.

While no modern scribe could match Wilde's description of the place as viewed in 1849, one can understand how the scene evoked his eloquent response. From our vantage point we could see the wooded, green hills overlooking dark Lugaree Pool, with wintry sunshine glinting off the river's constant torrent pouring over the horseshoe weir into the foaming cauldron beneath the falls. This vista, combined with muted roar of cascading Boyne water, provided sensory stimulation capable of inspiring the most prosaic person to become a poet, if only for the moment. Eastwards, the river tumbles over shallows below the weir, and then rushes headlong round the great bend into the gorge winding between the wooded heights of Stackallan and Dollardstown.

Though its beauty is hard to surpass, the crumbling old mills, disused canals and detritus of a wasteful society give pause for thought, providing stark reminders of the havoc sometimes visited by progress upon ancient settings. In addition, the so-called Celtic Tiger era failed to spare the landscape of Stackallan. Should one turn away reluctantly from the river and view the southern aspect, the escarpment above this beautiful location is occupied mostly by a vast quarry, stretching from Coyle's Corner to the ringfort, supposedly once the ancient royal House of Cletty.

Seamus Heaney's endeavours to explore the mysteries of the derelict navigation in 1978 were recorded by accompanying British journalist, Anthony Bailey. He scribed an article, entitled *A walk along the Boyne*, published by *the New Yorker* in June 1980. From which the following is a short excerpt:

> At Stackallan Bridge, the next landmark, about half way to Slane, we rashly assumed from the map that the path shifted, as the canal did, to the north bank; apparently, the towing horses would be loaded aboard the barges, and then barges, cargo, and horses would be poled across the river and into the lock on the other side. We therefore crossed the bridge. Heaney, parched, went to get a drink of water at a nearby

house, and brought back the information that it should be possible to reach Slane on this bank, but no promise of how easy it would be.

In fact, the path was soon densely overgrown. An unknown plant, a cross between mammoth dock and giant rhubarb, had settled here in thick colonies, rising to five or six feet and spreading out huge, salad-bowl leaves. It had to be beaten aside. Over these plants we glimpsed a fine ruined mill, on the south bank, next to a splendid horseshoe-shaped weir. Then we were within a few feet of the river itself but couldn't see it. A short clearing gave us hope, but we were at once in jungle again. My boots were soaking from the wet grass. Heaney and I took turns in the van, bashing away at the plant life – not just the Triffid-like things but briars, thorns and saplings. I broke off one of the last to use as a device for parting the way ahead. We needed Machetes. We needed more energy than we had. We were being turned green by the Irish Jungle.

The unknown Triffid-like plants, described by the author, might be the dreaded Hogweed, noxious plants imported from exotic shores to enhance demesnes in times past. The fine mill mentioned is obviously the old cotton mill. Reference to towing horses taken aboard and the barges poled across the river is interesting and sourced in Boyne folklore, but in my opinion gives rise to some speculation. Perhaps this method was used at several downstream crossings, nevertheless it would not have provided a safe and reliable means to progress the navigation at Stackallan, or, as mentioned previously, at Blackcastle in Navan. During that era, Stackallan Mills were in use concurrently with the canal, thereby creating a strong river current setting towards the weir and millrace, which current could have swept unpowered (and untethered) barges into the falls. Moreover, it seems improbable that one or even two men could 'pole' a heavily laden barge (40 to 60 dead-weight tons) upriver against the said current.

Richard Evans chose Stackallan originally for the crossing point because of the strategic location of the bridge. The river crossing; therefore, was made here by taking the horses across the adjacent Broadboyne Bridge, then down along the towing path on the northern riverbank, as shown on the OS maps. This procedure was used in reverse on the upriver passage. In addition, to enable a safer transit for barges across the river, upstream of the lock, it is probable that a cable/rope system was employed to haul vessels across the Boyne.

Other crossings with no bridges may have used similar cable systems, with the horses taken by barge or perhaps relays of draught horses used on either riverbank; indeed, it is possible that the horses were simply walked across the tops of some weirs during suitable river conditions.

Tom Crinion of Roestown provided an interesting insight, which may throw some light upon the methods used to work draught hoses on the navigation.[7] He tells of how his grandfather, Thomas Mc.Cullagh from nearby Rushwee, was a bargeman working the Boyne Navigation, circa 1910 to 1915. And how his grandmother brought two fresh horses to meet the barge at Stackallan, where the fresher beasts took over the tow and the tired horses were taken home to be foddered and prepared for the next exchange. This gem of information, pertaining to a long lost local tradition, tends to support the earlier suggestion that such horse relays operated elsewhere along the navigation.

The reach of the River Boyne between Broadboyne Bridge and Slane is one of the steepest and most dramatic parts of the Boyne descent. The OS Benchmark on the upriver bridge at Stackallan indicates a level of 102.9 feet (above sea level), while the datum mark on Slane Bridge is at elevation 67.5 feet; indicating that the terrain falls about 35ft over this relatively short stretch of about three miles. Here the river flows between high, beetling bluffs constricting its passage, thereby increasing the water velocity; these difficulties were compounded by several mill weirs, rapids and shallows, making the natural stream totally unnavigable.

To overcome this multifaceted problem, four lateral canals of varying length, together with five locks were built alongside the northern riverbank, in addition to increasing the height of Carrickdexter Weir. These canal sections were interspersed with deeper stretches of the river, the whole forming a navigable reach between Stackallan and Slane, thus connecting the upper and lower parts of the Boyne Navigation.

Engineering problems encountered on this reach of the Boyne, together with political shenanigans, driven by the vested interests of riparian landowners, downriver mill operators and fisheries, contributed to the forty-year delay in the navigation reaching Navan.

Old records show upwards of £20,000 expended on attempts to extend the navigation from Carrickdexter to Navan and Trim during this earlier period (c.1748-1770), and later during completion of the Upper Boyne Navigation from c.1792 to 1800. Several sections of the Trim/Navan extension were cut and finished to a certain degree. These included Ludlow Lock and bridge in Navan (1792-1799), a c.1 KM. cutting at Gainstown and Curraghtown, a similar cutting at Rataine near Robinstown and two lateral canal sections, complete with locks, linking Trim to Rathnally and Bective.[8] But the project was never completed, being abandoned in the early years of the 19th century due to lack of Parliamentary support and funding.

The navigation, from Carrickdexter to Stackallan (Lugaree) Weir, was first constructed in the 1750s by Dutch engineer Thomas Omer (who was involved in the Shannon Navigation also).[9] The works were badly executed e.g. with wooden floors and lock cills (sills), and the too thin ramparts built from rough-hewn stone and clay. Charles Vallencey's engineering report of 1771 indicated that although rarely used, the canal was ruinous by then. David Jebb's 1779 engineering report corroborated these findings, and commented thus on Stackallan Guard Lock's single pair of gates:

> This wretched contrivance to preserve the works from being injured by the floods puts an almost total stop to the navigation for the gates can hardly be opened above five months in the year. Wherever it is necessary to place a guard lock it must have two pairs of gates. (sic)

All the locks including the guard lock; therefore, required total reconstruction in the period 1790 to 1798, with much broader ramparts built of stone to withstand river erosion.

This Boyne reach, probably the most sylvan and picturesque riverscape in Ireland, is sparsely described in other writings, perhaps because of its relative remoteness and inaccessibility. In addition, the area played host to the most rugged and complex part of the former Boyne Navigation. I will put the reader in the picture by first describing the various lateral canals, built during the reconstruction phase from 1792 to 1800, and give an account of some walks along the towpath in the spring of 2013-2014 – followed by a boat journey down this memorable river reach.

Shackleton pic. –Stackallan Cotton-Woolen Mill *c.* 1896

The combined river and canal navigation passed through the riparian parts of four townlands on the northern riverbank between Broadboyne Bridge and Slane, namely, Stackallan, Cruicetown, Carrickdexter and Slane Castle Demesne. The towpath commenced from the road just north-west of Broadboyne Bridge, and joined the riverbank upstream of Lugaree Pool. From here it followed the various lateral canals and sections of river navigations to Carrickdexter Lock, below which it transferred across the Boyne to the opposite bank downstream of Beauparc House. These canal sections had a single bridge, once providing access to Cruicetown Tuck Mill (Carney's Mill); the other river ramparts were accessed via footbridges across the lock gates.

The above *wretched contrivance*, namely, Stackallan floodgate or old guard

lock, is where the upper section of the four lateral canals locked-out to the river at the summit of Stackallan or Lugaree Weir. It was replaced by a proper guard lock with double sets of gates during reconstruction of this Upper Boyne Navigation section 1792-1798. Although the new lock was built of ashlar-type stonework, complete with chamber (unlike other guard locks ['turf locks'] downstream of Slane), it had no lifting/lowering function, its main purpose being to protect the canal from flood damage. The uppermost (Deerpark) lateral canal took the navigation across Lugaree (Martin's Mill) Weir and some rapids/shallows further downstream. This lock had no dedicated Lock-house, as the gates were normally open except during times of flooding, when they were closed, probably by the Lockkeeper resident at Deerpark Lock.

Shackleton pic. -Stackallan - note Stackallan guard lock to left

The new guard lock was designed by Richard Evans and built by Thomas Martin at a cost of £241-15s-6d. The OS Benchmarks on the new lock's upper and lower gates are shown at elevation 86.6ft, the approximate pound level of the lateral canal between the guard lock and Deerpark Lock downstream. The lock's lower gate led into the first of the four original lateral canal sections taking the navigation from here to Carrickdexter Lock, circa three miles downriver near Slane. None of the other lateral canals on this reach were provided with guard locks.

The canal followed the river's course for approximately a half mile, to where it locked-out into the open river at Deerpark Lock above Dollardstown Mill Weir. This lock had a lift/drop of about 8.2ft to the navigable river; the attendant Lockkeepers' house being occupied in 1854 by Bridget Crinion, together with the 2.6 acres rampart between the upper and lower locks. Griffith's shows that this house was owned by the Boyne Navigation Co. and had a rateable valuation of 15s., with the river rampart at R.V. £1-10s. The OS Benchmark on the Deerpark Lock gate's stonework is shown at elevation 84ft.

The 1837 OS map shows two quarries on the northern riverbank between Stackallan and Deerpark Lock, probably utilised to supply the stonework for the locks and other structures on the navigation hereabouts.[10]

The next cutting is a short section of lateral canal taking the navigation past the mill weir at Dollardstown; it commences approximately two hundred yards downstream from Deerpark Lock, with Dollardstown Mill sited on the opposite shore. The canal is 15/20ft wide and about 350 yards long, it locked-out into the open river at Castlefin (*the White Castle J.O.D. 1836*) or Reilly's (Rileys) Lock, located at the lowermost end of the cut. The river rampart is built mostly of stone and approximately 10ft wide (2ft thick stone walls in the 1750s edition). According to Griffith's, the Lock-house for this lock, with offices and a small garden, was occupied by Catherine Maguire at R.V. 10s. The 1911 map indicates a boathouse on the riverbank immediately downstream from the lock; this building can be confused with the Lock-house.

There is some discrepancy in the described location of the Lock-house for Castlefin or Reilly's Lock, which acquired the latter name from a family named Reilly who later resided there at the turn of the 19th century. This subject is discussed in greater detail later in the chapter.

The OS Benchmark on the lock's stonework is marked at elevation 76.8ft, representing the approximate pound level of the unflooded, navigable river between Castlefin Canal and the upstream Deerpark Lock fairway. The level was controlled by a combination of Dollardstown Mill Weir and Castlefin Lock, which lock had a lift/drop of circa 5.2ft. This section of canal can be very difficult and confusing to research, because, while most of the canal is located in Stackallan Townland, Castlefin Lock and Lock-house are sited within Cruicetown.

The next lateral canal is located about two hundred yards further downstream from Castlefin Lock fairway, and was built originally to enable the navigation circumvent the drop across the mill weir at Cruicetown. Indeed, the upriver half of this canal (total length circa 450 yards), included the mill headrace leading from the head of the weir to the mill.

Cruicetown Mill Weir impounded the river water, thereby making the Boyne navigable from Castlefin Lock to Cruicetown Canal. It formerly provided a water-head to power Carney's Tuck Mill, located on the northern rampart about midway along this lateral canal. The long defunct mill straddled the waterway (the millwheel being located in the building's centre), with the tailrace falling into the Boyne about 20 yards below the mill building. As at Dollardstown Weir upstream, the main weir is built askew to the river, but in the opposite direction; it is slanted towards the northern bank, which suggests that it was built initially as a mill weir. This indicates that Cruicetown Tuck Mill was very old indeed and predated the navigation works which commenced here in the 1750s.[11]

The single lock is located some distance below the tuck mill, at the downstream end of the cut where the canal section locked-out to the open river. The Lockkeeper's house is situated about mid-way between the two gates on the landward side of the towpath. Griffith's shows the Lock-house occupied in 1854 by Patrick Maguire at R.V. 10s. The OS Benchmark on the lock stonework is at elevation 71.5ft. An indication that the lock had a lift/drop of circa 5ft from/to the unflooded, navigable river or pound level of approximately 66.6ft upstream of Carrickdexter Weir, located a mile further downstream below Beauparc.

Cyril Ellison's book references David Jebb's report on the navigation in 1779, which recommended that Carney's Tuck Mill be purchased and demolished as part of the upcoming reconstruction of the Upper Boyne Navigation. It is difficult to determine when this proposal was accepted and executed, as the 1837 OS map shows the mill and its associated buildings, together with the other canal works on this section. Although shown on the map of 1837 and indeed upon the map accompanying the valuation, no records of this tuck mill could be found in Griffith's Valuation of 1854.

The photograph on page 102 of Ellison's book, in fact, depicts remnants of Cruicetown Tuck Mill and the former stone bridge across the canal. As the photograph (captioned *The Boyne Navigation near Stackallan*) is part of the 1894 *Shackleton Collection*, it is evident; therefore, that the ruins of the mill and the arch of the bridge, though crumbling, had survived until then. The 1911 OS map; however, shows that no bridge spanned the canal in the early years of the 20th century, indicating that the mill bridge at Cruicetown collapsed or was taken down during the interim period. This map indicates the outlines of the bridge landward abutments and the old mill, with no buildings shown nearby on the riverbank other than the two Lock-houses.

The 1854 valuation records the Lock-house, occupied by Patrick Maguire, standing opposite the upper gate of Cruicetown Lock; with the other Lock-house occupied by Catherine Maguire sited just upstream of the mill at Cruicetown. The 1911 map places the No. 1 milestone of the Upper Navigation alongside the towpath immediately adjacent to the latter house.

These two Lock-houses were the only occupied dwellings recorded by the valuation adjacent to the lateral canals of Castlefin and Cruicetown; therefore, we will revisit the previously mentioned anomaly in the location of Reilly's Lock-house.

Popular local legends say that the Reilly family lived in a tiny building straddling a small stream at the Castlefin Lock, and several tales are woven around this location, now regarded as the site of Castlefin Lock-house. While some of the family did indeed live in this building in the later era of the navigation, it is my belief that this was not the Lockkeepers' residence originally, but the former workshop or carpenters shop where some of the lock gates were constructed for the original canal. In my opinion, the house beside No. 1 milestone, occupied by Catherine Maguire in 1854, was the original residence for the Castlefin Lockkeeper, and that Castlefin Lock was operated from this location during the navigation's earlier years.[12]

The Cruicetown canal and tuck mill were accessed by a roadway or lane leading off the Navan to Slane road from the Slane side of Wicker's Crossroads. Nowadays part of this old mill road provides an entry to Doherty's Quarry. According to the old maps, this roadway ran to the edge of Cruicetown Wood, where it turned to run due east for some distance, before veering southwards to meet the canal towpath directly opposite the mill bridge. The OS maps show that this lane formed the towpath for some distance to the east. Opposite Beauparc boathouse, it turned northwards and re-joined the Navan to Slane road, forninst a large dwelling in Pighill Townland; shown by Griffiths to be occupied by Catherine Kelsh (descendant of Squire Kelch 1798?). Baronstown House stands on this site nowadays.

The OS maps show a house located at the southern end of this laneway near the Boyne (in Sans Souci Wood); which the 1854 valuation lists as a caretaker's house, held in fee by the Marquis of Conyngham, together with c.11.76 acres.[13] Local tradition holds that a man named Brady (or Brien) lived in this house at the turn of the 19th century, and that he worked at Beauparc House across the river, hence commuted to and from work in a Boyne Corracle or Currach.

The last lateral canal section on this reach is at Carrickdexter, located downstream of the narrow, twisting gorge through which the river winds on this navigable stretch. The canal was built to circumvent Carrickdexter or Horseshoe Weir. Some mystery attaches to the origins of this weir i.e. whether it was built solely as a navigation weir or on the footprint of an existing fish-weir. It is unlikely a mill weir, as I can find no record of any mill in the locality. Records of the Boyne Navigation suggest the weir was the summit level of the Lower Boyne Navigation from 1763 until the late 1790s when the Upper Navigation opened to traffic.

Carrickdexter Lock was rebuilt by John Mulvany & Co. c.1792, the most important single contract of the eight supposedly awarded for the entire Upper Boyne project. The necessity for rebuilding the lock might suggest the original structure was one of those built by Thomas Omer in the 1750s, with wooden cills and rough-hewn stone walls. The new lock, as indeed all the locks now in existences on the navigation, are of ashlar-stone-block type construction, providing a lasting tribute to the skill and craftsmanship of the period. A remarkable feature of the defunct canals is how well most of these locks and bridges have survived the ravages of time and nature's assault, with little or no maintenance on the system for over a century. The OS Benchmark is at elevation 66.5ft on the stonework of both gates; indicating that Carrickdexter Lock had a lift/drop of circa 6ft to the navigable, unflooded river level of 61.1ft, impounded by the lock and weir at Slane Castle.

A Lockkeepers' house was located near the eastern end of the little island (0.584 acre) formed by the river rampart; with access to the island gained via footbridges on the lock gates. Griffith's indicates that the Lock-house, together with 3 roods 25 perches of land (the island) was occupied by Peter Lanny in 1854 at R.V. £1-10s. Carrickdexter Lock is located in Slane Castle Demesne, not within the townland of Carrickdexter.[14]

The 1837 OS map and 1852 revision show the head of the weir and canal fairway located in Carrickdexter Townland, with the lock and Lock-house sited within the boundaries of Slane Castle Demesne; whereas, the map of 1911 indicates all of these located within the demesne, which, indeed, occupies a much larger footprint in later times.

Cyril Ellison refers to Ligpulse Lock in the context of David Jebb's 1779 engineering report, which recommended that Carrickdexter Weir be raised to

Master Elmes, John Donnelly, Jimmy Collins, Concannon, Ned Comiskey, Willie R..... Liam Donnelly, Tommy Duffy.
Danny Synott, Dickie Tallon, John Lawlor, P Carey, Sonny Watters, Gerry Carolan, Jack Arbutnot, John Byrne.
John Mongey, Frank Donnelly, Joe McGrane, C Watters, Kit Brien, Peter Hughes, Jimmy Ward, Eric Quinn, Tommy Carey.
Circa 1929

Yellow Furze School Photo *c.* 1929

give a lift/drop of 7.5ft to/from the river to enable removal of Ligpulse lateral canal and lock.

OS Benchmarks on Carrickdexter Lock gates indicate a lift/drop of c. 6ft only, this was apparently sufficient to render the river navigable between Cruicetown and Carrickdexter. I have found no further reference to this lock system (Ligpulse) in reports or on the OS maps but if removed in the 1780s, as proposed; it was long gone previous to the first Ordnance Survey in the 1830s.[15]

ENDNOTES

1   The three wooden lighters moored at Stackallan were named *Teltown, Saint Patrick of Navan (Naomh Padraig Nuachonghbail)* and *Tara*. These were the vessels constructed by James McCann at Navan Lightering Works in 1902 and 1903 – some of their history and that of the Lightering Works is recounted in the Navan and District Historical Society's Vol. 2 Journal, *Navan – Its People and its Past* (2013).

2   The valuation correctly records this lock located in Stackallan Townland – the name Deerpark evolves from Stackallan Deerpark.

3   A list of Lockkeepers, compiled for Meath Co. Council's Road Committee in 1913 during a review of the navigation's proposed liquidation, names Mrs. John Murphy as keeper at this lock (Stackallan), and shows that she was in receipt of a quarter-annual salary of 10s-6d.

4   As noted, this lateral canal ran from Stackallen via Taaffe's and Rowley's Locks to the summit level at Metge's Lock above the 'V' weir in Navan (OS Benchmark at elevation113.8ft above sea level) – this was the final part of the Upper Boyne Navigation to be completed (circa 1798-1800). The Navan weir, Metge's Lock and adjacent dry-dock were demolished or buried by the OPW during the arterial drainage scheme, officially launched at Bellinter Bridge in 1968.

5   Another Longfield Map, No. 21F. 15 (57), surveyed by John Brownrigg in 1791, depicts part of Ardmulchan and is captioned: "a map of the mill and parts of the land at Ardmulchan intended for use of the Boyne Navigation, part of the estate of Lord Boyne – tenant John Martin." An inscribed note shows that the land purchased by the company was one acre & one rood.

6   Anthony (Dean) Cogan's ecclesiastical history of Meath *The Diocese of Meath, ancient and modern*, mentions that the above well was dedicated to the Blessed Virgin Mary and that Dollardstown Church had disappeared by then (1862).

7   Tom receives further mention later, in the context of Roestown corn/tuck mill near Slane.

8   See also Rathnally Weir, Chapter 6. Construction of Ludlow Lock and bridge, and the cuttings at Gainstown, Curraghtown and Rataine (Balbraddagh) were supervised by Daniel Monks and executed c.1792-1799, but I have found no record for construction of the canal sections between Trim and Rathnally to date.

9   Castlefin or Cruicetown locks were not provided with Lock-houses at this time.

10 A list of Lockkeepers, compiled for Meath Co. Council's Road Committee in 1913 during a review of the navigation's proposed liquidation, names John Englishby as keeper at Deerpark Lock (known in the vernacular as Englishby's Lock), and shows that he was in receipt of a quarter-annual salary of 10s-6d.

11 A mill of unspecified usage is depicted graphically hereabouts on the Down Survey map of 1656.

12 A list of Lockkeepers, compiled for Meath Co. Council's Road Committee in 1913 during a review of the navigation's proposed liquidation, names Mrs. Eliza Reilly as keeper at Castlefin Lock (known in the vernacular as Reilly's Lock), and in receipt of a quarter-annual salary of £1-5s.-3d. The same list also shows a Mrs. Eliza Reilly as Lockkeeper

of Cruicetown Lock, and in receipt of a quarter-annual salary of £1 for her services. An engineer's note on the said report states that the Lock-house at Cruicetown Lock was in poor condition and unoccupied in 1914 – which tends to support the proposition that Castlefin and Cruicetown locks were operated by a single keeper. David Jebb's 1779 report recommended provision of Lock-houses at Castlefin and Cruicetown, indicating that these houses were constructed or acquired in the period 1792-1798.

13 On a visit to Sans Souci Wood in April 2014, we came upon the ruins of this old stone house beside a modern duck pond; this was dug in recent times just upstream from the site of a larger pond depicted on the 1911 OS map. The old ruin is almost entirely obscured by wildwood, except for two openings facing towards the Boyne. These apertures are topped by a combination of pointed and semi-circular profiled arches, constructed from brick and stone. Local tradition holds that this was the abode of the ferryman who ran the river ferry, but discussions with members of the Sailor Reilly's family (supposed operator of this ferry boat), failed to elicit confirmation of this story. As shown on the 1911 map, the old laneway leading to the Slane road has disappeared.

14 A list of Lockkeepers, compiled for Meath Co. Council's Road Committee in 1913 during a review of the navigation's proposed liquidation, names Edward Reilly as keeper at Carrickdexter Lock (known in the vernacular as Carrick Lock), and shows that he was in receipt of a quarter-annual salary of £1-3s-3d. I believe that this Reilly family were cousins of the Reillys residing at Cruicetown and Castlefin Locks further upstream – the Reillys at Carrickdexter were known colloquially as 'the Sailor Reillys,' perhaps because of their supposed involvement in the old private ferry plying across the river at Beauparc?

15 Research suggests that Ligpulse Lock was part of the ill-fated system erected by Thomas Omer, and that it was probably located between Carrickdexter and Cruicetown Locks, at the head of the narrow gorge below Beauparc House. Charles Vallency's 1771 engineering report mentions that Thomas Omer attempted to build a horse bridge across the river narrows here in the 1750s – the pillars of which, he stated, caused such an obstruction to river flow that they could not withstand winter floods. When Richard Evans took charge of the Upper Boyne project in the 1790s, he demolished the remnants of the bridge and Ligpulse Lock This part of the project included raising Carrickdexter Weir to increase the pound level between it and the upstream weir at Cruicetown. N.B., Markes Plunkett, in his Parliamentary submission of 1710, mentions a place which may be the lost location of Ligpulse Lock, he described it thus: the grand pool of Lagpolse is a fit abode and rest for ships, 'being large, round, deep and sheltered, surrounded with steep rocks, safe from all tempests and storms and also fit for a main sluice.'(sic)

Broad boyne Bridge at sundown

14

The lost Navigation
Rambles from Broadboyne
to Cruicetown and Carrickdexter

Boyne Lighters' last mooring – springtime walks from Broadboyne, in search of Reilly's & Cruicetown Locks, Carney's Tuck Mill and Carrickdexter (Sailor Reilly's) Lock.

We had more success exploring the previously described sections of lateral canals in April 2013, than Seamus Heaney and Anthony Bailey in 1978, largely due to assistance provided by a local man named James Doherty.

Additionally, a combination of a long, dry spell and a late spring; caused mostly by the coldest month of March in living memory, conspired to provide perfect conditions for our riverside trek. The ground was firm underfoot, with a dearth of weeds, briars and river sedge, and no trace of the Triffid-like plants that so obstructed Heaney and Bailey in the past.

The road access to the towpath is blocked off nowadays, so Marie and I, together with sister-in-law Pauline, made our entry to the bottomlands through a gap in the hedge at the northern end of the bridge. The river here is deep and flows sluggishly eastwards towards Lugaree Pool and the great weir, with the bridge and old Lock-house, nestled beneath the higher, wooded escarpment, providing a splendid backdrop.

Walking along the riverbank, we came to the place, directly opposite Thomson's Lock, described by Connor Brennan as the last mooring of the Boyne Lighters. Because of the lack of greenery on the riverbank, I observed

Clockwise from top: Search for Navan Lighters June 2013
Lighter bow post rubbing strake protruding from Boyne at Stackallan
Recovered parts of lighters

several fitments of the vessels protruding from the water and loamy soil, including parts of the rudder mechanisms and a metal-clad rubbing strake. Tangible reminders indicating that this was indeed the last resting place of these craft that plied the now dead navigation all those years ago.[1]

Continuing onwards, we joined the navigation towpath at its intersection with the riverbank about 100 metres above the weir, where the muted roar of water became the dominant sound. The river rampart wall leading to the canal lock is partly collapsed, thus extending the waterfall of the weir towards the lock. From where a vista of the falls unfolded, with the former Fagan's Sibin and crumbling cotton mill framing the scene to the south.

The lead-in (or fairway), from Lugaree Pool at the head of the weir, to Stackallan Guard Lock is mostly obstructed by weeds, silt, dead tree limbs and debris from the old lock gates, including metal supports and handrails of the lock footbridge.

While the upper gate survived in situ, it was obviously in poor enough condition when abandoned long ago; with several bolted-on galvanised-metal support patches included to bolster its strength. The sheeting, comprised of 6in. x 1.5 inch boards, has decayed badly and fallen off in places; however, the underlying framework and mitred loggerhead posts seem mostly intact but rotting away.[2] A deep layer of compacted silt is washed up against the upstream faces of the gates; therefore, no trace of the sluices (or paddles) is evident without resorting to some heavy digging, but the operating rods are visible within the mass of shrubbery clinging to the gates.

Lugaree weir & pool from Stackallan guard lock fairway

Stackallan Guard Lock upper gate

As elsewhere on the navigation, a concrete wall mimicking their shape is built tight to the gates' downstream face. The tell-tale pattern of the corrugated-iron shuttering used, indicating that this wall was probably constructed by Meath County Council when the navigation became defunct in the 1930s.[3] No sign of the No. 2 milestone was evident in the undergrowth on the landward side of the towpath near the upper gate, the site depicted for the marker on various navigation sketch maps.

Though the lower gate is gone and the lock flooded to a depth of a couple of feet, the remainder of the canal is relatively dry all the way downriver to Deerpark Lock. Apart from a small wash-out near its upper end, the river rampart is sound and though overgrown in places, it is possible to walk along most of the canal bed (which varies in width from about 25ft to 50ft) from the guard lock to Deerpark. A tiny but very deep stream flows down the centre of the cutting for the last few hundred yards to the lower lock.

The towpath, running alongside the canal to the lower lock at Deerpark, is sound underfoot on its passage through the tree-tunnel of Cocker's Wood. In several places, remnants of old drainage ditches are evident alongside the pathway, their purpose being to clear runoff water from the steeply rising woodlands to the north of the track.

About mid-way between the locks, a small fisherman's hut stands in the wildwood beneath the high bluff to the left of the towpath. Enhancing the woodland scene, where the sunlight cast bright speckles amongst the darker shadows.

Deerpark Lock is overgrown nowadays, its stonework mantled by a tangled mass of ivy, blackthorn and briar, woven through a natural framework of wildwood and secondary deadfall timber. The upper gate is partly intact, but the metal framework and other accoutrements of the footbridge lie in the

Left: The Boyne at Deerpark Lock - near 'the Flats' on Dollardstown riverbank
Right: The fishing hut near Deerpark

mud at the bottom of the fairway. While the lock is inundated to a depth of about 2ft, the stonework seems sound enough, with some of the lower gate still clinging to its ancient hingeposts. Searching through the woods in the spot indicated on the OS maps, I found no trace of Bridget Crinion's/ Englishby's Lock-house.

Continuing our trek along the towpath, hereabouts covered liberally with wild garlic and other herbs unknown to us, we came to a natural barrier about one hundred yards downstream of Deerpark Lock. This obstacle comprised a near impenetrable mass of new-growth timber entwined through several deadfalls, some still fresh and growing although lying in a horizontal position. Here the magic of mobile phones came to our aid; a prearranged call to James Doherty informing us the towpath was passable to Castlefin, should we manage to pass through the obstruction.

Encouraged by these words, we managed to overcome the various obstacles by dint of some minor mountaineering effort; emerging on the other side, we met with James, who led us on downriver towards Castlefin Lock.

Left: Deerpark Lock - remnants of lower gates
Right: Remnants of footbridge at entry to Castlefin Canal

Making our way through the overgrown towpath below Deerpark Lock, we could hear a dull roar carried upriver on the gentle breeze; the sound of Boyne water pouring over Dollardstown Weir. Here the river moves less swiftly in midstream to cascade in a continuous white sheet across the skewed weir. It flows much faster near the northern bank; gaining momentum to rush headlong into the channel that was once the fairway leading to Castlefin Canal and lock.

The densely overgrown dividing rampart between canal and river commences as a rounded (bullnosed) pier at the head of the weir, and runs the full length of the lateral canal to the lock at the lowermost end of the cut. This is an obviously man-made construction of hewn stonework, averaging about 7 to 10ft in width. The rotting remains of a footbridge still straddle the current rushing through the fairway; a contrivance, James Doherty informed us, erected many years earlier by his father as an aid to fishermen. The footbridge, complete with handrails, is illustrated on page 61 of Ellison's book.

This section of lateral canal was not blocked off by a concrete wall in the 1930s, but left exposed to the vagaries of nature, with just Castlefin Lock gates holding back the impounded river. The inevitable happened and the rotted gates were swept away by some flood, leaving this canal section as a very dangerous stretch for an unwary boatman or canoeist. The canal nowadays is a virtual tidal rip, with a torrent of white water tearing through the lock's enclosed space, the danger increased by remnants of the gates, and many sharp objects protruding from each bank.

James related a story of two German canoeists arriving at his door early one morning, stark naked, the canoe having been swept down through the lock and their bodies stripped of clothing during the passage – a thrill-seekers ride indeed, but one unlikely to be repeated deliberately by them.

Approximately three-quarters way along the cut, we came to a small stream flowing into the canal through a breach in the towpath. A study of the old maps shows that this stream, known locally as the Cruicetown River, had many interesting features along its banks. Rising in several capillaries near Causetown House to the north-west, it flowed south-eastwards between the former old school and church in the long gone Stackallan Village, and fed a network of ornamental gardens and fish ponds within the grounds of Boyne House. It passed beneath the Navan/Slane road near Tobar Patrick, and then

Left: Stream running through arch beneath Reilly's (Castlefin) Lock-house/old-workshop
Right: Tidal race through Reilly's Lock

formed the mereing between Stackallan and Cruicetown Townlands before flowing onwards to Castlefin Lock.

Here it was diverted to run alongside the landward side of the towpath, and flow beneath a stone arch supporting the carpenter's workshop alongside the lock (later Reilly's house). Just below the lower lock gate, the stream passed into the old boathouse, then turned at right angles and flowed to the Boyne through a stone built conduit beneath the towpath. This tunnel-like opening is about 6ft in width and enabled small boats pass to and fro between boathouse and river.

Crossing the little stream we entered Cruicetown Townland, just above the lock's upper gate. As described earlier, the chamber is open at both ends, with remnants of the gates hanging from the hingeposts. Although the lock seems sound enough, it is under constant threat of destruction from the seething mass of white water tearing through its constricting stonework; together with the more insidious menace from the trees and ivy taking root within its joints.

While most of the stream has found a new route to the canal cutting, a small rill remains on course, flowing beneath the old workshop/Lock-house and on through the boathouse to the Boyne. The origin of this old Lock-house is uncertain and a puzzle for those attempting to unravel the mysteries of the old navigation hereabouts.

The exact size of the structure is difficult to determine, as the remnants are totally overgrown; however, the ruins appear to be about 18ft square, with a single doorway opening onto the towpath midway between the two lock gates. The foundations are unusual, formed by an approximately 5ft wide, near semi-circular profiled stone arch straddling the little stream. This site and method of construction were chosen because of the navigation being restricted to the limited space available between the Boyne and the craggy heights of Cruicetown Wood.

Local tradition holds that the structure was built originally as a carpenter's workshop during the earlier construction of the navigation, perhaps in the 1750s. It later became the abode of the Reilly family, some of whom lived also in the Lock-house downriver of the former Cruicetown Mill.[4]

The origins and original ownership of the boathouse are similarly uncertain, but it was likely part of the navigation and used at one time for river and canal maintenance. This building is roofless nowadays; its ruins are c.15ft square and sound, though overgrown with ivy and brush. The landward end is high and dry and accessed through a doorway on the downstream wall – at least two boats could be accommodated within the dry part of the building; to be launched into the little stream and taken through the tunnel to the Boyne.

Left: Outlet from Reilly's Lock to the Boyne - Reilly's former vegetable garden was on the rampart (to left of the picture) opposite the outlet from boathouse
Right: View from the boathouse through the arch to the Boyne

Local folklore relates how members of the extended Reilly family residing across the river in Painestown, crossed over in Boyne coracles and passed into the boathouse. Where they 'parked' the boat, then made their way along the towpath to visit relatives at Cruicetown Lock; or perhaps walked up the old mill road to socialise with other folk living along the Slane road.

The towpath was badly overgrown downstream; therefore, following our inspection of the navigation facilities at Castlefin/Reilly's Lock, James Doherty guided us out of the wooded valley. We followed the course of the little stream through Cocker's Wood, and clambered up the steep slope, then passed through the quarry yard onto the long defunct road to Cruicetown Mill. Here, we boarded James' van and he took us to the car, parked at Broadboyne Bridge; thus ended a most enlightening walk down the long gone towpath from Broadboyne to Castlefin.

About a month later, in early May 2013, our next foray in search of the lost navigation took us to Cruicetown. This time we were accompanied by my brother Tom, and came more prepared to do battle with the tangling brush and briar of Cruicetown Wood; armed for the fray with a slash-hook and a light crowbar. The purpose of the latter implement being to use as a probe in search of some elusive post holes, reputedly carved into the stonework that once formed a paved yard, but now constitutes the overgrown wilderness fronting the old workshop/Lock-house at Reilly's Lock.

With kind permission of James Doherty, we parked at the bottom of the quarry road and walked down to the south-east corner of a field, adjoining the upper mereing of Cruicetown Wood. Climbing across the barbed-wire fence, we entered the steeply sloping wildwood; hereabouts comprised mostly of beech, oak, ash, birch, some willow, larch and lime trees. An occasional young elm clung to the craggy riverbank; rare survivors indeed of the *Dutch*

Track of old road leading to Cruicetown Mill

Elm Disease (DED), which decimated the once bountiful elm tree, especially since the arrival of the more virulent strain on these shores in the late 1960s.

Our difficulties were increased by larger trees interwoven with a near impenetrable mass of undergrowth, formed by tangling briar, laurel, hazel and blackthorn; all descending in serried layers downslope towards the riverbank below. Finding some deer trails through the mass of wild shrubbery, we worked our way downwards and came to the ancient roadway leading towards the long disused mill at Cruicetown.

Although overgrown with second growth trees and brush, the old roadway is still visible, descending eastwards through the wood; its upper boundary hewn through rocky outcrops, with an occasional section buttressed by man-made dry stone walls. James Doherty's father told him of seeing grooves worn into the bedrock forming the surface of the old road; impressions made by iron shod cart and wagon wheels accessing the mill and towpath long ago.

Making our way through the brush and over many deadfall trees, we arrived at the place where the track turned at right angles towards the mill. Here are the remains of a house, a rectangle formed by some ivy covered low stone walls, the old homestead nowadays overshadowed by a large sycamore tree growing within its crumbled ruins. This building is marked on the 1837 OS map, but not on the 1911 edition. While I suspect that it was once the millers' house, I can discover no record of such or any mention thereof in local tradition.

As indicated on the old maps, the roadway led onto the towpath directly in line with the bridge leading across the canal to the mill, sited on the island or river rampart. The bridge is gone, but, following some vigorous work with the slash-hook, we found remnants of its landward abutments by the side of the canal. These old foundations indicated that the bridge was about 12ft wide and had a span of approximately 18ft across the canal.

Further upstream are the remains of the mill building, sited exactly as depicted on the Shackleton photograph of 1894, but now almost completely overgrown with luxuriant foliage such that it was almost invisible to the unknowing eye. We could see no trace of the iron cross, supposedly erected as a memorial to a child from England, who tragically drowned here long ago. No ready access to the island was available at this time, so we could not explore the mill.

Cruicetown Mill *c.* 1896 Shackleton collection

Hewing our way through the dense undergrowth covering the towpath, we made slow but steady progress eastwards towards the lock on the downriver end of the canal.

The canal hereabouts is about 25ft wide, its riverside rampart formed by rough-hewn stone walls, covered by trees and undergrowth. The old waterway is choked by a conglomeration of wild shrubbery entwined with ivy and briar, fallen trees and every imaginable type of natural detritus – the whole tangled mass sitting atop a bed of compacted river silt, through which tiny rivulets flowed, like irrigation ditches snaking through a desert.

We came to the lock fairway eventually, and observed yet another example of raw natural power; here demonstrated by tree roots displacing the heavy stones of the lock walls. Some have been knocked into the canal, others shoved aside like feathers, and now teeter on the edge ready to tumble into the chamber. Keeping a weather eye on these latter dodgy stones, we clambered into the fairway to inspect the upper gate; and discovered a veritable treasure trove of memorabilia for those interested in the workings of old lock gates.

The river and woodland debris was piled high against the upstream lock gates to their mid-level; with the upper part of the gates buried deep within

The author at Cruicestown Lock upper gate

the limbs of a fallen but still vigorously sprouting ash tree. Following some use of the slash-hook to clear a pathway through the ash, the piled debris provided a rather shaky platform from which to inspect the workings of the long disused gates.

Although in an advanced state of decay, these gates are the only set remaining on the entire navigation with the operating system intact; therefore, providing an accurate picture of their former workings. Additionally, as most of the footbridge mountings, stanchions and iron handrails were still in situ, with some of the boardwalks intact, these give an insight to the ironwork used on the original structure. The by now familiar concrete wall mimics the profile of Cruicetown Lock's upper gate; while its lower gate has mostly disappeared, apart from some rotting pieces of the hingeposts still clinging to the topmost hinge straps (stirrups).

The ruins of the Lock-house (the abode of Patrick Maguire in 1854), are located midway between the two lock gates, as depicted on the OS maps. Like elsewhere on this stretch of navigation, the roofless ruin is mantled in nature's green cloak; with pride of place taken by a large sycamore tree growing within the eastern gable wall. The dimensions of the house are difficult to determine without the assistance of a chainsaw, but the building appears to be c. 20/25ft long by about 18ft broad. While it is built to the north of the towpath, in alignment with the lock and tight to the steeply sloping hillside, I noted a track passing alongside the Lock-house rear wall, perhaps made by wandering deer.

Left: Pauline & Tom Holten at Cruicetown Lock-house ruins 2013
Right: Gap in Cruicetown millrace-canal rampart - from river aspect

As the towpath was impassable to the east of the lock, we turned back towards the mill to continue our search for the No. 1 milestone and Catherine Maguire's former abode.

Upstream from Cruicetown Mill, the channel leading downriver from Cruicetown Weir included both the canal and millrace; it was about 60ft wide originally, with the riverside dividing rampart formed by walls built of rough-hewn stones. The wider waterway commenced at the head of the weir, and ran for several hundred yards to the mill downstream; where it divided into two separate channels – one branch formed a millrace passing through an opening in the approximate centre of the building to drive the waterwheel; the other stream formed the canal fairway leading to the lock further downstream.

A large section of the dividing rampart has washed away just upstream of the mill's upriver façade. This breach constitutes a very dangerous set of rapids nowadays; where the Boyne waters pour through the restricted space like a tidal rip, a veritable maelstrom of white water to be avoided by less experienced boatmen.

On the north-western riverbank directly opposite the breached rampart, a small pond occupies the space between the towpath and the ancient road leading down through Cruicetown Wood to the mill. The pond is clogged by a profusion of wild sedge nowadays, but local anecdotes tell of its water being employed as a sheep-dip until recent times. The old towpath crosses the pond on a raised rampart, sound underfoot though choked with hogweed and briar. We came upon the No. 1 milestone about fifty yards above the pond; it is still in pristine condition, unencumbered by ivy and standing beneath the green canopy of riverside trees. The deeply engraved figure one (with flourish), declaring boldly that this place is one mile distant from the starting point of the Upper Navigation at Carrickdexter Lock.

On the edge of the towpath immediately behind this marker are the ivy covered ruins of a substantial stone building, which in 1854 I believe was home to Lockkeeper Catherine Maguire. Her 'small garden,' listed in that year's valuation, once comprised part of the now overgrown area located in a nook formed between the mill road and the pond,

Sitting on these ivy covered ruins, taking a rest in the sun dappled woods, I drifted off into a reverie. In this daydream I returned to Cruicetown's riverbank during its navigation days. My mind's eye conjuring up images of lighters, barges and rafts passing this way alongside the towpath – imagining hoof-thud of plodding horse, tow-rope creaking over gunwales, with an occasional cry and whip-crack as the bargeman urged greater effort from the toiling beast. The tillerman had little else to do besides sit at the helm contently smoking his pipe; until arrival at Reilly's Lock, where he might assist the Lock-keeper wind the handles and operate the gates.

Other echoes from the past flitted through my drowsy mind, intruding above the murmuring river and muted roar of Boyne water falling over weirs. This natural soundtrack punctuated by cries of Lockkeeper's children at play in the lonely woods, cackle of hens and occasional snorting of pigs from the crohans near the Lock-houses. But another and more persistent sound intruded on these musings, resonating from a long gone era prior to the Boyne Navigation. An all pervasive thumping wafting up the valley; the pulsating, rhythmic throb of water-driven wooden hammers in Carney's Tuck Mill, pounding local weavers' homespun cloth into frieze, a fabric used to produce the Boyneside cloak known as a Trusty.

When roused by a tap on the shoulder and my brother Tom saying "come on, it's time to get going," I became aware of my surroundings – a landscape very different to that of my daydream. On our first trek through Cruicetown a few weeks previously, we passed through a riverscape still covered by russet tones of winter, with scarcely a green leaf in sight except the occasional evergreen.

The scene was transformed by nature's response to the prolonged winter season. Described by Marie in more artistic terms – it was as though nature's dormant volcano had erupted; covering the landscape with a myriad of hues that even the greatest artist could not hope to capture on canvas. The surrounding wildwoods were alive with nature's resurgence. Freshly blooming trees competing to please the eye; soft tints of beech outdoing the softer sheen of new ash leaves, both contrasting with darker oak, sycamore and laurel. A veritable kaleidoscope enhanced by the yellow buttercup and primrose, vying with the many different shades of bluebells and Forget-me-not. An unforgettable scene enriched by beds of white flowered, pungent wild garlic.

The sounds had changed also; the constant murmur and gurgling of the river accentuating the valley's silence, making it seem more profound – we could hear the occasional crackle of a twig, possibly snapped by some deer lurking in the dense shrubbery nearby. The echoes from the past had disappeared, being merely a figment of my imagination, maybe brought to my consciousness by the loneliness of the location and my awareness of past events. Or were they present in another form; perhaps borne on the occasional *wind devils,* tiny gusts of wind rustling through the treetops and undergrowth, causing one to shiver in their cold draught even on the hot summer day.

Upstream of the milestone, the towpath was blocked by a mass of second growth timber, deadfalls and shrubbery, so we took to mountaineering once more. Here, the slash-hook and crowbar proved their worth as unconventional climbing aids; with Tom, our team leader, using them as anchors for us to traverse the craggy hillside.

Descending once more to the towpath, we came to a rocky bluff towering above the edge of the track-way, from which a green mass of drooping laurels overhung the path. Slashing our way through the laurels, we discovered a small rill cascading down the rockface, the area beneath encrusted with a thick layer of sedimentary limestone. In the midst of this darkened area could be seen the remains of a water catchment, or well, fashioned from the sediment and lined with wood; perhaps a contrivance to supply the Lockkeepers and their families with drinking water.[5]

Passing on upstream by the head of Cruicetown Weir, we noted a strong current flowing through the old canal and upper millrace; caused by the previously described breach in the ramparts just above the old mill. The weir runs askew across the river and is relatively short, with several small, sedge covered islets in the river just below its white water mark. The towpath hereabouts is choked with undergrowth, deadfalls and briar, through which we made slow progress towards Castlefin or Reilly's Lock.

Here we inspected and photographed the old boathouse, workshop/Lock-house and the remains of the lock.[6] Local tradition holds that four post holes were carved into the paving stones in front of the former workshop; their supposed purpose being to provide templates for construction of the lock gates on the various local canals. The apertures were perhaps used originally as slots for mooring posts, shown at this location on the 1911 OS map. As the Shackleton photographs of the 1890s indicate that these posts were of wooden construction, they may have rotted away long since.

Despite our best efforts, we were unsuccessful on this occasion due to heavy soil deposits and tangling briar; perhaps this little riddle will be solved in the future by someone equipped with more suitable implements than our crowbar and slasher.

Following these exertions, we traversed our previous route out through Cocker's Wood to Doherty's Quarry, then, followed the once well-trodden road from Cruicetown's ancient mill... homeward bound.

Towards the end of April 2014, James Doherty and I retraced the route to Cruicetown Mill with the intention of exploring its ancient interior. To achieve this objective, James carried a length of aluminium ladder down through the woods to the canal; where he placed it across the waterway, enabling me to cross, even with my infirm leg.

The island is overgrown with trees, heavily enmeshed in briar, dense shrubbery and hogweed-like vegetation. We made our way upstream to the breach, isolating the upper rampart section at the head of the weir from the mill island upon which we stood. From here we could see that the upper or lead-in section of canal is about 60ft wide, relatively clear and fast flowing as far as the breach; through which the Boyne thunders in a seething mass of white water. Because of the breach, the canal from here to the mill is almost entirely clogged by debris, trees and river sedge, with just a small stream flowing into the former canal and millrace.

The remains of the old mill are crumbling into oblivion. The walls of the section nearest the canal rise to a height of about 15ft and form a 20ft by 15ft oblong building, almost overgrown entirely both inside and outside.

Cruicetown Mill tailrace, with lozenge-shaped islet in background

A millrace about 4ft wide runs through the mill from its upstream façade to the downstream face of the building. Further sections of the structure on the river side of the millrace have fallen-in, but part of a sluice system is still evident on the downriver wall. The tailrace below the building is about 12ft wide and falls into the Boyne close by two little islands in the river.

These lozenge-shaped islets are about 20ft long, constructed from rough-hewn stone and are obviously man-made. Their former purpose give rise to some speculation, but following further research I suggest they were once part of a fish/eel weir in olden days.

The 1953 County Louth Archaelogical Journal records that the 1650s Civil Survey lists a fishing weir in the parish of Painestown. The Down Survey map of 1656 shows a weir upon the Boyne, crossing from the parish of Paynestown to the northern shore. The 1882 OS map depicts three islets where the later map of 1911 shows only two – this third islet was most likely demolished by floods in the interim period. Conor Brennan mentions in *Yellow Furze Memories* that local legends tell of several underwater pillars becoming visible hereabouts during low water levels, which in turn gave rise to the mystery

Carrickdexter Castle 2014 - Hill of Slane in left background

of 'the Nine Eyed Bridge.' I suggest that this myth derives from the ancient fish-weir of Paynestown, a structure perhaps consisting of a series of islets, linked by several footbridges (or foot stick fords) crossing the river, long since carried away and lost in the mists of time.

We found the iron cross just below the former bridge straddling the canal. The cross is about 2.5ft high by 1.5ft wide and is mounted on a dressed stone slab, set into the canal rampart wall. It is well made and probably crafted in some local Smithy, as the two arms are joined to the upright by a 'blacksmith's weld' or perhaps by brazing. The upright section is set into the stone and 'leaded-in' to prevent corrosion of the ironwork cracking the stone – a technique used on many of the parapet capstones on the older bridges. The history of this old cross (set in such a lonely location) is somewhat uncertain, but, as mentioned, some local tradition holds that a child from one of the Lock-houses drowned here in the canal during the early years of the 20th century; while other tales are told of a child on holidays from England perishing here.

As prevailing conditions prevented us from making a landing at Carrickdexter on the day we travelled downriver by boat in the winter of 2011; we took the opportunity of this visit to gain further insight into this section of beautiful riverbank. Next day (28-04-2014), my brother Tom and I made our way downhill through the fields from Baronstown Hill towards

Clockwise from top: Tom Holten & James Doherty at 'the Ferryman's House' 2014; Eastern gable of Carrick (Sailor Reilly's Lockhouse); A cold hearth by the river.

the wooded cleft of the Boyne valley. Passing by the old limekiln and onwards through the huge field, we noted that both Snowfield Clump and the Dark Wood[7] have disappeared entirely. However, the impressive growth of ivy mantling Castle Dexter had increased, such that it appears to be in danger of collapsing under the sheer weight of greenery.

We passed through the western end of the Glen Wood and on to the former canal towpath – where we paused to admire and photograph the beautiful 'horseshoe weir,' then followed the towpath leading eastwards

461

Left: Phyllis Dunne - Edward Reilly's (1914 Lockeeper at Carrickdexter) daughter and her niece - 2014   Right: At the Sailor Reilly's Lockhouse Tom holds up a sun-dappled roofing slate while James looks on

alongside Carrickdexter Canal to the small hydro plant at the lock. The canal is heavily silted up and overgrown with river sedge, the upper lock gate replaced by a pair of sluices and a screen (or rack) system to control and filter the water powering the hydro plant. This plant is located in a concrete structure straddling the old ashlar built lock chamber, which is open to the river downstream, with no trace of the lower gates remaining. The electric transformer stands atop a concrete pillar, occupying pride of place to the east of the lock; like some piece of modern art sculpted in the gothic style.

Access to the island and Lockkeeper's house, formerly gained via the lock gates, is now provided by two concrete footbridges, which are part of the hydro scheme. The former Lock-house is situated on the island (or rampart), adjacent to the location of the upper lock gate, and is heavily overgrown by wildwood and scrub timber. The old building is in a sorry state. Battling through the brush and briar growing within its ancient walls, we noted that the roof has disappeared together with the internal walls. The fire hearth that provided warmth for the Lanney and 'Sailor Reilly' families now merely a black opening in the upstream gable, its bright glow quenched forever.

Reflecting on the meaning of the word 'progress,' we made our way upriver to inspect the old caretaker's house in the woods close by Beauparc Ferry. And came to a location which evoked even sadder reflections – the place where gamekeeper, Timothy Kidman, was so callously murdered during the 1980s, and I pondered again upon the injustices of this world.

ENDNOTES

1 A full account of our search for these lighters is included in Volume 2 of the Navan & District Historical Society's Journal (2013); *Navan – Its People and its Past* – the title of this article is 'Echoes along the Boyne.'

2 A term used to describe opposing sections of lock gates i.e. their principle of operation depended on the angle of contact, as the greater the pressure exerted from upstream, the tighter they sealed.

3 Some anecdotes tell of these concrete walls being built across the canal locks as part of a defensive line along the river during 'The Emergency' of the 1940s, together with the more common Pillboxes which still dot the riverbank here and there. However, these walls were constructed as flood barriers to prevent the canal works from washing out following closure of the waterway in the 1930s.

4 Note mention in previous chapter of Catherine Maguire's Lock-house at No.1 milestone and Patrick Maguire's Lock-house at Cruicetown Lock.

5 Deliah Reilly, a member of the Reilly family from the nearby Reilly's Lock, born at the Lock-house in 1930, told me that this surmise is indeed correct. The family had a wooden cask installed beneath the waterfall, which they used as their water supply during her childhood by the Boyne. The little rill was/is sourced from a spring located in a field south of the Slane/Navan road and north-east of Doherty's Quarry – this spring was known as St. Bridget's Well, and it outflowed to the Boyne through a field called 'the Drain Field.'

6 Reilly's small vegetable garden was located on the river rampart beside lower gate of the lock.

7 These woods are referenced in Chap. 15 (in the context of Carrickdexter) during our downriver boat journey in the winter of 2011.

15

The Middle Reaches
Stackallan to Slane

Dollardstown Weir & Mills – Cruicetown Weir – Beauparc Ferry & Sans Souci Wood – Beauparc's natural mirror – Croppies of '98 & Lambert's Herd – Carrickdexter Wood, Castle and Lock – Carrickdexter Weir – Hydro for the castle – Glen Wood – old Parish of Painestown – Maiden Rock – Fennor – Slane sawing mill – Mullaha Corn Mill – Tom Crinion & Roestown Corn & Tuck Mill – Slane Castle Demesne – William Wilde on Slane Castle 1849 – Seamus Heaney in Slane Castle 1978 – Captains Lightfoot & Thunderbolt – Lady Well & The hermitage of Erc – the Lower Navigation & Slane Mill Weir.

Resuming the downriver journey, the RIBs approached the big drop across Stackallan Weir. Our boat remained in the centre of Lugaree Pool while the other craft sought out the best route. Choosing the direct approach eventually; they drove the craft straight across the centre of the salmon-leap amidst much whooping and glee. As the guinea pig survived, albeit having shipped some water, we used the same approach and crossed the weir safely, then followed the river's main course. Rounding the great bend, where the Boyne turns north-eastwards to flow past Cocker's Wood, then over the white water rapids we went; the two boats heading into the wide gorge leading downriver towards Slane.

Over Lugaree Weir, 2011

Below Deerpark Lock the navigation utilised the main river as described; the raised level maintained by a weir located further downstream. Dollardstown Weir is curved and crosses from the north bank at Stackallan to Dollardstowm, it is skewed towards the southern shore and built originally to power Dollardstown Mills, located on the south-side.

In the earlier years of the navigation, Sir Richard Gorges Meredyth (Meredith) owned Dollardstown estate, of which the mill site formed part. I found references to a man named Mooney associated with this mill in the 1790s,[1] perhaps the miller at that time. Griffith's shows that in 1854, a house, offices, corn and tuck mill at Dollardstown, together with c.18.76 acres were leased by Sir M. Somerville Bart' to Jane Mooney at R.V. £30. On the same property, John Mooney is shown as owner of a vacant house with a rateable valuation of 6s.[2]

The weir was modified during reconstruction of the navigation in the 1790s. The rounded (bullnosed) pillar and stone rampart were constructed at the head of the weir as an integral part of Castlefin lateral canal, sited across the Boyne opposite Dollardstown Mills. The remains of these mills are almost totally obscured by wildwood, and lie near the weir's southern end, where a few crumbling stone walls run landwards from the old millrace to merge with the outcropping bluff. It is truly amazing that any of the structure

Left: Dollardstown Millrace
Above: Dollardstown Weir

survived, as countless floods thundered through the gorge's narrow confines throughout the years. Similar to Cruicetown Mill across the Boyne, these mills may have been bought-out to enable improvements of the navigation during the period 1790 to 1800?

The 1837 OS and Larkin's map indicate a roadway leading to the mill from the old Navan to Drogheda road, with a hamlet of six houses located about midway between road and mills. In 1854, two of these houses were leased from Rev. Robert Nixon and occupied by Peter Dowdall and Patrick Connolly. To the east of Cottonmill Road, the old mill site is now accessed by a laneway known as Dollardstown Lane; which terminates in a farm track or cow-pass leading towards an area named 'the flats' in the vernacular. I walked down the old track but found no trace of the former hamlet, then rambled along the riverside fisherman's path to the remains of Mooney's Mill.[3]

Back on the boat – fortunately for our wellbeing, the old footbridge across the entrance to Castlefin Canal prevented us taking the previously described thrill seekers route down the tidal rip of the lock, so we followed normal procedure by sending the other boat across the weir as a scout. But the large drop capsized the craft and its crew was thrown into 'the washing machine,' as the River Rescue lads so described the turbulent waters beneath the weirs. This created great merriment, especially for us in the second boat, who had a bird's eye view of the event. We supernumeraries disembarked and walked along the southern riverbank, through the ruins of the old mill and waded across the remnants of the mill tailrace to board the RIB below the weir.

Nobody was injured, some suffering merely the indignity of wet arses and bruised egos, with several items of loose equipment lost overboard; which were recovered further downstream.[4]

Departing the troubled waters below Dollardstown Weir and passing alongside the remains of Cruicetown Wood on the left bank; we travelled along the secluded river reach towards the next weir a short distance downstream.

Cruicetown Weir nowadays is a very tricky and dangerous part of the river to negotiate. The post 1968 arterial drainage scheme, thankfully, left this stretch of the Boyne untouched, the river; therefore, remained as it was before the canal made it navigable in the late 18th century. The safest passage through the remnants of the weir and lateral canal system is difficult to fathom as one makes the approach on the fast-flowing current. Hence, when our guinea pig hung up on the centre of the weir, to avoid a similar fate our craft shot at speed down the throat of the old millrace that once powered Carney's Tuck Mill. Using oars, Hopper and Pa. succeeded in keeping clear of the jagged wall until we found a clean break in the stonework, which allowed Martin to manoeuvre back through some rapids to the relative safety of the open river below the weir. From where we had a fish eye view of our 'guinea pig' being extricated from the clutches of the weir; following our reunion, both craft continued the voyage of discovery downriver towards more placid waters at Beauparc.[5]

The open river transit, from Cruicetown towards Carrickdexter, leads through a rocky portal, once known as Beauparc Rocks, and so named after two beetling bluffs, one located on each shore. These craggy riverbanks form

Left: Lozenge-shaped islets at Cruicetown Lock - possible remains of ancient fish-weir
Right: Hung up on Cruicetown Weir.

Clockwise from top left:
Ruins of Cruicetown Mill May 2014; Cruicetown mill Canal and gap in rampart 2014
An old iron cross by Cruicetown Mill and canal; Cruicetown Millrace and millwheel housing 2014.

a gorge below Beauparc House, which stands atop an escarpment to the south, overlooking a most spectacular part of the River Boyne. The house, a Palladian-style mansion designed by Richard Cassells, was built c.1755 and occupied in times past by Gustavus Lambert Esq. – MP for County Westmeath and listed as juror number four in the Meath Grand Jury of 1803. While researching for *On Ancient Roads*, I noted Lambert named as one of six overseers for *the King's Road*, a colloquial name for the Ashbourne to Slane road; supposedly straightened to enable King George IV to more rapidly visit his mistress, Lady Conyngham, in Slane Castle. Like many such tales, this yarn doesn't stand the test of close scrutiny; a different version of the story is related in the other book.

The name Beau Parc derives from the French language, and translates to 'the handsome park,' perhaps an indicator that the Lamberts were great admirers of things French.

On the earlier maps (1837 OS & Larkin's), the name Beaupark applied only to the house and grounds in its immediate vicinity, and did not extend to the greater area of Painestown Townland. Although the extensive grounds are shown covered by woodlands, the area is not marked as a demesne. The 1911 OS map; however, indicates several changes, with the house and immediate environs named Beau Parc, and the name Beau Parc Demesne applied to a much greater area of Painestown.

When tourist trips operated on the navigation (c. early 1890s to 1911), steam launches plied the river from the tidal lock at Oldbridge and disembarked passengers at the boat landing beside Beauparc House. The tourists ascended the many-tiered steps leading to the house, and returned to Drogheda from nearby Beauparc Railway Station. Photographs in the Lawrence and Shackleton collections provide various insights to these now long disappeared scenes of leisure upon the Boyne. One photo depicts the steam powered vessel, *S.S. Ros Na Righ,* passing beneath Maiden Rock;[6] another shows a canopy-draped, unpowered and unnamed passenger tender being towed through the canal by a steam powered tug-boat. I suspect the latter snapshot may be of the elusive *S.S. Wasp,* part of the James McCann canal fleet of later times.

Beauparc House -Shackleton Collection *c.* 1896 (left) and from boat - Nov. 2011 (right)

The OS maps show some interesting features in the vicinity of Beauparc House, including the location of the copper mines, which worked rich ore seams here for several years and closed down in 1914. A private ferry operated from the boat landing to the northern riverbank; where, at the north-eastern end of Sans Souci Wood, a laneway once led northwards, connecting the navigation towpath to the Navan/Slane road in Pighill Townland. This lane passed by an area of woodland named 'the Dark Wood.'

Sans Souci Wood is a 6 acre area of woodland running alongside the northern riverbank, from the defunct lane to just west of Carrickdexter Wood.[7]

Looking back upstream while traversing the river reach above Beauparc, one had the impression of the darkening riverscape receding rearwards. The low winter's sun creating erratic patterns on the river below Cruicetown Weir, and causing a blinding glare when reflecting from the disturbed water of the boat's wake. A contrasting vista unfolded downriver; where inverted images of Palladian Mansion, tiered steps, rocky outcrops and the oak, beech and lime trees of Sans Souci Wood were mirrored from the river's dark, still water. If the Boyne could portray such enchanting images in the depths of winter, I wondered what it might present to downriver travellers when covered in summer's green foliage or autumn's golden tints.

Local folklore tells of several Croppies being rowed to safety across the river in 1798; these were part of the previously encountered Wexford Insurgent Colum that marched from Wexford in July 1798 following the earlier defeat at Vinegar Hill. Richard Murphy, a native of Kilbeggan County Westmeath, served as a Garda in Slane from 1935 until his retirement from the force in 1957. During his time in Slane, he interviewed many older local residents, recording their recollections of folklore pertaining to the summer of 1798 and the activities surrounding the arrival of the insurgents in the district – the following is one of many tales related to him at the time:

Traditional account of the Croppies who were in Carrickdexter and Beauparc in 1798 given by John Gallaher, Slane, on 9th June, 1950, to Guard R. Murphy, Slane.

I am 67 years of age and was born in Slane on 27th May, 1883. I knew old Mickey Southwell of Barristown, Slane, very well. He was 90 years of age when he died in 1948. I often heard him talk about the Croppies of '98. He said that a large number of them were hiding in a ditch (a deep channel) on the North side of the River Boyne opposite Beauparc house at that time. There was a Herd named Denis Rourke in the employment of Lambert of Beaupark then. When this Herd was on his rounds looking after the cattle in the evening he came across those Croppies who were resting in the deep ditch. He arranged to bring them across the Boyne that night. Some time later on that same evening, or the following morning, he rowed them across the river to the South side. When across, he brought them to his own house where he kept them for about two hours until they had taken some food. He then accompanied them for some distance and showed them the direction they were to take for Wexford.

Some years afterwards Denis Rourke had occasion to go to Wexford on business affairs. He used to travel by a float drawn by two horses. As far as I can remember he was going to the residence of some gentleman whose name I cannot remember when something happened to the float. A crowd collected amongst whom were some of the men he had rowed across the Boyne at Beauparc in 1798. When they saw the name of Lambert on the float they asked him some questions and to their delight they recognised him as the man who had befriended them. No sooner was this known than they took the horse from under the float and pulled it themselves into the next town, (I think it was Gorey) and lavishly they dispensed with "the cup that cheers."

There was a man locally known as the Squire Kelch who lived in Pighill in 1798. He gave information about some Croppies whom he found hiding somewhere about Carrickdexter. I cannot say what happened to the insurgents he informed on.

Signed John Gallagher. Senior
Witness Richard R. Murphy. Gda
June 9th 1950 (sic)[8]

Entering the winding gorge and leaving Beauparc astern, we glided on downriver through this dramatic landscape, with Carrickdexter Wood covering the northern bank just below the final bend of the narrows. The dull roar carrying upriver on the freshening east wind created by Boyne water cascading over Carrickdexter Weir.

A dark ivy covered ruin dominated the green hillside to our left, high above our mid-river vantage point; the great pile of Carrickdexter Castle overlooking the Boyne from its lofty perch above the northern bank. It is said that the castle was once occupied by the Flemings, a Norman family who later owned the precursor of nearby Slane Castle, but were dispossessed following the rebellion of 1641. The origins of the structure are uncertain, but Wilde suggested that although perhaps occupied by the Flemings at some period, it was possibly built by the D'Exeter family, who hailed from Connaught (MacJordan Clan) and once bore the name de Exoniis. The older part of the castle is comprised of a four storeyed tower house, probably dating from the 12th century, with the newer section based more on comfort than defence and reflecting a later period of architecture.

The 1911 OS map locates the castle in a very large field (176.387 acres), close by a spinney named Snowfield Clump and situated in Slane Castle Demesne (the extended demesne noted earlier). The 1837 OS map; however, shows the castle in a much smaller field and sited within Carrickdexter Townland on its boundary with Slane Castle Demesne. Both maps indicate Baronstown wayside cross situated in Carrickdexter Townland, adjacent to the Navan to Slane road.

Left: Carrickdexter - Horseshoe Weir   Right: Salmon leap and vortex at Carrickdexter Weir

The name Carrickdexter translates to 'the Rock of Dexter' or Dexter's Rock, which in my opinion derives from another riverside feature located across the Boyne in Fennor.

Being mindful of the earlier dunking at Dollardstown, we made the approach to Carrickdexter or Horseshoe Weir with caution. The weir is shaped more like a fishhook than a horseshoe; with the hook's shank skewed towards the south-eastern bank, where a sluice, possibly once a fish pass, ties it to the riverbank. The business (or sharp) end of the imaginary hook leads into Carrickdexter lateral canal, with a salmon leap bridging the gap between the two arms of the weir. This weir was probably built originally for navigation purposes and is perhaps the steepest remaining on this reach of the Boyne.

As noted, a hydro turbine generator, installed on the site of the canal works in the 1930s, supplied high tension electric current to power Slane Castle. Tradition holds that apart from being shut down for a major refit in 1959, this system supposedly worked continuously until contemporary times, when

Carrickdexter Lock - *c.* 1894 - from Shackleton Collection

Top, left to right: A Gothic hydro transformer - Hydro building in background;
Tom French at Carrick Weir. Bottom: Going over Carrick Weir - Courtesy Tom French

it was knocked out of commission by a lightning strike; a bolt from the blue, not the trade union version of such a strike.[9]

Discretion being the better part of valour, the River Rescue boys requested us to vacate the boat and walk along the south-eastern riverbank, while they took the boats across the steep drop.

Re-boarding our boat, we set off once more along the Boyne, north-eastwards from Carrickdexter towards Slane. Just below the castle, it turns and flows in a south-easterly direction to Slane Bridge and Rosnaree. The salient of land enclosed within this great curve is part of Fennor, referred to in the 1836 Field Notes as *Finnabhair, white plain, whitish spot.*

The dramatic riverscape continued below Carrickdexter, with the Boyne's deep, dark waters gliding between high woodlands rising steeply and towering above the riverside; the once cultivated woods of old demesnes, now tangled wildwood, mirrored from the river's glass-like surface. Here the woodland on our left flank is shown on the 1911 OS map as 'the Glen Wood.' This part of the main river was navigable during the era of the canal, its level controlled by the weir opposite Slane Castle, immediately upstream of Slane Mill Weir.

The map indicates also that the navigation towpath, heretofore running alongside the north-western riverbank from Stackallan Guard Lock, changed to the southern bank below Carrickdexter Weir. Here a small stream enters the Boyne from the south-east.

This little river is an important landmark, because it forms the eastern mereing of the ancient parish of Painestown (Paynestown) with Fennor Parish. It rises in marshy bottomlands to the south of McGruder's Crossroads on the Slane to Dublin road. Painestown Parish included the riparian sections of Dollardstown, Painestown and Thurstianstown Townlands. These are located on the Boyne's south-eastern bank, from downstream of Stackallan Weir to Fennor, including Beauparc Demesne. As the stream seems to be unnamed, I suggest 'the Painestown River' as a suitable title.

Below the confluence, a small wooded islet (shaped like a spear) bisects the river which briefly forms two channels in its vicinity. Downstream from the island, the wood on the southern bank is named Rock Wood on the old maps, as it is so named nowadays. This name would appear to derive from one of the most spectacular natural landmarks upon the River Boyne, known in local legends as Maiden Rock or Lover's Leap.

This is the rock formation mentioned previously, referred to by Wilde as 'the Rock of Fennor,' which in my opinion provides the source of the name Carrickdexter, or 'the Rock of Dexter.' Many legends are woven around this rock formation towering above the river; one such tale is of a maiden who cast herself from its lofty height because of unrequited love. I am unsure of the name's derivation and cannot discover a definitive story in local folklore, but it seems to be rooted in more recent times because Wilde refers to the outcrop by the older title.

The limestone formation rises perpendicularly above the south-eastern riverbank and is capped with small trees. An interesting insight into the changing landscape is provided should one compare photographs taken in older times with contemporary pictures. A photo from the Lawrence collection of the 1890s shows a white rock formation, standing out boldly from the surrounding woodland. The rock is draped with dark ivy and its summit covered by fir trees, and the adjacent riverside walk is obviously well tended.

Nowadays the rock is almost totally hidden by scrub timber and tinted a dirty grey (possibly caused by acid rainfall); with most of its surface obscured by withered ferns, moss and other woodland detritus. The former riverside

Maiden Rock - Shackleton Collection *c.* 1896

walk/towpath is overgrown. Nonetheless, Maiden Rock, whatever the derivation of its name, and though it could do with a facelift, provides the most dramatic natural feature alongside the River Boyne.

Irish landscape artist, James George O'Brien (1779-1819), known also as Oben, painted a famous watercolour of Maiden Rock circa 1800. I believe this artist portrayed several other views of the Boyne hereabouts, some of which were in the Slane Castle collection at one time.

The riverscape changes yet again downstream from the rock. To the south, the previously steep banks lessen below Fennor to flatter bottomlands, with rolling, undulating hillsides forming the horizon above the valley. The denser wildwood is replaced by open parklands, where clumps, spinneys and individual trees intermingle with grassland. Rounding a slight curve, our attention is drawn from the changing landscape of the southern shore by the grey bulk of Slane Castle, glimpsed through thinning woodlands on the higher northern riverbank.

Upriver from the castle a small stream enters the Boyne close by a boat house. Following the winding course of this stream (as shown on the 1911 map) up through the castle demesne and on past 'the Little Glen Wood,' a

Small cascade at site of Slane Castle sawmills (Harlinstown River)

saw-mill is depicted beside a mill pond. Here the brook flows beneath the Navan/Slane road at the bottom of Baronstown Hill, beside the castellated gatehouse. In 1854, Griffith's records Slane Sawing Mill, house, offices and land totalling c.182 acres at R.V. £130. The old mill has largely disappeared, its ruins standing in a wooded nook beside the little stream, which flows over a waterfall before passing beneath a pointed arched stone avenue bridge and onwards to the Boyne.

This stream, known to some as the Harlinstown River, is sourced from a series of small rills and streams rising in the marshy land near the townlands of Mullagha and Rochestown, to the north-west of Gormalough Crossroads (crossroads of the Lough *J.O.D. 1836*). The 1837 OS map indicates that the little river powered a corn mill within the grounds of Mullagha House, and then passed south-eastwards through Rochestown and into Roestown. Here it once powered a corn mill, shown on Griffith's as occupied by John Andrews in 1854. Other records indicate a tuck mill located on the same site, now occupied by Tom Crinion.

The little river meandered south-eastwards, receiving several more streams on its onward journey; winding through Castlepark and Harlinstown, before flowing beneath the Slane/Navan road to the mill pond close by the saw-mill at Slane Castle.

In these times of dwindling oil resources and increasing environmental pollution, the stream provides a fine example of how 'renewable green energy' was extracted from natural sources in bygone days. Though only a minor brook, it powered upwards of four mills along its modest course. Of particular interest is the layout of the mill(s) in Roestown, where Tom Crinion pointed out the ingenuity used in times past to maximise the energy inherent within the little stream. The mill builders diverted water from other streamlets to the mill pond through long and complex headraces, which, though now gone, can still be traced on the surrounding landscape.

I discovered the former existence of Roestown Corn Mill several years ago during previous research, and when visiting the site, noticed an unusual millstone standing by the roadside wall of the old house. I lost contact for several years, but revisited the site recently, and found the millstone had disappeared. It was not stolen, but moved to a safer location and is now embedded as a decorative feature in the paved patio to the front of the new house.

Tom Crinion's Millstone and detail of the drive collet.

Tom has a keen interest in history and a virtual treasure trove of historical family records; including an extensive collection of memorabilia from his own antecedents and the Andrews' family who owned the mill in bygone days. This collection includes old photographs and letters from family members who emigrated to the USA in post famine times.

During these visits I obtained a glimpse of a remarkable lineage, linking at least three families in County Meath, namely, the Crinions, Cassidys and Andrews. These families providing a connection between three watermills widely dispersed across the county, from Scurlockstown (Cassidy's Mill), Roestown or Andrews' Mill and Clatterstown Mill near Ardcath. The last mill was operated also by a member of the Andrews' family in times past. A wealth of local history is available should some enterprising person take an interest in visiting Tom and reviewing his treasure trove.

Many eminent historians have written tomes about Slane Castle and village, its ecclesiastical sites, and, of course, Saint Patrick and the Paschal Fire. I will provide only a brief description of the castle and its environs; therefore, as seen by Wilde and Seamus Heaney in different eras during their visits.

In 1849, Wilde seemed more impressed by the magnificent setting than the castle, which he describes thus:

> Slane Castle, the seat of the Marquis of Conyngham, and memorable in modern times, from its being visited by King George IV., stands on a swelling bank of verdant green-sward, rising gradually from the river. It is a large castellated mansion, with towers and embattled parapets, but not boasting much beauty of architectural design. It is principally the surrounding scenery, the combination of sylvan beauty formed by its own extensive demesne, blending with that of Beauparc, the neighbouring woods of other seats, the charming associations awakened by the ancient ruins standing on the romantic shores of its noble river, and the highly cultivated landscape on all sides, which claim for Slane Castle the eulogiums of its modern describers.

Anthony Bailey, who accompanied Seamus Heaney in his rambles along the Boyne in 1978, wrote a less poetic but more informative account of the castle and its history, the following is a short excerpt:

> After dinner, Henry gave us a tour of the interior. Slane castle is mostly a product of the late eighteenth century. Henry's ancestors, the Conynghams, were a Scottish family who came to Donegal in 1611. Sir Albert Conyngham fought for King William at the Boyne in 1690. On James ll side fought Christopher Fleming, the twenty second Lord Baron of Slane, whose family had held the estates from 1175 until 1641, when they were confiscated and sold to the Conynghams. Bits of the old Fleming castle are believed to have been incorporated in the Gothic Revival house that James Wyatt, the architect, designed here, with mock battlements and corner towers, and set on a rocky bastion overlooking a bend of the Boyne. Francis Johnson oversaw its completion. Capability Brown did the stables.[10]

I have my own youthful memories of Slane Castle. In 1954/55, part of the film *Captain Lightfoot* (released in 1956), was filmed in the area, with some major scenes set within the precincts of the castle and demesne. The movie starred Rock Hudson, Barbara Rush, John Morrow and Kathleen Ryan. It was set in post 1798 Ireland, with Hudson playing the part of Michael Martin, a fictional young rebel of the times, whose immediate sidekick was named Captain Thunderbolt. A film or series of the same name, *Thunderbolt and Lightfoot*, reappeared during the 1970s.

I recall viewing Captain Lightfoot at the Palace (or Lyric) Cinema in Navan, probably about 1957, because current movies were slow in arriving during that less urgent era. How I thrilled at the occasional visit to the cinema in those rare old times; the magical action scenes with the beautiful backdrop of the Boyne Valley impinged on my psyche such that I can still remember many of them today. One sequence I recollect vividly is of how Michael Martin (Hudson) escapes the clutches of dastardly redcoats, and descends a rope from the castle battlements. Then dashes down the steps, across the swelling hillside (described so eloquently by Wilde), and runs headlong towards the river; where he is saved by a bunch of rebel musketeers firing from across the weir. Yes indeed, those were the days of simplicity... would they were with us still.

Some other fleeting recollections are of visiting the castle during my teenage years in the early 1960s. Not, I may add, to hobnob with his Lordship like Bailey and Heaney, but to visit Lady Well on the banks of the Boyne near the castle weir. If my memory serves, ceremonies took place at the well during those times. I believe the castle is open to the public about the 15th of August each year and that a ceremony (or pattern) is held at the well around this date. I viewed the castle interior for the one and only time while attending a birthday party in 1977.

The crumbling remains of an old building are located within the castle demesne, close by the riverbank between Lady Well and the bridge of Slane. The ruin is referred to as 'the Hermitage,' and set upon a more ancient site, supposedly occupied by Saint Erc, first Bishop of Slane, who, legend says, was consecrated by Saint Patrick and died circa 514 AD. Ancient annals contain many stories about this saint, including his penchant for immersing his person up to the elbows in the Boyne while reading from missals placed on

Left:
Slane Castle from an unusual angle

Below:
Slane Castle Weir

the riverbank, and his rather odd diet of one and a half duck eggs per day. It is said also that in 1512, Christopher Fleming, Baron of Slane, granted the site to a pair of Franciscan Friars named Malachy and Donald(t) O'Brien (natural brothers), who lived there as recluses for a number of years thereafter; perhaps an explanation for the derivation of the name. History records also that the two brothers transferred to the Franciscan Friary atop the Hill of Slane when it was built in later times.

The castle weir, crossing the river from the demesne to the southern bank at Fennor, provided the next obstacle to a smooth downriver passage. Originally a fish-weir or dam built at 90 degrees to the river, it enhances the location by providing a stretch of deeper, placid water below the castle's high eminence. A lawsuit supposedly took place in 1459 involving the manor of Slane and its associated salmon weir (a possible reference to the castle weir).[11]

Here, the navigation switched from the navigable river to the southern bank once again, where a canal was cut across the promontory jutting from the low lying floodplain of Fennor; around which point the Boyne flows towards Slane Bridge to the south-east. The canal cutting bypasses the weir and is very short, merely a few hundred yards in extent, with a lock built on its lower or eastern end taking the canal barges into and out of the navigable river section above Slane Mill Weir. Known as the Castle Canal (or Fennor Canal), it was perhaps built originally in the period 1748 to 1763, as part of the works executed for the Lower Navigation. The surviving lock may have been rebuilt during construction of the Upper Navigation in the 1790s.

A plan of the Lower Boyne Navigation was drawn from a survey conducted by John Yeats C.E. in 1834.[12] The chart contains some interesting features, including: the lower navigation is shown extending from Carrickdexter Lock to 'the Bridge of Drogheda' and the canal lock opposite Slane Castle is listed as 1st lock.

Griffith's shows that in 1854 the Boyne Navigation Co. owned the navigation works hereabouts, including a two acre island, 10.76 acres of land and canal banks and a Lock-house. The Lock-house and island were occupied by Laurence Maguire, with the house listed at R.V. 13s., the island at R.V. £1-8s., the canal and banks at R.V. £1-8s. Other sources record the Lock-

Remains of the Lock-house at the castle weir in Fennor

house occupied by Richard Noble in 1788 and Joseph Holmes in 1834. The above two acre island is formed by the portion of land isolated by the canal cutting.

The Lock-house is located a short distance to the south of the lock and towpath, where a building is shown on the valuation map and 1837 OS map. The house is adjacent to a small wood, situated between the canal and a larger area of woodland, named Dean's Wood on the 1911 OS map. This map shows also the No. 12 milestone, the last of the series on the Lower Navigation (12 miles upriver from St. Mary's Bridge Drogheda). It is located about mid-way along the cutting, above the upper lock gate and slightly west of the Lock-house.

On a visit to the site in Nov. 2012, I noted that the old lock is in an advanced state of decay. Traces of the gates remain, but the chamber wall on the Fennor bank hosts several ash trees which have displaced the stonework. Destruction of the lock will be completed eventually by the fast-flowing stream tearing through the canal cutting. On the island, the opposite wall of the chamber is overgrown, such that it is impossible to see what lies beneath the greenery, but no doubt similar destructive forces are at work there also.

The No. 12 milestone is uprooted and now lies on the floodplain between the former towpath and the wooded escarpment of Fennor. The stone, though in good condition, is fortunate to have survived, perhaps doing so only because of its remote location and weight.

Similar to the lock, the old Lock-house is in poor condition, its remains now standing within a wood on the riverbank. The house is built tight to the steep hillside rising towards the heights of Fennor, almost totally obscured from the nearby riverbank. This was a two storey or dormer type building, but the upper floor and roof have mostly fallen in; however, what remains of the roof indicates that it was of fairly ornate construction with a large overhang to the gables. Some of the surviving window architraves, together with remnants of the stove and hobs, suggest that this was a cosy and well-appointed dwelling during the days of the navigation. The house was once accessed via a raised rampart across the narrow floodplain, connecting it to the lock and navigation towpath.[13]

The OS Benchmark on the stonework of the Castle Lock gates is at elevation 61.6ft; indicating a lift/drop of circa 2.5ft from and to the impounded,

Postcard Boyne at Slane Bridge

unflooded navigable river level (circa 59.1ft) above Slane Mill Weir. Reconstruction and raising of the mill weir by 2ft in 1763 allowed the removal, or partial removal of the castle weir, as referenced in Charles Vallency's report of 1771 (the stonework from this weir supposedly was used to build the guard lock at Slane in 1785).

Some confusion exists between the Vallency report (1771) and that of David Jebb in 1779, as quoted in Cyril Ellison's book. It is difficult; therefore, to determine when this short section of canal in Fennor first came into being, but, as noted above, it was probably constructed originally in the period 1748 to 1763.

Slane Castle weir nowadays creates merely a minor ripple on the placid waters, which we crossed with ease. Navigating around the islands and rounding the curve, a new vista unfolded towards the south-east.

To our left, high wooded banks of the old demesne towered above, obscuring both Hermitage and village, with lofty trees reflecting from the darkened water beneath. While the opposite riverbank of Fennor, denuded of summer's greenery, mirrored only the occasional sally or scraggy hawthorn. Beyond this stretch, we glimpsed the medieval Bridge of Slane appearing from the gathering winter's gloom.

Marie, Tony and Skylar at Slane floodgates

But looking upstream towards the castle, the spell of this beautiful riverscape is spoiled somewhat by ragged, high metal fences surrounding the demesne, erected to prevent non-paying guests from gate crashing rock concerts held at the castle nowadays. Yes indeed, progress and modernity frequently invade the most tranquil of settings.

Our boats passed along this beautiful reach of the Boyne, heading towards Slane Mill Weir, the murmur of falling water increasing to a dull roar as we approached. This is the longest mill weir remaining on the Boyne and runs askew across the river, from Fennor's bank towards the north-western or village side of the great bridge. The two arches on the village bank conduct Slane Mill headrace/canal under the former Great North Road (N2).

Development of the Lower Boyne Navigation commenced at Oldbridge Lock near Drogheda circa 1748. The lower navigation was completed to Slane in or about 1763/65, concurrent with the start-up of Jebb's Mill (Slane Mill). We encounter the next part of this navigation on the Fennor or south-western bank immediately above Slane Mill Weir.

This lateral canal section, together with the towpath atop the river rampart, runs parallel to the riverbank, beneath Slane Bridge (note, the towpath crossed the road) and through the floodplain of Fennor, to re-enter the

Boyne at Rosnaree Lock, over a mile further downstream. It was completed originally without an upstream guard lock, the only lock then being located at Rosnaree. This exposed the waterway to many floods, which ravaged the canal works from time to time. In 1785; however, David Jebb, owner of Slane Mill and engineer for the navigation, oversaw construction of Fennor Guard Lock. As mentioned, stones taken from partial demolition of the castle weir were supposedly used to build this lock, which cost about £1800 and is still in situ.[14]

It is very similar in construction to the guard lock at Stackallan, with two sets of gates and an ashlar-type stone chamber.[15] The upper gate is replaced by a chevron-shaped concrete wall, which, in addition to protecting remnants of the waterway, provides a footbridge for the riverside pathway. Although the lock stonework is in good condition, the rampart carrying the former towpath has not fared so well, with extensive breaches where the canal swings eastwards towards the bridge. It is noteworthy that this lock functioned as a guard lock only, having no lift or lowering function; and that its orientation is partly invert to the river's flow. The OS Benchmark is shown on the maps at elevation 59.1ft, the approximate pound level from here to the upper lock gate at Rosnaree.

During his tour of Ireland in June 1776, Arthur Young wrote thus of Slane Mill Weir and mill entry canal/headrace:

> Returning to Slane, dined with Mr. Jebb, and viewed the mill, which is a very large edifice, excellently built; it was begun in 1763, and finished in 1766. The water from the Boyne is conducted to it by a wear of 650 feet long, 24 feet base, and 8 feet high, of solid masonry; the water let into it by very complete flood-gates.
>
> The canal is 800 feet long, all faced with stone, and 64 feet wide; on one side is a wharf completely formed and walled against the river, whereon are offices of several kinds, and a dry dock for building lighters. (sic)[16]

Nowadays the skewed weir has a salmon leap across its upper end near the southern bank, above which three stone piers stand out boldly from the fast-flowing water. These piers were once part of a flood control system, comprising two sets of wooden gates and sluices; used to bypass water around the head of the weir, thereby lessening the impact of elevated water levels on mill operations. While perhaps employed in later times as a fish-pass, the piers are now showing the effects of time and constant erosion by Boyne water.

This weir presented a formidable obstacle, so the boys of the River Rescue used the by now well tested routine, sending the first boat across as the guinea pig. Using the direct approach, they shot across the drop next to the stone piers and arrived safely beyond the turbulent water of the washing machine; so Martin drove our boat straight across in the same place.

Arriving safely on the other side, I gazed upriver in admiration of the beautiful vista presented by the mighty river pouring across the weir... and saw the following words printed on a plastic sign adorning the central pillar, boldly declaring: 'Slane Bridge Fishing Club Private Waters Members Only.' Yes indeed, we were upon the Boyne Water in truly progressive times.

Crossing the remains of the salmon leap, we steered left of the long, narrow, fish-shaped and sedge covered island (0.569 acre). Taking the narrow channel between this islet and the high weir to our left, Martin, Hopper and Pa. manoeuvred our boat beneath the ancient arches of the great bridge, holding her in position while we discussed, examined and photographed the structure for future reference.

Beyond the bridge, we paused to take pictures of Jebb's famous mill, then, in the gathering gloom, headed across river to berth the boats on the southwestern shore near the canal; where we scrambled ashore across the mud and silt covered riverbank. Here, Kieran Maguire took group photographs and the River Rescue boys pulled the boats ashore, placed them on the trailers to be hauled back to their base in Navan. Another memorable and exciting trip down the Boyne completed.

ENDNOTES

1 The 1656 Down Survey Barony of Duleek map depicts two mills (one tuck and one corn mill) in Dollardstown – sited on the approximate location of the mill ruins.

2 The Somerville connection is logical because Sir Richard's daughter, Lady Mary Ann Meredyth, married Marcus Somerville, MP for County Meath and owner of nearby Somerville Demesne. The Meredyth ancestral home, Dollardstown House (famed for its Queen Anne style), was designed by Richard Cassells in 1734.

3 I am of the opinion that the old roadway, now Dollardstown Lane, once connected via a river ford to the now defunct road leading on through Doherty's Quarry to the Navan/ Slane Road. Traces of this old road system can be discerned on the old maps, and, indeed could still be seen on the landscape in Rushwee and Roestown until relatively recent times. James Doherty mentioned that in the 1930/40s, his grandfather, Paddy Hamil, drove carts loaded with hay across the River Boyne below Cruicetown, to fodder his cattle on leased land in Beauparc Estate. These shallows, together with the previously mentioned 'foot stick ford' at Painestown Fish-Weir, was the most likely main river crossing hereabouts prior to construction of Stackallan/Broadboyne Bridge in the early 1700s. Raising of Carrickdexter Weir further downstream during construction of the Upper Boyne Navigation (both phases c.1750/1798), would have raised the water level here, such that it was shallow only in times of low water or when Carrickdexter sluices were open.

4 The narrow dividing rampart between the river and lateral canals alongside the northern riverbank has been breached by the ravages of time and floodwaters. Consequently, during our passage downriver we were able to weave through the broken-down dividing stone walls – unfortunately, because of the densely wooded shoreline, we could not see most of the canal works, lock systems or Lockkeepers' houses. But we had enough to keep us occupied, because the fast-flowing river, together with overhanging tree branches, presented an ever-present hazard to life and limb – an unwary passenger could easily be knocked from the boat into the turbulent waters.

5 During our later walks along the riverbank in Cruicetown Wood, I noted that the gap in the stone rampart, through which we passed that day, was the previously described breach in the rampart of Cruicetown Canal and old millrace.

6 This craft was operated originally in 1905 by Boyne Valley Launch Co., and plied the river and canals between Oldbridge, Slane and Beauparc. In 1906 it was taken over and operated by John Spicer and Edward Crinnion, with the tourist trips extended to take in the Boyne Valley between Oldbridge and Navan. The scheduled trips were: on Mondays, Wednesdays and Fridays the launch ran from Drogheda and on Tuesdays, Thursdays and Saturdays it started from Navan. Unfortunately, the enterprise proved to be financially unviable, and the service closed down for good in 1911. (Meath Chronicle Jun. 16th 1906 – Irish Ind. Jun. 12th 1906 – Courtesy Mairéad Crinion)

7 The name Sans Souci derives from a French phrase translating to 'without concern' or 'carefree,' and may originate from the title given in 1747 to *Frederick the Great's* (King of Prussia) Sansussi Palace in Potsdam; if true, emphasising the French influence amongst the Irish gentry in the area.

8 I came across several versions of this tale, one stating that Denis Rourke travelled to Wexford to collect tree shoots from a nursery for planting in Beauparc Demense – this lends authenticity to the tale, because country demesnes development was at its height then.

9 Note previous mention of Snowfield Clump, Carrickdexter Lock and hydro in Chap 14. The installed power unit is a single stage Francis water turbine with an output capacity of 50 K.W. – the unit could operate throughout the year yielding an average output of about 30 K.W. It was indeed put out of commission in 2001 when the generator/transformer was damaged by the said lightning strike. Local man, Tom Doggett, maintained the equipment in more recent times, he told me that his father looked after the plant before his time.

10 Launcelot (Capability) Brown, a renowned and much sought-after landscape gardener/designer of 18th century England, is said to have designed the fine (but long gone) haw-haw in the former Dowdstown Demesne above Navan. I have seen other records; however, stating that he never performed any design works in Ireland. The nickname, Capability, supposedly derived from his frequent use of this term in the context of his client's estates' potential for improvement.

11 A weir is shown hereabouts on the 1656 Down Survey Barony of Slane map.

12 As the sketch map is headed "4th Annual Report On Public Works .. Ireland .. 1836.," it was likely initiated by the Commissioners of Public Works following their takeover of the Lower Boyne Navigation in c.1834.

13 A list of Lockkeepers, compiled for Meath Co. Council's Road Committee in 1913 during a review of the navigation's proposed liquidation, names Mrs. J. Given as keeper at Fennor Lock. It shows her in receipt of a quarter-annual salary of £1-5s. N.B., the higher salary perhaps reflected that the keeper here may have been in charge of the Slane Guard Lock further downstream.

14 Records of the Boyne Navigation Company show that a William Monghey was employed as a mason on the new lock at Slane Weir (Fennor Guard Lock) in June/July of 1785. He was in charge of a group of workers, including carpenters, masons and labourers, paid £12-0s-0d for working a six day week at building this lock. William was a member of a local family of stonemasons – masons from this family, I believe, were involved at many building projects in the locality, including: Slane Castle reconstruction, Boyne Navigation and Slane Mill. I believe also that family members took part in construction of the floodgate piers at the head of Slane Weir. All these structures still stand on the Boynes's landscape… an enduring testament to the skilled craftsmen of long ago. Courtesy of Thomas Mongey, author of *The Mongey Family Tree* (2000).

15 Yeats' 1834 sketch map delineates a red line running parallel to the Boyne, from the upstream Castle Lock to the canal at Fennor Guard Lock. Perhaps part of a plan, intended to eliminate the navigable river section at the castle from the main canal route to Navan, with Fennor Guard Lock providing side entry to Slane Mill only.

16 It is interesting to note that at this time (1776), boat building and dry docking facilities existed at Slane as they did over a century later at Navan in 1902. I cannot find any trace of such a feature marked on the 1837 or 1911 OS maps.

16

The Middle Reaches
Bridge of Slane

Upstream aspect – Upriver Facade – Widening in times past – Downriver Façade – Original Width – Peter O'Keefe & Tom Simington – Grace's Annals & Laud Manuscript – Great Flood of 1330 – Medieval connection with Trim & Babes Bridge – Evolution of present Bridge – Francis Ledwidge Plaque – Battle Of The Boyne connections – Bushmills in the Boyne.

This is a remarkable bridge from many different perspectives. Approaching from upriver, the structure appears gradually out of the hazy countryside, its stonework merging with surrounding riverscape, in harmony with and complementing winter's greyish shades. The bridge is orientated north-east to south-west, with the best upstream view obtained from midstream, immediately above the weir. The structure is about five hundred feet in length, from shore to shore, at ground level it is well-nigh impossible; therefore, to capture the entire bridge in a single photograph – except from an angle, thereby distorting the image and failing to depict accurately the many different aspects of this unique bridge.

Our view of the bridge changed dramatically when we crossed the weir; from here the red brick outline of Slane Mill's chimney-stack could be seen towering above the parapets, forming a contrasting backdrop to the symmetry of the ancient stone bridge. This view, together with endless

Slane Bridge and mill from upstream. Courtesy Aubrey Martin

torrents of water pouring across the skewed weir, presents the most perfect setting imaginable; a gem to squirrel away for the mind's eye to recall on darker days.

The upriver façade comprises the following: starting at the north-eastern or village riverbank, the mill headrace and access canal passes beneath two differently sized arches to the left of the weir. The abutment or No. 1 arch next to the north-eastern bank is the largest, once allowing barges access to and from the mill; the other, No. 2 forming the smallest span on the entire bridge.

The weir abuts the pillar separating No. 2 arch (lesser millrace), and No. 3, the first arch spanning the main river course below the weir. The three openings, No. 3, 4 & 5, become progressively larger to where No. 5 abuts the inter-arch pillar connecting to the first of four near equally-sized river arches No. 6, 7, 8 & 9. The most south-western river arch, No. 10, is smaller and located beyond a section of retaining wall much wider than the bridge inter-arch pillars – this span is of segmental rounded profile, it was probably added c.1763 as part of a flood control system associated with construction and operation of the mill weir and access canal. Two flood arches, No. 11 & 12 are located near the south-western end, at the extremity of the flood plain and close by the newer Lower Navigation canal bridge. Except for the larger mill canal elliptical span, all the upstream arches, though of varying size as described, are of near semi-circular profile and not of a pronounced segmental design – the inter-arch pillars are faced by triangular cutwaters, with conical/rounded cappings terminating at lower spandrel level.

On closer inspection, it became apparent that the bridge was widened in

Top: Upstream aerial of Slane Br. - L to R - No's 1 & 2 millrace (canal) arches - No's 3 to 9 river arches - No 10 flood control - No's 11 & 12 flood arches & No 13 canal Br. Courtesy Aubrey Martin

Center, left to right: Elliptical profiled Mill-canal arch (No. 1) & upstream extension rounded profiled arches No's. 2, 3 , 4 & 5; upstream extension rounded profiles on arch No's 6,7,8 & 9 - Note silouettes of downstream pointed arches

Bottom, left to right: Detail of upstream extension; upstream rounded profiles on extensions to No's 11 & 12 flood arches - Canal Br. *c.* 1763. Courtesy Aubrey Martin

times past; an upriver extension of about eight feet in width having been added to the original structure. When we passed through to the downstream side, the bridge presented an entirely different aspect. Gone was the beautiful upstream symmetry; here, a mixture of various sized and shaped arches formed the eastern-facing façade.

The downriver face of the bridge is comprised as follows:
counting from the village or north-eastern riverbank:

No. 01 Arch.

large millrace/canal arch of multi-centred segmental profile (near elliptical) as per upstream.

No. 02 Arch.

lesser millrace arch with a near-semi-circular profile as per upstream – inter-arch pillar with stone built breakwater extending for about 4 metres downstream – millrace rampart/wall abutting bridge.

No 03,04 & 05 arches.

Three varying size river arches, with near-semi-circular profiles as per upstream: arches No. 02, 03, 04 and 05 have triangular-shaped keystones and are symmetrical, increasing progressively in height towards the bridge centre. They are separated by pillars circa 6/8ft wide, faced by triangular cutwaters with conical/rounded cappings terminating at mid-spandrel level. No's 4 and 5 appear to be of a slightly different construction to the two other rounded arches – this may be significant in the context of anecdotes relating that part of the bridge was 'thrown down' prior to the Battle of the Boyne in 1690.

No. 06,07,08 & 09 arches.

Four varying size segmental pointed profile river arches, with inter-arch pillars similar in detail to previous – c. 25ft buttressed retaining wall with cutwater profile.

No. 10 arch.

Downstream view of Slane Br. - R to L - No 1 (elliptical) & 2 millrace (canal) arches - No's 3,4 & 5 rounded profile arches - No's 6,7,8, & 9 pointed arches - No 10 flood control.
Courtesy Aubrey Martin

Near-semi-circular profiled river arch (may once have been a flood-control arch) as per upstream – multi-buttressed retaining wall/embankment, extending to two flood arches on the bridge's south-western extremity.

No. 11 & 12 arches.

Two flood arches with segmental pointed profiles, separated by pillar with triangular cutwater and conical/rounded capping terminating at lower spandrel level.

In summary, the downstream façade contains twelve arches plus the extra canal bridge, making a total of thirteen spans, including the Boyne Navigation canal passage – others have said that the bridge comprises thirteen eyes plus the navigation canal bridge, but there are only twelve plus the navigation span, as listed sequentially above.

An opening in the upstream parapet provides access to the former canal wharf and towpath. A similar opening in the downstream parapet once permitted two-way passage for the draught horses across 'the Great North Road,' and provided an access to and from Rosnaree Lock further downstream. These openings are located between the flood arches and navigation canal bridge, which forms the south-western end of the main structure.

The bridge was approximately 16ft in width (including parapets) prior to addition of the 8ft upstream extension; increasing the road width from circa 12ft to 20ft. The extension is butt jointed to the original bridge and seems

From top: R to L - No's 1 & 2 mill canal, 3, 4 & 5 rounded profile arches - 6, 7, 8 & 9 pointed profile arches - rounded profile flood control arch;

The two profiles of No 7 arch from upstream;

Downstream pointed profile of No's 11 & 12 flood arches.

to have absorbed the ancient cutwaters. On the older segmental pointed arches, the joint is clearly visible because of the different curvature in the ring stones. New, low profiled cutwaters were included on the extension, but not extended upwards to include pedestrian refuges as at Poolboy, Kilcarn and Stackallan Bridges. All the downriver cutwaters are also low profiled and not extended upwards to the parapets.

The four segmental pointed river arches of the older structure are not symmetrical; being sized and shaped differently, which mars their aesthetics somewhat. But this effect is countered by the two flood arches which seem to be in perfect harmony of shape.

The foregoing data indicates that 'the Bridge of Slane' incorporates features from different eras, and includes in its ancient structure evidence pointing to the evolving techniques used by stonemasons over several centuries. I consider; therefore, that some time and space could be well used in exploring the mysteries posed by this remarkable stone bridge; commanding an important crossing point of the River Boyne.

Peter O'Keefe and Tom Simington include details of Slane Bridge in their *Irish Stone Bridges*. Space does not permit inclusion of the full content, but the following are some points taken from the book (paraphrased and not listed in order of priority):

a. Little information is available from ancient annals indicating that Slane was an important crossing point of the Boyne. For instance, none of the adjacent townlands reflect this in their names, such as in other places like Assey (Asigh) and Athlumney, named after fords on the Boyne.

b. Grand Jury records from 1760 to 1890, with a few exceptions due to loss of Query and Presentments books, do not include entries for the bridge.

c. The bridge was widened in the past.

d. Local tradition, according to C. E. F. Trench's book of 1975, says the bridge was widened in 1812.

e. The bridge is shown on Moll's Map of 1714.

f. Two arches were supposedly broken down by the Jacobite Army prior to the Battle of the Boyne in 1690.

g. Hugh O'Neil intended to use the bridge for an invasion of The Pale in 1599; but chose to take his army to Munster, where he was defeated at the Battle of Kinsale.

h. Edward Bruce (brother of Robert the Bruce) supposedly took his army southwards across the bridge in 1317, during the ill-fated 'Bruce Invasion.'

i. Reference to the Laud Manuscript which states that all bridges upon the Boyne, except Babes were destroyed by a great flood in 1330.

j. That the river at Slane is tidal; therefore, any wooden bridges in olden times might not last longer than a decade or two because of attack from the Terredo or shipworm.

k. That the bridge contains seven segmental pointed arches, five in the river channel and two flood-arches.

l. That both the bridge in Trim (the town bridge) and Slane Bridge were newly built soon after the great flood of 1330 – and that perhaps Slane Bridge was re-built to the pattern of Trim Bridge, possibly by the same master stonemasons hired by the Flemings.

m. That perhaps the forms, or frames, used to build the pointed arches at Trim, were floated downriver and re-used to build the bridge at Slane.

n. That Trim Bridge is built upon a rock foundation and the bridge at Slane is most likely built on a foundation of glacial till or boulder clay – which accounts for the stone paving on the riverbed beneath the bridge arches at Slane.

o. That the riverbed was possibly paved during construction of the upstream extension.

p. That segmental pointed arches provided more headroom for small boats and in addition saved circa 10% masonry.

The book provides much more historical data and construction details for Slane Bridge. Regarding point j. above: the OS maps show the maximum excursion of 'ordinary' tides reaching Oldbridge Weir, close by the River Mattock. The OS Benchmark at the nearby Curly Hole is 25.2ft (above mean sea level) while that on Slane Bridge reads 67.7ft; representing a difference of over forty feet. It is difficult to envisage; therefore, how the river at Slane is deemed to be tidal, even allowing for discrepancies in the OS markings. During prehistoric times, circa 3000 B.C., I believe the elevated sea level extended to just above Newgrange.

Referring to point i. above: this snippet from the *Laud Manuscript* (Peterborough Chronicle) is quoted extensively in the context of the bridges upon the River Boyne; together with a similar record from *Grace's Annals* (Annals Hibernia), perhaps sourced from the aforesaid Manuscripts.

The reference (page 116/117 of Grace's Annals) states:

1330. Most violent storms, by which a house was blown down which killed the wife of Milo Verdon and his daughter. There was also a great flood, especially of the Boyne, by which all the bridges on that river, except Babe's, were carried away, and other mischief done at Trim and Drogheda. (sic)

A footnote in Latin, (included on page 116), when translated, indicates that three great storms occurred in the winter of 1330, on Nov. 25th - Dec. 6th and Dec. 25th – perhaps indicating that the catastrophic flood may have taken place on or shortly after Christmas Day in 1330. It is my opinion that these notes should be treated with caution and examined more critically, because many later assumptions are predicated upon their veracity, which cannot be readily proven in other ways.

Very few stone bridges spanned the Boyne in the year 1330. It is probable that the only stone bridges on the river at the time were located at Trim, Kilcarn, Babes and Slane. The reference to 'all' the bridges being carried away could have meant the stone bridges at Trim, Kilcarn and Slane; together with wooden structures elsewhere on the river. I have an abiding recollection of the great flood on the 8th Dec. 1954, the greatest flood on the Boyne within living memory. Significantly, although this flood carried away parts of several stone bridges on lesser rivers within the Boyne catchment area, the arches of some remained partly intact. In this context, it is noteworthy that the downstream or medieval part of the old Bridge of Dowdstown, that once carried the Dublin to Navan turnpike road across the River Skein (Skane), was swept away by the flood in 1954. But the upstream extension (built circa 1729) remained intact and in use for a year or more thereafter (see *On Ancient Roads*, Chapter 8, pp. 107-109).

I believe it is by no means certain that the flood of 1330 swept away the Boyne's bridges in their entirety. A cogent argument could be made supporting the proposition that Trim Bridge may have survived, because the volume of water above Trim would have been much less than at Kilcarn and further downstream. Many smaller tributaries fall into the Boyne below Trim, including: Knightsbrook, Boycetown, Versheen, Clady, Bonfield, Abainne Na Sceali, Skein and Gabhra, Follistown or Gilltown, Swan, the Butter Stream, Leighsbrook and the River Blackwater at Navan. In 1330, some of these, together with many other lesser streams, would have swollen the river at Kilcarn and below Navan as they did in 1954.

Other factors worthy of consideration are the various drainage schemes on the Upper Boyne executed from the 1840s and prior to 1954. Our downriver journey through these upper reaches shows that vast changes took place during the interim period. The various main tributaries including the Yellow/Mongagh Rivers, Clonard, Deel, Kildare Blackwater, Stonyford and Tremblestown rivers were straightened and widened – thus allowing their waters escape to the Boyne more rapidly instead of being retained in the bog-lands as previously. Moreover, the various upriver bridges had their free waterway (or hydraulic capacity) increased greatly consequential to these drainage works. But Trim Bridge remained unaltered, with no increase in its hydraulic capacity until the Arterial Drainage Scheme of the 1970s. Hence, when the great flood hit the structure on Dec. 8th 1954, it was probably the greatest test of its integrity throughout the centuries, due to the increased velocity and volume of water released sooner from the uplands... but it withstood the test, as I believe it may have done in 1330 because it was founded upon rock.

Presuming that stone bridges did exist at Trim, Kilcarn and Slane, it is possible that, as stated above, Trim Bridge survived in its entirety and in addition, parts of the structures at Kilcarn and Slane survived the flood of 1330; and may indeed form part of these bridges spanning the river nowadays. I will introduce the following hypothesis; therefore, in support of this proposition, which perhaps explains the multi-faceted aspects of Slane Bridge.

My alternative view is: the main structure of Trim Bridge did, in fact, survive the great flood of 1330 and although part of Kilcarn Bridge was swept away, much of it survived also. Below Navan, Babes Bridge survived as described in the old manuscripts. I suggest that although part of Slane Bridge carried away in 1330, some of it remained in situ; perhaps including the two segmental flood-arches on the south-western riverbank, most (if not all) of the buttressed, walled embankment section and the four segmental pointed river arches. The remainder of the bridge, from the river's centre to the north-eastern bank collapsed, thereby relieving pressure on the surviving structure. The original bridge failure mechanisms cannot be determined definitively; therefore, the above postulation is as logical as any reviewed during research.

Possible evolutionary path of Slane Bridge.
Unlike more recently built bridges, no inscribed plaque stone is mounted on this ancient structure to inform us of its history and origins. However, a bronze plaque once adorned the parapet wall close by the entrance to Slane Mill. Designed by Seamus Murphy of Cork; the plaque was commissioned in 1962 by the Slane guild of Muinter na Tire in remembrance of well-known local poet, Francis Ledwidge. More recently, the original bronze plaque was transferred to the nearby Ledwidge Museum at the poet's ancestral cottage. Known by some as 'the Peasant's Poet' or 'Poet of the Blackbirds,' Ledwidge died at the Battle of Ypres in July 1917 during WWl and is buried in Passchendaele. The inscription includes a verse from his poem commemorating fellow poet, Thomas MacDonagh, executed following the rising of 1916:

> He shall not hear the bittern cry
> In the wild sky, where he is lain.
> Nor voices of the sweeter birds
> Above the wailing of the rain.

In the absence of hard evidence and conclusive proof to the contrary, it is possible to draw the following conclusions from the above hypothesis; which is, I must stress, my own view on the subject.

Presuming Trim and Slane stone bridges were built in the same period, circa 1200 AD, and to a similar pattern and possibly by the same master stonemasons, these bridges were in existence for over a century prior to the great flood of 1330. The main difference in their construction (apart from length and width) is that Trim Bridge was built upon a rocky foundation; whereas Slane Bridge was probably founded on the less stable glacial till or boulder clay – yet another point supporting the proposition that Trim survived the flood and Slane partly collapsed.

It is most unlikely that during those frugal times, any remaining parts of the damaged bridge at Slane were demolished to make way for a new structure. A brief study of Grace's Annals shows that in the years preceding the great flood of 1330, warfare was rife in the countryside, with feuds amongst the native clans and, indeed, outright mayhem between Gaelic Chieftains and Norman invaders – note previous reference to the Bruce Invasion (circa 1315-1318). It is fairly certain; therefore, that demolition of existing structures was not foremost in the minds of those craftsmen employed to restore the crossing at Slane. Moreover, as pointed out by Peter O'Keefe and Tom Simington, construction of segmental pointed arches is extremely difficult in a river environment; so it is likely they chose the simpler semi-circular design during those stressful times.

I suggest that some of, or indeed all six remaining segmental pointed arches in the eastern façade may be survivors of the original stone bridge, built circa 1200 AD. And that the four semi-circular arches, No. 2,3,4 & 5, were first erected following the 1330 flood, to replace the swept-away section.

It is interesting to note that in addition to abutting the river pillar between No. 2 and No. 3 arches, the inclined section of Slane Weir continues on beneath No. 3 arch. Downstream of the bridge, the weir structure forms part of the mill canal/millpond wall for about 10 metres, then merges with the wider rampart/island separating the millpond from the main river. The form of this structure raises the possibility that No. 2 and 3 arches were dismantled to allow construction of the weir in the 1760s, and then reconstructed atop the weir during building of the mill canal elliptical arch. An inspection beneath No. 3 arch revealed that the section of weir under the arch had been coated with a layer of concrete. As this effectively covered any visible joint, this riddle of Slane Bridge remains to be solved.

R to L No's 1 & 2 mill canal, 3, 4 & 5 rounded profile arches -
No's 6,7,8 & 9 pointed profile arches

The larger headrace/mill canal No. 1 arch was erected about 1763, during construction of Jebb's Mill and weir. It is possible (and very likely) that the previously described semi-circular arch No. 10, was part of the flood control system, built in conjunction with the mill weir and access canal. A suggestion supported by the following facts:

- Flood-gates were installed at the upper end of the mill weir, adjacent to the south-western riverbank.
- A clearly defined channel still exists between the fish-shaped island and the same riverbank.
- An upriver cutwater was not included on the retaining wall between the most south-westerly pointed river No. 9 arch and this opening, listed as No.10 arch above.
- A massive cutwater still spans the downstream side of this retaining wall – built, I suggest, to avoid undercutting/scouring same when the floodgates were opened.

In my opinion, the original mill canal (weir bypass) control system included a separate channel running from the floodgates to No. 10 arch. The channel was probably formed by a rampart or dyke connecting between the floodgates river pillar and the bridge; thus explaining the lack of a cutwater on the retaining wall between No. 9 & 10 arches. This rampart possibly washed away over the intervening years, with the long, narrow island being the sole evidence of its former existence.

Manipulation of the floodgates and mill sluices enabled unpowered barges to progress more easily along the mill canal – especially on exiting the mill against the millrace current setting towards the millwheel (with the floodgates closed and mill sluices open). The deep rope furrows in the upstream flanking parapet coping (on the village side of the mill canal arch), illustrates the above points. These grooves were worn into the stonework by ropes restraining the barges from being swept into the smaller millrace arch, and helped guide them beneath the larger elliptical opening.

Cross referencing the 1837 OS map with that of 1911, indicates the salmon leap weir did not exist in earlier times, and that the said island was much longer, extending almost to the floodgates.

Clockwise from top: James Doherty at No. 3 arch; rope furrows on village-end parapet wall; The Slane Weir from No. 3 arch

Traditionally, part of the bridge at Slane was demolished prior to the Battle of the Boyne in 1690. Two or three arches were 'thrown down' by the Jacobite Army to defend King James' left flank against an upriver sortie by Williamite forces. A futile tactic; however, because the Williamites crossed the river further downstream at Rosnaree Ford, the decisive manoeuvre in the battle. Mentions are made of the bridge 'being broken,' in *The Battle of the Boyne*, written by Demetrius Charles Boulger and another book *The Boyne Water*, by Peter Berresford Ellis.

Downstream facade from boat

From a military perspective, it is likely the destroyed arches were some of the four semi-circular (No. 2, 3, 4 & 5) spans on the bridge's north-eastern sector. Removal of these would prevent the enemy gaining control of the bridge, thereby leaving the crossing more easily defended. The supposedly destroyed section was probably re-built soon after cessation of hostilities and forms part of the present day bridge.

The foregoing hypothesis purports to explain some aspects of the multi-faceted Slane Bridge, which, in my opinion, were not apparent from previous descriptions of this historically unique bridge.

The bridge spanning the navigation canal was built as a separate entity during development of the Lower Boyne Navigation. Construction of the Lower Navigation commenced at Oldbridge tidal lock c. 1748, and it was completed to Slane about 1763. Construction of the south-eastern canal arch coincided with that of the larger headrace/mill canal (No. 01) arch on the north-eastern end.

An accurate date for widening of Slane Bridge has not been definitively established; therefore, it is still a moot subject. In my view, the upstream bridge extension was most likely built during one of the following periods:

(a) c. 1750 to 1785 – During this period, massive changes and developments occurred in and around Slane Village, including:

Downstream facade from boat

- Reconstruction of Slane Castle.
- Probable removal of the Dublin to Derry road from the Castle Demesne, which was rerouted up the Mill Hill through the village.
- Construction of the Lower Boyne Navigation and Slane Mill.
- Construction of the Gothic Gate across the old road line.
- Development of the 'Octagonal Village' on the site of Market Square.

(b) *c.* 1809 to 1815 – As part of conversion of 'the Great North Road' (Dublin to Derry) to a post road; work largely executed during this period.

The following data supports proposition (**a**): both the navigation elliptical arch and the similar arch bridging the mill access canal seem to be of integral construction i.e. there appear to be no joints indicating that these were widened similar to the other arches. David Jebb, together with his coteri of business supporters, were all very influential and powerful men, and most were members of the Grand Jury. The cost of the extension would have been miniscule (c. £350 to £500) in comparison to the amount expended on the other projects e.g. £20,000 to £30,000 for the mill and c. £70,000 for the Lower Navigation. The widened bridge would have suited the mill operations – giving direct access to the canal basin for smaller cargoes; thus curtailing expenses by avoiding two extra river crossings.

The following data supports proposition (b): the new Dublin to Slane 'post road' line via Ashbourne, known in the vernacular as 'the King's Road' or 'the straight road', was surveyed by William Larkin (of Larkin's Map fame) – the survey was completed circa 1810 and the road cut and opened by 1815; it is reasonable to suggest; therefore, that the bridge was widened in the interim period (1810 to 1815). During research, I noted that the Grand Jury (County at Large) Presentment Books covering the period c.1810 to 1816 were unobtainable and perhaps had not survived. Should this prove to be the case, the records for widening the Bridge of Slane may be lost if, in fact, this work was completed during that period.

If the bridge was widened at the later date, each of the two canal arches (the abutment arches for the main bridge), could have been reconstructed and integrated at this stage. This effectively bonded the two structures, thus providing much stronger abutments to counter lateral thrust. N.B., for more information on 'the King's Road, refer to *On Ancient Roads,* Chap. 17.

While the Bridge of Slane enhances the landscape of the Boyne Valley, it is also the scene of many tragedies over the years. A row of twenty-three white crosses line the eastern wall of the steep hill, which forms the bridge approach to and from Slane Village. Stark reminders of how beauty can cast its mantle over tragic events lurking in our midst. These crosses commemorate the number of people killed in road traffic accidents here; very often caused by vehicle brake failure on the steep descent. Despite strenuous lobbying by locals and others, all efforts to construct a bypass around the village have failed to date.

I will conclude on a lighter note by relating the tale of 'Bushmills in the Boyne.' The story begins in May 1969, with a truck laden with Bushmills and Cream of the Barley Whiskey en route from Antrim to Dublin. The truck's brakes failed on the steep descent, causing it to collide with the bridge parapet wall and topple over into the Boyne. Resulting in thousands of whiskey bottles ending up in the river, many smashed to smithereens in the process.

I recall the event well, because some local members of a Dublin based sub-aqua club became involved in diving operations to salvage the whiskey from the Boyne. I understand the divers recovered over four hundred bottles intact; some from the immediate vicinity of the wreck, and many others from further downriver at a location named 'the salmon hole.' The divers assisted also in removing the crashed truck from the river. Legends abound about the event, it is said that people came from far and near to get a piece of the action and that one could not purchase a drink of whiskey within a several mile radius of Slane for years thereafter; as local tradition holds that over two thousand bottles of 'the hard stuff' were recovered eventually.

The happening gave rise to a local song *Whiskey in the Boyne*, or *Bushmills in the Boyne*, the full original wording of which I have not as yet traced. However, a newer version goes thus:

> Oh yes 'tis true, the mountain dew, a lorry load in all
> Like Jack and Jill came down the hill and ran into the wall
> It then nosedived and soon arrived down where the water flowed
> And the festival of Slane began down on the Dublin road

> The Garda and the Sergeant said the cratur we must mind
> For if you lift this whiskey, in the courthouse you'll be fined
> But the natives came in hundreds and like vultures
> stood their ground
> Saying, come on give us whiskey if you don't want to be drowned

Several more verses followed, which cannot be included, but I hope the above few bars give a flavour of this unusual and exciting happening upon the Boyne's banks in the comparatively recent past.

Bridge of Slane
Aerial view from downstream, left to right:

Boyne Navigation Canal Bridge, with access ramp to Lower Boyne Navigation towpath leading towards Rosnaree – in background are canal wharf/basin and partly filled-in canal leading from Slane Mill (or Guard) Lock.

No. 11 & 12 pointed profile flood arches – Long buttressed embankment.

No. 10 rounded profile flood control arch; in background are remnants of flood channel leading from flood control gates at the head of Slane Mill Weir (Note fish-shaped islet separating this from main river channel)

C. 20ft buttress/embankment with cutwater profile.

Four segmental pointed profile arches, No. 09, 08, 07 & 06 – Three rounded profile arches No. 05, 04, & 03; in background are Slane Mill Weir & floodgates.

Two mill canal arches, smaller is of rounded profile and larger is of multi-segmental elliptical profile; the foreground is comprised of the millrace/canal, the 'Rack' and footbridge , the dividing rampart, the overgrown mill headrace/millpond, with the background formed by the millrace/canal above the weir.

To the right of the bridge is the lodge at the entrance to Slane Mill, the 'Mill Hill ' leading to Slane Village - N.B., the Gothic Gate, built across the earlier line of 'the Great North Road,' stands to the left of the newer road leading up Mill Hill.

Photograph courtesy of Aubrey Martin

Bridge of Slane.
Aerial view from upstream, left to right;
Slane Mill headrace/canal, with salmon leap indicated by white water to bottom right, Fish-shaped islet and remnants of flood control channel.
The background is comprised of Slane Mill and the Boyne Valley downriver towards Rosnaree and 'the big bend.'
In the right backgroud is the N. 2 (former Great North Road from Dublin to Derry), winding downhill through Fennor to the Bridge of Slane.
Courtesy of Aubrey Martin

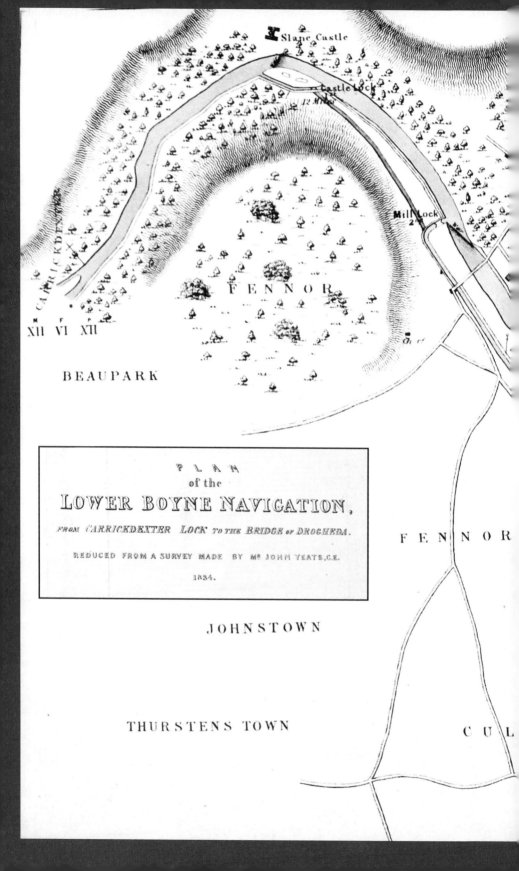

Slane Castle

Castle Lock

12 Miles

Mill Lock
2ML.

CARRICKDEXTER

FENNOR

XII VI XII

BEAUPARK

PLAN
of the
LOWER BOYNE NAVIGATION,
FROM CARRICKDEXTER LOCK TO THE BRIDGE OF DROGHEDA.

REDUCED FROM A SURVEY MADE BY Mr JOHN YEATS, C.E.

1834.

FENNOR

JOHNSTOWN

THURSTENS TOWN

CUL

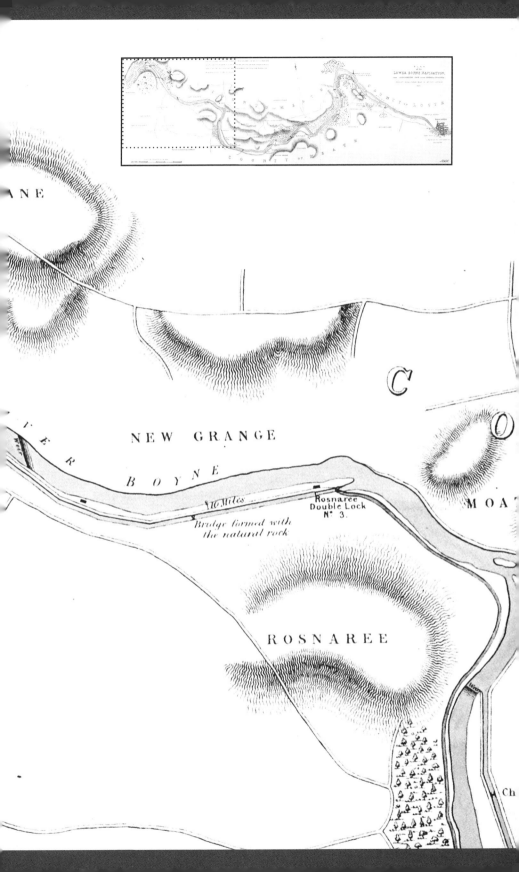

17

The Lower Reaches
Slane to the Big Bend

Arthur Young on Jebb's Mill – Boyneville Hotel – Fennor Castle & church
– The Cherry Island Fish-weir – A walk along the towpath – Scraggy Arch
– Rosnaree Lock & Lock-house – The Big Bend – Adventures in a Ford-ten
Van – Broe Weir – Broe Canal & Bridge – Rosnaree Ford & ancient roads
– Browny's Fish-weir & other Monastic Fisheries – The Seven Ways – Sir
Neal O'Neal & Battle of the Ford – Johnston's Mill & Sean Óg the Donkey.

Our Boyne Journey continued from Slane Bridge on Dec. 28th 2011; a
cloudy, bright day with a fresh wintry breeze blowing upriver from the east.
The group assembled beside the canal at 9 a.m., the two River Rescue boats
were launched from upriver of the bridge and we set off at 10 a.m. We noted
ongoing repairs to the collapsed retaining wall near the south-western end,
then passed beneath the ancient structure, heading eastwards towards the big
bend.

   The most notable feature on the north-eastern riverbank is Slane Mill.
Built as a corn mill in the period 1763 to 1766 by David Jebb, supported
financially by Blaney Townley Balfour, of Townley Hall and William Burton;
all three supposedly investing the sum of £1,500 each to the initial enterprise.
The 14 acre property, reputedly located on the site of an older mill, was leased
from Viscount Conyngham, owner of Slane Castle. In later years, during a

Slane (Jebb's) Mill *c.* 1763

dispute with the Canal Commissioners, David Jebb claimed that the mill cost £30,000 to develop fully.

The mill operated for about 200 years thereafter under several different owners, performing diverse functions, including: corn drying, treating and grinding, flax scutching; linen, jute and rayon weaving. A comprehensive description of the facility is given by Arthur Young on his visit there in June 1776 and recorded in his work *A Tour in Ireland*. The following are some excerpts from same:

> The mill is 138 feet long, the breadth 54, and the height to the cornice 42, being a very large and handsome edifice, such as no mill I have seen in England can be compared with. The corn upon being unloaded, is hoisted through doors in the floors to the upper story of the building, by a very simple contrivance, being worked by the water-wheel, and being discharged into spacious granaries which hold 5,000 barrels. From thence it is conveyed, during seven months in the year, to kilns for drying, the mill containing two, which will dry 80 barrels in 24 hours. From the kiln it is hoisted again to the upper story, from thence to a fanning machine for re-dressing, to get out dirt, soil, etc. And from thence, by a small sifting

machine, into the hoppers, to be ground, and is again hoisted into the bolting mills, to be dressed into flour, different sorts of pollard and bran. In all which progress, the machinery is contrived to do the business with the least labour possible: it will grind with great ease 120 barrels, of 20 stone each, every day. Beginning in 1763, for a few years, about 13,000 barrels per ann., were ground, of late years up to 17,000 barrels. It may be observed, that this mill is very different from the English ones, they not being under the necessity of kiln-drying or dressing. The expense per barrel of the drying in coals and labour is 3d., and the waste is one-twentieth in the weight; but the contrivance reduces the cost of dressing to a trifle. The whole charge of manufacturing the wheat into flour in mere labour is 9d. a barrel, and the 3d. drying makes 1s. The barrel weighs 20 stone, 14 pounds to the stone of which

Flour..14st. 8lb.
Bran..4st.

Pollard }
Dirt, waste, grinding and dressing..............1st. 6lb.
on average of the year...............................20st.

The corn is brought to the mill from all the country round to the distance of 10 miles. The farmers send it in, and leave the price to be fixed. Raising the mill and offices complete cost £20,000, and has established, in a fine corn country, a constant market; and has preserved the tillage of the neighbourhood, which would have declined from the premium on distant carriage.

The flour is sent to Dublin, and the manufacturing country to the north about Newry, &c. It employs constantly from 10 to 12 hands, the common ones, 6s. 6d., a week. *(sic)*

During its heyday, Slane Mill was the largest corn and flour mill in the entire country. In later years, towards the end of WWI, the mills were bought by a Northern Irish firm, who renovated the buildings and installed a water

Top: Slane Mill from river aspect and, below, Slane Mill tailraces

turbine, together with flax scutching equipment. The Slane Manufacturing Company was set up in the 1930s as a subsidiary of Thos. Taylor & Bro. Ltd. to manufacture cotton cloth for flour bags. It was bought out in 1946 by J. & L. F. Goodbody Ltd., jute manufacturers, for weaving of cotton and rayon.

The new weaving factory was built in 1955, with 200 automatic looms installed – a spinning mill, added in 1959, increasing the workforce to over 400. Goobody's sold out in 1965 to Messers. Ashton Bros., who in turn were taken over by Courtaulds in 1967. At the time, the Slane Manufacturing Company was the only surviving factory in Ireland manufacturing from raw cotton to the finished product.

To the north-east of the mill stands the miller's house, at one time occupied by David Jebb, it later became the Boyneville Hotel. This hostelry became a favourite watering place for tourists in general, and passengers from steamers and other craft plying the Boyne Navigation during its heyday.[1]

Standing high above the floodplain on the south-eastern bank, the remains of Fennor Castle include parts of an ancient tower house combined with those of a more modern dwelling. Wilde considered these ruins unworthy of major attention in 1849. Little is known of its former occupants, although some local legends associate the castle with the early Fleming dynasty. Francis Ledwidge wrote the following verse about an unknown singer from Fennor:

> Sweetest voice of vale and hill.
> Kneaded with thine own today – my soul with rapture fill!
> Etheral maid of Fennor Plain
> Yearn I to hear, to hear thee sing again.

Immediately below the castle are the ruins of Fennor Church. Inside the gate of the attendant graveyard is a stone bearing the date 1548; perhaps the date for construction of the old church, of which John O'Donovan's 1836 OS Field Notes say:

> *The old church and ruined Castle of Fennor are in this parish, which is a rectory in the diocese of Meath. The rectory is entirely impropriate in Mr. Balfour of Townley Hall, to whom are payable the tithes amounting to £104.*

Anthony (Dean) Cogan says of Fennor Church in 1862: Abbey – Finnabhair – Abna "Bright field of the River." And that its patron was Saint Neachtain, a disciple of Saint Patrick.

Downstream of the bridge, the riverscape is similar to that upstream, with low, rolling hillsides enclosing the valley from riverbank to horizon. Northwards, the ground rises steeply towards the distant ridge, along which the Navan to Drogheda road (N51) passes onwards through Monknewtown; the scrub-covered hillside dotted here and there with remains of old limekilns. To the south of the main road in the townland of Cashel (near the later site of Francis Ledwidge's ancestral cottage), the 1837 OS map depicts a large quarry and attendant limekiln, which area it names Limekiln Hill. This place name seems to have fallen into disuse; however, as it does not appear on the 1911 map.

These maps show two larger country houses on the hillside below the quarry, Janeville Cottage to the west, with Crewbane House further east and closer to the riverbank. Southwards is a much wider floodplain; carrying the navigation towards Rosnaree, the surrounding hillsides rising abruptly towards the heights of Fennor further to the south-east.

The riverbank is recessed below the mill and lined by a stone wall, pierced by three semi-circular arches taking the outflow from the various tailraces back to the river. Directly opposite the mill, on the southern riverbank, Yeats' 1834 plan indicates the location of navigation milestone No.11, not shown on the 1911 map. Several small islets are located alongside the northern riverbank near the tailraces, and one or two further downstream.

Left: The Cherry Island fish weir from upstream
Right: The Cherry Island weir downstream extension

Below these we came to an old eel/fish-weir, known locally as 'the Cherry Islands.'[2] The old maps depict this as a skewed weir crossing the river; with tiny islets dotted at intervals across the entire breadth of the Boyne. Though covered by scrub timber nowadays, these were perhaps once adorned by cherry trees, thereby explaining the origins of the name. It is possible also, that in former days, footbridges may have linked the islands, making this one of the crossing points known as 'foot stick fords.' This may be the place, described by Williamite Chaplin, George Story, where King William's infantry crossed the river to outflank the Jacobite army during the Battle of the Boyne in 1690.

Threading our way through the maze of islands, we headed downriver towards Rosnaree. Suddenly, when hearing a commotion astern, I looked back to see the cause. Two of the River Rescue lads from the second boat were paddling around in the water, having been swept overboard by low hanging branches. Following some mighty craic, they re-boarded the boat and headed after us in hot pursuit, such is the life of the rescue boys.

Below Cherry Island, another old fish-weir is depicted clearly on the 1911 OS map, running longitudinally in midstream, but in times past it may have formed part of a downriver extension to the Cherry Island Weir. This weir combination may be the fish-weir located in Fennor, as so recorded in the 1650s Civil Survey. Most of the above weir extension lies south of the Slane Barony boundary within Fennor, as shown on the 1837 OS map.

In May 2013, a small group including Pascal Marry, my brother Tom and his wife Pauline, Marie and I travelled along the towpath from Slane Bridge to Rosnaree Lock; located about one and a half miles further downstream. From its upper end at Slane Bridge, the narrow towpath runs south-eastwards upon a raised rampart traversing the centre of the broad floodplain, with the weed and sedge clogged canal alongside to the south-west. Several old stone gate piers adorn the towpath entrance near the bridge, another memento left by skilled craftsmen of olden times; unfortunately, we have not shown the same zest in preserving these for posterity.

The elevated pathway provided a greatly improved view of the green hillside, sweeping steeply upwards towards the old castle and church of Fennor. Viewed from the riverside aspect on the lower edge of this escarpment, one can better

Left to right: Terracettes at Fennor; Rock (Scraggy) Arch - with Author beneath

observe an unusually clear example of what we knew in childhood as 'cattle' or 'sheep ridges' i.e. parallel rows of tracks etched along the steep slope; grassy tiers formed over many years by livestock grazing the lush foliage. These ground anomalies are described in geological terms as Terracettes, created by a combination of grazing animals and gravity causing the moist soil to creep downhill.

Across the valley to the north-east, Slane Village and mill enhance the splendid vista of ancient bridge overlooking island-dotted river and sedgy bottomlands.

Downstream from the ridged hillside, the towpath swings eastwards to converge with the river about midway along Cherry Island Weir; where the floodplain narrows and the southern riverbank becomes less steep. Here, we had a much clearer view of the weir and island complex than that presented to us from the boat during the downriver trip.

The upper section of weir is formed mostly by weed covered banks, the long, continuous mid-section consisting of tree and scrub encrusted rocks, with the last section, near the southern bank, formed by several little islets with alder and willows clinging limpet-like to their rocky surfaces. The gaps between the latter islands, perhaps once home to the fish-traps, now provide a path for the fast-flowing Boyne water. Below the weir, the mid-river elongated fish-weir is now a long, narrow island covered by weeds and river sedge.

Here the navigation runs close by the southern riverside, constricted between the Boyne and the encroaching hillside, with the towpath running atop the dividing rampart. Further downstream, the canal is hewn through a rocky outcrop covered by scrub timber, described variously as Rock Arch, The Tunnel or The Scraggy Arch. Although this rocky outcrop is known to some as Fennor Rock, it is located just within Rosnaree Townland.

Two islands occupy much of the river opposite the arch, leaving a narrow channel through which our boats passed on the southern side during the earlier downriver passage. According to the 1911 OS map, the No.10 milestone was/is located beside the towpath just below Rock Arch; indicating this place is ten miles distant from the starting point of the Lower Boyne Navigation at 'the Bridge of Drogheda.' We could find no trace of the marker; perhaps it is hidden in the lush vegetation growing alongside the towpath or indeed departed to some unknown destination.

From upstream of Rock Arch, the canal makes its onward passage via a rock cutting made through the edge of the escarpment. The cutting continues most of the way to Rosnaree Lock; therefore, the southern canal bank is formed hereabouts by a layered, shale-like rock face, in places rising to a considerable height above the waterway. This craggy bank, covered nowadays by dense brush, presents a more rugged aspect of the landscape than the section closer to Slane. The underlying rock face can be observed; however, on some of the 1894 Shackleton photographs.

The Scraggy Arch is quarried through a small rock formation, outcropping further from the surrounding escarpment and across the line of the canal. My brother Tom, who once worked at tunnelling in Canada, concluded that the arch was not blasted, but cut using hand tools only; pointing out traces of the many hand-drilled holes in the very uneven and rugged arch profile. A ledge, lined with cut stone slabs, carries the old horse path beneath the arch, making it unnecessary to uncouple the towing horse from the lighter during the transit from Slane to Rosnaree Lock. Thought the arch/outcrop rises steeply above the towpath, some adventurous fishermen use it to cross the canal, as evidenced by its polished surface and a length of rope dangling down from the dense undergrowth crowning its rugged flank.

Rosnaree Lock is located on the southern riverbank, where the Boyne sweeps around in a great curve taking the river south-eastwards towards 'the Big Bend,' which incorporates the prehistoric royal cemetery of *Brugh na Boinne*. Here the riverscape performs yet another of its myriad changes, the wide floodplain narrowing, with the banks rising more abruptly towards the horizon. To the north is a steep, scrub-covered ridge, while further downstream on the southern horizon, the woods of Rosnaree (the King's Wood or Headland) rise from the water's edge. Although not so dramatic as Beauparc, the scenery is beautiful, enhanced by weirs and many islets.

Back on the boat and continuing our mid-winter trip from Cherry Island, we rounded the upstream end of the sweep and saw the high arch of the lock bridge peeping through undergrowth on the southern riverbank. Which shrubbery, though mostly devoid of greenery in winter, grows profusely hereabouts and smothers the old canal works.

Mooring the boats in the old fairway where the canal once locked-out to the river, we scrambled ashore through the tangling river sedge to survey the

From top: Negotiating the lock c.1890s. Negotiating the lock – Upper lock chamber full - note pristine Lock-house – Courtesy Meath County Library

scene. Rosnaree Lock is the only double lock on the entire Boyne Navigation i.e. it consists of two chambers, the lowermost compartment with a lift of approximately 6.4ft, the upper providing a lift of about 8ft. The combined lift of circa 14.4ft raised the waterway to the pound level taking barges and lighters into the navigable river above Slane Mill Weir. The upper gate OS Benchmark is at 56.6ft, with the Benchmark at elevation 48.6ft on the lower

Rosnaree Lock Shackleton collection c. 1896 - Courtesy Chris Corlett and Jonathan Shackleton

gate. The open (unflooded) river or pound level of circa 42.2ft, between Rosnaree lower lock chamber (empty) and Broe Upper Lock or floodgate, was controlled by a combination of Broe Lower Lock and Broe Navigation Weir further downstream.

Left: Lock-house porch 2013; Pa Reilly with Hopper at Rosnaree Lock Bridge

Nowadays the lock gates are missing, but the magnificent stonework is intact, a monument to the work of skilled craftsmen who built the chambers in the 1750s. The upper chamber is closed off by the usual concrete wall mimicking the pattern of the gates; but leaking sufficient water to provide a scenic waterfall cascading down the several crafted rock tiers of the lock cill. Larkin's Map of 1812 depicts a bridge at this location; therefore, the present horse-bridge, supposedly built by the Board of Works in 1834, may have replaced an earlier bridge.

The Lockkeepers' house stands on the riverbank between towpath and Boyne, adjacent to the upper lock chamber. The structure, the outer walls of which are built of cut-stone (including ornamental cornices), consists of two rooms, with a scullery to the rear and a porch opening onto the towpath to the front. This is the only single storey Lock-house we encountered on the lower navigation; the remaining three between here and Drogheda are two storeyed and of much larger construction.

Griffith's shows that Hugh Morgan occupied the lock-house, offices and canal banks, owned by the Commissioners of Boyne Navigation; the property attracted a rateable valuation of £2-5s. Other sources (Ellison) show that David Crampton occupied the premises in 1788 and Mary Morgan resided there in 1900.[3]

One can only imagine what a wonderful setting this location provided during the heyday of the waterway. Nowadays the tiny abode is minus its roof, with elder trees growing within the brick and stone structure; which appears to be held together by ivy and coming apart gradually. The cut and finely dressed stone porch lintel arch, such a striking feature on the 1894 Shackleton photograph, is falling down; due to the handiwork of some thief or vandal as evidenced by the crowbar scratch marks. Unless taken in charge, it will soon join the other overgrown detritus of the navigation works at Rosnaree Lock.

Cyril Ellison's book notes the first cargo arriving at Rosnaree Lock in August 1763, consisting of a consignment of coal from the Tyrone collieries borne on a 40 ton vessel. Though no record exists of commercial coal production, exploration mining took place during the late 18th century in the nearby 'Slane coal seams,' located in a townland to the north of Slane named Coal Pits.

A small bight or bay indents the riverbank directly across the Boyne from Rosnaree Lock.[4] Below this, the towpath transfers to the northern shore and the navigation uses the main river once more; the towpath following the same course downriver to Broe. The river level on this section was raised and controlled by the weir further downstream at Broe (Breo/Brow), which weir will be discussed presently. The name Broe would appear to be a derivation of *Brugh*. From mid-river the mound of Knowth can be seen commanding the two islets, nestled in the crook of the abrupt bend where the Boyne turns 90 degrees and runs due south for several hundred metres; the start of 'the Big Bend,' home to *Brugh na Boinne* or *Cemetery of the Kings*.

The Big Bend is a title often used to describe an area of the Boyne Valley wherein lies the cluster of Stone Age mounds, once used as a royal cemetery for the high kings. I believe its status as such was first recognised in William Wilde's *The Beauties of the Boyne and Blackwater*. Because so many renowned historians, archaeologists and anthropologists have written vast tomes about the ancient location, I am content with a brief description of its topographical location relative to the Boyne.

The tumuli of Knowth, Newgrange and Dowth stand upon a salient, around which the Boyne flows on its journey to the sea beyond Drogheda. The substrata is formed from carboniferous shales, overlaid by glacial till, hard substances that caused the river to seek an easier onward path. Turning 90 degrees to flow southwards, it then sweeps in a curve through Rosnaree and towards the east; finally flowing north-eastwards to Oldbridge, where it turns again to head south-eastwards.

The area enclosed within this great loop, from Knowth on its western extremity, past Newgrange to Dowth near the River Mattock, includes most of the historical site of *Brugh na Boinne*. Much of the enclosed area was once the property of nearby Mellifont Abbey; a Cistercian institution which flourished from pre-Norman times (1142) to the dissolution of the monasteries in the mid-16th century. This explains the inclusion of Grange (or monastic farm) in many of the local townland names i.e. Newgramge, Roughgrange, Littlegrange and Sheepgrange.

I became aware of this ancient site after Dad acquired our first motor transport back in 1956, when I was a child aged eleven years.[5] Dad was very interested in the historical sites around Meath and surrounding counties, so following our acquisition of the van and long before they became widely popular, we visited the Loughcrew Cairns, the Seven Wonders of Fore, Old Mellifont Abbey, the High Crosses at Monasterboice and the ancient sites of Newgrange, Dowth and Knowth.

Newgrange was deserted then and we had difficulty finding our way to the site. When we arrived eventually, no interpretative centre was there to greet us, just the great mound standing in the field, all overgrown by weeds and bushes. A little hut stood across the road; however, occupied by the caretaker, an older man with a droopy black hat… the interpretative centre then. The history of the place limited only by the scope of one's imagination and the old man's vivid sense of perspective.

On our first visit he took his bicycle flash lamp and some candles, then brought us across the road, through a little green wicket gate and over to the mound. Outside, beside the great stones, he regaled us with his own version of their history and then unlocked the gate. I recall looking into the great maw of darkness and shivering, it was the first cave I had ever seen and the dank smell, together with the darkened interior was very scary. The old man reached inside and clicked a switch, then, we could see up along the crooked gallery. The huge stone passageway stretched into the distant gloom, now illuminated by a few weak light bulbs suspended from ordinary brown flex; it was intensely cold inside but dry as a bone.

After negotiating the tortuous passageway and arriving at the chambers, we were entertained by more yarns, followed by his version of the big stone basin with the indented impressions in its base. Although I cannot recall most of what he said, at this remove, they seemed to be good yarns at the time.

Departing the gloomy, eerie place, we were happy to be back outside, though blinded by the bright sunlight. Not another tourist could be seen, just a few sheep and cattle grazing on the lush grass. The old man locked the gate, bade us good day and returned to his little hut. On subsequent visits when not feeling too good, he handed the flash lamp and keys to Dad, saying: "make sure youse switch off the lights on the way out, sure it's supplied from my own meter."

This little tale illustrates the difference between then and now. In the 1950s, very few people visited the site, whereas nowadays an ultra-modern interpretative centre greets thousands of visitors from many parts of the world; not Bob Hickey, the auld fellow with the slouched hat.

Visiting the high crosses at Monasterboice was likewise a memorable experience. Here an older man conducted private tours around the graveyard, the round tower and crosses. Though he wore a hat, no flash lamp was required, like at Newgrange, as everything was out in the open. The two older men were ringers for each other and I wondered at the time if they were brothers; the main difference being their attire, the man at Newgrange having a black hat and coat, while at Monasterboice the 'in colour' was brown.

The high crosses are adorned with incredibly detailed, graphic carvings and this man had yarns about them all. I can still recall vividly how he pointed to the depiction of Satan herding the lost souls off to hell on judgement day, prodding them on their way with a big trident fork. Though I cannot recollect the exact story he told, it impressed my young mind, because for the next few months thereafter, I told all my sins in confession, both real and imaginary.

Returning to our boat upon the River Boyne on a cold day in December 2011; we passed by the two islands and turned the big bend beneath Knowth Tumulus on its craggy escarpment, to head due south towards the weir at Broe. This is yet another scenic reach of the river, with the eastern (left-hand) bank, rising sharply from a narrow floodplain, covered by woodland, which is named Knowth Fox Covert on the 1911 OS map. The most prominent feature on this stretch is a ringfort, located below the No 9 navigation milestone, about midway between the bend and the weir.

The opposite floodplain is much broader, with green fields rising gradually towards Fennor and the higher esker of Mount Aikin (at Cullen House) in the distance. To the south and directly ahead, the wooded ridge of Rosnaree marks the place where the river commences its sweep towards the south-east.

Broe Weir was a navigation weir i.e. built to deepen the river for the navigation, rather than for fishing purposes or providing water-head to power a mill. The weir forms a slight curve across the river, with a kink where it joins the riverbank to the south-west. From just below this weir, to the next navigation weir downriver at Roughgrange, the Boyne's course is very difficult. It splits into many channels; with a multitude of little islets, streamlets, rapids, shallows, fish-weirs, millraces and 'foot stick fords' forming a complex network, well-nigh impossible to navigate. It is best described section by section, starting with Broe Canal on the north-eastern bank.

This lateral canal section begins immediately above Broe Weir and follows

Clockwise from top: Negotiating Broe weir; Broe upper lock gate chamber - Small building is on islet at 'The 7 ways' fish traps; Remains of Upper Broe lower gate - Looking east.

the Boyne's curvature to a point opposite Roughgrange, where it locks-out to the river at Lower Broe Lock. The canal here was/is scarcely one kilometre long, with a towpath on both sides; it bisects the south-western sector of the Big Bend, from Knowth to below Newgrange. There is no lock above the weir at Broe, but following the line of the cut, we encounter the upper lock a few hundred metres downriver, described variously as Upper Broe guard lock or flood-gate and on Yeats' plan of 1834 as a check gate.

The navigation has largely merged with the landscape, but the remains of Upper Broe Lock provide proof of its existence hereabouts. This lock was included about 1788 to prevent floods damaging the canal cutting; it is named on the 1837 OS map as a flood gate, but shown on later maps as a lock. The title of flood gate is more appropriate; however, because no stone chamber exists here, or any lift, as evidenced by the OS Benchmark on its stonework at elevation 42.2ft.

This is the approximate pound level of the section, including the canal from Broe Lower Lock and the navigable river from above Broe Weir to Rosnaree Lock. The lock chamber consisted of earthen banks, now crumbled away and enclosing only a muddy pond between two unconnected sets of gates. The wooden gates have disappeared long since; but the coping stones, lead-in breast walls and piers survived intact. The upper gate opening is blocked by a concrete wall forming a footbridge, while the lower gate's stone structure is threatened by ash trees taking root within its joints.

Apart from the lower lock, this canal would seem to be constructed in a similar fashion to the lateral canals built originally by Thomas Omer below Stackallan in the 1750s; destroyed by the elements and requiring full reconstruction in later years. Because Broe lateral canal caused so many problems, plans were drawn up for its replacement by a new cutting on the southern bank, running between Rosnaree Lock and Upper Stalleen Lock. This canal line would have dispensed with two river crossings; however, the estimated cost of £6,000 proved prohibitive, so the status quo remained (to the detriment of all concerned) until the demise of the entire waterway.

On a point of historical interest, these plans were developed by the Commissioners of Public Works following a survey completed when they took charge of the Lower Boyne Navigation in 1834. The Commissioners took over because of belated enforcement of a clause in the 1790 Act of

From top:

Broe Br. Upstream elevation.

Broe Br. downstream elevation 2013

Unusual dowelling on Broe Br. Parapet coping stones

Parliament. This clause stipulated that the Lower Boyne revert to public ownership should the navigation not reach Trim within five years of its completion to Navan; which momentous event occurred in 1800.

Following the cut downstream, we come to a bridge spanning the canal just upstream of Broe House. This bridge carried the ancient right of way from the main road at Monk Newtown, across the waterway to the 'paved' ford on the Boyne at Rosnaree. Legends say that this ancient road was once the route of *An Slight Mhidhluchra* or the road to Ulster, one of the five ancient roads of Tara. My own research has established that this place can indeed be linked; via the older road network, to the ancient road running north-eastwards from the hilltop at Tara (see *On Ancient Roads* Chap. 12).

The canal bridge at Broe was built during the early construction phase of the navigation circa 1750. My wife Marie and I visited the location on March 14th 2012 and with kind permission of the property owners, viewed and photographed the ancient structure. The bridge and canal section are located a few metres south of Broe House, mostly hidden in a grove of sycamore, beech and chestnut trees. The width of the old roadway between the northern parapet walls is approximately 12ft, but reduces to circa 9ft on the bridge section spanning the canal. The parapets splay outwards at the southern end, forming a wider area to allow vehicular traffic make the sharp turn onto and off the bridge.

Immediately south of the crossing, the now defunct roadway turns 90 degrees to the east on a stone-faced embankment running alongside the canal, and then turns southwards towards the ancient ford on the Boyne. The bridge has two stone arches, the wider opening for the canal and a smaller arch (circa 5.5ft high by 5ft wide) for the towpath. Both arches are of segmental profile and spring from vertical side walls; while they are in good condition, the parapet walls are crumbling in places and require attention to prevent their collapse.

The coping stones are smoothly dressed and in good condition also. Although not secured by iron dowelling like many old road bridges, they are tied together with unique diamond-shaped stone tenons or dowels. The OS Benchmark is shown at elevation 52ft (bridge battlement) on the map accompanying Griffith's Valuation.

The canal cutting is still clearly defined at the bridge, but partly filled by fallen trees and other detritus. We were unable to examine Broe Lower Lock on this occasion because of failing daylight.

Following the navigation, as depicted on the 1911 OS map, below Broe House we pass by a sluiceway (canal to river), then the canal bends slightly northwards at the No 8 milestone, beyond which we come to Lower Broe Lock. The lock seems to be named 40.th Lock on the 1837 OS map; however, this anomaly is caused by a map reference point placed such that it appears to be part of the lock name.

Here, the canal locked-out into the navigable Boyne section between Broe and Stalleen Upper Lock. Lower Broe (upper gate) benchmark was at elevation 40.5ft, indicating a lift of circa eight feet from the river (unflooded) operating, or pound level of approximately 32ft, controlled by Stalleen Lower Lock and the Navigation Weir just downstream of Stalleen Upper Lock. In 1854, the lock house at Broe Lower, owned by the Boyne Navigation Co., was exempt from rates and occupied by Patrick Fowler. Other sources indicate the premises occupied by Andrew Hall in 1788, William Martin in 1793 and Pat Fowler in 1912.[6]

Tom French and I visited the lock and Lock-house at Lower Broe in Sept. 2012, and inspected the site with the kind permission of the owners. The riverside location is accessed via a private laneway leading off the ancient roadway between Newgrange tumulus and Broe House. This narrow country road follows the approximate route of *An Slighe Mhidhluchra*, one of the ancient five roads supposedly leading from Tara to Ulster. As stated; this route crossed the ford at Rosnaree, from where its erratic course wound past Newgrange Tumulus to Monknewtown (Rossin). In more modern times, the road branched beyond Newgrange, and then ran through Dowth and Proudfootstown to join the Slane/Drogheda road close by the Curly Hole.

The 1911 OS map shows that this lock and Lock-house were accessible only via the towpath from Broe Bridge, perhaps an indication of the private laneway being added at some later date. The house is two storeyed and occupied at time of writing; it is built of dressed stonework and similar in construction to others situated at Stalleen and Oldbridge Locks. Extensions to front and rear appear to be added since the house was constructed originally in c.1750/60s, with the older main building recently extended northwards, but blending well with the original stonework.

The navigation No 8 milestone is shifted from its map position, to a small patch of lawn east of the Lock-house. The lock chamber is partially dried up, with the ashar-type stonework in good condition generally, but several medium-sized ash trees, rooted in the joints, will destroy the work of the stonemasons eventually. The gates have disappeared, but traces of their metal hinges (stirrups) remain as a reminder of their former presence.

The overgrown chamber is another reminder of how we set our sights so firmly on progress; yet cast aside and fail to cherish much of our more recent heritage, such as the old navigation, a potentially invaluable amenity in our fast maddening world.

The Boyne's course takes the river through a maze of islets below Broe Navigation Weir. From just downstream of the weir, to Rosnaree Mill, I counted twenty such on the 1911 OS map, varying in size from 6.87 acres to some too small for measurement. These natural features are complicated further by man-made obstructions such as weirs, millraces and fords, the whole forming a complex near impossible to negotiate.

Similar to Roughgrange further downriver, two separate and distinct fish-weirs existed close by Rosnaree in times past. The first we encounter, Brugh or Broe fish-weir, is named *Browny's Were* in older records. This starts immediately below the navigation weir, at the south-eastern bank, and runs downstream for several hundred feet, linking some of the islets. It terminates near the opposite riverbank beside Upper Broe Lock (flood gate); where the main channel veers sharply southwards, forming a chicane-like twist. The current flows through here at great speed like a tidal rip; this is the probable location of the former fish traps and perhaps source for the legend of the seven traps.

The larger island is formed by a narrow channel running from here, parallel to the canal and downriver to where it re-enters the mainstream near Broe Canal Bridge. The channel, which can be discerned on Bernard Scale's map of 1776, is so regular it may well have been man-made. Perhaps once used as part of the fisheries or maybe a millrace for the long lost Broe Mill or Newgrange Tuck Mill; as ancient

Above:
Lower Broe Lock-house with Nav. No. 8 milestone to fore

Below:
Shackleton photo of Lower Broe Lock lower gate

records list these Mellifont operated mills within the area. Access to the large island, and several other islets, was provided by 'foot stick fords.'

The other weir, Rosnaree fish-weir, starts from the north-eastern riverbank and runs askew for several hundred feet, to link with a narrow islet close by the south-eastern bank; upstream of the mill and opposite Broe Canal Bridge. This islet was the starting point for the headrace powering Rosnaree Mill on the south-eastern riverbank.

The millrace was formed by two long, narrow islets connected by a spill weir, perhaps the former site of the fish traps. This is probably the fish-weir known in times past as Monkneton/Monketon Were (old spellings), and named Rosnaree Fishery in more modern times. The mill tailrace fell into the main river just downstream from the mill.

The above fish-weirs (salmon) at Brugh/Broe and Rosnaree are possible survivors of those built by the monks of Mellifont during the 12th century; recorded by their older titles of Browny's Were and Monkneton (Monketon) Were in ancient records. Rosnaree Weir and fishery were worked under lease from the monastery, which took its fee or toll in a percentage of the fish caught by the lessee. The record shows that in 1541, following the dissolution

Remnants of Rosnaree fish weir

in 1539, Mellifont fisheries were leased to Lawrence Townley for a period of twenty-one years.

The former route using the ancient ford of Rosnaree is depicted on the 1911 map, crossing the Boyne and running between two islets at the mid-point of the mill tailrace, then, heading back upriver alongside its southern edge, to re-join the road east of the old mill. Rosnaree Ford, a paved crossing, was supposedly in regular use until the early years of the 20th century. The legend of the ford and burial of King Cormac Mac Airt at Rosnaree is reflected in the following verses:

> There came a breath of finer air
> That touched the Boyne with ruffling wings,
> It stirred him in his sedgy lair
> And in his mossy moorland springs.
>
> At morning on the grassy marge
> Of Rosnaree the corpse was found,
> And shepherds at their early charge
> Entombed it in the peaceful ground.
> From "The Burial of King Cormac" by Samuel Ferguson.

During *The Battle of the Boyne* on July 1st 1690 (Julian Cal.), history records that part of the Williamite cavalry crossed the Boyne at Rosnaree to outflank Jacobite positions at Oldbridge and Donore.[7] Although many conflicting versions of this event are recounted, it seems that a large Williamite contingent crossed the ford almost unopposed, and fought skirmishes with Jacobite forces in the bottomlands between here and Roughgrange. Traditionally, Patrick Sarsfield led a contingent of King James' cavalry in a belated attempt to repel the crossing, which proved decisive in winning the day for King Billy.

The ford was defended by Sir Neale O'Neal and 480 Irish Dragoons armed with two light field guns. Although heavily outnumbered by Count Schomberg's ten thousand-strong cavalry and infantry; O'Neal's men held the crossing for over an hour until the Count's heavy artillery arrived. O'Neal received a mortal wound during the engagement and died several days later. An interesting footnote to this military engagement shows that Count

Left to right: Remains of Millwheel hub Rosnaree Mill; Millstone set in patio at Rosnaree

Meinhard Schomberg, whose father, the 80 years old Duke of Schomberg, was killed at Oldbridge on the same day, later became the Duke of Leinster and Baron of Tarah (old spelling).

The river is navigable and clear of islands from below the mill to the canal weir located downstream at Upper Stalleen Lock, situated in the townland of Roughgrange.

Practical difficulties make it almost impossible to determine the exact layout from the river perspective nowadays, but cross-referencing the 1911 OS map with the OSI ortho' 2005 (aerial photography), indicates that although several changes have taken place since 1911, the Boyne's main course remains largely unaltered through Rosnaree. Some of the changes noted included alterations to the mill head and tailraces and several of the smaller islets seem to have merged with the riverbank. Both long fish-weirs are still evident, the chicane-like twist and long, narrow channel remain as previously described, but the largest island has been divided again by a newer channel.

Rosnaree Mill (called Broe Mill by some) occupies the supposed site of a 12th century mill operated by Cistercian monks from nearby Newgrange; although its earlier history cannot be traced accurately, this supposition is reasonable.[8] The property consisting of a house, offices, corn mill and kiln, together with about 41.3 acres is recorded by Griffith's as occupied by Walter Johnston at R.V. £41-10s., with the fishery leased from the Rev. Charles Osborne at R.V. £8-10s.

I recall the old stone building with the low-arched doorway, standing by

Rosnaree Mill from the river

the Boyne, when travelling the road in our 10cwt van during the 1950s: and the decaying, moss covered millwheel we could see while walking by the riverside in those days of our youth. But I cannot remember the ancient pagan symbol, Sheela na Gig, which once adorned the arched lintel, perhaps it was not considered appropriate for our young eyes to behold in those more innocent times. I believe this rather erotic carving was taken away for safe-keeping by some local person. Its former presence on the building; however, lends credence to the legend of the site's antiquity. The mill was occupied by the Johnston family down through the years with the area known colloquially as Molly Johnstons.

I viewed the outside of Johnston's Mill from terra firma during a visit to the site (April 11th 2012), accompanied by local historian Paschal Marry. The old mill was bought in recent times and tastefully converted to a private dwelling. Several old millstones are set up as garden features, one embedded in the front patio; however, pride of place is given to a 'bedstone' (the lower fixed millstone), complete with wooden bearing, driving-gear, mace-head and rind (or rynd).

As noted previously at Boardsmill, an interesting feature of the mills on the Boyne and its tributaries is that the shape of the above rinds/rynds varies between locations. The millstones observed so far on the Lower Boyne, e.g. Rosnaree, Roughgrange and Stalleen, having a four-spoked or cruciform-shaped profile, while those at Boardsmill, Bective, Kilcarn Upper and the ancient King's Mill in Lismullen (on the River Gabhra) had triple-spoked rynds for driving their 'runner stones.' At Rosnaree, a stack of millstones to the front includes a segmented French burr-type stone complete with shrunk-on hoops, and another with patented cast-iron balance weights embedded in its plaster of Paris coating.

The Boyne flows placidly by the old building nowadays, unperturbed by the ravages visited upon this ancient site by progress. The water wheel that powered the ancient grindstones is now gone, the rusting remains of its eight-spoked hub and axle, protruding from the mill's riverside wall beside the apron-board grooves. A tangible reminder that this place once provided a source of employment and social interaction upon the riverbank close by King Cormac's mythical resting place. Some river islets are gone, and the millraces are dried up because parts of the upstream weir were removed deliberately and by the many floods tearing through the valley. One wonders where progress is taking us, as the river hereabouts, which once drove at least four watermills, is now unused and incapable of illuminating even one lamp because of modern neglect.

Following a friendly nip on my forearm from Sean Óg, the resident donkey, Paschal and I departed the ancient site by the Boyne; taking the winding road by the river to visit the remains of McCullagh's old mill downstream at Stalleen.

On a later visit, the incumbent mill owner kindly conducted my wife Marie and I on a tour of the building to assist in our research. Inside, the former working deck that once housed the millstones and other operating plant, is now a homely, low-ceilinged combined kitchen and living room. Its north-facing window provides a splendid view across the old millwheel towards Broe on the other side of the Boyne.

In the basement below, much of the driving gear is intact (mostly of wooden construction), including the crown or pit-wheel, the big spur gearwheel for driving the stones, and most of the associated gearing. An interesting feature is a lay-shaft protruding through the western wall at ground level, driven by a pinion from the pit-wheel. This turned a pulley wheel on the outside of the building and may have been an auxiliary drive for a hoist or some other machinery. One grindstone drive shaft remains in situ, accessed through a hatch in the living room floor; which also provides a convenient escape route for the family cat through the machinery space beneath the building.

While drinking tea at the kitchen table, I visualised what a hive of activity the old building must have been in its working days. I could almost hear the millwheel thumping and splashing outside, the whirring of wooden gearwheels and rumbling grindstones, punctuated by occasional shouts from the miller to his assistant… sounds no longer heard at Rosnaree Mill and indeed, which may never echo across the Boyne again.

Leaving the scene on this occasion, Sean Óg bid us farewell, not by a friendly nip on the arm, but by an equally friendly hee-haw over the open half-door of the building across the road; once used to house the drying kiln for Johnston's Mill.

ENDNOTES

1   A basin or wharf was/is located on the south-western canal bank alongside the former towpath just above Slane Bridge. This allowed on and off loading of cargoes, and provided a means for tourists to access Slane Village and its historic environs. Several wrought iron mooring rings are still attached to the canal-side coping stones. Cargoes bound for Slane Mill, such as coal and corn, were taken direct to the mill via Fennor Guard Lock, then across the river above the weir, to be offloaded at the mill wharf sited alongside the headrace/access canal.

2   The 1656 Down Survey Barony of Duleek map depicts a weir upon the Boyne at this location.

3   A list of Lockkeepers, compiled for Meath Co. Council's Road Committee in 1913 during a review of the navigation's proposed liquidation, names Owen Morgan as keeper at this lock (Rosnaree), and shows that he was in receipt of a quarter-annual salary of 12s. Although the Lower Boyne Navigation reverted to public ownership in 1834, and was taken in charge by the newly formed Office of Public Works, Griffith's records all the other canal property on this section under the title of Boyne Nav. Co. in 1854. The works at Rossnaree is the one exception I could find included under ownership of the Commissioners.

4   The 1656 Down Survey Barony of Duleek map depicts a 'straight' weir (or bridge?) crossing the Boyne hereabouts, from 'Knockhamon' (Knockcommon) to the northern shore.

5   A Ford 10cwt van with a side-valve engine; which model, together with its companion, the Ford 5cwt, revolutionised transport for the ordinary folk of Ireland. As many a Blacksmith can confirm, in so doing they displaced the pony trap as a means of transport, thereby putting most of the local Smithies out of business.

6   A list of Lockkeepers, compiled for Meath County Council's Roads Committee in 1913 during a review of the Navigation's proposed liquidation, names Mrs. A. Callan as keeper at Broe Lock. It shows also that she was in receipt of 12s-2d as a quarterly salary.

7   See 'Battle of the Boyne' in Chapter 19.

8   A mill is depicted at this location on the 1656 Down Survey Barony of Duleek map.

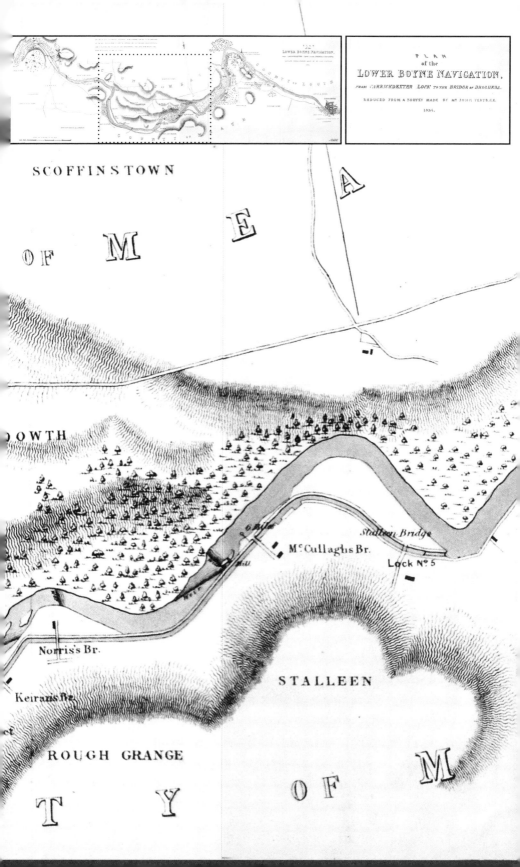

PLAN
of the
LOWER BOYNE NAVIGATION,
FROM CARRICKDEXTER LOCK TO THE BRIDGE OF DROGHEDA.
REDUCED FROM A SURVEY MADE BY Mr JOHN YEATS, C.E.
1834.

SCOFFINSTOWN

OF M E A

DOWTH

6 Rise

Stalleen Bridge

McCullaghs Br.

Lock No 5

Norris's Br.

STALLEEN

Keirans Br.

ROUGH GRANGE

TY OF M

18

The Lower Reaches
Broe to the Mattock River

Over Broe Weir & through The Seven Ways – Stalleen Navigation Weir –
Lougher's two riparian fields & Gilltown's single pasture – Proposed canal
from Rosnaree Lock to Roughgrange – Stalleen Canal Upper Guard Lock –
Kiernan's Bridge & Roughgrange – Norris' Bridge, Mill & Millstones – The
Leck – Roughgrange & Ballinacrad (Dowth) Fish-weirs – Craud Village,
'The Scoffing Town' – Under the new footbridge at Brugh Na Boine –
Dowth Castle, Netterville Institute & John Boyle O'Reilly – Stalleen &
Sharman Crawford Connection – A visit to Stalleen Mill, Miller's house
& a walk along the Canal Ramparts – McCullagh's Bridge – A Titanic
Moment – Stalleen Lower Lock, Lock-house & Horse Bridge – The Cottage
– Glenmore & Farm – a Race Course in Dowth & Proudfootstown Ford.

Resuming our journey, we approached Broe Weir with caution. The River
Rescue boys decided it was too dangerous to make the transit with the craft
fully laden, so we were ejected from the boat once more, to walk along the
riverbank. This provided an opportunity to photograph the event, which
took place without major incident, the boat merely taking on some extra
water-ballast during the crossing. Re-boarding below the weir, we headed on
downriver to where the complex of islets impeded our onward passage.

Crossing Broe Weir

This area is known as 'the seven ways' or 'the seven traps,' because there are supposedly seven different paths through the maze of ancient fish traps. Here the two boats landed on the north-eastern shore, next to a small cutting leading towards the partially filled-in remains of Broe canal. While the rescue boys debated our best route, Tom French and I walked across to Upper Broe Lock and surveyed the surroundings from this aspect.

Broe canal cuts across a broad floodplain adjoining the north-eastern riverbank, from above Broe Weir to the lower lock below Newgrange Tumulus; where the floodplain narrows again and the riverbank becomes steeper. At Broe the floodplain merges with higher ground rising gradually northwards to Knowth and eastwards towards Newgrange; Dowth Tumulus lies further eastwards nearer the River Mattock. Rosnaree House occupies the wooded heights on the opposite bank, from its eminence commanding the ancient ford, the mill and narrower floodplain of the south-eastern shore.

The rescue boys having decided to use the direct approach once more, we re-boarded and headed towards one of the seven ways. Where we crossed the downstream end of *Brugh* or *Browny's* fish-weir (at the former fish traps), and passed through the vortex of fast flowing water tearing through the chicane.

Following a bumpy ride, our boat emerged in calmer waters and passed

Clockwise from top: Stalleen upper navigation weir - in Roughgrange Townland - Newgrange in background; Upper Stalleen Nav. weir - in Roughgrange; Boyne at Roughgrange; Upper Stalleen 'flood gate' (Turf Lock) & towpath.

along a deeper stretch of river flowing to the south-east towards the lower fish-weir. This reach once led into the original approach to Rosnaree Mill headrace, which has been filled in as described.

We crossed *Monkneton* or *Rosnaree* fish-weir at its easternmost end, and carried on downriver, past the renovated mill standing on the southern riverbank, and onwards towards Stalleen. Rounding a slight curve, we left Broe Lower Lock in our wake, then, passed by remnants of a large limekiln on the northern bank. Our boat entered the deeper reach above Stalleen's navigation weir, built at 90 degrees to the river and now in poor repair. Here, the navigation once crossed the short, navigable river section to the southern bank, where the waterway cutting leaves the river immediately above the weir.

Stalleen Canal is shown commencing in Roughgrange Townland on the 1837 OS map, but the 1911 OS map marks it starting within Lougher Townland. Closer perusal of both maps indicates the likelihood of the rampart being extended, sometime between the surveys, by .030 of an acre; shown as a tiny spit of land extending upstream on the 1911 map.

Lougher and Gilltown Townlands have very small areas of river frontage immediately upstream of the cutting; Lougher with two fields totalling 10.1 acres and Gilltown with one field of 3 acres, as shown on the 1911 map. One might well wonder what political shenanigans occurred in times past to achieve these boundaries.

Berthing the boats and scrambling ashore through the sedges, we stood on the riverbank surveying the scene. The great mound of Newgrange dominates the horizon to the north of the river, with green fields descending in serried rows towards Broe Canal and the narrowing floodplain opposite our vantage point. I noted how the modern white façade stands out boldly from the surroundings, and reflected on its contrast to the nettle and briar covered mound of my childhood days.

The towpath on which we stood runs for several hundred metres upriver, through Lougher's two fields (now one), then turns due south. It passes alongside the mereing of Lougher and Gilltown Townlands, to meet with the nearby road (old Navan/Drogheda road) beside the modern car park. This access is shown on the 1837 and later OS maps.

Yeats' 1834 plan of the lower navigation depicts a red line running alongside the Boyne from Stalleen Upper Guard Lock to Rosnaree Lock. Though this is recorded as a pathway on the 1834 survey, it was not part of the towing path, because we know that this followed the navigation on the opposite riverbank to service Broe Canal. Perhaps it was used to shuttle towing horses between Rosnaree and Stalleen, with another horse relay in operation at Broe. Alternatively, the red line may represent the proposed route of the previously-mentioned lateral canal, being mooted at the time to replace Broe Canal.

The floodplain widens on the Roughgrange side, with marshy bottomlands extending to the road, beyond which the ground rises steeply to a high ridge framing the valley.

Upper Stalleen Lock is not in Stalleen Townland, but located in Roughgrange, so also is Stalleen Navigation Weir. The name is intended to denote the canal section; however, rather than the townland, as this part of the navigation is known as Stalleen Canal. Perhaps because its construction commenced further downstream at Stalleen Lower Lock.

Like Upper Broe, the lock here is located some distance down from the river, and is of similar construction, with earthen banks, no lift, double sets of gates and is approximately twice the width of the canal. It could be described as a guard lock or floodgate. Although long defunct, both upper and lower gates were mounted on cut stone piers, attached to approach walls at each end of the lock; these walls are about 25ft long, with curved lead-in abutments from the canal at their outer ends. They each have a stone built gate recess and terminate at the inner (or lock end) in a section curving outwards to the earthen banks forming the chamber.

The lock is not shown on the 1837 OS map and is depicted, but not named, on the 1911 map. Yeats' plan of 1834 names it a check gate and shows its location much closer to the river. The map in Griffith's (1852 revision) shows the benchmark on "stone work of New Lock" at elevation 32.6ft (at Upper Stalleen). Whereas, the benchmark at the lower gate of Stalleen Lower Lock is at 31.1ft; representing a difference of 1.5ft over the three miles of pound level between upper and lower locks.

The above mention of the benchmark on the "stone work of the New Lock," suggests the original single check gate was replaced by the current arrangement (with two sets of gates) sometime between 1834 and 1852. This might explain the additional spit of land added to the canal entry, as shown

Kiernan's Br. at the waterworks in Roughgrange

on the 1911 map. Nowadays the wooden gates are missing, with a concrete footbridge spanning the lower end of the lock; this includes a sluice system feeding the old canal, now a fast-flowing river supplying the pumping station at Roughgrange.

Crossing the canal weir without incident, we continued on downriver past a couple of islands and came to a low fall, scarcely noticeable from the boat. This is shown variously on the OS maps as a ford or weir, but no signs of any approach track is evident on either the landscape or maps. Just below the ford, an aqueduct carries the canal across a small stream flowing down through Roughgrange to the Boyne. This stream is known as the Lougher River, formed by several capillaries sourced variously in Cullen, Rathdrinagh, Knockcommon and Lougher Townlands.

Perhaps this little river is the same one, mentioned in various accounts of the Battle of the Boyne, which caused so much confusion during the skirmishes at Roughgrange following Schomberg's crossing at Rosnaree Ford.

On the opposite or north-eastern slopes, a small ringfort and standing stone can be seen in the fields from mid-river. Yeats' 1834 plan indicates the 7th milestone located just below the aqueduct, upstream of the present day pumping station; however, its omission from the 1911 OS map perhaps means it had disappeared by then.

Here, a horse-bridge spans the waterway to the rampart, which carried the towpath between the canal and Boyne. The bridge is about 8ft in passage width and named Kieran's Bridge on the navigation sketch in Ellison's book and Keiran's Bridge on Yeats' plan of 1834. It provides access from the pumping station to the former towpath, which now forms part of the Boyne Walk. This path crosses over the station's outflow sluiceway via a concrete bridge, and then continues eastwards past Bru Na Boinne to Stalleen Lower Lock.

The Boyne Currach Centre is located across the road from the station, on the corner of the small road leading to the Commons of Duleek.

Further downstream we come to the big, sweeping bend taking the river around the tip of Roughgrange; which stretch is almost as complicated as that at Rosnaree, with a maze of islets, fish-weirs and millraces forming a complex series of obstructions, difficult to navigate.

The canal takes a near right-angled turn here, and runs almost due east to the present day site of the Interpretive Centre. The portion of land, cut off by the navigation, forms a sector of a circle, within which lies a graveyard, several buildings and the site of a corn mill. The mill is shown on the 1837 OS edition but not on the 1911 map. The site was once accessed via Norris' Bridge; which is bypassed, the old laneway now crossing the filled-in canal and leading onwards to some houses and the old graveyard of Leck.

Cyril Ellison's book contains several references to a period in the 1780s when a cotton/linen mill supposedly occupied a site on the river at Roughgrange e.g.:

> The foundations of an extensive cotton manufactory had been laid at Roughgrange. The mill, powered by water, would cost over £4000. (sic)

Another reference, which may refer to this cotton mill, states:

> John Coulter of Drogheda had to be threatened with legal action for choosing this time to open sluices in the river bank above Oldbridge weir to drive a 6 foot wide wheel in aid of his linen mill. (sic)

The latter reference is made in the context of low water levels in the Boyne causing difficulty to canal operations in 1788. I cannot find further references to a cotton mill at Roughgrange in earlier times, but, as stated, the 1837 OS map indicates a corn mill on the site. Griffith's records that this mill, together with house, offices and land totalling circa 37 acres were leased from the reps' of Thomas McDermott and occupied by William Norris in 1854 at R.V. £44-10s. The head and tailrace for this mill form a narrow channel running across the sweeping bend at Roughgrange; this isolates several parcels of land, nowadays forming islands in the main river course.

The area immediately adjacent to Norris' Mill is known as 'the Leck,' with the graveyard called Leck Graveyard or 'Graveyard of The Leck.' Other places in Ireland include Leck in their titles e.g. Kilnaleck in County Cavan; which name translates to 'the church of the flagstone.' The name probably derives from the Welsh 'llech' (pronounced cleck), with its Irish equivalent spelled variously Leac, Lack, Leck and League. The name is associated also with Cromlech, a stone circle or burial chamber. The translation to English can mean variously monumental stone, flat stone, slab, hard surface, tombstone or flagstone; therefore, the name is relevant to the location which contains most of these features.

Paschal Marry and I visited 'the Leck' during April 2012 and with kind permission of the Gogan family, viewed the graveyard and adjacent site of Norris' Mill. The burial ground is obviously very old, with two fine cut-stone piers (each adorned with a small iron cross) supporting the wrought iron gate. There are several old tombstones inside the walled cemetery, including one remarkable monumental tomb hidden beneath the overhanging trees. Nicholas Wall of the Slane History & Archaeology Society compiled a list

Left to right: Peter - Sammy & their Mum standing on a mill stone upon site of Norris' Mill - With Leck Graveyard in background 2012; The Gogans & Paschal Marry discussing millstones - to left is the covered bridge spanning the former millrace - background is the Boyne at Ballinacrad Weir

of graves in the cemetery – the oldest grave I can find on this list is recorded as the final resting place of Michael Finnegan, who passed away on January 22nd 1776.

Though no traces of Norris' Mill remain; a memento of its former existence can be found on the riverbank directly opposite Ballinacrad Weir. A matched-pair of millstones lie on the grassy riverbank close by the old millrace; with the 'bedstone' fully exposed, while the 'runner stone' lay partly buried beneath a layer of topsoil.

The two boys, Peter and Sammy, attacked the clay covering with gusto and soon the old millstone lay exposed, such that we could see the cruciform-shaped rynd drive slots. The interest shown by the two youngsters was most gratifying in these times of computer games and gadgetry; the lads noting down details as we explained how the millstones worked. Pat Gogan, a native to the area, told us he never saw any ruins that might confirm the existence of a cotton or linen mill, as suggested by the excerpt from Cyril Ellison's book.

The 1911 OS map indicates a 'footstick' or footbridge spanning the defunct millrace at the site of the long gone corn mill. This is now replaced by an open-ended steel container, providing a covered access to the network of islets; a remarkable feature in the Irish landscape, more characteristic of covered bridges in New England.

Two separate and distinct fishing weirs existed on the Boyne close by Roughgrange in times past. Slightly upriver from the mill headrace (Norris' Mill), the 1837 OS map shows a fish-weir running from the north-eastern bank, (opposite the present day pumping station) and linking to several islets in the main river channel. The 1911 OS map indicates it terminating downriver, on the Roughgrange side, in a series of narrow openings or slots that held the former wickerwork fishing traps. This may have been the fish-weir of Newgrange in earlier times as it is located within that townland, which shares a mereing with Dowth a few metres further downriver. Perhaps it was once "the weir in the Grange," mentioned in records of 1554 and 1558 as being leased for twenty years to Henry Draycott. In later times it became known as Roughgrange Fishery. Griffith's shows the fishery at Roughgrange leased from the reps' of Thomas McDermott by William Norris at R.V. £8 in 1854.

Further downstream in Dowth and opposite Roughgrange, another fish-weir links several islets in the river; this weir terminates in a series of traps on the Dowth side of the Boyne. The 1911 OS map indicates it served also as a 'footstick-ford' in times past. We know from other sources that long ago the weir was part of Dowth Fisheries; later known as Ballinacrad Fishery, and in regular use until relatively recent times (c. 2005). It is attached to the nearby Ballinacrad Cottage, occupied by Joe Mc.Donald nowadays; who informed me that the property has been in his family for several generations, and that he operated the fish-traps until about seven years ago.

The origin of the name Ballinacrad is uncertain; it is not listed as a townland or parish in the late Jack Fitzsimons' *The Plains of Royal Meath*, and not shown on the 1837 OS map or listed in Griffith's Valuation of 1854. The 1911 OS map; however, shows Ballinacrad House to the south-west of Dowth Castle, sited within a large field together with three mounds.

Perhaps this name is associated with a place named Craud, located close by to the north-west and shown on both of the above OS maps; research indicates that Craud was listed as a hamlet or village in the 17th century.

The 1836 Field Notes record the following about Craud Village:

> Baile na Craide, town of the scoffing.
> "There is a village in Dowth called Crawd, so spelled to me, the meaning of which it was told me is The Coffin Town." – Lt. H. Tucker, R.E.
> Scoffing town – <u>not</u> Coffin town. J. O'D.
> In the west part of the td., 5 miles west from Drogheda.
> This is a hamlet of about 12 ground-floor, thatched mud houses. It is 28 perches north of the road that traverses the td. from west to east. At the back of one of the houses, Hugh Brien's, is a large mass of Green – stone, one of the erratic blocks. (sic)[1]

On William Larkin's 1812/17 Map of County Meath, this place name is shown as *Scoffingstown*.

Ballinacrad, formerly Dowth salmon weir, was 'not' the property of Mellifont Abbey and, according to ancient records it was seized by the crown in 1381, but restored to Luke Netherville of Dowth following legal action. It is said that in earlier times this weir became the subject of a lawsuit, resulting in the abbot of the BVM in Duleek being jailed for 'throwing down a weir owned by Nicholas de Nethervil.'

Whatever its previous history, this complex of little islands provided a formidable obstacle to river navigation in olden times, as it does nowadays. The River Rescue lads, having communicated with the Boyne River Rescue Service in Drogheda, decided to make our run via the north-eastern channel, the other passage through the old millrace being deemed impassable for our boats.

Encountering the first big island in mid-river just below the pumping station, we ran the gauntlet of little islets, probable remnants of the old fish-weir at Grange. Following a thrill seekers' ride, our boat entered the long, narrow stretch of clear water leading around the great sweep at Roughgrange. Passing by several mid-river islands on our right, we came to the necklace of small islets forming the fish traps of Ballinacrad Salmon Weir. Running this narrow passage, we entered the long, curved reach upstream of the Interpretive Centre, barely visible in the distance towards the north-east; its new metal footbridge gleaming in the bright winter's sunshine.

The riverscape changes again in the vicinity of Ballinacrad Weir; where the north-eastern riverbank slopes upwards from the water's edge, rising in grassy ridges to a low escarpment overlooking the curving Boyne. Though mid-winter, some small ponies and several clusters of sheep foraged on grasslands between the occasional clumps of brush and trees dotting the hillsides. The opposite shoreline encompasses the enclave of 'the Leck,' below which the floodplain narrows and the canal is partly filled in, with the area beyond the navigation enclosed by wooded hillsides rising towards Stalleen.

Passing beneath the footbridge leading from the Interpretive Centre to Newgrange, we noticed that the canal hereabouts is in an advanced state of decay, with the old waterway almost completely overgrown and filled with detritus. This neglect does not sit well against the backdrop of the state of the art modern facility. While it is laudable that our ancient prehistoric sites are well maintained; the less ancient Boyne Navigation is also a unique part of our heritage and should be preserved for future generations.

Below the footbridge, the north-eastern floodplain broadens as the river sweeps towards the great bend at Stalleen. The hillsides to the north-east are dotted with several old and interesting sites, including: Dowth Tumulus,

Dowth Castle, the former Netherville Institute and Dowth Hall. Because, like Newgrange, the Tumulus at Dowth is much written about by many renowned historians and others, I will devote this spac e to the lesser-known sites.

Dowth Castle stands to the east of the tumulus and was the ancestral home to the Netherville dynasty; granted these lands by the Baron of Slane during the early years of the Norman Conquest (circa 1300), and who operated some fisheries hereabouts in later times. The castle was vacated about the mid-18th century, when the Nethervilles moved to the adjacent and newly built Dowth Hall.

In later times it was the birthplace of renowned Fenian John Boyle O'Reilly (1844-1889). Close by the old building, a monument stands in memory of this remarkable man, described as one of our great patriots. His father was a teacher in the school attached to the castle, a tower house combined with an unfortified dwelling, now restored. At the rear of the castle is the ancient church and graveyard overlooking the Boyne.

One of the castle's most noted residents was the Right Hon. Nicholas Netherville, 5th Viscount Netherville, elected to the office of Grand Master to Ireland's Grand Lodge of Freemasons in 1732. Shortly thereafter, Navan's first Masonic Lodge was established in the town (lodge No. 107); this establishment being granted a warrant on 6th May 1739, followed by Lodge No. 197 at Oldcastle in October 1749. The rapid growth of Freemasonry within County Meath is attributed to the said Nicholas Netherville. His mother, Francis, was daughter of Richard Parsons, Earl of Rosse (Ross), the first recorded Grand Master to *The Grand Lodge of Ireland*, reputedly the second most senior Freemason's lodge in the world.

In 1826, the 6th Viscount Netherville (John Netherville) bequeathed Dowth Castle and some land to be used as a charitable home for destitute widows and orphans. The 15th century tower house was modified to suit this purpose, and used as such until these services were transferred to the magnificent brick building adjoining the castle's eastern boundary. Designed by noted architect George Ashlin; it was built in 1877 as a Charitable Almshouse and known as the Netherville Institute. It closed down in 1960 and had several owners in the interim period; being restored in 1998 and operated as a guest house for some time. I recall the premises in use during my youth as a nursing home, but it is now a private residence.

Further east stands Dowth Hall, former home to the Netherville (Netterville) dynasty. The family lost their property during the Cromwellian confiscations, but regained them later when the incumbent Netherville appealed to Parliament. In later years, Dowth Hall was owned by the Gradwells, then by the Camerons and in contemporary times, I believe, is the property of the Pidgeon family.

The mansion was planned contemporaneously with development of Dowth Demesne, which began c.1727 and perhaps finished about 1750. Built in the Palladian-style, some historians maintain that the residence was designed originally by George Darley of Drogheda. The manor's first occupant would appear to be the 6th Viscount Netherville, John Netherville. He was a supposed recluse, one of whose reputed eccentricities involved building a tea house atop the great tumulus, from which eminence he 'attended' Sunday Mass; participating in the ceremony through the lens of his telescope!

On the opposite riverbank, the townland named Stalleen has several different spellings, I have; therefore, spelled it as recorded on the OS maps to avoid confusion. John O'Donaovan's 1836 Field Notes on the townland record the following:

Sta Lin.
Sta is the Norse form of Teach, signifying 'a house'
Lin is the genitive case of Lion, meaning 'flax'

Sta Lin = **Teach Lin** = **the flax house**

Stalleen .... J. O' D.
.... N. Coddington, Esq
.... Edwd. Ray, Mearsman
Stallen .... Sur. & Val. Report 1824
Staleing .... Civil Survey 1654 – 56

It contains 792a. 1r. 26p. , including 13a. 3r. 17p. of the R. Boyne. It is the property of Wm. S. Crawford, esa. , and is well cultivated and supports a numerous tenantry. There are on it Stalleen House, a house called The Cottage and a corn mill. (sic)

Note the inclusion of *Mearsman*, a title for the official in charge of boundaries or mereings/mearings in the area.

The Crawford family owned Stalleen estate from early times, and I note that O'Donovan states also that Stalleen was the occasional residence of William S. Crawford, whose full title was William Sharman Crawford. A William Sharman Crawford (1781-1861), perhaps the same man, was an Irish politician with liberal and radical vision; who supported Catholic Emancipation and the rights of tenants. He was High Sheriff of County Down in 1811 and MP for Dundalk from 1835 to 1837 and for Rochdale from 1841 to 1852. The Crawford Dynasty hailed from Scotland originally and moved to a place named Crawfordsburn in County Down, perhaps during the Ulster Plantation. William Crawford 1 of Crawfordsburn had a son named John, whose daughter Mabel married William Sharman; hence the name Sharman Crawford.[2]

We came to remnants of the old fishing and mill weir at Stalleen just a short distance downstream from the Interpretive Centre; which weir is visible from the footbridge. The 1837 OS map shows the weir starting from the north-eastern riverbank, and running askew for several hundred feet towards the opposite bank near Stalleen Corn Mill. The 1911 map gives more details; indicating a series of slots for fishing boxes at the weir's mid-point, and below these a spill weir slanting towards the north-eastern bank.

The weir leads into the headrace powering the mill further downstream. Just below the mill, the navigation's No. 6 milestone was located on the rampart close by Mc.Cullagh's Bridge, but I could find no trace of the marker stone during my most recent site visit. This bridge provided access from the Donore road to the mill and towpath running along the rampart between the river and canal, now part of the Boyne Walk.

Griffith's shows that in 1854, Stalleen Corn Mill, house, offices, kiln and land totalling circa 40.75 acres were leased from William S. Crawford and occupied by Peter Mc.Cullagh at R.V. £46-5s. The attendant fishery was leased also by Peter Mc.Cullagh from William S. Crawford at R.V. £7-10s. More ancient records show that at the dissolution of Mellifont Abbey in the mid-16th century, Hugh Dodall was in possession of Stalleen fishing-weir, then valued at 60s.

Pauline Fulham and the author at Stalleen Miller's house.

Paschal Marry and I called to the miller's thatched house in Stalleen on April 11th 2012 and met the incumbent resident, Pauline Fulham; who informed us that her family have occupied the house for at least one hundred years. Local legends tell of bread being baked upon the hobs in the older part of the house, to help feed Jacobite soldiers during the Battle of the Boyne in 1690. Here again we observed an old millstone embedded in a patio; this measured circa 4.5ft in diameter and had a four-spoked rynd drive profile. We heard also that some of the millstones and machinery were moved upriver to Johnston's Mill when Stalleen Mill ceased operations many years ago.

Following a lengthy chat, and with Pauline's kind permission, we set off through the well-tended farmyard, and crossed the canal bridge to view the remains of the old corn mill standing beside the canal banks nearby.

Mc.Cullagh's Bridge is of segmental arch profile, which reduces the bridge's humped-backed effect, and has a passage width of approximately 12ft. These details, together with the 'skid stones' on its western end, indicates that it was constructed for vehicular traffic to access the corn mill. The skid stones were fitted to prevent cart and wagon wheels snagging the parapet while making the sharp turn onto the canal ramparts, or indeed, back onto the bridge. These stones can still be seen mounted at arched laneways in Navan; mementos of times when horse-drawn transport was king of the roads. The

Above:
McCullagh's Br. over canal
near Stalleen

Left:
Remnants of McCullagh's Mill
& millrace

bridge is in good condition, apart from a couple of arch ring stones/voussoirs missing from the downriver facade.

This is one of the most beautiful settings imaginable, the early spring sunshine dappling through newly blossoming trees, enhanced by the ever-present birdsong and sound of Boyne's water rippling across hidden weir.

We came to the mill some little distance above the bridge, the old building straddling the millrace to our right, below the rampart level. Not much remains of the ancient structure, just some stone walls supporting remnants of the crumbling roof; the remaining structure seemingly held together by ivy. Though a door provided access, we could not enter because it was locked; so we bade farewell to this old mill, supposedly occupying the site where Mellifont monks built one of their several corn mills during medieval times.

On the earlier downriver journey in Dec. 2011, we discovered that the remains of the ancient fish-weir at Stalleen form a network of islets, and pose much the same navigation hazards as those encountered further upstream. We made our approach down the right hand or south-eastern channel, once the headrace for the mill. The other boat, acting as guinea pig, went several metres ahead into the narrowing mouth of the old millrace. Suddenly, Martin, realising we were in the wrong channel and heading into dangerous waters, yelled at Hopper and Brendan to wheel the boat hard aport into one of the old fishing slots – then we experienced our *Titanic Moment*.

The two lads jumped into the water to manoeuvre the boat through the channel, but it was too late as the craft had gained too much momentum in the fast-flowing water and refused to respond – we ploughed into branches of a fallen tree protruding from one of the islets, knocking me flat on my backside into the bilges. Then I heard Hopper calling: "quick, quick Martin, get her into the bank, she's going down." It looked ominous as I scrambled back out of the bilges to place my newly wetted arse on the gunwale, the nose of our craft dipping underwater and the bilge level increasing rapidly. But nobody panicked, the two boys in the water guiding the RIB through the weir and across to the north-eastern bank, where we all scrambled ashore to review the situation from the safer aspect of terra firma.

An inspection revealed the problem caused by some underwater obstruction (possibly a tree branch), puncturing two of the boat's air filled compartments. Our crew decided to complete the trip in the undamaged boat, while the others would beach the damaged craft downriver at the Curly Hole and return to base in Navan. The transfer operation took place amid some slagging between the respective crews; Hopper and Brendan meanwhile receiving much good-humoured banter about their attempt to *do a Titanic* on the supposedly unsinkable RIB.

The changeover complete, we set off downriver through yet another beautiful reach of the Boyne water. A short distance below Stalleen Weir and mill, both river and canal turn 90 degrees to head due east; the Boyne flowing in a great curve around Stalleen, then winding through a gorge-like cleft. The navigation following almost the same course alongside, but hidden in the wildwoods of the steeper southern riverbank. Beyond the last river curve of this section, the Boyne turns sharply to head due north for a short distance, and then veers slightly north-eastwards through wooded terrain.

Above:
Stalleen Lower horse-
bridge

Left:
Lock-house at Stalleen
Lower (Neary's) Lock
2012

The navigation returned to the river at Stalleen Lower Lock, located in a little bay on the eastern riverbank, where the river turns northwards at the above bend. We were unable to land because of the problems with the boat, so could not view the canal works from terra firma on this occasion.

The canal hereabouts is accessed from the old Navan/Drogheda road via a lane leading to the horse-bridge spanning the waterway. This bridge allowed the towing horses to cross the canal, and then continue along the towpath to Oldbridge Guard Lock further downstream. The OS Benchmark is shown on the map at elevation 33.7ft on the bridge battlements.

The Lockkeeper's house is located c.150 metres upstream from Stalleen Lock, to the west of the bridge. Griffith's shows that in 1854, this house was held by the Boyne Navigation Co. in fee, with no occupant's name specified.

The valuation shows also that William S. Crawford owned the house named 'the Cottage' on the attendant map, and located close by the canal's access laneway. Other references indicate the Lockkeepers' house occupied by Pat Matthews in 1788, Peter Mc.Cullagh in 1860 (Stalleen Miller?) and by Mary Matthews in 1900.[3]

On a visit to the site in April 2012, I noted that 'the Cottage' is occupied and well-tended and the former Lock-house, built of dressed stone, is in good condition and lived-in from time to time. The bridge has a very pronounced humped back and is about eight feet in passage width, the canal bed beneath being mostly dried out and planted with flowers and shrubbery. A small stream passes beneath the canal between the Lock-house and the horse-bridge, and continues across the bottomlands to the Boyne.[4]

The lock gates are long gone, but the chamber, though overgrown, is mostly in good condition; however, its stone blocks are cracked here and there, providing footholds for the ever-present ivy and ash trees to take root and hasten its destruction in the future. The OS Benchmark on the lower gate stonework is at elevation 31.1ft; indicating that the lock provided a lift/drop of circa 10ft to the pound level of the unflooded river between here and

Partly cleared Stalleen Lower Lock - Dowth in background - 2013

Oldbridge Navigation Weir. This level was impounded by a combination of the navigation weir and Oldbridge tidal lock.

Passing along the muddy, overgrown towpath towards Oldbridge, one of the pillboxes, built during The Emergency (1939-1945) can be seen in the wildwood to the right of the old track-way. Altogether, apart from the well-tended cottage, Lock-house and bridge area, Stalleen Lower Lock has returned to nature and is being absorbed gradually into the wild riverscape.[5]

The Boyne is navigable from here to the navigation weir just upstream of the River Mattock. The said weir, built at right angles across the Boyne, deepened the river and effectively controlled the water level such that it remained sufficient to enable barges and lighters make the transit between Drogheda and Navan. The entry to the Oldbridge canal section is located just upstream of the weir. The towpath runs atop the rampart alongside the south-eastern riverbank from Stalleen to Oldbridge, hidden from the river amidst dense wildwood.

Leaving Stalleen Lock, our boats set off downriver, gliding through yet another scenic reach of the Boyne. The reed and sedge-covered riverbank on our left broadening to green floodplain dotted with trees that once formed

The Boyne at Stalleen

the Deerpark of Dowth, nowadays framed by the wooded hillsides of Townley Hall further to the north-east. To our right, the eastern riverbank rises steeply to an escarpment crowned by a wildwood known in times past as Glenmore Fox Covert.

The towpath hereabouts is obscured by the same woodlands, which encroach to the water's edge. It is noteworthy that this long navigable reach is located between the No. 3 and No. 5 milestones – while various sketches mark the distances along this stretch, I could not find the No. 4 and No. 5 milestones marked on the 1911 OS map. Perhaps the markers had disappeared by then or maybe they are still in situ, but hidden beneath the dense undergrowth of the riverbank.

The long, deep stretch of river tempted Martin to open the throttle, our boat responding in style, her nose rising almost like a speedboat. But the easterly wind provided a harsh reminder that we were not in tropical waters; whipping cold river-spray into our faces and forcing us to seek non-existent shelter. The lads in the other boat responded by dragging the damaged nose from the water, and tearing past us like sprinters in a race for the finishing line – perhaps their temporary solution could be described as a nose-job or maritime version of a facelift.

Following this harmless fun, we noted a large ruined building atop the high ridge on the south-eastern riverbank; but knew nothing of its name or history. Researching the 1911 OS map indicates this building was named Glenmore House, hence the high woodlands being called Glenmore Fox Covert.

Further research; however, shows this residence named Farm on the 1837 map and described as such on Griffith's Valuation in 1854. Larkin's Map of County Meath, surveyed for the Meath Grand Jury between 1804 and 1810, depicts Farm, together with a network of roads winding through Oldbridge and Sheephouse. Wilde mentions Farm Demesne in his account of the Battle of the Boyne and states that some Jacobite artillery was shown on Story's (Williamite Army Chaplain) map of 1693, mounted close by in anticipation of attempts by Williamite troops to cross the ford near the Mattock River.

Griffith's records Farm in Oldbridge Townland and owned by the Coddington family, but I cannot find references to the house or its occupants. The big house was obviously part of a well-developed demesne in former days, with enclosed gardens and stables within its curtilage. In 1854 the area seems to have been leased out in many small holdings, too numerous to mention. How and when the name was changed to Glenmore I have as yet been unable to discover.

Downstream from Glenmore (Farm), we pass by Glen Cottage; from here the Boyne sweeps in a series of curves taking it almost due north towards the great elbow known as the Curly Hole. The valley narrowing to almost a gorge, with the wooded heights of Townley Hall enclosing the rushy, sedgy riverbanks to the north-west; while the forested, craggy southern shore broadens to encompass Oldbridge Demesne.

On the north-western bank of the Boyne, directly opposite Glen Cottage, is a large 57 acres field; shaped like an arrowhead with the tip pointing due west and its base forming the curved riverbank. At *Cloghalea* mound, the road from Dowth Castle (once known as 'the great avenue'), makes the first of three acute right-angled turns taking it around the perimeter of the enclosed field; which is devoid of buildings except for a gate lodge on its north-eastern boundary. Nowadays, one might well wonder why this road takes such a torturous path to cross the New Bridge over the Mattock and run on to its junction with the Slane/Drogheda road near Townley Hall. Cross-referencing the 1837 and 1911 OS maps shows that it was configured thus to circumvent a racecourse sited within the confines of this oddly shaped field.

Further research elicited little more information about this ancient race-course or when and by whom it was used. An estate map in Geraldine Stout's *Newgrange and the Bend in the Boyne* names the field boundary at the zig zagged road The Paddock Wall. It would appear that 'the paddock,' the later site of the race-course, was developed as a feature of Dowth Hall Demesne in the period 1727 to 1750.

During other research, I noted several mentions of Proudfootstown Ford, no trace of which Boyne crossing exists now. The following excerpt describing this ford is taken from Wilde's description of the Battle of the Boyne:

> At the weir, where the tide ends, near the entrance of the Mattock river, the Boyne is fordable in dry weather, but with difficulty, and the right bank rises rather precipitously immediately beyond its margin.

Pratt's map of 1702 and Moll's 1714 map show the road from Dowth to Drogheda crossing the Boyne at Proudfootstown, then passing through Oldbridge Demesne and re-crossing the river at Oldbridge Ford to link with the Slane/Drogheda road. Because the map's scale is so small, no road is shown on the Boyne's southern bank leading through Rathmullan to Drogheda. This map gives the impression that two river crossings were necessary to travel from Dowth to Drogheda; whereas an alternative route existed via the old road leading from Proudfootstown Ford through Sheephouse and onwards by the high road through Rathmullan to Drogheda.

Larkin's Map of County Meath shows the main road through Dowth starting from the ford at Rosnaree and running north-eastwards across the Big Bend to Dowth. It branches here towards Monknewton (Rossin), with another line running across the Mattock towards Townley Hall. This map, while it gives many clues to the older road network on the Meath side, unfortunately does not cover the local road network on the County Louth riverbank. Extensive improvements to these roads were carried out in the early part of the 19th century, including building the New Bridge across the Mattock at Proudfootstown, cutting a new road from there to Townley Hall, and onwards via the Curly Hole to Waterunder.

The exact location of this long gone ford is very difficult to determine at this remove, but it was likely located above the maximum tide level. It perhaps connected the race-course avenue in Dowth, to the old road leading through Sheephouse, Whitehall and Rathmullan to Drogheda on the south-eastern riverbank. This places the crossing above the ancient fish-weir of Oldbridge, which might explain why, though not affected by normal tides; it was extremely difficult to cross as so described by William Wilde.

The Boyne Navigation Stalleen to Oldbridge pound level leaves the river above Oldbridge Navigation Weir, and passes through the demesne as a lateral canal to the tidal lock beside Yellow Island.

ENDNOTES

1   My understanding is that the above-mentioned Green-stone was laid down much later in geological time than underlying limestone – hence it concentrated in cracks, faults and fissures of the bedrock and became known to some as trap rock. It is associated with glacial transportation, generally crystalline and dark green in colour. The 1837 OS map indicates a Large Stone in the garden of a house on the eastern end of the village. See also references to *The Witch's Stone* at Carrick Hill, Co. Kildare, in Chap. 2.

2   The Crawford family have a connection with Cork City – the elder William Crawford's grandson, also named William Crawford, came to Cork in 1792 and teamed up with William Beamish to build the famous Beamish and Crawford brewery. The family-endowed Sharman Crawford Institute was built alongside the street formerly named Fitton Street, re-named Sharman Crawford Street. This institute housed several different schools over the years, including the Marine Engineering facility and Cork Institute of Technology. The Crawford College of Art and attendant gallery now occupies the beautiful brick building, where my daughter Anna Marie studied art in the 1990s and I attended marine engineering school during my sea going days in the 1970s.

3   A family named Neary were the last known permanent occupiers of the Lock-house in Lower Stalleen – they were in residence there until relatively recent times. A list of Lock-keepers, compiled for Meath Co. Council's Road Committee in 1913 for the liquidation of the waterway, shows Christopher Neary as the keeper at Stalleen, and that he was in receipt of a quarter-annual salary of 7s-4d.

4   While the stream is shown on the 1837 OS map, the 1911 map does not show an aqueduct or the stream flowing into the Boyne. These later omissions might give the erroneous impression that this was a feeder stream for the waterway.

5   On a later visit in April 2013, I noted that work had commenced on restoring the lock – the ivy and ash trees were cleared away, leaving the old lock with a much brighter aspect and a great vista across the Boyne to Dowth Hall.

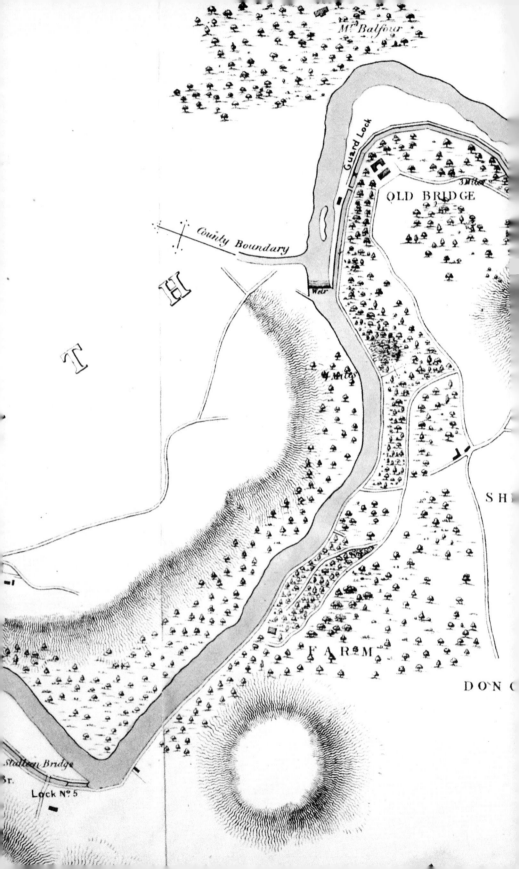

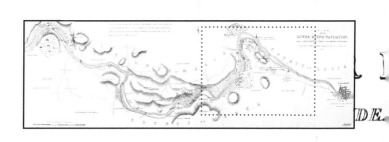

REDUCED FROM

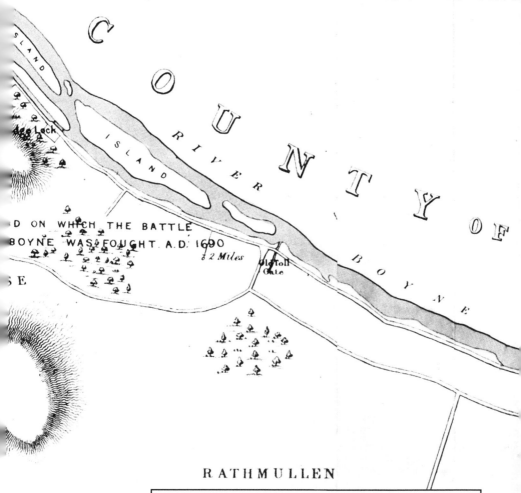

ISLAND

C O U N T Y   O F

R I V E R

I S L A N D

B O Y N E

...deo Lock

D ON WHICH THE BATTLE
BOYNE WAS FOUGHT A.D. 1690

2 Miles

Old Toll Gate

R A T H M U L L E N

PLAN
of the
LOWER BOYNE NAVIGATION,
FROM CARRICKDEXTER LOCK TO THE BRIDGE OF DROGHEDA.

REDUCED FROM A SURVEY MADE BY MR JOHN YEATS, C.E.

1834.

19

The Lower Reaches
River Mattock – Oldbridge

River Mattock & its Mills – Devlin River –Rossin & Monknewton Mill – Mattock Bridge – Mary Elcock's Mill – Proudfootstown Castle & Mill – Oldbridge Navigation Weir – Oldbridge Canal, Half-lock & Horse Bridge – Canal road bridge, Ford & Road network in olden times – Tidal Lock or Tiernan's Lock – Thomas Steers – Summary of Boyne Navigation, Canal & Locks on the system – Oldbridge Ancient Fish-weir.

The River Mattock rises in County Louth to the west of Collon and for much of its course forms the boundary between Counties Meath and Louth. As spelled on the various maps, Mattock is a Middle English name (old English Mattuc) for a pickaxe with a cross-cutting blade shaped like an adze. One might wonder how such a name was given to this small river in North-east Leinster; a riddle perhaps solved by John O'Donovan's mention in his 1836 OS Field Notes that the Gaelic name *Maiteog* means an overflowing river

The river takes its source from a series of little streams and rills coalescing in Ballymacan Townland, then flowing to the east beneath Phoenixtown Bridge. The developing river flows eastwards from here to Ballyboni, west of Collon; where the 1837 OS map depicts it feeding a large millpond, which drove a corn and a flax mill. Continuing eastwards, it formed another millpond powering a corn mill in Collon, just east of the Slane road, where

left to right: Devlins Br. spanning Devlin River in Higginstown
and Higginstown Corn Mill, converted to modern dwelling - Devlin Br. in background, 2013

it is first named Mattock River on the 1911 map. Flowing south-eastwards, the river formed another millpond driving a corn mill upstream from Boyds' Bridge, and then passed beneath this bridge, to feed a millpond that powered a flax mill in Starinagh Townland. Hereabouts the river turns to flow south-westwards and on past 'Victoria Drummond's Gate'[1] in Monasterboice, then swings southwards towards Mellifont Bridge.

The river coalesces with the Devlin River, and turns to flow south-eastwards in a circuitous path taking it close by Old Mellifont Abbey, through Rossin (Monknewtown) before meeting the Boyne beside Oldbridge Weir.

Watermills on the Upper Mattock River
from Ballyboni to Devlin River.[2]

No. 01 – Collon Townland Co. Louth (Ballyboni)
(1837) millpond, corn & flax mills – (G.V.1854) Lot 60a house, mill, offices and land totalling c.159 acres, leased by Mary Anne Traynor from Viscount Massereene & Ferrard (<u>Fosters</u>) @ R.V. £100.

No. 02 – Collon Townland (south of village) Co. Louth
(1837) millpond & corn mill – (G.V.1854) Lot 149 Ba corn-mill, offices

and land totalling c.139 acres, leased by Margaret Shekelton from Viscount Massereene & Ferrard @ R.V. £112.

No. 03 – Collon Townland (above Boyds' Br.) Co. Louth

(1837) millpond & corn mill – (G.V.1854) Lot 131a corn-mill, offices and land totalling circa 32 acres, leased by Luke Givney from Viscount Massereene & Ferrard @ R.V. £58.

No. 04 – Starinagh Townland
(below Victoria Drummond Gate) Co. Meath:

(1837) millpond & flax mill – (G.V.1854) Lot 42a house, offices, flax mill and land totalling circa 3.2 acres, leased by Patrick Byrne from Viscount Massereene & Ferrard @ R.V. £7-10s.

No. 05 on Devlin(s) River
– Higginstown Townland (at Devlins' Br.) Co. Meath

(1837) corn mill – (G.V.1854) Lot 2a house, offices, corn-mill and land totalling circa 36 acres, leased by Patrick Byrne from William White @ R.V. £62-10s.

The following is a more detailed description of the mills located on the last three miles or so of the Mattock River, upstream of its confluence with the Boyne.

Although a watermill once stood alongside the River Mattock just north-east of Mellifont Bridge, no trace of it remains on the contemporary landscape. Another mill downstream from the old abbey, depicted on the 1837 OS map as a corn mill, is located within the small townland of Mellifont Park or Louth Hill, which mill is not listed as such on Griffith's Valuation.

The valuation accounts for the townland's full area of 129 acres 1 rood 1 perch as follows: Lot No. 1 (91 acres of land only) leased by Nathanial A. Nicholson from the Marquis of Drogheda at R.V. £43 – Lot No. 2a, consisting of a house, offices and land totalling 38 acres 1 rood 1 perch, leased by Edward Tiernan from Nathaniel A. Nicholson at R.V. £35-10s. The smaller lot includes the buildings shown as a corn mill on the 1837 map (and appear also on the valuation's own map), but are not listed as a mill. These records suggest that the buildings, indicated on the earlier map to be a corn mill, were being used as a dwelling and out-offices in 1854, and that the mill; therefore, was defunct as such.

A short distance to the south of the mill site, the bridge carrying the Tullyallen to Kellystown road across the Mattock is named Wood Mill Bridge on the 1911 OS map. An indication that the old mill was perhaps used as a sawmill during the period between 1854 and 1911.

It is possible that this mill was very old and may indeed have been part of the monastic establishment of Mellifont in early times. The long headrace is taken from the River Mattock just downstream from the old abbey; while the entire workings were situated within Mellifont Park, which attached to the abbey grounds. These buildings were restored in recent times by members of a well-known local bakery family.

Further downstream we come to the great mill of Monknewtown, known colloquially as Rossin Mill. In 1825, the lease for construction of this mill, together with three acres of land upon which to site the attendant millpond and dam was granted by the Earl of Sheffield (John Baker Holroyd) to one Townley Blackwood Hardman. The original structure was built adjacent to the medieval church ruins and in operation by 1828. A weir, located upstream on the Mattock, supplied the millpond. This pond fed a long headrace that powered the millwheels, the tailrace falling back into the river upstream of Mattock Bridge on the Slane/Drogheda road. Steam power was added at a later date to power the three sets of grindstones during times of low water; hence the tall brick chimney that still enhances the mill's surviving structure.

While earlier records show that a Mr. Rogers operated the mill; Griffith's indicates that in 1854, the property consisting of a corn & flour mill, stores and land totalling 9.3 acres, was occupied by Richard R. Hill and leased from William Rodgers at R.V. £140.

The name Rossin perhaps derives from the Gaelic equivalent of Little Wood, and is described by some as an 'unofficial place name. 'It comprises an area including parts of Monknewtown, Balfaddock and Dowth Townlands. During childhood rambles with Dad in our 10cwt van, he referred to the location as 'Mitchell's of Rossin.' I have an abiding memory of the strange place; with two Wellington-boot-clad stumps protruding from a wooden barrel standing by the roadside, my child's mind pondering over this odd

Rossin (Monknewtown) Mill

spectacle presented to my wondering eyes.

For the reader seeking more enlightenment on this area, the book *Rossin, Couny Meath An unofficial place* (written by Bryn Coldrick), provides a most informative insight on the subject.

Geraldine Stout's *Newgrange and the Bend of the Boyne*, reveals that Mattock Bridge was built circa 1764, because the Grand Jury query book of that year includes a presentment made by David Jebb, William and Benjamin Burton in the sum of £167, for construction of the Meath section of this triple-arched structure.

This section comprises a single stone arch of segmental profile; while the other two arches on the Louth side are almost semi-circular. The varied shapes may reflect a differing design concept between the Grand Juries of Meath and Louth, or perhaps show that the two sides were built in different periods. The semi-circular design; however, caused the structure to have a higher elevation on the Louth side, accounting for the bridge having a more obvious humped back in days gone by. On the breast wall of the bridge is mounted a plaque commemorating local Volunteer, Philip Clarke, who died in the Easter Rising of 1916.[3]

Mattock Br. at Rossin 2013

Below the bridge, we follow the river's wandering course through Dowth Townland to the site of the long gone corn mill. The headrace, supplemented by a small stream flowing from the direction of Craud, was taken from upstream of a skewed weir on the Mattock and followed a winding course downstream to the mill. The tailrace passed by the White Well to re-enter the main river further downstream.

On the 1837 OS map, a minor road or laneway is shown running northwards from the 'Pound' opposite Dowth Castle, and crossing the millrace on a bridge close by Dowth Corn Mill. Here it linked with another road or laneway leading from Craud Village, which crossed the millrace on a bridge to the west of the corn mill. Beyond the mill, the combined roads continued northwards through Littlegrange to join the Slane/Drogheda road east of the old schoolhouse in Littlegrange.

The 1911 map indicates river fords replacing the former bridges near the corn mill, while the 2005 ortho' shows the road from Dowth Pound defunct as a through road, with a cul de sac at both ends and the road from Craud Village shown as a track. Local people tell of this old laneway being used as a shortcut, from the area adjacent to Rossin to the old post office near Dowth Hall. The layout of the mill and water conduits can be seen clearly on the earlier maps; however, while the millraces are traceable on the 1911 map, the mill building is not depicted. The former path of the head and tail races can be traced by the boundary ditches on the 2005 OS ortho' but the mill site is obscured by woodland.

References in the Civil Survey of 1656 show a tuck mill in Dowth but I cannot find any later data on this ancient mill. Other sources (Stout) record the corn mill of Dowth owned by Susanna Smith in 1734, and that it was occupied by her family for several years previously. The sources show also that Luke Elcock owned the mill in 1775. Griffith's records that Dowth Corn Mill was vacant in 1854, but owned by Mary Elcock and assessed at R.V. £1. I believe that a millstone could be seen on the mill site until relatively recent times.

The 1836 Field Notes describe the White Well thus:

> In the N.E. part of Dowth td. 5¼ miles from Drogheda. It is a good spring well neatly enclosed by a stone-and-lime wall. It is arched over . . . A ground floor, thatched building in good repair. A millrace from the Mattock river supplies the driving power. The mill has one over shot wheel.

The long headrace shown on the maps explains the overshot wheel, which requires greater water elevation to drive.

Following the Mattock's meandering course, we encounter another weir which once supplied water-head to power Proudfootstown Corn Mill, located within one of the river's many loops further downstream. The millrace is taken from the main stream immediately below the tailrace from Dowth Corn Mill, to the west of Proudfootstown Castle ruins, and follows the twisting course of the river to the mill site. The tailrace re-entered the Mattock just above 'the New Bridge' on the Dowth/Drogheda road. The layout of Proudstown Mill and attendant millraces is outlined on the two OS maps and can be traced by the boundary hedgerows on the 2005 ortho.'

Griffith's records this mill, together with house, offices and land totalling 42.5 acres occupied by James Drew; with the property leased from Ambrose Cox at R.V. £76. This higher valuation suggests that the mill was perhaps in use at the time. Other records indicate that Nicholas Hillock was in possession of this mill in 1734.

The 1836 Field Notes describe Proudfootstown Corn Mill thus:

In the N. part of Proudfootstown td., 4 miles W. from Drogheda.
A ground-floor, thatched building in good repair. It is 12 perches east
of the Mattock River, a mill race from which supplies the mill. There
is a good supply of water during the whole year. It has one wheel, an
overshot, 13 feet in diameter and 5 feet broad, which drives two pairs
of stones. (sic)

And describe the castle as follows:

about ¼ mile above "the New Bridge" on the Mattock river.
Of this castle all that remains is a tower, which appears to have been a
Flanking Tower on the N.E. angle of the structure. (sic)

The Mattock falls into the Boyne a short distance north-east of Proudfootstown
Mill, about midway along the ancient fish-weir of Oldbridge. The 1911 OS
map shows the following note inscribed close by the confluence: 'highest
point to which ordinary tides flow,' indicating that this is the maximum tidal
reach of the Boyne – except during extreme conditions which might cause
the tidal floods to penetrate some little distance further upriver.

Resuming our journey down the Boyne, we made the approach to the
navigation weir at Oldbridge; where the lateral canal section commences its
passage through Oldbridge Demesne. Because the area is multi-faceted and
extremely complex, it is best portrayed in individual sections, starting with
the navigation.

The navigation weir is built at right angles to the river's course, to deepen
the Boyne, thereby providing sufficient draught for heavily laden vessels
making the transit upriver towards Stalleen. The cutting starts immediately
above the weir and follows the Boyne's course around the great elbow formed
by Oldbridge Demesne. It ends at the sea or tidal lock (No. 1 lock) opposite
Yellow Island; circa 1.3 miles distant from its starting point upriver. This is
a lovely stretch of the canal, passing through wildwood between the tideway
of the Boyne and the now neatly manicured lawns of Oldbridge House. The
area is home to a colony of a rare species of bat, known as the *Lesser Horseshoe
Bat* (Rhinolophus Hipposideros), because of its uniquely shaped nose, which
creature is reputedly the world's smallest bat.

Like the lateral canals elsewhere on the system, Oldbridge Canal has no upper lock immediately adjacent to the river, but following the cutting, we come to a bridge spanning the waterway some little distance down from the Boyne. This is known as 'Horse Bridge' and, as the title suggests, it allowed towing horses to cross over to the towpath running along the rampart between the lateral canal and river. The bridge has an approximate passage width of 8ft and is in good condition; except where some stonework beneath the arch-springers was gouged out on both sides, possibly in an attempt to erect a barrier.

Oldbridge horsebridge

Upper Oldbridge Lock, known to some as 'the half-lock,' is sited immediately below the bridge. The upper gate hingestones are directly beneath its downstream façade and the gate structure is tied in to the bridge abutments. Though shown on the 1837 OS map, the lock is unnamed and no gates are indicated; it is constructed in a similar fashion to Upper Stalleen and Upper Broe, with no lift included in its function. Yeats' plan of 1834 records it as a flood gate while the sketch map in Ellison's book names it Oldbridge Upper and indicates two sets of gates.

From the above, one can deduce that it was erected as a check gate for prevention of damage during heavy flooding. Both gates are long gone, but the stonework of the lead-in walls and gate recesses are in good condition. The canal is blocked by a concrete wall at the upper gate, which incorporates a sluice, controlled by a ratchet mechanism mounted on the parapet wall. The OS Benchmark atop the bridge battlements is at elevation 33.3ft.

Oldbridge Guard Lock ('the Half Lock')

Following the navigation around the great curve of Oldbridge, we pass by the former site of No. 3 milestone and Oldbridge boathouse, then come to the narrow roadway leading to a stone arched bridge. This once carried the road from the Metal Bridge (Obelisk Bridge) across the waterway and onwards to Drogheda. The older stone arch was demolished recently to provide access to Oldbridge House, and replaced by a modern concrete structure.

The older bridge enabled draft horses to cross over the canal and access the towpath, which ran alongside the south-side of the canal and estuary from here to Drogheda. This was not its sole purpose; however, as explained by the following synopsis of the old road system hereabouts.

A very different road network existed in the area prior to construction of the earlier wooden bridge and later metal-latticed bridge across the Boyne at Oldbridge in 1869. The Slane/Drogheda road was realigned in the vicinity of Townley Hall and the Curly Hole in the late 18th and early 19th centuries. Analysis of the old maps suggests that the original bridge, similar to the bridge at Broe, was built across the canal circa 1750 to access the ancient ford on the Boyne.

The 1837 OS map shows an old road (now long defunct) leading down from the Slane/Drogheda road to the northern riverbank, almost directly in line with the canal bridge on the southern bank. The former 'Y' shaped ford of Oldbridge is delineated crossing the river just upstream of Grove Island; the easterly leg of the ford leading towards the canal bridge, the other

The Metal Br. & Boyne obelisk at Oldbridge - Oldbridge House in left background - *c.* 1890s
Courtesy Paschal Marry

towards Oldbridge. Traces of another old road can be observed upon the map south of the canal bridge, which led through Sheephouse and Oldbridge Demesne towards Farm (Glenmore) and Proudfootstown Ford. The present day road from King William's Glen to the metal bridge was merely a track in the 1830s, running from the Slane/Drogheda road to the Boyne Obelisk.

Studying the area from the OS ortho' perspective, all the above features can be noted in outline, including the old ford, its former path etched by white water shallows. The towpath morphed to become the roadway leading from the metal bridge, crossing the stone arch, then running alongside the canal and on past Oldbridge Lock towards Drogheda.

Thomas Steers constructed the original Oldbridge Lock from a mixture of stone and wood during the period 1748 to 1750. Steers reputedly served as a foot-soldier under Brigadier General Trelawney during the Battle of the Boyne. One of Britain's most noted navigation engineers, he has been ranked with such as Stevenson and Brunel, but unlike them, seems to have sunk to near oblivion. His many engineering achievements included design of Liverpool's Mersey Docks and construction of the Newry Canal, the latter being completed between 1736 and 1741. On the political front, he became

Oldbride canal Br. 2013 - new concrete flat deck constructed on old stone abutments; this will be a major impediment to larger craft using the canal.

elected Mayor of Liverpool in 1739. Thomas Steers died in Nov. 1750, soon after completion of Oldbridge Lock.

This lock proved troublesome during earlier years because of many fresh water springs beneath its foundations. The Commissioners of Public Works rebuilt it entirely from stone in the period 1834-1837. It is difficult to ascertain a precise level from the OS Benchmark on the lower gate's stonework, marked on the old maps at either elevation 10.2ft or 19.2ft. As the lower figure is inconsistent with that noted on the next lock upstream at Stalleen Lower (31.2ft) and the overall lift to Navan, I will opt for the higher number of 19.2ft. This would reflect the pound level taking the canal section into the open river above Oldbridge navigation weir, and then to Stalleen Lower Lock; with minor discrepancies explained by variations in the river levels. The lift/drop at Oldbridge Lock varied because of tidal conditions, with the lock chamber receiving upstream bound, laden vessels only at a minimum of half maximum tide.

According to Griffith's, the Boyne Nav. Co. held c.19.6 acres of canal and banks in fee at Oldbridge; together with the attendant Lockkeepers' house at R.V. £2-10s. The Lock-house is located on a small site across the road (0.393

Oldbridge Sea Lock - 2012

acre), and has been extended and modernised. The house is two storeyed and was originally of similar construction to the Lock-houses at Stalleen Lower and Broe, perhaps reflecting a different ethos during initial construction of the Lower Boyne waterway.

The valuation does not name an occupant in 1854; however, other records indicate the house being occupied by James Farnan in 1788, Michael Tiernan in 1834, Joseph Tiernan in 1860 and Nicholas Tiernan in 1900. The Tiernan family's long occupancy explains why the lock is known colloquially as Tiernan's Lock.[4] In contemporary times, Joe Tiernan of the Lock-house sponsors a perpetual trophy, known as the Tiernan Cup, for which Boyne anglers competed over the years. Oldbridge Lock has been restored by canal enthusiasts and was due to re-open in summer 2012.

In summary, the Lower and Upper Boyne Navigations had a total of nineteen locks during their operational life. As noted earlier, another lock named Ligpulse seems to have existed for a time but was perhaps demolished in the 1790s.

The locks were divided into two categories; namely, lift/lowering locks and guard locks, the latter were to protect the waterway from floods or potential damage caused by failure of the lower gates or rampart wash-out. Starting at the tideway, the lifting/lowering locks are named Oldbridge Lower (or Sea Lock), Stalleen Lower, Broe Lower, Rosnaree (double), Slane Castle Weir, Carickdexter, Cruicetown, Castlefin or Rileys (Reilly's), Deerpark, Stackallan or Thomson's, Taaffe's and Rowley's. Ruxton Lock is located in Navan but did not increase the overall navigation lift, because it provided side access only, from the main canal to the Boyne below the Blackwater confluence at Navan.

From upriver, the guard locks were named Metge's (see other references in the chapter on the Navan/Dunmoe section), Stackallan, Slane/Fennor, Upper Broe, Upper Stalleen and Upper Oldbridge.

Discounting the lift at Oldbridge Sea Lock and working from its Benchmark at 19.2ft (full), the navigation provided a total lift of circa 94.6ft., from this level to the Benchmark at 113.8ft on the upper lock gate at Metge's Lock in Navan. Although the rise varied somewhat at each lock, the total figure represents an average lift of about 7.8ft on each of the 12 lift/drop locks from Oldbridge to the summit level at Navan. The shortest single lock measured 86ft. and the longest 141ft., with the double lock at Rosnaree having a length of 208.75ft. The breadth of the narrowest lock was 14ft. 11in. with the widest being 15ft. 2in. These dimensions suggest that no vessel in excess of circa 80ft. long by 14.5ft wide could make the full transit to Navan.

Other lock names on the Lower Boyne, such as Roughgrange, Newcomen's, Knowth and Fennor are mentioned in Cyril Ellison's book, these were perhaps altered to the above-listed names, as they are not depicted on maps or sketches.

Back on the main river, we encounter Oldbridge Fish-weir (nowadays known as Marry's Weir) below the navigation weir at Oldbridge. Starting from the approximate mid-point of the navigation weir in County Meath; it runs slantwise downriver to link with the Meath riverbank, just across from the Mattock River confluence in County Louth. The weir nowadays poses much the same hazards to river navigation as does its counterparts upstream at Stalleen, Dowth and Rosnaree; the Boyne hereabouts forming several channels winding between a maze-like series of islets. The complexity of the older network is increased by submerged concrete walls added-on to the system as eel traps in more recent times; some of which run across the mouth of the Mattock. Here again can be seen the narrow passes, or slots, described previously at the upriver fishing weirs; they run from mid-river, opposite the Mattock, to the Meath riverbank at Oldbridge.[5]

Similar to the upstream fish-weirs, this weir is very old, the original dating from early Norman times and owned by the monks of Mellifont from c.1200 AD until dissolution of the monasteries in the mid-16th century. Ancient records show the monks were granted a new charter for their possessions in the area in 1203, including their fisheries on the River Boyne. At the dissolution about 1539, the old records show that Mellifont Abbey had 16 Boyne corracles or corrachs in operation at Oldbridge, which were valued at £13-6s. Like the fishery at Ballinacrad, the fish-weir in Oldbridge appears to have a troublesome and strife-torn history; the following extract is quoted from an account published in 1953 by the County Louth Archaeological Society:

On 18th September, 1349 the King confirmed all and every grant made from time to time to this abbey. A few years later, in 1358, the Abbot obtained judgement in his favour in an action regarding his three fishing weirs at Rosnaree, Knowth and Staghlyn. At this time Reginald Lynagh was abbot and in 1366 he was indicted at Trim for erecting a weir in the river Boyne at Oldbridge. The jury found That from the time of the arrival of the English, the King had a certain free passage in that river from the town of Drogheda to the bridge at Trim, usually called a watersarde, 24 feet in breadth from the bank on each side of the river, according to the discretion of twelve honest men, six of the neighbourhood of one side and six of the other, and that through that aperture, boats called corraghs, with timber for building and flores had liberty to pass constantly free from Drogheda to the bridge of Trim; they also found that no weir had been erected there for upwards of thirty years; the court then ordered the weir to be totally removed for the said breadth of twenty-four feet and the abbot to be committed to gaol. (sic)[6]

The record goes on to tell of the abbot being released subsequently upon payment of a fine amounting to £10. This punishment had little effect; however, because his successor was indicted for a similar offence three years later. In more modern times, Griffith's shows the fishery at Oldbridge leased by William Malone from Henry Coddington at R.V. £45 in 1854 – the tideway fishery was leased by Richard Rourke from George Ball at R.V. £30 in the same year.[7]

ENDNOTES

1   Decorative, castellated gatehouse erected c.1858 and named after mother of William Drummond Delap, owner of Monasterboice House.

2   The Devlin or Devlins River coalesces with the Mattock just above Rossin Mill. This tributary rises in a series of rills that coalesce in Creewood Townland and flow south-eastwards through Sallygardens to Higginstown (where it powered a corn mill), then passed beneath Devlins' Br. on the Slane/Collon road, and onwards to its confluence with the Mattock in Keerhan Townland.

3   The Down Survey Barony of Ferrard (Co. Louth) map depicts a bridge on this location – the structure, named Matoge Bridge, is detailed by two parallel lines and is an indication that this was an ancient crossing.

4   A list of Lockkeepers, compiled for Meath Co. Council's Road Committee in 1913 for the liquidation of the waterway, shows the Reps. of P. Tiernan, Deceased, as the keepers at Oldbridge, and that they were in receipt of a quarter-annual salary of £2-2s. As at other locations upriver, the higher caretaker's salary here may reflect that the keeper was in charge of the guard lock, located a considerable distance upriver from the Lock-house.

5   Yeats' plan of 1834 and the 1911 map show a building sited on a spit of land upstream of the Horse Bridge – a walk along the riverbank revealed its ivy covered ruins hidden in the wildwood near the old fish traps. Perhaps it formed part of Oldbridge fisheries in bygone days.

6   Records such as these led to the myth of the Boyne being navigable between Drogheda and Trim. I suggest; however, that they merely signify extension of the King's Writ to the river between these towns – and, as outlined in Chapter 6, reflected local usage of boats for conveyance upon the river, rather than suggesting that the Boyne was navigable between Trim and the sea.

7   The 2012 book entitled *The Boyne Currach* by Claidhbh O Gibne, includes some more recent history of Oldbridge Fisheries.

20

Journey's End
The Tideway

Mattock Confluence – Oldbridge or Marry's Weir – Curly Hole & Townley Hall – King William's Glen – Oldbridge House – The Metal or Obelisk Bridge – The Boyne Obelisk & its demise – Fords & Road Network – Oldbridge Village – Battle of the Boyne – Grove & Yellow Islands – Drybridge (the mill) Ford & 'Pass if you can' – Estuary Waters – The Bridges of Drogheda – A Tale of Navan Divers & a Boat – The Boyne Viaduct – Concrete Boats – Estuary mills in Co. Louth & a modern 'limekiln' – Last watermill on Boyne – 'the Colpe' – Stameen corn-mill & windmill – Maiden's Tower & Lady's finger.

Crossing Oldbridge Navigation Weir we continued on downriver towards the Mattock confluence, now passing into the tidal reaches or tideway of the River Boyne. Here we pulled the boats ashore upstream from the tributary; providing an opportunity for the River Rescue lads to discuss our passage onward through the maze. While the navigators plotted the course ahead, we researchers surveyed our surroundings and marvelled at the wonderful landscape.

The boys decided to manhandle the boats across the weir, then we all trogged along the partly submerged concrete wall, across the mouth of the Mattock River to re-board our craft in County Louth. Passing through the narrow channel between Oldbridge Fish-weir and Louth's shore, we could

586

Boyne Corracles at Oldbridge - *c.* early 1900s

see the big bend downstream at 'the Curly Hole.' Gliding down the long, still reach towards our rendezvous, we were ever watchful for the many snags reported to be lying in wait beneath the tidal waters of the Boyne.

The Curly Hole is so named because of the effects tidal movements and river currents have on the Boyne water; where it turns abruptly through 90 degrees to head due east towards Drogheda. This enormous elbow creates current eddies which form whirlpool-like conditions on the river, thus giving rise to the unusual place name. The Navan to Drogheda road passes close by the river here and several tragic accidents occurred at this spot during the years.

We landed in the alder grove now growing on the riverbank at the Mullaroo Stream,[1] to be greeted by the River Rescue support team and some family members. While the team loaded the damaged boat onto the trailer, the rest of us had a soggy-sandwich lunch while discussing our exciting run down the river; meanwhile, the River Rescue boys from our boat received some more slagging concerning their *Titanic* moment. The interlude provided a welcome respite in which to stretch cramped muscles and observe the scenery from this picturesque setting in the Boyne Valley.

Across the road from where we stood are the gates of Townley Hall, once the densely wooded demesne and Georgian residence of the Townley Balfour dynasty. Griffith's records the property leased from the Marquis of Drogheda

Tiernans former Lock-house at Oldbridge Lock

at R.V. £490 in 1854; it consisted of house, offices, gate lodges and land totalling about 545 acres.[2] The lessee, Blaney Townley Balfour, held an additional 305 acres of plantation in fee at R.V. £185.

Townley Hall was built in the period from 1794 to 1798 for Blaney Balfour Townley lll and is famous for its Georgian Architecture; most notably the magnificent staircase. Of which feature Country Life magazine once noted: "There is nothing lovelier in the Georgian architecture of these islands than the rotunda and staircase of Townley Hall." The hall was designed by Francis Johnston, designer of the GPO in Dublin and foremost Irish architect of his era.

In contrast to the splendour of the building… local lore tells of a resident of this noted manor who suffered from eternal flatulence. Supposedly, the condition became so bad he took to his bed and could not be persuaded to arise by anyone, including his eminent family physician – and his retainers outside heard him pleading incessantly "Townley Hall… Townley Hall… doctor, I'll give you Townley Hall for a fart… just one little fart!"

Nowadays the old wooded demesne is a State-owned forest park of about sixty acres, and the magnificent building used as an event centre.

Northern abuttment & Iron latticework detail of the Obelisk Br. Dec 2011

The other crew having departed for Navan with the damaged RIB, we boarded our boat and headed off downriver to complete the journey to the estuary.

The Boyne Valley broadens below the Curly Hole, with the riverbank on the high northern or Louth shoreline covered by the great woodlands of Townley Hall. These woods extend downriver to King William's Glen; a deep defile named after King Billy, through which runs a stream and the road leading northwards towards Tullyallen and old Mellifont Abbey.[3] In olden times this glen was known as *An Alt* (or 'the Alt Ravine'), a name I believe derives from Ulster Gaelic and means a mountain glen or deep ravine. The 1911 OS map indicates a place named *Mill of Alt* located on the right side of the glen, several hundred yards up from the Drogheda road; although a building is not shown on the said map, this may have been the site of a mill in times past. Beyond the glen, the floodplain widens and the hillsides become less steep towards the M1 motorway and Drybridge.

On the southern, or Meath shore, Oldbridge House and demesne dominate the riverscape; the house was supposedly built originally by Dixie Coddington c.1750. This property is now owned by the Irish State and used as an Interpretive Centre commemorating The Battle of the Boyne. The floodplain is much wider and less steep on this side, with neatly manicured lawns rising gradually towards the house; which overlooks the navigation and the Boyne Bridge from its lofty perch atop the green hillside.

From top:

The Obelisk Shackleton Collection *c.*1896

The Obelisk rock Dec. 2011

This unusual bridge is named variously the Metal Bridge or Obelisk Bridge, because it is of wrought iron construction and crosses the river adjacent to the site of the former obelisk commemorating the said battle. The bridge is of the through-girder type, formed of top and bottom members and double layers of closely spaced diagonal latticing. It consists of two main girder sections, each forming a load-bearing frame weighing 28 tons originally, with inner edges of flanges spaced at 16ft; effectively limiting the road width to c.14ft. To allow for expansion and consequent movement, the single span of 120ft rests on 4 inch diameter rollers, bearing upon iron plates mounted on limestone abutments.

The south-western abutment is part of an older bridge, while the north-eastern abutment extended 28ft further into the river to reduce the free span. In 1869, the metal structure replaced an older wooden bridge, swept away by floods about 1867. The sections of ironwork, prefabricated in 1868 by Thomas Grendon & Co. in Drogheda, were then floated upriver on pontoons. Thomas Grendon operated a large engineering complex in Drogheda, reputedly employing about 800 persons in the 1840s. The facility included an iron foundry, locomotive and weighing scales manufactory, together with general metal fabrication and boat building yards.

Construction of this bridge was a joint venture between the Meath and Louth Grand Juries, the responsible authority then prior to the formation of County Councils in 1899. Samuel Searancke, Meath County Surveyor and John Neville, Louth County Surveyor, shared the responsibility for design of the structure; with Alexander Tate the civil engineer for Grendon & Co. Another engineer, named William George Strype, whose father managed Grendon & Co., became newly appointed chief engineer to the company c.1868 and worked on the project.

I note that of all the above engineers, Neville's name is the only one engraved on the bridge plaque; perhaps a reflection on the structure being built in County Louth and the intense local rivalry between the two counties. A trawl through the Grand Jury presentment books might disclose the cost of the project and name the stonemasons who built the new north-eastern abutments. During my youthful ramblings, I observed that the white-painted ironwork played host to much graffiti; including some less than complimentary nicknames for King Billy and the Pope, together with terms of endearment exchanged between lovers and wishful greetings to absent friends.

Passing beneath the bridge, I noticed a metal gantry hanging from the structure like a bird perch, slung there for maintenance purposes. Going on downriver, we came upon a single, white-hued large rock outcropping from the grassy riverbank immediately downstream of the northern abutment. Its ivy covered summit crowned by ragged remnants of a cut-stone plinth, pointing towards the grey, wintry sky. This is all that remains of the obelisk which dominated the Boyne's landscape hereabouts for almost two hundred years; standing 110ft (or 130ft) tall above the river in commemoration of King Billy's victory here in 1690.

The inscription on the plinth proclaimed the supremacy of King William, and included a declaration that Lionel Sackville, Duke of Dorset, Lord Lieutenant of the Kingdom of Ireland, laid the foundation stone in MDCCXXXVI (1736).

Although King Billy's admirers were loud in proclaiming the virtues of the Dutch-born monarch, their verbosity was not matched by an equal laxity of pocket for maintenance of the monument – as evidenced by the following excerpt from *The Journal of the Royal Society of Antiquaries of Ireland;* Fifth Series, Vol. 5 No. 2 (Jun. 1895), pp. 180-181.

For some years past the obelisk had been in a dangerous condition for want of pointing. There was a serious crack running through several courses of the stones; grass was growing between the stones at the basement, and dislodging them; the monument had the appearance of having been struck by lightening, and had evidently suffered from the effects of frost. I had been assured by Sir T. Deane that if no steps were taken to preserve it, the monument would fall.

As the Board of Works were unable to undertake the charge of the monument, Col. Coddington and I made ourselves responsible for the work, which is being executed by Mr. Faulkner, electrician, from Manchester, under the superintendence of Mr. Fuller.

We require a little over £100, and if any of our Members are disposed to assist in the preservation of this historical monument, I shall be happy to receive their contributions.

We have carefully avoided giving the matter a political or sectarian aspect – B. R. Balfour, Townley Hall, Drogheda, June 22nd, 1895.

The destruction of the monument, just over a quarter century later, is shrouded in myth and legend, which give varying accounts of the date and affiliation of those responsible. One article researched mentions July 1921, another June 1923 as the date when the granite obelisk bit the dust. However, the most likely date is 2nd June 1923, although the Meath Chronicle 100 Year Book reported it happening in May that year.

For many years it was widely believed that the Old IRA destroyed the monument; some even blaming Irregulars (anti-treaty forces) during the Irish Civil War. Another story tells of how, in the 1970s, retired officers of the Irish Army admitted responsibility for the deed, executed while they were serving members of the Irish Free State Army in June 1923. Supposedly, they were part of the local garrison in Drogheda at the time, and blew up the symbol of Protestant supremacy in retaliation for organised, sectarian attacks on Catholic communities in Derry and Belfast.

While further research might establish the exact date of the monument's destruction, I doubt that the full truth will ever emerge at this remove; because of the many myths and conflicting accounts surrounding the event to this day. Like General Tom Barry stated in his biography regarding the number of Old IRA active in the field during the War of Independence (1918-1922):[4]

> that during the actual fighting, scarcely a couple of hundred Volunteers participated, but when it came to claiming pensions, sure you could fill Croke Park with the numbers signing up. *(paraphrased)*

Another colloquial story tells of events reputedly occurring on the night of the big bang all those years ago. An old gentleman named Heeney, nicknamed 'the Pope' and occupier of the property upon which the obelisk stood, lived just a short distance away alongside the Slane to Drogheda road. On the night in question, armed men knocked on his door and requested him to leave his home, because they intended to blow up the spike and were fearful lest he get injured. Luckily he took them at their word, as all his windows were blown out (or in) by the resultant blast, heard for miles around, some say even as far distant as Slane. The explosion lifted the monument from its plinth, and dropped it across the road, some of it falling into the Boyne to the west of the bridge. It is somewhat ironic that pieces of the carved plaque, extolling the virtues and invincibility of King Billy, were to be found scattered all over the Pope's field until recent times.[5]

Griffith's shows that in 1854 the site upon which the obelisk stood was part of a property of 133.76 acres, leased by Judith Heeny from Catherine O'Neill at R.V. £140. The same Judith Heeny held other properties in the area; including a house and forge sub-leased to one Patrick Taafe at R.V. 15s. This forge was one of the few Smithies denoted on the 1837 OS map by a horseshoe symbol; it was sited further along the road towards Drogheda, just beyond the junction where once the access road to Oldbridge Ford on the Boyne branched from the Slane to Drogheda road.

During drainage work in the summer of 1837, an ancient boat (Boyne Cott) was found buried beneath the mud and shingle near the obelisk. The craft, carved from a single section, was about 18.75ft long, 2.25ft wide and flattened at bow and stern. Though no oars were discovered, grooves found fore and aft provided evidence that the boat was propelled by sculls.

Below the Obelisk rock we come to the ford of Oldbridge, once the main theatre of operations during the Battle of the Boyne. The ford was located midway between the bridge and the westernmost tip of Grove Island. Griffith's shows this island of 5.76 acres held in fee by Henry B. Coddington at R.V. £3-5s. In olden times, the route across this 'Y' shaped ford turned eastwards and ran alongside the south side of the Boyne to Rathmullan and Drogheda. I suspect that another branch led southwards towards Sheephouse and Donore, (perhaps the *lane* mentioned in various accounts of the battle at Oldbridge in 1690) and branched again to head westwards towards Farm and the ford at Proudfootstown.

As described in the previous chapter, the stone arched bridge beside the entrance gateway to Oldbridge House, once carried the route from the ford across the canal, but this has been replaced by a modern structure in recent times. The now defunct road would have passed through Oldbridge Village, some buildings from which have been identified and re-structured on their original foundations as part of the Oldbridge heritage project.

The bodies of Reinard, Duke of Schomberg and Colonel Callemote (Callimotte), leader of the Protestant French (Huguenots), were reputedly buried between the site of the old village and the gate lodge of Oldbridge House. Both men were killed at the river crossing on July 1st 1690 (old Julian calendar). Various elements of the Williamite army crossed at the main ford, the westernmost tip of Grove Island and the shallows at Grove and Yellow Islands, with King Billy crossing further east near Drybridge.

This brings us to the Battle of the Boyne. It is with reluctance that I delve further into this event, but, like the elephant in the room, it cannot be ignored.

Though, in military terms, 'the Battle' was scarcely more than a series of skirmishes, its consequences resonated throughout the land for many generations. Indeed, it can still be heard on 'the green, grassy slopes of the Boyne,' when the rattle of musketry and thunder of cannon echo along the valley during commemorative occasions at Oldbridge.

Studying such events from the past, one should be ever mindful of the old adage: "to the victor go the spoils." However, the equally valid corollary, that: "the victor also writes most of the history books," is seldom quoted. The many, varied and sometimes contradictory accounts of the battle; therefore, often reflect more the hubris of the victors in the aftermath, rather than factual events of the engagement.[6]

To place the event in its military and historical context, I will quote from Wilde, who studied the battle in great detail, and indeed, unlike several other authors, explored the topography upon which it was fought. These writings were recorded during the 1840s; in times closer to the conflict; therefore, more relevant than what we observe nowadays through the misty window of history, clouded further by revisionism and more recent happenings.

The following are several short excerpts constituting a brief synopsis of the battle as recorded in *The Boyne and the Blackwater* (2nd edition):

> Heretofore, the descriptions of the battle of the Boyne have been almost all one-sided, being, for the most part, written by violent partisans, pandering to the vanity of one party and exciting the sensitiveness of the other. The authorities from which the historians drew were nearly all Williamite; but within the last few years the gleaners in this department of Irish history have had access to documents written by officers in the Irish army and others in every way worthy of credit, and which must now induce the calm searcher after truth to very much modify some, and altogether reject other statements put forward by the former, and which have been generally received as facts. To give these latter their fair share of merit, and to weigh and discuss the adverse statements of both parties, would not suit the intention of the present work, and would require a more critical examination of the subject than our space would warrant.

> We should like, 'tis true, to fight this battle in detail, and to record the gallant deeds of the O'Neals and Schombergs, – the Callimottes and Sarsfields – of Berwick, Sidney, Ginkle, Geraldine, Hamilton, and others who have left material for many a tribute to their fame. But this, at present, is denied us; perhaps some other day we'll try our hand at this "grievous battle," so bravely fought by a comparatively young, but experienced general – gallant in the field and wise in council, with a highly disciplined army, a part of which had been trained in many a hard contested battle in France and Flanders, then the great battleground of European warfare, – against a weak and vacillating

prince, advanced in years, and borne down by misfortune, neither wise in council nor gallant in action, remaining in the rere of, but not commanding an army, which, however great its devotion, was totally unable to cope with its opponent.

The army of King William amounted, according to the most moderate calculation, to 36,000 men; some authorities make it upwards of 40,000; all well-disciplined soldiers; numbers of them tried veterans, whose prowess had been tested and their courage schooled in many a well-fought field in Europe; hardy warriors, well-appointed, and comprised of the greatest number of nations that ever fought for or against the crown of England before or since – Danes, Dutch, Swedes, and Flemings, Swiss, French Huguenots, English, Scotch, Anglo-Irish, and Germans, – led by some of the most esteemed officers of the day, the two Schombergs, Douglas, Sidney, and La Mellionere, and commanded by one of the greatest generals of the age, personally brave, energetic, and well-skilled in war. The Williamite force, being chiefly composed of mercenaries, was less likely to be influenced by any feelings of loyalty towards the deposed sovereign than if it had been entirely English.

To this was opposed an army scarcely three and twenty thousand strong, a large portion of which, the French excluded, was composed of raw levies; undisciplined, and but ill supplied with arms and money; under generals no doubt brave and skilful, but whose interests were so constantly clashing that it was with great difficulty they could ever be brought to act in unison; and moreover commanded by a Prince whose weakness, imbecility, and bigotry, had already lost him a crown, who was totally unskilled in war, and whose heart was not in the country nor the cause of the men who fought for him. Either in order to secure a retreat, or fearing the issue of the engagement, James sent off all the baggage, and six of his twelve field guns, to Dublin, the night before the battle, and dispatched a trusty messenger to the south to prepare a vessel for his departure.

Wilde goes on to summarise the battle casualties and examine its symbolism as follows:

> The numbers killed at the battle of the Boyne were not considerable, when we take into account the amount of the belligerents, and that the engagement and retreat lasted nearly twelve hours. On the Irish side it is stated to have been upwards of a thousand, and upon the English above four hundred. The orange and green have long been party words in Ireland; – are our readers aware of the fact, that while the Irish troops wore pieces of white paper, the livery of France, every English soldier was decorated with a branch of green.

Oldbridge House has been acquired by the Irish State and restored; the site used nowadays to commemorate the battle of 1690. It is ironic; therefore, that during these post Celtic Tiger frugal times, when our elderly citizens and children are deprived of vital medical assistance and hospital wards are closing almost daily; hard-pressed Irish taxpayers are contributing unwittingly towards the costs of celebrating a defeat. Although the battle of July 1st 1690 was only one of several fought during the so-called Williamite War to determine which foreign king wore the crown of England; defeat of King James had a huge negative impact on the predominantly Catholic population of Ireland. It led to the demise of the Catholic Stuart dynasty, thereby reinforcing Protestant supremacy within the ruling elite in Ireland.

Preceded by Cromwell's savage campaign following the 1641 rebellion; defeat at the Boyne led to the slaughter at Aughrim in 1691 and the Treaty of Limerick, broken shortly thereafter by the said ascendancy. Over one hundred and thirty years of religious persecution ensued during the new penal law era (c.1695-1829). These unjust 'laws' provided the background to the rising of 1798, our loss of national sovereignty through the Act of Union in 1801 and Emmet's 1803 rising. There followed the Great Hunger, or ethnic cleansing of the Cottier class (1845-1850); the Fenian uprising and land war era, the Easter Rebellion in 1916, the Anglo Irish War of Independence, including the Black and Tan terror campaign (1918-1922); the Anglo Irish Treaty and Irish Civil War.

The more recent events in Ulster can trace their lineage to the happenings on the Boyne in July 1690. So what are some Irish people celebrating at Oldbridge… is it the defeat of a previously deposed foreign monarch at the head of, but not leading a rag-tag army of mostly raw recruits – or the victory of a Dutch-born king, whose army, comprised mostly of foreign professional mercenaries, won the English crown. Maybe it is neither; perhaps we Irish are once more demonstrating our inability or reluctance to learn the lessons of history? I believe that in this context, the current proposal to rebuild the Boyne Obelisk, especially following the events of the past several years, sadly, tends to indicate that we have learned little from our bloodstained back trail.

Local legends tell of the former battleground becoming a veritable Mecca for treasure hunters in succeeding years. The discarded weaponry and accoutrements, buried in pits close by the river, became much sought-after souvenirs, which, it is said, led to virtual grave-robbing of the various sites. In the early to mid-1800s, a great flood on the Boyne stripped much of the soil from the floodplain, exposing the remains for all to see.

Passing over the shallows at the ford and through the main channel around the north of Grove Island, we came to Yellow Island. This island of c.16.26 acres is shown by Griffith's to be occupied by John Roche and leased from Henry B. Coddington at R.V. £9-10s. It shows also that the adjacent Oldbridge Demesne, including buildings and land totalling about 600 acres was held in fee and occupied by the said H. B. Coddington at R.V. £735. These two larger islands are almost indiscernible from the river aspect nowadays, but can be traced clearly on the OS maps. The main river channel passes to the north of Grove, then winds to the south of Yellow Island; between the two are several smaller islets impeding the river passage.

An unusual feature is shown on the OS maps at the junction of the river road with the road leading down through Sheephouse from Donore Village. On the north-western corner, the maps show a series of ten plots or allotments on a rectangular site next to the junction. These are recorded on Griffith's 1854 valuation as leased from H.B. Coddington and occupied variously by John Mullins, William Reynolds, James Nugent, William Malone, Thomas Magennis, Owen Maguire, James Lynch, Thomas Mc.Cullagh and Laurence Mc.Donnel. Six sites are listed with house, offices and gardens, two with house and gardens and two with gardens only. This is interesting from an historical aspect, as the little cluster (traditionally known as 'the Street') is located only a short distance to the east of the former older village of Oldbridge, the epicentre of the battle in 1690. Several modern dwellings occupy this site nowadays.

Continuing the downriver journey, we passed through a gap in the islets and along the main channel south of Yellow Island, then onwards by Oldbridge Lock. Below the lock, we come to a laneway leading up through the woods on the southern riverbank to Oldbridge Concrete Products, a firm much advertised as 'located beside 'the New Bridge.' The OS maps show this lane providing access to some dwellings, including a place named Crockfean.[7]

We went onwards beneath the new M1 Motorway or Millennium Bridge (renamed the Mary McAleese Bridge), supposedly the longest suspension bridge in Ireland, to pass the site of the navigation's No. 2 milestone and come to the old ford on the Boyne near Drybridge. Known to some as the Mill Ford, it was perhaps named after a mill nearby on the Kinneas River. This is the place where King Billy reputedly crossed the Boyne on July 1st 1690. These type fords were sometimes called 'pass if you can,' as they were treacherous and uncertain crossing places, passable only during specific times and river conditions – perhaps explaining why this area was known as Pass in older times.

The Taylor and Skinner road maps of 1778 show fords named such in various places throughout Ireland, most notably near Kilsallaghan in North County Dublin, where a place retains that name to the present day. Drybridge is located on the Slane to Drogheda road, and probably derives its name from a crossing point on a stream (Kinneas or Kenny's River) flowing from the north-west of Barnattin (near Red Mountain), past *Tobar na Solas* and beneath the bridges at Waterunder and Drybridge to the Boyne through 'the Aills Ravine. The old ford on the Boyne was located near where the higher road from Rathmullan swings down to the southern riverbank. Traces of the old road system can be discerned on the older OS maps, between the Slane/Drogheda road and the northern riverbank.

The navigation towpath continued from here to Drogheda, following the southern riverbank to the town. Yeats' plan of 1834 shows an 'old toll gate' at the place where the previously-mentioned high road from Rathmullan swings down to the river and runs alongside the Boyne to Oldbridge. This might suggest that the navigation track-way was subject to a toll in days gone by; or, as it was located at 'the Mill Ford,' it may have been one of the many cess and toll collection points mentioned in D'Alton's 1844 history of Drogheda.

This section of defunct towpath nowadays provides a beautiful riverside walk leading to Drogheda. The 1911 OS map indicates the No. 1 navigation milestone located on the towpath below the salt marsh, directly in line with Mell School on the opposite riverbank. This marker stone was supposedly sited one mile upriver from the Bridge of Drogheda (St. Mary's Bridge). Griffith's shows the Boyne Nav. Co. held circa 2.75 acres of track-way in fee at Rathmullan, which was exempt from charges.

Our river journey has taken us to the historic town of Drogheda, of which so much was written by many noted historians, it is beyond my compass to add further to the fount of knowledge. I will end our Boyne journey by taking the reader downriver and under the bridges of the ancient town, to where we left the estuary, seaward of the famous railway viaduct.

Below Drybridge, the river valley broadens further into the estuary proper. The high northern shore of Waterunder and Mell is altered completely nowadays, buried beneath a network of roads servicing the new motorway; with the landscape mostly denuded of woodlands and pock-marked by development. Likewise, the high-ridged southern aspect of Rathmullan and Ballsgrove provide further testament to the crazy days of Celtic Tiger Ireland's 'build over everything' approach to planning. Fortunately, the riverside walk along the southern shore compensates somewhat for the ravages inflicted upon the landscape over the past several years.

The river morphs gradually to an appendage of the Irish Sea while passing through this ever-changing scene. The upriver aspect of bog-lands, wooded hills, falls, weirs and turbulent rapids, where the Boyne rushes through gorges and then meanders lazily between pastoral parklands; now becomes a broader expanse sandwiched between scrub and reed-covered mudflats, sandbanks and shingle-encrusted shoreline. The river sounds change also, muted roar of weir and rapids; gurgle and ripple of rill, replaced by traffic noise drifting across the broader estuary reaches; punctuated by frantic, shrill cries of sea-birds seeking sustenance from the river, and diving for scraps thrown by children from the riverside pathway. A freshening sea-breeze and swelling tide forms wavelets on the placid waters; with spindrift carrying aft to sting eyes and caress one's lips with the salty tang of the sea.

Brendan and Hopper, made near redundant by the changing conditions; now became mere passengers like us, a welcome respite indeed from the arduous task of hauling our craft across the many obstacles along the Boyne's winding course – meantime, Martin opened up the throttle to maintain headway against the incoming tide.

The first bridge encountered at Drogheda is called 'the Peace Bridge' or Bridge of Peace, built in the mid-1970s. It was named in honour of 'the Women's Peace Movement of Northern Ireland,' whose members made valiant efforts to stem the tide of violence threatening to overwhelm Ulster during the period euphemistically referred to as 'the troubles.' In more recent times; however, this bridge has become famous for art/graffiti festivals and murals decorating its concrete abutments.

Further downstream we come to St. Dominic's Bridge, a low-level iron girder structure that once carried vehicular traffic, but nowadays is used for pedestrians only. John Neville, involved in design and construction of the Obelisk Bridge, designed this bridge which was completed in 1863. The bridge spans the river where, in 1783, Edward Cheshire was licensed to operate a passenger and goods ferry, plying between the Linenhall and Ballsgrove, whose ancient decorative gateway stands close by on the southern riverbank.

The bridge being so low and lacking in headroom, we had to lie almost flat to pass beneath on the rising tide. This casts some doubt on the popular belief that the lighters and barges on the navigation transhipped their cargos directly from ships moored at the docks. In my opinion, from 1863 onwards, goods bound upriver to Navan, may have required road transport from the docks to upstream of St. Dominic's Bridge; there to be loaded onto the barges that could not pass beneath the bridge on a high tide. Or perhaps fully laden lighters passed under the bridge at low tide, to await the rising tide, needed to navigate the river to Oldbridge.

Further downstream near the centre of the town, we passed beneath the Haymarket or John's St. Bridge; a modern structure overlooked by Celtic Tiger era apartments, a reminder of many upriver trips to Far-Eastern cities during my seagoing days.

Drogheda translates to Droichead-atha in Gaelic, which means 'the Bridge of the Ford.' Some historians believe that a bridge existed here before the coming of the Normans circa 1170s, and that the invaders either improved the old structure or built their own. Old annals record 'the Bridge of Drogheda' collapsing in Sept.1472 and being replaced by a wooden bridge supported on

From top: Under 'the Peace (Grafitti) Br.' Drogheda Dec. 2011
From Laurence Collection - Tall ships at North Quay Drogheda - date c. 1860 - 1883 -
Courtesy C. Ryan

stone piers, which was opened to traffic in 1506. This structure caused many problems over the following years and was replaced by a stone arched bridge, completed in 1722; it was supposedly constructed by Stephen Price of Clones and John Bencher at a cost of £3,000. This bridge was widened circa 1814, and later replaced by the stone arched St. Mary's Bridge in 1868. John Neville was involved also in the design and erection of this bridge; which in turn fell victim to the heavy traffic of the great north road and was replaced by a modern structure in recent years. One might well wonder what spectacle 'the Bridge of the Ford' will provide for future generations.

The journey through the near-empty docklands, once a heartland of industry, commerce and shipping, was a strange experience in the new millennium. Considered to be one of Ireland's busiest ports in days gone by, the docks of Drogheda provided also an escape route for many families fleeing 'the Great Hunger' of the 1840s and for several years thereafter. Perhaps, like the cathedral in Cobh, County Cork, the Boyne Estuary provided the last tangible memory of Irish shores for emigrants leaving to start new lives in England, America and Australia.

During the mid-1960s, I had a short flirtation with a boat in Drogheda prior to commencing my career as a marine engineer. A group of diving enthusiasts from Navan Subaqua Club purchased an old thirty-foot wooden trawler (built originally by Tyrrell's of Arklow), intending to use her for diving on some offshore wreck. The old Perkins engine being kaput, they acquired an equally old B.M.C. diesel, which they asked me to install and commission.

I recall those working on the boat at Kilcarn Waterworks were: Sean Donohoe, Donal Bradley, Davey Byrne, Robin Byrne, Paul Geraghty, Dermot Byrne, Joe Murray, Sylvester Roe and John Bradley. Part of the rebuild included a half deck and wheelhouse – Jack Sarsfield, a local carpenter and wheelwright, worked on this part of the project with the Subaqua Club lads. Jack was quite a character, who lived in a small bungalow at the Athlumney end of old Kilcarn Bridge, he was known to call this house Swamp Villa, because it was frequently inundated when the Boyne rose in flood.

The craft was launched eventually about the summer of 1968 and moored alongside Merchant's Quay in Drogheda. We cruised up and down the Boyne on her shakedown trip, and beneath the railway viaduct to the estuary;

everything went ok, but being all landlubbers then, we hadn't the nerve to take her out to sea. While I am uncertain of her voyages thereafter, I heard that she ran aground somewhere along the coastline.

I recalled this interlude of earlier days while passing beneath the latest version of St. Mary's Bridge and under the new futuristic looking footbridge (Hugh De Lacy Bridge)

We headed on downriver through the docklands, with Merchant and Steam Packet Quays to port and the Bull Ring, South Quays and former industrial heartland of the town to starboard. I passed along this reach of the river many years ago, when visiting the port several times on a tanker named the Rathowen (formerly the M.V. Alk) while serving with Dublin Shipping in the late 1970s. The few vessels owned by this company were popularly known as 'the Rat Boats,' not, I may add, that they were infested by rodents, but because their names all started with Rath.

This area is overlooked from the southern aspect by the 1808 Martello Tower of Millmount (now a museum), perched atop its high, green mound, reputedly the tomb of the druid, Amergin Mac Miled, bard of the Milesians. But looking eastwards towards the sea, the estuary is dominated by the massive and imposing bulk of the railway viaduct towering high above the river.

Like so many other features of the Boyne Valley, this structure is surrounded by myth and legend. The viaduct once carried the twin tracked Dublin to Belfast Railway across the Boyne Estuary (now single track configuration). The Dublin and Belfast railway (later the Great Northern Railway/GNR) line from Dublin to Drogheda was completed by 1844 and from the northern riverbank to Dundalk by 1849. But the gap formed by the estuary remained unbridged for several years thereafter. During the interim period, passengers wishing to complete the full journey in either direction were required to detrain and make the transit across the river via St. Mary's Bridge, then re-embark at the opposite terminus.

The many engineering challenges posed by the wide, muddy estuary, were exacerbated by the British Admiralty's requirement of 90ft headroom beneath for marine transport. The crossing; therefore, required enormous approach embankments and construction of a high bridge or viaduct, which commenced in 1851 and was completed in 1855. The structure consisting

From top: Inward bound Steamer about to pass beneath Viaduct c. early 1900s. Courtesy Paschal Marry; Aerial of viaduct - Courtesy Aubrey Martin 2016

6 of Southern arches on Boyne Viaduct - From Marsh Road Drogheda, 2011
Courtesy Pauline Holten

eventually of twelve 61ft span limestone approach arches on the south side, three latticed wrought iron girder spans across the river, and three limestone approach arches abutting the northern riverbank. The latticed sections comprised a 141ft span on either side of a 226ft central span; these were supported by enormous limestone free-standing pillars founded on more solid ground beneath the mud-line of the river. I believe the cut-stones forming the lighter-coloured arch rings were sourced from the White Quarry in Ardbraccan County Meath, with additional stonework obtained from a local quarry and another in Skerries.

Construction of the pillars in the riverbed caused a major delay to the project; and in turn gave rise to the long-lasting and prevailing myth that the Boyne Viaduct is 'built upon wool.' Normal construction of such piers necessitated the use of cofferdams or caissons to provide a reasonably dry habitat for the work and workers. Such containments were used for construction of piers 13 & 14, the main supports for the iron-latticed sections of the Boyne Viaduct. These caissons were rendered more watertight by use of woollen bales, vast quantities of which were employed in the project, thus giving rise to the urban legend, believed by some even in contemporary times.

Unfortunately, the bridge builders encountered an unexpected soft spot at the location of pier No. 14, where the oozy mud went deeper and no solid foundation existed at the expected depth. The railway company was under pressure to run trains on the line from Belfast to Dargan's Great Industrial Exhibition in Dublin, scheduled for May 1853. Consequently, the construction scaffolding was strengthened and the track-bed laid across the temporary structure. I believe the first train from Belfast crawled across the viaduct on May 11th 1853, its speed limited to 4 m.p.h. because of 'the temporary little arrangement.'

A solid foundation was found later for pier No.14 at a depth of circa 45ft below the mud-line (Evans had supposedly excavated to 30ft), with the pier being completed early in 1855 and the viaduct officially opened on April 5th of that year.

The concept for the viaduct's stone arched section is attributed to John Benjamin Macneill 1795-1880, engineer in charge, who also designed the rail viaduct at Navan. James Barton and A. Schaw were responsible for design of the lattice girder section. The £68,000 construction contract was awarded to William Evans in May 1851. The costly delays, caused mostly by the problems with pier No. 14, made Evans bankrupt and the project was completed by the railway company, with James Barton as engineer in charge of the works. The chairman of the company, Lord Charlemont, laid the foundation stone amidst much pomp and ceremony following completion of the structure; the original contract cost of £68,000 having risen to £123,000 by then.

A sequel to the story indicates the safety and strength of the viaduct being questioned as early as 1860 and again in 1900, when a speed limited of 20 m.p.h. was imposed. An inspection in the late 1920s revealed that the wrought-iron latticework was corroded, with the bridge; therefore, deemed to be unsafe. The GNR, with George Howden as chief engineer, constructed a new steel latticed bridge within the original structure; this work being executed without major impediment to rail traffic. The newer design is reflected in the arched top truss, or 'bowstring strut,' which in addition to giving extra strength to the structure, enhances the aesthetic quality of the viaduct as viewed from terra firma.

While gliding beneath the viaduct and close by pillar No. 14, I reflected that although its construction made William Evans bankrupt, he continued working in the bridge and railroad building industry. He took charge of the Canada Works in Birkenhead, established to build equipment for the Canada

Grand Trunk Railway (G.T.R.), which operated in Quebec and Ontario together with several states in the north-eastern USA. This railway system was precursor to the contemporary Canadian National Railways.

Below the bridge, we passed the spot where the hulk of an old concrete-hulled boat (Ferrow Concrete Boat or F.C.B.) lay upon the shingle-covered shoreline for several years during my younger days – this has disappeared and I wondered where it ended its days. Such concrete-built vessels have a surprisingly lengthy history, the first known being built in Southern France by Joseph Louis Lambot in 1848. These type boats were employed extensively during the steel shortages in both World Wars; most notably in the Mulberry docking systems used to support the Normandy landings in 1944. A fine example of these craft can still be seen in the River Moy near Ballina County Mayo.

There were several watermills located on the northern riverbank alongside the estuary between the viaduct and the bar. Two of these mills were near the former village of Wallace's Row in the townland of Yellowbatter, on an unnamed stream that rises near Killeneer and falls into the estuary at Greenhills. Details of these mills are as follows:

Upper Mill
Yellowbatter Townland Co. Louth: (1837) millpond & corn mill – (1911) Yellowbatter Mills – corn (G.V.1854) Lot 45a house, offices, mill and land totalling circa 2.6 acres, leased by Isaiah Moore from Henry Smythe @ R.V. £2-10s.

Lower Mill
Yellowbatter Townland Co. Louth: (1837) millpond & corn mill – (1911) not shown on OS map – millrace possibly demolished during construction of Newfoundwell Railway Br. (G.V.1854) Lot 43a house, offices, mill and land totalling circa 4.1 acres, leased by Thomas Moore from Henry Smythe @ R.V. £14-5s.

A third mill was located in Newtownstalaban Townland (detached part of Tullyallen), further downstream near the Boyne – detailed as follows:

Stalaban Townland Co. Louth: (1837) corn mill (1911) Newfoundwell Mill (corn) (G.V. 1854) Lot 37Aa house, offices, mill and land totalling circa 82 acres, leased by George McCarthy from Henry Smythe @ R.V. £185. N.B., a windmill 'in ruins' is depicted on the 1837 & 1852 maps, but not indicated on the map of 1911 – immediately downstream, the 1852 map indicates a large area denoted as a 'Cotton Weaving Factory,' marked on the 1911 map as Boyne Mills.

Downstream from here, just above Tom Roe's Point, we pass what once constituted 'the ultimate limekiln,' the former site of the Irish Cement Factory, which once spewed vast quantities of inert (and noxious) gasses into the sky above Drogheda. As a youngster, I recall standing on the Hill of Skryne, observing the white plume of gasses rising above the clearly visible stack silhouetted against the darker backdrop of the Coolee Hills... and wondering what it was all about. In more recent times; however, this concern was replaced by Premier Periclase, which extracts Magnesium from seawater taken from the estuary. According to well-documented internet blogs by local groups, this enterprise covers the environs of Drogheda with constant showers of white dust and other particulate matter. During my various worldwide rambles, I have seen many such messy industrial operations, usually sited in barren areas of India or Western Australia, but not in former beauty spots like the Boyne Estuary.

Passing on by Beaulieu (Bewley) Demense and its famous house, we come to the site of the last watermill on the Boyne, the furthest downstream from the first such mill located near the river's source in Carbury Co. Kildare. This mill was located in Banktown Townland near Braghan Bridge, on a small unnamed tributary that falls into the estuary at Baldoyle just above Baltray – the following are details gleaned from the maps and valuation:

> Banktown Townland Co. Louth: (1837) mill dam-pond & corn mill
> – (1911) buildings only & river ford (G.V.1854) Lot 3b – vacant mill,
> with no land attached owned by Joseph Wright @ R.V. £7-10s.

The most notable feature on the County Meath or southern shore of the estuary is an area named Colpe/Colp, reputedly named after Colpa, a son of Milesius, who drowned here in the Boyne during the mythological Milesian invasion in times past. Towards the end of the 12th century, Hugh DeLacy

Windmill stump at Stammeen

set up an Augustinian Monastery at Colpe, in this Diocese of Meath parish, situated within the Barony of Duleek and dedicated to St. Mary. The unmarked site of the monastic settlement is located in Colpe-east Townland, in a field behind Colpe House (Colpe Storage), to the south of the intersection of the contemporary Colpe Road and Mill Road.

Mill Road is named after a watermill and windmill combination, located several hundred metres north of the intersection, in the townland of Stameen. The windmill stump (known as Colpe Windmill) is well preserved and clearly visible from the roadway, but the watermill has disappeared entirely from the landscape. While I believe that mention is made of the windmill (complete with four sails) in Davis Ducart's engineering report to the Boyne Navigation Co. in 1766/67, I can find no record of the watermill on Griffith's 1854 valuation.

The watermill was powered by a small stream taking its rise to the west near Bryanstown Townland, and then flowing through Colpe to Stameen Townland. Here it formed a millpond to the west of Mill Road, with a weir or dam located immediately above the bridge. The tailrace re-entered the stream, which flowed by St. John's Well and on past 'Little Mornington' (Donacarney House) to fall into the estuary above the pier at Mornington Village.[8]

The 1837 OS map depicts the corn mill located in the glen to the east of the bridge. The 1911 map; however, shows no trace of the mill, but depicts the

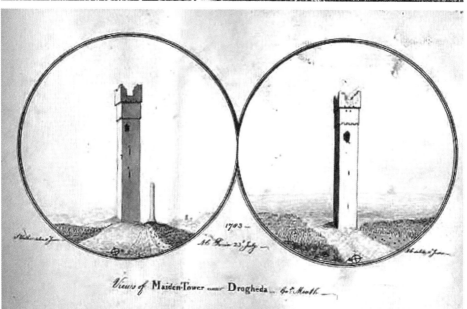

From top: Maiden Tower - From *Penny Journal*. Courtesy M.C.L.
Sighting line for bar using Maiden Tower and Lady's Finger - 1783 Courtesy M.C.L.

Steamer (with side paddle wheel) passing by Lifeboat house and Maiden Tower - name of vessel unknown, but it was perhaps the *PS Iverna* in the early 1900s - Courtesy M.C.L.

contemporary Glen House in the parkland to the south. At time of writing, a search of the wooded glen, by Paschal Marry, Tom French and me, failed to discover any trace of this long gone mill, the last such watermill upon the Boyne's fair banks within County Meath. The following are details gleaned about Stameen Corn Mill:

> Stameen Townland Co. Meath: (1837) mill dam, pond & corn mill
> – (1911) gate-lodge & avenue to buildings at site of windmill stump,
> with no millpond or corn mill indicated. Stameen House is depicted
> close by the former pond site on opposite side of roadway. Griffith's
> 1854 valuation records the site of the former corn mill thus: Lot 4a
> Herd's house, offices and land totalling circa 32 acres, leased by Francis
> Chadwick from Reps. of Thomas Wade @ R.V. £43-15s.

We end our journey with a brief visit to the mouth of the Boyne, the great maw of which opens between Baltray in County Louth and Mornington (or Mariners town) in County Meath.

Standing near the extremity of the South Bull peninsula are two stone edifices, one a circa 60ft high square tower, with castellated parapets, known as 'Maiden (Mayden) Tower' – the other a round, obelisk-like spire, topped in similar fashion to the round towers of old, and known as the Lady's Finger. While these towers are shrouded in myth and legend, it is likely that the Maiden Tower was constructed as a watchtower during the reign of Elizabeth l (early/mid-16th century), and the Lady's Finger at a later date. It is believed that their combination provided triangulation points to align ships with the channel through the bar and entry to the river, previous to construction of the river walls in the 1760s. To the north-west of Maiden Tower is the Victorian era Lifeboat House, closed in 1926 and now a private residence.

Returning upriver, the old town of Drogheda stood out against the lowering sun through the great spans of the viaduct as Martin turned our boat toward the slipway on the southern shore. Here we landed at the new Boyne River Rescue Base and packed up the boat. Then enjoyed the hospitality of the spanking new facilities over hot cups of soup; before departing homewards with wonderful recollections of our days spent resolving a few mysteries and rediscovering some lost history of the unexplored Boyne.

ENDNOTES

1 This stream rises in a pond NW of Townley Hall. It flows down through the Mullaroo Ravine ('the Old Glen' on 1911 map) – the ravine is one of three such defiles mentioned regarding deployment of the Willamite Army in 1690.

2 The incumbent Earl in 1854 was Henry Moore (1825-1892), 3rd Marquess of Drogheda.

3 I believe this road was constructed under the auspices of the Grand Jury in the period c. 1775 to 1800.

4 *Tom Barry: IRA Freedom Fighter* by Meda Ryan.

5 The Pope was so named because he was a member of the Irish Brigade that fought on the Papal side during the Garibaldi campaigns against the Papal States (wars for Italian re-unification) in the second half of the 19th century.

6 Another version of this adage says: "the oppressor writes the history whilst the oppressed compose the songs."

7 This lane may once have connected to Cloughpatrick (or Barrack) Lane on the northern riverbank, via another fording point on the Boyne at the eastern end of Yellow Island.

8 The 1656 down Survey Barony of Duleek map shows two watermills located on this stream in the vicinity of Mornington Village.

Postscript

Kilcarn Bridge – September. 2016
Mairéad Crinion & the Author
Damage and defects at several Boyne bridges were noted during various river trips while researching this book (2011-2015). Of particular concern were the public safety issues caused by the severe cracks in the pedestrian refuges at Bective Bridge, the degradation and impact damage at Old Kilcarn Bridge and a diagonal crack on 'the New Bridge' in Navan. These were reported to the relevant authority in a timely manner. 'The New Bridge' in Navan was repaired and maintained in July – Aug. 2015, Kilcarn Bridge is still under repair in Aug. – Sept. 2016 and the hazardous situation at Bective Bridge has not been addressed at time of writing in Sept. 2016.

In response to the ongoing damage, caused by the environment but exacerbated by lack of action in addressing the issues at Old Kilcarn Bridge, Navan and District Historical Society (N&DHS) agreed that two of its members, Mairéad Crinion and the author, research the issues involved and lobby the relevant authorities and other interested parties – this included several meetings. Due to poor results obtained from this process, a letter was dispatched to the editor of the *Meath Chronicle*. Most of its content was published as an article (entitled *Save Kilcarn Bridge – round two*) in their Sat. Feb 20th 2016 issue.

The said article included inter alia the following assessment of the bridge in 2015.

'Old Kilcarn Bridge consists of two free-standing structures, built side by side; it has been neglected for many years. The lack of care/maintenance is obvious in every aspect of the structure:

- Blocking up of the millrace and its two arches.
- Trees/ivy and shrubbery growing from within the joints.
- Failure to underpin river-arch pillars, similar to the bridges in Navan, Bellinter, Bective and Trim.
- Failure to repair gaps/cracks in barrel vaults stonework (intrados) and to point/plaster or spray-concrete same.
- Failure to repair and point stonework of parapets, copings, pedestrian refuges and spandrel walls.
- Failure to point/repair arch ringstones/voussoirs.
- Delays in removing flotsam/trees blocking arches."

It suggested the following course of action to preserve the bridge for posterity:

1. Repair all damaged cutwaters.
2. Underpin in concrete all pillars not previously so protected – complete same as per Trim Bridge.
3. Restore all the neglected stonework.
4. Erect a plaque/label stone detailing the history of the bridge.'

Remedial work on Old Kilcarn Bridge 2016

Previous descriptions of Old Kilcarn Bridge (in this book), list No. 01 arch and pier nearest to the Balreask or western riverbank; therefore, this convention is followed here to avoid confusion.

Meath County Council commissioned engineering consultants, Roughan and O'Donovan (ROD), as project supervisors – this firm prepared a preliminary work scope based on reports generated by consultant engineer Nicholas O'Dwyer (2012), and examinations/inspections conducted by

Meath Co. Co. engineers c.2014. The preliminary survey included a full inspection of the structure, together with a Bathymetric Survey profiling the sub-structure and underlying rock base. The preliminary work scope included inter alia the following: isolate the structure by stone causeways (bunds) constructed upstream and downstream of the bridge – pump out the work area – carry out archaeological survey – clear/rake out loose debris from each arch vault – remove calcite deposits (calcium carbonate or lime) from footings and bedrock – de-vegetate structure and arch barrel vaults – 'fabriform' concrete mats to fill scour channels at pillar footings so affected – construct reinforced concrete collars (anti-scour collars) around each of the nominated piers – repair damaged cutwaters – repair/replace missing stonework on arch barrel vaults – pressure grout all repaired piers and point all critical stonework. N.B., the initial scope did not include piers No. 01 & 02 at western riverbank, as low level concrete collars were installed on these (and a partial collar on pier No. 03) c.1980s by the OPW. It included one half of an anti-scour collar on the river-facing side of pier No. 09 (c.20ft wide buttressed retaining wall) but did not include any underpinning on pier No. 10 nearest to eastern bank.

The contract was awarded to Glass Civil Engineering and work commenced on the eastern end of the bridge in early Aug. 2016.

The work was conducted in two distinct phases:

Phase 01
This work was tackled from the eastern riverbank, and involved building temporary stone causeways/bunds from this bank both upstream and downstream of the bridge. The bunds converged on pier No. 05 (between arches No. 05 & 06 - as per our numbering). The River Boyne's full flow was diverted through the c. 11ft span western arches No. 01, 02 , 03, and the two c. 22ft span central arches No. 04 & 05 – these arches had an aggregate hydraulic capacity of approximately 78ft. This enabled completion of the full work scope on arches 09 to 06 inclusive – work scope on piers 09, 08, 07 and 06 was completed in this phase.

Phase 02

Due to wildlife habitat considerations, work access to the riverbank at this end of the bridge was confined to the new boat landing slip below the bridge. Towards the end of Aug. or early Sept. 2016, two temporary stone causeways/ bunds were constructed from the western riverbank and converged on pier No. 06 (between arches No. 06 & 07 - as per our numbering). The River Boyne's full flow was diverted through the c. 11ft span easternmost arches No. 09 & 08 and the c. 22ft span central arch No. 07 – these arches had an aggregate hydraulic capacity of approximately 45ft. This enabled completion of the full work scope on arches 01 to 05 inclusive, and any outstanding tasks on arch No. 06 – work scope on western abutments and piers 01, 02, 03. 04 and 05 was completed during this phase.

Site visits

Meath Co. Co. kindly facilitated us to visit the site and observe the work in progress. We were greatly impressed by the obvious professional approach used and the attention to detail evident in the planning and execution of this historic work. During these visits we examined the full bridge, observed both phases of the project and had informal discussions with the archaeologists and engineers on site.

The following notes are based on these discussions, previous research and our on-site observations:

1 We noted the stonework damage/defects as listed in the ROD scope of work.

2 That the underlying riverbed profile did not conform to that depicted on the Bathymetric survey (the bedrock here is at OS Benchmark level c. 32.5/33 metres above mean sea level).

3 That heavy calcite deposits were evident at footings level on all the piers – together with some evidence of mortar application higher up on the footings.

4   Heavy scouring in way of these mortar and calcite deposits – the scouring appeared to be more severe at piers No. 07 & 06 (our numbers).

5   When cleared of calcite depositions and lime mortar, it was evident that piers No. 04, 05, 06 & 07 (supporting the four older [1680/1720] c. 13 -13.5ft wide larger central spans), were founded upon broader stone-built footings. In some cases these footings were used to level the uneven underlying rocky shoals forming the base – this is perhaps a good indication that the earlier builders were aware of the effects of water scouring on such structures.

6   It was equally evident that different techniques were used on the 1729 upstream extension piers. These were largely founded on looser, rubble-type rock. As noted elsewhere, the upstream extension spans were constructed as free-standing entities, with no obvious interconnecting joints evident. The extensions were generally constructed from smaller stones, and their corbel stones protruded c. 2.5ft higher than those on the older structure.

7   In places, some mortar-type deposits were evident in the open joint, while these could indicate that the two bridge sections were once bonded by mortar, they may be the result of leaching from the unsealed spandrels and arch crowns.

8   Pier stub discovered beneath central arch No. 06. This was likely part of a pier supporting one of the spans of an earlier bridge, six of which were replaced by the existing four c. 22ft span central arches about 1680/1720. The jagged remains of the pier are roughly rectangular in shape with a triangular cutwater pointing upriver towards the south – the main rectangle (about 2 metres wide by c.1½ metres long) is located beneath the older downstream section, while the cutwater extends upriver into the space occupied by the extension on the other piers. Thus it would appear that the 1729 extension absorbed the original upriver cutwaters. The remnants of this pier prove beyond doubt that an earlier bridge, with smaller central arches, spanned the river at Kilcarn. It could originate from the Early

Norman Period nine arched bridge (c. 1180/1200), part of which was supposedly swept away by the great flood of 1330 – or indeed formed part of its post 1330 nine (or 11) arched replacement bridge.

9 No. 01, 02 & 03 arches and piers No. 01, 02 & 03 nearest Balreask/ Ballybatter end of bridge: as stated elsewhere in this book, the older (pre 1729) c.13.5ft wide section of these three arches and piers are likely survivors of the original Early Norman Period bridge. Previous research shows that in the early to mid-1400s, Parliament passed a 'Bridge Act' prescribing that all new bridges built thereafter were broad enough to carry roadways of 18-20ft. As the pre-1729 Kilcarn Bridge had a face to face width of c.13 - 13.5ft (exclusive of cutwaters), and carried a roadway c. 10.5ft wide, it was most likely built previous to this Act of Parliament. When examined in detail, the stonework on these three arches and pillars is different to that on the remainder of the structure. For example, the vertical risers, barrel vaults (intrados) and spandrel walls appear to be constructed from unquarried or 'field' stones. These aspects, together with the difference in the arch ringstones and the dearth of corbel stones, suggest that this section was built at a different (and earlier) period to the remainder of the pre-1729 structure. The arches here are similar in construction to the flood arch at the village end of Bective Bridge, which arch may indeed be the remnants of an earlier bridge. Unfortunately, as no archaeological survey seems to have been conducted prior to the earlier underpinning work, a definitive date for construction of this section may never be determined.

Artefacts found

The following artefacts were found within the immediate precincts of the bridge:

- Three bronze Gannesh (Hindu) statuettes (c. six inches tall) – source unknown.
- Several round musket balls – source unknown.
- Several flattened musket balls – source unknown.
- Several larger pieces of round shot – could be canister or grape shot – source unknown.

- A ring – source unknown.
- Section of a metal-winged trinket – source unknown.
- Several flattened pieces of lead – could be fishing weights.
- Part of an unidentified triangular shaped trinket – source unknown.

C. 16th century extension/Millrace arches

In his *The Dublin to Navan Road and Kilcarn Bridge* (c.1991), Peter O'Keefe concludes that Kilcarn Bridge was extended eastwards by construction of four c.11ft span segmental arches and three piers. He opines that this extension was built circa late 16th century, and that it coincided with construction of the corn mill at Lower or Greater Kilcarn. This effectively increased the length of the post 1330 nine arched replacement bridge to a thirteen arched structure.

The eastwards extension included the contemporary No. 11, 10, 09 and 08 arches, together with piers No. 10, 09 and 08 (our numbers). Piers 10 and 08 are c.7.5ft wide, while pier 09 is circa 20ft in width – as such it could be described more accurately as a buttressed retaining wall or short embankment. On the northern façade it is faced by a vertical buttress with an inclined top matching the other downstream cutwaters, while the southern façade is faced by an extra-large cutwater with a pedestrian refuge at parapet level. Arch No. 09 has a unique (for Kilcarn Bridge) string course running just above the arch crown on its northern facade, while arch No. 08 has a single flat slab deployed in similar fashion above its eastern sector – the purpose for these is hard to define, but they may have been used to reinforce the spandrel walls and parapets.

Others have said that the wider pier/buttressed retaining wall was necessitated by and built atop a small islet in the river – but it was more likely part of the embankment/causeway leading onto the eastern end of the original shorter and narrower bridge. It is possible the four arched extension was built in two phases and at slightly different times, or, indeed, that the post 1330 replacement bridge consisted of eleven arches and that the eastern extension was comprised of the two mill tailrace (No. 10 & 11) arches only. The different construction details of the tailraces arches (evident in their older, downstream facades), supports this proposition. Which in turn suggests that the wider pier was employed as part of the tailrace rampart – there is considerable anecdotal and some cartographic evidence that the mill tailrace ran downstream from the bridge, to re-enter the river at the old eel/fish traps below Athlumney House (shown in graphic form but not named on the 1911 OS map). Its purpose being to enhance the differential water head across the waterwheel, thereby keeping the mill operational during elevated river levels – at nearby Rathfeigh (Delany's) Mill on the Hurley River, the tailrace returned to the main river about one kilometre below the mill. Unfortunately, the post 1968 arterial drainage scheme altered the riverbank hereabouts, so this remains a moot point at Kilcarn Mill.

Following on from our on-site discussions, Meath County Council decided to include the eastern half of pier No. 09 and the entire pier No. 10 within the scope of work, together with arches No. 10 and 11. The new work scope included inter alia: de-vegetation, repair/renewal of defective stonework and pressure grouting the refurbished piers. This should make them fit for purpose as flood arches only, because installation of anti-scour collars was not included at this stage.

While the original and increased work scope fulfils our initial aims and objectives to preserve the bridge for posterity, it falls somewhat short of our final goal... to have the river realigned such that the Boyne flows through all eleven arches. The following is an excerpt from a letter we wrote to Meath County Council in 2016:

'... I have witnessed the Boyne in its many phases; from the great flood of Dec. 8th 1954 to its half flood earlier this year. In 1954, even though the two mill tailrace arches were open, several of the smaller arches were covered completely and 'suck- holes' (or water vortexes) formed – I am of the opinion that the bridge survived only because of its large hydraulic capacity. In this context, I believe that the hydraulic capacity of the bridge should be guarded jealously to enhance its survival prospects. Recent installation of the anti-scour collars necessitated losing approximately 22ft of its throughput capacity at normal to lower flood levels – thus the overall hydraulic capacity of the bridge is reduced by circa 44ft when the closed off mill tail race arches are considered...'

We thank the following for their assistance and courtesy during our work site visits: Meath Co. Co. staff, especially engineer Paul Mc'Nulty – Gerry White and his staff (of Glass Civil Engineering), and the consulting archaeologists on site. A special thanks to Councillor Joe Reilly, who took the trouble to meet us at Kilcarn Bridge, April 2014 – and for his support of this book's publication.

Final notes on Kilcarn Bridge

Extensive research of the older road network for the books, entitled *Where Tollroads Meet* and *On Ancient Roads*, and more recent studies of Kilcarn Bridge, led me to form the following opinions on the ancient river crossing at Kilcarn:

The exact location and importance of this river crossing has been lost in the mists of time. In pre-medieval and later times, fords on the Boyne hereabouts allowed passage for several of the five great roads and their offshoots, radiating across the landscape from Tara. These fords included Ballyna or Bective – Ath Sidhe or Assey – Ardsallagh or Ath Sallagh – Ballagh/Ballybatter (opposite Kilcarn) and the Ford of Athlumney. N.B., while many consider that Athlumney Ford crossed the Boyne at Kilcarn, I believe that Athlumney (Navan) Ford was located in Limekilnhill Townland at (or close by) a place known as 'the Slip' (see details in Chap. 09) – and that another ford was sited upstream of Old Kilcarn Bridge. This ford probably crossed the Boyne between the later sites of the Kilcarn new bridge and Lower Kilcarn Mill, and was the probable source of the old townland names of Ballagh (114 acres - 37 perches) and Ballybatter (92 acres - 22 perches).

The relative angle of the contemporary Old Kilcarn Bridge to the river's flow, suggests that the Boyne's main channel was once located in the floodplain closer to the western Ballagh/Ballybatter riverbank ridge. The present, and more easterly river line, was created by redevelopment of the mill at Lower or Greater Kilcarn i.e. from a modest corn mill in the late 16th century to 'the Big Mill' (flour) of the early 1700s. It later diversified to become a dual purpose mill, scutching flax and producing flour. These phases of development necessitated construction of the great weir, the head and tailrace river ramparts, the two easternmost arches on Old Kilcarn Bridge and probably the tailrace rampart downstream to Athlumney eel/fish traps.

These developments totally altered the original riverscape and eliminated all traces of the ford hereabouts.

Old Kilcarn Bridge probable evolutionary path
The recent examination of the old bridge has reinforced my views that the present structure possibly evolved in the following phases:

1 Pre-Norman
   Possible combined Pace and Cesdroichet (wickerwork bridge)

2 Early Norman (1180 – 1200)
   First stone bridge (uncertain parameters)

3 Post 1330
   Replacement narrow bridge of 09 (or 11) arches

4 Late 1500s
   Eastwards extension/mill tailrace arches – Narrow bridge with 13 spans

5 Late 1600s/early 1700s
   Replacement of six c.11ft spans by contemporary four c.22ft central spans
   – Narrow bridge with 11 arches

6 C.1729
   Upstream extension added for turnpike status –
   Contemporary structure of 11 spans

From top:
Stub of pillar from earlier bridge – possibly Early Norman.
No. 03 arch downstream façade – Possibly Early Norman pre-1330

From top:
Phase 01 Aug. 2016 – Working on arches No. 07, 08 & 09 on eastern upstream end
Phase 02 Sept. 2016 – Working on No. 04 (c.22ft span) arch on western upstream end

From top:
Downstream façade – Phase 01 Aug. 2016

Upstream façade – Phase 01 Aug. 2016

One of the three bronze elephant
statuettes found beneath the bridge

From top:
Phase 02 Sept. 2016 - Beneath No. 06 arch (note upstream extension joint)

Phase 01 Aug. 2016 – Eastern footings of N0. 07 arch pillar: note, scouring,
differences in footings substrate & varying height of corbel stones

From top:
Sept. 2016 – Mairéad Crinion and the author beneath No. 04 arch Old Kilcarn Bridge

Part of c. 1820 Longfield map of Kilcarn estate – Note the many interesting features, including:
the mill tailrace, weir, headrace and sluices – Kilcarn Mill fronted by the old turnpike road
– the Steward's Garden and adjacent house (perhaps once a staging post or turnpike house)

From top:
Oct. 2016 – Refurbished upstream façade of Old Kilcarn Bridge
Refurbished downstream façade of Old Kilcarn Bridge

Notes on the text

Note 01 – use of (sic) and paraphrasing.

When first writing on history and quoting passages/extracts, I researched the usage of (sic). While it can be used solely to denote errors in quotations, it has a broader meaning and usage, the following explanation is taken from several dictionaries:

sic = "Thus, so Used to indicate that a quoted passage, especially one containing an error or unconventional spelling, has been retained in its original form or written intentionally."

Several quotations used in this work contain abbreviations, unusual/unconventional spelling, together with strange phraseology and occasional mistakes; therefore, I used (sic) to resolve this conundrum. Its use in this context (as above defined) also avoids conflict with contemporary writings, in which research reveals errors (including errors of fact) – thus putting the reader on notice, so to speak.

When undertaking work of heritage and historical interest, the author carries the responsibility for its accuracy, I consider; therefore, that the use of (sic), as described in dictionaries, helps to attain this goal.

When paraphrasing or using a quotation in part only, I occasionally use the terms 'not verbatim' or 'paraphrased for clarity.'

Note 02 – vernacular words.

The *Meath Field Name Project* revealed that several words, commonly used in the vernacular and folklore, had fallen from everyday usage, including: mereing, forninst/fornenst, kesh etc. These and several other lost words were in regular usage during my early years; therefore, I have included them throughout the narrative, together with other vernacular terms such as rusticated limestone. According to the British Survey Office, the word 'mereing' still means 'a defined boundary:' Ref. Sheetlines, the journal of *The Charles Close Society* for the study of Ordnance Survey Maps – Sheetlines, 70 (August 2004), pp.8-9.

Note 03 – the 'box system.'

At several locations on our trip down the River Boyne, the journey is interrupted to give very detailed/complex descriptions of certain bridges, mills or events. To avoid distracting the reader, not overly interested in such detail, some passages are enclosed within a box-like outline delineated by a small leaf emblem. Thus, the outlined passages can be skipped and the journey continued by taking up the narrative at the end of the box.

Note 04 – Griffith's Valuation.

All references to Griffith's are to Sir Richard Griffith's Primary Valuation. The County Meath sections were recorded largely in 1852-1854. The abbreviation R.V. means rateable valuation.

Note 05 – Townlands.

With changing demographics people are becoming much less aware of the townland as a specific entity – I believe that the recent change in the postal address (to a numbered, coded system) will hasten this process. As the River Boyne flows through a myriad of townlands, from its source to the sea, I have endeavoured to record as many as possible of its riparian townlands, including some of those along the tributaries. Hopefully, this will help preserve these names, which once added context and relevance to the Boyne's local landscape.

Historical Notes:

The Irish Pale

Some dictionaries provide two definitions of areas known as 'the Pale'. The first concerns a restricted area in Imperial Russia, where Jews were allowed to settle. The second, and more pertinent description to these writings reads as follows:

Pale, Part of Ireland under English rule: The area of Ireland, based around Dublin, that was controlled by England, from the 12th century, until the final conquest of the entire country in the 16th century.

The seaboard of the Irish (or English) Pale extended from south of Dublin northwards to Dundalk in County Louth: the defensive perimeter of The Pale spread westward in a salient, or bulge, enclosing large areas in the later-day counties of Louth, Meath, Kildare and Dublin, including much of the Boyne Valley and parts of other counties in Leinster. In the early days of their conquest the Normans built large flat-topped Mottes, upon which eminences they constructed wooden castles for defence. Later, settlements sprang up around the Mottes and these became centres of commerce. Later still, when things were more settled, stone castles were built close by, varying in size and layout from massive stone built moated-castles to the smaller tower houses and even smaller watchtowers – these various sized structures became known as 'the castles, tower houses and watchtowers of The Pale. Several were constructed alongside the Boyne and its environs, especially at the fords and later bridges, and were the target of attacks by the fiercely independent Gaelic chieftains. In later times, some were besieged during the Rebellion of 1641 (known also as 'the Confederate Wars' and 'Wars of the Three Kingdoms') and the following Cromwellian campaign. Many of the castles changed hands several times during the turbulent years of the rebellion and the land confiscations that followed the conflicts. It is said that in 1429, King Henry V1 offered grants of £10 to any person building specified sized castles within some areas of The Pale.

Selected Bibliography

Some of my principle sources of reference for this work are the following:

Maps

- Ordnance Survey Maps of 1837, 1882, 1911. (6 & 25 inch), including 2005 Ortho.
- Ordnance Survey 1958 river basin map of Boyne catchment (including tributaries).
- William Larkin's Map of County Meath, 1812 – 1817.
- Revised OS map accompanying Griffith's 1854 valuation.
- Molls, H., *Map of Ireland, 1714,* in Nat. Lib. of Ireland.
- Pratt's map of 1702, In Nat. Lib. of Ireland.
- Petty, Sir William, (1685), *Hibernia Delineatio: Atlas of Ireland,* (Newcastle upon Tyne, 1968).
- Down Survey Barony & County maps (1644-1656), (copies in M.C.L.).
- Longfield estate maps of Dowdstown, Kilcarn, Bective & Stackallen c. 1810/1822, Nat. Lib. of Ireland.
- Taylor, G. and Skinner, A. *Maps of the Roads of Ireland,* (Shannon, 1969) (Facsimile reprint of 2nd ed. 1783). (M.C.L.).
- Beaufort, Daniel Augustus, *Map of the diocese of Meath, 1797. (Meath County Library).*
- Taylor, J., *'County of Meath'* (engraved map), 1802. (M.C.L.)
- The Preston Bellinter Maps – Prepared from a survey of the Estates of Lord Tara (John Preston), conducted in 1810 by James Vaughen from Athboy. Courtesy of the late George Briscoe.
- Estate map of Ardsallagh – Draughted by J.J. Byrne in1843, Meath County Library.
- Yeats C.E. – 1834 plan of Lower Boyne Navigation (M.C.L.).
- Williams, Thomas, *Sketch map of Navan Town* 1756 (Meath Co. Library Navan).
- Google Sat. Imaging.

Note: I came across many inaccurate maps in circulation on the internet. Some of these may derive from deliberate errors inserted on original maps as copyright protection. The most reliable maps are OS originals.

Books and Papers

- Broderick, David, *The First Toll Roads: Irelands Turnpike Roads 1729-1858* (Cork, 2002).
- Doyle, Eamon, *The Wexford Insurgents of '98 and Their March in to Meath* (Enniscorthy, 1997), including second edition.
- Duffy, Sean (ED) *Atlas of Irish History,* (Dublin, 1997).
- Ellison, Cyril, *The Waters of the Boyne and Blackwater: A Scenic and Industrial Miscellany,* (Dublin, 1983).
- Fitzsimons, Jack, *The Plains of Royal Meath* 1978, (Meath Co. Library Navan).
- Griffith, Richard, *General Valuation of Rateable Property in Ireland,* [Meath volumes] (Dublin, 1852-54) – Valuation Cancellation Books. (www.askaboutireland.ie).

- Hickey, Elizabeth, *Skryne and the Early Normans,* (Navan, 1994).
- *Meath Grand Jury Presentment & Query Books 1790 - 1830* (National Archives, Four Courts).
- O'Donovan, John, *Ordnance Survey Field Names Books 1835-37* (typescripts Meath County Library).
- *Ordnance Survey Letters Meath,* edited by Michael Herity (Dublin, 2001).
- O'Keefe, Peter, *The Dublin to Navan Road and Kilcarn Bridge* (The Author 1994). Available M.C.L.
- O'Keefe, Peter & Tom Simington, *Irish Stone Bridges* (Meath Co. Library Navan).
- Petrie, George, (1790-1866) *On the History and Antiquities of Tara Hill*, 1837 (Paper) and, *Ecclesiastical Architecture anterior to the Norman Invasion* (Paper).
- Reynolds, Jim, *A Life by the Boyne (M.C.L.).*
- Simington, Robert, *The Civil Survey A.D. 1654-1656 County of Meath Vol. V,* (Dublin, 1940).
- Wilde, Sir William, *The Beauties of the Boyne and Blackwater* (Dublin, 1849) 2nd edition.
- *Commissioners of Public Works 17th Report* (1848), Southampton University.
- *1938-1940, Drainage Commission Report* (Meath Co. Library).
- Young, Arthur, *A Tour in Ireland* (1776) (Meath Co. Library).
- Boulger, Demetrius Charles, *The Battle of the Boyne* (Meath Co. Library).
- Beresford Ellis, Peter, *The Boyne Water* (Meath Co. Library).
- Brennan, Conor, *Yellow Furze Memories* (Meath County Library).
- *The Laud Manuscript/Peterborough Chronicles* (Meath Co. Library).
- Holten, Anthony, *On Ancient Roads & Where Toll Roads Meet* (Meath Co. Library).
- Louth Archaeolgical Society, 1953 Paper on Boyne fisheries (Meath Co. Library.
- Brady, Byrnes, Cooney & O'Sullivan – An Archaeological Study of the *Battle of the Boyne* at Oldbridge (completed for Dúchas c. 2003) (Paper).
- Stout, Geraldine, *Newgrange and the Bend of the Boyne.*
- Crinion, Mairéad – *A history of Oldbridge, Sheephouse and Donore* (Paper) NUI Maynooth.
- Fagan, Martin - *From Grinding Corn to Grinding Halt* – Dissertation – a local study of the milling industry along the Meath Boyne c. 1650/1900.
- Augustus Grimble – *The Salmon Rivers of Ireland* (1913). M.C.L.
- *Hall's Ireland* – Mr. and Mrs. Hall on County Meath pre-famine (1844).
- *Thomson's Statistical Survey* (1802) In M.C.L.
- *Slater's and Piggots Directories* (Various).
- D'Alton 1844, *History of Drogheda.*
- Trench, C.E.F. *Slane town trail – Newgrange.*
- Cogan, Anthony (Dean), *The Diocese of Meath Ancient and Modern* (1862).
- Coldrick, Bryn, *Rossin, County Meath – An unofficial place.*
- McKeever, Edward, *History of Kilmessan – And its environs.*
- Murphy, Richard R. (Garda), Typescripts on the Wexford Croppies of 1798 (activities in the Slane area) – Meath County Library.
- Moore, Doctor Beryl, Typescripts in Meath County Library.

Types
of Mill
Wheels

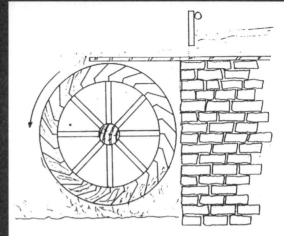

1. Overshot Wheel

2. Breast Shot Wheel

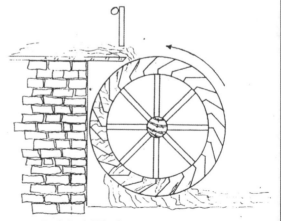

3. Pitch Back Wheel

Watermills on the River Boyne & tributaries

Carbury to Baltray (Excluding town of Drogheda)

River	Townland/location	County	Type of mill
Little Boyne	(on source from Carbury Bog)	Kildare	2 x corn-mills
Little Boyne	Newbury Pond	Kildare	flax mill
Little Boyne	Clonkeen T/L	Kildare	corn-mill
Little Boyne/Garr R.	Kilmore T/L	Kildare	ruined mill
Little Boyne/trib.	Waterstown/Monasteroris	Offaly	corn-mill/windmill
Glash River	Garrisker T/L	Kildare	corn-mill
Glash River	Ballyonan/Bunglass	Kildare	corn-flour mill
Yellow River	Derryiron T/L	Offaly	corn-mill
Mongagh River	Caslejordan	Meath	corn-mill
River Boyne/trib.	Ballyboggan T/L	Meath	Old mill
River Boyne/trib.	Ticroghan	Meath	Old mill
Clonard/Kilwarden R.	Hightown T/L	W. Meath	corn-mill
Clonard/Kilwarden R.	Rattin T/L	W. Meath	corn-mill
River Deel	Carrick T/L	W. Meath	corn-mill & kiln
River Deel	Cummerstown T/L	W. Meath	corn-mill
River Deel	Gormanstown T/L	W. Meath	corn & tuck mill
River Deel	Glenidan T/L	W. Meath	corn-mill & kiln
River Deel	Grangetown T/L	W. Meath	corn & tuck mill
River Deel/trib.	Killagh Br.	W. Meath	corn & tuck mill
River Deel	Raharney-Little T/L	W. Meath	corn-mill
Riverstown River	Mill Land T/L	W. Meath	flour-mill
Riverstown River	Cushenstown T/L	W. Meath	corn-mill & kiln
River Deel	Ballyadams/T/L Killyon	Meath	windmill/corn-mill & kiln
Kildare Blackwater	Gilltown T/L	Kildare	corn-mill
Fear English R.	Johnstown Br.	Kildare	corn-flour-mill
Kildare Blackwater	Clonguiffin T/L	Meath	corn-mill
Kildare Blackwater	Inchamore/Lionsden	Meath	corn-mill
Stonyford River	Diamore T/L	Meath	corn-mill & kiln
Stonyford R. trib.	Archerstown T/L	W. Meath	corn-mill & kiln
Stonyford River	Killacroy T/L (Killallon)	Meath	corn-mill
Stonyford River	Ballynadrimna T/L	Meath	corn (Misset's) mill

River	Townland/location	County	Type of mill
Stonyford River	Corballis T/L	Meath	corn (Earl's) mill
Tromman River	Killballyporter T/L	Meath	(Kill Mill-corn)-windmill stump
Tromman R.	Brannockstown/Boardsmill	Meath	corn-mill & kiln
Boyne/trib.	Bellewstown/Higginsbrook	Meath	(the Factory) tuck mill
Tremblestown R.	Martinstown T/L	Meath	corn-mill & kiln
Athboy River	Athboy Town	Meath	(Newmans) corn & flour mill
River Boyne	Kilnagross T/L	Meath	(Mitchell's) corn-mill
River Boyne	Newhaggard T/L	Meath	corn & flour mill
River Boyne	Townspark-North Trim	Meath	(Kennedy's) corn & tuck mills
River Boyne	Friarspark 1st Div. Trim	Meath	(Smart's) tuck mill
River Boyne	Iffernock T/L	Meath	(Kiely's/Shiel's) tuck & corn mills
River Boyne	Loganstown T/L	Meath	corn-mill
Knightsbrook R.	Iffernock T/L - Knock	Meath	(overshot) corn & flour mills
Boycetown R.	Scurlockstown T/L	Meath	(Cassidy's) corn mill
River Boyne	Rathnally	Meath	corn-flour mills/kilns
River Boyne	Bective	Meath	corn/saw mill
Versheen R.	Ballina/Ballyna	Meath	site of old corn-mill
Versheen River	Trubley T/L	Meath	(Harvey's) Old corn-mill
River Boyne	Asigh (Assey)	Meath	site of ancient mill
River Boyne	Ardsallagh T/L	Meath	corn-mill/eel weir
River Skein	Knockmark T/L	Meath	corn-mill
River Skein	Leshemstown T/L	Meath	corn-mill
River Skein	Clowanstown T/L	Meath	(Teelins)corn-mill (overshot)
River Skein/trib.	Dunsany/Ganzey Village	Meath	corn-mill
River Skein	Kilmessan	Meath	(Arnold's) corn-mill
River Gabhra	Lismullin T/L	Meath	(the King's Mill) corn-mill
River Gabhra	Blundelstown T/L	Meath	(Dillon's Br.) old tuck mill site
River Gabhra	Castletown Tara	Meath	(Larkin's Map) old mill site
River Boyne	Upper/Little Kilcarn	Meath	corn-mill
River Boyne	Lower/Greater Kilcarn	Meath	(big mill) corn & flax mill
River Boyne	Navan/Academy St.	Meath	Murphy's Distillery
River Boyne	Navan/Ludlow St.	Meath	corn-mill & kiln
River Boyne	Navan/Ludlow St.	Meath	(downstream) corn-mill

Carbury to Baltray (Excluding town of Drogheda) continued

River	Townland/location	County	Type of mill
River Boyne	Navan/Athlumney	Meath	Boyne Mills 2 mills corn & flour
Blackwater R.	Navan – Abbeyland-south	Meath	(Mill Brook) paper & woollen mill
Blackwater R.	Navan – Abbeyland-south	Meath	(Fay's/Skelly's) corn-mill/distillery
Blackwater R.	Navan – Abbeyland-south	Meath	(Forde's at Mollies) wool mill
Blackwater R.	Navan – Abbeyland-south	Meath	(Bradley's) corn-mill
Blackwater R.	Navan-Blackcastle/Poolboy	Meath	(Morgan's) distillery-two corn-mills

Upper Blackwater mills – source to Lough Ramor

Blackwater R.	Crocknahattan T/L	Cavan	two corn-mills
Blackwater R.	Galbolie T/L	Cavan	flax & bleach mills
Blackwater R.	Cleffin T/L	Cavan	corn & tuck mills
Blackwater R.	Greagadossan T/L	Cavan	flax mill
Park River	Correagh Glebe	Cavan	corn-mill
Park River	Fintawan T/L	Cavan	corn-mill
Burreen River	Ballaghanea T/L	Cavan	corn & tuck mills

Lower Blackwater mills – Lough Ramor to Liscartan

Blackwater R.	Ryefield T/L	Cavan	(Ryefield Cross) corn-mill
Blackwater R.	Pottlereagh T/L	Meath	(Daly's Cross) corn-mill
Blackwater R	Castlepole T/L	Meath	corn & tuck mills
Blackwater R.	Cakestown Glebe	Meath	old corn-mill
Blackwater R.	Martry T/L	Meath	(Tallon's) corn-mill
Blackwater R.	Teltown T/L	Meath	corn-mill
Blackwater R.	Tankardstown T/L	Meath	Old mill
Blackwater R.	Liscartan T/L	Meath	corn-mill
Yellow R.	Wilkinstown	Meath	corn-mill
River Boyne	Athlumney	Meath	(Aylesburys') flour-flax & corn-mill
River Boyne	Athlumney	Meath	(Chadwicks') corn-mill (overshot)
River Boyne	Dunmoe T/L	Meath	corn-mill
River Boyne	Ardmulchan T/L	Meath	(Martin's/Dunne's) corn-mill
River Boyne	Ardmulchan T/L	Meath	Coxon's-Clayton's cotton/woollen
Boyne/trib.	Hays-Carnuff T/L	Meath	corn-mill

River	Townland/location	County	Type of mill
River Boyne	Cruicetown T/L	Meath	(Carney's) tuck mill
River Boyne	Dollardstown T/L	Meath	corn & tuck mills
Harlinstown R.	Mullaha T/L	Meath	corn-mill
Harlinstown R.	Roestown T/L	Meath	corn & tuck mills
Harlinstown R.	Slane Castle Demesne	Meath	saw-mill
River Boyne	Slane	Meath	(Jebb's Mill) corn & flour mill
River Boyne	Rosnaree	Meath	(Molly Johnston's) corn-mill
River Boyne	Roughgrange T/L (Leck)	Meath	(Norris') corn-mill
River Boyne	Stalleen T/L	Meath	(McCullagh's) corn-mill
River Mattock	Collon/Ballyboni	Louth	corn & tuck mills
River Mattock	Collon Village	Louth	corn-mill
River Mattock	Collon T/L	Louth	corn-mill
River Mattock	Starinagh T/L	Louth	flax mill
River Devlin	Higginstown T/L	Meath	(Devlins Br.) corn-mill
River Mattock	Monknewton/Rossin	Meath	corn & flour mills
River Mattock	Dowth T/L	Meath	(Elcock's) corn-mill (overshot)
River Mattock	Proudfootstown T/L	Meath	corn-mill (overshot)
Boyne/trib	Tullyallen T/L (King.W.Glen)	Louth	(Mill of Alt/site) unspecified
Boyne/trib	Tullyallen/Kinneas R.	Louth	unspecified

Estuary mills – Northern shore

River Boyne/trib.	Yellowbatter T/L	Louth	mill (unspecified)
River Boyne/trib.	Yellowbatter T/L	Louth	mill (unspecified)
River Boyne/trib.	Newtownstalaban	Louth	(windmill ruins) - mill (unspecified)
River Boyne/trib.	Banktown T/L	Louth	mill (unspecified)

Estuary Mills – Southern shore

River Boyne/trib.	Stameen T/L	Meath	corn-mill/windmill stump
River Boyne/trib.	Mornington	Meath	Two mills on 1656 D.S. Map

Total for River Boyne and tributaries c. 140 Watermills – 04 Windmills – 03 Distilleries.

Bridges on the Boyne – from source to sea

Compiled 2012 to 2014

01   Newbury Park – c.3ft stone built gullet under R403 Co. Kildare

02   River Bridge – Clonkeen, rectangular profiled concrete bridge
      c. 1890/1900. Co. Kildare

03   Kishawanny Metal Rail Br. 1877 (now defunct) * Kildare/Offaly

04   Kishawanny New Br. c. 2003 Kildare/Offaly

05   Kishawanny Br. stone c.1848, now pedestrian Kildare/Offaly

06   Boyne Bridge Near Ballygibbon House Kildare/Offaly

07   Kinnafad Br. Single stone arch Kildare/Offaly

08   Ballyboggan Br. Stone arch c. 1850s + 1 flood Kildare/Meath

09   M4 Br. Concrete c. 2004 Kildare/Meath

10   Leinster Br. 3 x 25/30ft stone arches 1831 Kildare/Meath

11   Ashfield Br. - stone 3 + 1 + 3 - centre span c.1849 Kildare/Meath

12   Rail Br. 3 elliptical arches - M.G.W.R. 1840s Meath

13   Royal Canal Aqueduct - John Evans 1804 Longwood/Meath

14   Stonyford Br.   Large single span c. 45/50ft built O.P.W. c. 1849 + 1 x c.18ft &
      several smaller arches high & dry on left bank.

15   Inchamore Br. (known as Inny Br.) Large single span c. 45/50ft –
      1837 OS map shows 7 arches – present Br. c 15ft road width, built c.1849 by O.P.W.

16   Scariff Br. 60ft centre span O.P.W. 1849 + 4 dry arches on left or N/E bank,
      survivors from older 1761 Br.

17   Derryinydaly Br. Large centre span c.35/40ft O.P.W. 1849, 2 x narrower arches each side –
      survivors of 1760s Br. Several iron tie bars in place to strengthen structure, possibly late 19th cent.

18   Foot Br – West of Trim c. 2001/2004.

19   New Watergate Br. c. 2005 (metal & concrete)

20   Bridge of Trim 4 x pointed stone arches – perhaps c. late 12th or early 13th century

21   Foot Br. (Millenium Br.) built in c. 1999.

22   New Br. Maudlins to Porch Field Trim c.1970s

23   Newtown Br. c. 15th century 5 x stone arches

24   Tribley Rail Br – built c. 1860s demolished 1960s*

25   Bective Br. c. 1690s to 1710 - 11 x stone arches +1 millrace arch

26 Asigh Rail Viaduct – 6 x stone arches c. 1860.

27 Bellinter Br. – 6 x stone arches + I millrace arch - built by Grand Jury 1812.

28 M3 Br. – Dowdstown to Ardsallagh 2005

29 New Kilcarn Br. Concrete opened 1977

30 Kilcarn Br. 11 x stone arches 4 central c.1600s 3 on west side perhaps medieval – 2 on eastern end for millrace c. mid-1500s.

31 Concrete Bridge (at Swan Br.) - Limekilnhill to Athlumney, opened c.2005

32 'The New Br.' or Bridge of Navan, originally 8 but now 6 x stone arches c.1735-1756, one arch on town end entombed for relief road c.1980s – one arch buried on Athlumney end at Andy Brennan Park.

33 Stackallan or Broadboyne Br. 6 x stone arches + one dry arch - c.1714 + I canal arch (Thomson's Br.) 1792, Richard Evans.

34 Slane Br 12 x stone arches + I canal arch c.1763 – widened c.1810 – 6 surviving medieval pointed arches downstream façade

35 Footbridge at Newgrange c.1990s

36 Oldbridge metal Br. built in 1869

37 M1 bridge c.2000

38 Bridge of Peace in Drogheda – opened 1976

39 St Dominic's Br. built 1863 now pedestrian

40 Haymarket Br. c. 1990s

41 New St. Mary's or *Bridge of Drogheda* c.2004

42 Footbridge – Hugh de Lacy Br. c.2000

43 Boyne Viaduct Rail Br opened 1854

Note 1 The list does not include c. 5ft Skewed Br. at the old Carbury Corn Mill, and several private bridges spanning the *Little Boyne* on the reach between Carbury and the Yellow River.

Note 2 The rail bridges at Kishawanny & Tribley, were demolished.

Note 3 The list excludes the long gone medieval *Bridge of the Grange* (Tribley) and Babes Bridge at Donaghmore.